Robert J. Carbaugh, PhD
Professor of Economics
Central Washington University

FIFTH EDITION

International Economics

SOUTH-WESTERN College Publishing

An International Thomson Publishing Company

HV60EA

Copyright © 1995
by South-Western College Publishing Co.
Cincinnati, Ohio

ISBN 0-538-84427-2

4   5   6   MT   9   8   7   6

Printed in the United States of America

Acquisitions Editor: *Ken King*
Production Coordinator: *Robin Schuster*
Production: *Cecile Joyner*
Manuscript Editor: *Margaret C. Tropp*
Cover Design: *Stuart Patersen, Image House, Inc.*
Internal Design: *Terri Wright Design*
Internal Art: *Carl Brown*
Marketing Manager: *Denise Carlson*
Typesetting: **T·H** *Typecast, Inc.*

Library of Congress Cataloging-in-Publication Data

Carbaugh, Robert J., 1946–
   International economics / Robert J. Carbaugh.
—5th ed.
      p.   cm.
   Includes bibliographical references and index.
   ISBN 0-538-84427-2
   1. International economic relations.   I. Title.
HF 1359.C37   1994
337—dc20 94-13411
                                                CIP

*This book is printed on
acid-free recycled paper.*

International Thomson Publishing
South-Western is an ITP Company. The ITP
trademark is used under license.

To Cathy, Julie, Mary, Alice, and Emily

Preface

My belief is that the best way to motivate students to learn a subject is to demonstrate how it is used in practice. The first four editions of *International Economics* reflected this belief and were written to provide a serious presentation of international economic theory with an emphasis on current applications. Adopters of these editions strongly supported the integration of economic theory with current events. This edition has been revised with an eye toward improving this presentation and updating the applications as well as toward including the latest theoretical developments.

Like its predecessors, this edition is intended for use in a one-quarter or one-semester course for students who have no more background than principles of economics. This book's strengths are its clarity and organization and its applications, which demonstrate the usefulness of theory to students. The revised and updated material in this edition emphasizes current applications of economic theory and incorporates recent theoretical and policy developments in international trade and finance. Among the new, or substantially revised, topics in the fifth edition are the following:

- What is international competitiveness?
- Comparative advantage with money
- International competitiveness in the U.S. auto and steel industries
- Health care costs and comparative advantage
- Specific factors trade model

- Jet aircraft competition: Boeing and Airbus
- Sugar import quotas
- Minivan dumping
- Smith Corona's antidumping victories
- Trade remedy laws
- Industrial policies of the United States and other nations
- Strategic trade policy
- OPEC's incentive to cheat
- The North American Free Trade Agreement
- Government procurement policies of the European Community
- Direct exporting, foreign direct investment, and licensing
- Japanese automobile transplants
- Interest arbitrage
- Foreign exchange speculation
- Law of one price
- Exchange rate overshooting
- Exchange rates, costs, and prices
- European currency crisis of 1993
- Exchange rate stabilization and monetary policy
- International economic policy coordination
- International lending risk

The fifth edition contains a new chapter, Chapter 17, which discusses international economic policy and international policy coordination. A substantially revised Chapter 7 emphasizes the role of industrial policy for the United States and other nations.

Although instructors generally agree on the basic content of the international economics course, opinions vary widely about what arrangement of material is appropriate. This book is structured to provide considerable organizational flexibility. The topic of international trade relations is presented before international monetary relations, but the order can be reversed by instructors who choose to start with monetary theory. Instructors can begin with Chapters 11–18 and conclude with Chapters 2–10. Those who do not wish to cover all the material in the book can omit Chapters 7–10 and Chapters 16–18 without loss of continuity.

An *Instructor's Manual* accompanies the fifth edition. It contains (1) brief answers to end-of-chapter study questions, (2) multiple-choice questions for each chapter, and (3) suggestions for further readings. It is available both as a book and on disk.

To accompany this fifth edition, Professor Jim Hanson of Willamette University has prepared a student *Study Guide*. The guide provides a review of the text's main topics and provides practice problems, true-false and multiple-choice questions, and short-answer questions.

I am pleased to acknowledge those who aided me in preparing the fifth edition. Helpful suggestions and often detailed reviews were provided by Robin Klay, Hope College; Darwin Wassink, University of Wisconsin, Eau Claire; Terutomo Ozawa, Colorado State University; Jim Hanson, Willamette University; Farhad Rassekh, University of Hartford; Eleanor Craig, University of Delaware; Bun Song Lee, University of Nebraska, Omaha; Byron Brown, Southern Oregon State College; G. Rod Erfani, Transylvania University; Al Gutowsky, California State University, Sacramento. I would also like to thank Wolfgang Franz of Central Washington University for his advice and help while I was preparing the manuscript. I am also indebted to Barbara Hodges, who assisted in the manuscript's preparation. It has been a pleasure to work my editor Ken King, as well as Jason Moore, Peter Cochran, Margaret Tropp, Terri Wright, and Carl Brown. Special thanks and recognition are given to Cecile Joyner, who orchestrated the production of this text. Finally, I am grateful to my students who commented on the revisions included in this new edition.

I would appreciate any comments, corrections, or suggestions that faculty or students wish to make so I can continue to improve this text in the years ahead. Thank you for permitting this text to evolve to a fifth edition!

Robert J. Carbaugh
Department of Economics
Central Washington University
Ellensburg, Washington 98926
(509) 963–3443

Contents

Part One
International Trade Relations 15

CHAPTER THREE

Modern Trade Theory: Demand and the Terms of Trade 51

CHAPTER FOUR

Trade Model Extensions and Applications 67

CHAPTER FIVE

Tariffs   106

CHAPTER SIX

Nontariff Trade Barriers   143

C H A P T E R   S E V E N

Trade Regulations and Industrial Policies   182

C H A P T E R   E I G H T

Trade Policies for the Developing Nations   223

C H A P T E R   N I N E

Preferential Trading Arrangements   246

CHAPTER TEN

International Factor Movements and Multinational Corporations 271

Part Two
International Monetary Relations 303

CHAPTER ELEVEN

The Balance of Payments 305

CHAPTER   TWELVE

Foreign Exchange   320

CHAPTER   THIRTEEN

Exchange-Rate Determination   350

CHAPTER SEVENTEEN

International Economic Policy   438

CHAPTER EIGHTEEN

International Banking: Reserves, Debt, and Risk   455

List of Essays

CHAPTER *1*

The International Economy

In today's world, no nation exists in economic isolation. All aspects of a nation's economy—its industries, service sectors, levels of income and employment, living standard—are linked to the economies of its trading partners. This linkage takes the form of international movements of goods and services, labor, business enterprise, investment funds, and technology. Indeed, national economic policies cannot be formulated without evaluating their probable impacts on the economies of other countries.

The high degree of **economic interdependence** among today's economies reflects the historical evolution of the world's economic and political order. At the end of World War II, the United States was economically and politically the most powerful nation in the world. It was sometimes stated that "when the United States sneezed, the economies of other nations caught a cold." But with the passage of time, the U.S. economy became increasingly integrated into the economic activities of foreign countries. The formation of the European Community (EC) during the 1950s, the rise in importance of the multinational corporation during the 1960s, and the market power in world oil markets enjoyed by the Organization of Petroleum Exporting Countries (OPEC) during the 1970s all resulted in the evolution of the world community into a complicated system based on a growing interdependence among nations.

In recent years, the character of global economic interdependence has become much more sophisticated. Rather than emphasizing only the economic issues of the industrial countries, world conferences are now recognizing and incorporating into their discussions the problems of the less developed nations. For resources such as energy and raw materials, the Western industrial nations rely on the less developed nations for a portion of their consumption requirements. However, this reliance varies among nations. For Europe and Japan, dependence on foreign energy and materials is much more striking than for the United States. On the other hand, the livelihood of the developing nations' economies greatly depends on the exports of the industrial nations.

Recognizing that world economic interdependence is complex and its effects uneven, the economic community has made efforts toward *international cooperation.* Conferences devoted to global economic issues have explored the avenues through which cooperation could be fostered between the industrial and the less developed nations. The efforts of the less developed nations to reap larger gains from international trade and to participate more

1

fully in international institutions have been hastened recently by the impact of the global recession on manufacturers, industrial inflation, and the burdens of high-priced energy.

Interdependence among nations also applies in the case of *foreign debt*. Throughout the 1970s, the growth of middle-income developing nations (such as Brazil) was widely viewed as a great success story. Of particular importance was their success in increasing exports of manufactured goods. However, much of this success was due to the availability of loans from industrial nations. Based on overly optimistic expectations about export earnings and interest rates, these nations borrowed excessively to finance growth. Then, with the impact of world recession on export demand, high interest rates, and tumbling oil prices, countries such as Argentina and Mexico found they had to make annual payments of principal and interest that exceeded their total exports of goods and services. The reluctance of creditor nations to lend as much as in the past meant that debtor nations were pressed to cut imports or expand exports, in spite of a worldwide recession. It was recognized that failure to repay the debt could result in a serious disruption of the international financial system.

During the past decade, the world's market economies have become integrated as never before. Exports and imports as a share of national output have reached unprecedented levels for most industrial nations, while foreign investment and international lending have expanded more rapidly than world trade. This closer linkage of economies can be mutually advantageous for trading nations. It permits producers in each nation to take advantage of specialization and economies of large-scale production. A nation can consume a wider variety of products at a cost less than that which could be achieved in the absence of trade. Despite these advantages, demands have grown for protection against imports. For industrial nations, protectionist pressures have been strongest during periods of rising unemployment caused by economic recession. Moreover, developing na-

tions often maintain that the so-called liberalized trading system called for by industrial nations works to the disadvantage of developing nations. Their reason: Industrial nations can control the terms (prices) at which international trade takes place.

Economic interdependence also has direct consequences for a student taking an introductory course in international economics. As consumers, we can be affected by changes in the international values of currencies. Should the Japanese yen or German mark appreciate against the U.S. dollar, it would cost us more to purchase Japanese television sets or German automobiles. As investors, we might prefer to purchase British securities if overseas interest rates rise above U.S. levels. As members of the labor force, we might want to know whether the president plans to protect U.S. workers producing steel or television sets from foreign competition.

In short, economic interdependence has become a complex issue in recent times, often resulting in strong and uneven impacts among nations and among sectors within a given nation. Business, labor, investors, and consumers all feel the repercussions of changing economic conditions or trade policies in other nations. Today's global economy requires cooperation on an international level to cope with the myriad issues and problems.

THE UNITED STATES AS AN OPEN ECONOMY

It is generally agreed that the U.S. economy has become increasingly integrated into the world economy in recent decades. Such integration involves a number of dimensions, including trade of goods and services, financial markets, the labor force, ownership of production facilities, and dependence on imported materials.

One type of dependence on the rest of the world concerns the damage that could be done to the U.S. economy—and possibly to national security—by loss of access to foreign supplies

Foreign Competition and Deconcentration in the U.S. Auto Industry

U.S. Automobile Market: Market Shares

Manufacturer	Market Share	
	1985	1991
General Motors	43	36
Ford	18	19
Chrysler	13	8
Honda	5	10
Toyota	6	9
Nissan	4	4
Mazda	2	3
VW-Audi	3	1
Subaru	1	1

SOURCE: U.S. Department of Commerce, *U.S. Industrial Reports* (Washington, D.C.: Government Printing Office, 1993).

The history of the U.S. automobile industry can be divided into the following distinct eras: the emergence of Ford Motor Company as a dominant producer in the early 1900s; the shift of dominance to General Motors in the 1920s; and the rise of foreign competition in the 1970s.

As a share of the U.S. market, auto imports expanded from 0.4 percent in the late 1940s to more than 30 percent in 1990s. Foreign producers have been effective competitors for the U.S. auto oligopoly, which used to be largely immune from market pressures (such as costs and product quality). Increased competitiveness has forced U.S. auto companies to alter price policies, production methods, work rules, and product quality. Japanese firms are the largest source of the competition.

The competitive success of foreign manufacturers in the U.S. market has led to the deconcentration of the domestic industry. Although the Big Three (GM, Ford, Chrysler) controlled more than 90 percent of the U.S. market in the 1960s, their collective market share has greatly diminished because of import competition; by the early 1990s, the Big Three accounted for less than 70 percent of U.S. auto sales. In particular, foreign manufacturers have emphasized the small-car segment of the market; their impact on U.S. auto company deconcentration has been greatest in this segment.

or foreign markets. Table 1.1 illustrates the increasing U.S. dependence on foreign sources of supply for several vital minerals and metals. Because termination of the supply of these resources could impair the health and security of the United States, the United States maintains strategic stockpiles of most of these products in case of international crisis and future shortfall. Similarly, the United States has stockpiled some 500 million barrels in its strategic

T A B L E 1. 1 / U.S. Imports of Selected Minerals and Metals as a Percentage of Domestic Consumption

Mineral	Percentage of Domestic Consumption	Major Foreign Sources
Manganese	100	South Africa, France, Gabon
Bauxite	100	Australia, Guinea, Jamaica
Asbestos	95	Canada, South Africa
Platinum	88	United Kingdom, Russia
Cobalt	82	Zaire, Zambia, Canada
Tungsten	75	China, Bolivia, Canada
Nickel	74	Canada, Norway, Australia
Potassium	67	Canada, Israel, Russia
Cadmium	54	Canada, Australia, Mexico
Selenium	52	Canada, United Kingdom, Japan
Zinc	30	Canada, Mexico, Peru
Gypsum	30	Canada, Mexico, Spain

SOURCE: U.S. Department of Commerce, *Statistical Abstract of the United States* (Washington, D.C.: Government Printing Office, 1992).

petroleum reserve to cope with possible future shortages.

The openness of the U.S. economy is more widespread than indicated by these commodities. Table 1.2 shows exports of goods and services as a percentage of gross domestic product (GDP) for selected nations. As of 1992, the United States exported about 10 percent of its GDP; in 1970, this figure stood at 5 percent. Although the U.S. economy has been increasingly tied to international trade, this tendency is even more striking for many other nations. As shown in Table 1.2, the Netherlands exported a whopping 56 percent of its GDP in 1992! It may come as a surprise to find that in 1992 Japan exported only 11 percent of its GDP; from reading the newspapers, one might get the erroneous impression that Japan's exports constitute a much larger share of its national output than they actually do.

The significance of international trade for the U.S. economy is even more noticeable when specific products are considered. For example, we would have fewer personal computers without imported components, no aluminum if we did not import bauxite, no tin cans without imported tin, and no chrome bumpers if we did not import chromium. Students taking an 8:00 a.m. course in international economics might sleep through the class (do you really believe this?) if we did not import coffee or tea. Moreover, many of the products we buy from foreigners would be much more costly if we were dependent on our domestic production. Table 1.3 illustrates the share of the U.S. market captured by foreign producers of manufactured goods.

With which nations does the United States conduct trade? As seen in Table 1.4, Canada and Japan head the list. Other leading trading

TABLE 1. 2 / *Exports of Goods and Services as a Percentage of Gross Domestic Product (GDP), 1992*

Country	Exports as a Percentage of GDP
Netherlands	56
Norway	45
Germany	39
Portugal	36
Switzerland	35
Canada	24
United Kingdom	24
France	23
Japan	11
United States	10

SOURCE: International Monetary Fund, *International Financial Statistics,* July 1993.

TABLE 1. 3 / *Import Penetration Ratios for Selected U.S. Industries, 1992*

Product	Imports as a Percentage of Shipments*
Luggage	72
Footwear	70
Crude oil	37
Machine tools	32
Textiles	31
Plywood	27
Electronic components	25
Lumber	18
Farm machinery	15
Industrial instruments	14
Paper	12
Aerospace	7

* Ratio of imports to new supply (product shipments plus imports).

SOURCE: U.S. Department of Commerce, International Trade Administration, *U.S. Industrial Outlook* (Washington, D.C.: Government Printing Office, 1993).

partners of the United States include Mexico, Germany, and the United Kingdom. The newly industrializing countries (such as Hong Kong and South Korea) have also emerged as major trading partners of the United States in the 1980s and 1990s.

The United States has become increasingly tied to the rest of the world in finance and banking. Foreign ownership of U.S. financial assets has risen since the 1960s. During the 1970s, the OPEC nations recycled many of their oil dollars by making investments in U.S. financial markets. The 1980s also witnessed major flows of investment funds to the United States as Japan and other nations, with dollars accumulated from trade surpluses with the United States, acquired U.S. financial assets, businesses, and real estate. Consuming more than it was producing, by the late 1980s the United States had become a net borrower from

the rest of the world to pay for the difference. Increasing concerns were raised about the interest cost of this debt to the U.S. economy and about the impact of this debt burden on the living standards of future U.S. generations.

The process of globalization has also increased in financial markets. U.S. banks developed worldwide branch networks in the 1960s and 1970s for loans, payments, and foreign-exchange trading. In the 1970s, U.S. securities firms began to establish operations in Europe and Tokyo. Foreign securities firms subsequently expanded into the United States. By the 1970s, foreign exchange became a 24-hour market, with major banks conducting business with one another in the United States, the Far East, the Middle East, and Europe. Table 1.5 profiles the world's top banks and securities

*T A B L E 1. 4 / Leading Trading Partners of the United States, 1992**

Country	Value of U.S. Exports (billions of dollars)	Value of U.S. Imports (billions of dollars)
All countries, total	105.1	148.1
Canada	19.8	26.5
Japan	12.0	26.8
Mexico	9.6	8.9
Germany	5.3	7.5
United Kingdom	4.9	5.8
Hong Kong	2.3	7.0
South Korea	3.9	5.1
France	3.8	3.7
Singapore	2.2	2.8
Netherlands	2.3	1.6

* Third quarter.

SOURCE: *Direction of Trade Statistics* (Washington, D.C.: International Monetary Fund, March 1993).

firms; notice the financial dominance of Japanese banks.

By the 1980s, U.S. government securities were traded on virtually a 24-hour basis. Foreign investors purchased U.S. treasury bills, notes, and bonds, and many desired to trade during their own working hours rather than those of the United States. Primary dealers of U.S. government securities opened offices in such locations as Tokyo and London. Stock markets became increasingly internationalized, with companies listing their stocks on different exchanges throughout the world. Financial futures markets also spread throughout the world, with market acronyms such as SIMEX for Singapore and LIFFE for London.

In the area of banking, foreign banks have increased their presence in the United States throughout the 1980s and early 1990s, reflecting (1) the multinational population base of the United States, (2) the size and importance of U.S. markets, and (3) the role of the U.S. dollar

as an international medium of exchange and reserve currency. Today, more than 250 foreign banks operate in the United States; in particular, Japanese banks have been the dominant group of foreign banks operating in the United States.

CONSEQUENCES OF INCREASED OPENNESS

What implications does increased international economic interdependence have for the domestic economy? Opening the economy to foreign trade tends to curtail *inflationary pressures* at home. From 1981 to 1985, for example, the U.S. dollar became more expensive in terms of foreign currencies. This was largely due to high interest rates in the United States, caused by a tight monetary policy, an expansionary fiscal policy, and a low domestic savings rate. The high interest rates attracted foreign investment

TABLE 1. 5 / *Profiles of the World's Largest Banks and Financial-Services Firms, 1991*

Banks	Assets
1. Dai-Ichi Kangyo Bank (Japan)	$480 billion
2. Sakura Bank (Japan)	458
3. Sumitomo Bank (Japan)	458
4. Sanwa Bank (Japan)	452
5. Fuji Bank (Japan)	448
6. Mitsubishi Bank (Japan)	428
7. Industrial Bank of Japan (Japan)	325
8. Credit Agricole (France)	307
9. Credit Lyonnais (France)	306
10. Deutsche Bank (Germany)	295

Securities Firms	Capital
1. Nomura Securities (Japan)	$18 billion
2. Daiwa Securities (Japan)	12
3. Salomon (U.S.)	11
4. Nikko Securities (Japan)	10
5. Yamaichi Securities (Japan)	10
6. Merrill Lynch (U.S.)	9
7. Goldman Sachs (U.S.)	7
8. Dean Witter (U.S.)	6
9. Shearson Lehman Brothers (U.S.)	6
10. Morgan Stanley (U.S.)	5

SOURCE: "World Business," *The Wall Street Journal,* September 24, 1992, p. R-27.

general wage level. The practice of *wage concessions,* or givebacks, has occurred in industries facing intense foreign competition. With their members becoming unemployed, unions feel compelled to renegotiate compensation levels and work rules in order to save jobs.

Another result of increased openness is the reduction or elimination of the *crowding out* of private investment that was predicted to occur as a result of the growth in U.S. budget deficits in the 1980s. Budget deficits were expected to lead to increased money demand and higher interest rates. Because firms would find it more expensive to undertake investment projects, they would decrease investment spending. As it turned out, the expansionary fiscal policy and tight monetary policy of the early 1980s triggered flows of foreign investment funds into the United States. The investment inflow increased the supply of funds in U.S. financial markets and held domestic interest rates below expected levels, thus mitigating the crowding-out problem.

Increased openness makes the domestic economy *vulnerable to disturbances* initiated overseas, as seen in the oil crises of the 1970s. But increased openness also helps to dissipate the disturbances that occur in the domestic economy. During periods of domestic recession, the rest of the world may operate somewhat like a sink into which excess domestic output can be poured (although foreigners may initiate international dumping complaints). Conversely, the output of the rest of the world may satisfy domestic consumption during eras of shortages. This situation occurred in 1959, when a strike by U.S. steelworkers shut down domestic production for a number of months; an increase in steel imports fulfilled consumption requirements and greatly reduced the effects of the strike on the American economy.

Greater openness also affects *fiscal policy* (taxes and government spending). Suppose domestic residents spend more on imports out of each dollar of income earned. An expansionary fiscal policy, which increases the income

to the United States, which increased demand for the dollar and bid up its price. With the dollar more expensive in terms of foreign currencies, foreign imports into the United States became cheaper in terms of the dollar. Import prices fell by 14 percent between 1981 and 1985, which contributed to a lower inflation rate in the United States.

Increased foreign competition places constraints on those sectors (such as steel and autos) in which wages get out of line with the and spending of domestic residents, will leak overseas more quickly, thus lessening the fiscal policy's impact on the domestic economy.

SOME ARGUMENTS FOR AND AGAINST AN OPEN TRADING SYSTEM

The **benefits of international trade** accrue in the forms of lower domestic prices, development of more efficient methods and new products, and a greater range of consumption choices. In an open trading system, a country will import those commodities that it produces at relatively high cost while exporting commodities that can be produced at relatively low cost. Because resources are channeled from uses of low productivity to those of high productivity, trade permits higher levels of consumption and investment. Competition from imports tends to hold down the prices of domestic substitutes while promoting efficiency among home producers.

Although the benefits of an open trading system are widely understood, several conditions give rise to arguments against international trade. It is sometimes maintained that import protection should be extended to preserve or strengthen industries that produce strategic goods and materials vital to the nation's security. During periods of national emergency or war, political and military objectives may dominate over the goals of economic efficiency. Arguments against an open trading system also arise during eras of high unemployment and low plant utilization. Displaced labor and capital may find it costly and time-consuming to shift to new industries. Their demands for protection are often stated more effectively than the demands of consumers for a better range of products and lower prices. Imports that might be welcomed during periods of high employment become increasingly condemned as a main cause of domestic unemployment during periods of excess production capacity. To the average citizen, such arguments are often very appealing, even though the gains to a nation from international trade may more than outweigh the losses to particular domestic firms and workers.

WHAT MAKES A COMPANY "AMERICAN"?

During the 1980s and 1990s, many calls have been advanced for U.S. companies to revitalize their international competitiveness. But wait! What is an "American" company? Are General Motors, IBM, and Whirlpool "American" companies? What about Toyota, Honda, or Sony? Consider two hypothetical corporations. First is ABC Computers, headquartered in San Francisco. Its managers, directors, and stockholders are U.S. citizens. However, most of ABC's employees are South Korean because the firm conducts its product design and manufacturing in South Korea. Many of these computers are exported to the United States. The second firm is XYZ Computers, headquartered in Germany. Its managers, directors, and stockholders are German citizens. But most of XYZ's employees are Californians who design and manufacture computers, many of which are exported to Germany. Which of these firms is the "American" corporation? Which is more important for the U.S. economic welfare?

As Robert Reich notes,[1] we have witnessed an increasing number of corporations like ABC and XYZ as the U.S. economy has become internationalized. Reich notes that the U.S. corporation is typically perceived as the main vehicle for improving U.S. competitiveness. He speculates that most people would designate ABC Computers as the "American" corporation.

But in the 1990s, the competitiveness of U.S.-owned corporations is no longer the same as "American" competitiveness. Consider International Business Machines, Inc. More than 40 percent of IBM's employees are foreign. Its Japanese subsidiary employs more than 18,000 Japanese workers and is one of Japan's leading exporters of computers. Or consider Whirlpool, which employs more than 43,000 people

Even the Pontiac Le Mans and Boeing 767 Aren't All American

1991 Pontiac Le Mans Cost Breakdown

Country	Operation	Amount
South Korea	Assembly operations	$3,000
Japan	Advanced components (engines, transaxles)	1,850
Germany	Styling and design engineering	700
Taiwan, Japan, Singapore	Small components	400
United Kingdom	Advertising and marketing	250
Ireland and Barbados	Data processing	50
United States	Final assembly, etc.	3,750
		$10,000

SOURCE: Data from Robert Reich, "The Myth of Made in the U.S.A.," *The Wall Street Journal,* July 5, 1991.

Economic interdependence is reflected in many products that embody worldwide production. In our global economy, it is increasingly difficult to say what is a "U.S." product. Years ago, products had distinct national identities. Regardless of where products were traded, their country of origin (the name of which was generally imprinted on them) was never in doubt. But in today's world, goods are produced efficiently in many different locations and combined in all sorts of ways to fulfill buyer needs in many places. What is traded between nations is less often finished goods than research and development, management, design, marketing, advertising, and financial and legal services, as well as materials and components.

When a U.S. resident purchases a Pontiac Le Mans from General Motors, she engages in an international transaction. Of the $10,000 paid to General Motors for a 1991 Le Mans, the portion of the vehicle manufactured overseas accounted for more than $6,000; less than $4,000 was accounted for by U.S. production. The cost breakdown of the Le Mans is shown in the preceding table. The owner of the Le Mans is likely ignorant of having purchased so much from overseas. Of course, General Motors conducted the trading within its global network.

Another example of a truly international product is the Boeing 767 jet aircraft, which was first produced in 1981. Some 29 nations manufacture parts and components included in this aircraft. For example, wing parts and the nose tip are produced in Italy; the plane's rear section is produced in Canada; the front windshield and some engines are produced in the United Kingdom; the largest part of the plane, the fuselage, is produced in Japan. As for the United States, Boeing employees design the plane, manufacture its wings and cockpit, and conduct final assembly.

around the world in 45 countries. Another example is Texas Instruments, which conducts most of its research and development, product design, and manufacturing in East Asia.

Reich argues that in an economy of increasing international investment, foreign-owned XYZ Computers, with its manufacturing presence in the United States, is far more significant to U.S. economic welfare than U.S.-owned ABC Computers, with its staff of South Korean workers. Reich defines "American competitiveness" as the capacity of U.S. workers to add value to the international economy, irrespective of the nationality of the company that employs them. U.S. competitiveness is thus not the profitability or market share of U.S.-owned corporations. Indeed, the interests of U.S.-owned firms may or may not coincide with those of the U.S. population.

So who represents the United States? Reich maintains that it is represented by the U.S. work force, the people, but not necessarily the U.S.-owned corporation. U.S. ownership of a corporation is less significant for U.S. economic well-being than the training, skills, and knowledge attained by U.S. workers—workers that are increasingly hired by foreign-owned firms.

The policy implications of this view are clear. If the United States desires to revitalize its competitiveness, it must invest in people, not in nationally defined corporations. The United States must open its boundaries to foreign investors instead of favoring firms that may simply fly the U.S. flag. And government should increase investment in education, training, research, and infrastructure, so that the United States becomes a good location to set up shop for any international firm seeking talented employees.

Reich notes that, in reality, the U.S. government often does the opposite of what he advocates. Namely, it identifies national interest with the self-interest of home-based corporations. For example, in 1989 the U.S. government criticized Japan for excluding Motorola from the Tokyo market for telephone equip-

ment and speculated about retaliation. But Motorola designs and manufactures much of its telephone equipment in Kuala Lumpur. Most of the U.S. workers who manufacture telephone equipment in the United States for export to Japan are hired by Japanese-owned firms. If Reich is correct, the U.S. allegiance to a Texas Instruments or an IBM should be conditional instead of merely patriotic, just as America's affection for Toyota and Honda should be based on what they bring to the United States.

WHAT IS INTERNATIONAL COMPETITIVENESS?

By the late 1980s, Japan was widely characterized as being more competitive than Europe or the United States. But what does "more competitive" mean? And why has Japan been the leader? Does competitiveness refer to Japan's total exports? Germany's total exports are larger. Does it refer to Japan's performance in certain industries, such as steel or automobiles? If so, what criteria for performance should be used?

International competitiveness is fairly easy to define at the level of the individual firm. A *firm* is competitive if it can produce goods or services of higher quality or lower cost than its domestic and international rivals. Competitiveness is thus synonymous with a firm's long-run profit performance and its ability to compensate its employees and provide superior returns to its owners.

For a *nation*, there are many ways of defining international competitiveness. However, they all have a common factor: a nation's competitiveness depends on its ability to take advantage of opportunities in the world market. International competitiveness is the ability of a nation, under free and fair market conditions, to design, produce, and market goods and services that are better and/or cheaper than those of foreign nations. Competitiveness is fundamental to a nation's living standard and is basic to the expansion of employment opportunities and the ability to meet international obligations.

It is unlikely that all of a nation's sectors will be equally competitive in world markets. Japan, for example, is highly competitive in automobiles, while its agriculture sector experiences competitive disadvantage. A nation thus reaps benefits by expanding its most efficient industries.

Competitiveness is not a zero-sum game. Nations benefit from and depend on the economic growth of other nations. As Europe grows, it generates larger export markets for U.S. products as well as low-cost sources of supply for goods which the United States cannot produce efficiently. The United States can purchase low-cost goods from other nations and reallocate its own resources to higher-productivity uses. The objective of competitiveness is not to generate disadvantages for one's trading partners, but to enhance and better facilitate the advantages the home country has at its command.

A nation's productivity (generally expressed as output per worker hour), relative to that of other nations, is the most important determinant of international competitiveness. If a nation's productivity increases at a faster rate than the productivity of its trading partners, its per-unit costs will decrease relative to foreign per-unit costs (when measured at a constant exchange rate); the nation's competitiveness is thus enhanced. A nation can maintain its international competitiveness only if its productivity performance keeps pace with that of other nations. If a nation's productivity growth lags behind that of its trading partners, its per-unit costs rise relative to foreign unit costs, and its competitiveness declines.

Many factors affect productivity, including skills of workers and managers, investment in plant and equipment, the scale of operations, technology, management-labor relations, the organization of the workplace, and economic infrastructure. The relative importance of these factors varies for each nation and tends to change over time.

A distinction needs to be made between competitiveness resulting from internal efficiency of an enterprise (such as implementation of robotics) and competitiveness that is enhanced or impaired by national environments (such as government health/safety/environmental regulations). Moreover, some factors have an immediate effect on competitiveness (for example, labor productivity), whereas others have a longer-run effect (for example, research and development). Some factors can be influenced by entrepreneurs (for example, work rules), while others are beyond an entrepreneur's control (for example, natural resource endowments).

To what degree are national environments conducive or detrimental to the domestic and worldwide competitiveness of firms operating in those nations? Each year the *World Competitiveness Report* presents the comparative rankings of national competitiveness. As seen in Table 1.6, the ranking covers 23 industrial nations and measures 330 criteria contributing to competitiveness. These data are combined with perceptions of business executives on the competitiveness of their countries drawn from yearly surveys. Eight major categories governing competitiveness are identified: domestic economic strength, internationalization or openness, government policies, finance markets, infrastructure, management, science and technology, and people.[2] The comparative rankings for each competitiveness factor are presented in the table. The composite competitiveness ranking of the 23 industrial nations, indicated in column 1, is based on a weighted average of these factors. It comes as no surprise that in 1991 the most competitive nations were Japan, the United States, and Germany.

The fundamentals that underlie the competitiveness of the top industrial nations are widely recognized. They include a strong emphasis on good infrastructure, continuous technological flow, conservative fiscal and monetary

**T A B L E 1. 6 / *International Competitiveness Factors:*
*Comparative Rankings for 23 Industrial Nations in 1991***

Competitiveness Factor Rankings

	Composite Ranking	Domestic Economic Strength	Internationalization	Government	Finance	Infrastructure	Management	Science/Technology	People
Australia	16	17	20	14	18	4	17	18	12
Austria	6	4	10	9	10	16	9	14	6
Belgium/Lux.	11	14	6	15	8	14	6	10	14
Canada	5	10	16	6	11	2	11	17	5
Denmark	8	11	8	13	7	13	8	16	8
Finland	9	8	15	10	13	12	12	5	10
France	15	12	17	18	15	8	7	8	16
Germany	3	2	2	4	6	6	3	4	4
Greece	22	23	22	21	22	23	21	22	22
Hungary	23	22	23	23	23	22	23	21	23
Ireland	13	15	7	11	14	17	15	12	11
Italy	17	7	12	22	16	19	13	11	19
Japan	1	1	1	2	1	5	1	1	1
Netherlands	7	13	4	12	5	15	5	7	13
New Zealand	18	21	19	8	19	9	20	19	17
Norway	14	5	21	16	17	3	14	13	7
Portugal	21	20	14	17	21	21	22	20	15
Spain	19	9	13	20	20	20	18	15	21
Sweden	12	18	11	19	12	7	10	6	9
Switzerland	4	3	3	3	2	10	2	3	3
Turkey	20	19	18	5	9	18	19	23	20
United Kingdom	10	16	5	7	3	11	16	9	18
United States	2	6	9	1	4	1	4	2	2

SOURCE: International Institute for Management Development, *The World Competitiveness Report 1991*, 11th Edition (Lausanne, Switzerland: 1991), p. 165.

policy, stable sociopolitical environment, and a dynamic international orientation. A significant competitiveness determinant involves education and social values. The top competitive nations share strong educational systems that appear to place less emphasis on creating geniuses than on upscaling the average competence of the general population. Their people tend to have a system of values founded upon work, loyalty, and team spirit. An increasingly important factor is the strong linkage between mass communication and the international production processes within a nation's firms.

Since the mid-1980s, Japan has consistently been ranked as the most competitive nation in the world. In 1991 it ranked first in six of the eight competitiveness categories shown in Table 1.6. The *World Competitiveness Report* indicated that Japan's competitiveness was founded on manufacturing excellence and technology. The Japanese led the world in factory automation (including industrial robots). A labor force receptive to automation contributed to high Japanese manufacturing productivity. The Japanese also mastered the application of basic research, turning innovations into successful products at a rate without comparison elsewhere in the world; this occurred despite the fact that the United States outspent Japan in research and development. Japanese competitiveness was supported by its people, who exhibited high levels of worker motivation, good relationships with companies, a high degree of economic literacy, and strong technical skills. Japan's competitiveness has changed dramatically in recent years; many industries in which it has a leading competitive edge in the 1990s (such as semiconductors) were only small parts of its competitive portfolio two decades earlier.

The United States ranked second in the international competitiveness rankings of 1991. Among its strengths were a government policy permitting business freedom to make decisions in a market-driven economy and infrastructure, including natural resources, transportation, and information systems; contributing to U.S. competitiveness weakness were financial constraints caused by budget deficits and a relatively low national savings rate. Building on the education effect, commentators have increasingly attributed much of the large U.S. trade deficit (excess of imports over exports) to the fact that U.S. workers cannot compete with their Northern European and Japanese counterparts on the

factory floor. It is widely agreed that the U.S. literacy rate is significantly lower than that of Japan. Moreover, Pacific Rim students typically outperform U.S. students on international science and mathematics achievement tests. As jobs in the international trade area require increasing levels of basic literacy and technological know-how, the educational handicap soon translates into competitive handicap.

If Japan's international competitiveness is so strong, as Table 1.6 suggests, then why doesn't Japan produce all the chemicals, transportation equipment, machinery, and food it wants so that the Japanese would not have to buy these goods from the United States? The answer is that nations have different quantities and qualities of economic resources and different ways of combining them; each nation can thus produce certain products at relatively lower costs than others. As long as *relative (comparative)* production costs of two goods differ in two countries, there are gains to be made from specialization and trade. This principle is the famous *law of comparative advantage*, which will be discussed in the next chapter.

THE PLAN OF THIS BOOK

This book examines the functioning of the international economy. Although it emphasizes the theoretical principles that govern international trade, it also gives considerable coverage to empirical evidence of world trade patterns and to trade policies of the industrial and developing nations. The book is divided into two major parts. Part I deals with international trade and commercial policy, whereas Part II stresses the balance of payments and adjustment in the balance of payments.

Chapters 2–4 deal with the theory of comparative advantage, as well as theoretical extensions and empirical tests of this model. This topic is followed by a treatment of tariffs, nontariff trade barriers, and contemporary trade policies of the United States in Chapters 5–7. Discussion of trade policies for the developing nations, preferential trading arrangements, and international factor movements in Chapters 8–10 completes the first part of the text.

The treatment of international financial relations begins with an overview of the balance of payments, the foreign-exchange market, and exchange-rate determination in Chapters 11–13. Balance-of-payments adjustment under alternate exchange-rate regimes is discussed in Chapters 14–16. Chapter 17 considers international economic policy, and Chapter 18 analyzes the international banking system.

SUMMARY

1. Throughout the post–World War II era, the world economies have become increasingly interdependent in terms of the movement of goods and services, business enterprise, capital, and technology.
2. The United States has seen growing interdependence with the rest of the world in its trade sector, financial markets, ownership of production facilities, and labor force.
3. Largely owing to the vastness and wide diversity of its economy, the United States remains among the countries for which exports constitute a small fraction of national output.
4. Proponents of an open trading system contend that international trade results in higher levels of consumption and investment, lower prices of commodities, and a wider range of product choices for consumers. Arguments against free trade tend to be voiced during periods of excess production capacity and high unemployment.

STUDY QUESTIONS

1. What factors explain why the world's trading nations have become increasingly interdependent, from an economic and political viewpoint, during the post–World War II era?
2. What are some of the major arguments for and against an open trading system?
3. What significance does growing economic interdependence have for a country like the United States?
4. What factors influence the rate of growth in the volume of world trade?

Part One

International Trade Relations

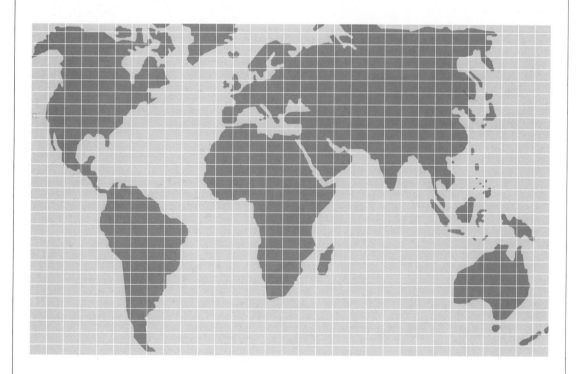

Foundations of Modern Trade Theory

Modern trade theory seeks to answer the following questions: (1) What constitutes the **basis for trade**—that is, why do nations export and import certain products? (2) At what **terms of trade** (relative prices) are products exchanged in the world market? (3) What are the **gains from international trade** in terms of production and consumption? This chapter addresses these questions, first by summarizing the historical development of modern trade theory and next by presenting the contemporary theoretical principles used in analyzing the effects of international trade.

HISTORICAL DEVELOPMENT OF MODERN TRADE THEORY

Modern trade theory is the product of an evolution of ideas in economic thought. In particular, the writings of the mercantilists, Adam Smith, and David Ricardo have been instrumental in providing the framework of modern trade theory.

The Mercantilists

During the period 1500–1800, a group of writers appeared in Europe who were concerned with the process of nation building. According to the **mercantilists**, the central question was how a nation could regulate its domestic and international affairs so as to promote its own interests. The solution lay in a strong foreign-trade sector. If a country could achieve a *favorable trade balance* (a surplus of exports over imports), it would enjoy payments received from the rest of the world in the form of gold and silver. Such revenues would contribute to increased spending and a rise in domestic output and employment. To promote a favorable trade balance, the mercantilists advocated government regulation of trade. Tariffs, quotas, and other commercial policies were proposed by the mercantilists to minimize imports in order to protect a nation's trade position.[1]

By the eighteenth century, the economic policies of the mercantilists were under strong attack. According to David Hume's **price-specie-flow doctrine**, a favorable trade balance was possible only in the short run, for over time it would automatically be eliminated. To illustrate, suppose England were to achieve a trade surplus that resulted in an inflow of gold and silver. Because these precious metals would constitute part of England's money supply, their inflow would increase the amount of money in circulation. This would lead to a rise in England's price level relative to that of its trading partners. English residents would therefore be encouraged to purchase foreign-produced goods, while England's exports would decline. As a result, the country's trade surplus would eventually be eliminated. The Hume price-specie-flow mechanism thus showed that mercantilist policies could provide at best only short-term economic advantages.[2]

The mercantilists were also attacked for their *static view* of the world economy. To the mercantilists, the world's economic pie was of constant size. This meant that one nation's gains from trade came at the expense of its trading partners; not all nations could simultaneously enjoy the benefits of international trade. This view was challenged with the publication of Adam Smith's *Wealth of Nations* in 1776. According to Smith, the world's economic pie is not a fixed quantity. International trade permits nations to take advantage of specialization and the division of labor, which increase the general level of productivity within a country and thus increase world output. Smith's dynamic view of trade suggested that *both* trading partners could simultaneously enjoy higher levels of production and consumption with free trade. Although the mercantilists' view of regulated trade has been subject to attacks by free-trade proponents, their policies are certainly in evidence today. This topic is discussed in Chapters 5 and 6.

Why Nations Trade: Absolute Advantage

The next stage in the development of modern trade theory is found in the writings of the classical economist Adam Smith. Smith was a leading advocate of **free trade** (open markets) on the grounds that it promoted the international division of labor. With free trade, nations could concentrate their production on goods they could make most cheaply, with all the consequent benefits of the division of labor.

Accepting the idea that *cost differences* govern the movement of goods among nations, Smith sought to explain why costs differ among nations. Smith maintained that *productivities* of factor inputs represent the major determinant of production cost. Such productivities are based on natural and acquired advantages. The former include factors relating to climate, soil, and mineral wealth, whereas the latter include special skills and techniques. Given a natural or acquired advantage in the production of a good, Smith reasoned that a nation would produce that good at lower cost, becoming more competitive than its trading partner. Smith thus viewed the determination of competitive advantage from the *supply side* of the market.[3]

TABLE 2. 1 / *A Case of Absolute Advantage When Each Nation Is More Efficient in the Production of One Good*

Nation	Output per Labor Hour	
	Wine	Cloth
United States	5 bottles	20 yards
United Kingdom	15 bottles	10 yards

Adam Smith's concept of cost was founded upon the **labor theory of value,** which asserted that within each nation, (1) labor is the only factor of production and is homogeneous (of one quality), and (2) the cost or price of a good depends exclusively upon the amount of labor required to produce it. For example, if the United States uses less labor to manufacture a yard of cloth than the United Kingdom, U.S. production cost will be lower.

Smith's trading principle was the **principle of absolute advantage:** in a two-nation, two-product world, international trade and specialization will be beneficial when one nation has an absolute cost advantage (that is, uses less labor to produce a unit of output) in one good and the other nation has an absolute cost advantage in the other good. For the world to benefit from international division of labor, each nation must have a good that it is absolutely more efficient in producing than its trading partner. A nation will *import* those goods in which it has an absolute cost *disadvantage;* it will *export* those goods in which it has an absolute cost *advantage.*

An arithmetic example helps illustrate the principle of absolute advantage. Referring to Table 2.1, suppose workers in the United States can produce 5 bottles of wine or 20 yards of cloth in an hour's time, while workers in the United Kingdom can produce 15 bottles of

wine or 10 yards of cloth in an hour's time. Clearly, the United States has an absolute advantage in cloth production; its cloth workers' productivity (output per worker hour) is higher than that of the United Kingdom, which leads to lower costs (less labor required to produce a yard of cloth). In like manner, the United Kingdom has an absolute advantage in wine production.

According to Smith, each nation benefits by specializing in the production of the good which it can produce at a lower cost than the other nation, while importing the good it produces at a higher cost. Because the world uses its resources more efficiently as the result of specializing according to the principle of absolute advantage, there occurs an increase in world output which is distributed to the two nations through trade.

Why Nations Trade: Comparative Advantage

According to Adam Smith, mutually beneficial trade required that each nation be the *least-cost producer* of at least one good that it could export to its trading partner. But what if a nation is more efficient than its trading partner in the production of *all* goods? Dissatisfied with this looseness in Smith's theory, David Ricardo (1772–1823) developed a principle to show that mutually beneficial trade could occur when one nation was absolutely more efficient in the production of all goods.[4]

Like Smith, Ricardo emphasized the supply side of the market. The immediate basis for trade stemmed from cost differences between nations, which were underlaid by their natural and acquired advantages. Unlike Smith, who emphasized the importance of absolute cost differences among nations, Ricardo emphasized *comparative* (relative) cost differences. Ricardo's trade theory thus became known as the **principle of comparative advantage.**

According to Ricardo's comparative-advantage principle, even if a nation has an

Do Rising Health-Care Costs Lead to Competitive Disadvantage?

Ford Motor Company 1989 Health-Care Costs per Individual Employee: Ford U.S. Compared with Ford Foreign Subsidiaries

Ford's Assembly Plant Location	Total Health-Care Cost per Employee	Total Health-Care Cost as a Percentage of Payroll
United States	$4,532	17%
Canada	1,856	6
Belgium	1,673	8
Germany	1,582	4
France	1,231	5
Mexico	516	3
United Kingdom	190	1

NOTE: These figures exclude health-care payments funded from general tax revenues. Thus, the higher per-contract health-care costs in the United States are offset to some extent by lower tax rates on U.S. corporations and individuals.

SOURCE: Ford Motor Company, as found in Harvard Business School case study N9-792-015, January 15, 1992.

In the 1980s and 1990s, U.S. manufacturers increasingly maintained that rising U.S. health costs adversely affected their international competitiveness. Chrysler corporation has been one of the most vocal proponents of the linkage between health-care costs and competitive disadvantage. In 1992, Chrysler contended that its direct health-care expenditures for employees and dependents added approximately $1,000 to the cost of a Chrysler vehicle produced in the United States, whereas competitors in other nations did not have such high costs. Similarly, calculations made by Ford Motor Company concluded that the firm's health-care costs in the United States accounted for 17 percent of its total payroll, while the comparable figures for its foreign subsidiaries were substantially less, as seen in the table above.

Why don't firms, such as Chrysler or Ford,

absolute cost disadvantage in the production of *both* goods, a basis for mutually beneficial trade may still exist. The *less efficient* nation should specialize in and export the good in which it is relatively less inefficient (where its absolute disadvantage is least)! The *more efficient* nation should specialize in and export that good in which it is relatively more efficient (where its absolute advantage is greatest)!

To demonstrate the principle of comparative advantage, Ricardo formulated a simplified model based on the following assumptions: (1) only two nations and two products; (2) free trade; (3) product quality does not vary among nations; (4) in each nation, labor is the only factor of production and is homogeneous (the labor theory of value); (5) labor can move freely within a nation, but is incapable of moving simply add rising health-care costs to the prices of their products? In many cases, they do. But if a product is manufactured in more than one nation and has a global price, this may not be feasible—especially if foreign competitors are not burdened by the same increases in direct health-care costs. U.S. industry leaders have contended that rising health-care costs hinder the U.S. ability to produce competitively priced products. This is especially true for large U.S. companies that pay sizable health benefits per employee, compared to small U.S. companies that do not.

The Big Three auto producers of the United States have maintained that Japanese companies with plants in the United States have lower health and pension costs because they employee a younger work force. In 1993, the Big Three suggested that the U.S. government should levy a tax on autos sold in the United States, with the proceeds going to defray Big Three health and pension costs.

There are those who disagree with the linkage between a firm's direct health-care costs and its competitiveness. They maintain that all nations somehow finance health care for their labor force and overall population; to assert that British, German, or Japanese auto companies have no health-care costs is incorrect. Their health costs are simply financed differently (governmental systems financed by taxes)

than in the United States (private-sector financing). Moreover, the price of labor as a factor of production must be viewed in terms of an employee's total compensation, including both cash wages and fringe benefits. The mix of cash wages and fringe benefits is negotiable between management and labor; to blame one component of total compensation (health-care costs) as the factor causing competitive disadvantage is incorrect.

Economists at the University of Pennsylvania have analyzed the relationship between U.S. health-care costs and competitiveness. They found the impact of increasing health-benefit costs on total compensation, and thus on prices and trade flows, to be positive, but quite small in magnitude. For example, U.S. import volume in the 1980s rose by 125 percent, but only 0.14 percent could be explained by rising health-benefit costs. During this same period, U.S. export volume rose by 75 percent, although health-care costs accounted for a negative influence of 0.16 percent.

Source: "Do U.S. Health Care Costs Affect U.S. International Competitiveness?" U.S. International Trade Commission. *Industry Trade and Technology Review*, October 1992; pp. 15–20. See also David Brailer et. al, "Study Project on Health Care Reform and American Competitiveness," The Wharton School of the University of Pennsylvania, November 8, 1991.

between nations; (6) costs do not vary with the level of production and are proportional to the amount of labor used; (7) no technological change; (8) no transportation costs; (9) perfect competition in all markets.

Table 2.2 illustrates Ricardo's comparative-advantage principle when one nation has an absolute advantage in the production of both commodities. Assume that in one hour's time U.S. workers can produce 40 bottles of

wine or 40 yards of cloth, while U.K. workers can produce 20 bottles of wine or 10 yards of cloth. According to Smith's principle of absolute advantage, there is no basis for mutually beneficial specialization and trade, because the United States is more efficient in the production of both goods.

Ricardo's principle of comparative advantage, however, recognizes that the United States is four times as efficient in cloth production

TABLE 2. 2 / *A Case of Comparative Advantage When the United States Has an Absolute Advantage in the Production of Both Goods*

Nation	Output per Labor Hour	
	Wine	Cloth
United States	40 bottles	40 yards
United Kingdom	20 bottles	10 yards

(40 / 10 = 4) but only twice as efficient in wine production (40 / 20 = 2). The United States thus has a *greater absolute advantage* in cloth than in wine, while the United Kingdom has a *lesser absolute disadvantage* in wine than in cloth. Each nation specializes in and exports that good in which it has a comparative advantage—the United States in cloth, the United Kingdom in wine. The output gains from specialization will be distributed to the two nations through trade.

Concerning U.S. trade patterns during the 1980s and 1990s, in which the United States realized large trade deficits (imports exceeded exports) with Japan, some doomsdayers appeared to believe that Japan could outproduce the United States in virtually everything. Those who foresaw a flood of imports from Japan causing the United States to deindustrialize and become a nation of fast-food restaurants seemed to be suggesting that the United States did not have a comparative advantage in anything.

It is possible for a nation not to have an absolute advantage in anything; but it is not possible for one nation to have a comparative advantage in everything and the other nation to have a comparative advantage in nothing. That's because comparative advantage depends on *relative* costs. As we have seen, a nation having an absolute disadvantage in all goods would find it advantageous to specialize in the production of the good in which its absolute disadvantage is *least!* There is no reason for the United States to surrender and let Japan produce all of everything. The United States would lose, and so would Japan, because world output would be reduced if U.S. resources were left idle. The idea that a nation has nothing to offer confuses absolute advantage and comparative advantage.

Comparative Advantage in Money Terms

Although Ricardo's comparative-advantage principle is used to explain international trade patterns, people are not generally concerned with which nation has a comparative advantage when they purchase something. A person at a candy store does not look at Swiss chocolate and U.S. chocolate and say, "I wonder which nation has the comparative advantage in chocolate production?" The buyer relies on price, after allowing for quality differences, to tell which nation has the comparative advantage. It is helpful, then, to illustrate how the principle of comparative advantage works in terms of money prices.

Refer again to the Ricardian comparative-advantage example of Table 2.2, which assumes that labor is the only input and is homogeneous. Recall that (1) the United States has an absolute advantage in the production of both cloth and wine; and (2) the United States has a comparative advantage in cloth production, while the United Kingdom has a comparative advantage in wine production. This information is restated in Table 2.3. As we shall see, even though the United Kingdom is absolutely less efficient in producing both goods, it will export wine (the product of its comparative advantage) when its money wages are sufficiently lower than those of the United States so as to make wine cheaper in the United Kingdom! Let us see how this works.

Suppose the wage rate is $20 per hour in the United States, as indicated in Table 2.3. If U.S. workers can produce 40 yards of cloth in an hour, the average cost of producing a yard of

T A B L E 2. 3 / Ricardo's Comparative Advantage Principle Expressed in Money Prices

Nation	Labor Input	Hourly Wage Rate	Cloth (yards)		Wine (bottles)	
			Quantity	Price	Quantity	Price
U.S.	1 hour	$20	40	$0.50	40	$0.50
U.K.	1 hour	£5	10	£0.5	20	£0.25
U.K*	1 hour	$8	10	$0.80	20	$0.40

* Dollar prices of cloth and wine, when the prevailing exchange rate is $1.60 = £1.

cloth is $0.50 ($20 / 40 yards = $0.50 per yard); similarly, the average cost of producing a bottle of wine in the United States is $0.50. Because Ricardian theory assumes that markets are perfectly competitive, in the long run a product's price equals its average cost of production. The prices of cloth and wine produced in the United States are shown in the table.

Suppose now that the wage rate in the United Kingdom is 5 pounds (£5) per hour. Again, the average cost (price) of producing a yard of cloth in the United Kingdom is £0.50 (£5 / 10 yards = £0.50 per yard), and the average cost (price) of producing a bottle of wine is £0.25. The prices, in pounds, of U.K. cloth and wine are indicated in Table 2.3.

Is cloth less expensive in the United States or the United Kingdom? In which nation is wine less expensive? When U.S. prices are expressed in dollars and U.K. prices are expressed in pounds, we cannot answer this question. We must therefore express all prices in terms of one currency—say, the dollar. To do this, we must know the prevailing *exchange rate* at which the pound and dollar trade for each other.

Suppose the dollar/pound exchange rate is $1.60 = £1. In Table 2.3, we see that the U.K. hourly wage rate (£5) is equivalent to $8 at this exchange rate (£5 × $1.60 = $8). The average

dollar cost of producing a yard of cloth in the United Kingdom is $0.80 ($8 / 10 yards = $0.80 per yard), while the average dollar cost of producing a bottle of wine is $0.40 ($8 / 20 bottles = $0.40 per bottle). Compared to the costs of producing these products in the United States, we see that the United Kingdom has lower costs in wine production but higher costs in cloth production. The United Kingdom thus has a comparative advantage in wine!

We conclude that even though the United Kingdom is not as efficient as the United States in the production of wine (or cloth), its lower wage rate (in terms of dollars) more than compensates for its inefficiency. At this wage rate, the U.K. average (dollar) cost of producing wine is less than the U.S. average cost. With perfectly competitive markets, the U.K. selling price is lower than the U.S. selling price, and the United Kingdom exports wine to the United States.

INTERNATIONAL COMPETITIVENESS: AUTOS AND STEEL

In the news media, international trade is characterized as a race for competitiveness in which firms strive to minimize production costs.

Recall that Adam Smith and David Ricardo emphasized labor cost as a determinant of competitiveness. Material cost, depreciation expense, and interest expense are other costs of production. Consider the following international cost comparisons for auto and steel manufacturers.

Auto Manufacturing Costs

From the 1950s to the 1990s, the Big Three auto firms of the United States (General Motors, Ford, and Chrysler) saw their position in the North American market steadily diminish. This trend accelerated in the late 1970s as Japanese firms moved aggressively to increase their market share, first by exporting and then by assembling autos in their own plants in North America. These actions resulted in plant closures, decreased market share, and reduction in production levels for U.S. firms.

Throughout this era, the Big Three were plagued by problems such as poor fuel economy, poor quality, poor customer service, high interest rates, and domestic economic recession. What's more, the Big Three had significant material and parts, labor, capital, and productivity cost disadvantages. Industry analysts estimated that the Big Three faced an average cost disadvantage of more than $2,000 per car compared to their Japanese competitors in 1982. Indeed, observers contended that the Big Three had become a classic example of how not to do things.

Nothing remains constant, of course. During the 1980s and 1990s, both U.S. and Japanese firms realized productivity gains, and there were changes in many cost factors. As seen in Table 2.4, by 1992 the competitiveness of the Big Three had greatly improved.

Comparing production costs on a current operating basis, the Big Three had become world-class competitors. Although the Big Three had higher labor costs than Japanese producers, their parts and components were the least expensive in the world; to hold costs down, Ford and Chrysler sourced much of their parts production abroad and built cooperative, longer-term relationships with parts suppliers. As a result, Ford became the low-cost manufacturer of autos in 1992. It maintained a $527 per car advantage over Toyota, who was widely regarded to be the best of the Japanese; moreover, Ford had a $990 advantage over the average Japanese manufacturer.

Although the Big Three could compete in terms of running ongoing operations, they faced cost disadvantages in other areas. (1) Big Three capacity utilization in 1992 averaged 80 percent versus 93 percent in Japan; lower levels of capacity utilization resulted in a cost disadvantage that averaged $400 per car for the Big Three. (2) Loss of market share to imports resulted in plant closures and massive layoffs in the United States. However, pensions, health care, and unemployed worker benefits had to be paid. With fewer active workers and fewer units of production over which to spread the burden, these "adjustment costs" penalized the Big Three by $600 per car. (3) Relatively high costs of capital burdened the Big Three by $325 per car. These cost disadvantages neutralized the operating cost advantages of the Big Three; General Motors, in particular, faced a sizable competitive disadvantage.

Steel Manufacturing Costs

During the 1960s and 1970s, the relatively low production costs of foreign steelmakers encouraged their participation in the U.S. market. In 1982, the average cost per ton of steel for integrated U.S. producers was $685 per ton—52 percent higher than for Japanese producers, the highest of the Pacific Rim steelmakers. This cost differential was largely due to a strong U.S. dollar and higher domestic costs of labor and raw materials, which accounted for 25 percent and 45 percent, respectively, of total cost. Moreover, domestic operating rates were relatively

T A B L E 2. 4 / Comparison of U.S. and Japanese Production Costs for a Small Car, 1992

	Average U.S. Firm	Average Japanese Firm
CURRENT OPERATING COST		
Labor Costs		
Wage rate/hour	$18.76	$21.72
Benefits/hour	$13.21	$4.06
Total compensation/hour	$31.97	$25.78
Labor hours per car	64	42
Total labor costs*	$2,046	$1,083
Components and materials	$4,202	$4,818
Other manufacturing costs	$1,188	$1,412
Total production cost	$7,436	$7,313
OTHER COSTS (e.g., interest, depreciation)	$1,617	$226
TOTAL COST**	$9,053	$7,539

* The product of labor-hours-per-car times total-compensation-per-hour.

** For U.S. firms, the total cost of producing a small auto in 1992 was: Ford, $7,558; General Motors, $10,353; Chrysler, $8,173. For Japanese firms, the total cost of producing a small auto was: Honda, $7,592; Mazda, $7,658; Nissan, $7,772; Toyota, $6,990.

SOURCE: C. Prestowitz and P. Wilen, *The Future of the Auto Industry: It Can Compete, Can It Survive?* (Washington, D.C.: Economic Strategy Institute, 1992), pp. 16, 21.

low, resulting in high fixed costs of production for each ton of steel.

The cost disadvantage encouraged U.S. steelmakers to initiate measures to reduce production costs and regain competitiveness. Many steel companies closed obsolete and costly steel mills, coking facilities, and ore mines. They also negotiated long-term contracts permitting materials, electricity, and natural gas to be obtained at lower prices. Labor contracts were also renegotiated, with a 20 to 40 percent improvement in labor productivity.

By the early 1990s, the U.S. steel industry had substantially reduced its cost of producing a ton of steel, as seen in Table 2.5. U.S. steelworker productivity was estimated to be higher than that of most foreign competitors, a factor that enhanced U.S. competitiveness. But semi-industrializing nations, such as South Korea and Brazil, had labor cost advantages because of lower wages and other employee costs. Overall, the cost disadvantage of U.S. steel companies narrowed considerably from the 1980s to the 1990s.

Transformation Schedules

David Ricardo's law of comparative advantage suggested that specialization and trade can lead to gains for both nations when comparative advantage exists. His theory, however, depended on the restrictive assumption of the labor theory of value, in which labor was

T A B L E 2. 5 / *Cost per Ton of Steel, March 1993*

Cost Components	United States	Japan	South Korea	Brazil
Labor cost				
LH/ton*	5.1	5.1	7.5	9.2
Employee cost/hour	$30.0	$30.0	$12.0	$8.0
Labor cost**	$153	$153	$90	$74
Material costs	$320	$322	$294	$329
Depreciation expense	$26	$76	$112	$83
Interest expense	$15	$22	$15	$52
Total cost/ton	$514	$573	$511	$538

* LH refers to labor hours.

** The product of LH/ton times employee cost/hour; labor cost has been rounded off.

SOURCE: Data from Peter F. Marcus and Karlis M. Kirsis, "World Steel Dynamics," *Cost Monitor #15*, March 1993. See also U.S. International Trade Commission, *Steel: Semiannual Monitoring Report*, various issues.

assumed to be the only factor input. In practice, however, labor is only one of several factor inputs.

Recognizing the shortcomings of the labor theory of value, modern trade theory provides a more generalized theory of comparative advantage. It explains the theory using a **transformation schedule**, also called a **production possibilities schedule**.[5] This schedule shows various alternative combinations of two goods that a nation can produce when *all* of its factor inputs (land, labor, capital, entrepreneurship) are used in their most efficient manner. The transformation schedule thus illustrates the maximum output possibilities of a nation. Note that we are no longer assuming labor to be the only factor input as did Ricardo!

Figure 2.1 illustrates a hypothetical transformation schedule for the United States. By fully using all available inputs with the best available technology during a given time period, the United States could produce either 60 bushels of wheat or 120 autos or certain combinations of the two commodities.

Just how does a transformation schedule illustrate the comparative-cost concept? The answer lies in the transformation schedule's slope, which is referred to as the **marginal rate of transformation** (*MRT*). The *MRT* shows the amount of one product a nation must sacrifice to get one additional unit of the other product:

$$MRT = \frac{\Delta \text{ Wheat}}{\Delta \text{ Autos}}$$

This rate of sacrifice is sometimes called the *opportunity cost* of the product. Because this formula also refers to the slope of the transformation schedule, the *MRT* equals the absolute value of the transformation schedule's slope.

In Figure 2.1, the *MRT* of wheat into autos gives the amount of wheat that must be sacrificed for each additional auto produced. Movement from point *A* to point *B* along the trans-

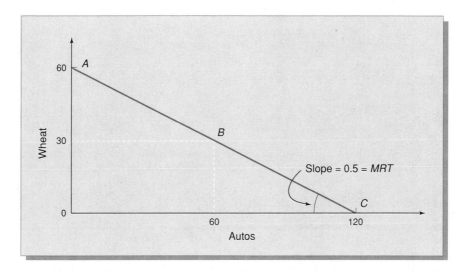

F I G U R E 2. 1 Transformation schedule. A transformation schedule (production possibilities schedule) illustrates the maximum output possibilities for a nation. It assumes that a nation utilizes all available resources with the available technology. The slope of a transformation schedule indicates the opportunity cost of producing a particular good.

formation schedule shows that the comparative cost of producing 60 additional autos is the sacrifice of 30 bushels of wheat. This means that the opportunity cost of each auto produced is ½ bushel of wheat sacrificed—that is, the $MRT = ½$.

TRADING UNDER CONSTANT-COST CONDITIONS

This section illustrates the principle of comparative advantage assuming **constant opportunity costs.** Although the constant-cost case may be of limited relevance to the real world, it serves as a useful pedagogical tool for analyzing international trade. The discussion focuses on two questions. First, what is the *basis for trade* and the *direction of trade?* Second, what are the potential *gains from free trade,* for a single nation and for the world as a whole?

Constant Costs

In Figure 2.2, the hypothetical transformation schedules for the United States and Canada illustrate the capacities of these nations to produce two commodities, autos and wheat. If the United States fully used all of its resources in the most efficient manner possible, it could produce a maximum of 60 bushels of wheat or 120 autos or any combination in between along its transformation schedule. Canada, on the other hand, could produce 160 bushels of wheat or 80 autos or some combination in between, if it used all of its factor inputs in the most efficient way. Note that in this example the transformation schedules for both countries are drawn as *straight lines* because we are assuming constant-cost conditions. Constant opportunity costs suggest that the relative cost of one product in terms of the other will remain the same, no matter where a nation chooses to locate on

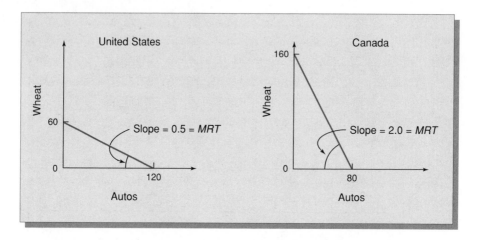

F I G U R E 2. 2   *Transformation schedules: constant opportunity costs.* Given constant opportunity-cost conditions, the relative cost of producing one good in terms of the other good remains the same, no matter where a nation chooses to locate along its transformation schedule. Constant opportunity costs lead to linear transformation schedules.

its transformation schedule. In Figure 2.2, we can see that for the United States, the relative cost of each auto produced is ½ bushel of wheat. For Canada, the relative cost of producing each additional auto is 2 bushels of wheat.

There are two explanations of constant costs. First, the factors of production are perfect substitutes for each other. Second, all units of a given factor are of the same quality. As a country transfers resources from the production of wheat into the production of autos, or vice versa, the country will not have to resort to resources that are less well suited for the production of the commodity. Therefore, the country must sacrifice exactly the same amount of wheat for each additional auto produced, regardless of how many autos it is already producing.

The constant-cost concept can also be illustrated in terms of a *supply schedule*. Remember that the law of supply reasons that a producer's supply price rises as the producer offers more of the commodity for sale on the market. This means that the supply schedule slopes upward from the quantity axis. The factor

underlying the law of supply is the tendency for marginal production costs to increase as the level of output rises. But what if a producer faces constant-cost conditions? What then would be the shape of the supply schedule?

Based on the transformation schedules in Figure 2.2, Figure 2.3 illustrates the supply schedules of autos and wheat for the United States and Canada. Note that on the vertical axes, the prices of the commodities are measured in opportunity-cost terms rather than in monetary terms. The transformation schedules of the two countries suggest that the relative price of producing each extra auto is ½ bushel of wheat for the United States, whereas it is 2 bushels of wheat for Canada. Because constant-cost conditions imply that these prices (costs) do not change with the level of production, the supply schedules of autos are drawn as *horizontal* lines at the respective supply prices. Wheat production provides similar results. The production conditions are such that the relative price of producing an extra bushel of wheat is 2 autos for the United States and ½ auto for Canada.

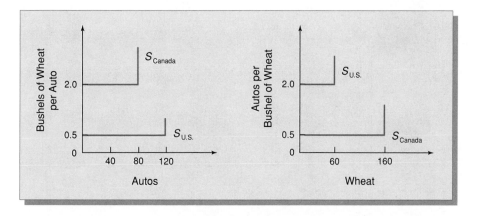

F I G U R E 2. 3 *Supply schedules: constant opportunity costs.* With constant opportunity costs, a product's supply schedule is drawn horizontally at its supply price, suggesting that unit costs do not change with the level of output. There are two explanations for constant opportunity costs: (1) resources are perfect substitutes for each other; (2) all units of a given resource are of the same quality. The vertical portion of the supply schedule of autos (wheat) corresponds to the endpoint of the transformation schedule of Figure 2.2, where all resources are devoted to auto (wheat) production.

The Basis for Trade and Direction of Trade

In **autarky** (the absence of trade), a country's transformation schedule represents the possible points along which its *production* as well as *consumption* will occur. This is because a country can consume only that combination of goods that it can produce. Based on Figure 2.2, Figure 2.4 depicts the output possibilities of the United States and Canada under constant-cost conditions. Assume that the United States prefers to produce and consume at point *A* on its transformation schedule, with 40 autos and 40 bushels of wheat. Assume also that Canada produces and consumes at point *A'* on its transformation schedule, with 40 autos and 80 bushels of wheat. The *slopes* of the two countries' linear transformation schedules give the *relative cost* of one product in terms of the other. The relative cost of producing an additional auto is only ½ bushel of wheat for the United States but is 2 bushels of wheat for Canada. According to the principle of compar-

ative advantage, this situation provides a basis for mutually favorable trade owing to the differences in the countries' relative costs. As for the direction of trade, we find the United States specializing in and exporting autos and Canada specializing in and exporting wheat.

Production Gains from Specialization

The law of comparative advantage asserts that with trade, each country will find it favorable to specialize in the production of the commodity of its comparative advantage and will trade part of this for the commodity of its comparative disadvantage. In Figure 2.4, the United States moves from production point *A* to production point *B*, totally specializing in auto production. Canada totally specializes in wheat production by moving from production point *A'* to production point *B'*. Taking advantage of specialization can result in **production gains** for both countries.

Looking at Figure 2.4, we find that in autarky, the United States produces 40 autos and 40 bushels of wheat. But with complete

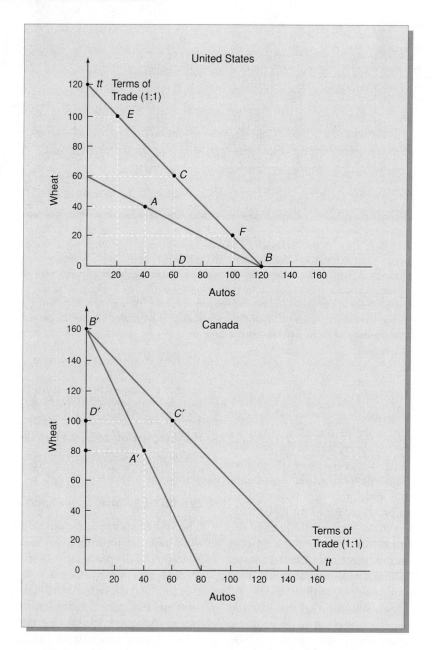

F I G U R E 2. 4 *Trading under constant opportunity costs.* With constant opportunity costs, a nation will specialize in the product of its comparative advantage. The principle of comparative advantage implies that with specialization and free trade, a nation enjoys production gains and consumption gains. A nation's trade triangle denotes its exports, imports, and terms of trade. In a two-nation, two-product world, the trade triangle of one nation equals that of the other nation; one nation's exports equal the other nation's imports, and there is one equilibrium terms of trade.

T A B L E 2. 6 / Production Gains from Specialization: Constant Opportunity Costs

	Before Specialization		After Specialization		Net Gain (Loss)	
	Autos	*Wheat*	*Autos*	*Wheat*	*Autos*	*Wheat*
United States	40	40	120	0	80	-40
Canada	40	80	0	160	-40	80
World	80	120	120	160	40	40

specialization, the United States produces 120 autos and no wheat. As for Canada, its production point in autarky is at 40 autos and 80 bushels of wheat, whereas its production point under complete specialization is at 160 bushels of wheat and no autos. Combining these results, we find that both nations together have experienced a net production gain of 40 autos and 40 bushels of wheat under conditions of complete specialization. Table 2.6 summarizes these production gains.

Consumption Gains from Trade

In autarky, the consumption alternatives of the United States and Canada are limited to points *along* their domestic transformation schedules. The exact consumption point for each nation will be determined by the tastes and preferences in each country. But with specialization and free trade, two nations can achieve posttrade consumption points *outside* their domestic transformation schedules. Clearly, this would be a more desirable consumption point than that attainable without trade.

The set of posttrade consumption points that a nation can achieve is determined by the rate at which its export product is traded for the other country's export product. This rate is known as the **terms of trade**. The terms of trade defines the relative prices at which two products are traded in the marketplace.

Under constant cost conditions, the slope of the transformation schedule defines the domestic rate of transformation (domestic terms of trade), which represents the relative prices at which two commodities can be exchanged at home. For a country to consume at some point *outside* its transformation schedule, it must be able to exchange its export good internationally at a terms of trade more favorable than the domestic terms of trade.

Assume that the United States and Canada achieve a terms-of-trade ratio that permits both trading partners to consume at some point outside their respective transformation schedules (Figure 2.4). Suppose that the terms of trade agreed on is a 1:1 ratio, whereby 1 auto is exchanged for 1 bushel of wheat. Based on these conditions, let line *tt* represent the international terms of trade for both countries (note that the terms-of-trade line is drawn with a slope having an absolute value of 1).

Suppose now that the United States decides to export, say, 60 autos to Canada. Starting at postspecialization production point *B*, the United States will slide along its international terms-of-trade line until point *C* is reached. At point *C*, 60 autos will have been exchanged for 60 bushels of wheat, at the terms-of-trade ratio of 1:1. Point *C* then represents the U.S. *posttrade consumption point*. Compared with autarky consumption point *A*, point *C* results in a *net consumption gain* for the United States

TABLE 2.7 / Consumption Gains from Trade: Constant Opportunity Costs

	Before Trade		After Trade		Net Gain (Loss)	
	Autos	Wheat	Autos	Wheat	Autos	Wheat
United States	40	40	60	60	20	20
Canada	40	80	60	100	20	20
World	80	120	120	160	40	40

of 20 autos and 20 bushels of wheat. The triangle *BCD* showing the U.S. exports (along the horizontal axis), imports (along the vertical axis), and terms of trade (the slope) is referred to as the **trade triangle**.

Does this trading situation provide favorable results for Canada? Starting at postspecialization production point *B'*, Canada can import 60 autos from the United States by giving up 60 bushels of wheat. Canada would slide along its international terms-of-trade line until it reached point *C'*. Clearly, this is a more favorable consumption point than autarky point *A'*. With free trade, Canada experiences a net consumption gain of 20 autos and 20 bushels of wheat. Canada's trade triangle is denoted by *B'C'D'*. Note that in our two-country model, the trade triangles of the United States and Canada are identical; one country's exports equal the other country's imports, which are exchanged at the equilibrium terms of trade. Table 2.7 summarizes the consumption gains from trade for each country and the world as a whole.

Distributing the Gains from Trade

The preceding example assumed that the terms of trade agreed to by the United States and Canada resulted in both trading partners' benefiting from trade; both were able to achieve posttrade consumption points outside their domestic transformation schedules. Note that the consumption gains from trade are not always distributed equally between countries.

The closer the international terms-of-trade line is located to the U.S. transformation schedule, the smaller are the U.S. consumption gains from trade. At the extreme, if the international terms of trade were to coincide with the U.S. domestic rate of transformation, the United States would not realize any gains from trade. This is because the U.S. posttrade consumption point would lie along its transformation schedule. The United States could not achieve a higher level of consumption with trade than could be attained in the absence of trade; it would no longer desire to trade with Canada! The same reasoning also applies to Canada.

The domestic transformation rates of the United States and Canada clearly represent the *limits* within which the international terms of trade must fall. But where will the international terms of trade ultimately fall? As we explain in the next chapter, the actual location depends on the relative demand of the two nations for the products in question.

Complete Specialization

One implication of the foregoing trading example was that the United States totally specialized in auto production, whereas Canada produced only wheat. To see why **complete specialization** in production occurs under constant-cost conditions, consider Figure 2.5. The figure depicts the autarky cost conditions and production points for the United States and Canada based on the trading example of Figure 2.4. The

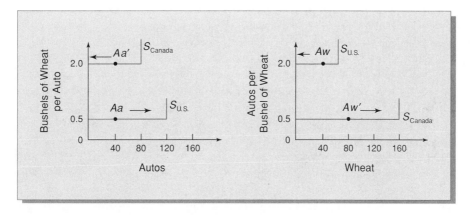

F I G U R E 2. 5 *Complete specialization under constant costs.* According to the principle of comparative advantage, complete specialization occurs under constant opportunity costs. Because production costs do not change with the level of output, a nation does not lose its comparative advantage (disadvantage) as it produces more (less) of a product.

United States is assumed to have the cost advantage in auto production, whereas Canada is more efficient in the production of wheat.

As the United States increases and Canada reduces the production of autos, both countries' unit production costs remain constant. Since the relative costs never equalize, the United States does not lose its comparative advantage, nor does Canada lose its comparative disadvantage. The United States, therefore, totally specializes in the production of autos. Similarly, as Canada produces more wheat and the United States reduces its wheat production, both nations' production costs remain the same. Canada totally specializes in the production of wheat without losing its advantage to the United States.

PRODUCTIVITY AND COMPARATIVE ADVANTAGE

The comparative advantage developed by manufacturers of a particular product can vanish over time when productivity growth falls behind that of foreign competitors. In the post–World War II era, for example, many U.S. steel companies produced steel in aging plants in

which productivity increases lagged behind those of foreign manufacturers. This contributed to U.S. steel companies' loss of market share to foreign firms. Other U.S. industries that went the way of steel were automobiles, machine tools, and consumer electronics. By the 1990s, Japanese computer suppliers had begun to compete effectively with U.S. producers in markets including printers, floppy-disk drives, and dynamic random-access memory chips. This was particularly disturbing to those who considered computers to be a treasure of U.S. technology and a hallmark of U.S. competitiveness.

Losing Competitiveness

If productivity in the Japanese computer industry grows faster than it does in the U.S. computer industry, the opportunity cost of each computer produced in the United States increases relative to the opportunity cost of the Japanese. U.S. computers become less competitive in international markets because Japanese manufacturers can sell computers at lower prices.

Figure 2.6 illustrates the transformation schedules, for computers and automobiles, of

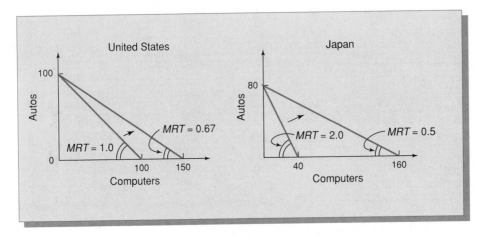

F I G U R E 2. 6 *Losing competitiveness.* If productivity in the Japanese computer industry grows faster than it does in the U.S. computer industry, the opportunity cost of each computer produced in the United States increases relative to the opportunity cost of the Japanese.
U.S. computers become less competitive in international markets.

the United States and Japan under conditions of
constant opportunity cost. Note that the *MRT*
of automobiles into computers initially equals
1.0 for the United States and 2.0 for Japan. The
United States thus enjoys a comparative advantage in the production of computers.

Over a number of years, suppose both
nations experience productivity increases in
computer manufacturing but no productivity
change in the manufacturing of automobiles.
Also assume that U.S. productivity in computer
manufacturing increases by 50 percent (from
100 to 150 computers) but that Japan increases
its computer manufacturing productivity by
400 percent (from 40 to 160 computers).

As a result of these productivity gains, the
transformation schedule of each country *rotates
outward and becomes flatter.* More output can
now be produced in each country with the same
amount of resources. Referring to the new
transformation schedules, the *MRT* of automobiles into computers equals 0.67 for the United
States and 0.5 for Japan. The comparative cost
of a computer in Japan has thus fallen below
that in the United States. For the United States,

the consequence of lagging productivity growth
is that it loses its comparative advantage in
computer production! The lesson of this example is that producers who fall behind in research
and development, technology, and equipment
tend to find their competitiveness dwindling in
world markets.

For domestic workers, what are the consequences of lost competitiveness in particular
export markets? Not only do they lose jobs to
foreign workers, but their wages tend to decrease relative to wages of competing workers
abroad. Some domestic workers with specialized skills that are not transferable to other
industries may face lasting reductions in income.

It should be noted, however, that all countries enjoy a comparative advantage in some
product or service. For the United States, the
growth of international competition in industries such as steel and autos may make it easy to
forget that the United States continues to be a
major exporter of aircraft, paper, instruments,
plastics, and chemicals. But putting the comparative-advantage principle into operation can

be difficult, since workers are often reluctant to retrain and relocate to areas of the country where industries are expanding. Workers in import-competing industries often demand trade restrictions (such as tariffs or quotas) to preserve their jobs and wages.

Is the United States Losing Its Productivity Edge?

The 1970s, '80s, and '90s have been bruising decades for many U.S. manufacturers. During this era, the "Made in USA" label vanished as foreign manufacturers came to dominate entire industries. In 1970, U.S. manufacturers produced 90 percent of the nation's machine tools, 88 percent of its automobiles, and 82 percent of its television sets; by the early 1990s, they had given up almost one-third of the auto market, one-half of the domestic machine-tool market, and almost all of the television market. Although manufacturing comprised about one-fifth of total U.S. output, much of that reflected growing numbers of foreign-owned (transplant) plants in the United States. It was widely felt that the U.S. technological edge had been reduced, or eliminated, in many industries.

Available evidence suggests that the United States traditionally has been a leader in manufacturing productivity. During the 1950s and 1960s, countries in Europe and elsewhere complained that superior know-how due to scientific and technological achievement in the United States allowed U.S. manufacturers to penetrate European markets in electronics, aircraft, and computers. Other factors that supported the U.S. productivity edge included the U.S. educational system, management quality, research and development (R&D) expenditures, and the combining of R&D with production and marketing.

By the 1970s and 1980s, the U.S. technological advantage had been reduced. Table 2.8 shows that manufacturing productivity growth in the United States tended to lag behind productivity growth in many of its trading partners during this era. In industries such as autos and steel, the United States yielded its technological advantage to other countries, especially Japan. Analysts maintained that part of the U.S. problem was that its companies did not imitate and build on the technological advances of their rivals as cheaply and quickly as Japan.

Based on interviews with scores of U.S. business leaders, analysts have concluded that to survive in the competitive environment of the 1990s, U.S. companies must restructure their managerial methods. Among the recommendations, companies must (1) streamline factory processes to slash production costs, inventories, and material costs; (2) pare management layers to force designers, engineers, production workers, and marketers to work as teams; (3) harness computer technology to make small batches of customized products at low cost; (4) pounce on breakthrough discoveries, such as superconductivity, that will revolutionize entire businesses; (5) cultivate a work force that is less specialized and continuously learning; (6) accept labor representatives as valued partners in the innovation process; and (7) not be excessively concerned with short-term profits.

TRADE RESTRICTIONS

The preceding analysis suggests that trading nations will achieve the greatest possible gains from trade when they completely specialize in the production of the commodities of their comparative advantage. One factor that limits specialization is the restrictions governments impose on the movement of commodities among nations. By reducing the overall volume of trade, trade restrictions tend to reduce the gains from trade.

Assume that, for reasons of national security, the United States establishes restrictions on the amount of oil that can be imported from the OPEC (Organization of Petroleum Exporting Countries) cartel. Rather than importing all of its oil from OPEC, which is assumed to have a

The Race in Research and Development

National Research and Development Expenditures as a Percentage of Gross Domestic Product

	United States	France	Germany	Japan	United Kingdom
Total R&D					
1975	2.2%	1.8%	2.2%	2.0%	2.1%
1980	2.3	1.8	2.4	2.2	2.1
1985	2.8	2.3	2.8	2.8	2.3
1990	2.7	2.3	2.9	3.0	2.0
Nondefense R&D					
1975	1.6	1.5	2.1	2.0	1.5
1980	1.7	1.4	2.3	2.2	1.5
1985	2.0	1.8	2.5	2.8	1.6
1990	1.9	1.8	2.8	3.0	1.6

SOURCE: U.S. Department of Commerce, *Statistical Abstracts of the United States,* various issues.

During the 1980s, international competition forced the United States to learn anew how to compete on cost and quality in products such as steel, autos, and electronics. By the 1990s, the United States faced stiffer challenges in science and invention as well. The table above shows research and development (R&D) expenditures as a percentage of gross domestic product for selected nations.

In total dollar terms, the United States still spends the most on R&D by far. Among the U.S. corporations with the largest R&D budgets are GM, IBM, AT&T, Digital Equipment, DuPont, Hewlett-Packard, Eastman Kodak, and United Technologies. In addition, U.S. law permits cooperative R&D ventures among U.S. companies. They range from the Electric Power Research Institute, dedicated to helping utilities generate and deliver electricity, to the Automotive Emissions Cooperative Research Program, established by U.S. auto companies and oil companies.

It is widely felt, however, that although the United States has been the source of many brilliant ideas—the big breakthroughs that win Nobel Prizes—it has taken a beating when it comes to practical innovation, in which inventions are translated into products. In addition, a cash-rich Japan and a unifying Europe were spending more and more on R&D in the early 1990s, reducing the U.S. advantage in science and technology.

comparative advantage in oil production, suppose the United States wishes to produce some oil itself. The United States chooses to produce some of the commodity of its comparative disadvantage in return for a greater degree of national security!

Figure 2.7 illustrates this trading situation between the United States and OPEC. Because the United States has the comparative advantage in the production of manufactured goods, it would benefit by specializing in manufactured-goods production. The United States thus

TABLE 2. 8 / *Annual Indexes of Manufacturing Productivity*

Country	Output per Hour (1982 = 100)			
	1960	1970	1980	1990
Canada	51.6	76.9	99.9	121.8
Japan	18.6	52.0	92.1	138.0
Belgium	24.2	44.3	87.5	140.5
Denmark	32.4	57.2	98.0	105.5
France	30.7	58.5	90.6	127.7
Germany	38.6	67.0	98.4	126.2
Italy	29.1	54.6	95.5	138.8
Netherlands	26.5	52.9	93.9	129.4
Norway	47.8	74.5	96.3	127.1
Sweden	36.2	69.1	96.4	118.2
United Kingdom	49.4	70.8	89.9	145.0
United States	58.4	77.2	94.4	125.7

SOURCE: U.S. Bureau of Labor Statistics, *Monthly Labor Review,* various issues.

moves its production location from autarky point *A* to point *B*. By exporting, say, 175 manufactured goods at the international terms of trade *tt*, the United States would import 275 barrels of crude oil. At posttrade consumption point *C*, the U.S. consumption gains from trade total 125 manufactured goods and 100 barrels of crude oil.

Suppose instead that, for national security reasons, the United States wishes to produce some crude oil as well as some manufactured goods. Assume that the United States locates at point *D*, producing 75 barrels of crude oil and 275 manufactured goods. Given terms of trade *tt'* (assumed to be the same as terms of trade *tt*), the United States will achieve a lower posttrade consumption point than would exist under free trade. The U.S. posttrade consumption point will now lie along *tt'* (note that *tt'* is drawn parallel to *tt*)—say, at point *E*. Clearly, point *E* is inferior to point *C*.

TRADING UNDER INCREASING-COST CONDITIONS

The preceding section illustrated the comparative-advantage principle under constant-cost conditions. But in the real world, a good's opportunity cost may *increase* as more of it is produced. The principle of comparative advantage must be illustrated in a slightly modified form.

Increasing Costs

Increasing opportunity costs give rise to a transformation schedule that appears *concave*, or bowed outward from the diagram's origin. In Figure 2.8, with movement along the transformation schedule from *A* to *B*, the opportunity cost of producing autos becomes larger and larger in terms of wheat sacrificed. Because the real cost of producing autos rises as more autos are produced, the auto supply schedule is *positively* sloped. Auto producers will offer more autos on the market only if they are compensated for their rising costs of production. Changes in the quantity supplied and product price are therefore directly related. This is shown in the lower part of Figure 2.8.

Increasing costs mean that the *MRT* of wheat into autos *rises* as more autos are produced. Remember that the *MRT* is measured by the absolute slope of the transformation schedule at a given point. With movement from production point *A* to production point *B*, the respective tangent lines become *steeper*—their slopes increase in absolute value. The *MRT* of wheat into autos rises, indicating that each additional auto produced requires the sacrifice of increasing amounts of wheat.

Increasing costs represent the usual case in the real world. In the *overall economy*, increasing costs may result when inputs are imperfect substitutes for each other. As auto production rises and wheat production falls in Figure 2.8, inputs that are less and less adaptable to autos are introduced into that line of production. To produce more autos requires more and more of

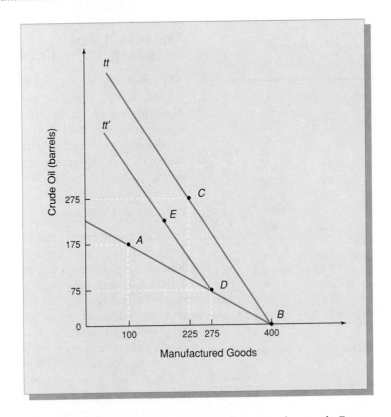

F I G U R E 2. 7   *Trade restrictions and the gains from trade.* For a
nation to achieve the greatest possible gains from trade, it is necessary
that it specialize completely in the production of the commodity of its
comparative advantage. Trade restrictions reduce the production and
consumption gains from specialization and trade by decreasing the extent
of specialization and the volume of trade.

such resources and thus an increasingly greater
sacrifice of wheat. For a *particular product,*
such as autos, increasing cost is explained by
the principle of diminishing marginal productivity. The addition of successive units of labor
(variable input) to capital (fixed input) beyond
some point results in decreases in the marginal
production of autos that is attributable to each
additional unit of labor. Unit production costs
thus rise as more autos are produced.

Under increasing costs, the slope of the

concave transformation schedule varies as a
nation locates at different points on the schedule. Because the domestic *MRT* equals the
transformation schedule's slope, it also will be
different for each point on the schedule. In addition to considering the *supply factors* underlying the transformation schedule's slope, one
must also account for the role of tastes and preferences (*demand factors*), for they will determine the point along the transformation schedule at which a country chooses to consume.

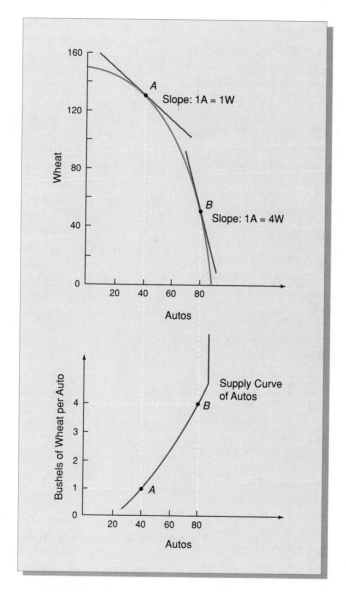

F I G U R E 2. 8 Transformation and supply schedules under increasing-cost conditions. Increasing opportunity costs lead to a transformation schedule that is concave, viewed from the diagram's origin. The marginal rate of transformation equals the (absolute) slope of the transformation schedule. Under increasing costs, a product's supply schedule is upward sloping, suggesting that unit costs rise with the level of output. The vertical portion of the auto supply schedule corresponds to the endpoint of the transformation schedule at which all resources are devoted to auto production.

Increasing-Cost Trading Case

Figure 2.9 gives the transformation schedules of the United States and Canada under conditions of increasing costs. Assume that in autarky the United States is located at point *A* along its transformation schedule, producing and consuming 5 autos and 18 bushels of wheat. Assume also that in autarky Canada is located at point *A'* along its transformation schedule, producing and consuming 17 autos and 6 bushels of wheat. For the United States, the opportunity cost of wheat into autos is indicated by the slope of line $t_{U.S.}$, tangent to the transformation schedule at point *A* (1 auto = 0.33 bushels of wheat). In like manner, Canada's opportunity cost of wheat into autos is denoted by the slope of line t_C (1 auto = 3 bushels of wheat). Because line $t_{U.S.}$ is *flatter* than line t_C, autos are relatively cheaper in the United States and wheat is relatively cheaper in Canada. According to the law of comparative advantage, the United States will export autos and Canada will export wheat.

As the United States specializes in auto production, it slides downward along its transformation schedule from point *A* toward point *B*. The opportunity cost of autos (in terms of wheat) rises, as implied by the increase in the (absolute) slope of the transformation schedule. At the same time, Canada specializes in wheat. As Canada moves upward along its transformation schedule from point *A'* toward point *B'*, the opportunity cost of autos (in terms of wheat) decreases, as evidenced by the decrease in the (absolute) slope of its transformation schedule.

The process of specialization continues in both nations until (1) the opportunity cost of autos is identical in both nations and (2) U.S. exports of autos precisely equal Canada's imports of autos, and conversely for wheat. Assume that this occurs when both nations' domestic rates of transformation (domestic terms of trade) converge at the rate given by line *tt*. At this point of convergence, the United States produces at point *B*, while Canada produces at point *B'*. Line *tt* becomes the international terms-of-trade line for the United States and Canada; it coincides with each nation's domestic terms of trade. The international terms of trade are favorable to both nations since *tt* is steeper than $t_{U.S.}$ and flatter than t_C.

What are the **production gains** from specialization for the United States and Canada? Comparing the amount of autos and wheat produced by the two nations at their autarky points with the amount produced at their postspecialization production points, we see that there are production gains of 3 autos and 3 bushels of wheat. The production gains from specialization are illustrated in Table 2.9.

What are the **consumption gains** from trade for the two nations? With trade, the United States can choose a consumption point along international terms-of-trade line *tt*. Assume that the United States prefers to consume the same number of autos as it did in autarky. It will export 7 autos for 7 bushels of wheat, achieving a posttrade consumption point at *C*. The U.S. consumption gains from trade are 3 bushels of wheat, as shown in Figure 2.9 and also in Table 2.10. The U.S. *trade triangle*, showing its exports, imports, and terms of trade, is denoted by triangle *BCD* in Figure 2.9.

In like manner, Canada can choose to consume at some point along international terms-of-trade line *tt*. Assuming that Canada holds constant its consumption of wheat, it will export 7 bushels of wheat for 7 autos and wind up at posttrade consumption point *C'*. Its consumption gain of 3 autos is also shown in Table 2.10. Canada's *trade triangle* is depicted in Figure 2.9 by triangle *B'C'D'*. Note that Canada's trade triangle is identical to that of the United States.

Partial Specialization

One feature of the increasing-cost model analyzed here is that trade generally leads each country to specialize only partially in the production of the good in which it has a comparative advantage. The reason for **partial special-**

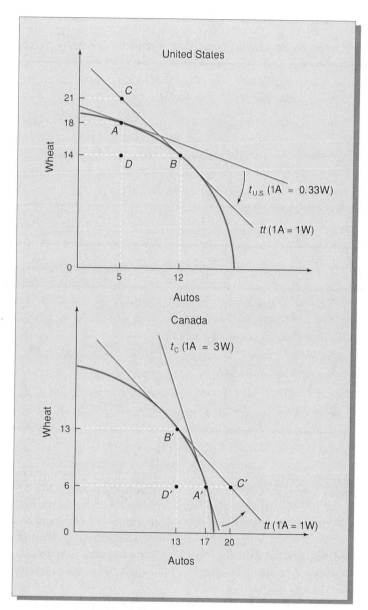

F I G U R E 2. 9   *Trading under increasing opportunity costs.*
With increasing opportunity costs, comparative product prices in each
country are determined by both supply and demand factors. This is
unlike the case of production under constant opportunity costs, in
which comparative product prices are determined solely by supply factors; changes in demand do not affect unit production costs and prices
under constant-cost conditions.

T A B L E 2. 9   /   *Production Gains from Specialization: Increasing Opportunity Costs*

	Before Specialization		After Specialization		Net Gain (Loss)	
	Autos	Wheat	Autos	Wheat	Autos	Wheat
United States	5	18	12	14	7	-4
Canada	17	6	13	13	-4	7
World	22	24	25	27	3	3

T A B L E 2. 10   /   *Consumption Gains from Trade: Increasing Opportunity Costs*

	Before Trade		After Trade		Net Gain (Loss)	
	Autos	Wheat	Autos	Wheat	Autos	Wheat
United States	5	18	5	21	0	3
Canada	17	6	20	6	3	0
World	22	24	25	27	3	3

ization is that increasing costs constitute a mechanism that forces costs in two trading nations to converge. When cost differentials are eliminated, the basis for further specialization ceases to exist.

Figure 2.10 assumes that in autarky the United States has a comparative cost advantage in auto production, whereas Canada is relatively more efficient at producing wheat. With trade, each country produces more of the commodity of its comparative advantage and less of the commodity of its comparative disadvantage. Given increasing-cost conditions, unit costs rise as both nations produce more of their export commodities. Eventually, the cost differentials are eliminated, at which point the basis for further specialization ceases to exist.

When the basis for trade is eliminated, there exists a strong probability that both nations will produce some of each good. This is because costs often rise so rapidly that a country loses its comparative advantage vis-à-vis the other country before it reaches the endpoint of its transformation schedule. In the real world of increasing-cost conditions, partial specialization is a likely result of free trade.

COMPARATIVE ADVANTAGE EXTENDED TO MANY PRODUCTS AND COUNTRIES

In our discussion so far, we have used a trading model in which only two goods are produced and consumed and in which trade is confined to two countries. This simplified approach has permitted us to analyze many essential points about comparative advantage and trade. But

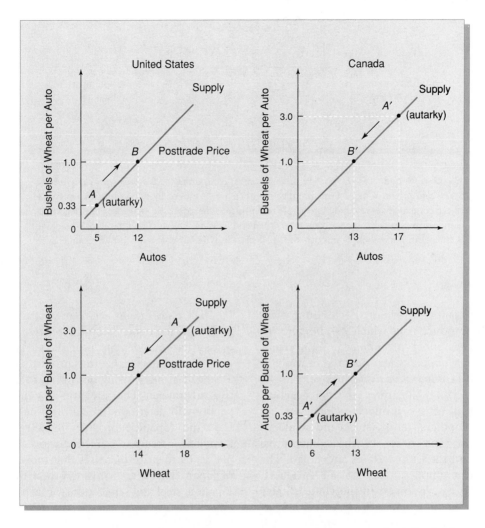

F I G U R E 2. 10 *Partial specialization: increasing opportunity costs.* Specialization in production tends to be partial in the case of increasing costs. This is because unit costs rise as each nation produces additional amounts of its export good. As the cost differentials among nations are eliminated, the basis for continued specialization disappears.

the real world of international trade involves more than two products and two countries; each country produces thousands of products and trades with many countries. To move in the direction of realism, it is necessary to understand how comparative advantage functions in a world of many products and many countries. As we will see, the conclusions of comparative

advantage hold when more realistic situations are encountered.

More Than Two Products

When a large number of goods are produced by two countries, operation of comparative advantage requires that the goods be ranked by the

F I G U R E 2. 11   *Hypothetical spectrum of comparative advantages for the United States and Japan.* When a large number of goods are produced by two countries, operation of the comparative-advantage principle requires that the goods be ranked by the degree of comparative cost. Each country exports the product(s) in which its comparative advantage is strongest. Each country imports the product(s) in which its comparative advantage is weakest.

degree of comparative cost. Each country *exports* the product(s) in which its *comparative advantage is most pronounced*. Conversely, each country *imports* the product(s) in which it has *greatest comparative disadvantage*.

Figure 2.11 illustrates the hypothetical arrangement of six products—chemicals, jet planes, computers, autos, steel, and semiconductors—in rank order of the comparative advantage of the United States and Japan. The arrangement implies that, of all products, chemical costs are lowest in the United States relative to Japan, whereas the U.S. cost advantage in jet planes is not quite as pronounced. Japan enjoys its greatest comparative advantage in semiconductors, and so forth.

The product arrangement of Figure 2.11 clearly indicates that with free trade the United States will produce and export chemicals while Japan will produce and export semiconductors. But where will the *cutoff point* lie between what is exported and what is imported? Between computers and autos? Or will Japan produce computers and the United States produce only chemicals and jet planes? Or will the cutoff point fall along one of the products rather than between them—so that computers might be produced in both Japan and the United States?

The cutoff point between what is exported and imported depends on the relative strengths of international demands for the various products. One can visualize the products as beads arranged along a string according to comparative advantage. The strength of demand and supply will determine the cutoff point between U.S. and Japanese production. A rise in the demand for steel and semiconductors, for example, leads to price increases that move in favor of Japan. This leads to rising production in the Japanese steel and semiconductor industries.

More Than Two Countries

When many countries are included in a trading example, the United States will find it advantageous to enter into *multilateral trading relationships*. Figure 2.12 illustrates the process of multilateral trade for the United States, Japan, and OPEC. The arrows in the figure denote the directions of exports. The United States exports jet planes to OPEC, Japan imports oil from OPEC, and Japan exports semiconductors to the United States. The real world of international trade involves trading relationships even more complex than this triangular example.

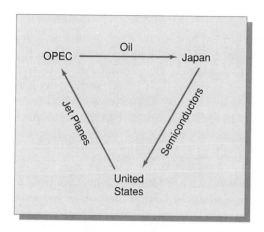

F I G U R E 2. 12 Multilateral trade among the United States, Japan, and OPEC. When many countries are involved in international trade, the home country will likely find it advantageous to enter into multilateral trading relationships with a number of countries. This figure illustrates the process of multilateral trade for the United States, Japan, and OPEC.

This example casts doubt on those who suggest that *bilateral balance* should pertain to any two trading partners. What would be the effect if all countries entered into bilateral trade agreements that balanced exports and imports between each pair of countries? The volume of trade and specialization would be greatly reduced, and resources would be hindered from moving to their highest productivity. Exports would be brought into balance with imports, but at the level of whichever was least. The gains from trade would be lessened.

EXIT BARRIERS

According to the principle of comparative advantage, an open trading system results in resources' being channeled from uses of low productivity to those of high productivity. Competition forces high-cost plants to exit, leaving the lowest-cost plants to operate in the long run. In practice, the restructuring of inefficient companies can take a long time because they often cling to capacity by nursing along antiquated plants. Why do companies delay plant closing when profits are subnormal and overcapacity exists? Part of the answer lies in the existence of **exit barriers,** which are various cost conditions that make lengthy exit a rational response by companies.

Consider the case of the U.S. steel industry. Throughout the 1980s and early 1990s, industry analysts maintained that overcapacity was a key problem facing U.S. steel companies. Overcapacity was caused by factors such as imports, reduced demand for steel, and installation of modern technology that allowed greater productivity and increased output of steel with fewer inputs of capital and labor. It was estimated that if steel capacity utilization could be increased, given existing prices, significant cost reductions would occur, bringing the industry to a position of profitability.

Traditional economic theory envisions hourly labor as a *variable* cost of production. However, the U.S. steel companies' contracts with the United Steel Workers union make hourly labor a *fixed* cost instead of variable cost, at least in part. The contracts call for unemployment benefits, health and life insurance, pensions, and severance pay (employee benefits) when a plant is shut down. From a business perspective, it may be rational to keep a plant operating even if it is losing money if labor costs remain fixed. For example, in 1980 Kaiser Steel decided to keep more than 11,000 workers employed because closing an aging plant would have cost the company more than $350 million in employee benefits!

Besides employee benefits, other exit costs tend to delay the closing of antiquated steel plants. These costs include raw-material supply contract-termination penalties and expenses associated with writing off undepreciated plant assets. Steel companies also face environmental costs associated with plant closures because they are potentially liable for cleanup costs at their abandoned treatment, storage, and disposal facilities. Such cleanup costs can easily amount to hundreds of millions of dollars. Also, steel companies cannot depend on high resale values of plant assets to cover the high closing expenses. The equipment is unique to the steel industry and is of little value for any purpose other than producing steel. What's more, the equipment in a closed plant is generally in need of major renovation because the former owner allowed the plant to become antiquated prior to closing.

U.S. steel companies have maintained that they face cost disadvantages when they attempt to reduce plant capacity relative to their foreign competition. They point out that foreign companies often receive government assistance for closing obsolete plants. Two frequently mentioned examples have been the Japanese steel companies that receive financing from the Bank of Japan to assist in restructuring and the European steel companies that receive subsidies for plant closures from their national governments.

In summary, the existence of exit barriers *delays* the market adjustments that occur according to the principle of comparative advantage. Indeed, the movement of resources from uses of low productivity to those of high productivity may take considerable time.

EMPIRICAL TESTING OF RICARDO'S COMPARATIVE-ADVANTAGE THEORY

David Ricardo's theory of comparative advantage provides a useful framework for analyzing international trade. But is Ricardo's theory a good fit to the real world? Does it accurately predict trade patterns?

The first empirical test of the Ricardian model was made by the British economist G. D. A. MacDougall in 1951.[6] Comparing the export patterns of 25 separate industries for the United States and the United Kingdom for the year 1937, MacDougall tested the Ricardian prediction that nations tend to export goods in which their labor productivity is relatively high.

In each industry that MacDougall studied, U.S. labor productivity exceeded that of the United Kingdom, giving the United States a cost advantage. However, the average U.S. wage rate was twice as high as the average U.K. wage rate, giving the United States a cost disadvantage. MacDougall maintained that production costs would be lower in the United States in those industries where U.S. workers were *more than twice* as productive as British workers! These would be the industries in which the United States has a comparative advantage and undersells the United Kingdom in the world market. In those industries where British workers were *more than half* as productive as U.S. workers, the United Kingdom would have a comparative advantage and undersell the United States in the world market!

Table 2.11 summarizes MacDougall's results. Of the 25 industries studied, 20 fit the predicted pattern: the United States had the larger share of world exports when its labor productivity was at least twice the British productivity! The MacDougall investigation thus supported the Ricardian theory of comparative advantage. Subsequent studies by Balassa and Stern also confirmed Ricardo's conclusions.[7]

Although there is empirical support for the Ricardian model, it is not without limitations. Labor is not the only factor input. Allowance should be made where appropriate for production and distribution costs other than direct labor. Differences in product quality also explain trade patterns in industries such as automobiles and footwear. One should therefore proceed with caution in explaining a nation's competitiveness solely on the basis of labor productivity and wage levels.

*T A B L E 2. 11 / United States and United Kingdom Output per Worker
and Quantity of Exports to Third Countries in 1937*

Product	U.S. Exports Compared to U.K. Exports (Ratio)
U.S. OUTPUT PER WORKER MORE THAN TWICE THE U.K. OUTPUT	
Wireless sets and values	8:1
Pig iron	5:1
Motor cars	4:1
Glass containers	3½:1
Tin cans	3:1
Machinery	1½:1
Paper	1:1
U.S. OUTPUT PER WORKER LESS THAN TWICE THE U.K. OUTPUT	
Cigarettes	1:2
Linoleum	1:3
Hosiery	1:3
Leather footwear	1:3
Coke	1:5
Rayon weaving	1:5
Cotton goods	1:9
Cement	1:11
Rayon making	1:11
Beer	1:18
Men's/boys' coats	1:23
Margarine	1:32
Woolen and worsted	1:250

Exceptions (U.S. output per worker more than twice the U.K. output, but U.K. exports exceed U.S. exports):
electric lamps, rubber tires, soap, biscuits, watches.

SOURCE: G. D. A. MacDougall, "British and American Exports: A Study Suggested by the Theory of Comparative Costs," *Economic Journal* 61 (1951).

SUMMARY

1. Modern trade theory is primarily concerned with determining the basis for trade, the direction of trade, and the gains from trade.
2. Current explanations of world trade patterns are based on a rich heritage in the history of economic thought. Among the most important forerunners of modern trade theory were the mercantilists, Adam Smith, and David Ricardo.
3. To the mercantilists, stocks of precious metals represented the wealth of a nation. The mercantilists contended that the government should adopt trade controls to limit imports and promote exports. One nation could gain from trade only at the expense of its trading partners because the stock of world wealth was fixed at a given moment in time and because not all nations could simultaneously have a favorable trade balance.
4. Adam Smith challenged the mercantilist views on trade by arguing that, with free trade, international specialization of factor inputs could increase world output, which could be shared by trading nations. All nations could simultaneously enjoy gains from trade. Smith maintained that each nation would find it advantageous to specialize in the production of those goods in which it had an absolute advantage.
5. David Ricardo argued that mutually gainful trade is possible even if one nation has an absolute disadvantage in the production of both commodities compared with the other nation. The less productive nation should specialize in the production and export of the commodity in which it has a comparative advantage.
6. Modern trade theory reasons that if in the absence of trade the comparative costs (prices) of two products differ between nations, both nations can benefit from international trade. The gains from trade stem from increased levels of production and consumption brought about by the international division of labor and specialization.
7. Comparative costs can be illustrated with the transformation schedule, also called the production possibilities schedule. This schedule indicates the maximum amount of any two products an economy can produce, assuming that all resources are used in their most efficient manner. The slope of the transformation schedule provides a measure of the marginal rate of transformation, which indicates the amount of one product that must be sacrificed per unit increase of another product.
8. Under constant-cost conditions, the transformation schedule is a straight line. Domestic relative prices are exclusively determined by a nation's supply conditions. Complete specialization of a country in the production of a single commodity may occur in the case of constant costs.
9. In the real world, nations tend to experience increasing cost conditions. Transformation schedules thus are drawn concave to the diagram's origin. Relative product prices in each country are determined by both supply and demand factors. Complete specialization in production is improbable in the case of increasing costs.
10. The comparative advantage accruing to manufacturers of a particular product in a particular country can vanish over time when productivity growth falls behind that of foreign competitors. Lost comparative advantages in foreign markets reduce domestic companies' sales and profits as well as the jobs and wages of domestic workers.
11. When a large number of goods are produced by two countries, operation of comparative advantage requires that the goods be ranked by the degree of comparative cost. Each country exports the product(s) in which its comparative advantage is most pronounced, while importing the product(s) in which its comparative advantage is weakest. When many countries are involved in international trade, the home country likely finds it advantageous to enter into multilateral trading relationships.
12. According to the comparative-advantage principle, competition forces high-cost producers to exit from the industry. In practice, the restructuring of an industry can take a long time because high-cost producers often cling to capacity by nursing along obsolete plants. Exit barriers refer to various cost conditions that make lengthy exit a rational response by high-cost producers.
13. The first empirical test of Ricardo's theory of comparative advantage was made by G. D. A. MacDougall. Comparing the export patterns of the United States and the United Kingdom, MacDougall found that wage rates and labor productivity were important determinants of international trade patterns. His findings supported Ricardo's theory.

STUDY QUESTIONS

1. Identify the basic questions with which modern trade theory is concerned.
2. How did Adam Smith's views on international trade differ from those of the mercantilists?
3. Develop an arithmetic example that illustrates how a nation could have an absolute disadvantage in the production of two goods while having a comparative advantage in the production of one of them.
4. Both Adam Smith and David Ricardo contended that the pattern of world trade is determined solely by supply conditions. Explain.
5. How does the comparative-cost concept relate to a nation's transformation schedule? Illustrate how differently shaped transformation schedules give rise to different opportunity costs.
6. What is meant by constant opportunity costs and increasing opportunity costs? Under what conditions will a country experience constant or increasing costs?
7. Why is it that the pretrade production points have a bearing on comparative costs under increasing-cost conditions but not under conditions of constant costs?
8. What factors underlie whether specialization in production will be partial or complete on an international basis?
9. The gains from specialization and trade are discussed in terms of *production gains* and *consumption gains*. What do these terms mean?
10. What is meant by the term *trade triangle*?
11. With a given level of world resources, international trade may bring about an increase in total world output. Explain.
12. Assume that the maximum amount of steel or aluminum that Canada and France can produce if they fully use all the factors of production at their disposal with the best technology available to them is shown in Table 2.12. Assume that production occurs under constant-cost conditions. On graph paper, draw the transformation schedules for Canada and France; locate aluminum on the horizontal axis and steel on the vertical axis of each country's graph. In the absence of trade, assume Canada produces and consumes 600 tons of aluminum and 300 tons of steel, while France produces and consumes 400 tons of aluminum and 600 tons of steel. Denote these autarky points on each nation's transformation schedule.

TABLE 2. 12 / *Steel and Aluminum Production*

	Canada	France
Steel (tons)	500	1200
Aluminum (tons)	1500	800

a. Determine the *MRT* of steel into aluminum for each nation. According to the principle of comparative advantage, should the two nations specialize? If so, which product should each country produce? Will the extent of specialization be complete or partial? Denote each nation's specialization point on its transformation schedule. Compared to the output of steel and aluminum that occurs in the absence of trade, does specialization yield increases in output? If so, by how much?
b. Within what limits will the terms of trade lie if specialization and trade occur? Suppose Canada and France agree to a terms-of-trade ratio of 1:1 (1 ton of steel = 1 ton of aluminum). Draw the terms-of-trade line in the diagram of each nation. Assuming that 500 tons of steel are traded for 500 tons of aluminum, are Canadian consumers better off as the result of trade? If so, by how much? How about French consumers?
c. Describe the trade triangles for Canada and France.
13. The hypothetical figures in Table 2.13 give five alternate combinations of steel and autos that Japan and South Korea can produce if they fully use all factors of production at their disposal with the best technology available to them. On graph paper, sketch the transformation schedules of Japan and South Korea. Locate steel on the vertical axis and autos on the horizontal axis of each nation's graph.
a. The transformation schedules of the two countries appear concave, or bowed out, from the origin. Why?

TABLE 2. 13 / *Steel and Auto Production*

Japan		South Korea	
Steel (tons)	Autos	Steel (tons)	Autos
520	0	1200	0
500	600	900	400
350	1100	600	650
200	1300	200	800
0	1430	0	810

b. In autarky, Japan's production and consumption points along its transformation schedule are assumed to be 500 tons of steel and 600 autos. Draw a line tangent to Japan's autarky point and from it calculate Japan's MRT of steel into autos. In autarky, South Korea's production and consumption points along its transformation schedule are assumed to be 200 tons of steel and 800 autos. Draw a line tangent to South Korea's autarky point and from it calculate South Korea's MRT of steel into autos.

c. Based on the MRT of each nation, should the two nations specialize according to the principle of comparative advantage? If so, in which product should each nation specialize?

d. The process of specialization in the production of steel and autos continues in Japan and South Korea until their relative product prices, or MRTs, become equal. With specialization, suppose the MRTs of the two nations converge at MRT = 1. Starting at Japan's autarky point, slide along its transformation schedule until the slope of the tangent line equals 1. This becomes Japan's production point under partial specialization. How many tons of steel and how many autos will Japan produce at this point? In like manner, determine South Korea's production point under partial specialization. How many tons of steel and how many autos will South Korea produce? For the two countries, do their combined production of steel and autos with partial specialization exceed their output in the absence of specialization? If so, by how much?

e. With the equilibrium relative product prices in each nation now at 1 ton of steel equal to 1 auto (MRT = 1), suppose 500 autos are exchanged at this terms of trade.
   (1) Determine the point along the terms-of-trade line at which Japan will locate after trade occurs. What are Japan's consumption gains from trade?
   (2) Determine the point along the terms-of-trade line at which South Korea will locate after trade occurs. What are South Korea's consumption gains from trade?

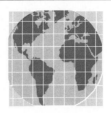

CHAPTER 3

Modern Trade Theory: Demand and the Terms of Trade

This chapter examines how **demand** affects the basis for trade, the mix of products consumed, and the gains from trade. The indifference-curve technique is introduced to analyze these topics. Analysis then turns to the role that demand plays in establishing the equilibrium terms of trade. The chapter also discusses how the terms of trade is measured empirically.

INDIFFERENCE CURVES

Modern trade theory contends that the pattern of world trade is governed by international differences in *supply conditions* and *demand conditions*. Therefore, the role of demand must be developed and introduced into the trade model. Economic theory reasons that an individual's demand curve is based on several underlying determinants, among them (1) the level of disposable income and (2) personal tastes and preferences. Discussion of income as a determi-

nant of demand is undertaken in Chapter 4. Here we consider the role of personal tastes and preferences in demand analysis.

The role of tastes and preferences can be illustrated graphically by a consumer's indifference curve. An **indifference curve** depicts the various combinations of two commodities that are equally preferred in the eyes of the consumer—that is, yield the same level of satisfaction. The term *indifference curve* stems from the idea that the consumer is indifferent among the many possible commodity combinations that provide identical amounts of satisfaction. Figure 3.1 illustrates a consumer's indifference curve. The consumer is just as happy consuming, say, 6 bushels of wheat and 1 auto at point *A* as consuming 3 bushels of wheat and 2 autos at point *B*. All combination points along an indifference curve are equally desirable because they yield the same level of satisfaction. Besides this fundamental characteristic, indifference curves have several other features.

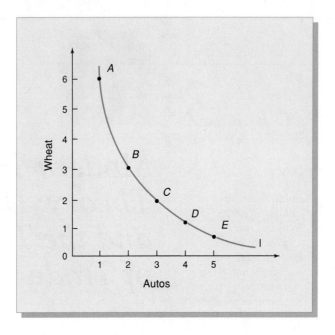

F I G U R E 3. 1   A consumer's indifference curve. An indifference curve depicts various combinations of two goods that are equally satisfactory to the consumer. An indifference curve tends to be sloped downward to the right and bowed in to the diagram's origin. The marginal rate of substitution is indicated by the (absolute) slope of an indifference curve.

Inspection of Figure 3.1 reveals that an indifference curve tends to be negatively sloped —that is, sloped downward to the right. This is assured by the assumption that a consumer always desires more of a commodity than less of it. Because each combination of goods along an indifference curve provides the same level of satisfaction, it follows that a consumer who increases auto holdings must decrease wheat intake by some amount if the initial level of satisfaction is to be maintained. If the wheat holdings are not decreased, the new market basket would include more of the combined amount of both commodities, resulting in a higher level of satisfaction. Because changes in the consumption of one commodity are inversely related to changes in the amount consumed of another for

a given level of satisfaction to be maintained, it follows that an indifference curve slopes downward to the right.

Indifference curves are also generally convex (bowed in) to the diagram's origin. The negative slope of an indifference curve indicates that, for any given level of satisfaction, some amount of one good must be sacrificed if more of another is to be acquired. The rate at which the substitution occurs is called the **marginal rate of substitution** (*MRS*). In terms of Figure 3.1, the marginal rate of substitution indicates the extent to which a consumer is willing to substitute autos for wheat (or vice versa) while maintaining a given level of satisfaction. The marginal rate of substitution of autos for wheat is expressed algebraically as

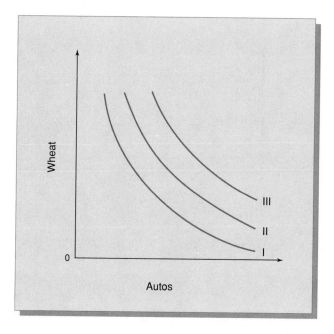

F I G U R E 3. 2 *A consumer's indifference map.* An indifference map is a graph that illustrates an entire set of indifference curves. Each higher indifference curve represents a greater level of satisfaction for the consumer. A community indifference curve denotes various combinations of two goods that yield equal amounts of satisfaction to the nation as a whole.

$$MRS = \frac{\Delta \, Wheat}{\Delta \, Autos}$$

The marginal rate of substitution is equal to an indifference curve's absolute slope. As we move downward along the indifference curve, autos become relatively plentiful while wheat becomes relatively scarce. With less wheat and more autos, each additional auto becomes less valuable to the consumer. For each additional auto consumed, the consumer is willing to sacrifice smaller amounts of wheat. This means that the marginal rate of substitution of autos for wheat decreases as more autos are consumed—hence the convex nature of an indifference curve.

An indifference curve shows the various combinations of two commodities that yield equal amounts of satisfaction to a consumer. An **indifference map** is a graph that illustrates an entire set of indifference curves. Figure 3.2 illustrates a consumer's indifference map. Although the figure contains only three indifference curves, an infinite number can be drawn. Note that each higher indifference curve denotes a greater amount of satisfaction. This is because any point on a higher indifference curve suggests at least the same amount of one commodity plus more of another commodity.

Having developed an indifference curve for a single person, can we assume that the

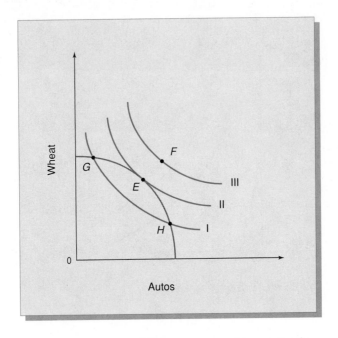

F I G U R E 3. 3   *Indifference curves and international trade.* A nation achieves autarky equilibrium at the point where its community indifference curve is tangent to its transformation schedule. At this point, the nation experiences the highest attainable level of satisfaction given the constraint of its transformation schedule, which limits the amount of goods available for consumption.

preferences of all consumers in the entire nation could be added up and summarized by a **community indifference curve**? Strictly speaking, the answer is no, because it is impossible to make interpersonal comparisons of satisfaction. For example, person A may desire a lot of coffee and little sugar, whereas person B prefers the opposite. The dissimilar nature of individuals' indifference curves results in their being noncomparable. Despite these theoretical problems, a community indifference curve can be used as a pedagogical device that depicts the role of consumer preferences in international trade. But keep in mind its shortcomings and limitations.

AUTARKY EQUILIBRIUM

Beginning once again with the assumption of autarky, what is the optimal level of production and consumption for a nation? In other words, at what point on its transformation schedule will a country choose to locate in the absence of trade?

Assuming that a nation wishes to maximize satisfaction, it will attempt to consume some combination of goods on the highest indifference curve that it can reach. But an indifference curve only tells what a consumer would like to do. Given the availability and quality of resources and the level of technology, there is a constraint on how many goods will actually be available to consume. For a nation, this production constraint is represented by its transformation schedule. A nation in autarky will maximize satisfaction if it can reach the highest attainable indifference curve, given the production constraint of its transformation schedule. Because there are an infinite number of indifference curves in an indifference map, this will occur when the transformation schedule is *tangent* to an indifference curve.

Figure 3.3 illustrates the transformation schedule and indifference map for a single country. In autarky, the country will maximize satisfaction if it produces and consumes at point *E*, where indifference curve II is tangent to its transformation schedule. Any point on a higher indifference curve—say, *F*—is unattainable because it is beyond the economy's capacity to produce. Any point on a lower indifference curve, such as *G* or *H*, does not represent maximum satisfaction. This is because a higher indifference curve can be reached with the existing transformation schedule. Point *E*, then, represents the **autarky equilibrium** of production and consumption.

BASIS FOR TRADE, GAINS FROM TRADE: A RESTATEMENT

Using indifference curves, let us now develop a trade example to restate the basis-for-trade and gains-from-trade issues. Figure 3.4 depicts the trading position of the United States. Assuming that the United States attempts to maximize satisfaction, its autarky location of production and consumption will be at point *A*, where the U.S. transformation schedule is just tangent to indifference curve I. At point *A*, the U.S. relative price ratio is denoted by line $t_{U.S.}$.

Suppose that the United States has a comparative advantage vis-à-vis Canada in the production of autos. The United States will find it advantageous to specialize in auto production until the two countries' relative prices of autos equalize. Suppose this occurs at production point *B*, where the U.S. price rises to Canada's price, depicted by line *tt*. Also suppose that *tt* becomes the international-terms-of-trade line. Starting at production point *B*, the United States will export autos and import wheat, trading along line *tt*. The immediate problem the United States faces is to determine the level of trade that will maximize its welfare.

Suppose that the United States exchanges 6 autos for 50 bushels of wheat at terms of trade *tt*. This would shift the United States from production point *B* to posttrade consumption point *D*. But the United States would be no better off with trade than it was in autarky. This is because in both cases the consumption points are located along indifference curve I. Trade volume of 6 autos and 50 bushels of wheat thus represents the *minimum* acceptable volume of trade for the United States. Any smaller volume would force the United States to locate on a lower indifference curve.

Suppose instead that the United States decides to trade 22 autos for 183 bushels of wheat. The United States would move from production point *B* to posttrade consumption point *E*. With trade, the United States would again locate on indifference curve I, resulting in no gains from trade. From the U.S. viewpoint, trade volume of 22 autos and 183 bushels of wheat therefore represents the *maximum* acceptable volume of trade. Any greater volume would find the United States moving to a lower indifference curve.

Trading along terms-of-trade line *tt*, the United States can achieve *maximum welfare* if it exports 15 autos and imports 125 bushels of wheat. The U.S. posttrade consumption location would be at point *C* along indifference curve II, the highest attainable level of satisfaction. Comparing point *A* and point *C* reveals

Customer Satisfaction and the U.S. Automobile Industry

Customer Satisfaction Index: Product Quality and Dealer Service

Year	Domestic	Japanese Imports	European Imports	Industry Average
1986	94	119	106	100
1987	98	119	102	104
1988	102	122	110	108
1989	112	130	111	118
1990	116	138	124	122
1991	121	139	127	127
1992	123	139	127	129

SOURCE: J. D. Power and Associates, *The Power Report,* various issues.

As discussed in this chapter, a person's (nation's) indifference curve represents the level of satisfaction that is achieved when consuming various combinations of two products. An application of the satisfaction concept is the customer satisfaction index for automobiles.

During the 1980s and 1990s, numerous comparisons have been made between U.S.- and foreign-manufactured automobiles. In 1986, J. D. Power and Associates, a market research organization, began to compile its annual index of "Customer Satisfaction with Product Quality and Dealer Service" (CSI). The index includes measures of vehicle repair and reliability, as well as customer service.

As seen in the table, in 1992 Japanese-origin vehicles (such as Honda, Toyota, and Nissan)

achieved the highest ranking by U.S. customers, leading U.S.-manufactured autos by 16 CSI points and European imports (such as Volvo and Porsche) by 12 CSI points. The Japanese autos scored highest in both the vehicle repair/reliability and customer-service categories.

Competitive pressure by foreign automakers provided incentive for U.S. manufacturers to improve product quality. Throughout the late 1980s and early 1990s, the CSI scores continued on an upward trend for domestic and foreign manufacturers. By 1989, U.S. autos had edged European imports out of second place in the CSI rankings; however, this ranking was reversed in 1990. Despite their gains, U.S. autos were unable to erase the satisfaction gap when compared with Japanese autos.

that with trade the United States consumes more wheat, but fewer autos, than it does in the absence of trade. Yet point C is clearly a preferable consumption location. This is because

under indifference curve analysis, the gains from trade are measured in terms of total satisfaction rather than in terms of number of goods consumed.

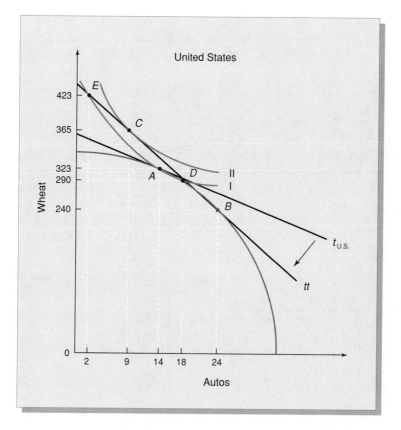

F I G U R E 3. 4 *Basis for trade, gains from trade.* A nation benefits
from international trade if it can achieve a higher level of satisfaction (indifference curve) than it can attain in autarky. Maximum gains from trade
occur at the point where the international terms-of-trade line is tangent to a
community indifference curve.

THE CLASSICAL EXPLANATION OF THE TERMS OF TRADE

A major shortcoming of the Ricardian principle
of comparative advantage was its inability to
explain fully the *distribution* of the gains from
trade among trading partners. The best description of the gains from trade that Ricardo could
provide was the *outer limits* within which the
equilibrium terms of trade would fall. This is
because the Ricardian theory did not recognize

the role that demand plays in setting market
prices.

To appreciate the limitations that Ricardian theory faced in explaining the distribution
of the gains from trade, consider Figure 3.5,
which depicts the domestic cost conditions of
the United States and Canada. Note that we
have translated the domestic cost ratio, given
by the negatively sloped transformation schedule, into a positively sloped price-ratio line. In
both diagrams, the relative costs or prices of

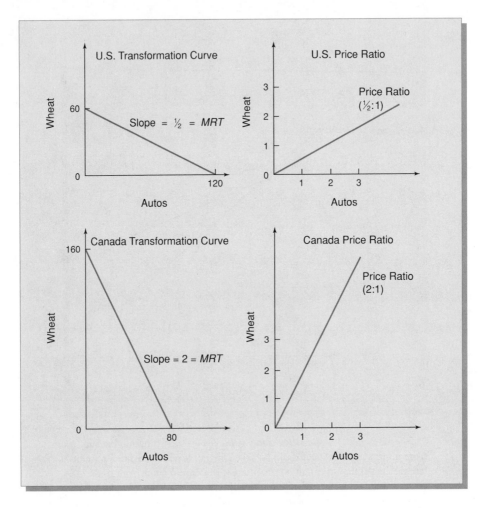

F I G U R E 3. 5   *Relative prices of autos and wheat: constant-cost conditions.* The domestic cost ratio, indicated by the negatively sloped transformation schedule, can be translated into a positively sloped price-ratio line, which illustrates the outer limits for the equilibrium terms of trade.

autos for wheat are the same. As seen in the figure, the relative price of each auto produced equals ½ bushel of wheat for the United States. For Canada the relative price of producing each auto is 2 bushels of wheat. The United States therefore has the comparative advantage in autos, whereas Canada has the comparative advantage in wheat. Figure 3.6 combines the

results of Figure 3.5 and illustrates both the U.S. and Canadian domestic price ratios for autos and wheat.

According to Ricardo, the domestic price ratios set the **outer limits for the equilibrium terms of trade.** If the United States is to export autos, it would not be willing to accept any terms of trade less than a ratio of 1/2:1, indi-

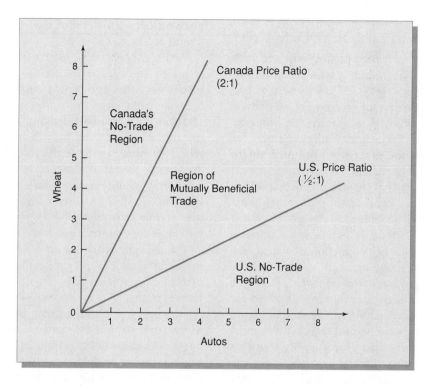

F I G U R E 3. 6 Equilibrium terms-of-trade limits. The supply-side analysis of Ricardo describes the outer limits within which the equilibrium terms of trade must fall. The domestic price ratios set the outer limits for the equilibrium terms of trade. Mutually beneficial trade for both countries occurs if the equilibrium terms of trade lies between the two countries' domestic price ratios.

cated by its domestic price line. Otherwise, the U.S. posttrade consumption point would lie inside its domestic transformation schedule. The United States would clearly be better off without trade than with trade. The U.S. domestic price line therefore becomes its *no-trade boundary*. Similarly, Canada would require a minimum of 1 auto for every 2 bushels of wheat exported, as indicated by its domestic price line; any terms of trade less than this rate would be totally unacceptable to Canada. The no-trade boundary line for Canada is thus defined by its domestic price-ratio line.

Because the Ricardian theory relied only on supply analysis, it could define only the outer limits within which the equilibrium terms of trade must fall. It was recognized that for international trade to exist, a nation would have to achieve a posttrade consumption location at least equivalent to its autarky point along its domestic transformation schedule. Any acceptable international terms of trade would have to be more favorable than or equal to the rate defined by the domestic price line. The **region of mutually beneficial trade** is thus bounded by the cost ratios of the two countries. But where will the equilibrium terms of trade actually lie? It was not until John Stuart Mill developed his theory of reciprocal demand that this question could be answered.

THEORY OF RECIPROCAL DEMAND

By bringing into the picture the relative strengths of the trading partners' demands, John Stuart Mill (1806–1873) was able to formulate the **theory of reciprocal demand**.[1] According to Mill, if we know the domestic demands expressed by both trading partners for both products, the exact equilibrium terms of trade can be defined. The theory of reciprocal demand suggests that the actual price at which trade takes place depends on the trading partners' *interacting demands*.

Suppose Canada, which has a comparative advantage in the production of wheat, expresses an enormous demand for autos, both domestically produced and imported. It will be willing to pay a high price in terms of wheat for those autos demanded. As can be seen in Figure 3.7, the United States would then achieve most of the gains from trade, because its terms of trade would improve. Starting at point A in the figure, where the gains from trade are evenly divided between the two countries, an improving U.S. terms of trade suggests that a given quantity of auto exports buys larger amounts of wheat imports. The United States would achieve a posttrade consumption point farther outside its transformation schedule. At the outer extreme, the Canadian auto demand could be so enormous that the terms of trade would settle along its domestic price-ratio line. The United States would then enjoy *all* of the gains from trade.

Again starting at point A in Figure 3.7, suppose the United States expresses an enormous demand for wheat, both domestically produced and imported. Because the price the United States is willing to pay for wheat would rise, Canada would enjoy most of the gains from trade. As Figure 3.7 illustrates, an improving Canadian terms of trade suggests that a given amount of wheat exports buys increasing amounts of auto imports. At the extreme, the terms of trade could settle at the U.S. domestic price ratio, at which *all* of the gains from trade would accrue to Canada.

Mill's theory reasons that the equilibrium terms of trade depends on the Canadian demand for autos and wheat, as well as on the U.S. demand for the same products. The stronger the Canadian demand for autos relative to the U.S. demand for wheat, the closer the terms of trade will settle to the Canadian domestic price ratio. The reverse is equally true. The reciprocal-demand theory thus contends that the equilibrium terms of trade depends on the *relative strength of each country's demand* for the other country's product.

Although Mill's theory of reciprocal demand provides a useful explanation of the terms of trade, it explains only a portion of international trade. The reciprocal-demand theory applies best when both nations are of *equal economic size,* so that the demand of each nation has a noticeable effect on market prices. Given two nations of *unequal economic size,* it is possible that the relative demand strength of the smaller nation will be dwarfed by that of the larger nation. In this case, the domestic price ratio of the larger nation will prevail. Assuming the absence of monopoly or monopsony elements working in the markets, the small nation can export as much of the commodity as it desires, enjoying large gains from trade.

Consider trade in crude oil and autos between Venezuela and the United States before the rise of the OPEC (Organization of Petroleum Exporting Countries) oil cartel. Venezuela, as a small nation, accounted for only a very small share of the U.S.–Venezuelan market, whereas the U.S. market share was overwhelmingly large. Because Venezuelan consumers and producers had no influence on market price levels, they were in effect price takers. In trading with the United States, no matter what the Venezuelan demand was for crude oil and autos, it was not strong enough to affect U.S. price levels. As a result, Venezuela traded according to the U.S. domestic price ratio, buying and selling

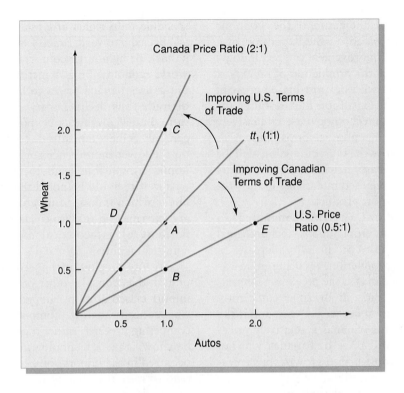

F I G U R E 3. 7 *Movements in the terms of trade.* According to the theory of reciprocal demand, the actual price at which trade occurs depends on the trading partners' interacting demands. The theory of reciprocal demand best applies when both trading partners are of equal economic size so that demand conditions in each country have a noticeable effect on the world price.

autos and crude oil at the price levels existing within the United States.

The preceding example implies the following generalization: If two nations of approximately the same size and with similar taste patterns participate in international trade, the gains from trade will be shared about equally between them. However, if one nation is significantly larger than the other, the *larger* nation attains *fewer* gains from trade, while the *smaller* nation attains *most* of the gains from trade. This situation is characterized as the **importance of being unimportant.** What's more, when nations are very dissimilar in size, there

is a strong possibility that the larger nation will continue to produce its comparative-disadvantage good, because the smaller nation is unable to supply all of the world's demand for this product.

ECONOMIC GROWTH AND THE TERMS OF TRADE

Does a nation necessarily become better off when it produces more? Does economic growth enhance domestic welfare? Precisely how a country's welfare is affected by economic growth depends on the nature of the economic growth. Growth based on the expansion of a resource (or an improvement in technology) used intensively in the production of an export commodity is known as **export-biased growth.** Growth based on expansion of a resource (or an improvement in technology) used intensively in the import-competing sector is known as **import-biased growth.** Our discussion will be restricted to the case in which growth occurs only in the resource used intensively in the production of the export product.

Consider Brazil, heavily committed to bananas, an export crop. Suppose technological improvements lead to productivity increases in Brazil's banana production, resulting in an excess supply of bananas at the prevailing international terms of trade. If Brazil is sufficiently large to be able to affect world price and if the foreign demand for bananas is relatively price-inelastic, the world price of bananas will fall substantially. Export-biased growth thus *worsens* Brazil's terms of trade.

Export-biased growth has two opposing effects for Brazil's welfare. Brazil gains because it can produce more, but it loses because it receives a lower price for its exports. Whether the benefits of rising output more than outweigh the losses due to the deterioration of the terms of trade will determine if Brazil is better off or worse off as a result of growth. If the negative terms-of-trade effect outweighs the positive effect of increased output, the technological improvement that generated this outcome is known as **immiserizing growth.**

Figure 3.8 illustrates the possibility of immiserizing growth. The figure shows Brazil's transformation schedules for bananas (export sector) and computers (import sector). Initially, Brazil produces at point A and exports bananas for computers at the terms-of-trade ratio denoted by tt_0. With trade, Brazil achieves a welfare level indicated by indifference curve I and attains a posttrade consumption point at B.

Because of the technological improvements in banana production, Brazil's transformation

schedule shifts rightward; as drawn, the growth is "biased" toward Brazil's export sector (bananas). Being a large country, compared to the world economy, Brazil's increased banana output causes banana prices to fall; Brazil's terms of trade thus decline to tt_1. At this exchange ratio, Brazil continues to export bananas, but it can only achieve a posttrade consumption point on the lower indifference curve II. Brazil's economic growth thus leads to *reduced* Brazilian welfare! It should be noted that the conditions under which immiserizing growth could occur are extreme and that it is usually considered to be more of a theoretical possibility than an empirical reality.[2]

Before concluding that economic growth is undesirable, consider other possibilities such as import-biased growth. Suppose Brazil's growth was concentrated in computers, its import-competing product, rather than bananas. It can be shown that a technological advantage that occurred in the import-competing sector would tend to raise the price of the export good relative to the price of the import-competing good and thus improve Brazil's terms of trade. It is left to more advanced texts to illustrate this point.

MEASURING THE TERMS OF TRADE

The gains a nation enjoys from its foreign trade consist of a larger income owing to a wider range of goods available to consumers and the favorable influence trade has on productivity levels. Estimating these gains at a particular time would be extremely difficult, for it would require knowledge of what a nation's imports would have cost had it produced them itself instead of purchasing them from a less expensive foreign source. Instead, economists have attempted to measure the direction of these gains over time. This is accomplished by calculating changes in the terms of trade.

The **commodity terms of trade** (also referred to as the *barter terms of trade*) is the

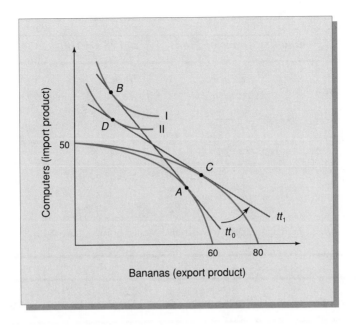

FIGURE 3. 8 *Immiserizing growth.* Prior to economic growth, Brazil achieves a posttrade consumption point *B* along indifference curve I. Export-biased growth shifts out Brazil's transformation schedule; as drawn, the growth is biased toward bananas. If the resulting increased volume of trade substantially reduces Brazil's terms of trade, the country's posttrade consumption point D may end up on indifference curve II, which lies below indifference curve I.

most frequently used measure of the direction of trade gains. It measures the relationship between the prices a nation gets for its exports and the prices it pays for its imports. This is calculated by dividing a nation's export price index by its import price index, multiplied by 100 to express the terms of trade in percentages:

$$Terms\ of\ Trade = \frac{Export\ Price\ Index}{Import\ Price\ Index} \times 100$$

An *improvement* in a nation's terms of trade requires that the prices of its exports rise relative to the prices of its imports over the given time period. A smaller number of export goods sold abroad is required to obtain a given

number of imports. Conversely, a *deterioration* in a nation's terms of trade is due to a rise in its import prices relative to its export prices over a time period. The purchase of a given number of imports would require the sacrifice of a greater number of exports.

Table 3.1 gives the commodity terms of trade for selected countries. With 1985 as the base year (equal to 100), the table shows that by 1992 the U.S. index of export prices had risen to 115, an increase of 15 percent. During the same period, the index of U.S. import prices rose by 18 percent, to a level of 118. Using the terms-of-trade formula, we find that the U.S. terms of trade *fell* by 2 percent [(115/118) × 100 = 98] over the 1985–1992 period. This

T A B L E 3. 1 / *Commodity Terms of Trade, 1992 (1985 = 100)*

Country	Export Price Index	Import Price Index	Terms of Trade
Japan	77	55	140
Germany	104	79	132
Sweden	125	104	120
United States	115	118	98
Australia	118	125	94
Singapore	79	87	91

SOURCE: *IMF Financial Statistics* (Washington, D.C.: International Monetary Fund, June 1993).

T A B L E 3. 2 / *The Commodity Terms of Trade: Annual Changes, in Percentages*

Year	Industrial Countries	Oil-Exporting Countries	Non-Oil-Exporting Developing Countries
1974–1983 (average)	-1.3%	14.3%	-2.0%
1984	0.6	0.7	3.2
1986	8.6	-40.3	2.7
1988	1.3	-17.0	1.1
1990	-0.7	14.4	-2.5
1992	1.1	-3.3	0.8
1993	-0.8	0.8	-0.1

SOURCE: International Monetary Fund, *Annual Report* (Washington, D.C.: International Monetary Fund), various issues. See also International Monetary Fund, *World Economic Outlook (World Economic and Financial Surveys)* (Washington, D.C.: International Monetary Fund), various issues.

means that to purchase a given quantity of imports, the United States had to sacrifice 2 percent *more* exports; or for a given number of exports, the United States could obtain 2 percent fewer imports.

Table 3.2 shows historical movements in the commodity terms of trade for the industrial countries, oil-exporting countries, and non-oil-exporting developing countries. The real-world significance of changes in the terms of trade is especially apparent when considering the experience of the oil-exporting countries. (Chapter 8 discusses the terms-of-trade issue for the non-oil-exporting developing countries.)

Throughout the 1960s, the terms of trade decreased marginally each year for the oil-exporting countries, as oil export prices stagnated and import prices rose by less than 2 percent a year. From 1970 to 1973, oil exporters' terms of trade improved, largely owing to moderate increases in petroleum prices. From 1973 to 1974, the oil-exporting countries dramatically increased the price of oil from $3.60 to $11.45 per barrel, leading to a 150-percent improvement in their terms of trade. In effect, these countries realized a 150-percent increase for each barrel of oil that was exported. The standard of living of the oil-exporting countries improved at the expense of the oil-importing countries. Another dramatic change in the terms of trade occurred in 1979–1980, when oil prices leaped from $17 to $29 per barrel. From their peak of $33 in 1982, oil prices progressively eroded in subsequent years, hitting a low of $12 in 1986.

Although changes in the commodity terms of trade indicate the direction of movement of the gains from trade, their implications must be interpreted with caution. Suppose there occurs an increase in the foreign *demand* for U.S. exports, leading to higher prices and revenues for U.S. exporters. In this case, an improving terms of trade implies that the U.S. gains from trade have increased. However, suppose the cause of the rise in export prices and terms of trade is falling *productivity* of U.S. workers. If this results in reduced export sales and less revenue earned from exports, we could hardly say that U.S. welfare has improved.[3] Despite its limitations, the commodity terms of trade is a useful concept. Over a long period, it illustrates how a country's share of the world gains from trade has changed and gives a rough measure of the fortunes of a nation in the world market.[4]

SUMMARY

1. Demand and supply conditions determine the basis for trade and direction of trade. Demand also helps establish the international terms of trade—that is, the relative prices at which commodities are exchanged between nations.

2. A community indifference curve depicts a nation's tastes or preferences. Community indifference curves illustrate the various combinations of two commodities that yield equal satisfaction to a nation. A higher indifference curve indicates more satisfaction. Community indifference curves are analogous to an individual's indifference curve. The slope of a community indifference curve at any point indicates the marginal rate of substitution between two goods in consumption. This shows the amount of one good a nation is willing to sacrifice in order to gain an additional unit of another good while still remaining on the same indifference curve.

3. The introduction of community indifference curves into the trade model permits a restatement of the basis for trade and the gains from trade.

4. In the absence of trade, a nation achieves equilibrium when its community indifference curve is tangent to its transformation schedule. The domestic relative commodity price is denoted by the common slope of these two curves at their point of tangency. When the relative commodity prices of two nations differ, a basis for mutually beneficial trade exists.

5. A nation will benefit from trade when it is able to reach a higher indifference curve (level of satisfaction) than could be achieved without trade. Gains from trade will be maximized when a nation's posttrade consumption point is located where the international terms-of-trade line is tangent to a community indifference curve.

6. Because Ricardian trade theory relied solely on supply analysis, it was not able to determine precisely the equilibrium terms of trade. The solution was first provided by John Stuart Mill in his theory of reciprocal demand. This theory suggested that before the equilibrium terms of trade can be established, it is necessary to know both countries' demands for both products.

7. The commodity terms of trade is often used to measure the direction of trade gains. It indicates the relationship between the prices a nation gets for its exports and the prices it pays for its imports over a given time period.

T A B L E 3. 3 / Export Price and Import Price Indexes

Country	Export Price Index		Import Price Index	
	1985	1994	1985	1994
Japan	100	150	100	140
Canada	100	175	100	175
Ireland	100	167	100	190

STUDY QUESTIONS

1. What advantages are provided by introducing community indifference curves into the trade model?

2. What is the difference between the marginal rate of transformation and the marginal rate of substitution?

3. Even though the production conditions of two nations are identical, gainful trade may still occur if demand conditions are dissimilar. Demonstrate this fact by using community indifference curves.

4. Why is it that the gains from trade could not be determined precisely under the Ricardian trade model?

5. What is meant by the theory of reciprocal demand? How does it provide a meaningful explanation of the international terms of trade?

6. How is the international terms of trade influenced by changing supply and demand conditions?

7. Why is it that the domestic cost ratios of two countries provide limits to the equilibrium terms of trade?

8. How does the commodity-terms-of-trade concept attempt to measure the direction of trade gains?

9. What problems do we encounter when attempting to interpret the commodity terms of trade?

10. Table 3.3 gives hypothetical export price indexes and import price indexes (1985 = 100) for Japan, Canada, and Ireland. Compute the commodity terms of trade for each country for the 1985–1994 period. Which country's terms of trade improved, worsened, or showed no change?

11. Will export-biased growth lead to improvements in the home country's welfare? Why or why not?

12. What is meant by *immiserizing growth,* and what implications does it have for a country's welfare?

Trade Model Extensions and Applications

Our analysis so far has stressed the importance of relative price differentials among nations as the immediate basis for trade. Because relative prices are underlaid by supply and demand conditions, an account should be made of factors such as resource endowments, technology, tastes and preferences, and income levels. In this chapter, we first consider the leading theories that attempt to explain what underlies relative price differentials. We then turn our attention to the role of transportation costs and their impact on trade flows.

FACTOR-ENDOWMENT THEORY

What is the underlying determinant of comparative advantage? According to David Ricardo, as explained in Chapter 2, comparative advan-

tage depends on relative differences in labor productivity. However, his analysis sheds little light on what underlies these differences.

In the 1920s, Eli Heckscher and Bertil Ohlin formulated a theory to explain why different nations have comparative advantages in producing different goods. Because Heckscher and Ohlin maintained that factor (resource) endowments underlie a nation's comparative advantage, their theory became known as the **factor-endowment theory**.[1]

The factor-endowment theory states that comparative advantage is explained exclusively by differences in relative national *supply conditions*. In particular, the Heckscher–Ohlin theory highlights the role of nations' *factor endowments* (such as land, labor, capital) as the key supply factor underlying comparative advantage. Like all theories, the Heckscher–Ohlin theory relies on several simplifying assumptions: (1) nations have the same tastes and preferences (demand conditions), (2) they use factor inputs that are of uniform quality, and (3) they use the same technology.

According to the factor-endowment theory, relative price levels differ among nations because (1) the nations have different relative endowments of factor inputs and (2) different commodities require that the factor inputs be used with differing intensities in their production. Given these circumstances, a nation will *export* that commodity for which a large amount of the relatively *abundant* (cheap) input is used. It will *import* that commodity in the production of which the relatively *scarce* (expensive) input is used. That is why land-abundant nations (such as Canada and Australia) export land-intensive goods such as wheat and meat, while labor-abundant nations (such as South Korea and Hong Kong) export labor-intensive goods such as textiles and shoes.

The factor-endowment theory is illustrated in Figure 4.1. which shows the transformation schedules of France and Germany. Assume that auto production is capital-intensive, requiring much capital and little land; wheat production is assumed to be land-intensive, requiring much land and little capital. Suppose that capital is relatively abundant in Germany while land is relatively abundant in France. The abundance of capital in Germany causes its transformation schedule to be biased toward the auto axis, while the abundance of land in France causes its transformation schedule to be biased toward the wheat axis.

According to the factor-endowment theory, demand conditions are assumed to be identical for each nation. This is illustrated in Figure 4.1 by the community indifference curves (curve I and curve II), which are common for both France and Germany. In the top portion of the figure, the points where community indifference I is tangent to the transformation schedules of Germany and France indicate the autarky equilibrium locations for the two countries. In autarky, Germany locates at point G on its transformation schedule and France at point F on its schedule. The relative price ratios at these points suggest that Germany has the comparative advantage in auto production and France has the comparative advantage in producing wheat.

The preceding example depicts the following assertion of the Heckscher–Ohlin theory: Given identical demand conditions and input productivities, differences in the relative abundance of resources determine relative price levels and the pattern of trade. Capital is relatively cheaper in the capital-abundant country, and land is relatively cheaper in the land-abundant country. The capital-abundant country thus exports the capital-intensive product, and the land-abundant country exports the land-intensive product.

Refer now to the lower part of Figure 4.1. With trade, each nation continues to specialize in the production of the commodity of its comparative advantage until its commodity price equalizes with that of the other nation. Specialization in production continues until France reaches point F' and Germany reaches point G'—the points at which the transformation schedules of the two nations are tangent to the common relative price line t_1.

With trade, France maximizes its welfare by exchanging 10 bushels of wheat for 12 autos, and achieves posttrade consumption at point H along community indifference curve II. Similarly, Germany exchanges 12 autos for 10 bushels of wheat, and achieves posttrade consumption at point H. With trade, both nations achieve a higher level of satisfaction (community indifference curve II) than that which occurs in the absence of trade (community indifference curve I).

Factor-Price Equalization

Recall that free trade tends to equalize commodity prices among trading partners. Can the same be said for factor prices?[2] A nation with trade

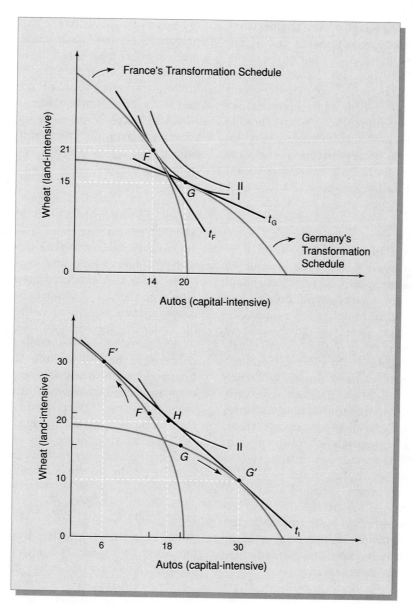

FIGURE 4. 1 *Comparative advantage according to the factor-endowment model.* The factor-endowment model asserts that the pattern of trade is explained by differentials in resource endowments. A capital-abundant nation will have a comparative advantage in a capital-intensive product, while a labor-abundant nation will have a comparative advantage in a labor-intensive product.

finds output expanding in its comparative-advantage industry, which uses a lot of the cheap, abundant factor. As a result of the rise in demand for the abundant factor, its price increases. The expensive, scarce factor is simultaneously being released from the comparative-disadvantage industry; producers will not be induced to employ this factor unless its price falls. Because this process occurs at the same time in both nations, there occurs in each nation a *rise in its price of the abundant factor* and a *fall in the price of the scarce factor*. Trade therefore leads toward an equalization of the relative factor prices in the two trading partners.

In the preceding example, the French demand for inexpensive German autos results in an increased German demand for its abundant factor, capital; the price of capital thus rises in Germany. As France produces fewer autos, its demand for capital decreases, and the price of capital falls. The effect of trade is thus to equalize the price of capital in the two nations. Similarly, the German demand for cheap French wheat leads to France's demanding more land, its abundant factor; the price of land thus rises in France. With Germany producing less wheat, its demand for land decreases, and the price of land falls. With trade, the price of land tends to equalize in the two trading partners. We conclude that by redirecting demand away from the scarce factor and toward the abundant factor in each nation, trade leads toward **factor-price equalization**. In each nation, the cheap factor becomes more expensive, while the expensive factor becomes cheaper.

In the real world, differences in factor prices do exist. For example, the average salary of unskilled labor in the United States is higher than in Korea. That resource prices may not fully equalize between trading partners can be explained, in part, by the fact that the assumptions underlying the factor-endowment theory are not completely met in the real world. For example, to the extent that different countries use different technologies or that markets are not perfectly competitive, factor prices may

only partially equalize. The existence of transportation costs and trade barriers may prevent product prices from becoming equal. Such market imperfections reduce the volume of trade, limiting the extent to which commodity prices and factor prices can equalize.

An example of the tendency toward factor-price equalization is provided by the U.S. auto industry. By the early 1980s, the compensation of the U.S. autoworker was roughly double that of the Japanese autoworker. In 1981, the average General Motors worker earned hourly wages and benefits of $19.65, compared to the $10.70 earned by the average Japanese autoworker. Owing to the domestic recession, high gasoline prices, and other factors, the demand for U.S.-produced autos deteriorated. However, the U.S. consumer continued to purchase Japanese vehicles up to the limit permissible under the prevailing quota system. To save its members' jobs with struggling U.S. auto companies, the United Auto Workers (UAW) union reluctantly accepted wage cuts so that the companies could remain in business. It is no wonder that the UAW pushed for trade legislation to further restrict foreign autos entering the United States, thereby insulating the wages of domestic autoworkers from the market pressure created by foreign competition.

Trade and the Distribution of Income

It has been shown how free trade can increase the level of output and income for trading nations. Not only does trade affect a nation's aggregate income level, however; it also affects the internal *distribution of income* among resources.

The factor-endowment theory states that the export of commodities embodying large amounts of the relatively cheap, abundant factors makes those factors less abundant in the domestic market. The increased demand for the *abundant* factor leads to an *increase* in its return. At the same time, returns to the factor used intensively in the import-competing product (the *scarce* factor) *decrease* as its demand falls. The increase in the returns to each country's abundant factor thus comes at the expense of the scarce factor's returns.

To the extent that free trade and import competition impose hardship on suppliers of the scarce factor, they may desire tariffs or quotas on imports. This may explain why segments of the U.S. labor force (such as steelworkers or autoworkers) favor protection against import competition; labor is scarce relative to capital in the United States compared with the rest of the world.

ARE ACTUAL TRADE PATTERNS EXPLAINED BY THE FACTOR-ENDOWMENT THEORY?

The first attempt to investigate the factor-endowment theory empirically was undertaken by Wassily Leontief.[3] It had been widely recognized that in the United States capital was relatively abundant and labor was relatively scarce. According to the factor-endowment theory, the United States should export capital-intensive goods, while its import-competing goods should be labor-intensive.

In 1954, Leontief tested this proposition by analyzing the capital/labor ratios for some 200 export industries and import-competing industries in the United States; in the study, he used 1947 trade data. As shown in Table 4.1, Leontief found that the capital/labor ratio for U.S. export industries was lower (about $14,000 per worker year) than that of its import-competing industries (about $18,000 per worker year). Leontief concluded that exports were *less* capital-intensive than import-competing goods! These findings, which contradicted the predictions of the factor-endowment theory, became known as the **Leontief paradox.**

Some economists maintained that 1947 was not a normal year, since the World War II reconstruction of the global economy had not been corrected by that time. To silence his critics, Leontief repeated his investigation in 1956, using 1951 trade data. Leontief again determined that U.S. import-competing goods were more capital-intensive than U.S. exports, as seen in Table 4.1.

Since Leontief's time, many other studies have tested the predictions of the factor-endowment model. Although the tests conducted thus far are not conclusive, they seem to provide support for a more generalized factor-endowment model that recognizes many subvarieties of capital, land, and human factors and that factor endowments change over time as a result of investment and technological advance.

The upshot of a generalized factor-endowment model can be seen by looking at some recent trading patterns. Tables 4.2 and 4.3 compare relative resource endowments with trade patterns for six of the world's leading industrial nations.

Table 4.2 shows the shares of world resources for six industrial countries. Reading across a row for a given country reveals its endowments of six resources, expressed as a percentage of the world's resources. For each resource, a higher value (percentage) indicates a greater relative abundance as compared with the country's endowment of all resources in the far-right column.

Consider the resource endowments of the United States. Table 4.2 indicates that the U.S. share of the world's total resources (far-right column) is 28.6 percent. Compared with its other productive inputs, physical capital is relatively abundant in the United States (33.6 percent of world capital). In like manner, the United States is relatively well endowed with research and development scientists (50.7-percent share) and arable land (29.3-percent share); relative scarcities occur in semiskilled labor (19.1-percent share) and unskilled labor (0.19-percent share).

Because the United States has a larger share of physical capital and R&D scientists than of world resources in total, the factor-endowment model predicts that the United

T A B L E 4. 1 / Factor Content of U.S. Trade: Capital and Labor Requirements per Million Dollars of U.S. Exports and Import Substitutes

Empirical Study	Import Substitutes	Exports	Import/Export Ratio
Leontief (1954)			
Capital	$3,091,339	$2,550,780	
Labor (person years)	170	182	
Capital/person years	$18,184	$14,015	1.30
Leontief (1956)			
Capital	$2,303,400	$2,256,800	
Labor (person years)	168	174	
Capital/person years	$13,726	$12,970	1.06

SOURCE: W. Leontief, "Domestic Production and Foreign Trade: The American Capital Position Re-examined," *Economia Internazionale,* February 1954, pp. 3–32, and "Factor Proportions and the Structure of American Trade: Further Theoretical and Empirical Analysis," *Review of Economics and Statistics,* November 1956, pp. 386–407.

T A B L E 4. 2 / Shares of World's* Resource Endowments, 1980, for Six Industrial Nations (Each Nation's Resource Endowment as a Percentage of World Total)

Country	Physical Capital	Skilled Labor	Semi-Skilled Labor	Unskilled Labor	Arable Land	R&D Scientists	All Resource. Combined (1982 GNP)
United States	33.6%	27.7%	19.1%	0.19%	29.3%	50.7%	28.6%
Canada	3.9	2.9	2.1	0.03	6.1	1.8	2.6
France	7.5	6.0	3.9	0.06	2.6	6.0	6.0
West Germany	7.7	6.9	5.5	0.08	1.1	10.0	7.2
Japan	15.5	8.7	11.5	0.25	0.8	23.0	11.2
United Kingdom	4.5	5.1	4.9	0.09	1.0	8.5	5.1
Rest of world	27.3	42.7	53.0	99.3	59.1	0.0	39.3
	100.0%	100.0%	100.0%	100.0%	100.0%	100.0%	100.0%

* Computed from a set of 34 countries that accounted for more than 85 percent of gross domestic product among market economies.

SOURCE: John Mutti and Peter Morici, *Changing Patterns of U.S. Industrial Activity and Comparative Advantage* (Washington, D.C.: National Planning Association, 1983); and World Bank, *World Development Report 1984* (Washington, D.C., 1984), Appendix Table I.

T A B L E 4. 3 / Export/Import Ratios (Net Exports) *in Leading Industrial Nations, 1979*

Product	Export/Import Ratios					
	United States	Japan	West Germany	Canada	France	United Kingdom
Technology-intensive	1.52	5.67	2.4	0.77	1.38	1.39
Standardized	0.39	1.09	0.84	1.38	1.03	0.76
Labor-intensive	0.38	1.04	0.59	0.20	0.86	0.71
Services	1.50	0.72	0.82	0.49	1.22	1.28
Primary products	0.55	0.04	0.29	2.21	0.52	0.81

SOURCE: John Mutti and Peter Morici, *Changing Patterns of U.S. Industrial Activity and Comparative Advantage* (Washington, D.C.: National Planning Association, 1983). See also P. Morici, *Meeting the Competitive Challenge: Canada and the United States* (Washington, D.C.: Canadian-American Committee, 1988).

States should have a comparative advantage in goods and services that embody more scientific know-how and physical capital. This prediction is consistent with Table 4.3, which shows the export/import ratios for the six industrial countries referred to in Table 4.2, as of 1979. The U.S. export/import ratios are greater than unity (that is, the United States is a net exporter) for technologically intensive manufactured goods (such as transportation equipment) and services (such as financial services and lending) that reflect U.S. technological know-how and past accumulation of physical capital. The United States is a net importer (the export/import ratio is less than unity) of standardized and labor-intensive manufactured goods (such as footwear and textiles). The situation represented in Table 4.3 is probably not much different today, except that the export/import ratio for standardized and labor-intensive products may be less than unity for all six nations, and Japan's comparative advantage in technology-intensive goods is now even more pronounced.

Not all recent empirical tests support the predictions of the factor-endowment theory.

One test was based on the notion that international trade in goods (such as autos) was in fact an indirect way of trading factor inputs (such as labor). According to the Heckscher–Ohlin analysis, if one were to measure the factor inputs embodied in a country's imports and exports, one should find that the country is a net importer of the factor inputs in which it is relatively poorly endowed and is a net exporter of the factor inputs in which it is relatively abundantly endowed.

Table 4.4 illustrates the results of a test based on 12 factor inputs and 23 countries. In their investigation, the researchers determined the ratio of each country's endowment of each factor input to the world supply. Then they compared these ratios with each country's share of world income from each factor. If the factor-endowment theory is correct, a country would always be an exporter of factor inputs for which its factor input share was greater than its factor income share; a country would be an importer of factor inputs for which the reverse was true. It was found that for almost half of the 12 factor inputs analyzed, international trade ran in the predicted direction less than

TABLE 4. 4 / *Testing the Factor-Endowment Model*

Factor Input	Predictive Success (%)*
Pasture land	78
Arable land	71
Forest	67
Agricultural workers	67
Managerial workers	60
Capital	55
Labor	51
Service workers	44
Sales workers	44
Production workers	40
Clerical workers	37
Professional workers	22

* Percentage of countries for which net export of factor input is consistent with the prediction of the Heckscher–Ohlin theory.

SOURCE: Harry Bowen, Edward Leamer, and Leo Sveikauskas, "Multicountry, Multifactor Test of the Factor Abundance Theory," *American Economic Review* (December 1987), pp. 27–33.

half the time! The results of this test challenge the predictive accuracy of the factor-endowment theory.

SPECIFIC FACTORS: TRADE AND THE DISTRIBUTION OF INCOME IN THE SHORT RUN

The factor-price-equalization theory assumes that factor inputs are completely mobile among industries within a nation and completely immobile among nations. Although factor mobility among industries may occur in the long run, many factors are immobile in the short run. Physical capital (such as factories and machinery), for example, is generally used for specific purposes; a machine designed for computer production cannot suddenly be used to manufacture jet aircraft. Similarly, workers often acquire certain skills suited to specific occupations and cannot immediately be assigned to another occupation. The so-called **specific-factors theory** analyzes the income-distribution effects of trade in the *short run* when factor inputs are *immobile* among industries—in effect, a short-run version of the factor-price-equalization theory.

Referring to Figure 4.2, suppose the United States produces steel and computers using labor and capital. Labor is perfectly mobile between the steel and computer industries, but capital is industry-specific: steel capital cannot be used in computer production, and computer capital cannot be used in steel production. Also assume that the total U.S. labor force equals 30 workers.

In each industry, labor is combined with a fixed quantity of the other factor (steel capital or computer capital) to produce the good. Labor is thus subject to diminishing marginal productivity, and the labor demand schedule in each industry is downward sloping.[4] The computer industry's labor demand schedule is denoted by $D_{L(C)}$, while $D_{L(S)}$ denotes the labor demand schedule in the steel industry. Because labor is the mobile factor, it will move from the low-wage industry to the high-wage industry until wages are equalized. Let the equilibrium wage rate equal $15 per hour, seen at the intersection point A of the two labor demand schedules. At this wage, 14 workers are hired for computer production (reading from left to right) while 16 are used in steel production (reading from right to left).

Suppose the United States has a comparative advantage in computer production. With free trade and expanded output, the domestic price of computers increases, say, from $2,000 to $4,000 per unit, a 100-percent increase; the demand for labor in computer production increases by the same proportion as the computer price increase and is denoted by demand

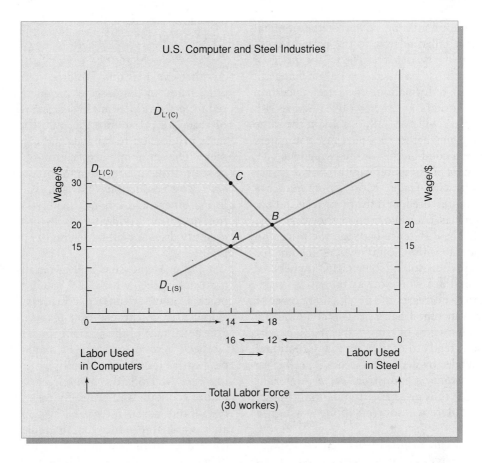

F I G U R E 4. 2   Relative prices and the specific-factors model. The computer labor demand schedule increases in proportion to the rise in the price of computers (100 percent); however, the wage rate increases less than proportionately (33 percent). Labor is transferred from steel to computer production. Output of computers thus increases, while steel output falls.

schedule $D_{L'(C)}$.[5] The result of the demand increase is a shift in equilibrium from point *A* to point *B*.

As the result of the increased demand for labor in computer production, two facts emerge. First, the equilibrium wage rate rises, from $15 to $20, which is a lesser increase (33 percent) than the computer price increase (100 percent). Second, the increased labor demand in computer production draws workers away from steel production. At the new equilibrium

point *B*, 18 workers are employed in computer production and 12 workers are employed in steel manufacturing; compared to equilibrium point *A*, 4 workers are shifted from steel to computers. Output of computers thus rises, and steel output falls.

How does trade affect the *distribution of income* for the three groups: workers, owners of computer capital, and owners of steel capital? Workers find that although their nominal wages are higher than before, their real wages (that is, the purchasing power of the nominal wage) have fallen relative to the price of computers but have risen relative to the price of steel (which is assumed to be unchanged). Given this information, we are uncertain whether workers are better off or worse off. Their welfare will rise, fall, or remain the same depending on whether they purchase computers or steel or a combination of the two goods.

Owners of computer capital, however, are better off with trade. More computers are being manufactured, and the price received per computer has risen more than the wage cost per unit. The difference between the price and the wage rate is the capital owners' income for each computer sold. Conversely, owners of steel capital are worse off as the rise in computer prices decreases the purchasing power of any given income (that is, real income falls).[6] In general, owners of factors specific to *export* industries tend to *gain* from international trade, while owners of factors specific to *import-competing* industries *suffer*. International trade thus gives rise to potential conflict between different resource suppliers within a society.

The specific-factors theory helps to explain Japan's rice policy. Japan permits only small quantities of rice to be imported, even though rice production in Japan is more costly than in other nations such as the United States. It is widely recognized that Japan's overall welfare would rise if free imports of rice were permitted. However, free trade would harm Japanese farmers. Although rice farmers displaced by imports might find jobs in other sectors of Japan's economy, they would find changing employment to be time-consuming and costly. Moreover, as rice prices decrease with free trade, so would the value of Japanese farming land. It is no surprise that Japanese farmers and landowners strongly object to free trade in rice; their unified political opposition has influenced the Japanese government more than the interests of Japanese consumers.

ECONOMIES OF SCALE AND SPECIALIZATION

Another explanation of trade patterns involves efficiencies of large-scale production, which reduce a firm's per-unit costs. Such **economies of scale** are pronounced in industries that use mass-production techniques and capital equipment. The economic justification of economies of scale is that a large organization may experience cost reductions through specialization in machinery and labor, assembly-line production operations, utilization of by-products, and quantity discounts obtained on the purchase of inputs.

For example, steel mills generally find that a steel furnace, which can produce twice as much as another furnace, costs less than twice as much to construct. Auto plants are able to take advantage of the assembly line, where each worker (or robot) performs a single operation on a car as it moves by. Multiplant operations, like the McDonald's hamburger chain, also realize economies of scale. By operating many restaurants as an integrated system, McDonald's is able to produce food ingredients at centralized kitchens and train its managers at its "Hamburger University." McDonald's also enjoys economies of scale in advertising, marketing, and finance.

How large a production run must a plant realize to exhaust its economies of scale? Table 4.5 furnishes estimates of scale economies for the motor vehicle industry. The table indicates the **minimum efficient scale** of plant size (that is, the volume of output required to minimize per-unit cost) for various production processes.

How do economies of scale underlie a nation's comparative advantage? Adam Smith gave the answer in his 1776 classic, *The Wealth of Nations*, which stated that the division of labor is limited by the size of the market. By widening the size of a firm's market, international trade permits the firm to take advantage of longer production runs, which lead to

Have U.S. Manufacturers Forgotten the Basics?

Invented in the United States, Manufactured Elsewhere

U.S.-Invented Technology	U.S. Producers' Share of U.S. Market (%) *		
	1970	1980	1992
Phonographs	90	30	1
Color TVs	90	60	10
Audiotape recorders	40	10	0
Videotape recorders	10	1	1
Machine-tool centers	99	79	35
Telephones	99	88	25
Semiconductors	88	65	64
Computers	NA	94	74

*1 - (value of imports / value of product shipments + value of imports)
SOURCE: U.S. Department of Commerce, *U.S. Industrial Outlook* (Washington, D.C.: Government Printing Office, 1993).

By many indicators, the United States should be competitive in many manufactured goods. The United States has an abundance of engineers and scientists who have won more Nobel Prizes than the rest of the world combined. U.S. companies have large R&D budgets. Foreign students rush to U.S. universities for the best training in engineering, mathematics, and science. The United States remains a bastion of technology, ideas, and innovation.

The United States is the nation that invented the integrated circuit, the tape recorder, the color television, and many other products. But today, U.S. manufacturers enjoy only a small share of the U.S. market for many goods, and an even smaller share of the world market. It has become painfully clear that there is more to innovation than large R&D budgets and Nobel Prizes.

Industry analysts have increasingly recognized that a good deal of the U.S. competitive problem lies in *manufacturing*—translating ideas into products good enough to be marketed overseas at competitive prices. Too many U.S. companies have forgotten that successful innovation requires small but steady improvements in products, not just major breakthroughs. It was incremental innovation in the auto industry that replaced manual transmissions with automatics and resulted in power brakes and power steering.

In contrast, the Japanese have become masters at incremental innovation and making tiny product improvements in "a thousand places." Such gradualism results in a steady flow of higher-quality products at low prices. The Japanese consumer electronics industry provides an example of Japanese innovation at its best. Today, U.S. homes are filled with electronic gadgets that have been upgraded continuously and that keep on getting better and cheaper.

TABLE 4.5 / *Plant Economies of Scale:*
Minimum Efficient Plant Size in the Motor Vehicle Industry

Production Process	Volume of Production per Year Required to Minimize Unit Production Cost
Final assembly	200,000–250,000
Engine casting	1,000,000
Other casting	100,000–750,000
Power-train machining and assembly	600,000
Axle machining and assembly	500,000
Body-panel pressing	1,000,000–2,000,000
Painting	250,000

SOURCE: UNCTNC, *Transnational Corporations in the International Auto Industry* (New York: United Nations, 1983), p. 73.

increasing efficiency. An example is Boeing, Inc., which has sold about half of its jet planes overseas in recent years. Without exports, Boeing would have found it difficult to cover the large design and tooling costs of its jumbo jets, and the jets might not have been produced at all.

Figure 4.3 illustrates the effect of economies of scale on trade. Assume that a U.S. auto firm and a Mexican auto firm are each able to sell 100,000 vehicles in their respective countries. Also assume that identical cost conditions result in the same long-run average cost curve for the two firms, *AC*. Note that scale economies result in decreasing unit costs over the first 275,000 autos produced.

Initially, there is no basis for trade, because each firm realizes a production cost of $10,000 per auto. Suppose that rising income in the United States results in demand for 200,000 autos, while the Mexican auto demand remains constant. The larger demand allows the U.S. firm to produce more output and take advantage of economies of scale. The firm slides downward along its cost curve until its cost equals $8,000 per auto. Compared to the Mexican firm, the U.S. firm can produce autos at a lower cost. With free trade, the United States will now export autos to Mexico.

Economies of scale thus provide additional cost incentives for *specialization* in production. Instead of manufacturing only a few units of each and every product that domestic consumers desire to purchase, a country specializes in the manufacture of large amounts of a limited number of goods and trades for the remaining goods. Specialization in a few products allows a manufacturer to benefit from longer production runs, which lead to decreasing average costs.

How might trade operate with economies of scale? Figure 4.4 represents the transformation schedules of the United States and South Korea for computers and steel. Note that the two countries' transformation schedules are *bowed inward* (convex from the diagram's origin), indicating *decreasing* opportunity costs.

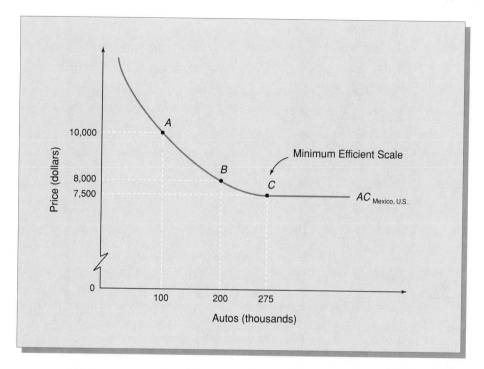

F I G U R E 4. 3 Economies of scale as a basis for trade. By adding to the size of the domestic market, international trade permits longer production runs by domestic firms, which can lead to greater efficiency and reductions in unit costs.

At each point, the (absolute) slope of the transformation schedule reflects the opportunity cost of steel. Along a convex transformation schedule, this cost decreases as more steel is manufactured: smaller and smaller amounts of computers are sacrificed for each additional ton of steel as one slides down the schedule. A similar argument holds for computers.

Without trade, suppose South Korea and the United States desire both computers and steel. Both countries would have to manufacture some of each good at inefficient points, such as point *A* for South Korea and point *B* for the United States. Reflecting the (absolute) slopes of the transformation schedules at these points, South Korea has a comparative advantage in steel, while the United States has a comparative advantage in computers. The two countries should not remain for long at these inefficient production points. They can reduce costs by *specializing completely* in the production of the goods of their comparative advantage.

As South Korea moves to the right of point *A* along its transformation schedule, the relative cost of steel continues to decrease until South Korea totally specializes in steel production at point *C*. Similarly, as the United States moves to the left of point *B* along its transformation schedule, the relative cost of computers continues to fall until the United States totally specializes in computer production at point *D*. With trade, U.S. computers are exchanged for South Korean steel at the equilibrium terms of trade (not illustrated); both countries can attain

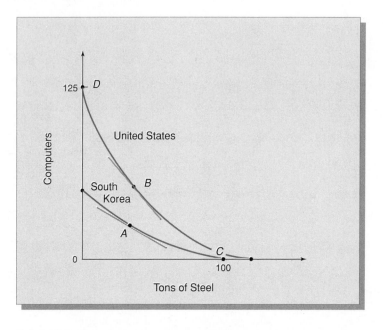

FIGURE 4. 4   *Trade and specialization under decreasing costs (economies of scale).* With decreasing costs, a country has the cost incentive to specialize completely in the product of its comparative advantage. Devoting additional resources to steel (computer) production results in economies of large-scale production and falling unit cost. With specialization, South Korea produces 100 tons of steel at point C, while the United States produces 125 computers at point D.

consumption points that are superior to those attained in the absence of trade.

THEORY OF OVERLAPPING DEMANDS

The relationship between demand conditions and international trade patterns has been analyzed by Staffan Linder.[7] According to Linder, the factor-endowment theory has considerable explanatory power for trade in primary products (natural resources) and agricultural goods, but not for trade in manufactured goods. This is because the main force influencing manufactured-good trade is domestic demand conditions. Because much of international trade involves manufactured goods, *demand conditions* play an important role in explaining overall trade patterns.

Linder states that firms within a country are generally motivated to manufacture goods for which there is a large domestic market. This determines the set of goods that these firms will have to sell when they begin to export. The foreign markets with greatest export potential will be found in nations with consumer tastes similar to those of domestic consumers. A nation's exports are thus an extension of production for the domestic market.

Going further, Linder contends that tastes of consumers are conditioned strongly by their income levels. Thus, a country's average, or per capita, income will yield a particular pattern of tastes. Nations with high per capita incomes will demand high-quality manufactured goods (luxuries), while nations with low per capita incomes will demand lower-quality goods (necessities).

The Linder hypothesis explains which types of nations will most likely trade with each other. Nations with similar per capita incomes will have overlapping demand structures and will likely consume similar types of manufactured goods. Wealthy (industrial) nations will likely trade with other wealthy nations, while poor (developing) nations will likely trade with other poor nations. The Linder hypothesis is thus known as the **theory of overlapping demands.**

Linder does not rule out all trade in manufactured goods between wealthy and poor nations. Because of unequal income distribution within nations, there will always be some overlapping of demand structures: some people in poor nations are wealthy, while some people in wealthy nations are poor. But the potential for trade in manufactured goods is small when the extent of demand overlap is small.

Linder's theory is in rough accord with the facts. A high proportion of international trade in manufactured goods takes place among the relatively high income (industrial) nations: Japan, Canada, the United States, and the European nations. Moreover, much of this trade involves the exchange of similar products: each nation exports products that are much like the products it imports. However, detailed empirical support for the theory has not been found.

INTRAINDUSTRY TRADE

The trade models considered so far have dealt with **interindustry trade**—the exchange between nations of products of different industries; examples include computers and aircraft traded for textiles and shoes, or finished manufactured items traded for primary materials. Interindustry trade involves the exchange of

goods with *different* factor requirements. Nations having large supplies of skilled labor tend to export sophisticated manufactured products, while nations with large supplies of natural resources export resource-intensive goods. Much of interindustry trade is between nations having vastly different resource endowments (such as developing countries and industrial countries) and can be explained by the principle of comparative advantage (the Heckscher–Ohlin model).

Interindustry trade is based on *interindustry specialization*: each nation specializes in a particular industry (say, steel) in which it enjoys a comparative advantage. As resources shift to the industry with a comparative advantage, certain other industries having comparative disadvantages (say, electronics) contract. Resources thus move geographically to the industry where comparative costs are lowest. As a result of specialization, a nation experiences a growing *dissimilarity* between the products that it exports and the products that it imports.

Although some interindustry specialization occurs, this generally has not been the type of specialization that industrialized nations have undertaken in the post–World War II era. Rather than emphasizing entire industries, industrial countries have adopted a narrower form of specialization. They have practiced *intraindustry specialization*, focusing on the production of particular products or groups of products within a given industry (for example, subcompact autos, rather than autos). With intraindustry specialization, the opening up of trade does not generally result in the elimination or wholesale contraction of entire industries within a nation; however, the range of products produced and sold by each nation changes.

Advanced industrial nations have increasingly emphasized **intraindustry trade**—two-way trade in a similar commodity. For example, computers manufactured by IBM are sold abroad, while the United States imports computers produced by Hitachi of Japan. Table 4.6

High-Tech Muscle

The Ten Strongest High-Tech Companies

Company (Headquarters Country)	Number of U.S. Patents 1991	Current Impact Index 1991	Technological Strength 1991
Toshiba (Japan)	1156	1.45	1677
Hitachi (Japan)	1139	1.43	1633
Canon (Japan)	828	1.45	1201
Mitsubishi Electric (Japan)	959	1.24	1190
Eastman Kodak (U.S.)	887	1.34	1186
IBM (U.S.)	680	1.71	1161
General Motors (U.S.)	863	1.32	1139
General Electric (U.S.)	923	1.16	1069
Fugi Photo Film (Japan)	742	1.42	1056
Motorola (U.S.)	631	1.54	969

SOURCE: "Global Innovation: Who's in the Lead?" *Business Week*, August 3, 1992, pp. 68–73.

As an indicator of high-tech strength, *Business Week* and CHI Research, Inc., have developed the so-called *current impact index*, which shows how often a firm's patents are cited in other patents (a measure of how frequently they are used as the foundation for other inventions). In this table, the 1.45 rating for Toshiba suggests that its patents are cited 45 percent more often than its competitors'. *Technological strength*, derived by multiplying the current impact index by the number of patents, is the basis for the overall ranking.

This table does not tell the entire story,

because it includes only U.S. patents. Although most important foreign inventions are also patented in the United States, this is not always true. Moreover, to keep some research confidential, some technologically strong firms restrict the number of patents they file.

In spite of these caveats, the table illustrates the technological power of Japanese companies. In 1991, Japan held down the first four slots, led by Toshiba's technological-strength rating of 1677. These rankings challenge the stereotype that the Japanese are mere copycats.

provides examples of intraindustry trade for the United States. As the table indicates, the United States is involved in two-way trade in many manufactured goods, such as chemicals and electronics.

The existence of intraindustry trade appears to be incompatible with the models of comparative advantage previously discussed. In the Ricardian and Heckscher–Ohlin models, a country would not simultaneously export and

TABLE 4. 6 / *Intraindustry Trade Examples: Selected U.S. Exports and Imports, 1992 (in Millions of Dollars)*

Category	Exports	Imports
Telephone equipment	$2,458	$4,327
Sawmill products	2,523	2,327
Textiles	3,918	6,875
Pulp	2,926	2,423
Chemicals	44,480	23,500
Steel	4,212	9,200
Electronic components	18,250	18,940
Semiconductors	12,000	12,820
Machine tools	1,746	2,909
Power-driven hand tools	644	2,347
Construction machinery	5,175	2,650
Farm machinery	3,085	2,259
Laboratory instruments	5,342	2,918
Photographic equipment	4,900	5,346
Computer equipment	27,800	29,320
Aircraft	40,733	13,950

SOURCE: U.S. Department of Commerce, International Trade Administration, *U.S. Industrial Outlook*, 1992.

import the same product. However, California is a major importer of French wines as well as a large exporter of its own wines; the Netherlands imports Lowenbrau beer while exporting Heineken. Intraindustry trade involves flows of goods with *similar* factor requirements: nations that are net exporters of manufactured goods embodying sophisticated technology also purchase these goods from other nations. Much of intraindustry trade is conducted among industrial countries, especially those in Western Europe, whose resource endowments are similar. The firms that produce these goods tend to be oligopolies, with a few large firms constituting each industry.

Intraindustry trade includes trade in homogeneous goods as well as differentiated products. For *homogeneous goods*, the reasons for intraindustry trade are easy to grasp. A nation may export and import the same product because of *transportation costs*. Canada and the United States, for example, share a border whose length is several thousand miles. To minimize transportation costs (and thus total costs), a buyer in New York may import cement from a firm in Quebec, while a manufacturer in Washington sells cement to a buyer in British Columbia. Such trade can be explained by the fact that it is less expensive to transport cement from Quebec to New York than to ship cement from Washington to New York.

Another reason for intraindustry trade in homogeneous goods is *seasonal*. The seasons in the Southern Hemisphere are opposite those in the Northern Hemisphere. Brazil may export seasonal items (such as agricultural products) to the United States at one time of the year while importing them from the United States at another time during the same year. Differentiation in time also affects electricity suppliers. Because of heavy fixed costs in electricity production, utilities attempt to keep plants operating close to full capacity. This may mean that it is less costly to export electricity at off-peak times, when domestic demand is inadequate to ensure full-capacity utilization, and import electricity at peak times.

Although some intraindustry trade occurs in homogeneous products, available evidence suggests that most intraindustry trade occurs in *differentiated products*. Within manufacturing, the levels of intraindustry trade appear to be especially high in machinery, chemicals, and transportation equipment. A significant share of the output of modern economies consists of differentiated products within the same broad product group. Within the automobile industry, a Ford is not identical to a Honda, a Toyota, or a Chevrolet. Two-way trade flows can occur in differentiated products within the same broad product group.

For industrial countries, intraindustry trade in differentiated manufactured goods often occurs when manufacturers in each country produce for the "majority" consumer tastes within their country while ignoring the "minority" consumer tastes. This unmet need is fulfilled by imported products. For example, most Japanese consumers prefer Toyotas to General Motors vehicles; yet some Japanese consumers purchase vehicles from General Motors, while Toyotas are exported to the United States. Intraindustry trade increases the range of choices available to consumers in each country, as well as the degree of competition among manufacturers of the same class of product in each country.

Intraindustry trade in differentiated products can also be explained by overlapping demand segments in trading nations. When U.S. manufacturers look overseas for markets in which to sell, they often find them in countries having market segments that are similar to the market segments in which they sell in the United States (for example, luxury automobiles sold to high-income buyers). Nations with similar income levels can be expected to have similar tastes, and thus sizable overlapping market segments, as envisioned by Linder's theory of overlapping demand; they would be expected to engage heavily in intraindustry trade.

Besides marketing factors, economies of scale associated with differentiated products also explain intraindustry trade. A nation may enjoy a cost advantage over its foreign competitor by specializing in a few varieties and styles of a product (for example, subcompact autos with a standard transmission and no other optional equipment), while its foreign competitor enjoys a cost advantage by specializing in other variants of the same product (subcompact autos with automatic transmission, air conditioning, cassette player, and other optional equipment). Such specialization permits longer production runs, economies of scale, and decreasing unit costs. Each nation exports its particular type of auto to the other nation, resulting in two-way auto trade. In contrast to interindustry trade, which is explained by the principle of comparative advantage, intraindustry trade can be explained by *product differentiation* and *economies of scale*.

With intraindustry specialization, fewer adjustment problems are likely to occur than with interindustry specialization, because intraindustry specialization requires a shift of resources within an industry instead of between industries. Interindustry specialization results in a transfer of resources from import-competing to export-expanding sectors of the economy. Adjustment difficulties can occur when resources, notably labor, are occupationally and geographically immobile in the short run; massive structural unemployment may result. In contrast, intraindustry specialization often occurs without requiring workers to exit from a particular region or industry (as when workers are shifted from the production of large-size automobiles to subcompacts); the probability of structural unemployment is thus lessened.

PRODUCT CYCLES

The underlying explanations of international trade presented so far are similar in that they presuppose a given, unchanging state of technology. The basis for trade was ultimately attributed to such factors as differing labor productivities, factor endowments, and national demand structures. In a dynamic world, technological changes occur in different nations at different rates of speed. Technological innovations commonly result in new methods of producing existing commodities, in the production of new commodities, or in commodity improvements. These factors can affect comparative advantage and the pattern of trade.

Recognition of the importance of *dynamic* changes has given rise to another explanation of international trade in manufactured goods: the **product life cycle theory**. This theory focuses on the role of technological innovation as a key determinant of trade patterns in manufactured products. According to this theory, many manufactured goods, such as electronic products and office machinery, undergo a predictable *trade cycle*.[8] During this cycle, the home country initially is an exporter, then loses its competitive advantage vis-à-vis its trading partners, and eventually may become an importer of the commodity. The stages that many manufactured goods go through include the following:

1. Manufactured good is introduced to home market.
2. Domestic industry shows export strength.
3. Foreign production begins.
4. Domestic industry loses competitive advantage.
5. Import competition begins.

The introduction stage of the trade cycle begins when an innovator establishes a technological breakthrough in the production of a manufactured good. At the start, the relatively small local market for the product and technological uncertainties imply that mass production is not feasible. The manufacturer will likely operate close to the local market to gain quick feedback on the quality and overall appeal of the product.

During the trade cycle's next stage, the domestic manufacturer begins to export its product to foreign markets having similar tastes and income levels. The local manufacturer finds that, during this stage of growth and expansion, its market becomes large enough to support mass-production operations and the sorting out of inefficient production techniques. The home-country manufacturer is therefore able to supply increasing amounts to the world markets.

As time passes, the manufacturer realizes that, to protect its export profits, it must locate production operations closer to the foreign markets. The domestic industry enters its mature stage as innovating businesses establish branches abroad. A reason for locating production operations abroad is that the cost advantage initially enjoyed by an innovator is not likely to last indefinitely. Over time, the innovating nation may find its technology becoming more commonplace and transportation costs and tariffs playing an increasingly important role in influencing selling costs. The innovator may also find that the foreign market is large enough to permit mass-production operations.

Although an innovating nation's monopoly position may be prolonged by legal patents, it tends to break down over time because knowledge tends to be a free good in the long run. The benefits an innovating nation achieves from its technological gap are short-lived, as import competition from foreign producers begins. Once the innovative technology becomes fairly commonplace, foreign producers begin to imitate the production process. The innovating nation gradually loses its comparative advantage, and its export cycle enters a declining phase.

The trade cycle is complete when the production process becomes so standardized that it can be easily used by all nations. The technological breakthrough therefore no longer benefits only the innovating nation. In fact, the innovating nation may itself become a net importer of the product as its monopoly position is eliminated by foreign competition. Textiles and paper products are generally considered to have run the full course of the trade cycle. The spread of automobile production into many parts of the world implies that its production process is close to becoming standardized.

The experience of U.S. and Japanese radio manufacturers illustrates the product life cycle model. Following World War II, the radio was a well-established product. U.S. manufacturers dominated the international market for radios because vacuum tubes were initially developed in the United States. But as production technologies spread, Japan used cheaper labor and captured a large share of the world radio market. The transistor was then developed by U.S. companies. For a number of years, U.S. radio

Pocket Calculators

Pocket calculators provide an illustration of a product that has moved through the stages of the international product cycle. This product was invented in 1961 by engineers at Sunlock Comptometer, Inc., and was marketed soon after at a price of approximately $1,000. Sunlock's pocket calculator was more accurate than slide rules (widely used by high school and college students at that time) and more portable than large mechanical calculators and computers that performed many of the same functions.

By 1970, several U.S. and Japanese companies had entered the market with competing pocket calculators; these firms included Texas Instruments, Hewlett-Packard, and Casio (of Japan). The increased competition forced the price down to about $400. As the 1970s continued, additional

companies entered the market. Several began to assemble their pocket calculators in foreign countries, such as Singapore and Taiwan, to take advantage of lower labor costs; these calculators were then shipped to the United States. Steadily improving technologies resulted in product improvements and falling prices; by the mid-1970s, pocket calculators sold routinely for $10 to $20, sometimes even less.

It appears that by the late 1970s, pocket calculators had reached the standardized-product stage of the product cycle, with product technology available throughout the industry, price competition (and thus costs) of major significance, and product differentiation widely adopted. In a period of less than two decades, the international product cycle for pocket calculators was complete.

manufacturers were able to compete with the Japanese, who continued to use outdated technologies. Again, the Japanese imitated the U.S. technologies and were able to sell radios at more competitive prices.

DYNAMIC COMPARATIVE ADVANTAGE: INDUSTRIAL POLICY

David Ricardo's theory of comparative advantage has influenced international trade theory and policy for almost 200 years. It implies that nations are better off by promoting free trade and allowing competitive markets to determine what should be produced and how.

Ricardian theory emphasizes specialization and reallocation of existing resources found

domestically. It is essentially a *static* theory that does not consider a dynamic change in comparative advantage or disadvantage of industries over the course of several decades. The theory overlooks the fact that additional resources can be made available to the trading nation because they can be created or imported.

Ricardian theory also suffers from its assumption of increasing costs, in which additional use of limited resources results in rising unit costs as resources become fully used. Although this principle holds in the short run, empirical evidence suggests that unit costs may *decrease* over time—partly because firms learn to be more efficient and partly because of economies of large-scale production.

The remarkable postwar economic growth of the East Asian countries appears to be based on a modification of the static concept of comparative advantage. The Japanese were among the first to recognize that comparative advantage in a particular industry can be created through the mobilization of skilled labor, technology, and capital. They also realized that, in addition to the business sector, government can establish policies to promote opportunities for change through time. Such a process is known as **dynamic comparative advantage**. When government is actively involved in creating comparative advantage, the term **industrial policy** applies.

In its simplest form, industrial policy is the initiation of a strategy to revitalize, improve, and develop an industry. Proponents maintain that government should enact policies that encourage the development of emerging, "sunrise" industries (such as high-technology) and hasten the phasing out of declining, "sunset" industries. This requires that resources be directed to industries in which productivity is highest, linkages to the rest of the economy are strong (as with semiconductors), and future competitiveness is important. Presumably, the domestic economy will enjoy a higher average level of productivity and be more competitive in world markets as the result of such policies.

A variety of government policies can be used to foster the development and revitalization of industries; examples are antitrust immunity, tax incentives, R&D subsidies, loan guarantees, low-interest-rate loans, and trade protection. Creating comparative advantage requires government to identify, or target, "the winners" and encourage resources to move into industries with the highest growth prospects.

To better understand the significance of dynamic comparative advantage, one might think of it in terms of the classic example of Ricardo's theory of comparative advantage. His example showed that, in the eighteenth century, Portugal and England would each gain by specializing respectively in the production of wine and cloth, even though Portugal might produce

both cloth and wine more cheaply than England. According to static comparative-advantage theory, both nations would be better off by specializing in the product in which they had an existing comparative advantage.

By adhering to this prescription, however, Portugal would sacrifice long-run growth for short-run gains. Instead, if Portugal adopted a dynamic theory of comparative advantage, it would specialize in the growth industry of that time (cloth). The Portuguese government (or Portuguese textile manufacturers) would thus initiate policies to foster the development of its cloth industry. This strategy would require Portugal to think in terms of acquiring or creating strength in a "sunrise" sector instead of simply accepting the existing supply of resources and using that endowment as productively as possible.

Every industrialized country, and many less developed countries, today uses industrial policies that encourage the development or revitalization of basic industries, including steel, autos, chemicals, transportation, and other important manufactures. While each of these industrial policies differ with regard to character and approach, common to all is an active role for government in the economy. Usually, industrial policy is a strategy developed collectively by government, business, and labor through some sort of tripartite consultation process.

Advocates of industrial policy typically cite Japan as a nation that has been highly successful in penetrating foreign markets and achieving rapid economic growth. Following World War II, the Japanese were the high-cost producers in many basic industries (such as steel). In this situation, a static notion of comparative advantage would require the Japanese to look to areas of "lesser disadvantage" that were more labor-intensive (such as textiles). Such a strategy would have forced Japan into low-productivity industries that would eventually compete with other East Asian nations having abundant labor and modest living standards.

Instead, the Japanese invested in basic industries (steel, autos, and later electronics, including computers) that required intensive employment of capital and labor. From a short-run, static perspective, Japan appeared to pick the wrong industries. But from a long-run perspective, those were the industries in which technological progress was rapid, labor productivity rose fast, and unit costs decreased with the expansion of output. They were also industries in which one would expect rapid growth in demand as national income increased.

These industries combined the potential to expand rapidly, thus adding new capacity, with the opportunity to use the latest technology and thus promote a strategy of cost reduction founded on increasing productivity. Japan, placed in a position similar to that of Portugal in Ricardo's famous example, refused to specialize in "wine" and chose "cloth" instead. Within three decades, Japan became the world's premier low-cost producer of many of the products for which it initially started in a high-cost position.

Critics of industrial policy, however, contend that the causal factor in Japanese industrial success is unclear. They admit that some of the Japanese government's targeted industries—such as semiconductors, steel, shipbuilding, and machine tools—are probably more competitive than they would have been in the absence of government assistance. But they assert that Japan also targeted some losers, such as petrochemicals and aluminum, for which the returns on investment were disappointing and capacity had to be reduced. Moreover, there are examples of successful Japanese industries that did not receive government assistance—motorcycles, bicycles, paper, glass, and cement.

Industrial-policy critics contend that if all trading nations take the route of using a combination of trade restrictions on imports and subsidies on exports, a "beggar-thy-neighbor" process of trade-inhibiting protectionism would result. They also point out that the implementation of industrial policies can result in "pork-barrel" politics, in which politically powerful industries receive government assistance. Finally, it is argued that in a free market, profit-maximizing businesses have the incentive to develop new resources and technologies that change a country's comparative advantage. This raises the question of whether the government does a better job than the private sector in creating comparative advantage.

Silicon Valley and Industrial Policy

In the 1970s, the Japanese began undercutting U.S. competitors in consumer electronic goods. The strategy eventually brought Japanese dominance in products including television sets, stereos, and videocassette recorders. By the 1990s, U.S. business executives contended that the same was happening with microchips, and the consequences could be more severe. Semiconductors, they maintained, would be the enabling technology underpinning advances in every field of science and technology for decades to come. If the U.S. semiconductor industry surrendered to foreign competition, telecommunications and the rest of the electronics field would not be far behind—including supercomputers. Moreover, the U.S. Department of Defense asserted that virtually all future U.S. war-making capability was dependent on the microchip industry. Should the United States obtain microchips from unreliable foreign suppliers, its national security could be jeopardized.

From California's Silicon Valley to Route 128 in Massachusetts, scores of U.S. executives called for a new strategic partnership between the government and the electronic industry. Computer makers, microchip producers, telecommunications companies, and software houses urged the federal government to formulate a high-tech industrial policy to battle the Japanese.

It was argued that a coherent industrial policy should recognize that developing new technology has become very expensive. Efforts should be made to decrease the cost of capital by promoting additional savings, reducing the federal deficit, and discouraging consumer and business debt. Next is blocking imports that use predatory pricing designed to drive U.S. competitors out of the market. Then come such measures as indexing the capital gains tax to promote longer-term investments and eliminating double taxation on dividends. U.S. antitrust laws could also be reformed so that U.S. companies could share the huge capital burden of commercializing new technology and collaborate on manufacturing as well as research. The Clinton administration was considering these and other measures at the publication date of this book.

Not all semiconductor executives called for a high-tech industrial policy. They argued that government subsidies would likely favor the largest and most politically powerful microchip makers, while the smaller companies would be left sitting on the sidelines. Moreover, allowing consortiums of manufacturers could result in their using predatory pricing practices to eliminate smaller, startup companies. They also pointed to past federal government channeling of private-sector resources that produced such expensive duds as the U.S. Synthetic Fuels Corporation, which squandered billions of dollars trying to draw synthetic oil from coal.

Jumbo Jet Aircraft Competition: Boeing and Airbus

The world's manufacturers of large commercial jet aircraft operate in an imperfectly competitive market that has been dominated by Boeing, Inc., of Seattle; McDonnell-Douglas, Inc., is the other U.S. producer of jumbo jets. The largest non-U.S. manufacturer is Airbus Industrie, which was created in 1966 when four European nations pooled their resources to form an aircraft company to compete with the United States. Table 4.7 illustrates the sources of competitive advantage in the world aircraft industry.

The members of the Airbus consortium are France's Aerospatiale S.A. (38-percent ownership), Germany's Messerschmitt, Boelkow and Bloom (38 percent), British Aerospace PLC (20 percent), and Construcciones Aeronauticas S.A. of Spain (4 percent). These companies cooperate in the manufacturing of jumbo jets, although they compete against each other in other aircraft products. During the mid-1970s, Airbus sold less than 5 percent of the world's jumbo jets; by 1992 it captured 31 percent of the world market.

Throughout the 1980s, the United States complained that Airbus received unfair subsidies from the governments of the four partners, placing U.S. aircraft manufacturers at a disadvantage. The Airbus consortium allegedly received loans from European governments for the development of new aircraft; these loans were made at below-market interest rates and amounted to 70–90 percent of an aircraft's development cost. Rather than repaying the loans according to a prescribed timetable, as typically would occur in a free market, Airbus was allowed to repay them as it delivered an aircraft. Airbus was also alleged to benefit from debt forgiveness when it suffered losses. In short, the United States maintained that Europe's treatment of Airbus was tantamount to an industrial policy in which a government targets a producer for subsidization to ensure its competitiveness.

Critics of these subsidies contended that conventional economic theory could not be used to analyze Airbus, since it was motivated by factors other than just profits. For example, Airbus had a stated objective of keeping its production lines in operation, irrespective of profits, to provide jobs for European workers. Because government subsidies lessened/eliminated financial risks for Airbus, the firm did not have to base its decisions to launch new aircraft

T A B L E 4. 7 / *Sources of Competitiveness in the Aerospace Industry*

	United States	Europe
Technology		
Design	+	+
Manufacturing	+	+
R&D	+	+
Test facilities	0/+	0
Management		
Project management	+	+
Integration	+	+
Technology team management	0	0
Market forecasting	+	0
Human resource management	-	+
Finance		
Ability to secure new project financing	0	+
Export sales financing	-	+
Military spending	+	+
Direct government support	-	+

+ Strong, 0 Moderate, - Weak

SOURCE: D. Cravens and others, "Global Competition in the Commercial Aircraft Industry," *Columbia Journal of World Business* 26, no. 4 (Winter 1992), p. 52.

types solely on profits/losses. Airbus's financial statements showed that it did not generate a profit during the 1970s–1990s; without subsidies, the firm would have gone bankrupt.

Airbus defended its subsidies on the grounds that they prevented the United States from holding a worldwide monopoly in commercial jet aircraft. In the absence of Airbus, European airlines would have to rely exclusively on U.S. companies as suppliers. Fears of dependence and the loss of autonomy in an area on the cutting edge of technology motivated European governments to subsidize Airbus. Airbus also argued that U.S. commercial aircraft producers benefitted from government assistance. Rather than receiving direct governmental subsidies like Airbus, U.S. firms received indirect subsidies. For example, governmental research organizations (such as the National Aeronautics and Space Administration) sup-

ported aeronautics and propulsion research that was shared with U.S. aircraft manufacturers. Support for commercial aircraft innovation also came from military-sponsored research and military procurement. Research financed by the armed services yielded indirect but important technological spillovers to the commercial aircraft industry, most notably in aircraft engines and aircraft design.

As a result of the Boeing/Airbus conflict, in the late 1980s the United States and Europe negotiated the issue of aircraft subsidies. In 1992, the nations agreed on terms to curb subsidies for Airbus and its U.S. rivals. The principal element of the accord was a variable 30- to 33-percent cap on the amount of government subsidies that the United States and European aerospace industries could receive for product development. In addition, the indirect subsidies (spillover benefits from military contracts) would be limited, under a complicated formula, to 5 percent of a firm's civil-aeronautics revenue. The pact also required Europe and the United States to report more clearly what public funds are used to support civilian-aircraft development.

ENVIRONMENTAL REGULATORY POLICIES AND INTERNATIONAL COMPETITIVENESS

Beginning in the early 1960s, the U.S. government became increasingly concerned with the quality of life for its people—the conditions under which goods and services are produced, the effect of production on society, and the physical characteristics of the products themselves. This led to government regulation, known as **social regulation**, that promoted safer and better products, less pollution, better working conditions, and greater equality of opportunity. Although the objectives of these regulations were widely recognized as laudable, it was apparent that they added to a business's costs and prices. Table 4.8 illustrates the costs of pollution-abatement equipment for U.S. manufacturers.

Questions have arisen as to whether *differing efforts* by individual nations to improve the quality of life distort international trade patterns. It has been argued that because the United States is a more litigious society than many of its foreign competitors, U.S. companies are burdened with relatively high regulatory costs that hinder their international competitiveness. Because most of the cost of U.S. social regulations has been attributed to environmental policy, it is worth examining the trade effects of **environmental regulation** separately.

In an *unregulated market*, producers can impose costs on society from pollution (such as emissions into the air) but do not bear these costs. Profit-maximizing manufacturers desire the least-cost combination of inputs and attempt to bear only unavoidable costs. They find it profitable to dump solid waste into rivers instead of paying for expensive pollution-abatement equipment. By enjoying lower production costs than if they had not polluted the environment, manufacturers can sell their products more cheaply, increase output, and earn larger profits. The polluting manufacturer's supply schedule lies too far to the right because it does not include the cost that society absorbs in the form of environmental decay. This results in an *overallocation* of resources to the pollution-yielding commodity.

When environmental neglect affects the domestic economy, international trade also becomes affected. Because the prices of pollution-yielding goods do not include their full costs to society, such goods receive a subsidy equal to the "unpaid" use of economic resources for pollution-control, "paid" for by the victims of pollution in the producing country. A change in competitiveness in international trade could occur if an industry in one country enjoyed substantially lower pollution control costs than the same industry in other countries. Similarly, the location of industry is influenced by the lack of recognition given to pollution costs in private investment decisions.

The distinction between *production pollution* and *consumption pollution* is important for international trade. For industries that pollute (for example, paper companies that discharge into the water), meeting environmental regulations generally requires their paying for pollution-abatement equipment. Costs are thus raised for the producer, leading to price increases for the consumer and a reduction in competitiveness for exporting and import-competing companies. For consumption pollution, meeting environmental regulations generally involves product design and operating standards. Such standards include the composition of a product (such as phosphates in detergents), emissions or design (as with motor vehicle exhaust and noise), and product use (rate of aircraft climb to avoid noise). The increase in price resulting from environmental product standards thus reflects a changed or altered product, whereas price increases due to production

TABLE 4.8 / *Pollution-Abatement Capital Expenditures, 1990: U.S. Industries* (Millions of Dollars)

Selected Industries	Total	Air	Water	Solid Waste
Food	$249	$65	$163	$21
Tobacco	6	4	1	1
Textile	46	19	25	2
Lumber	105	58	10	37
Furniture	24	19	2	2
Paper	1075	414	510	152
Printing	68	56	4	7
Chemicals	1851	596	994	261
Petroleum	917	426	401	90
Rubber	94	69	11	14
Leather	8	1	7	1
Stone	128	94	20	14
Primary metals	499	279	167	54
Fabricated metals	171	53	61	57
Machinery	107	46	41	20
Electric	178	93	58	26
Transportation	395	207	143	46
Instruments	92	58	26	8

SOURCE: U.S. Department of Commerce, Current Industrial Reports, *Manufacturers' Pollution Abatement Capital Expenditures and Operating Costs,* January 1992.

pollution result from the increased costs of pollution-abatement equipment used in producing the good.

Figure 4.5 illustrates the *trade consequences* of pollution regulations imposed on the production process. Assume a world of two steel producers, South Korea and the United States. The supply and demand schedules of South Korea are indicated by $S_{S.K._0}$ and $D_{S.K._0}$, and those of the United States by $S_{U.S._0}$ and $D_{U.S._0}$. In the absence of trade, South Korean producers sell 5 tons of steel at $400 per ton, while 12 tons of steel are sold in the United States at $600 per ton. South Korea thus enjoys a cost advantage in steel production. With free trade, South Korea moves toward greater specialization in steel production, while the United States produces less steel. Under increasing cost

conditions, South Korea's costs and prices rise, while prices and costs fall in the United States. The basis for further growth of trade is eliminated when the two countries' prices equalize at $500 per ton. At this price, South Korea produces 7 tons, consumes 3 tons, and exports 4 tons, while the United States produces 10 tons, consumes 14 tons, and imports 4 tons.

Now suppose that the production of steel results in discharges into waterways, leading the U.S. Environmental Protection Agency to impose pollution regulations on U.S. steel producers. Meeting these regulations adds to production costs, resulting in a shift in the U.S. supply schedule for steel to $S_{U.S._1}$. Assuming that the South Korean government does not initiate environmental regulations, South Korean producers enjoy an additional competitive

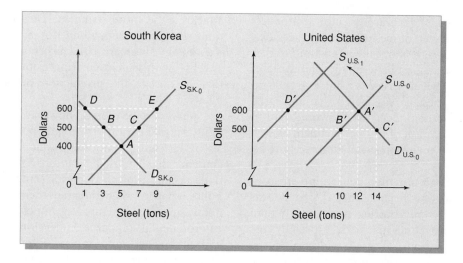

FIGURE 4. 5 *Trade effects of pollution-control regulations.* The imposition of pollution-control regulations on U.S. steel companies leads to higher costs and a decrease in market supply. This detracts from the competitiveness of U.S. steel companies and reduces their share of the U.S. steel market.

advantage. As South Korean producers expand steel production—say, to 9 tons—higher production costs result in a rise in steel prices to $600. At this price, South Korean consumers demand only 1 ton. The excess supply of 8 tons is earmarked for sale to the United States. As for the United States, 12 tons of steel are demanded at the price of $600, as determined by South Korea. Given supply schedule $S_{U.S.,1}$, U.S. firms now produce only 4 tons of steel at the $600 price. The excess demand, 8 tons, is met by imports from South Korea. For U.S. steel companies, the costs imposed by pollution regulations lead to further competitive disadvantage and a smaller share of the U.S. market.

A widespread concern expressed by environmentalists is that trade liberalization may result in a lowering of environmental standards. First, there is the concern that trade and investment liberalization might result in pressure on domestic regulatory authorities to loosen enforcement or lower standards so as to preserve domestic jobs and income. Second, environmentalists sometimes perceive efforts to

remove trade barriers and equalize regulatory burdens on producers as undermining the goal of environmental protection. They fear that efforts to create uniformity in environmental regulation through the harmonization of standards may result in a lowest-common-denominator approach.

During the early 1990s, the United States, Canada, and Mexico negotiated a North American Free Trade Agreement (NAFTA), designed to phase out trade barriers among the three nations (see Chapter 9). Environmental activists in these nations, however, expressed concerns that a free-trade agreement would encourage many U.S. companies that pollute to move to Mexico, where enforcement of environmental regulations was considered to be more lenient. They further argued that the competition for investment among the nations in a free-trade area could push environmental standards and enforcement to the lowest common denominator. Some environmental groups even asserted that NAFTA would encourage the importation into the United States of environmentally unsafe products (such as agricultural products with high levels of pesticides). Furthermore, there was concern about the impact of NAFTA on the border region between the United States and Mexico, which serves as a home to foreign-owned factories; it was feared that increased volumes of trade under NAFTA would lead to further degradation of this environment as well as the overall environment, of all three NAFTA nations.

Sporadic information concerning environmental regulation suggests that U.S. standards have often been more stringent and costly than those of its trading partners, especially the developing nations. These regulatory costs, however, are not large enough to negate the general findings of other researchers concerning the importance of capital, raw materials, labor skills and wages, and R&D as determinants of trade performance. One study found that in most cases environmental-regulation costs amounted to only 2 to 5 percent of total production costs for U.S. producers.[9]

U.S. air and water pollution-control standards are similar to those of other industrial nations today. There is, however, one environmental standard that the United States enforces more strictly than other industrial nations: the generation, transportation, and disposal of hazardous waste (such as toxic chemicals). The United States has a hazardous-waste law for which there is no counterpart abroad: the Environmental Response, Compensation, and Liability Act of 1976, known as the **Superfund law**. This law is designed to ensure that potentially harmful abandoned hazardous-waste sites are identified and cleaned up, often at a cost exceeding $30 million per site. To the extent that the United States has a competitive disadvantage due to pollution-control regulations, it is probably because the United States has a Superfund law while its industrial-nation competitors do not.

Relative to the environmental standards of many *developing nations*, the standards of the United States (and other industrial nations)

appear to be more stringent. Developing nations such as Mexico, South Korea, Brazil, and Taiwan have been criticized as being "pollution havens" with lenient environmental standards that encourage the production of pollution-intensive goods.

It should be noted, however, that most industrialized nations are greater polluters than less industrialized nations. Developing nations contend that industrial nations, rather than undertaking radical domestic environmental policy changes that threaten their own economic growth, attempt to impose stringent environmental standards on developing nations without any assistance in paying for them; lack of compensation lessens the opportunity for less industrialized nations to grow.

One hotly debated issue is the protection of rain forests, mostly in Latin America, which help reduce carbon dioxide in the air and provide biological diversity. Industrialized nations have moved to prevent wood imports from Brazil, for example, in order to reduce deforestation in that nation. Developing nations argue that industrialized nations should provide compensation for the benefits they receive from rain-forest maintenance.

Why would less industrialized, developing nations adopt less stringent environmental policies than industrial nations? Poorer nations may place a higher priority on the benefits of production (more jobs and income) relative to the benefits of environmental quality than wealthy nations; as income rises, however, demand for environmental quality tends to increase. Moreover, less industrialized nations may have greater environmental capacities to reduce pollutants by natural processes (such as Latin America's rain-forest capacity to reduce carbon dioxide in the air) than do industrial nations, which suffer from the effects of past pollution. Less industrialized nations can thus tolerate higher levels of emissions without increasing pollution levels. Finally, the introduction of a polluting industry into a sparsely populated developing nation will likely have less impact on the capacity of the environment to reduce pollution by natural processes than it would have in a densely populated industrial nation.

To the extent that environmental costs are ignored, producers in developing nations have a competitive advantage compared to those of the industrial nations. The fact that environmental costs remain hidden means that developing nations may be able to attract more investment to exportable manufactured goods than they would under a more rigorous system of environmental control.

There is some evidence of relocation by business firms because of national differences in environmental standards. For example, during the 1970s and 1980s, several U.S. copper smelters and asbestos plants were reported have located production abroad in order to avoid stringent U.S. environmental laws. Another example is General Motors, which announced in 1992 that it would move its 56-year-old truck assembly plant out of Mexico City because of tighter emission standards.

On a world scale, however, evidence does not suggest that cost differences due to environmental standards have significant investment effects on firm location. Perhaps the most important reason is that environmental-compliance costs in most industries are a relatively small fraction of total costs and can easily be dwarfed by other relative cost differences, such as raw materials and wages. Moreover, there is always the risk that a nation with low environmental standards will raise them in the future; such revisions potentially entail expensive retrofits of plant and equipment. Finally, firms are increasingly finding that marketing their goods to environmentally conscious consumers as environmentally "safe" or "clean" enhances their competitiveness. This means that technical changes and innovations induced by strict environmental regulations help position the leaders to compete more effectively in the long run, even if they reduce competitiveness in the short run.

Some experts maintain that trade and environmental concerns not only complement each other, but can actually be mutually beneficial. It is argued that stringent environmental standards can foster the creation and upgrading of competitive advantage. They force companies to improve quality, upgrade technology, and provide features in important areas of customer and social concern. Especially beneficial are stringent environmental regulations that precede the adoption of similar standards in other nations.

To the extent that domestic producers do lose competitiveness because of stringent environmental regulations, what might be done? Government could provide *subsidies* to domestic producers to offset production-cost disadvantages caused by environmental regulations. However, subsidies must be financed by higher taxes and may not be in the national interest. International differences in the costs of environmental regulations could also be neutralized through tariffs (taxes) applied to imports of goods produced by polluting industries overseas. Such a policy, however, could invite tariff retaliation by foreign governments.

The *international harmonization of environmental policies* is another way of minimizing adverse effects of environmental regulations on trade patterns. The United States has acknowledged the need for such harmonization in the Federal Water Pollution Control Act, which requires the U.S. government to work in cooperation with other nations to develop similar pollution standards. Although there has been some success in negotiating international environmental policies, the main obstacle has been the lack of a supranational authority that can require nations to initiate pollution-abatement programs to improve global welfare. International harmonization of environmental policies is undertaken voluntarily only if a nation believes there is an equitable distribution of the costs and benefits among participating nations.

The international environmental policy of the United States and other industrial nations is founded on the **polluter-pays principle**. It states that the cost of pollution prevention and control measures should be incorporated into the prices of goods and services that cause pollution in the production process or consumption. This approach is intended to provide producers the incentive to develop more efficient pollution-control techniques and production processes that do not pollute as much and to find substitute goods whose use is less polluting. Subsidies for pollution control are seen as weakening these incentives. But exceptions to the polluter-pays principle do exist. All industrial countries, including the United States, have offered some government assistance to help domestic companies finance the costs of pollution abatement. The U.S. government, for example, has used industrial revenue bonds that allow companies to borrow money at subsidized interest rates.

TRADE IN BUSINESS SERVICES

The trading of products among countries is not confined to the exporting and importing of manufactured goods, but also includes a group of activities known as **business services**.[10] In many cases, business services are nonstorable, in that they must be consumed as they are produced (for example, management consulting); unlike manufactured goods, business services cannot be maintained in inventories by producers. Examples of internationally traded business services include the following:

TRAVEL AND TRANSPORTATION

Tourism

Passenger transportation (for example, airlines)

Shipping transportation (for example, freight and port facilities)

PROPRIETARY RIGHTS

The use and sale of intangible property or rights (for example, fees and royalties paid for the use of technology, patents, and copyrights)

OTHER BUSINESS SERVICES

Construction, architecture, engineering, consulting, brokerage, communications, management and technical services, R&D assessments, banking, finance, insurance, information management, medical, and legal

In recent years, business services have become an important item on national and international policy agendas; Table 4.9 shows the world's leading exporters and importers of business services. The reasons for this growing interest are easy to identify. In many countries, business-service activities account for the largest share of employment and national production. Most of the job creation in industrial countries in the past two decades has been in the service sector. Technological innovations are creating many new services and making many types of services tradeable across national boundaries. These innovations have gone hand in hand with changes in the organization of production; the production and trade of goods and services have become increasingly linked.

Does the theory of comparative advantage apply to trade in business services? The theory suggests that trade between two countries creates mutual economic gains, provided that such trade is based on a competitive market. As a theoretical statement, the theory of comparative advantage should be equally valid whether the products involved are tradeable merchandise (such as aircraft) or tradeable services (such as accounting services). The wine and cloth in Ricardo's classic example of comparative advantage could easily have been replaced by wine and insurance policies without altering the validity of the comparative-advantage doctrine.

Similar to manufactured goods, business services are produced by combining resources to create something of value that can be bought or sold in the market. One would expect that

T A B L E 4. 9 / Leading Exporters and Importers of Commercial Services, 1990
(Billions of Dollars)

Exporters	Value	Importers	Value
United States	$119	Japan	$89
France	82	United States	88
United Kingdom	55	Germany	82
Germany	52	France	65
Japan	42	United Kingdom	44
Italy	41	Italy	39
Netherlands	30	Netherlands	29
Spain	29	Belgium	27
Belgium	28	Canada	23
Austria	23	Sweden	17
Switzerland	17	Spain	16
Canada	15	Switzerland	16
Singapore	15	Taiwan	15
Hong Kong	14	Yugoslavia	15
Sweden	14	Australia	14

SOURCE: General Agreement on Tariffs and Trade, *International Trade: 1990–1991*, vol. 2, p. 4.

the production and sale of services would follow a pattern of economic behavior similar to the production and sale of manufactured goods. The majority of researchers who have examined the applicability of the comparative-advantage principle to services have indicated that there is nothing in the theory that intrinsically makes it less applicable to services than to goods.

One problem of applying comparative-advantage theory to trade involving business services is that many services—being intangible, nonstorable, and nontransportable—cannot be traded without the physical relocation of providers or receivers. International trade in services (such as construction) requires the consumer and the producer to be at the same place at the same time because the production and consumption activities are exactly the same process.

Applying the comparative-advantage principle to services is also difficult because they are such a heterogeneous group. The clear differences that exist between, say, banking services, air freight, and architecture services have led many to question whether the theory of comparative advantage can be a useful empirical guide for all service sectors. The heterogeneous nature of services makes it impossible to think of them as a single entity or for a nation to think of itself as having a competitive advantage in all services, any more than it can have a cost advantage in all manufactured goods.

It is unlikely that a single theory can encompass all the characteristics of international trade in services. But the same holds true for trade in goods. Some characteristics of trade in particular goods have led to the development of partial theories (such as overlapping demand theory, which applies to manufactured goods).

In like manner, partial theories will likely have to be developed for single services or groups of services having common characteristics.

Although there is no single theory involving trade in business services, empirical research has identified a number of determinants underlying a nation's competitiveness in various services:

Skills and capabilities of employees and employee wages

A business's ability to organize a cooperative effort among workers with the right complementary skills

Abundance of equipment, including communications facilities, data processing, and computers

The institutional support provided by the legal system, practices, and traditions found in each nation

The potential economies of scale afforded by a market's size

Of these determinants, the cost of capital and labor and physical proximity depend on a nation's current endowment of resources. The other determinants—institutional environment, organization, and personal skills—can be acquired.

The export advantage in many services, as revealed by existing patterns of trade in services, appear to lie substantially with the developed countries. Empirical evidence suggests that many traded services tend to be intensive in the use of technology and of capital, whether human or physical. This seems to give the developed countries a competitive edge. The United States, for example, has often been characterized as having a comparative advantage in business services; this reflects the longstanding position of the United States as a net exporter of technology and know-how.

TRANSPORTATION COSTS

Because the movement of goods among nations involves economic distance, the effects of trans-portation costs cannot be ignored. **Transportation costs** refer to the costs of moving goods, including freight charges, packing and handling expenses, and insurance premiums. The introduction of transportation costs into the analysis modifies the trade model in two ways. First, the trade effects of transportation costs are a lower volume of trade, higher import prices, and thus lower gains from trade. Second, transportation costs affect the location of industry and the geographic pattern of trade.

Trade Effects

The trade effects of transportation costs can be illustrated with a conventional supply-and-demand model based on increasing-cost conditions. Figure 4.6 illustrates the supply and demand curves of autos for the United States and Canada. Reflecting the assumption that the United States has the comparative advantage in auto production, the U.S. and Canadian equilibrium autarky locations are at points E and F, respectively. In the absence of trade, the U.S. auto price, $4,000, is lower than that of Canada, $8,000.

When trade is allowed, the United States will move toward greater specialization in auto production, whereas Canada will produce fewer autos. Under increasing-cost conditions, the U.S. cost and price levels rise, and Canada's price falls. The basis for further growth of trade is eliminated when the two countries' prices equalize at $6,000. At this price, the United States produces 6 autos, consumes 2 autos, and exports 4 autos; Canada produces 2 autos, consumes 6 autos, and imports 4 autos. Thus, $6,000 becomes the equilibrium price for both countries because the excess auto supply of the United States just matches the excess auto demand in Canada.

The introduction of transportation costs into the analysis modifies the conclusions of the preceding example. Suppose the per-unit cost of transporting an auto from the United States to Canada is $2,000, as shown in Figure 4.7. The United States would find it advantageous to

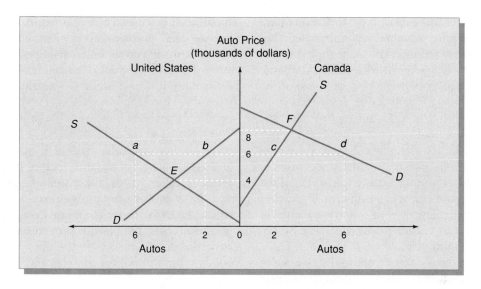

FIGURE 4. 6   *Free trade under increasing-cost conditions.* In the absence of transportation costs, free trade results in the equalizing of the prices of the traded goods, as well as resource prices, in the trading nations.

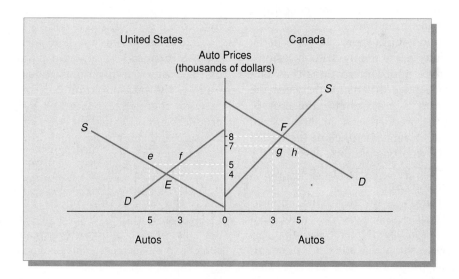

FIGURE 4. 7   *Trade effects of transportation costs.* With the introduction of transportation costs, the low-cost exporting country produces less, consumes more, and exports less. The high-cost importing country produces more, consumes less, and imports less. The degree of specialization in production between the two countries decreases, as do the gains from trade.

produce autos and export them to Canada until its relative price advantage is eliminated. But when transportation costs are included in the analysis, the U.S. export price reflects domestic production costs *plus* the cost of transporting autos to Canada. The basis for trade thus stops growing when the U.S. auto price plus the transportation cost rises to Canada's auto price level. This occurs when the U.S. auto price rises to $5,000 and Canada's auto price falls to $7,000, the difference between them being the $2,000 per-unit transportation cost. Instead of a single price ruling in both countries, there will be two domestic auto prices, differing by the cost of transportation.

Compared with free trade in the absence of transportation costs, when transportation costs are included the high-cost importing country will produce more, consume less, and import less. The low-cost exporting country will produce less, consume more, and export less. Transportation costs, therefore, tend to reduce the volume of trade, the degree of specialization in production among the nations concerned, and thus the gains from trade.

The inclusion of transportation costs in the analysis modifies our trade-model conclusions. A product will be traded internationally as long as the pretrade price differential between the trading partners is *greater than* the cost of transporting the product between them. When trade is in equilibrium, the price of the traded product in the exporting nation is *less than* the price in the importing country by the amount of the transportation cost.

Transportation costs also have implications for the factor-price-equalization theorem presented earlier in this chapter. Recall that this theorem suggests that free trade tends to equalize commodity prices and factor prices so that all workers will earn the same wage rate and all units of capital will earn the same interest income in both nations. Free trade permits factor-price equalization to occur because factor inputs that cannot move to another country are implicitly being shipped in the form of com-modities. Looking at the real world, however, we see U.S. autoworkers earning more than South Korean autoworkers. One possible reason for this differential is transportation costs. By making low-cost South Korean autos more expensive for U.S. consumers, transportation costs reduce the volume of autos shipped from South Korea to the United States. This reduced trade volume stops the process of commodity- and factor-price equalization before it is complete. In other words, the prices of U.S. autos and the wages of U.S. autoworkers do not fall to the levels of those in South Korea. Transportation costs thus provide some relief to high-cost domestic workers who are producing goods subject to import competition.

Transportation Costs and U.S. Imports

Imports are shipped to the United States by land, water, and air. Air transportation is generally the most costly of the three. In recent years, the share of imports shipped to the United States by water has equaled roughly 70 percent; by land, 20 percent; and by air, 10 percent.

How important are transportation costs for U.S. imports? The most common measure of the cost of transporting goods in foreign trade is the transportation cost of a product between countries expressed as a share of the product's import value (the *freight factor*). This measure indicates how much transportation costs hinder international trade.

Since the 1960s, the cost of international transportation has decreased significantly relative to the value of U.S. imports. From 1965 to 1981, transportation costs as a percentage of the value of all U.S. imports decreased from 10 percent to 4.5 percent. This decline in the relative cost of international transportation made imports more competitive in U.S. markets and contributed to a higher volume of trade for the United States. It is estimated that decreasing international transportation costs resulted in a 14-percent increase in U.S. imports from 1976 to 1981. Table 4.10 shows transportation costs

TABLE 4. 10 / *Transportation Costs as a Share of Value for Selected U.S. Imports* (in Percentages)

Commodity	1965	1981
Live animals	3%	1.7%
Motor vehicles	11	4.5
Office machines	4	2.5
Iron or steel	13	8.0
Wool	7	8.1
Rubber	11	8.1
Plywood	19	11.1
Cocoa	7	6.8
Nails, screws, bolts	11	6.6
Electrical machinery	6	2.5
Hides, skins, leather	5	4.9

SOURCE: U.S. International Trade Commission, *Transportation Costs of U.S. Imports*, USITC Publication 1375 (Washington, D.C.: Government Printing Office, 1983), p. 7.

as a percentage of import values for selected U.S. imports.

Why did the relative cost of international transportation for most U.S. imports fall during the late 1970s and early 1980s? One reason is technological improvements, including the development of large dry-bulk containers, large-scale tankers, containerization, and wide-bodied jets. During the recession years, ocean freight rates for manufactured goods fell as a result of weak demand for shipping. Relative transportation costs for petroleum products decreased because of excess capacity in the world tanker fleet and the rapid increase in the price of petroleum products. At the same time, the United States reduced its petroleum purchases from the Middle East and increased purchases from nearby countries, including Mexico and the United Kingdom. The reduction in the average haul length of crude oil reduced the demand for tankers, and hence shipping rates.

Partially offsetting these cost-reducing factors were rising fuel prices, which contributed to transportation cost increases.

Domestic transportation costs also affect the international competitiveness of import-competing industries. For example, U.S. steel and auto producers tend to concentrate production in the midwestern states. Because of land transportation costs, import penetration for these industries is much higher in areas that are farther away from Midwest production centers. Thus, foreign auto sales in the United States have been strongest in the Pacific Coast states and weakest in states bordering the Great Lakes.

Location of Industry

Besides having trade effects, transportation costs affect the **location of industry**. A profit-seeking business recognizes the costs of transporting raw materials and final products as well as the costs of production. A business will achieve its best location when it can minimize its total operating costs, including both production and transportation costs. In terms of location theory, production can be classified into three categories: (1) resource- or supply-oriented, (2) market- or demand-oriented, and (3) footloose or neutral.

Resource-oriented industries, such as steel and lumber, are generally *weight-losing*. Because the final product is so much less weighty or bulky than the materials from which it is made, the industry will find it advantageous to undertake production near the resource supplies. This is because the cost of transporting finished products is substantially lower than the cost of transporting the inputs used in their manufacture. A firm's transportation costs thus decrease if it locates near the supply of resources.

Industrial processes that add weight or bulk to the commodity are likely to be located near the product market to minimize transportation costs. An industry tends to be

market-oriented when its production process is *weight-gaining*. This is because the cost of shipping the final product exceeds the cost of transporting the raw materials that go into its production. A firm's transportation costs are minimized if it locates close to its product market. A prominent example of weight gaining occurs in the case of Coca-Cola and Pepsi-Cola. These companies transport syrup concentrate to plants all over the world, which add water to the syrup and bottle it. Another example is the U.S. auto industry, which has located assembly plants near regional and even foreign markets. This is because it is cheaper to ship the unassembled auto parts than to ship the finished automobile.

Footloose industries are those that do not find their manufacturing operations pulled close to the resource supplies or the location of market demand. This may occur (1) when a product is extremely valuable, such as electronic products, so that transportation costs are a very small portion of the product's total costs or (2) when the product is neither weight-gaining nor weight-losing. Given these circumstances, the industry tends to be quite mobile, locating wherever the availability and cost of factor inputs permit total production costs to be minimized. Because transportation costs are not of particular significance in a footloose industry, production costs are the key determinant of industry location.

Transportation Costs and the U.S. Steel Industry

Transportation costs for steel products are an important factor affecting the competitive position of U.S. manufacturers and foreign companies that export steel to the United States. Because steel has a low value per unit, transportation costs are a significant part of the cost to end users. To minimize transportation costs, U.S. steel companies have generally located production close to either their main sources of raw materials or their large-volume customers.

The geographic pattern of steel consumption and production in the United States contributes to the high transportation costs faced by shippers of steel products. Most U.S. steel mills are located in Indiana, Ohio, Pennsylvania, and Illinois. The cost of transporting steel, via truck or rail, to other locations in the United States can be sizable. Customers in many locations may be closer to a foreign manufacturer's port of entry than to a U.S. steel mill. The cost of transporting steel within the United States via rail and truck—which is often high compared to ocean freight rates—may thus reduce the competitiveness of U.S. steel firms. This is especially true for West Coast steel manufacturers who compete with foreign firms for sales in the eastern part of the United States.

Steel from Brazil, Japan, South Korea, Germany, and France (the major steel exporters to the United States) is shipped to the United States exclusively by ocean freight. Of these nations, Brazil has generally enjoyed the lowest transportation cost on shipments to the United States.

Steel transportation costs also vary by port of entry into the United States, because of port facilities and the distance from the foreign steel mill. The five exporting nations previously mentioned generally ship steel to the U.S. port where transportation costs will make up the lowest percentage of total costs. As seen in Table 4.11, South Korea and Japan in 1986 sent the largest portion of their U.S. shipments to the West Coast; France and Germany shipped the largest portion of their steel exports to the Great Lakes; and Brazil shipped the majority of its steel exports to the East Coast.

T A B L E 4. 11 / Transportation Cost and Port Shipments: Shipping Cost as a Percentage of Total Cost of Steel Sheet and Strip Products Imported into the United States, 1986

Exporting Nation	Primary Port of Entry	Unit Value (dollars/ton)	Transportation Cost as a Percentage of Unit Value
Brazil	East Coast	$324.47	6%
South Korea	West Coast	386.66	7
Japan	West Coast	386.66	8
France	Great Lakes	436.57	8
Germany	Great Lakes	470.78	8

SOURCE: U.S. International Trade Commission, *U.S. Global Competitiveness: Steel Sheet and Strip Industry* (Washington, D.C.: Government Printing Office, January 1988), pp. 3–48.

SUMMARY

1. The immediate basis for trade stems from relative commodity price differences among nations. Because relative prices are determined by supply and demand conditions, such factors as resource endowments, technology, and national income are important determinants of the basis for trade.

2. The Heckscher–Ohlin theory suggests that differences in relative factor endowments among nations underlie the basis for trade. The theory asserts that a nation will export the commodity in the production of which a relatively large amount of its abundant and cheap resource is used. Conversely, it will import commodities in the production of which a relatively scarce and expensive resource is used. The theory also states that with trade the relative differences in resource prices between nations tend to be eliminated.

3. Contrary to the predictions of the Heckscher–Ohlin model, the empirical tests of Wassily Leontief demonstrated that for the United States exports are labor-intensive and import-competing goods are capital-intensive. His findings became known as the Leontief paradox.

4. By widening the size of the domestic market, international trade permits firms to take advantage of longer production runs and increasing efficiencies (such as mass production). Such economies of large-scale production can be translated into lower product prices, which improve a firm's competitiveness.

5. Staffan Linder offers two explanations of world trade patterns. Trade in primary products and agricultural goods conforms well to the factor-endowment theory. But trade in manufactured goods is best explained by overlapping demand structures among nations. For manufactured goods, the basis for trade is stronger the more similar the structure of demand in the two nations—that is, the more similar are the nations' per capita incomes.

6. Besides interindustry trade, the exchange of goods among nations includes intraindustry trade—two-way trade in a similar product. Intraindustry trade occurs in homogeneous goods as well as differentiated products.

7. One dynamic theory of international trade is the product life cycle theory. This theory views a variety of manufactured goods as going

through a trade cycle, during which a nation initially is an exporter, then loses its export markets, and finally becomes an importer of the product. Empirical studies have demonstrated that trade cycles do exist for manufactured goods at some times.

8. Dynamic comparative advantage refers to the creation of comparative advantage through the mobilization of skilled labor, technology, and capital; it can be initiated by either the private or public sector. When government attempts to create comparative advantage, the term *industrial policy* applies. Industrial policy seeks to encourage the development of emerging, sunrise industries through such measures as tax incentives and R&D subsidies.

9. The environmental laws of national governments can affect the competitive position of their industries. These laws often result in cost-increasing compliance measures, such as the installation of pollution-control equipment, which can detract from the competitiveness of domestic industries.

10. International trade includes the flow of services between countries as well as the exchange of manufactured goods. As with trade in manufactured goods, the principle of comparative advantage applies to service trade.

11. Transportation costs tend to reduce the volume of international trade by increasing the prices of traded goods. A product will be traded only if the cost of transporting it between nations is less than the pretrade difference between their relative commodity prices. Transportation costs also influence the location of industry.

STUDY QUESTIONS

1. What are the effects of transportation costs on the location of industry and on the volume of trade?

2. Explain how the international movement of products and of factor inputs promotes an equalization of the factor prices among nations.

3. How does the Heckscher–Ohlin theory differ from Ricardian theory in explaining international trade patterns?

4. The Heckscher–Ohlin theory demonstrates how trade affects the distribution of income within trading partners. Explain.

5. How does the Leontief paradox challenge the overall applicability of the factor-endowment model?

6. According to Staffan Linder, there are two explanations of international trade patterns—for manufacturers and for primary (agricultural) goods. Explain.

7. Do recent world trade statistics support or refute the notion of a product life cycle for manufactured goods?

8. How can economies of large-scale production affect world trade patterns?

9. Distinguish between intraindustry trade and interindustry trade. What are some major determinants of intraindustry trade?

10. What is meant by the term *industrial policy?* How do governments attempt to create comparative advantage in sunrise sectors of the economy? What are some problems encountered when attempting to implement industrial policy?

11. How can environmental regulatory policies affect an industry's international competitiveness?

12. International trade in services is determined by what factors?

13. Table 4.12 illustrates the supply and demand schedules for calculators in Sweden and Norway. On graph paper, draw the supply and demand schedules of each country.

   a. In the absence of trade, what are the equilibrium price and quantity of calculators produced in Sweden and Norway? Which country has the comparative advantage in calculators?

   b. Assume there are no transportation costs. With trade, what price brings about balance in exports and imports? How many calculators are traded at this price? How many calculators are produced and consumed in each country with trade?

   c. Suppose the cost of transporting each calculator from Sweden to Norway is $5. With

T A B L E 4. 12   /   Supply and Demand Schedules for Calculators

| | Sweden | | | Norway | |
| | Quantity | Quantity | | Quantity | Quantity |
Price	Supplied	Demanded	Price	Supplied	Demanded
$ 0	0	1200	$ 0	—	1800
5	200	1000	5	—	1600
10	400	800	10	—	1400
15	600	600	15	0	1200
20	800	400	20	200	1000
25	1000	200	25	400	800
30	1200	0	30	600	600
35	1400	—	35	800	400
40	1600	—	40	1000	200
45	1800	—	45	1200	0

trade, what is the impact of the transportation cost on the price of calculators in Sweden and Norway? How many calculators will each country produce, consume, and trade?

d. In general, what can be concluded about the impact of transportation costs on the price of the traded product in each trading nation? The extent of specialization? The volume of trade?

Tariffs

The conclusion of the trade models presented so far is that free trade leads to the most efficient use of world resources. When nations specialize according to the comparative-advantage principle, the level of world output is maximized. Not only does free trade enhance world welfare, but it can also benefit each participating nation. Every nation can overcome the limitations of its own productive capacity to consume a combination of goods that exceeds the best it can produce in isolation.

Despite the power of the free-trade argument, however, free trade policies meet major resistance among those companies and workers who face losses in income and jobs because of import competition. Policymakers are torn between the appeal of greater global efficiency made possible by free trade and the needs of the voting public whose main desire is to preserve short-run interests such as employment and income. The benefits of free trade may take years to achieve and are spread out over wide segments of society, whereas the costs of free trade are immediate and fall on specific groups (for example, workers in the import competing industry).

In today's world, restrictions on the flow of goods and services in international trade are widespread. This chapter considers one type of restriction, tariffs, and their impact on trade.

THE TARIFF CONCEPT

Tariffs are simply taxes (duties) levied on products when they cross national boundaries. The most widespread tariff is the *import tariff,* which is a tax levied on an imported product. A less common tariff is an *export tariff,* which is a tax imposed on an exported product. Export tariffs have often been used by developing nations. For example, cocoa exports have been taxed by Ghana and oil exports have been taxed by the Organization of Petroleum Exporting Countries (OPEC) in order to raise revenue or promote scarcity in global markets and hence increase the world price.

Did you know that the United States cannot levy export tariffs? When the U.S. Constitution was written, Southern cotton-producing states feared that Northern textile-manufacturing states would pressure the federal government into levying export tariffs to depress the price of cotton: an export duty would lead to decreased exports and thus a falling price of cotton within the United States. As the result of negotiations, the Constitution was worded so as to prevent export taxes: "No Tax or Duty shall be laid on Articles exported from any State."

Tariffs may be imposed for protection or revenue purposes. A **protective tariff** is designed to insulate import-competing producers from foreign competition. Although a protective tariff generally is not intended to totally prohibit imports from entering the country, it does place foreign producers at a competitive disadvantage when selling in the domestic market. A **revenue tariff** is imposed for the purpose of generating tax revenues and may be placed on both exports and imports.

Over time, tariff revenues have decreased as a source of government revenue for industrial nations including the United States. In 1900, tariff revenues constituted more than 41 percent of U.S. government receipts; by 1990, the figure had fallen to 1.6 percent. However, many developing nations currently rely on tariffs as a major source of government revenue. Table 5.1 shows the percentage of government revenue resulting from tariffs for selected nations.

Specific, Ad Valorem, and Compound Tariffs

Tariffs can be specific, ad valorem, or compound, as seen in Table 5.2. A **specific tariff** is expressed in terms of a fixed amount of money per physical unit of the imported product. For example, a U.S. importer of a German computer may be required to pay a duty to the U.S. government of $100 per computer, regardless of the computer's price. An **ad valorem tariff,** like a sales tax, is expressed as a fixed percentage of the value of the imported product. Suppose that an ad valorem duty of 15 percent is levied on imported trucks. A U.S. importer of a Japanese truck valued at $20,000 would be required to pay a duty of $3,000 to the government ($20,000 × 15% = $3,000). A **compound tariff** is a combination of a specific and an ad valorem tariff. For example, a U.S. importer of a television might be required to pay a duty of $20 plus 5 percent of the value of the television.

What are the relative merits of specific, ad valorem, and compound tariffs?

Specific tariff. As a fixed monetary duty per unit of the imported product, a specific tariff is relatively easy to apply and administer, particularly to standardized commodities and staple products. A main disadvantage of a specific tariff is that the degree of protection it affords domestic producers varies *inversely* with changes in import prices. For example, a specific tariff of $1,000 on autos will discourage

**T A B L E 5. 1 / *Tariff Revenues as a Percentage of Government Revenues, 1990:*
*Selected Countries***

Developing Countries	Percentage	Industrial Countries	Percentage
Tunisia	75.3%	Iceland	13.5%
Cameroon	61.2	Switzerland	7.7
Solomon Islands	56.7	Ireland	7.1
Tonga	50.6	Australia	4.6
Mali	47.2	Canada	3.8
Seychelles	45.4	United States	1.6
Bangladesh	42.6	Norway	0.5
Senegal	41.9	United Kingdom	0.1

SOURCE: International Monetary Fund, *Government Finance Statistics Yearbook* (Washington, D.C.: Author, 1991).

TABLE 5. 2 / *Selected U.S. Tariffs*

Product	Duty Rate
Watch cases	15 cents each
Mercury	16.5 cents/kg
Safety fuses	$1.18 per 1,000
Machine screws	1 cent/kg
Frozen hams	2.2 cents/kg
Squash	2.4 cents/kg
Cough drops	3.9% ad valorem
Auto tires	4% ad valorem
Ski gloves	3.5% ad valorem
Plywood	8% ad valorem
Station wagons	2.5% ad valorem
Babies' T-shirts	21% ad valorem
Woven fabrics	48.5 cents/kg + 38% ad valorem
Ethyl alcohol	6.6 cents/kg + 3% ad valorem
Men's overcoats	77.2 cents/kg + 20% ad valorem
Wool gloves	33.1 cents/kg + 7.4% ad valorem
Boys' shirts	52.9 cents/kg + 21% ad valorem
Hedge shears	1 cent each + 2.8% ad valorem

SOURCE: U.S. International Trade Commission, *Tariff Schedules of the United States* (Washington, D.C.: Government Printing Office, 1992).

imports priced at $15,000 per auto to a greater degree than those priced at $20,000. During times of inflating import prices, a given specific tariff loses some of its protective effect. On the other hand, a specific tariff has the advantage of providing domestic producers more protection during a business recession, when cheaper products are purchased.

Ad valorem tariff.   Ad valorem tariffs usually lend themselves more satisfactorily to manufactured goods, because they can be applied to products with a wide range of grade variations. As a percentage applied to a product's value, an ad valorem tariff can distinguish among small differentials in product quality to the extent that they are reflected in product price. Under a system of ad valorem tariffs, a person importing a $20,000 Datsun (Nissan) would have to pay a higher tariff duty than a person importing a $19,900 Toyota. The person would likely pay the same duty under a system of specific tariffs.

Another advantage of an ad valorem tariff is that it tends to maintain a constant degree of

protection for domestic producers during periods of changing prices. If the tariff rate is 20
percent ad valorem and the imported product
price is $200, the duty is $40. If the product's
price increases, say, to $300, the duty collected
rises to $60; if the product price falls to $100,
the duty drops to $20. An ad valorem tariff
yields revenues proportionate to values, maintaining a constant degree of relative protection
at all price levels. An ad valorem tariff is similar
to a proportional tax in that the real proportional tax burden or protection does not change
as the tax base changes. In recent decades, ad
valorem duties have been used more often than
specific duties in response to global inflation
and the rising importance of world trade in
manufactured products.

Determination of duties under the ad valorem principle at first appears to be simple, but
in practice it has suffered from administrative
complexities. The main problem has been trying to determine the value of an imported product, a process referred to as **customs valuation.**
Import prices are estimated by customs appraisers, who may disagree on product values.
Moreover, import prices tend to fluctuate over
time, which makes the valuation process rather
difficult.

Another customs-valuation problem stems
from the variety of methods used to determine a
commodity's value. For example, the United
States has traditionally used **free-on-board
(FOB) valuation,** whereby the tariff is applied
to a product's value as it leaves the exporting
country. But European countries have traditionally used a **cost-insurance-freight (CIF) valuation,** whereby ad valorem tariffs are levied as a
percentage of the imported commodity's total
value as it arrives at its final destination. The
CIF price thus includes transportation costs
such as insurance and freight.

Compound tariff. Compound duties are often
applied to manufactured products embodying
raw materials that are subject to tariffs. In this
case, the "specific" portion of the duty neutral-

izes the cost disadvantage of domestic manufactures that results from tariff protection granted
to domestic suppliers of raw materials, and the
"ad valorem" portion of the duty grants protection to the finished-goods industry. In the
United States, for example, there is a compound duty on woven fabrics (for example, 50
cents per kilogram plus 20 percent). The specific portion of the duty (50 cents) compensates
U.S. fabric manufacturers for tariff protection
granted to U.S. cotton producers, while the ad
valorem portion of the duty (20 percent) provides protection for their own woven fabrics.

Effective Rate of Protection

A main objective of an import tariff is to protect domestic producers from foreign competition. By increasing the domestic price of an
import, a tariff serves to make home-produced
goods more attractive to resident consumers.
Output in the import-competing industry can
thus expand beyond what would exist in the
absence of a tariff. The degree of protection
afforded by a tariff reflects the extent to which
domestic prices can rise above foreign prices
without the home producers' being priced out
of the market.

The **nominal tariff rate** published in a
country's tariff schedule give us a general idea
of the level of protection afforded the home
industry. But it may not always truly indicate
the actual or effective protection given. For
example, it is not necessarily true that a 25-
percent import tariff on an automobile provides
the domestic auto industry a protective margin
of 25 percent against foreign producers. This is
because the nominal tariff rates apply only to
the total value of the final import product. But
in the production process, the home import-
competing industry may use imported material
inputs or intermediate products that are subject
to a different tariff than that on the final product; in this case, the **effective tariff rate** will differ from the nominal tariff rate.[1]

T A B L E   5. 3   /   The Effective Rate of Protection

Foreign Radio Import	Cost	Domestic Competing Radio	Cost
Component parts	80	Component parts	80
Assembly activity (value added)	20	Assembly activity (value added)	30(?)
Nominal tariff	10	Domestic price	110
Import price	110		

The effective tariff rate is an indicator of the actual level of protection that a nominal tariff rate provides the domestic import-competing producers. It signifies the *total increase in domestic productive activities (value added) that an existing tariff structure makes possible,* compared with what would occur under free-trade conditions. The effective rate tells us how much more expensive domestic production can be relative to foreign production and still compete in the market.

Assume that the domestic radio industry adds value to imported inputs by assembling component radio parts imported from abroad. Suppose the imported components can enter the home country on a duty-free basis. Suppose also that 20 percent of a radio's final value can be attributed to domestic assembly activities (value added), the remaining 80 percent reflecting the value of the imported components. Furthermore, let the cost of the radio components be the same for both the domestic country and the foreign country. Finally, assume that the foreign country can produce a radio for $100.

Suppose the home country imposes a nominal tariff of 10 percent on finished radios, so that the domestic import price rises from $100 to $110 per unit (Table 5.3). Does this mean that home producers are afforded an effective rate of protection equal to 10 percent? Certainly not! Because the imported component parts enter the country duty-free (at a nominal tariff rate less than that on the finished import

product), the effective rate of protection is 50 percent. Compared with what would exist under free trade, domestic radio producers can be 50-percent more costly in their assembly activities and still be competitive!

To see this, examine Table 5.3. Under free trade (zero tariff), a foreign radio could be imported for $100. To meet this price, domestic producers would have to hold their assembly costs down to $20. But under the protective umbrella of the tariff, domestic producers can afford to pay up to $30 for assembly and still meet the $110 domestic price of imported radios. The result is that domestic assembly costs could rise to a level of 50 percent above what would exist under free-trade conditions:

$$(\$30 - \$20)/\$20 = 0.5$$

In general, the effective tariff rate is given by the following formula:

$$e = \frac{n - ab}{(1 - a)}$$

where

e = the effective rate of protection

n = the nominal tariff rate on the final product

a = the ratio of the value of the imported input to the value of the final product

b = the nominal tariff rate on the imported input

When the values from the radio example are plugged into the formula, we obtain

$$e = \frac{0.1 - 0.8(0)}{1 - 0.8}$$

$$= 0.5$$

The nominal tariff rate of 10 percent levied on the final import product thus affords domestic production activities an effective degree of protection equal to 50 percent—five times the nominal rate.

Two consequences of the effective-rate calculation are worthy of mention. First, the degree of effective protection increases as the value added by domestic producers declines (the ratio of the value of the imported input to the value of the final product increases). In the formula, the higher the value of *a*, the greater the effective protection rate for any given nominal tariff rate on the final product. Second, a tariff on imports used in the production process reduces the level of effective protection. The higher the value of *b*, the lower the effective protection rate for any given nominal tariff on the final product. In the formula, as *b* rises, the numerator of the formula decreases, and hence *e* decreases.

Generalizing from this analysis, *when material inputs or intermediate products enter a country at a very low duty while the final imported commodity is protected by a high duty, the result tends to be a high protection rate for the domestic producers.* The nominal tariff rate on finished goods thus understates the effective rate of protection. But should a tariff be imposed on imported inputs that exceeds that on the finished good, the nominal tariff rate on the finished product would tend to overstate its protective effect. Such a situation might occur if the home government desired to protect raw material suppliers more than domestic manufacturers.

Tariff Escalation

As illustrated in Table 5.4, in many industrialized nations the effective rate of protection is several times the nominal rate. The apparently low nominal tariffs on the final import products may thus *understate* the effective rate of protection, which takes into account the effects of tariffs levied on raw materials and intermediate goods. In addition, the industrialized nations' tariff structures have generally been characterized by an escalation of tariff rates to permit higher degrees of protection on intermediate and finished products than on primary commodities. This is commonly referred to as **tariff escalation**. Although raw materials are often imported at zero or low tariff rates, the nominal and effective protection increases at each stage of production. Many industrialized nations afford a relatively high degree of protection to their manufacturing sector, as suggested in Table 5.5.

The tariff structures of the industrialized nations may indeed discourage the growth of processing and manufacturing industries in the less developed nations. The industrialized nations' low tariffs on primary commodities encourage the developing nations to expand operations in these sectors, while the high protective rates levied on manufactured goods pose a significant entry barrier for any developing nation wishing to compete in this area. From the point of view of the less developed nations, it may be in their best interest to discourage disproportionate tariff reductions on primary commodities. The effect of these tariff reductions is to magnify the discrepancy between the nominal and effective tariffs of the industrialized nations, worsening the potential competitive position of the less developed nations in the manufacturing and processing sectors.

OFFSHORE-ASSEMBLY PROVISION

An interesting feature of U.S. tariff policy is the **offshore-assembly provision** (OAP). Under OAP, when a finished component originating in the United States (such as a semiconductor) is sent overseas and there assembled with one or

T A B L E 5. 4   /   Nominal and Effective Tariff Rates*

Product	United States		Japan		European Community	
	Nominal Rate (%)	Effective Rate (%)	Nominal Rate (%)	Effective Rate (%)	Nominal Rate (%)	Effective Rate (%)
Agriculture, forestry, fish	1.8	1.9	18.4	21.4	4.8	4.1
Food, beverages, tobacco	4.7	10.6	25.4	50.3	10.1	17.8
Textiles	9.2	18.0	3.3	2.4	7.2	8.8
Wearing apparel	22.7	43.3	13.8	42.2	13.4	19.3
Leather products	4.2	5.0	3.0	-14.8	2.0	-2.2
Footwear	8.8	15.4	15.7	50.0	11.6	20.1
Wood products	1.6	1.7	0.3	-30.6	2.5	1.7
Furniture and fixtures	4.1	5.5	5.1	10.3	5.6	11.3
Paper and paper products	0.2	-0.9	2.1	1.8	5.4	8.3
Printing and publishing	0.7	0.9	0.1	-1.5	2.1	-1.0
Chemicals	2.4	3.7	4.8	6.4	11.7	-0.7
Petroleum and related products	1.4	4.7	2.2	4.1	3.4	0.1

* Following the completion of the Tokyo Round of Multilateral Trade Negotiations in 1979.

SOURCE: Alan Deardorff and Robert Stern, "The Effects of the Tokyo Round on the Structure of Protection." In R. Baldwin and A. Krueger, *The Structure and Evolution of Recent U.S. Trade Policy* (Chicago: University of Chicago Press, 1984), pp. 368–377.

more other components to become a finished good (such as a television), the cost of the U.S. component is not included in the dutiable value of the imported assembled article into which it has been incorporated. U.S. import duties thus apply only to the *value added in the foreign assembly process,* provided that U.S.-made components are used by overseas companies in their assembly operations. In like manner, the OAP applies to U.S. metal articles processed abroad and returned to the United States for further processing. The OAP is used most frequently as a means for U.S. manufacturers to reduce their costs so as to be competitive with overseas producers.

In recent years, major manufactured products entering the United States under OAP have included motor vehicles, office machines, and television receivers. These articles are assembled primarily in Mexico and Germany. Aluminum cans and semiconductors are the main metal articles assembled abroad and returned for further processing in the United States under OAP. Japan, Canada, Mexico, and Malaysia account for most of these items shipped to the United States.

The OAP provides potential advantages for the United States and its trading partners. By reducing import tariffs on foreign-assembled goods embodying U.S. components, OAP provides incentives for foreign manufacturers desiring to export to the United States to purchase inputs from U.S. sources. The OAP also encourages U.S. consumers to purchase imports assembled by those foreign companies that use U.S. components. The OAP is especially significant

TABLE 5.5 / *Escalation of Tariff Protection by Production Stages: Nominal Tariffs**

Production Stages	United States (%)	Japan (%)	European Community (%)
Meat products			
Fresh and frozen meat	1.6	10.1	6.6
Prepared meat	2.3	22.5	17.9
Fruit			
Fresh fruit	1.1	21.5	7.7
Prepared fruit	20.3	21.8	16.6
Chocolate			
Cocoa beans	0.0	0.0	1.9
Powder and butter	0.1	2.9	9.0
Chocolate	0.1	24.3	0.1
Leather			
Hides and skins	0.8	0.0	0.0
Leather	3.7	8.5	2.4
Leather products	9.2	12.4	5.5

* Post–Tokyo Round tariffs.

SOURCE: J. Finger and A. Olechowski, eds., *The Uruguay Round* (Washington, D.C.: World Bank, 1987).

to developing nations that are striving to industrialize and require export markets for their goods. These nations' products can become more competitive in the United States if they use U.S. inputs in their assembly operations.

POSTPONING IMPORT DUTIES

Import duties may have unintended side effects for some businesses. For example, duties may discourage a company from importing goods in amounts large enough to take advantage of quantity discount pricing. Before imported goods are released by the U.S. Customs Service, import duties must be paid, or a bond must be posted to guarantee their payment. Up-front payment of these duties may impose financial hardships on importers.

Consider a U.S. assembler who uses imported components. By purchasing its annual requirement of components at one time and shipping it in bulk, the firm could reduce the cost of the imported components. Paying the import duty on the entire year's supply of components at one time, however, may be too expensive for the importer. U.S. trade laws mitigate the effects of import duties by allowing U.S. importers to postpone and prorate over time their duty obligations through bonded warehouses and foreign trade zones.

Bonded Warehouse

According to U.S. tariff law, dutiable imports can be brought into a customs territory and left in a **bonded warehouse**, duty-free. These storage facilities are operated under the lock and key of the U.S. Customs Service. Owners of storage facilities must be bonded to ensure that they will satisfy all customs duty obligations.

Imported goods can be stored, repacked, or further processed in the bonded warehouse. As long as the products are kept in the bonded warehouse, the duty obligation is postponed. The goods may be later sold duty-free overseas or withdrawn for domestic sale upon payment of import duties. When goods are processed in a bonded warehouse with additional domestic materials and enter the domestic market at a later date, only the import portion of the finished good is subject to customs duties.

Bonded warehouses are sometimes used for reexportation. Imported goods are stored in the bonded warehouse until suitable foreign markets can be found. If these goods are not stored in a bonded warehouse, the importer must pay duty on them when they enter the country. The importer can then claim a refund of 99 percent of the duties paid, referred to as a *drawback,* after they have been reexported. By using a bonded warehouse, however, a business can avoid the delay and costs associated with customs clearance and drawback application connected with reexport.

Foreign Trade Zones

Because of inspection and surveillance by the U.S. Customs Service, storage in bonded warehouses is generally more costly than in ordinary storage facilities. As a less expensive alternative, the U.S. government permits importers to use a **foreign trade zone** (FTZ). FTZs enlarge the benefits of a bonded warehouse by eliminating the restrictive aspects of customs surveillance and by offering more suitable manufacturing facilities.

An FTZ is a site within the United States where foreign merchandise can be imported *without* formal U.S. customs entry (payment of customs duties) or government excise taxes. FTZs are intended to stimulate international trade, attract industry, and create jobs by pro-

viding an area that gives users tariff and tax breaks. Merchandise in the zone can be stored, used in manufacturing or assembling a final product, or handled in several other ways.

In 1970, there were 17 FTZs in the United States; today, there are more than 240. Many are situated at seaports, but some are located at inland distribution points. Despite their growing importance, FTZs account for only about 2 percent of the merchandise exports and imports of the United States. Among the businesses that enjoy FTZ status are Caterpillar, Chrysler, Eli Lilly and Co., General Electric, and International Business Machines (IBM).

By offering cost savings to U.S. importers and exporters, FTZs encourage international competitiveness. Companies importing merchandise into an FTZ enhance their cash flow because they do not pay customs duties or federal excise taxes until the goods are shipped out of the zone to U.S. markets. If a good is shipped from an FTZ to a foreign country, no U.S. import duty is imposed on the good. For example, in an FTZ located in Seattle, optical equipment is assembled combining lenses from Japan, prisms from Germany, plastic castings from the United Kingdom, precision mechanisms from Switzerland, and control instruments from France. In an FTZ located in Kansas City, Kansas, pool tables and related equipment are produced using frames from the United States, slate from Italy, balls from Belgium, rubber from Japan, and cue sticks from Taiwan. U.S. Customs Service officials monitor the FTZs by performing audits and spot inspections.

Besides seeing FTZs as a mechanism to reduce costs on imported components through deferral of duty payment, manufacturers have sought FTZ status to obtain relief from "inverted" tariff schedules that place higher duty rates on imported inputs than on the industry's final product. Manufacturers in the FTZ can reduce tariff liability on components or raw materials with higher duty rates by zone processing or assembly into finished goods that enter the U.S. market at a lower duty rate. For example, Volkswagen of America pays only a 2.9-percent import duty on the Rabbit, which it assembles in its New Stanton (Pennsylvania) FTZ, instead of the 6-percent duty that would be levied on imported components.

TARIFF WELFARE EFFECTS: CONSUMER AND PRODUCER SURPLUS

To analyze the effect of trade policies on national welfare, it is useful to separate the effects on consumers from those on producers. For each group, a measure of welfare is needed; these measures are known as consumer surplus and producer surplus.

Consumer surplus refers to the difference between the amount that buyers would be willing and able to pay for a good and the actual amount they do pay. To illustrate, assume the price of a Pepsi is $.50. Being especially thirsty, suppose you would have been willing to pay up to $0.75 for a Pepsi. Your consumer surplus on this purchase is $.25 ($.75 - $.50 = $.25). For all Pepsis bought, consumer surplus is merely the sum of the surplus for each unit.

Consumer surplus can also be depicted graphically. Let us first remember that (1) the height of the market demand curve indicates the maximum price that buyers are willing and able to pay for each successive unit of the good, and (2) in a competitive market, buyers pay a single price (the equilibrium price) for all units purchased. Referring now to Figure 5.1, assume the market price of gasoline is $2 per gallon. If buyers purchase 4 gallons at this price, they spend $8, represented by area *ACED*. For those 4 gallons, buyers would have been willing and able to spend $12, as shown by area *ABCED*. The difference between what buyers must spend and the amount they were willing and able to spend is consumer surplus; in this case, it equals $4 and is denoted by area *ABC*. The size of consumer surplus is affected by the market price. A decrease in the market price will

lead to an increase in the quantity purchased and a larger consumer surplus. Conversely, a higher market price will reduce the amount purchased and shrink the consumer surplus.

Let us now consider the other side of the market: producers. **Producer surplus** is the revenue producers receive over and above the minimum amount required to induce them to supply the good. This minimum amount has to cover the producer's total variable costs. Recall that total variable cost equals the sum of the marginal cost of producing each successive unit of output.

In Figure 5.2, producer surplus is represented by the area above the supply curve of gasoline and below the good's market price. Recall that the height of the market supply curve indicates the least price at which producers will be willing to supply gasoline; this minimum price increases with the level of output because of rising marginal costs. Suppose the market price of gasoline is $2 per gallon, and 4 gallons are supplied. Producers receive revenues totaling $8, represented by area *ACDB*. The minimum revenue they must receive to produce 4 gallons equals total variable cost, which equals $4 and is depicted by area *BCD*. Producer surplus is the difference, $4 ($8 - $4 = $4), and is depicted by *ABC*.

If the market price of gasoline rises, more gasoline will be supplied, and producer surplus rises. It is equally true that if the market price of gasoline falls, producer surplus will fall.

In the following sections, we will use the concepts of consumer surplus and producer surplus to analyze the effects of import tariffs on the nation's welfare.

TARIFF WELFARE EFFECTS: SMALL-NATION MODEL

What are the effects of a tariff on a nation's welfare? Consider the case of a nation whose imports constitute a very small portion of the world market supply. This small nation would

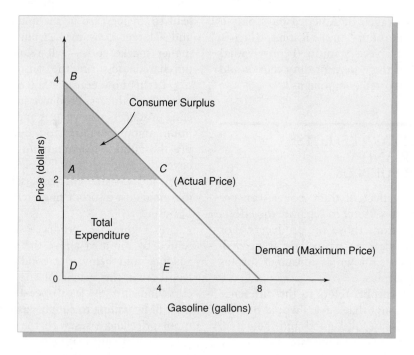

F I G U R E 5. 1　*Consumer surplus.* Consumer surplus is the difference between the maximum amount buyers are willing to pay for a given quantity of a good and the amount actually paid.　Graphically, consumer surplus is represented by the area under the demand curve and above the good's market price.

be a *price taker,* facing a constant world price level for its import commodity. This is not a rare case: many nations are not important enough to influence the terms at which they trade.

In Figure 5.3, the small nation before trade produces at market equilibrium point *E,* as determined by the intersection of its domestic supply and demand schedules. At equilibrium price $9,500, the quantity supplied is 50 units, and the quantity demanded is 50 units. Now suppose that the economy is opened to foreign trade and that the world auto price, $8,000, is less than the domestic price. Because the world market will supply an unlimited number of autos at price $8,000, the world supply schedule would appear as a horizontal (perfectly elastic) line. Line S_{d+w} shows the supply of autos available to the small-nation consumers from

domestic and foreign sources combined. This overall supply schedule is the one that would prevail in free trade.

Free-trade equilibrium is located at point *F* in the figure. Here the number of autos demanded is 80 units, whereas the number produced domestically is 20 units. The excess domestic auto demand is fulfilled by imports of 60 autos. Compared with the situation before trade occurred, free trade results in a fall in the domestic auto price from $9,500 to $8,000. Consumers are better off because they can import more autos at a lower price. However, domestic producers now sell fewer autos at a lower price than they did before trade.

Under free trade, the domestic auto industry is being damaged by foreign competition. Industry sales and revenues are falling, and workers are losing their jobs. Suppose manage-

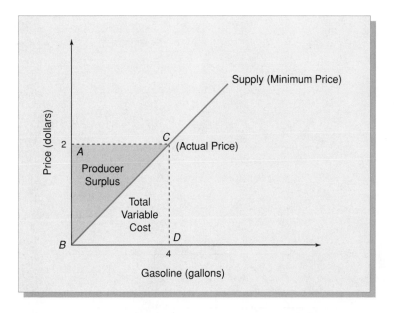

F I G U R E 5. 2 Producer surplus. Producer surplus is the revenue producers receive over and above the minimum necessary for production. Graphically, producer surplus is represented by the area above the supply curve and below the good's market price.

ment and labor unite and convince the government to levy a protective tariff on auto imports. Assume the small nation imposes a tariff of $1,000 on auto imports. Because this small nation is not important enough to influence world market conditions, the world supply price of autos remains constant, unaffected by the tariff. This means that the small nation's terms of trade remains unchanged. The introduction of the tariff raises the home price of imports by the full amount of the duty, and the increase falls entirely on the domestic consumer. The overall supply shifts upward from S_{d+w} to S_{d+w+t} by the amount of the tariff.

The protective tariff results in a new equilibrium quantity at point G, where the domestic auto price is $9,000. Domestic production increases by 20 units, whereas domestic consumption falls by 20 units. Imports decrease from their pretariff level of 60 units to 20 units. This reduction can be attributed to falling domestic consumption and rising domestic

production. The effects of the tariff are to impede imports and protect domestic producers. But what are the tariff's effects on the *national welfare?*

Figure 5.3 shows that before the tariff was levied, *consumer surplus* equaled areas $a + b + c + d + e + f + g$. With the tariff, consumer surplus falls to areas $e + f + g$, an overall loss in consumer surplus equal to areas $a + b + c + d$. This change affects the nation's welfare in a number of ways. The welfare effects of a tariff are classified as the revenue effect, the redistribution effect, the protective effect, and the consumption effect. As might be expected, the tariff provides the government with additional tax revenue and benefits domestic auto producers; at the same time, however, it wastes resources and harms the domestic consumer.

The tariff's **revenue effect** represents the duty collections of the government. Found by multiplying the number of imports (20 units) times the tariff ($1,000), government revenue

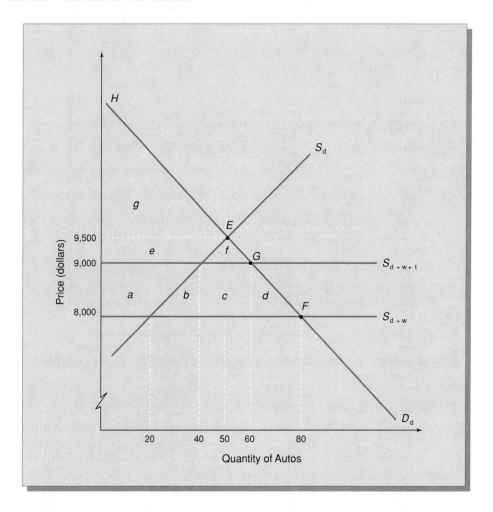

F I G U R E 5. 3 Tariff trade and welfare effects: small-nation model. For a small nation, a tariff placed on an imported product is shifted totally to the domestic consumer via a higher product price. Consumer surplus falls as a result of the price increase. The small nation's welfare decreases by an amount equal to the protective effect and consumption effect, the so-called deadweight losses due to a tariff.

equals area *c,* or $20,000. This represents the portion of the loss of consumer surplus, in monetary terms, that is transferred to the government. For the nation as a whole, the revenue effect does *not* result in an overall welfare loss; consumer surplus is merely shifted from the private to the public sector.

The **redistribution effect** is the transfer of consumer surplus, in monetary terms, to the domestic producers of the import-competing product. This is represented by area *a,* which equals $30,000. Under the tariff, domestic consumers will buy from domestic firms 40 autos at a price of $9,000, for a total expenditure of

---

Calculating the Welfare Effect of a Tariff

Figure 5.3 presents the welfare effects of a tariff in dollar terms. For example, the dollar value of the consumption effect (area *d*) equals $10,000. It is easy to carry out the calculation of triangular area *d*. Recall from geometry that the area of a triangle equals (base x height)/2. The height of the triangle ($1,000) equals the price increase in autos due to the tariff; the base (20 autos) equals the reduction in domestic consumption due to the tariff. The consumption effect is thus

$$\frac{20 \times \$1,000}{2} = \$10,000$$

Similarly, the dollar value of the protective effect (area *b*) equals $10,000. The height of the triangle equals the increase in price due to the tariff ($1,000); the triangle's base (20 autos) equals the increase in domestic auto production due to the tariff. The protective effect is thus

$$\frac{20 \times \$1,000}{2} = \$10,000$$

The calculation of all such "triangular" welfare effects of tariffs (and other protectionist devices) is based on this formula. The reader will find the formula useful for calculating the welfare effects of trade barriers in response to the study questions at the end of chapters.

$360,000. At the free-trade price of $8,000, the same 40 autos would have yielded expenditures of $320,000. The imposition of the tariff thus results in home producers' receiving additional revenues totaling areas *a* + *b*, or $40,000 (the difference between $360,000 and $320,000). As the tariff encourages domestic production to rise from 20 to 40 units, however, producers must pay part of the increased revenue as higher costs of producing the increased output, depicted by area *b*, or $10,000. The remaining revenue, $30,000, area *a*, is a net gain in producer income. The redistribution effect, therefore, is a transfer of income from consumers to producers. Like the revenue effect, it does *not* result in an overall loss of welfare for the economy.

Area *b*, totaling $10,000, is referred to as the **protective effect** of the tariff. It illustrates the loss to the domestic economy resulting from wasted resources used to produce additional autos at increasing unit costs. As the tariff-induced domestic output expands, resources

that are less adaptable to auto production are eventually utilized, increasing unit production costs. This means that resources are used less efficiently than they would have been with free trade, in which case autos would have been purchased from low-cost foreign producers. A tariff's protective effect thus arises because less efficient domestic production is substituted for more efficient foreign production. Referring to Figure 5.3, as domestic output increases from 20 to 40 units, the domestic cost of producing autos rises, as shown by supply schedule S_d. But the same increase in autos could have been obtained at a unit cost of $8,000 before the tariff was levied. Area *b*, which depicts the protective effect, represents the loss to the economy.

Most of the consumer surplus lost because of the tariff has been accounted for: *c* went to the government as revenue; *a* was transferred to home suppliers as income; and *b* was lost by the economy because of inefficient domestic production. The **consumption effect** represented by area *d,* which equals $10,000, is the residual not accounted for elsewhere. It arises from the decrease in consumption resulting from the tariff's artificially increasing the price of autos from $8,000 to $9,000. A loss of welfare occurs because of the increased price and lower consumption of autos. Like the protective effect, the consumer effect represents a *real* cost to society, not a transfer to other sectors of the economy. Together, these effects equal the **deadweight loss** of a tariff.

As long as it is assumed that a nation accounts for a negligible portion of international trade, its levying an import tariff necessarily lowers its national welfare. This is because there is no favorable welfare effect resulting from the tariff that would offset the deadweight loss of consumer surplus. If a nation could impose a tariff that would improve its terms of trade vis-à-vis its trading partners, it would enjoy a larger share of the gains from trade. This would tend to increase its national welfare, offsetting the deadweight loss of consumer surplus. Because it is so insignificant relative to the world market, however, a small nation is unable to influence the terms of trade. Levying an import tariff, therefore, *reduces* a small nation's welfare.

TARIFF WELFARE EFFECTS: LARGE-NATION MODEL

Now consider the case in which an importing nation accounts for a significant portion of the world market. This large nation, as a consumer, is important enough to affect the terms at which it trades. Changes in a large nation's domestic economic conditions or trade policies, therefore, can influence the distribution of the gains from trade that affects its national welfare.

One of the justifications for an import tariff is that it may enable a nation to extract larger gains from trade. A tariff-levying nation is similar to a monopsonist who restricts the level of purchases to reduce the price of inputs.

By reducing the volume of imports with a tariff, a nation hopes to force down the prices it pays to foreign producers. This would improve the importing nation's terms of trade and result in larger gains from trade. But an importing nation would face a decline in its national welfare if the negative effects of a reduced volume of trade outweighed the positive effects of a favorable change in the terms of trade. This is like a monopolist who cuts back output too far and finds that price gains are more than offset by losses in volume.

Figure 5.4 illustrates the trade position of an importing nation. Line S_d represents the domestic supply schedule, and line D_d depicts the domestic demand schedule. *Autarky equilibrium* is achieved at point E. With free trade, the importing nation faces an overall supply schedule of S_{d+w}. This schedule shows the number of autos that both domestic and foreign producers together offer domestic consumers. The overall supply schedule is upward sloping rather than horizontal because the foreign supply price is not a fixed constant. The price depends on the quantity purchased by an importing country when it is a large buyer of the product. With free trade, our country achieves market equilibrium at point F. The price of autos falls to $8,000, domestic consumption rises to 110 units, and domestic production falls to 30 units. Auto imports totaling 80 units satisfy the excess domestic demand.

Suppose that the importing nation imposes a specific tariff of $1,000 on imported autos. By increasing the selling cost, the tariff results in a shift in the overall supply schedule from S_{d+w} to S_{d+w+t}. Market equilibrium moves from point F to point G, while product price rises from $8,000 to $8,800. The tariff-levying nation's consumer surplus falls by an amount equal to areas $a + b + c + d$. Area *a,* totaling $32,000, represents the *redistribution effect;* this amount is transferred from domestic consumers to domestic producers. Areas *d + b* depict the tariff's *deadweight loss*—the deterioration in national welfare because of reduced

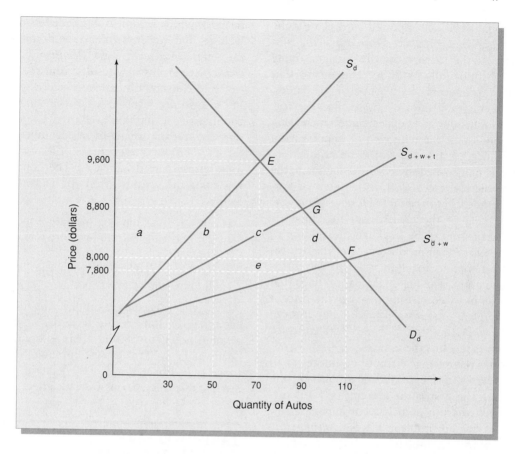

F I G U R E 5. 4 Tariff trade and welfare effects: large-nation model. For a large nation, a tariff on an imported product may be partially shifted to the domestic consumer via a higher product price and partially absorbed by the foreign exporter via a lower export price. The extent by which a tariff is absorbed by the foreign exporter constitutes a welfare gain for the home country. This gain offsets some (all) of the deadweight welfare losses due to the tariff's consumption effect and protective effect.

consumption (*consumption effect* = $8,000) and inefficient use of resources (*protective effect* = $8,000).

As in the small-nation example, a tariff's *revenue effect* is determined by multiplying the import tariff times the number of auto imports. This yields areas *c* + *e*, or $40,000. Notice that the tariff revenue accruing to the government now comes from foreign producers as well as domestic consumers. This is unlike the small-

nation case, in which the supply schedule is horizontal and the tariff's burden falls entirely on domestic consumers. The tariff of $1,000 is added to the free trade import price of $8,000. Although the price in the protected market will exceed the foreign supply price by the amount of the duty, it will *not* exceed the free-trade foreign supply price by this amount. Compared with the free-trade foreign supply price of $8,000, the domestic consumers pay only an additional $800 per imported auto. This is the *amount of the tariff shifted forward to the consumer*. At the same time, the foreign supply price of autos falls by $200. This means that foreign producers earn smaller revenues, $7,800, for each auto exported. Because foreign production takes place under increasing cost conditions, the reduction of imports from abroad triggers a decline in foreign production, and thus unit costs decline. The reduction in the foreign supply price, $200, represents that *portion of the tariff borne by the foreign producer*. The levying of the tariff raises the domestic price of the import by less than the amount of the duty as foreign producers lower their prices in an attempt to maintain sales in the tariff-levying nation. The importing nation finds that its terms of trade has improved if the price it pays foreign producers for auto imports decreases while the price it charges foreigners for its exports remains the same.

Thus the revenue effect of an import tariff in the large-nation case is made up of two components. The first is the amount of tariff revenue shifted from domestic consumers to the tariff-levying government; this is determined in Figure 5.4 by multiplying the level of imports (40 units) by the portion of the import tariff borne by domestic consumers ($800). The **domestic revenue effect** is depicted by area *c*, which equals $32,000. The second element is the tariff revenue extracted from foreign producers in the form of a lower supply price. Found by multiplying auto imports (40 units) by the portion of the tariff falling on foreign producers ($200), the **terms-of-trade effect** is shown as area *e*, which equals $8,000. Note that the terms-of-trade effect represents a redistribution of income from the foreign nation to the tariff-levying nation as a result of the new terms of trade. Together, the domestic revenue effect and the terms-of-trade effect equal the total revenue effect of the tariff.

A nation that is a major importer of a product is in a favorable trade situation. It may be able to use its tariff policy to improve the terms at which it trades, and hence its national welfare. But remember that the negative welfare effect of a tariff is the *deadweight loss* of consumer surplus that results from the protection and consumption effects. Referring to Figure 5.4, to determine if a tariff-levying nation can improve its national welfare, we must compare the overall impact of the deadweight loss (areas *b* + *d*) with the benefits of a more favorable terms of trade (area *e*). The conclusions regarding the welfare effects of a tariff are as follows:

1. If *e* > (*b* + *d*), national welfare is increased.
2. If *e* = (*b* + *d*), national welfare remains constant.
3. If *e* < (*b* + *d*), national welfare is diminished.

In the preceding example, the domestic economy's welfare would have declined by an amount equal to $8,000. This is because the deadweight welfare losses, totaling $16,000, more than offset the $8,000 gain in welfare attributable to the terms-of-trade effect.

TARIFF WELFARE EFFECTS: EXAMPLES

The previous section analyzed the welfare effects of import tariffs from a theoretical perspective. Now let us turn to some examples of import tariffs and examine estimates of their costs and benefits to the nation.[2]

Citizens Band Radios

In 1978, President Carter extended temporary relief to U.S. producers of citizens band (CB) radio transceivers when he raised import tariffs from 6 percent to 21 percent. Over the following three years, the tariffs were phased down annually—from 21 to 18 to 15 percent—until final termination. The president's action was taken in response to the government's finding that imports of CB radios were seriously hurting the domestic industry.

Costs to the Consumer of Preserving a Production Worker's Job

Saving Jobs: Consumer Costs

Industry	Year in Which Protectionist Program Began	Annual Cost to Consumers	
		Total (millions of dollars)	Per Job Saved (dollars)
Specialty steel	1976	520	1,000,000
Nonrubber footwear	1977	700	55,000
Color TVs	1977	420	42,000
Bolts, nuts, screws	1979	110	550,000
Mushrooms	1980	35	117,000
Automobiles	1981	5,800	105,000
Textiles and apparel	1982	27,000	42,000
Carbon steel	1982	6,800	750,000
Motorcycles	1983	104	150,000

SOURCE: Gary Hufbauer et al., *Trade Protection in the United States: 31 Case Studies* (Washington, D.C.: Institute for International Economics, 1986), Tables 1.1 and 1.2.

Although import restrictions may provide benefits to domestic firms and workers, they are, in effect, a tax on the consumers of the protected products. Trade restraints result in an increase in the price and a decrease in the quantity of imported goods, which in turn increases the consumption of domestically produced goods as well as domestic prices.

A striking fact about protection to preserve jobs is that each job often ends up costing domestic consumers more than the worker's salary! As seen in the table, the consumer cost of protecting each job preserved in the auto industry in the United States is estimated to be $105,000 a year; this is far above the salary a production employee in that industry would receive. The fact that costs to consumers for each production job saved are so high underpins the argument that an alternative approach should be used to help workers: workers departing from an industry facing foreign competition should be liberally compensated (subsidized) for moving to new industries or taking early retirement.

Over the period 1972–1976, U.S. demand for CB radios increased twentyfold to a level valued at $940 million. However, imports as a share of the U.S. market were also rising, from 78 percent to 90 percent. By 1977, the sales of U.S. producers had fallen by almost 40 percent, and domestic employment in the manufacture of CB radios was down considerably. These circumstances led to the president's decision to provide additional protection for U.S. producers.

TABLE 5. 6 / *Estimated Costs and Benefits
of an Increased Tariff
on CB Radios*

Welfare Effect	Cost/Benefit (in millions of dollars)
Losses to domestic consumers	48.8
Deadweight losses	
Consumption	10.7
Production	1.5
Increase in tariff revenues	33.6
Gains to domestic producers	3.0

SOURCE: Morris E. Morkre and David G. Tarr, *Effects of Restrictions on U.S. Imports* (Washington, D.C.: Federal Trade Commission, 1980), p. 71.

The first-year welfare effects of the tariffs, as estimated by the Federal Trade Commission (FTC), are summarized in Table 5.6. An increase in the tariff from 6 percent to 21 percent would be expected to result in an $8 increase in the price of CB radios, from $54 to $62 per unit. Domestic consumption would fall by 1.53 million units, whereas domestic production would expand by 221,000 units. The total reduction in consumer surplus, resulting from the losses of those consumers who would have to pay a higher price plus the losses of those forced out of the market owing to the higher price, would amount to $48.8 million. Of this sum, tariff revenues would rise by $33.6 million, and profits to U.S. producers would increase by $3 million. The deadweight losses to the U.S. economy would stem from a $1.5-million loss due to production inefficiencies and a $10.7-million loss due to consumption inefficiencies. Approximately 587 jobs would be created for U.S. workers—but at a cost to the U.S. consumer of some $83,000 per job created.

Based on these estimates, the FTC concluded that the tariff would yield only modest benefits to the domestic industry. At the same time, the U.S. consumer and the economy at large would face considerable costs, and employment and sales of companies distributing imported CB radios would drop.

Motorcycles

There have been approximately 150 manufacturers of motorcycles in the United States since the first commercially produced motorcycle was manufactured in 1901. By the 1980s, there were one U.S.-owned firm, Harley-Davidson Motor Co., and two Japanese-owned firms, Kawasaki and Honda, operating in the United States. Harley specializes in the production of heavyweight motorcycles (1000 and 1300 cc).

In the early 1970s, Harley had 100 percent of the U.S. market for heavyweight motorcycles; by the early 1980s, its market share was less than 15 percent. During this decade, Harley continually lost ground to Japanese competitors such as Suzuki, Yamaha, Honda, and Kawasaki. Being used to tough competition, these Japanese firms were able to undercut Harley by $1,500 to $2,000 per motorcycle. Industry analysts maintained that Harley was plagued by inefficient production methods and poor management and that its per-unit costs were higher than those of the U.S. plants of Honda and Kawasaki.

During this period, Harley was the victim of a Honda–Yamaha struggle for domination of the motorcycle market. In the early 1980s, both Japanese motorcycle manufacturers flooded the U.S. market with a variety of new competitive models. Bloated Japanese inventories, estimated to be a year-and-a-half supply of new motorcycles stashed in U.S. dealerships and warehouses, led to heavy price cuts and intense product promotion.

By 1982, Harley was rapidly approaching bankruptcy because of a recession and reduced demand for motorcycles, operating inefficiencies, and a massive debt problem. Harley was surviving on borrowed money from Citicorp, and the bank was becoming increasingly apprehensive about extending additional loans.

Harley suffered a huge buildup in motorcycle inventories throughout 1982, which led to declines in profits, wages, and employment. In 1980, Harley had more than 4,000 employees; by the end of 1982, it had 2,200.

Harley turned to the U.S. government for tariff protection that would result in reductions in Japanese motorcycle inventories and increases in the price of Japanese motorcycles, so that Harley could become more competitive. With massive layoffs of their members, union officials actively supported Harley's plea for protectionism. In hopes of forestalling possible trade restrictions, the Japanese motorcycle producers offered technical assistance and loan guarantees to Harley, who turned down the offers. Apparently, Harley felt that it could convince the government that import restrictions were justified.

In September of 1982, Harley petitioned the U.S. government for protectionist relief from the importation of heavyweight motorcycles. The government concluded that rising motorcycle imports from Japan were a substantial cause of a threat of serious injury to Harley and that temporary protectionism was justified to permit Harley to recover from its injuries and provide it time to complete a comprehensive program to fully compete with the Japanese.

On April 1, 1983, the U.S. government implemented a five-year tariff program for heavyweight (700-cc engines and larger) motorcycles. The import tariff was raised from 4.4 percent to 49.4 percent during the first year; during the second year, the tariff was reduced to 39.4 percent, followed by cuts of 15 percent, 5 percent, and 5 percent in the next three years. After the fifth year, the tariff was to revert back to 4.4 percent. The tariff hikes did not apply to motorcycle imports from Italy, Germany, and the United Kingdom, which accounted for less than 20 percent of U.S. imports of heavyweight motorcycles in 1982. The five-year tariff program was intended to allow Harley sufficient time to eliminate its excess inventories and to benefit from improved economies of scale obtained from increased sales and production.

The U.S. International Trade Commission (ITC) estimated the economic effects of the increased tariff on imported heavyweight motorcycles. During the first year of the tariff, motorcycle prices would increase 10 percent; prices would rise more than 12 percent during the second year as motorcycle inventories were reduced. The ITC felt that Harley would be restrained from raising prices to any significant degree by continued competition from motorcycles produced domestically by Honda and Kawasaki, as well as from imports. The ITC also estimated that during the first two years of the tariff program, overall motorcycle sales would fall by 20,000 units; however, sales of Harley-Davidson motorcycles would rise by more than 8,000 units. This would allow Harley to keep its plants operating.

But the substantial tariff looked much better on paper than it worked out in reality. Stung, Japanese motorcycle manufacturers reacted promptly to circumvent the tariff policy. They quickly downsized their 750-cc motorcycle engines to 699 cc, thus evading the tariff that applied to motorcycle imports having engines of 700 cc or more. The press dubbed these downsized models as "tariff busters." The downsized engine wiped out approximately half of the tariff's value to Harley.

Moreover, Kawasaki and Honda quickly increased production of heavyweight motorcycles in their U.S. plants. That left only Suzuki and Yamaha motorcycles, with engines over 1000 cc, subject to the tariff. And these manufacturers were permitted to ship 7,000–10,000 of these heavyweight motorcycles to the United States before they had to start paying the extra import duty.

Although the outcome of the tariff was disappointing to Harley, one of its important objectives was accomplished—an end to the escalation of U.S. motorcycle inventories by Japanese firms and liquidation of the large stock of motorcycles already in dealers' showrooms and warehouses. This liquidation, however, occurred at discounted prices, which put further competitive pressure on Harley.

As the 1980s continued, Harley's economic performance improved. By 1987, Harley enjoyed record profits of almost $18 million. It also enjoyed a 40-percent market share in the super-heavyweight motorcycle class, 11 percentage points ahead of its closest rival, Honda, and 17 points above its 1983 low of 23 percent. In March 1987, Harley announced that it no longer needed special tariffs to compete with the Japanese motorcycle firms. Harley indicated that, given temporary relief from predatory import practices, it had become competitive in world markets.[3]

EVALUATION OF TARIFF WELFARE EFFECTS

In earlier sections, we saw that a tariff affects a nation's welfare in two opposing ways: a terms-of-trade effect and a volume-of-trade effect.

Imposition of a tariff may result in an improvement in a nation's terms of trade (the rate at which products are exchanged in international trade). Because a tariff makes imports more expensive for, say, U.S. consumers, the number of imports demanded tends to decline. This makes it more difficult for foreigners to generate the revenues necessary to finance purchases from the United States. Foreigners may reduce their export prices in an attempt to enhance their capacity to finance purchases. So the tariff improves the U.S. terms of trade by lowering the prices the nation must pay for its imports. However, a reduced volume of imports due to the tariff results in a negative welfare effect for the United States in the form of a deadweight loss in consumer surplus. U.S. welfare thus improves if the favorable terms-of-trade effect outweighs the adverse trade-volume effect.

By modifying the relative prices at which nations exchange goods and services, a tariff results in a redistribution of the gains from trade among nations. A favorable terms of trade, yielding a larger share of the gains from trade for one nation, implies a smaller share for

the other nation; overall world welfare does not change because of the terms-of-trade effect. However, tariffs do produce a negative welfare effect: a reduction in the volume of world trade. For the world as a whole, tariffs thus reduce the level of welfare.

A single nation that is dissatisfied with the distribution of the world gains from trade may consider whether it should initiate a tariff on imports. But in an interdependent world, the nation realizes that this act would not be welcomed by its trading partners. The possibility of foreign tariff retaliation may be a sufficient deterrent for any nation considering whether to impose higher tariffs.

A classic case of a tariff-induced trade war was the implementation of the Smoot–Hawley tariff by the U.S. government in 1930. The tariff was initially intended to provide relief to U.S. farmers. However, senators and members of Congress from industrial states used the technique of vote trading to obtain increased tariffs on manufactured goods. The result was a policy that increased tariffs on more than 1,000 products, with an average nominal duty on protected goods of 53 percent! Viewing the Smoot–Hawley tariff as an attempt to force unemployment on its workers, 12 nations promptly increased their duties against the United States. U.S. farm exports fell to one-third of their former level, and between 1930 and 1933, total U.S. exports fell by almost 60 percent. Although the Great Depression accounted for much of that decline, the adverse psychological impact of the Smoot–Hawley tariff on business activity cannot be ignored.

HOW A TARIFF BURDENS EXPORTERS

The benefits and costs of protecting domestic producers from foreign competition, as discussed earlier in this chapter, are based on the direct effects of an import tariff. Import-competing businesses and workers can benefit from tariffs through increases in output, profits,

Effects of Eliminating Import Tariffs

Eliminating Import Tariffs: Gains and Losses

Import-Competing Industry	Millions of Dollars			
	Consumer Gain	Producer Loss	Domestic Tax Loss	Job Loss (in thousands)
Rubber footwear	$272.2	$44.1	$28.5	2.4
Women's footwear	325.1	54.6	38.0	3.5
Ceramic tile	90.0	10.0	11.6	0.4
Luggage	186.3	36.4	21.0	1.8
Women's handbags	134.4	25.7	15.5	1.6
Glasswear	185.8	77.2	14.8	2.5
Resins	93.1	45.1	5.8	1.1
Bicycles	38.1	10.0	4.0	0.6
Ball bearings	50.3	3.9	6.9	0.1
Canned tuna	61.3	35.0	3.2	0.8
Cedar shingles	25.3	11.5	6.1	0.1

SOURCE: U.S. International Trade Commission, *The Economic Effects of Significant U.S. Import Restraints, Phase 1: Manufacturing* (Washington, D.C.: Government Printing Office, October 1989), Tables ES-1 and ES-2.

What would be the effects if the United States unilaterally removed tariffs on imported products? On the positive side, tariff elimination lowers the price of the affected imports and may lower the price of the competing U.S. good, resulting in economic gains to the U.S. consumer. On the negative side, the lower price to import-competing producers, as a result of eliminating the tariff, results in profit reductions; workers become displaced from the domestic industry that loses protection; and the U.S. government loses tax revenue as the result of eliminating the tariff. The table gives estimates of the short-run effects that would occur in the first year after tariff removal.

jobs, and compensation. A tariff imposes costs on domestic consumers in the form of higher prices of protected products and reductions in consumer surplus. There is also a net welfare loss for the economy because not all of the loss of consumer surplus is transferred as gains to domestic producers and the government (the protective effect and consumption effect).

A tariff carries additional burdens. In protecting import-competing producers, a tariff leads indirectly to a reduction in domestic exports. *The net result of protectionism is to move the economy toward greater self-sufficiency, with lower imports and exports.* For domestic workers, the protection of jobs in import-competing industries comes at the expense of jobs in other sectors of the economy, including exports. Although a tariff is intended to help domestic producers, the economy-wide implications of a tariff are adverse for the export sector. The welfare losses due to restrictions in output and employment in the economy's export industry may offset the welfare gains enjoyed by import-competing producers.

Because a tariff is a tax on imports, the burden of a tariff falls initially on importers, who must pay duties to the domestic government. However, importers generally try to shift increased costs to buyers through price increases. There are at least three ways in which the resulting higher prices of imports injure domestic exporters.

First, exporters often purchase imported inputs subject to tariffs that increase the *cost of inputs*. Because exporters tend to sell in competitive markets where they have little ability to dictate the prices they receive, they generally cannot pass on a tariff-induced increase in cost to their buyers. Higher export costs thus lead to higher prices and reduced overseas sales.

Second, by increasing the price of imports, tariffs raise the *cost of living*. Workers thus have the incentive to demand correspondingly higher wages, resulting in higher production costs. Tariffs lead to expanding output for import-competing companies that in turn bid for workers, causing money wages to rise. As these higher wages pass through the economy, export industries ultimately face higher wages and production costs, which lessen their competitive positions in international markets.

Finally, import tariffs have *international repercussions* that lead to reductions in domestic exports. Tariffs cause the quantity of imports to decrease, which in turn decreases other nations' export revenues and ability to import. The decline in foreign export revenues results in a smaller demand for a nation's exports and leads to falling output and employment in its export industries.

To what extent do tariffs on imports impose higher costs on domestic exporters?

TABLE 5. 7 / *The Proportion of an Import Tariff Borne by Exporters*

Country	Period	Percentage of Import Tariff Borne by Domestic Exporters*
Chile	1959–1970	55
Uruguay	1966–1979	53
Argentina	1935–1979	57
El Salvador	1962–1977	70
Australia	1950–1980	70
Brazil	1950–1978	70
Colombia	1970–1978	95
Mean		66

* Indicates the share of any import protection that, because of relative prices, becomes an implicit tax on exports.

SOURCE: Kenneth W. Clements and Larry A. Sjaastad, *How Protection Taxes Exporters* (London: Trade Policy Research Centre, 1985), pp. 25–27.

Estimates have been made of the fraction of an import tariff that is transferred to domestic exporters in the form of higher costs. The results for seven countries are summarized in Table 5.7. These estimates suggest that at least one-half of a nominal tariff on imports is borne by the domestic export industries of the seven countries studied! Government officials cannot independently choose to protect import-competing producers without imposing significant cost burdens on domestic exporters.

If domestic export companies are damaged by import tariffs, why don't they protest such policies more vigorously? One problem is that tariff-induced increases in costs for export companies are subtle and invisible. Many exporters may not be aware of their existence. Also, the tariff-induced cost increases may be of such magnitude that some potential export companies are incapable of developing and have no tangible basis for political resistance.

TARIFF QUOTA: A TWO-TIER TARIFF

Another restriction used to insulate a domestic industry from foreign competition is the **tariff quota**. Although not widely used as a trade restriction, the tariff quota has been levied by the U.S. government to protect producers of such commodities as milk, cattle, fish, brooms, tobacco products, and coconut oil.

As its name suggests, a tariff quota displays both tariff-like and quota-like characteristics. This device allows a specified number of goods to be imported at one tariff rate (the *within-quota rate*), whereas any imports above this level face a higher tariff rate (the *over-quota rate*). A tariff quota can thus be thought of as a *two-tier tariff*. For example, during the early 1970s, the U.S. tariff quota on fluid milk was set at 3 million gallons a year. Milk imports within this limit faced a duty of 2 cents per gallon, but a duty of 6.5 cents per gallon was applied to any imports over this limit.

The tariff quota is generally viewed as a compromise between the interests of the consumer, who desires low-cost imports, and those of the domestic producer, who desires protectionism. The tariff quota attempts to minimize the adverse costs for the consumer through a modest within-quota rate, while still shielding home producers from severe import competition by means of a stiffer over-quota rate.

Figure 5.5 illustrates the welfare effects of a hypothetical tariff quota on steel. Assume that the U.S. demand and supply schedules for steel are given by $D_{U.S.}$ and $S_{U.S.}$, and the equilibrium (autarky) price of steel is $540 per ton. Assuming free trade, suppose the United States faces a constant world price of steel equal to $400 per ton. At the free-trade price, U.S. production equals 5 tons, U.S. consumption equals 40 tons, and imports equal 35 tons.

To protect its producers from foreign competition, suppose the United States enacts a tariff quota of 5 tons. Imports within this limit face a 10-percent tariff, but a 20-percent tariff is applied to imports in excess of the limit.

Because the United States is initially importing an amount exceeding the limit as defined by the tariff quota, both the within-quota rate and the over-quota rate would apply. This two-tier tariff results in a rise in the price of steel sold in the United States from $400 to $480 per ton. Domestic production increases to 15 tons, domestic consumption falls to 30 tons, and imports fall to 15 tons. Increased sales would permit the profits of U.S. steel producers to rise by an amount equal to area *e*. The deadweight losses to the U.S. economy, in terms of production and consumption inefficiencies, would equal areas *f* and *g*, respectively.

The interesting feature of the tariff quota is the revenue it generates. Some of it accrues to the domestic government as tariff revenue, but the remainder is captured by business as **windfall profits**.

In the preceding example, after enactment of the tariff quota, 15 tons of steel are imported. The U.S. government collects area *a*, found by multiplying the within-quota duty of $40 times 5 tons. Area *b* + *c* also accrues to the government, ascertained by multiplying the remaining 10 tons of imported steel times the over-quota duty of $80.

Area *d* in the figure represents windfall profits—a gain to business resulting from sudden or unexpected government policy. Under the tariff quota, the domestic price of the first 5 tons of steel imported is $440, reflecting the foreign supply price of $400 plus the import duty of $40. Suppose U.S. import companies are able to obtain foreign steel at $440. By reselling the 5 tons to U.S. consumers at $480, the price of over-quota steel, U.S. importers would capture area *d* as windfall profits. But this opportunity will not last long, because foreign steelmakers will want to capture the windfall gain. To the extent that they can restrict steel exports to the

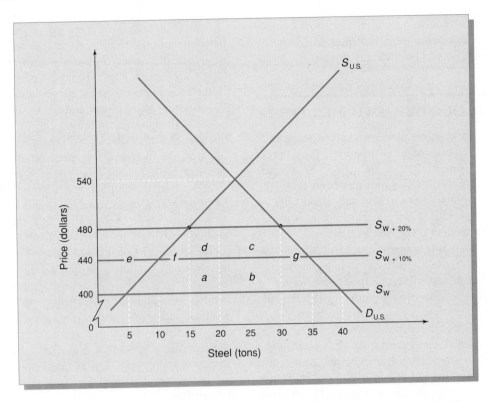

F I G U R E 5. 5 *Tariff quota trade and welfare effects.* A tariff quota is a two-tier tariff levied on imports. Its imposition leads to higher product prices and a decrease in consumer surplus for domestic buyers. Of the tariff quota's revenue effect, a portion accrues to the domestic government, while the remainder is captured by domestic importers or foreign exporters as windfall profits.

United States in a monopolistic fashion, foreign producers could force up the price of steel and expropriate profits from U.S. importers. Foreign producers conceivably could capture the entire area *d* by raising their supply price to $480 per ton. The portion of the windfall profits captured by foreign steelmakers represents an overall welfare loss to the U.S. economy.

ARGUMENTS FOR TRADE RESTRICTIONS

The **free-trade argument** is, in principle, persuasive. It states that if each nation produces what it does best and permits trade, over the long run all will enjoy lower prices and higher levels of output, income, and consumption than could be achieved in isolation. In a dynamic world, comparative advantage is constantly changing owing to shifts in technologies, input productivities, and wages, as well as tastes and preferences. A free market compels adjustment to take place. Either the efficiency of an industry must improve, or else resources will flow from low-productivity uses to those with high productivity. Tariffs and other trade barriers are viewed as tools that prevent the economy from undergoing adjustment, resulting in economic stagnation.

Do Trade Restraints Bolster Overall Employment?

Effects of Trade Restraints

Industry	Change in Employment	
	Percentage	Absolute
Job Gainers		
Primary metals (steel)	3.61	31,003
Mining	0.34	3,280
Utilities	0.14	1,244
Finance and insurance	0.11	6,108
Printing and publishing	0.09	1,234
Wholesale and retail trade	0.08	12,720
Services	0.07	16,177
Other		5,679
		77,455
Job Losers		
Motor vehicles and equipment	1.31	11,311
Furniture and fixtures	0.70	3,417
Machinery	0.67	16,914
Transportation equipment	0.63	6,497
Construction	0.59	15,763
Other		23,538
		74,440

SOURCE: Linda C. Hunter, "U.S. Trade Protection: Effects on the Industrial and Regional Composition of Employment," *Federal Reserve Bank of Dallas, Economic Review* (January 1990), pp. 1–13.

(continued)

Although the free-trade argument tends to dominate in the classroom, virtually all nations have imposed restrictions on the international flow of goods, services, and capital. Often proponents of protectionism say "Free trade is fine in theory, but it does not apply in the real world." Modern trade theory assumes perfectly competitive markets whose characteristics do not reflect real-world market conditions. Moreover, even though protectionists may concede that economic losses occur with tariffs and other restrictions, they often argue that noneconomic benefits such as national security more than offset the economic losses. In seeking protection from imports, domestic industries and labor unions seek to better their economic welfare. Over the years, a number of arguments have been advanced to pressure the president and Congress to enact restrictive measures.

Do Trade Restraints Bolster Overall Employment?

(continued)

The dramatic increase in the U.S. trade deficit in the 1980s fueled protectionist sentiment. Proponents of trade restrictions contended that U.S. workers were losing jobs to foreigners in key industries (such as electronics) and that trade barriers were necessary to bolster overall employment.

Trade restraints raise employment in the protected industry (such as steel) by increasing the price (or reducing the supply) of competing import goods. Industries that are primary suppliers of inputs to the protected industry also gain jobs. However, industries that purchase the protected product (such as motor vehicle manufacturers) face higher costs. These costs are then passed on to the consumer through higher prices, resulting in decreased sales. Thus, employment falls in these related industries.

Economists at the Federal Reserve Bank of Dallas have examined the effects of trade restrictions on the composition of employment in several U.S. industries: textiles and apparel, steel, and automobiles. They conclude that in an economy near full employment, trade protection will have little or no effect on the level of employment in the long run. Trade restraints tend to provide job gains for only a few industries, while they result in job losses spread across many industries.

The table illustrates the effects of trade restraints for the U.S. steel industry in 1984. The restraints provided an almost 4-percent increase in the number of U.S. steelworker jobs; the mining industry, a primary supplier to the steel industry, also experienced significant employment increases. The restraints, however, resulted in job losses for steel-using industries, including motor vehicles and equipment, furniture and fixtures, transportation equipment, and fabricated metal products.

Comparing the job gainers and losers, the trade restraints provided negligible employment gains for the U.S. economy. The economists at the Federal Reserve Bank of Dallas drew similar conclusions concerning the employment effects of trade restrictions in the textiles and apparel industry and the automobile industry.

Job Protection

The issue of jobs has been a dominant factor in motivating government officials to levy trade restrictions on imported goods. During periods of economic recession, workers are especially eager to point out that cheap foreign goods undercut domestic production, resulting in a loss of domestic jobs to foreign labor. Alleged job losses to foreign competition historically have been a major force behind the desire of most U.S. labor leaders to reject free-trade policies.

This view, however, has a serious omission: it fails to acknowledge the dual nature of international trade. Changes in a nation's imports of goods and services are closely related to changes in its exports. Nations export goods because they desire to import products from other nations. When the United States imports goods from abroad, foreigners gain purchasing power that will eventually be spent on U.S. goods, services, or financial assets. U.S. export industries then enjoy gains in sales and employment, whereas the opposite occurs in U.S. import-competing industries. Rather than promoting overall unemployment, imports tend to generate job opportunities in some industries as part of the process by which they decrease employment in other industries. However, the job gains due to open trade policies tend to be less visible to the public than the readily observable job losses stemming from foreign competition. The more conspicuous losses have led many U.S. business and labor leaders to combine forces in their opposition to free trade.

Protection against Cheap Foreign Labor

One of the most common arguments used to justify the protectionist umbrella of trade restrictions is that tariffs are needed to defend domestic jobs against cheap foreign labor. As indicated in Table 5.8, production workers in the United States have been paid much higher wages, in terms of the U.S. dollar, than workers in countries such as Mexico and South Korea. So it could be argued that low wages abroad make it difficult for U.S. producers to compete with producers using cheap foreign labor and that unless U.S. producers are protected from imports, domestic output and employment levels will decrease. Although this viewpoint may have widespread appeal, it fails to recognize the links among efficiency, wages, and production costs.

Even if domestic wages are higher than those abroad, if domestic labor is more productive than foreign labor, domestic labor costs may still be competitive. Total labor costs reflect not only the wage rate but the output per labor hour. If the productive superiority of domestic labor more than offsets the higher domestic wage rate, the home nation's labor costs will actually be less than they are abroad.

TABLE 5. 8 / *Hourly Compensation Costs in U.S. Dollars for Production Workers in Manufacturing, 1992*

Country	Hourly Compensation (dollars/hour)
United States	$16.17
Canada	17.02
Mexico	2.35
Australia	12.94
Korea	4.93
Taiwan	5.19
Austria	19.65
Finland	18.69
Germany	25.94
France	16.88
Norway	23.20
Sweden	24.23
Switzerland	23.26
United Kingdom	14.69

SOURCE: U.S. Department of Labor, Bureau of Labor Statistics, *International Comparisons of Hourly Compensation Costs for Production Workers in Manufacturing, 1992* (Washington, D.C.: Government Printing Office), April 1993.

Another limitation of the cheap-foreign-labor argument is that low-wage nations tend to have a competitive advantage only in the production of goods requiring much labor and little of the other factor inputs. This means that the wage bill is the largest component of the total costs of production, which include payments to all factor inputs. It is true that a high-wage nation may have a relative cost disadvantage compared with its low-wage trading partner in the production of labor-intensive commodities. But this does not mean that foreign producers can undersell the home country across the board in all lines of production, causing the overall domestic standard of living to decline. Foreign nations should use the revenues from their export sales to purchase the products in which the home country has a competitive advantage—that is, products requiring a large share of the factors of production that are abundant domestically.

Contemporary international trade theory suggests that as economies become integrated through trade, there is a tendency for resource payments to become equalized in different nations, given competitive markets. A nation with expensive labor will tend to import products embodying large amounts of labor. As imports rise and domestic output falls, the resulting decrease in demand for domestic labor will cause domestic wages to fall to the foreign level.

In automobile manufacturing, for example, there has been sufficient international competition to warrant such a process. This was seen in the 1980s, when high unemployment in the U.S. auto industry permitted General Motors and Ford to scale down the compensation levels of their employees as a means of offsetting their cost disadvantages against the Japanese. The adverse implications of resource price equalization for the wages of U.S. autoworkers could explain the United Auto Workers' (UAW) support for protectionism. By shielding U.S. wage levels from market pressures created by foreign competition, protectionism would result in the U.S. government's validating the high wages and benefits of UAW members. International price equity is thus negated by trade restrictions.

Fairness in Trade: A Level Playing Field

Fairness in trade is another reason given for protectionism. Business firms and workers often argue that foreign governments play by a different set of rules than the home government, giving foreign firms unfair competitive advantages. Domestic producers contend that import restrictions should be enacted to offset these foreign advantages, thus creating a **level playing field** on which all producers can compete on equal terms.

U.S. companies often allege that foreign firms are not subject to the same government regulations regarding pollution control and worker safety as U.S. companies; this is especially true in many developing nations (such as Mexico and South Korea), where pollution laws and enforcement have been lax. Moreover, foreign firms may not pay as high corporate taxes or have to comply with employment regulations such as affirmative action, minimum wage, and overtime pay. Also, foreign governments may erect high trade barriers that effectively close their markets to imports, or they may subsidize their producers so as to enhance their competitiveness in world markets.

These fair-trade arguments are often voiced by organized lobbies that are losing sales to foreign competitors. They may sound appealing to voters, because they are couched in terms of fair play and equal treatment. However, there are several arguments against levying restrictions on imports from nations that have high trade restrictions or place lower regulatory burdens on their producers.

First, there is a benefit to the domestic economy from trade even if foreign nations impose trade restrictions. Although foreign restrictions that lessen our exports may decrease our welfare, retaliating by levying our own import barriers (which protect inefficient domestic producers) decreases our welfare even more. Second, the argument does not recognize the potential impact on global trade. If each nation were to increase trade restrictions whenever foreign restrictions were higher than domestic restrictions, there would occur a worldwide escalation in restrictions; this would lead to a lower volume of trade, falling production and employment levels, and a decline in welfare. There may be a case for threatening to levy trade restrictions unless foreign nations reduce their restrictions; but if negotiations fail and domestic restrictions are employed, the result is undesirable. Foreign trade practices are seldom an adequate justification for domestic trade restrictions.

Maintenance of the Domestic Standard of Living

Advocates of trade barriers often contend that tariffs are useful in maintaining a high level of income and employment for the home nation. It is argued that by reducing the level of imports, tariffs encourage home spending, which stimulates domestic economic activity. As a result, the home nation's level of employment and income is enhanced.

Although this argument appears appealing on the surface, it merits several qualifications. It is apparent that all nations together cannot levy tariffs to bolster domestic living standards. This is because tariffs result in a redistribution of the gains from trade among nations. To the degree that one nation imposes a tariff that improves its income and employment, it occurs at the expense of its trading partner's living standard. Nations adversely affected by trade barriers are likely to impose retaliatory tariffs, resulting in a lower level of welfare for all nations. It is little wonder that tariff restrictions designed to enhance a nation's standard of living at the expense of its trading partner are referred to as *beggar-thy-neighbor* policies.

Equalization of Production Costs

Proponents of this argument, sometimes called the *scientific tariff*, seek to eliminate what they consider to be unfair competition from abroad. Owing to such factors as lower wage costs, tax concessions, or government subsidies, foreign sellers may enjoy cost advantages over domestic firms. To offset any such advantage, tariffs equivalent to the cost differential should be imposed. Such provisions were actually part of the U.S. Tariff Acts of 1922 and 1930.

In practice, the scientific tariff suffers from a number of problems. Because within a given industry costs differ from business to business, how can costs actually be compared? Suppose that all U.S. steelmakers were extended protection from all foreign steelmakers. This would require the costs of the most efficient foreign producer to be set equal to the highest costs of the least efficient U.S. company. Given today's cost conditions, prices would certainly rise in the United States. This would benefit the more efficient U.S. companies, which would enjoy economic profits, but the U.S. consumer would be subsidizing inefficient production. Because the scientific tariff approximates a prohibitive tariff, it completely contradicts the notion of comparative advantage and wipes out the basis for trade and gains from trade.

Infant-Industry Argument

One of the more commonly accepted cases for tariff protection is the **infant-industry argument**. This argument does not deny the validity of the case for free trade. However, it contends that for free trade to be meaningful, trading nations should temporarily shield their newly developing industries from foreign competition. Otherwise, mature foreign businesses, which are at the time more efficient, can drive the young domestic businesses out of the market. Only after the young companies have had time to become efficient producers should the tariff barriers be lifted and free trade take place.

Figure 5.6 illustrates the logic of the infant-industry argument. During its infant stage, shown as time period t_0–t_1, a new industry will not likely be able to compete against mature foreign industries. Not only are its operations too small to realize economies of scale, but its production methods may be untested and need further improvements. Only after these long-run adjustments have been made can the young industry prosper and become an efficient producer. This occurs during time period t_1–t_2 in

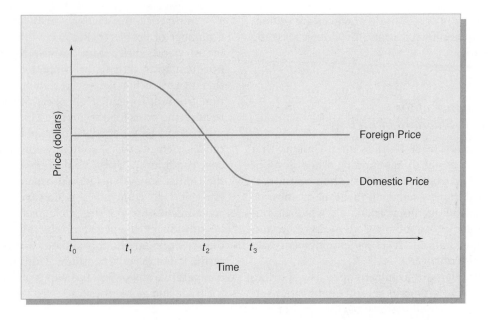

F I G U R E 5. 6   *Infant-industry argument for tariff protection.* According to the infant-industry argument, a new, emerging industry may not be able to compete against mature foreign producers. Temporary tariff protection granted to the infant industry will allow it to prosper and become competitive in the world market. When the infant industry matures and achieves international competitiveness, the tariff will be removed.

Figure 5.6. Eventually, the infant industry will mature and achieve its competitive advantage.

Although there is some truth in the infant-industry argument, it must be qualified in several respects. First, once a protective tariff is imposed, it is very difficult to remove, even after industrial maturity has been achieved. Special-interest groups can often convince policymakers that further protection is justified. Second, it is very difficult to determine which industries will be capable of realizing comparative-advantage potential and thus merit protection. Third, the infant-industry argument generally is not valid for the mature, industrialized nations such as the United States, Germany, and Japan. Finally, there may be other ways of insulating a developing industry from cutthroat competition. Rather than adopt a protective tariff, the government could grant a subsidy to the industry. A subsidy has the advantage of not distorting domestic consumption and relative prices; its drawback is that instead of generating revenue, as an import tariff does, a subsidy spends revenue.

Noneconomic Arguments

Noneconomic considerations also enter into the arguments for protectionism. One such consideration is *national security*. The national-security argument contends that a country may be put in jeopardy in the event of an international crisis or war if it is heavily dependent on foreign suppliers. Even though domestic producers are not as efficient, tariff protection should be granted to ensure their continued existence. A good application of this argument involves the major oil-importing nations, which saw several Arab nations impose oil boycotts on the West to win support for the Arab position against Israel during the 1973 Middle East conflict. The problem, however, is stipulating what constitutes an essential industry. If the term is defined broadly, many industries may be able to win protection from import competition, and the argument loses its meaning.

Another noneconomic argument is based on *cultural* and *sociological* considerations. New England may desire to preserve small-scale fishing; West Virginia may argue for tariffs on handblown glassware, on the grounds that these skills enrich the fabric of life; certain products such as narcotics may be considered socially undesirable, and restrictions or prohibitions placed on their importation. These arguments constitute legitimate reasons and cannot be ignored. All the economist can do is point out the economic consequences and costs of protection and identify alternative ways of accomplishing the same objective.

It is important to note that most of the arguments justifying tariffs are based on the assumption that the national welfare, as well as the individual's welfare, will be enhanced. The strategic importance of tariffs for the welfare of import-competing producers is one of the main reasons that reciprocal tariff liberalization has been so gradual. It is no wonder that import-competing producers make such strong and politically effective arguments that increased foreign competition will undermine the welfare of the nation as a whole, as well as their own. Although a liberalization of tariff barriers may be detrimental to a particular group, one must be careful to differentiate between the individual's welfare and the national welfare. If tariff reductions result in greater welfare gains from trade and if the adversely affected party can be compensated for the loss it has faced, the overall national welfare will increase. However, proving that the gains more than offset the losses in practice is very difficult.

THE POLITICAL ECONOMY OF PROTECTIONISM

Recent history indicates that increasing dependence on international trade yields uneven impacts across domestic sectors. The United States has enjoyed comparative advantages in such products as agricultural commodities, industrial machinery, chemicals, and scientific instruments. However, some of its industries have lost comparative advantages and suffered from international trade—among them, apparel and textiles, motor vehicles, electronic goods, basic iron and steel, and footwear. Formulating international trade policy in this environment is difficult. Free trade can yield substantial benefits for the overall economy through increased productivity and lower prices, but specific groups may benefit if government provides them some relief from import competition. Government officials must consider these opposing interests when setting the course for international trade policy.

Considerable attention has been devoted to what motivates government officials when formulating trade policy. As voters, we do not have the opportunity to go to the polls and vote for a trade bill. Instead, formation of trade policy rests in the hands of elected officials and their appointees. It is generally assumed that elected officials form policies to maximize votes, and thus remain in office. The result is a bias in the political system that favors protectionism.

The **protection-biased sector** of the economy generally consists of import-competing companies, the labor unions representing workers in that industry, and the suppliers to the companies in the industry. Seekers of protectionism are often established firms in an aging industry that have lost their comparative advantage. High costs may be due to lack of modern technology, inefficient management procedures, outmoded work rules, or high payments to domestic workers. The **free-trade-biased sector** generally comprises exporting companies, their workers, and their suppliers. It also consists of consumers, including wholesalers or retail merchants, who import goods.

Government officials understand that they will likely lose the political support of, say, the UAW if they vote against increases in tariffs on auto imports. They also understand that their vote on this trade issue will not be the key factor underlying the political support provided by many other citizens. This support can be retained by appealing to them on other issues while voting to increase the tariff on auto imports to maintain UAW support.

U.S. protection policy is thus dominated by special-interest groups that represent producers. Consumers generally are not organized, and their losses due to protectionism are widely dispersed, whereas the gains from protection are concentrated among well-organized producers and labor unions in the affected sectors. Those harmed by a protectionist policy absorb individually a small and difficult-to-identify cost. Many consumers, though they will pay a higher price for the protected product, will not associate the higher price with the protectionist policy and thus are unlikely to be concerned about trade policy. Special-interest groups, however, are highly concerned about protecting their industries against import competition. They provide support for government officials who share their views and lobby against the election of those who do not. Clearly, government officials seeking reelection will be sensitive to the special-interest groups representing producers.

The political bias favoring domestic producers is seen in the tariff escalation effect, discussed earlier in this chapter. Recall that the tariff structures of industrial nations often result in lower import tariffs on intermediate goods and higher tariffs on finished goods. For example, U.S. imports of cotton yarn have traditionally faced low tariffs, while higher tariffs have been applied to cotton fabric imports. The higher tariff on cotton fabrics appears to be the result of ineffective lobbying efforts of diffused consumers, who lose to organized U.S. fabric producers lobbying for protectionism. But for cotton yarn, the protectionist outcome is less clear. Purchasers of cotton yarn are U.S. manufacturers who want low tariffs on imported inputs. These companies form trade associations and can pressure Congress for low tariffs as effectively as U.S. cotton suppliers who lobby for high tariffs. Protection applied to imported intermediate goods, such as cotton yarn, is thus less likely.

Not only does the interest of the domestic producer tend to outweigh that of the domestic consumer in trade policy deliberations, but *import-competing producers tend to exert stronger influence on legislators than do export producers.* A problem faced by export producers is that their gains from international trade are often in addition to their prosperity in the domestic market; producers that are efficient enough to sell overseas are often safe from foreign competition in the domestic market. Most deliberations on trade policy emphasize protecting imports, and the indirect damage done by import barriers to export producers tends to be spread over many export industries. But import-competing producers can gather evidence of immediate damage caused by foreign competition, including falling sales, profits, and employment levels. Legislators tend to be influenced by the more clearly identified arguments of the import-competing industry and see that a greater number of votes are at stake among their constituents than among the constituents of the export producers.

The political economy of import protection can be analyzed in terms of supply and demand. Protectionism is supplied by the domestic government, while domestic companies and workers are the source of demand. The supply of protection depends on (1) the costs to society, (2) the political importance of the import-competing industry, (3) adjustment costs, and (4) public sympathy.

Enlightened government officials realize that although protectionism provides benefits to the domestic industry, *costs* are inflicted on society. These costs include the losses of consumer surplus because of higher prices and the resulting deadweight losses as import volume is reduced, lost economies of scale as opportunities for further trade are foregone, and the loss of incentive for technological development caused by import competition. The higher the costs of protection to society, the less likely it is that government officials will shield an industry from import competition.

The supply of protectionism is also influenced by the *political importance* of the import-competing industry. An industry that enjoys strong representation in the legislature is in a favorable position to win import protection. It is more difficult for politicians to disagree with 1 million autoworkers than with 20,000 copper workers. The national-security argument for protection is a variant on the consideration of the political importance of the industry. Thus, for example, the U.S. coal and oil industries were successful in obtaining a national-security clause in U.S. trade law permitting protection if imports threaten to impair domestic security.

The supply of protection also tends to increase when domestic businesses and workers face large costs of adjusting to rising import competition (for example, unemployment or wage concessions). This protection is seen as a method of delaying the full burden of *adjustment*.

Finally, as *public sympathy* for a group of domestic businesses or workers increases (for example, if workers are paid low wages and have few alternative work skills), a greater amount of protection against foreign-produced goods tends to be supplied.

On the demand side, factors that underlie the domestic industry's demand for protectionism are (1) comparative disadvantage, (2) import penetration, (3) concentration, and (4) export dependence.

The demand for protection rises as the domestic industry's *comparative disadvantage* intensifies. This is seen in the U.S. steel industry, which has vigorously pursued protection against low-cost Japanese and South Korean steel manufacturers in recent decades.

Higher levels of *import penetration*, suggesting increasing competitive pressures for domestic producers, also trigger increased demands for protection. A significant change in the nature of the support for protectionism occurred in the late 1960s when the AFL–CIO union abandoned its long-held belief in the desirability of open markets and supported protectionism. The shift in the union's position was due primarily to the rapid rise in import-penetration ratios that occurred during the 1960s in such industries as electrical consumer goods and footwear.

Another factor that may affect the demand for protection is *concentration* of domestic production. The U.S. auto industry, for example, is dominated by the Big Three. Support for import protection can be financed by these firms without fear that a large share of the benefits of protectionism will accrue to nonparticipating firms. Conversely, an industry that comprises many small producers (for example, meat packing) realizes that a substantial share of the gains from protectionism may accrue to producers who do not contribute their fair share to the costs of winning protectionist legislation. The demand for protection thus tends to be stronger the more concentrated the domestic industry.

Finally, the demand for protection may be influenced by the degree of *dependence on exports*. One would expect that companies whose foreign sales constitute a substantial portion of total sales (for example, Boeing Aircraft) would not be greatly concerned about import protection. Their main fear is that the imposition of domestic trade barriers might invite retaliation overseas, which would ruin their export markets.

SUMMARY

1. Even though the free-trade argument has strong theoretical justifications, trade restrictions are widespread throughout the world. Trade barriers consist of tariff restrictions and nontariff trade barriers.

2. There are three types of tariffs. An ad valorem tariff is stated as a fixed percentage of the value of an imported commodity. A specific tariff represents a fixed amount of money per unit of the imported commodity. A compound tariff combines a specific tariff with an ad valorem tariff.

3. Concerning ad valorem tariffs, several procedures exist for the valuation of imports. The free-on-board (FOB) measure indicates a commodity's price as it leaves the exporting nation. The cost-insurance-freight (CIF) measure shows the product's value as it arrives at the port of entry.

4. The effective tariff rate tends to differ from the nominal tariff rate when the domestic import-competing industry uses imported resources whose tariffs differ from those on the final commodity. Developing nations have traditionally argued that the tariff structures of many advanced nations on industrial commodities are escalated to yield an effective rate of protection several times the nominal rate.

5. U.S. trade laws mitigate the effects of import duties by allowing U.S. importers to postpone and prorate over time their duty obligations by means of bonded warehouses and foreign trade zones.

6. The welfare effects of a tariff can be measured by the following: protective effect, consumption effect, redistribution effect, revenue effect, and terms-of-trade effect.

7. If a nation is small compared with the rest of the world, its welfare necessarily falls by the total amount of the protective effect plus the consumption effect if it levies a tariff on imports. If the importing nation is large relative to the world, the imposition of an import tariff may improve its international terms of trade by an amount that more than offsets the welfare losses associated with the consumption effect and the protective effect.

8. Although tariffs may improve one nation's economic position, any gains generally come at the expense of other nations. Should tariff retaliations occur, the volume of international trade would decrease, and world welfare would suffer. Tariff liberalization is intended to promote freer markets so that the world can benefit from expanded trade volumes and international specialization of inputs.

9. Although not widely used as a trade restriction, tariff quotas have been used to protect certain industries. A tariff quota permits a limited number of goods to be imported at a lower tariff rate, whereas any imports beyond this limit face higher tariffs. Of the revenue generated by a tariff quota, some accrues to the domestic government as tariff revenue and the remainder is captured by producers as windfall profits.

10. Tariffs are sometimes justified on the grounds that they protect domestic employment, help create a level playing field for international trade, equalize the cost of imported products with the cost of domestic import-competing products, allow domestic industries to be insulated temporarily from foreign competition until they can grow and develop, or protect industries necessary for national security.

STUDY QUESTIONS

1. Describe a specific tariff, an ad valorem tariff, and a compound tariff. What are the advantages and disadvantages of each?

2. What are the methods that customs appraisers use to determine the values of commodity imports?

3. Under what conditions does a nominal tariff applied to an import product overstate or understate the actual or effective protection afforded by the nominal tariff?

4. Less developed nations sometimes argue that the industrialized nations' tariff structures dis-

courage the less developed nations from undergoing industrialization. Explain.

5. Distinguish between consumer surplus and producer surplus. How do these concepts relate to
a country's economic welfare?

6. When a nation imposes a tariff on the importation of a commodity, economic inefficiencies
develop that detract from the national welfare.
Explain.

7. What factors influence the size of the revenue,
protective, consumption, and redistribution
effects of a tariff?

8. A nation that imposes tariffs on imported goods
may find its welfare improving should the tariff
result in a favorable shift in the terms of trade.
Explain.

9. Which of the arguments for tariffs do you feel
are most relevant in today's world?

10. Although tariffs may improve the welfare of a
single nation, the world's welfare may decline.
Under what conditions would this be true?

11. What impact does the imposition of a tariff normally have on a nation's terms of trade and volume of trade?

12. In 1978, President Carter extended relief to the
U.S. CB radio industry when he increased
import duties for a three-year period. What
would be the likely effects of this policy for the
U.S. economy if it were continued?

13. Would a tariff imposed on U.S. oil imports promote energy development and conservation for
the United States?

14. A tariff quota is often viewed as a compromise
between the interests of the domestic consumer and those of the domestic producer.
Explain.

15. How does the revenue effect of a tariff quota
differ from that of an import tariff?

16. What is meant by the terms *bonded warehouse*
and *free-trade zone*? How does each of these
help importers mitigate the effects of domestic
import duties?

17. Assume that the nation of Australia is "small,"
unable to influence world price. Its demand and
supply schedules for TVs are shown in Table
5.9. On graph paper, plot the demand and supply schedules on the same graph.

a. Determine Australia's market equilibrium
for TVs in the absence of trade.
(1) What are the equilibrium price and
quantity?
(2) Calculate the value of Australian consumer surplus and producer surplus.

b. Under free-trade conditions, suppose Aus-

*TABLE 5. 9 / Demand and Supply:
TVs (Australia)*

Price of TVs	Quantity Demanded	Supplied
$500	00	50
400	10	40
300	20	30
200	30	20
100	40	10
0	50	0

tralia imports TVs at a price of $100 each.
Determine the free-trade equilibrium, and illustrate graphically.
(1) How many TVs will be produced, consumed, and imported?
(2) Calculate the dollar value of Australian consumer surplus and producer
surplus.

c. To protect its producers from foreign competition, suppose the Australian government
levies a specific tariff of $100 on TV
imports.
(1) Determine and show graphically the
effects of the tariff on the price of TVs
in Australia, the quantity of TVs supplied by Australian producers, the
quantity of TVs demanded by Australian consumers, and the volume of
trade.
(2) Calculate the reduction in Australian
consumer surplus due to the tariff-
induced increase in the price of TVs.
(3) Calculate the value of the tariff's consumption, protective, redistribution,
and revenue effects.
(4) What is the amount of deadweight
welfare loss imposed on the Australian
economy by the tariff?

18. Assume that the United States, as a steel-
importing nation, is large enough so that
changes in the quantity of its imports influence
the world price of steel. The U.S. supply and
demand schedules for steel are illustrated in
Table 5.10, along with the overall amount of
steel supplied to U.S. consumers by domestic
and foreign producers. On graph paper, plot the

TABLE 5. 10   /   *Supply and Demand:*
Tons of Steel: (United States)

Price/ Ton	Quantity Supplied (Domestic)	Quantity Supplied (Domestic + Imports)	Quantity Demanded
$100	0	0	15
200	0	4	14
300	1	8	13
400	2	12	12
500	3	16	11
600	4	20	10
700	5	24	9

supply and demand schedules on the same graph.

a. With free trade, the equilibrium price of steel is $_____ per ton. At this price, _____ tons are purchased by U.S. buyers, _____ tons are supplied by U.S. producers, and _____ tons are imported.

b. To protect its producers from foreign competition, suppose the U.S. government levies a specific tariff of $250 per ton on steel imports.

(1) Show graphically the effect of the tariff on the overall supply schedule of steel.

(2) With the tariff, the domestic price of steel rises to $_____ per ton. At this price, U.S. buyers purchase _____ tons, U.S. producers supply _____ tons, and _____ tons are imported.

(3) Calculate the reduction in U.S. consumer surplus due to the tariff-induced price of steel, as well as the consumption, protective, redistribution, and domestic revenue effects. The deadweight welfare loss of the tariff equals $_____ .

(4) By reducing the volume of imports with the tariff, the United States forces the price of imported steel down to $_____ . The U.S. terms of trade thus (improve/worsen), which leads to a(an) (increase/decrease) in U.S. welfare. Calculate the terms-of-trade effect.

(5) What impact does the tariff have on the overall welfare of the United States?

CHAPTER 6

Nontariff Trade Barriers

KEY CONCEPTS AND TERMS

Antidumping duty
Buy-national policies
Cost-based dumping
Domestic subsidy
Dumping
Export credit subsidy
Export quota
Export subsidy
Foreign sourcing
Global quota
Government procurement policies
Import quota
International price discrimination
Local content requirements
Margin of dumping

Multifiber Arrangement
Nonrestrained suppliers
Nontariff trade barriers
Orderly marketing agreement
Persistent dumping
Predatory dumping
Price-based dumping
Quota licenses
Selective quota
Sporadic dumping
Subsidies
Technical and administrative regulations
Trade diversion effect
Voluntary export restraints

This chapter considers policies other than tariffs that restrict international trade. Referred to as **nontariff trade barriers** (NTBs), such measures have been on the rise since the 1960s and have become the most widely discussed topics at recent rounds of international trade negotiations. Indeed, the post–World War II success in international negotiations for the reduction of tariffs has made remaining NTBs even more visible.

NTBs encompass a variety of measures. Some have unimportant trade consequences; for example, labeling and packaging requirements can restrict trade, but generally only marginally. Other NTBs significantly affect trade patterns; examples include import quotas, voluntary export restraints, subsidies, and do-

mestic content requirements. These NTBs are intended to reduce imports and thus benefit domestic producers.

Table 6.1 shows the *NTB trade coverage ratio* for major industrial nations in 1990. This ratio indicates the percentage of industrial-nation total imports (by value) subject to NTBs; for example, 35.9 percent of industrial-nation food imports were subject to NTBs in 1990. NTBs affect exports from developing nations to a larger degree than they do exports from industrial nations, especially for manufactured products; notice the high proportion of imports of textiles, clothing, and footwear subject to NTBs.

Why do countries use NTBs instead of tariffs? Several reasons have been suggested.

TABLE 6. 1 / *Import Coverage Ratios of Selected Nontariff Trade Barriers* Applied by Major Industrial Nations in 1990*

Product Group	Import Coverage Ratio
All food items	35.9%
Food and live animals	39.3
Oilseeds and nuts	7.4
Animal fats/vegetable oils	10.0
Agricultural raw materials	4.3
Ores and metals	17.9
Iron and steel	52.9
Nonferrous metals	0.8
Chemicals	10.8
Manufacturers, excluding chemicals	17.8
Leather	13.2
Textiles, yarn, and fabrics	38.7
Clothing	63.1
Footwear	19.7
Vehicles	54.9
All items, excluding fuels	18.5
All items	18.4

* Includes variable levies, quantitative restrictions, import surveillance, automatic licensing, and price control measures.

SOURCE: United Nations Conference on Trade and Development, *Trade and Development Report, 1991* (Geneva: UNCTAD, 1991). See also M. Kelly and A. McGuirk, *Issues and Developments in International Trade Policy,* International Monetary Fund, World Economic and Financial Surveys (Washington, D.C.: 1992).

Politicians may sometimes be reluctant to levy a tariff because it is an explicit tax on domestic consumers. As we will see, the adverse effects that NTBs exert on consumers tend to be more remote and less visible. Politicians may therefore perceive NTBs as being more acceptable to the voting public.

Another reason is the certainty of the restrictive impact of a protectionist instrument. For example, it may be much easier to show that a quota of 2 million tons restricts steel imports to 2 million tons than to show conclusively that a tariff of, say, $50 per ton would result in imports of only 2 million tons. Moreover, a rise in an import tariff may encourage the exporting nation to subsidize its exporting companies to make them more price-competitive, thus offsetting the tariff's restrictive impact. Such subsidies, however, would not alter the restrictive impact of an import quota.

Finally, many nations have adopted NTBs because they are not covered by the main body of rules of conduct in international trade, the General Agreement on Tariffs and Trade (GATT). Although GATT has succeeded in liberalizing tariffs in the post–World War II era, nations have circumvented GATT rules by using loopholes in the agreements and levying types of NTBs over which trade negotiations have failed.

IMPORT QUOTA

An **import quota** is a physical restriction on the quantity of goods that may be imported during a specific time period; the quota generally limits imports to a level below that which would occur under free-trade conditions. For example, the 1964 Meat Import Law requires the president to impose quotas on frozen, chilled, or fresh veal, mutton, beef, and goat meat when the secretary of agriculture determines that imports during a year will exceed 110 percent of an adjusted base quota. The adjusted base quota maintains imports at about 7 percent of domestic production. Although import quotas have been used primarily to provide protection to domestic producers, they have also been intended to help reverse balance-of-payments deficits as well as to stimulate domestic employment.

International trade agreements (General Agreement on Tariffs and Trade) have prevented

T A B L E 6. 2 / Selected Import Quotas of the United States

Imported Article	Quota Quantity* (yearly)
Milk and cream (New Zealand)	5.7 million L
Cheddar cheese (Australia)	1.2 million kg
Swiss cheese (European Community)	20.5 million kg
Chocolate (Ireland)	4.3 million kg
Chocolate (United Kingdom)	3.3 million kg
Animal feeds (New Zealand)	1.8 million kg
Animal feeds (Ireland)	5.4 million kg
Ice cream (Belgium)	0.9 million kg
Ice cream (Netherlands)	0.1 million kg
Wheat (Canada)	21.6 million kg
Cotton (Mexico)	4.0 million kg
Cotton (India and Pakistan)	0.9 million kg

* L = liters; kg = kilograms.

SOURCE: U.S. International Trade Commission, *Tariff Schedules of the United States* (Washington, D.C.: Government Printing Office, 1992).

the application of import quotas to manufactured goods from developing nations. Most import quotas are used to protect agricultural producers (as in the United States, the European Community, and Japan). Developing countries, in turn, have used import quotas to stimulate the growth of manufacturing industries. Table 6.2 gives examples of U.S. import quotas.

Import quotas are generally imposed *unilaterally* by the home government, without prior negotiation or consultation with other nations. They are levied and administered exclusively by the importing nation. Because of their unilateral nature, import quotas may be resented by other nations and may lead to retaliatory quotas.

One way of administering import limitations is through a **global quota**. This technique permits a specified number of goods to be imported each year, but does not specify where the product is shipped from or who is permitted to import. When the specified amount has been imported (the quota is filled), additional imports of the product are prevented for the remainder of the year.

In practice, the global quota becomes unwieldy because of the rush of both domestic importers and foreign exporters to get their goods shipped into the country before the quota is filled. Those who import early in the year get their goods; those who import late in the year may not. Moreover, goods shipped from distant locations tend to be discriminated against because of the longer transportation time. Smaller merchants, without good trade connections, may also be disadvantaged relative to large merchants. Global quotas are thus plagued by accusations of favoritism against merchants fortunate enough to be the first to capture a large portion of the business. For these reasons, global quotas are relatively uncommon, especially among industrial nations.

To avoid the problems of a global quota system, import quotas are usually allocated to specific countries; this type of quota is known as a **selective quota**. For example, the European Community might impose a global quota of 30 million apples per year, of which 14 million must come from the United States, 10 million from Mexico, and 6 million from Canada. Customs officials in the importing nation monitor the quantity of a particular good that enters the country from each source; once the quota for that source has been filled, no more goods are permitted to be imported.

Selective quotas suffer from many of the same problems as global quotas. Consider the case of Kmart, which ordered more than a million dollar's worth of wool sweaters from China in the 1980s. Before the sweaters arrived in the United States, the Chinese quota was filled for the year; Kmart could not bring them into the country until the following year. By that time, the sweaters were out of style and had to be sold at discounted prices. The firm estimated that it recovered only 60 cents on the dollar on these sweater sales.

Trade and Welfare Effects

Like a tariff, an import quota affects an economy's welfare. Figure 6.1 represents the case of cheese, involving the United States in trade with the European Community (the rest of the world). Suppose the United States is a "small" country in terms of the world cheese market. Assume that $S_{U.S.}$ and $D_{U.S.}$ denote the supply and demand schedules of cheese for the United States. S_{EC} denotes the supply schedule of the European Community. Under free trade, the price of European Community cheese and U.S. cheese equals $2.50 per pound. At this price, U.S. firms produce 1 pound, U.S. consumers purchase 8 pounds, and imports from the European Community total 7 pounds.

Suppose the United States limits its cheese imports to a fixed quantity of 3 pounds by imposing an import quota. Above the free-trade price, the total U.S. supply of cheese now equals

U.S. production plus the quota. In Figure 6.1, this is illustrated by a shift in the supply curve from S_{US} to S_{US+Q}. The reduction in imports from 7 pounds to 3 pounds raises the equilibrium price to $5; this leads to an increase in the quantity supplied by U.S. firms from 1 pound to 3 pounds and a decrease in U.S. quantity demanded from 8 pounds to 6 pounds.

Import quotas can be analyzed in terms of the same welfare effects identified for tariffs in the preceding chapter. Because the quota in our example results in a price increase to $5 per pound, U.S. consumer surplus falls by an amount equal to area $a + b + c + d$ ($17.50). Area a ($5) represents the *redistribution effect*, area b ($2.50) represents the *protective effect*, and area d ($2.50) represents the *consumption effect*. The *deadweight loss* of welfare to the economy resulting from the quota is depicted by the protective effect plus the consumption effect.

But what about the quota's *revenue effect*, denoted by area c ($7.50)? This amount arises from the fact that U.S. consumers must pay an additional $2.50 for each of the 3 pounds of cheese imported under the quota, as a result of the quota-induced scarcity of cheese. Where does this revenue go?

One outcome occurs when U.S. importers (for example, Safeway grocery stores) organize as buyers. Such importers might bargain favorably with European Community exporters and purchase cheese at the prevailing world price of $2.50 per pound, reselling the cheese to U.S. consumers at a price of $5 per pound. In this case, the quota's revenue accrues to the U.S. importers as profits. Alternatively, European Community exporters might organize as sellers and drive up the delivered price of cheese to $5 per pound, thereby capturing the quota's revenue effect. Still another outcome results if the U.S. government auctions import licenses to the highest bidder in a competitive market. Such auctions are intended to permit the government to recoup the quota revenue that would have accrued to importers in the form of monopoly profits (see box essay on page 148).

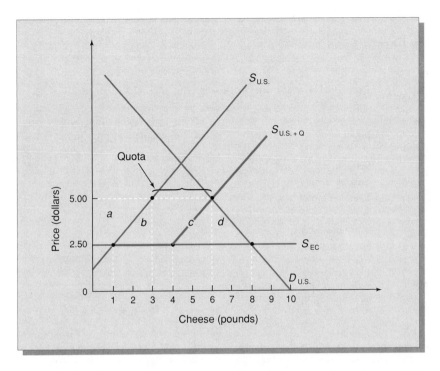

F I G U R E 6. 1   Import quota: trade and welfare effects. By restricting available supplies of an imported product, a quota leads to higher import prices. This price umbrella allows domestic producers of the import-competing good to raise prices. The result is a decrease in consumer surplus. Of this amount, the overall welfare loss to the importing nation consists of the protective effect, the consumption effect, and that portion of the revenue effect that is captured by the foreign exporter.

Sugar Import Quotas

The U.S. sugar industry provides an example of the impact of an import quota on a nation's welfare. Traditionally, U.S. sugar growers have received government subsidies in the form of price supports. Under this system, domestic sugar producers are provided a higher price than the free-market price; the difference between these two prices is the deficiency payment of the U.S. government. If the market price of sugar falls (rises), the government's deficiency payment rises (falls). To keep the market price of sugar close to the support price, and thus minimize its deficiency payments, the government has relied on import tariffs and

quotas. The price-support program ran into trouble when a glut of sugar in the world market sent the commercial price of sugar plunging to 6 cents a pound in 1982, compared with 41 cents a pound in 1980. This price was well below the 17-cents-a-pound support price of the federal government. Unless the government took action to prop up the commercial price paid to U.S. growers, the cost to the government of maintaining the support price of sugar would amount to an extra $800 million.

One way of boosting the U.S. commercial price of sugar was to raise the tariff on sugar imports. But, according to U.S. tariff codes, import duties could not exceed 50 percent of the world price of sugar. Although import

Allocating Quota Licenses

Potential Auction Revenues for the U.S. Government

Product	Revenue Estimate (millions of dollars)
Textiles and apparel	3,000
Carbon steel	1,270
Machine tools	320
Sugar	300
Dairy products	200
Specialty steel	60

SOURCE: C. F. Bergsten et al., *Auction Quotas and United States Trade Policy* (Washington, D.C.: Institute for International Economics, 1987), p. 49.

Because an import quota restricts the quantity of imports, usually below the free-trade quantity, not all domestic importers can obtain the same number of imports that they could under free trade. Governments thus allocates the limited supply of imports among domestic importers.

In oil and dairy products, the U.S. government has issued import licenses, which are rights to a stipulated quantity of imports, to U.S. importers on the basis of their historical share of the import market. But this method discriminates against importers seeking to import goods for the first time. In other cases, the U.S. government has allocated import quotas on a pro rata basis, whereby U.S. importers receive a fraction of their demand equal to the ratio of the import quota to the total quantity demanded collectively by U.S. importers.

The U.S. government has also considered using another method of allocating licenses among domestic importers: the auctioning of import licenses to the highest bidder in a competitive market. This technique has been used in Australia and New Zealand.

Consider a hypothetical quota on U.S. imports of textiles. The quota pushes the price of textiles in the United States above the world price, making the United States an unusually profitable market. Windfall profits can be captured by U.S. importers (for example, Sears, Wal-Mart) if they buy textiles at the lower world price and sell them to U.S. buyers at the higher price made possible because of the quota. Given these windfall profits, U.S. importers would likely be willing to pay for the rights to import textiles. By auctioning import licenses to the highest bidder in a competitive market, the government could capture the windfall profits (the revenue effect shown as area c in Figure 6.1). Competition among importers to obtain the licenses would drive up the auction price to a level at which no windfall profits would remain, thus transferring the entire revenue effect to the government. The auctioning of import licenses would turn a quota into something akin to a tariff, which generates tax revenue for the government.

The Trade Agreements Act of 1979 authorizes the U.S. government to auction import licenses on existing and newly imposed quotas; to date, such action has not been taken. The table here provides estimates of how much the federal government might collect from such auctions.

duties were raised to their legal maximum, the import duty system was deemed inadequate to protect U.S. growers from cheap foreign sugar as world prices fell throughout 1982. However, the government did impose quotas on imported sugar as a means of boosting domestic prices.

In 1982, the United States announced an import quota system that fixed nation-by-nation import allocations for 24 countries. Each nation's quota was based on its average sugar exports to the United States between 1975 and 1981, excluding the highest and lowest years. The total amount any nation could export to the United States was adjusted on a quarterly basis in light of changing market conditions. The quota for the first year of the system was 2.98 million tons, well below the 4.4–5.4 million tons that had entered the United States each year from 1976 to 1981.

By reducing sugar supplies, the quota was intended to force up the commercial price of sugar in the United States. The quota program thus transferred the cost of sugar support from the U.S. taxpayer to the U.S. sugar consumer.

Figure 6.2 illustrates the effects of the sugar quota during 1983, as estimated by the Federal Trade Commission. Note that the United States is assumed to be a "small" country with regard to the world sugar market. The world price of sugar, including transportation charges to the United States, was 15 cents a pound during 1983, denoted by curve S_W. In addition, the U.S. duty on sugar that year was 2.8 cents per pound. Therefore, the domestic market price was 17.8 cents, denoted by curve S_{W+T}. At this price, the United States imported 5.06 million tons of sugar (9.356 - 4.296 = 5.06).

Under the quota program, U.S. sugar imports were cut from 5.06 million tons to 2.98 million tons. The quota-induced scarcity of sugar drove the domestic price up from 17.8 cents per pound to 21.8 cents per pound. This price increase reduced the cost of maintaining sugar price supports for the U.S. government. It also led to a decrease in U.S. consumer surplus

equal to area $a + b + c + d$ ($735.2 million). Of this loss, the *redistribution effect* (area a) and the *protective effect* (area b) totaled $483.6 million, while the *consumption effect* (area d) equaled $13.2 million. The quota's *revenue effect* (area c) equaled $238.4 million. Because the sugar quota was administered by the exporting countries and U.S. importers operated as competitive buyers, the lion's share of the revenue effect was captured by foreign exporters.

The sugar price increases under the quota program hastened the development of sugar substitutes in the United States. In particular, high-fructose corn syrup and various artificial sweeteners were produced and sold to former U.S. sugar-using industries.

The sugar quotas also had international repercussions. About half of the U.S. sugar requirements are fulfilled with imported sugar, much of which comes from poorer, developing nations. The restricted market created financial problems for nations such as the Dominican Republic, where sugar accounted for almost 40 percent of its exports to the United States.

Like most regulations, the sugar quotas had loopholes waiting to be discovered. It turns out that when sugar comes into the United States blended with at least 65 percent of another sweetener, flavoring, or food, the government does not consider it sugar. Thus, the sugar quota does not apply. In 1981, the year before the implementation of the sugar program, only 300 tons of "blended sugar" were imported by the United States. In 1982, however, the amount rose to 13,000 tons, and by 1983, some 75,000 tons found their way into U.S.-made soft drinks, ice cream, and candy bars. The majority of blended-sugar imports came from Canada, because Canadian refiners could import sugar at low world prices and, despite U.S. tariffs, export to the United States at roughly 8 cents below the U.S. domestic refined price. Located adjacent to the United States, Canada also enjoyed the advantage of lower transportation costs compared with most other sugar-exporting nations.

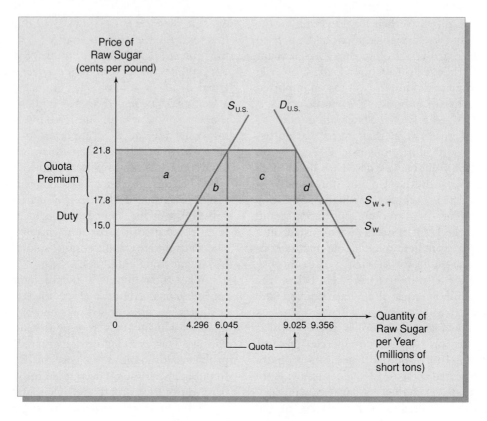

F I G U R E 6. 2   *The effects of a quota on sugar imports.* By forcing up the market price of sugar, an import quota reduces the costs to the U.S. government of maintaining price supports for domestic sugar producers. The higher market price of sugar, however, leads to decreases in welfare for U.S. consumers. SOURCE: D. Tarr and M. Morkre, *Aggregate Costs to the United States of Tariffs and Quotas on Imports* (Washington, D.C.: Federal Trade Commission, 1984).

Quotas versus Tariffs

Previous analysis suggests that the revenue effect of import quotas differs from that of import tariffs. These two commercial policies can also differ in the impact they have on the volume of trade. The following example illustrates how, during periods of growing demand, an import quota restricts the volume of imports by a greater amount than does an equivalent import tariff.

Figure 6.3 represents the trade situation of the United States in autos. The U.S. supply and demand schedules for autos are given by $S_{U.S._0}$

and $D_{U.S._0}$; S_{J_0} represents the Japanese auto supply schedule. Suppose the U.S. government has the option of levying a tariff or a quota on auto imports to protect U.S. companies from foreign competition.

In Figure 6.3(a), a tariff of $1,000 would raise the price of Japanese autos from $6,000 to $7,000; auto imports would fall from 7 million units to 3 million units. In Figure 6.3(b), an import quota of 3 million units would put the United States in a trade position identical to that which occurs under the tariff: the quota-induced scarcity of autos results in a rise in the price from $6,000 to $7,000. So far, it appears

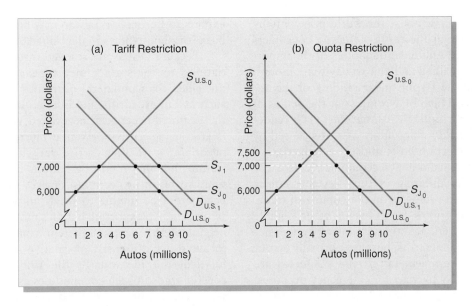

F I G U R E 6. 3 *Trade effects of tariffs versus quotas.* In a growing market, an import tariff is a less restrictive trade barrier than an equivalent import quota. With an import tariff, the adjustment that occurs in response to an increase in domestic demand is an increase in the amount of the product that is imported. With an import quota, an increase in demand induces an increase in product price. The price increase leads to a rise in production and a fall in consumption of the import-competing good, while the level of imports remains constant.

that the tariff and the quota are equivalent with respect to their restrictive impact on the volume of trade.

Now suppose the U.S. demand for autos rises from $D_{U.S._0}$ to $D_{U.S._1}$. Figure 6.3(a) shows that, despite the increased demand, the price of auto imports remains at $7,000. This is because the U.S. price cannot differ from the Japanese price by an amount exceeding the tariff duty. Auto imports rise from 3 million units to 5 million units. Under an import tariff, then, domestic adjustment takes the form of an increase in the *quantity* of autos imported rather than a rise in auto prices.

In Figure 6.3(b), an identical increase in demand induces a rise in domestic auto prices. Under the quota, there is no limit on the extent to which the U.S. price can rise above the Japanese price. Given an increase in domestic auto

prices, U.S. companies are able to expand production. The domestic price will rise until the increased production plus the fixed level of imports are commensurate with the domestic demand. Figure 6.3(b) shows that an increase in demand from $D_{U.S._0}$ to $D_{U.S._1}$ forces auto prices up from $7,000 to $7,500. At the new price, domestic production equals 4 million units, and domestic consumption equals 7 million units. Imports total 3 million units, the same amount as under the quota before the increase in domestic demand. Adjustment thus occurs in domestic *prices* rather than in the quantity of autos imported.

During periods of growing demand, then, an import quota is a more restrictive trade barrier than an equivalent import tariff. Under a quota, the government arbitrarily limits the quantity of imports. Under a tariff, the domestic price can rise above the world price only by the amount of the tariff; domestic consumers can still buy unlimited quantities of the import if they are willing and able to pay that amount. You might test your understanding of the approach used here by working out the details of two other hypothetical situations: (1) a reduction in the domestic supply of autos caused by rising production costs and (2) a reduction in domestic demand due to economic recession.

Besides differing in their revenue effects and restrictive impacts on the volume of trade, tariffs and quotas have several other notable differences. Quotas are administratively easier to manage than tariffs, but they normally do not provide government tax revenues. Quotas are relatively easy to enact for emergency purposes, whereas enactment of tariffs is a time-consuming process requiring statutory legislation.

ORDERLY MARKETING AGREEMENTS

In the past two decades, trading nations have witnessed an emerging form of protectionism that has moved alongside tariffs and import quotas as a major restrictive device. This protectionist measure is the so-called **orderly marketing agreement** (OMA), which essentially is a market-sharing pact negotiated by trading partners. Its main purpose is to *moderate* the intensity of international competition, allowing less efficient domestic producers to participate in markets that would have been lost to foreign producers that sell a superior product or price on a more competitive basis. OMAs involve trade negotiations between importing and exporting nations, generally for a variety of labor-intensive manufactured goods.

A typical OMA consists of voluntary quotas applied to exports. These controls are known as **voluntary export restraints** (VERs); they are sometimes supplemented by backup import controls to ensure that the restraints are effective. For example, Japan may impose limits on steel

exports to Europe, or Taiwan may agree to cutbacks on shoe exports to the United States.

Because OMAs are reached through negotiations, on the surface they appear to be less one-sided than unilateral protectionist devices such as import tariffs and quotas. In practice, the distinction between negotiated versus unilateral trade curbs becomes blurred. Trade negotiations are often carried out with the realization that the importing nations may adopt more stringent protectionist devices should the negotiators be unable to reach an acceptable settlement. An exporting nation's motivation to negotiate OMAs may thus stem from its desire to avoid a more costly alternative—that is, a full-fledged trade war. By the 1990s, OMAs covered trade in such commodities as television sets, steel, textiles, autos, and ships, as seen in Table 6.3.

As for the United States, the 1974 Trade Act gives the president the option of negotiating market-sharing agreements with other nations. As a result of economic recession and increased foreign competition, U.S. labor and business, as well as Congress, have become increasingly protectionist-minded. The result has been an aggressive pursuit by the United States of market-sharing agreements.

Orderly marketing pacts are viewed by their proponents as an escape valve for rising protectionist pressures from labor and business and are considered much less disruptive to international transactions than unilaterally imposed tariffs and quotas. Moreover, they avert the dangers of a trade war. Free-trade advocates oppose such accords, however, on the grounds that they create a misallocation of world resources. Because resources are being prevented from flowing to their most productive use, product prices are forced upward while world output levels are reduced.

Voluntary Export Restraints (VERs)

A typical OMA involves limitations on export sales administered by one or more exporting

Effects of Eliminating Nontariff Trade Barriers

Economic Effects of NTB Elimination

Category	Millions of Dollars			
	Consumer Gain	Producer Loss	Worker Income Loss	Job Loss (thousands)
Steel VERs	820.6	268.7	18.4	3.8
Specialty steel quotas	34.1	9.9	0.7	0.1
Machine tool VERs	48.0	11.3	1.9	0.4
Textile quotas under the MFA	883.1	303.6	86.8	6.3

SOURCE: U.S. International Trade Commission, *The Economic Effects of Significant U.S. Import Restraints, Phase 1: Manufacturing* (Washington, D.C.: Government Printing Office, October 1989), Tables ES-3 and ES-4.

This table provides estimates of the economic effects that would occur if the United States eliminated NTBs (and tariffs) on the products they covered in 1988. The removal of an NTB lowers the price of the affected import and may lower the price of the competing domestic good, yielding gains for domestic consumers. Such price reductions, however, result in lower profits in the import-competing domestic industry. Domestic workers tend to be displaced from the import-competing industry and thus suffer income losses.

nations or industries. What are the trade and welfare effects of such VERs?

Figure 6.4 illustrates these effects in the case of of trade in autos among the United States, Japan, and Germany. Assume that $S_{U.S.}$ and $D_{U.S.}$ depict the supply and demand schedules of autos for the United States. S_J denotes the supply schedule of Japan, assumed to be the world's low-cost producer, and S_G denotes the supply schedule of Germany.

Under free trade, the price of autos to the U.S. consumer is $6,000 per unit. At that price, U.S. firms produce 1 million autos, and U.S. consumers purchase 7 million autos, with imports from Japan totaling 6 million autos. Note that German autos are too costly to be exported to the United States at the free-trade price.

Suppose that Japan, responding to protectionist sentiment in the United States, decides to restrain auto shipments to the United States rather than face possible mandatory restrictions on its exports. Assume that the Japanese government imposes an **export quota** on its auto firms of 2 million units, down from the free-trade level of 6 million units. With the volume of imports constrained, U.S. consumers find the price of Japanese autos rising from $6,000 to $7,000. Consumer surplus falls by area $a + b + c + d + e + f + g + h + i + j + k + l$, an amount totaling $6 billion. Area $a + b$ ($2 billion) represents the transfer to U.S. auto companies as

TABLE 6.3 / *Orderly Marketing Agreement Examples*

Manufactured Good	Principal Nations	Accord Provisions
Specialty steel	U.S., European Community, Sweden, Japan, Canada	Japan negotiates export quota in U.S. market; U.S. imposes import quota on others.
Carbon steel	Japan, South Africa, Spain, European Community, South Korea	Japan voluntarily restrains exports to European Community; European Community requests export restraints by others.
TV sets	Japan, Benelux, Britain	Japan voluntarily limits exports to Britain and Benelux.
Ships	Japan, European countries	Japan enters into agreement with European countries to curb price competition.
Garments and textiles	41 exporting and importing nations	Export and import quotas; annual growth rates.
Autos	Japan, U.S.	Japan voluntarily restrains exports to the U.S.
Carbon steel, pipe, tubing	European Community, U.S.	European Community voluntarily limits exports to the U.S.

SOURCE: *Annual Report of the President of the United States on the Trade Agreements Program* (Washington, D.C.: Government Printing Office), various issues.

profits. The export quota results in a dead-weight welfare loss for the U.S. economy equal to the *protection effect,* denoted by area $b + c + i$ ($1 billion), and the *consumption effect,* denoted by area $f + g + l$ ($1 billion). The export quota's *revenue effect* equals area $d + e + j + k$ ($2 billion), found by multiplying the quota-induced increase in the Japanese price times the volume of autos shipped to the United States.

Remember that under an import quota, the disposition of the revenue effect is indeterminate: it will be shared between foreign exporters and domestic importers, depending on the relative concentration of bargaining power. But under a voluntary export quota, it is the foreign exporter who is able to capture the largest share of the quota revenue. In our example of the auto export quota, the Japanese exporters, in

compliance with their government, self-regulate shipments to the United States. This supply-side restriction, resulting from Japanese firms' behaving like a monopoly, leads to a scarcity of autos in the United States. Japanese automakers then are able to raise the price of their exports, capturing the quota revenue. For this reason, it is not surprising that exporters might prefer to negotiate a voluntary restraint pact in lieu of facing other protectionist measures levied by the importing country. As for the export quota's impact on the U.S. economy, the expropriation of revenue by the Japanese represents a welfare loss in addition to the deadweight losses of production and consumption.

Another characteristic of a voluntary export agreement is that it typically applies only to the most important exporting nation(s). This is in contrast to a tariff or import quota, which

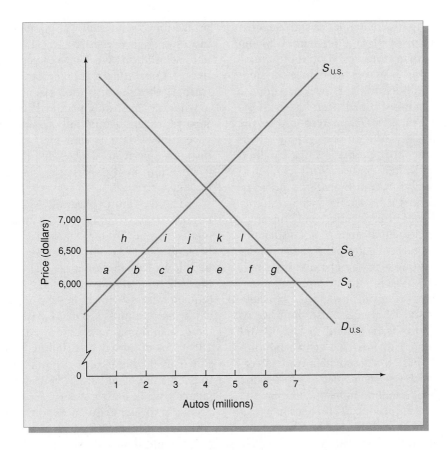

F I G U R E 6. 4 *Trade and welfare effects of a voluntary export quota.* By reducing available supplies of a product, an export quota (levied by the foreign nation) leads to higher prices in the importing nation. The price increase induces a decrease in consumer surplus. Of this amount, the overall welfare loss to the importing nation equals the protective effect, the consumption effect, and the portion of the revenue effect that is captured by the foreign exporter. To the extent that nonrestrained countries augment shipments to the importing nation, the overall welfare loss of an export quota decreases.

generally applies to imports from all sources. When voluntary limits are imposed on the chief exporter, exports of the **nonrestrained suppliers** may be stimulated. Nonrestrained suppliers may seek to increase profits by making up part of the cutback in the restrained nation's shipments. They may also want to achieve the maximum level of shipments against which to base any export quotas that might be imposed on

them in the future. For example, Japan was singled out by the United States for restrictions in textiles during the 1950s and in color TVs during the 1970s. Other nations quickly increased shipments to the United States to fill in the gaps created by the Japanese restraints. Hong Kong textiles replaced most Japanese textiles, and TVs from Taiwan and Korea supplanted Japanese TVs.

Referring to Figure 6.4, let us start again at the free-trade price of $6,000, with U.S. imports from Japan totaling 6 million autos. Assume that Japan agrees to reduce its shipments to 2 million units. However, suppose Germany, a nonrestrained supplier, exports autos to the United States in response to the Japanese cutback. Given an auto supply schedule of S_G, assume that Germany ships 2 million autos to the United States. With combined imports totaling 4 million units, auto prices to U.S. consumers rise to $6,500. The resulting deadweight losses of production and consumption inefficiencies equal area $b + g$ ($0.5 billion), less than the deadweight losses under Japan's export quota in the absence of nonrestrained supply. Assuming that Japan administers the export restraint program, Japanese companies would be able to raise the price of their auto exports from $6,000 to $6,500 and earn profits equal to area $c + d$ ($1 billion). Area $e + f$ ($1 billion) represents a **trade diversion effect**, which reflects inefficiency losses due to the shifting of 2 million units from Japan, the world's low-cost producer, to Germany, a higher-cost source. Such trade diversion results in a loss of welfare to the world because resources are not being used in their most productive manner.

When increases in the nonrestrained supply offset part of the cutback in shipments that occurs under an export quota, the overall inefficiency loss for the importing nation (deadweight losses plus revenue expropriated by foreign producers) is *less* than that which would have occurred in the absence of nonrestrained exports. In the preceding example, this amounts to area $i + j + k + l$ ($1.5 billion).

Japanese Auto Restraint

As previously discussed, the U.S. government in 1980 turned down the requests of the auto industry for additional protectionism in response to rising imports. However, by 1981 protectionist sentiment was gaining momentum in Congress as domestic auto sales plummeted, and legislation was introduced calling for import quotas. This momentum was a major factor in the administration's desire to negotiate a voluntary restraint pact with the Japanese. Japan's acceptance of this agreement was apparently based on its view that voluntary limits on auto shipments would derail protectionist momentum in Congress for more stringent measures.

The restraint program called for self-imposed export quotas on Japanese auto shipments to the United States for three years, beginning in 1981. First-year shipments were to be held to 1.68 million units, 7.7 percent below the 1.82 million units exported in 1980. In subsequent years, auto shipments were to be held to the same number plus 16.5 percent of any increase in domestic U.S. auto sales recorded in 1981. As it turned out, falling U.S. sales resulted in Japanese auto exports' being limited to 1.68 million units in 1982 and 1983. Still facing a weak auto industry, the United States was able to negotiate an export restraint pact with Japan for 1984, during which Japanese firms would limit auto shipments to the United States to 1.85 million units. In 1984, the United States released Japan from its formal commitment to the export agreement, but the Japanese government thought it imprudent to permit its automakers to export freely to the United States. The Japanese government has imposed its own export quotas on its auto manufacturers since the termination of the VER pact.

The purpose of the export agreement was to help U.S. automakers by diverting U.S. customers from Japanese to U.S. showrooms. As domestic sales increased, so would jobs for American autoworkers. It was assumed that Japan's export quota would assist the U.S. auto industry as it went through a transition period of reallocating production toward smaller, more fuel-efficient autos and adjusting production to become more cost-competitive. The restraint program would provide U.S. auto companies temporary relief from foreign competition so they could restore profitability and reduce unemployment.

Not all Japanese auto manufacturers were equally affected by the export quota. By requiring Japanese auto companies to form an export cartel against the U.S. consumer, the quota allowed the large, established firms (Toyota, Nissan, and Honda) to increase prices on autos sold in the United States. To derive more revenues from a limited number of autos, Japanese firms shipped autos to the United States with fancier trim, bigger engines, and more amenities such as air conditioners and deluxe stereos as standard equipment. Product enrichment also helped the Japanese broaden their hold on the U.S. market and enhance the image of their autos. As a result, the large Japanese manufacturers earned record profits in the United States.

The export quota was unpopular, however, with smaller Japanese automakers, including Suzuki and Isuzu. Under the restraint program, as administered by the Japanese government, each company's export quota was based on the number of autos sold in the United States three years prior to initiation of the quota. Smaller producers claimed that the quota forced them to freeze their U.S. dealer networks and abandon plans to introduce new models. It was argued that the quotas helped Nissan, which was floundering before the restraints, to become a dominant force in the U.S. market at the expense of smaller Japanese automakers. Table 6.4 depicts the estimated welfare effects for the United States of the Japanese export quota.

Multifiber Arrangement

The U.S. textile industry also has sought relief from foreign competition. In the early 1950s, the textile industry faced market-adjustment problems because of excess capacity in cotton textiles, a shift to synthetic fibers, technological changes, and increased imports. Cotton textiles from Japan accounted for more than 60 percent

TABLE 6. 4 / *Effects of Japanese Export Quota on Autos**

Effect	Amount
Price of Japanese autos sold in the the United States (increase)	$1,300
Price of U.S. autos sold in the United States (increase)	$660
Cost to U.S. consumers (increase)	$15.7 million
Number of Japanese autos sold in the United States (decrease)	1 million units
Japanese share of U.S. auto market (decrease)	9.6%
Sales of U.S.-produced autos (increase)	618,000 units
U.S. auto industry jobs (increase)	44,000

* These estimates apply to 1984, the fourth year of the export quota.

SOURCE: U.S. International Trade Commission, *A Review of Recent Developments in the U.S. Automobile Industry Including an Assessment of the Japanese Voluntary Restraint Agreements* (Washington, D.C.: Government Printing Office, February 1985).

of U.S. textile imports during this period. Despite domestic pressure for import quotas, the U.S. government refused to provide them, given its commitment to trade liberalization. Relief was finally granted to U.S. producers in 1957, when Japan agreed to place voluntary export controls on textile shipments to the United States. This assistance was of little help, however, because other suppliers such as Hong Kong were gaining stronger footholds in U.S. markets. By 1959, Hong Kong accounted for more than 28 percent of U.S. cotton textile imports.

To broaden the scope of the VERs, in 1962 the United States entered into a multilateral agreement known as the Long-Term Arrangement on Cotton Textiles (LTA). The LTA was a market-sharing pact that encouraged participating nations to adopt restraint in their export policies to avoid disruptive effects on import markets. Because the LTA applied only to cotton textiles, there were incentives for foreign producers to switch operation to artificial-fiber textiles. By 1970, U.S. imports of artificial-fiber textiles totaled 329 million pounds, up from 31 million pounds in 1961. This situation led to termination of the LTA in 1973.

What was needed was an arrangement that included trade in artificial-fiber textiles as well as cotton textiles. Such an expanded agreement was reached in 1974 by some 50 nations. This multilateral agreement was known as the **Multifiber Arrangement** (MFA), also referred to as the Arrangement Regarding International Trade in Textiles. The MFA is an orderly marketing pact that applies to trade in textile products manufactured from cotton, wool, and artificial fibers. The MFA attempts to prevent disruption of importing-nation textile markets by low-priced imports. Under the MFA, participating nations control textile and apparel imports through bilateral agreements that establish individual textile quotas for each restrained nation. Table 6.5 provides examples of U.S. textile and apparel imports under the MFA.

As of 1992, the United States had bilateral agreements limiting imports with 42 nations, accounting for more than 83 percent of total U.S. imports of textile and apparel products. These bilateral agreements included the three main suppliers of the United States—Hong Kong, Taiwan, and South Korea.

The bilateral agreement on textile shipments between Hong Kong and the United States provides an example of the MFA's operation. The U.S.–Hong Kong agreement assigns specific limits assigned to 34 categories of textiles and textile products. The limits for each of these product categories may be exceeded by either 5 or 6 percent annually, provided that a corresponding reduction is made in one of the other category limits. For all items not subject

TABLE 6. 5 / *U.S. Imports of Textiles and Apparel under the Multifiber Arrangement, 1991: Selected Examples*

Country	Value of Imports (millions of dollars)
Hong Kong	3.9
China	3.7
Taiwan	3.1
South Korea	2.4
Dominican Republic	1.0
Mexico	0.9
Thailand	0.7
Indonesia	0.7
Singapore	0.6
Malaysia	0.6
Pakistan	0.5
Bangladesh	0.5
Costa Rica	0.4
Turkey	0.3

SOURCE: U.S. International Trade Commission, *U.S. Imports of Textiles and Apparel Under the Multifiber Arrangement* (Washington, D.C.: September 1992).

to formal quotas, Hong Kong must obtain export authorizations as frequently as requested by the United States. The United States may request these authorizations when it appears that restrictions on further trade are necessary to eliminate a risk of market disruption.

The Hong Kong government allocates export quotas, without charge, to individual companies in Hong Kong. The quotas pertain to a specific calendar year and may be used at any time during that year. Export quotas apply to specific products, and the total amount of the quota for each product category is governed by the quota limit established in the bilateral agreement. A Hong Kong company wishing to export, say, cotton blouses to the United States must first apply for a license and designate the source of the quota against which the quantity of the textile exports will be deducted. The export quota system also permits transfers of quotas among companies. Thus, a Hong Kong exporter can accept a U.S. textile order even if it does not currently have sufficient quota authorization. Filling this order depends on the exporter's being able to obtain sufficient quota through transfer—and at a price that permits the exporter to still make a profit on its shipments to the United States.

Steel Export Restraints

In 1950, the U.S. steel industry dominated the world market. Accounting for almost half of global steel output, it produced almost 20 times as much steel as Japan and more steel than all of Europe combined. By 1959, the year of a four-month strike by U.S. steelworkers, the United States became a net importer of steel. Imports captured increasing shares of the U.S. steel market throughout the 1960s, reaching 16.7 percent in 1968. In that year, the U.S. government negotiated restrictions on certain steel products from the European Community and Japan. Import restraints of some type have been in force for most of the three decades since the implementation of those agreements in 1969 and have expanded to include additional steel products and other foreign suppliers.

With the imposition of trade restraints, the portion of U.S. steel imports from the European Community and Japan decreased during the 1960s–1990s. But South Korea, Spain, and other third-world nations shipped sizable amounts of steel into the U.S. market during this period. Reacting against surging imports, which skyrocketed to 26 percent of the U.S. market in 1984, the Reagan administration pressured 19 other nations and the EC to negotiate the Voluntary Export Restraint Agreements Program of 1984–1989.[1] In return, U.S. steelmakers agreed not to press a rash of antidumping suits against steel manufacturers of these nations. The goal of the VER program was to allow the U.S. steel industry time to

adjust and modernize so as to become competitive in the world market.

Under the VER program, U.S. imports of steel products were limited to about 21 percent of the market; VER nations were allocated an 18-percent market share, while nations without VERs were assumed to have a market share of about 3 percent. The VERs restricted exports to the United States of a variety of steel products, with product coverage varying by nation. In some cases, the program determined market-share limits as a percentage of projected U.S. consumption. In other cases, the program stipulated fixed quantitative limits. Some nations were subject to both types of restraints for various steel products.

The VER agreement was administered jointly by the United States and participating (constrained) nations. None of the covered steel products of a participating nation could enter the United States without an export certificate, issued by a foreign government and subsequently monitored by the U.S. Department of Commerce. To ensure that any quota premium resulting from increased domestic steel prices was not diverted to nonsteel endeavors, the U.S. government required most of the steel industry's cash flow to be reinvested in steel operations.

The VER agreement was more flexible than traditional import quotas in several respects. First, the VER quotas that were based on market shares permitted steel imports to vary with the level of U.S. consumption. Second, foreign nations that underfilled their quotas in one year were generally permitted to carry forward at least part of the unused portion to the following year. These two provisions permitted rising imports during eras of increased scarcity. Third, the VER agreement permitted waivers of import restrictions for steel products that were determined to be in short supply in the United States. From 1984 to 1989, 96 short-supply waivers were approved, totaling about 1.4 million tons of steel.

When VER quotas are *binding*, they reduce the volume of imports below the level that would enter in the absence of such quotas;

the quotas become filled before demand is satisfied. As domestic consumers compete against each other for the restricted supply, prices of foreign manufacturers increase. This encourages domestic consumers to substitute domestic and non-VER (nonrestrained supply) steel products for VER-nation-sourced steel products. Domestic suppliers, in turn, respond to the increased demand with higher prices and greater shipments.

Higher-priced steel results in rising production costs for domestic steel-using industries (such as autos and machinery). To the degree that steel-using industries attempt to cover their production cost increases by raising their product prices, they incur decreased sales, as domestic consumers switch to relatively cheaper imports and as foreign consumers decrease purchases of their exports. Moreover, because foreign competitors continue to have access to less expensive foreign steel, some domestic steel-using industries may choose to move their production facilities abroad in order to minimize the impact of the foreign price advantage. These efforts to enhance their competitiveness may result in job losses for domestic workers. It

is no wonder that domestic steel-using industries often view import restrictions as a "tax" that weakens their competitive position.

The Reagan steel quotas were binding throughout 1985 and 1986. Beginning in 1987, however, the VER quotas became *nonbinding* (that is, unfilled) thanks to an improvement in U.S. cost competitiveness, relatively strong steel demand in foreign markets, and the falling exchange value of the dollar against the currencies of the European Community and Japan. In 1987, only 94 percent of the total export ceiling established under the VER program was filled; this figure dropped to 90 percent in 1988 and 65 percent in 1989. By the late 1980s, the actual level of steel imports fell so significantly short of the ceilings that the price effects of the VERs were negligible. It appears that the VER quotas were most influential during 1985 and 1986, and less so thereafter.

Table 6.6 illustrates the economic effects of the steel VERs. By limiting steel imports, the VERs raised the price of imported steel. This price umbrella allowed U.S. steel companies to raise prices, though by a smaller amount. Although the increased steel prices benefited the

T A B L E 6. 6 / Estimated Effects of the Steel VER Agreement, 1985–1988

Effect	1985	1986	1987	1988
Effects on U.S. steel market (in percentages)				
Imports as a share of the U.S. market	25.7	24.7	21.8	21.4
Decrease in U.S. steel imports	6.9	16.2	15.8	2.0
Price increase for imported steel	1.7	4.3	4.2	0.5
Price increase for domestic steel	0.2	0.5	0.5	0.1
Effects on U.S. steel-using industries (in millions of dollars)				
Decrease in domestic sales	1665	4397	4106	478
Decrease in exports	258	673	699	95
Increase in imports	332	992	964	117

SOURCE: U.S. International Trade Commission, *The Effects of the Steel Voluntary Restraint Agreements on U.S. Steel-Consuming Industries* (Washington, D.C.: Government Printing Office, May 1989).

U.S. steel industry, they harmed other U.S. industries using steel as an input in production. Steel price increases were generally not as great for larger steel purchasers, such as General Motors, as for smaller purchasers, such as metal framers. Major steel purchasers typically negotiate long-term contracts (one year or longer) in which prices are established for the duration of a contract; smaller steel users often purchase steel on the "spot" market at prices prevailing at the time of sale. U.S. steel-consuming industries that openly complained about the price-increasing effects of the VER program included manufacturers of commercial windows, commercial food-preparation equipment, and material-handling equipment. The lower portion of Table 6.6 illustrates the effects of the steel VERs on U.S. steel-using industries.

Following implementation of the VERs, a shift in the U.S. import trade pattern occurred between VER nations and non-VER nations. *Nonrestrained* nations increased steel shipments to the United States from approximately 4 million tons in 1984 to more than 6 million tons in 1988, while U.S. imports from VER nations fell from 20 million to 15 million tons. Increased steel shipments to the United States by nonrestrained suppliers partially offset the restrictive impact of the VER quotas and led to the U.S. steel industry's demand for the U.S. government to expand the scope of the VER program.

Concerning U.S. steel imports from non-VER nations, another issue was the effect of steel exported from VER nations to non-VER nations for fabrication and reexport to the United States. Such a transformation would permit VER nations to circumvent the VER quotas. Throughout the Reagan quotas, the transformation of VER steel in non-VER nations and subsequent export to the United States was widespread. Examples of this practice included galvanized coils from New Zealand, wire products from Canada, and pipe from Thailand. In some cases, manufacturers from VER nations were involved in third-nation transformation ventures and supplied them with raw material, such as the partial ownership of Steel Tubes Company of Singapore by Japan's Kobe Steel Company.

In July 1989, the Bush administration announced its program for extending the steel VERs. Known as the Steel Trade Liberalization Program, the Bush objective was to provide a transition to a free, competitive steel market over a two-and-a-half-year period; during this period, the Bush administration attempted to achieve an international consensus to eliminate trade-distorting practices of foreign nations (such as subsidies). With the profitability of U.S. steel manufacturers improving by the late 1980s, the Bush quotas were less restrictive than those of President Reagan. The U.S. steel import share under the Bush VERs, including shipments from VER nations and nonrestrained nations, was projected to be 24 to 25 percent, as compared with a 21-percent market share under the Reagan administration. The Bush program thus afforded greater recognition to the needs of U.S. steel-using industries and consumers than did the Reagan program. In 1992, the steel VER program was terminated.

LOCAL CONTENT REQUIREMENTS

Although VERs help insulate domestic companies from sales of competitors abroad, they do not address the issue of **foreign sourcing**. In terms of the U.S. auto industry, foreign sourcing refers to the purchase of foreign components by a U.S. company for use in its domestic vehicle production. For example, General Motors has obtained engines from its subsidiaries in Mexico and Brazil, Chrysler has purchased ball joints from Japanese producers, and Ford has purchased cylinder heads from European companies. Foreign-sourcing commitments often reflect a desire to take advantage of lower costs overseas, including lower wage rates. They have also permitted U.S. automakers a rapid means of building up their capacity for small cars and

Caterpillar Opposes Extension of Steel Quotas

President Bush's decision to extend the steel VER agreement from 1989 until 1992 was widely opposed by steel-using manufacturers in the United States. Following are the reasons why Caterpillar, one of the nation's largest steel consumers, opposed the quota extension.

We believe more "protection" for the U.S. steel industry is unnecessary and carries tremendous costs. Prices of the primary steel products used by Caterpillar—plate and hot rolled bar—have risen approximately 20 percent from January 1988 to April 1989. By artificially restricting the supply of steel, quotas would create additional availability problems and provide U.S. steel producers increased leverage to demand higher prices. Caterpillar and its workers, dealers, and customers will be forced to "pay the price" for this protection.

For many Caterpillar products—including large tractors and off-highway trucks—steel comprises at least 20 percent of product cost. Since January 1988, prices for the primary steel products used by Caterpillar—plate and hot rolled bar—have increased approximately 20 percent. This price increase took place even though the cost to produce steel in the U.S. has dropped sharply in recent years.

Did quotas contribute to this price increase? Caterpillar believes the answer is clearly yes. At the time the company negotiated its 1988 plate price, U.S. mills were running flat out; the plate quota was 99.8 percent filled. Plate lead times in the United States were 14 to 16 weeks. Yet outside the United States, plate was in ample supply.

It's common knowledge that negotiating price during a time of shortage puts the buyer at a big disadvantage. Caterpillar's complaint with the quotas is that this program encourages—in fact, at times creates—shortages. Caterpillar estimates that had quotas not been in effect, its 1988 price increases would have been more in line with inflation (perhaps 4 to 8 percent).

Besides causing higher prices, steel shortages have hurt Caterpillar in other ways. In late 1987, for example, the company's U.S. facilities ran out of the large special section steel used to manufacture crawler-tractor track shoes. The consequence was incomplete products and inefficient factory operations. Because there were no U.S. producers of this type of steel . . . and quotas prevented Caterpillar from importing enough steel to satisfy its needs . . . the shortage was clearly quota-induced.

Quota-induced steel shortages, during 1987 and early 1988, further increased Caterpillar costs by forcing the company to: (1) temporarily resource products to countries where steel was available; (2) maintain expensive steel inventories to ensure steel is available during shortages; (3) purchase steel from warehouses at substantial premiums.

SOURCE: Excerpts from *Steel Import Quotas: Update*, April 1989, Caterpillar, Inc. Reprinted by permission.

trucks. Furthermore, a variety of foreign rules have required U.S. automakers with overseas assembly plants to use locally produced components for vehicles assembled overseas.

To limit the practice of foreign sourcing and to encourage the development of domestic industry, nations may impose **local** (domestic) **content requirements**. These requirements typically stipulate the percentage of a product's total value that must be produced domestically for that product to be sold domestically. Domestic content requirements have often been used by developing nations attempting to foster domestic production of some good. These nations are committed to the industrialization strategy of *import substitution*, in which domestic production gradually replaces the practice of importing goods from abroad.

Local content requirements have been used by Australia to support domestic industries as diverse as tobacco and broadcast commercials. To qualify for a relatively low duty on imported tobacco, Australian cigarette manufacturers must use at least 57 percent domestic tobacco leaf. In broadcasting, prior to 1992, Australia required that not more than 20 percent of any one television or radio advertisement could be foreign produced. As of 1992, not more than 20 percent of the advertisements shown on Australian television can be produced by non-Australians. This restriction applies to both live-action and animated commercials.

Figure 6.5 illustrates the welfare effects for the United States of a domestic content requirement applied to autos. In the upper diagram, S_0 represents the supply of autos offered by U.S. companies, and D_0 represents the U.S. demand schedule for autos. Under free-trade conditions, the foreign supply schedule of autos is denoted by S_1. Note that the United States is assumed to be a more costly producer of autos; accordingly, the U.S. supply price exceeds the foreign supply price at each possible quantity. Schedule S_2 depicts the combined supply of autos offered by U.S. and foreign producers; that is, S_2 is determined by adding the quantity of autos supplied by U.S. producers and by foreign producers at each possible price. Free-trade equilibrium occurs at point A, where schedule S_2 intersects schedule D_0. At the free-trade price, $9,000, U.S. consumers demand 27 autos. Of this total, 4 autos will be supplied by U.S. companies and 23 autos will be supplied by foreign producers.

Assume that the U.S. government, in order to provide U.S. producers relief from foreign competition, imposes domestic content requirements on autos sold in the United States. As a result, foreign auto companies decide to locate manufacturing operations in the United States to produce for the U.S. market. Because production costs are assumed to be higher in the United States than overseas (because of lower U.S. worker productivity, perhaps), locating production in the United States raises the costs of for-

eign auto companies. The cost increase results in a shift in the foreign supply schedule from S_1 to S_3, which leads to an upward shift in the total supply schedule of autos from S_2 to S_4. The U.S. auto market is now in equilibrium at point B. The content requirement results in an increase in auto prices from $9,000 to $15,000, while the number of autos sold in the United States falls from 27 to 21 units. Of this quantity, 8 autos are supplied by U.S. companies, and 13 autos are supplied by foreign companies located in the United States.

What are the welfare effects of the content requirement? Refer to the lower diagram of Figure 6.5, which summarizes the content-requirement analysis illustrated in the upper diagram (omitting supply schedules S_1 and S_3). By forcing up the costs of production, the content requirement leads to a $6,000 increase in auto prices and a decrease in U.S. consumer surplus equal to area $a + b + c + d + e$. Area a is transferred to U.S. producers as producer surplus. The protective effect is denoted by area b, and area e depicts the consumption effect. Area $c + d$ represents additional revenues accruing to foreign manufacturers as a result of the price increase. Of this amount, higher production costs capture area d; area c is captured by producer surplus of foreign manufacturers locating in the United States. Area d represents a deadweight welfare loss to the United States because of inefficient resource utilization. For the United States, then, the total deadweight loss as a result of the content requirement equals area $b + d + e$.

Throughout the early 1980s, as unemployment increased among U.S. autoworkers, the UAW pressured the U.S. government for protection against foreign-produced autos. Defending the interests of its members, the UAW maintained that domestic content legislation was needed to ensure that all companies selling autos in the United States would build a portion of each vehicle with U.S. parts and assembly. In 1982, the U.S. House of Representatives passed a domestic content bill entitled the Fair Practices in Automotive Products Act. The pro-

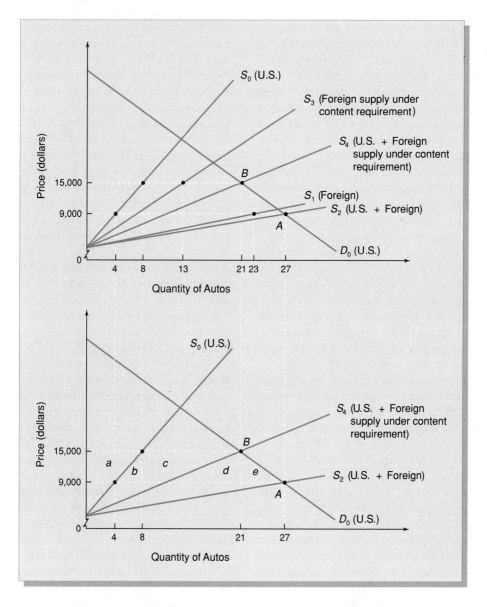

F I G U R E 6. 5   *Welfare effects of a domestic content requirement.* A domestic content requirement leads to rising production costs and prices to the extent that manufacturers are "forced" to locate production facilities in a high-cost nation. Although the content requirement helps preserve domestic jobs, it imposes welfare losses on domestic consumers.

posed legislation would have required all domestic and foreign manufacturers producing more than 100,000 vehicles for sale in the U.S. market to achieve minimal domestic content requirements on a scale that graduated along with increased U.S. sales. General Motors and Ford, for example, would have faced minimum content requirements (U.S.-added domestic value as a percentage of wholesale price) of 90 percent, whereas the requirement for Toyota would have been 71 percent. The bill was never passed by the U.S. Senate, however, and did not become part of U.S. trade policy.

SUBSIDIES

National governments sometimes grant **subsidies** to domestic producers to help improve their trade position. Such devices are an indirect form of protection provided to home businesses, whether they be import-competing producers or exporters. By providing domestic firms a cost advantage, a subsidy allows them to market their products at prices lower than their actual cost or profit considerations warrant. Governments wanting to see certain domestic industries expand may provide subsidies to encourage their development.

Government subsidies assume a variety of forms. In the simplest method, a government makes an outright cash disbursement to a domestic exporter after the sale has been completed. The payment may be according to the discrepancy between the exporter's actual costs and the price received or on the basis of a fixed amount for each unit of a product sold. The overall result is to permit the producer a cost advantage that would not otherwise exist. Such direct export subsidies when applied to manufactured goods have been prohibited by the General Agreement on Tariffs and Trade, as discussed in the next chapter.

Governments sometimes use indirect subsidies to achieve the same general result. For example, governments may give their exporters special privileges, including tax concessions, insurance arrangements, and loans at below-market interest rates. Governments may also sell surplus materials (such as ships) to domestic exporters at favorable prices. Governments may purchase a firm's product at a relatively high price and then dump it in foreign markets at lower prices. This has traditionally been the technique used by the U.S. government in conjunction with its farm-support programs. As with direct cash disbursements to domestic producers, indirect subsidies are intended to encourage the expansion of a nation's exports by permitting them to be sold abroad at lower prices. The Export-Import Bank of the United States encourages U.S. businesses to sell overseas by providing direct loans and guaranteed/insured loans to foreign purchasers of U.S. goods and services. Table 6.7 provides examples of government subsidies by a number of countries.

For purposes of our discussion, two types of subsidy can be distinguished: a **domestic subsidy**, which is sometimes granted to producers of import-competing goods, and an **export subsidy**, which is made to producers of goods that are to be sold overseas. In both cases, the recipient producer views the subsidy as tantamount to a negative tax: the government adds an amount to the price the purchaser pays rather than subtracting from it. The net price actually received by the producer equals the price paid by the purchaser plus the subsidy. The subsidized producer is thus able to supply a greater quantity at each consumer's price.

Domestic Subsidy

Figure 6.6 illustrates the trade and welfare effects of a subsidy granted to import-competing producers. Assume that the initial supply and demand schedules of the United States for steel are depicted by curves $S_{U.S._0}$ and $D_{U.S._0}$, so that the market equilibrium price is $430 per ton. Assume also that, because the United

T A B L E 6. 7 / *Examples of Governmental Subsidies*

Country	Subsidy Policy
Australia	Export market development grants extended to Australian exporters to seek out and develop overseas markets
Canada	Rail transportation subsidies granted to Canadian exporters of wheat, barley, oats, and alfalfa
China	Financial aid provided to unprofitable exporting factories and trade corporations
European Community	Export subsidies provided to many agricultural products, such as wheat, beef, poultry, fruits, and dairy products Financial assistance extended to Airbus Domestic subsidies granted to EC coal producers so as to allow EC coal to be competitive with imported coal
Finland	Financial incentives granted to the shipbuilding industry, such as research and development grants and preferential loans
Japan	Financial assistance extended to Japanese aerospace producers, including low-interest loans and R&D assistance
Pakistan	Exports encouraged through rebates of import duties, sales taxes, and income taxes
South Korea	Aid provided to commercial shipbuilding and repair firms in the form of equity infusions, preferential loans, and tax exemptions
United States	Export subsidies provided to U.S. producers of agricultural and manufactured goods via the Commodity Credit Corporation and the Expor-Import Bank

Source: Office of the U.S. Trade Representative, *Foreign Trade Barriers* (Washington, D.C.: Government Printing Office), various issues.

States is a small buyer of steel, changes in its purchases do not affect the world price of $400 per ton. Given a free-trade price of $400 per ton, the United States consumes 14 tons of steel, produces 2 tons, and imports 12 tons.

To partially insulate domestic producers from foreign competition, suppose the U.S. government grants them a production subsidy of $25 per ton of steel. The cost advantage made possible by the subsidy results in a shift in the U.S. supply schedule from $S_{U.S._0}$ to $S_{U.S._1}$. Domestic production expands from 2 to 7 million tons, and imports fall from 12 to 7 million tons. These changes represent the subsidy's trade effect.

The subsidy also affects the national welfare of the United States. According to Figure 6.6, the subsidy permits U.S. output to rise to 7 million tons. Note that, at this output, the net price to the steelmaker is $425—the sum of the price paid by the consumer ($400) plus the subsidy ($25). To the U.S. government, the total cost of protecting its steelmakers equals the amount of the subsidy ($25) times the amount of output to which it is applied (7 million tons), or $175 million.

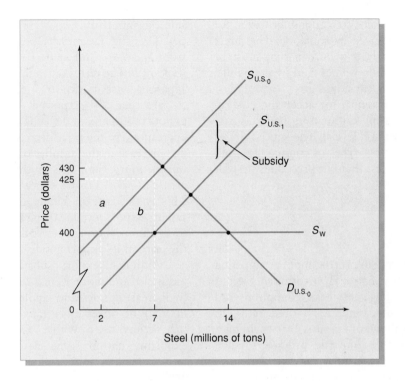

F I G U R E 6. 6 *Economic effects of a domestic subsidy.* A government subsidy granted to import-competing producers leads to increased domestic production and reduced imports. The subsidy revenue accruing to the producer is absorbed by producer surplus and high-cost production (protective effect). The subsidy imposes a deadweight welfare loss on the domestic economy equal to the protective effect.

Where does this subsidy revenue go? Part of it is redistributed to the more efficient U.S. producers in the form of producer surplus. This amount is denoted by area *a* ($112.5 million) in the figure. There is also a protective effect, whereby more costly domestic output is allowed to be sold in the market as a result of the subsidy. This is denoted by area *b* ($62.5 million) in the figure. To the United States as a whole, the protective effect represents a deadweight loss of welfare.

Attempting to encourage production by its import-competing producers, a government might levy tariffs or quotas on imports. But tariffs and quotas involve larger sacrifices in national welfare than would occur under an equivalent subsidy. Unlike subsidies, tariffs and quotas distort choices for consumers (resulting in a decrease in the domestic demand for imports), in addition to permitting less efficient home production to occur. The result is the familiar consumption effect of protection, whereby a deadweight loss of consumer surplus is borne by the home nation. This welfare loss is absent in the subsidy case. A subsidy tends to yield the same result for domestic producers as does an equivalent tariff or quota, but at a *lower* cost in terms of national welfare.

Subsidies are not free goods, however, for they must be financed by someone. The direct cost of the subsidy is a burden that must be financed out of tax revenues paid by the public. Moreover, when a subsidy is given to an industry, it is often in return for accepting government conditions on key matters (such as employee compensation levels). The superiority of a subsidy over other types of commercial policies may thus be less than the preceding analysis suggests.

Export Subsidy

Besides attempting to protect import-competing industries, many national governments grant subsidies, including special tax exemptions and the provision of capital at favored rates, to increase the volume of exports. By providing a cost advantage to domestic producers, such subsidies are intended to encourage a nation's exports by reducing the price paid by foreigners. Foreign consumers are favored over domestic consumers to the extent that the foreign price of a subsidized export is less than the product's domestic price.

The granting of an export subsidy yields two direct effects for the home economy: a *terms-of-trade effect* and an *export revenue effect*. Because subsidies tend to reduce the foreign price of home-nation exports, the home nation's terms of trade is worsened. But lower foreign prices generally stimulate export volume. Should the foreign demand for exports be relatively elastic, so that a given percentage drop in foreign price is more than offset by the rise in export volume, the home nation's export revenues would increase.

Figure 6.7 illustrates the case of an export subsidy applied to TV sets in trade between Japan and the United States. Under free trade, market equilibrium exists at point *E*, where Japan exports 1 million TVs to the United States at a price of $100 per unit. Suppose the Japanese government, to encourage export

sales, grants to its exporters a subsidy of $50 per TV. The Japanese supply schedule shifts from S_{J_0} to S_{J_1}, and market equilibrium moves to point *F*. The terms of trade thus turns against Japan because its export price falls from $100 to $75 per TV exported. Whether Japan's export revenue rises depends on how U.S. buyers respond to the price decrease. If the percentage increase in the number of TVs sold to U.S. buyers more than offsets the percentage decrease in price, Japan's export revenue will rise. This is the case in Figure 6.7, which shows Japan's export revenue rising from $100 million to $112.5 million as the result of the decline in the price of its export good.

Although export subsidies may benefit industries and workers in a subsidized industry by increasing sales and employment, the benefits may be offset by certain costs that fall on the society as a whole. Consumers in the exporting nation suffer as the international terms of trade moves against them. This is because, given a fall in export prices, a greater number of exports must be exchanged for a given dollar amount in imports. Domestic consumers also find they must pay higher prices than foreigners for the goods they help subsidize. Furthermore, to the extent that taxes are required to finance the export subsidy, domestic consumers find themselves poorer. In the previous example, the total cost of the subsidy to Japanese taxpayers is $75 million ($50 subsidy times 1.5 million TVs).

One type of export subsidy is the **export credit subsidy**. To encourage exporting by domestic producers, governments frequently extend loans to foreign customers. These loans are often awarded when private banks are unwilling to grant credit to importing businesses viewed as high risk. The interest rates charged on export credits have traditionally been less than those demanded by private banks on similar loans. Export credit subsidies transfer money from the domestic taxpayer to the subsidized export industry, the foreign purchaser, or both.

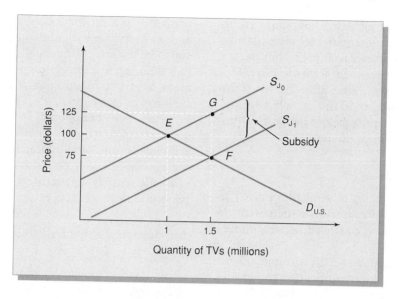

F I G U R E 6. 7 *Economic effects of an export subsidy.* To improve the competitiveness of domestic exporters, governments grant subsidies such as tax breaks and export credit subsidies. These cost reductions lead to a shift in the exporter's supply schedule to the right, and result in two effects: a terms-of-trade effect and an export revenue effect.

Export subsidies have been justified on a number of grounds. To the extent that credit subsidies lead to increased exports, the home nation's balance of trade is strengthened. Rising exports also result in higher levels of domestic employment. Thus, credit subsidies are often viewed as a relatively cheap alternative to unemployment and welfare payments. Credit subsidies have helped industries increase their scale of production and overcome inefficiencies or other presumed disadvantages. They have been used to encourage industrial sectors favored by the government. Finally, credit subsidies have been viewed as a kind of foreign aid because they help ease the debt burdens of the recipient developing nations.

To prevent nations from attaining unfair competitive advantage through export subsidies, guidelines have been established by the industrial nations; the interest rate, term, and down payment for credit programs are stipulated. By 1981, however, market interest rates had risen significantly above the minimum permissible interest rates on export credits, which had not been altered since 1975. Over this period, therefore, the extent of credit subsidization was rising. In 1981, 22 industrial nations agreed to raise the minimum export credit rate from an average of 7.75 percent to 10 percent. This move supported the principle that export credit interest rates should relate to the interest rates established by the private market in each nation. The result was a reduction in subsidies by almost 30 percent.

DUMPING

The case for protecting import-competing producers from foreign competition is bolstered by the antidumping argument. **Dumping** is recognized as a form of international price discrimination. It occurs when foreign buyers are charged lower prices than domestic buyers for an identical product, after allowing for transportation costs and tariff duties. Selling in foreign markets at a price below the cost of production is also considered dumping.

Forms of Dumping

Commercial dumping is generally viewed as either sporadic, predatory, or persistent in nature. Each type is practiced under different circumstances.

Sporadic dumping (distress dumping) occurs when a firm disposes of excess inventories on foreign markets by selling abroad at lower prices than at home. This form of dumping may be the result of misfortune or poor planning by foreign producers. Unforeseen changes in supply and demand conditions can result in excess inventories and thus in dumping. Although sporadic dumping may be beneficial to importing consumers, it can be quite disruptive to import-competing producers, who face falling sales and short-run losses. Temporary tariff duties can be levied to protect home producers, but because sporadic dumping has minor effects on international trade, governments are reluctant to grant tariff protection under these circumstances.

Predatory dumping occurs when a producer temporarily reduces the prices charged abroad to drive foreign competitors out of business. When the producer succeeds in acquiring a monopoly position, prices are then raised commensurate with its market power. The new price level must be sufficiently high to offset any losses that occurred during the period of cutthroat pricing. The firm would presumably be confident in its ability to prevent the entry of potential competitors long enough for it to enjoy economic profits. To be successful, predatory dumping would have to be practiced on a massive basis to provide consumers with sufficient opportunity for bargain shopping. Home governments generally are concerned about predatory pricing for monopolizing purposes, and may retaliate with antidumping duties that eliminate the price differential. Although predatory dumping is a theoretical possibility, economists have not found empirical evidence that supports its existence.

Persistent dumping, as its name suggests, goes on indefinitely. In an effort to maximize economic profits, a producer may consistently sell abroad at lower prices than at home. The rationale underlying persistent dumping is explained in the next section.

International Price Discrimination

Consider the case of a domestic seller who enjoys market power as a result of barriers restricting competition at home. Suppose this firm sells in foreign markets that are highly competitive. This means that the domestic consumer response to a change in price is less than that abroad; the home demand is less elastic than the foreign demand. A profit-maximizing firm would benefit from international price discrimination, charging a *higher* price at home, where competition is weak and demand is less elastic, and a *lower* price for the same product in foreign markets to meet competition. The practice of identifying separate groups of buyers of a product and charging different prices to these groups results in increased revenues and profits for the firm as compared to what would occur in the absence of price discrimination.

Figure 6.8 illustrates the demand and cost conditions of South Korean Steel Inc. (SKS), which sells steel to buyers in South Korea (less elastic market) and Canada (more elastic market); the total steel market consists of these two submarkets. Let D_{SK} be the South Korean steel demand and D_C be the Canadian demand, with the corresponding marginal revenue schedules represented by MR_{SK} and MR_C, respectively. D_{SK+C} denotes the market demand schedule, found by adding horizontally the demand schedules of the two submarkets; similarly, MR_{SK+C} depicts the market marginal revenue schedule. The marginal cost and average total

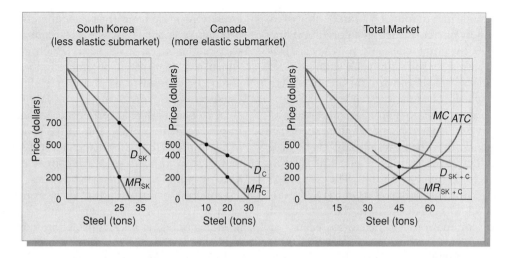

F I G U R E 6. 8 International price discrimination. A price-discriminating firm maximizes profits by equating marginal revenue, in each submarket, with marginal cost. The firm will charge a higher price in the less-elastic-demand (less competitive) market and a lower price in the more-elastic-demand (more competitive) market. Successful dumping leads to additional revenue and profits for the firm compared to what would be realized in the absence of dumping.

cost schedules of SKS are denoted, respectively, by *MC* and *ATC*.

SKS maximizes total profits by producing and selling 45 tons of steel, at which marginal revenue equals marginal cost. At this output level, ATC = $300 per ton, and total cost equals $13,500 ($300 × 45 tons). The firm faces the problem of how to distribute the total output of 45 tons, and thus set price, in the two submarkets in which it sells. Should the firm sell steel to South Korean and Canadian buyers at a uniform (single) price, or should the firm practice differential pricing?

As a *nondiscriminating* seller, SKS sells 45 tons of steel to South Korean and Canadian buyers at the single price of $500 per ton, the maximum price permitted by demand schedule D_{SK+C} at the *MR = MC* output level. To see how many tons of steel are sold in each submarket, construct a horizontal line in Figure 6.8 at the price of $500. The optimal output in each submarket occurs where the horizontal line intersects the demand schedules of the two nations. SKS thus sells 35 tons of steel to South

Korean buyers at a price of $500 per ton and receives revenues totaling $17,500. The firm sells 10 tons of steel to Canadian buyers at a price of $500 per ton and realizes revenues of $5,000. Sales revenues in both submarkets combined equal $22,500. With total costs of $13,500, SKS realizes profits of $9,000.

Although SKS realizes profits as a nondiscriminating seller, its profits are not optimal. By engaging in price discrimination, the firm can increase its total revenues without increasing its costs, and thus increase its profits. The firm accomplishes this by charging *higher* prices to South Korean buyers, who have *less elastic* demand schedules, and *lower* prices to Canadian buyers, who have *more elastic* demand schedules.

As a price-discriminating seller, SKS again faces the problem of how to distribute the total output of 45 tons of steel, and thus set price, in the two submarkets in which it sells. To accomplish this, the firm follows the familiar *MR = MC* principle, whereby the marginal revenue of each submarket equals the marginal cost at the profit-maximizing output. This can be shown in Figure 6.8 by first constructing a horizontal line from $200, the point where $MC = MR_{SK+C}$. The optimal output and price in each submarket is then found where this horizontal line intersects the MR schedules of the submarkets. SKS thus sells 25 tons of steel to South Korean buyers at a price of $700 per ton and receives revenues totaling $17,500. The firm sells 20 tons of steel to Canadian buyers at a price of $400 per ton and collects revenues of $8,000. The combined revenues of the two submarkets equal $25,500, which is $3,000 greater than in the absence of price discrimination. With total costs of $13,500, the firm realizes profits of $12,000, compared to $9,000 under a single pricing policy. As a price-discriminating seller, SKS thus enjoys higher revenues and profits.

Notice that the firm took advantage of its ability to price-discriminate, charging different prices in the two submarkets: $700 per ton to South Korean steel buyers and $400 per ton to Canadian buyers. For international price discrimination to be successful, certain conditions must hold. First, to ensure that at any price the demand schedules in the two submarkets have different demand elasticities, the submarkets' demand conditions must differ. Domestic buyers, for example, may have income levels or tastes and preferences that differ from those of buyers abroad. Second, the firm must be able to separate the two submarkets, preventing any significant resale of commodities from the lower-priced to the higher-priced market. This is because any resale by consumers will tend to neutralize the effect of differential prices and narrow the discriminatory price structure to the point at which it approaches a single price to all consumers. Because of high transportation costs and governmental trade restrictions, markets are often easier to separate internationally than nationally.

Excess Capacity

One reason underlying sporadic or distress dumping is that producers sometimes face reductions in demand that leave them with idle productive capacity. This *excess capacity* is of particular concern to a nation such as Japan, which has guaranteed lifetime employment to much of its industrial labor force. For many Japanese companies, therefore, labor comes close to being a fixed cost, because wages must be paid regardless of the company's production, sales, or profitability. Management thus has the incentive to compete vigorously for sales and to keep output high to generate revenues.

Should a firm find that its productive capacity exceeds the requirements of the domestic market, it may consider it more profitable to use the capacity to fulfill export orders at low prices than to allow the capacity to go idle. To keep exports high, a firm may be willing to sell abroad at a loss if necessary. Any profits generated by higher-priced domestic sales would help subsidize the goods that are dumped in foreign markets.

Consider the case of a radio producer under the following assumptions: (1) The producer's physical capacity is 150 units of output over the given time period. (2) The domestic market's demand for radios is price-inelastic, whereas foreign demand is price-elastic. Refer to Table 6.8. Suppose that the producer charges a uniform price (no dumping) of $300 per unit to both domestic and foreign consumers. With domestic demand inelastic, domestic sales total 100 units. But with elastic demand conditions abroad, suppose the producer cannot market any radios at the prevailing price. Sales revenues would equal $30,000, with variable costs plus overhead costs totaling $30,000. Without dumping, the firm would find itself with excess plant capacity of 50 radios. Moreover, the firm would just break even on its domestic market operations.

Suppose this producer decides to dump radios abroad at lower prices than at home. As long as all variable costs are covered, any price that contributes to overhead costs will permit larger profits (smaller losses) than those realized with idle plant capacity at hand. According

T A B L E 6. 8 / Dumping and Excess Capacity

	No Dumping	Dumping
Home sales	100 units @ $300	100 units @ $300
Export sales	0 units @ $300	50 units @ $250
Sales revenue	$30,000	$42,500
Less variable costs of $200 per unit	-20,000	-$30,000
	$10,000	$12,500
Less overhead costs of $10,000	-$10,000	-$10,000
Profit	$0	$2,500

to Table 6.8, by charging $300 to home consumers, the firm can sell 100 units. Suppose that by charging a price of $250 per unit, the firm is able to sell an additional 50 units abroad. The total sales revenue of $42,500 would not only cover variable costs plus overhead costs, but would permit a profit of $2,500.

With dumping, the firm is able to increase profits even though it is selling abroad at a price less than full cost (full cost = $40,000/150 = $267). Firms facing excess productive capacity may thus have the incentive to stimulate sales by cutting prices charged to foreigners—perhaps to levels that just cover variable production costs. Of course, home prices must be sufficiently high to keep the firm operating profitably over the relevant time period.

Antidumping Regulations

Despite the benefits that dumping may offer to importing consumers, governments have often levied stiff penalty duties against commodities they believe are being dumped into their markets from abroad. U.S. antidumping law is designed to prevent price discrimination and below-cost sales that injure U.S. industries. Under U.S. law, an **antidumping duty** is levied when the U.S. Department of Commerce determines that a class or kind of foreign merchandise is being sold at *less than fair value* (LTFV)

and the U.S. International Trade Commission (ITC) determines that LTFV imports are causing or threatening material injury (such as lost sales and profits and unemployment) to a U.S. industry. Such antidumping duties are imposed in addition to the normal tariff in order to neutralize the extent of price discrimination or below-cost sales.

The **margin of dumping** is calculated as the amount by which the foreign market value exceeds the U.S. price. Foreign market value is defined in one of two ways. According to the **priced-based definition**, dumping occurs whenever a foreign company sells a product in the U.S. market at a price below that for which the same product sells in the home market. When a home-nation price is not available (for example, if the good is produced only for export and is not sold domestically), an effort is made to determine the price of the good in a third market.

In cases where the price-based definition cannot be applied, a **cost-based definition** of foreign market value is permitted. Under this approach, the Commerce Department "constructs" a foreign market value equal to the sum of (1) the cost of manufacturing the merchandise, (2) general expenses, (3) profit on home-market sales, and (4) the cost of packaging the merchandise for shipment to the United States. The amount for general expenses must equal at least 10 percent of the cost of manufacturing, and the amount for profit must equal at least 8 percent of the manufacturing cost plus general expenses.

Antidumping cases begin with a complaint filed concurrently with the Commerce Department and the International Trade Commission. The complaint comes from an import-competing industry (such as a firm or labor union) and consists of evidence of the existence of dumping and data to demonstrate material injury or threat of injury.

The Commerce Department first makes a preliminary determination as to whether or not dumping has occurred, including an estimate of the size of the dumping margin. If the preliminary investigation finds evidence of dumping, U.S. importers must immediately pay a special tariff (equal to the estimated dumping margin) on all imports of the product in question. The Commerce Department then makes its final determination as to whether or not dumping has taken place, as well as the size of the dumping margin. If the Commerce Department rules that dumping did not occur, the special tariffs previously collected are rebated to U.S. importers. Otherwise, the International Trade Commission determines whether or not material injury has occurred as the result of the dumping.

If the International Trade Commission rules that import-competing firms were not injured by the dumping, the special tariffs are rebated to U.S. importers. But if both the International Trade Commission and the Commerce Department rule in favor of the dumping petition, a permanent tariff is imposed that equals the size of the dumping margin calculated by the Commerce Department in its final investigation.

Washington Apples

Not only have foreign producers dumped products in the United States, but U.S. firms have sometimes dumped goods abroad.

In 1989, the Canadian government ruled that U.S. Delicious apples, primarily those grown in Washington, were dumped on the Canadian market, causing injury to 4,500 commercial apple growers. As a result of the ruling, a 42-pound box of Washington apples could not be sold in Canada for less than $11.87, the "normal value" (analogous to the U.S. concept of "fair value") established by the Canadian government for regular-storage apples. Canadian importers purchasing U.S. apples at below-normal value had to pay an antidumping duty to the Canadian government so that the total purchase price equaled the established value. The antidumping order was for the period 1989–1994.

The Canadian apple growers' complaint alleged that extensive tree plants in the United States during the late 1970s and early 1980s had resulted in excess apple production. In 1987–1988, Washington growers experienced a record harvest and inventories that exceeded storage facilities. The growers dramatically cut prices in order to market their crop, leading to a collapse of the North American price of Delicious apples.

When Washington apple growers failed to provide timely information, the Canadian government estimated the normal value of a box of U.S. apples using the best information available. As seen in Table 6.9, the normal value for a box of apples in crop-year 1987–1988 was $11.87. During this period, the U.S. export price to Canada was about $9 a box. Based on a comparison of the export price and the normal value of apples, the weighted-average dumping margin was determined to be 32.5 percent.

The Canadian government determined that the influx of low-priced Washington apples into the Canadian market displaced Canadian apples and resulted in a loss to Canadian apple growers of $1 to $6.40 (Canadian dollars) per box during the 1987–1988 growing season. The Canadian government ruled that the dumped apples injured Canadian growers, and thus imposed antidumping duties on Washington apples.

Smith Corona Finds Antidumping Victories Are Hollow

Although antidumping duties are intended to protect domestic producers from unfairly priced imports, they can be an inconclusive weapon. Consider the case of Smith Corona, Inc., which won several antidumping cases in the 1970s–1990s but had little to show for it.

Trouble erupted for Smith Corona in the 1970s when it encountered ferocious competition from Brother Industries Ltd. of Japan, which flooded the U.S. market with its portable typewriters. Responding to Smith Corona's dumping complaint, in 1980 the U.S. government imposed antidumping duties of 49 percent on Brother portables. Smith Corona's antidumping victory proved hollow, however, because Brother realized that the antidumping ruling applied only to typewriters without a memory or calculating function. Through the tactic of *product evolution*, Brother evaded the duties by upgrading its typewriter to include a tiny computer memory. It took until 1990 for Smith Corona to get this loophole plugged by the federal court of appeals in Washington, D.C. By that time, Brother had found a more permanent method of circumventing antidumping duties: it began assembling portable typewriters in the United States from components manufactured in Malaysia and Japan. These typewriters were no longer "imported," and thus the 1980s duties did not apply.

Then competition shifted to another product, the personal word processor. By 1990, Smith Corona complained that Brother and other Japanese manufacturers were dumping word processors in the United States. This led the U.S. government to impose import duties of almost 60 percent on Japanese word processors in 1991. But that victory was also hollow, because it applied only to word processors manufactured in Japan; the Japanese firms' word processors were assembled in the United States.

Undeterred, Smith Corona filed another complaint, invoking a provision in U.S. trade law that was designed to deter foreign firms from evading antidumping duties by importing components and assembling them in the United States. Assuming that imported components would come from domestic (Japanese) factories, the provision did not cover components produced in third countries. Recognizing this loophole, Brother demonstrated that its imported components came from third countries, and therefore its word processors were not subject to antidumping duties. Needless to say, obtaining relief from foreign dumped goods was a difficult process for Smith Corona.

SOURCE: See Eduardo Lachica, "Anti-dumping Pleas Are Almost Useless, Smith Corona Finds," The *Wall Street Journal,* June 18, 1992, pp. A-1, A-11.

Minivans

In 1991, General Motors, Ford Motor Company, and Chrysler Corporation (the Big Three) filed an antidumping petition with the U.S. government charging injurious and unfair pricing of minivans imported from Japan into the United States. The petition alleged that minivan dumping by Japanese producers injured the U.S. industry, consumers, and workers. Domestic manufacturers were allegedly weakened by unfair pricing and thus were restricted in their ability to offer a broad range of model lines to serve consumer needs. Workers were denied security in their employment because domestic firms were unable to earn a fair return on their investment. As a result, shareholders were

T A B L E 6. 9 / *Normal Value and the Margin of Dumping: Delicious Apples, Regular Storage, 1987–1988**

U.S. FOB per Packed Box (42 pounds)	Normal Value (in dollars)
Growing and harvesting costs	5.50
Packing, marketing, and storing costs	5.49
Total costs	10.99
Profit (8% margin)	.88
Total normal value	11.87
Margin of dumping	*Percentage*
Range	0–63.44
Weighted-average margin	32.52

* The weighted-average dumping margin for controlled atmosphere–storage apples was 23.86 percent.

SOURCE: *Statement of Reasons: Final Determination of Dumping Respecting Delicious Apples Originating in or Exported from the United States of America,* Revenue Canada, Customs and Excise Division (December 1988).

injured, and the development of future product was retarded. It was also pointed out that dumping of automotive products in the United States was especially objectionable when it emanated from a nation (Japan) whose domestic automotive market was restricted against U.S. and all other foreign manufacturers.

The Big Three's dumping petition alleged that Toyota and Mazda of Japan sold new minivans in the United States below cost. In determining whether such dumping occurred, the U.S. Department of Commerce compared the price of Toyota and Mazda minivans exported to the United States with the foreign market value of similar minivans sold in Japan. Because it was determined that more than 90 percent of the minivans sold in Japan were sold at prices below the cost of production during the investigation period, the Commerce Department constructed a foreign market value (average cost) for minivans sold in Japan; the constructed value included the cost of materials, fabrication

of the merchandise, general expenses, and normal profit. Comparing the U.S. price of Toyota and Mazda minivans to the constructed cost of similar minivans in Japan, the Commerce Department determined that the average dumping margin was 12.7 percent for Mazda and 6.75 percent for Toyota.

In its dumping investigation, the Commerce Department included "transfer pricing" (see Chapter 10) issues. In this case, the investigation focused on whether Toyota paid its affiliated suppliers less for parts to be used in the Previa, the model intended for export to the United States, than for parts for the Estima, the model intended for domestic sales. The Big Three had contended that certain sweetheart deals that the Japanese auto manufacturers get from suppliers belonging to their corporate families had the effect of lessening their export costs, and thus were a form of dumping. The determination of dumping by the Commerce Department implied that Japanese automakers could not use such pricing practices to increase the competitiveness of their exports.

Upon the finding of minivan dumping by the Commerce Department, the case was sent to the U.S. International Trade Commission to determine if the Big Three were economically injured by the dumping. In a major blow to the Big Three, the International Trade Commission found that imported Japanese minivans did *not* significantly harm U.S. producers. The International Trade Commission apparently based its decision on the fact that, during the investigation period, Chrysler sold virtually all the minivans it could manufacture and that the slow minivan sales of Ford and General Motors were mostly attributable to the shortcomings of those products. Moreover, the Big Three controlled 85 percent of the U.S. minivan market. The International Trade Commission's determination meant that Mazda and Toyota minivans would not be subject to antidumping duties that could have raised the price of an imported minivan as much as $2,000. This was good news for the U.S. consumer, but a major disappointment to the U.S. auto industry.

OTHER NONTARIFF TRADE BARRIERS

Other NTBs consist of government codes of conduct applied to imports. Even though such provisions are often well disguised, they remain important sources of commercial policy. Let's consider two such barriers: government procurement policies and technical and administrative regulations.

Government Procurement Policies

Because government agencies are large buyers of goods and services, they are attractive customers for foreign suppliers. If governments purchased goods and services only from the lowest-cost suppliers, the pattern of trade would not differ significantly from what occurs in a competitive market. Most governments, however, favor domestic suppliers over foreign ones in the procurement of materials and products. This is evidenced by the fact that the ratio of imports to total purchases in the public sector is much smaller than in the private sector.

Governments often extend preferences to domestic suppliers in the form of **buy-national policies**. The U.S. government, through explicit laws, openly discriminates against foreign suppliers in its purchasing decisions. Although most other governments do not have formally legislated preferences for domestic suppliers, they often discriminate against foreign suppliers through hidden administrative rules and practices. Such governments utilize closed bidding systems that restrict the number of companies allowed to bid on sales, or they may publicize government contracts in such a way as to make it difficult for foreign suppliers to make a bid.

To stimulate domestic employment during the Great Depression, in 1933 the U.S. government passed the Buy American Act. This act requires federal agencies to purchase materials and products from U.S. suppliers if their prices are not "unreasonably" higher than those of foreign competitors. A product, to qualify as domestic, must have at least a 50-percent domestic component content and must be manufactured in the United States. As it stands today, U.S. suppliers of civilian agencies are given a 6-percent preference margin. This means that a U.S. supplier receives the government contract as long as the U.S. low bid is no more than 6-percent higher than the competing foreign bid. This preference margin rises to 12 percent if the low domestic bidder is situated in a labor-surplus area, and to 50 percent if the purchase is made by the Department of Defense. These preferences are waived when it is determined that the U.S.-produced good is not available in sufficient quantities or is not of satisfactory quality.

By discriminating against low-cost foreign suppliers in favor of domestic suppliers, buy-national policies are a barrier to free trade. Domestic suppliers are given the leeway to use less efficient production methods and to pay resource prices higher than those permitted under free trade. This yields a higher cost for government projects and deadweight welfare losses for the nation in the form of the protective effect and consumption effect.

Buy-national policies are generally defended on the grounds of fairness. In 1978 Conrail, the preeminent freight railroad system in the northeastern United States, indicated that it would purchase foreign-produced rail track spikes. This announcement contradicted its earlier decision to purchase steel from U.S. producers. Critics of the announcement argued that because U.S. taxpayers were providing $2.1 billion in subsidies to Conrail, Conrail had a moral obligation to support U.S. producers in its purchases.

The buy-American restrictions of the U.S. government have been liberalized with the adoption of the Tokyo Round of Multilateral Trade Negotiations (see Chapter 7). However, the pact does not apply to the purchase of materials and products by state and local government agencies. More than 30 states currently have buy-American laws, ranging from explicit prohibitions on foreign-product purchases to loose policy guidelines favoring U.S. products. Advocates of state buy-American laws usually maintain that the laws provide direct local economic benefit in the form of jobs; moreover, the threat of foreign retaliation is minimal at the state level.

The adoption of Minnesota's buy-American legislation provides an example of state feelings toward foreign competition. In 1978, the Minnesota Department of Transportation awarded a $3.7-million contract to a local firm to build a portion of a bridge. The winning firm's bid was lower than that of its nearest competitor largely because it embodied lower-cost Japanese steel instead of the U.S. steel contained in the second-place bid. The Minnesota AFL–CIO estimated that the award decision cost Minnesota steel fabricators some $750,000 in wages, a portion of which would have been paid back as taxes to the state. Local labor unions pressured the state government to prevent future occurrences of such loss. Three months later, the Minnesota legislature passed a tough buy-American law by a 91-to-33 vote.[2]

Technical and Administrative Regulations

Today, national governments impose a wide variety of technical and administrative regulations on imports. Even though not all such codes are intended to restrict international trade, they have the effect of doing so.

Marketing and packaging standards may be used to limit imports. For instance, a few nations refuse to allow a product to be marketed as "beer" unless it contains specified types and amounts of certain key ingredients. In Canada, the government stipulates container sizes for all imported canned goods.

Government health and safety standards also may modify international trade patterns. In the 1970s, the United States made efforts to restrict imports that did not meet U.S. pollution-control standards. Such was the issue in granting landing rights at Kennedy Airport to the Concorde supersonic plane produced by the French and British. Many New Yorkers contended that the noise level of the plane made it environmentally unsound. Mandatory antipollution-control devices on automobiles have also discouraged the sale of foreign autos in the United States. In short, government codes of conduct have often placed effective import barriers on foreign commodities, whether they are intended to do so or not.

SUMMARY

1. With the decline in import tariffs in the past two decades, nontariff trade barriers have gained in importance as a measure of protection. Nontariff trade barriers include such practices as (a) import quotas, (b) orderly marketing agreements, (c) local content requirements, (d) subsidies, (e) antidumping regulations, (f) discriminatory government procurement practices, and (g) safety standards.

2. An import quota is a government-imposed limit on the quantity of a product that can be imported. Quotas are imposed on a global (worldwide) basis or a selective (individual country) basis. Although quotas have many of the same economic effects as tariffs, they tend to be more restrictive. A quota's revenue effect generally accrues to domestic importers or foreign exporters, depending on the degree of market power they possess. If government desired to capture the revenue effect, it could auction import quota licenses to the highest bidder in a competitive market.

3. Orderly marketing agreements are market-sharing pacts negotiated by trading nations that generally involve quotas on exports and imports. Proponents of orderly marketing agreements contend that they are less disruptive of international trade than unilaterally determined tariffs and quotas.

4. Because an export quota is administered by the government of the exporting nation (supply-side restriction), its revenue effect tends to be captured by sellers of the exporting nation. For the importing nation, the quota's revenue effect is a welfare loss in addition to the protective and consumption effects.

5. Local content requirements try to limit the practice of foreign sourcing and encourage the development of domestic industry. They typically stipulate the minimum percentage of a product's value that must be produced in the home country for that product to be sold there. Local content protection tends to impose welfare losses on the domestic economy in the form of higher production costs and higher-priced goods.

6. Government subsidies are sometimes granted as a form of protection to domestic exporters and import-competing companies. They may take the form of direct cash bounties, tax concessions, credit extended at low interest rates, or special insurance arrangements. Direct production subsidies for import-competing producers tend to involve a smaller loss in economic welfare than do equivalent tariffs and quotas. The imposition of export subsidies results in a terms-of-trade effect and an export-revenue effect.

7. International dumping occurs when a firm sells its product abroad at a price that is (1) less than average total cost or (2) less than that charged to domestic buyers of the same product. Dumping can be sporadic, predatory, or persistent in nature. Idle productive capacity may be the reason behind dumping. Governments often impose stiff penalties against foreign commodities that are believed to be dumped in the home economy.

8. Government rules and regulations in areas such as safety and technical standards and marketing requirements can have significant impacts on world trade patterns.

STUDY QUESTIONS

1. In the past two decades, nontariff trade barriers have gained in importance as protectionist devices. What are the major nontariff trade barriers?

2. How does the revenue effect of an import quota differ from that of a tariff?

3. What are the major forms of subsidies that governments grant to domestic producers?

4. What is meant by voluntary export restraints, and how do they differ from other protective barriers?

5. Should U.S. antidumping laws be stated in terms of full production costs or marginal costs?

6. Which is a more restrictive trade barrier—an import tariff or an equivalent import quota?

7. Differentiate among sporadic, persistent, and predatory dumping.

8. A subsidy may provide import-competing producers the same degree of protection as tariffs or quotas but at a lower cost in terms of national welfare. Explain.

TABLE 6. 10 / *TV Supply and Demand: Venezuela*

Price/TV	Quantity Demanded	Quantity Supplied
$100	900	0
200	700	200
300	500	400
400	300	600
500	100	800

TABLE 6. 11 / *Computer Supply and Demand: Ecuador*

Price/ Computer	Quantity Demanded	Quantity Supplied
$ 0	100	—
200	90	0
400	80	10
600	70	20
800	60	30
1000	50	40
1200	40	50
1400	30	60
1600	20	70
1800	10	80
2000	0	90

9. Rather than generating tax revenue as do tariffs, subsidies require tax revenue. Therefore, they are not an effective protective device for the home economy. Do you agree?

10. In 1980, the U.S. auto industry proposed that import quotas be imposed on foreign-produced cars sold in the United States. What would be the likely benefits versus costs of such a policy?

11. Why did the U.S. government in 1982 provide import quotas as aid to domestic sugar producers?

12. Which tends to result in a greater welfare loss for the home economy, (a) an import quota levied by the home government or (b) a voluntary export quota imposed by the foreign government?

13. What would be the likely effects of export restraints imposed by Japan on its auto shipments to the United States?

14. Why might U.S. steel-using firms lobby against the imposition of quotas on foreign steel sold in the United States?

15. Concerning international dumping, distinguish between the price-based and cost-based definitions of foreign market value.

16. Table 6.10 illustrates the demand and supply schedules for TVs in Venezuela, a "small" nation that is unable to affect world prices. On graph paper, sketch Venezuela's demand and supply schedules of TVs.
   a. Suppose Venezuela imports TVs at a price of $150 each. Under free trade, how many TVs does Venezuela produce, consume, and import? Determine Venezuela's consumer surplus and producer surplus.
   b. Assume that Venezuela imposes a quota that limits imports to 300 TVs. Determine

the quota-induced price increase and the resulting decrease in consumer surplus. Calculate the quota's redistribution effect, consumption effect, protective effect, and revenue effect. Assuming that Venezuelan import companies organize as buyers and bargain favorably with competitive foreign exporters, what is the overall welfare loss to Venezuela as a result of the quota? Suppose that foreign exporters organize as a monopoly seller. What is the overall welfare loss to Venezuela as a result of the quota?
   c. Suppose that, instead of a quota, Venezuela grants its import-competing producers a subsidy of $100 per TV. In your diagram, draw the subsidy-adjusted supply schedule for Venezuelan producers. Does the subsidy result in a rise in the price of TVs above the free-trade level? Determine Venezuela's production, consumption, and imports of TVs under the subsidy. What is the total cost of the subsidy to the Venezuelan government? Of this amount, how much is transferred to Venezuelan producers in the form of producer surplus, and how much is absorbed by higher production costs due to inefficient domestic production? Determine the overall welfare loss to Venezuela under the subsidy.

17. Table 6.11 illustrates the demand and supply schedules for computers in Ecuador, a "small" nation that is unable to affect world prices. On

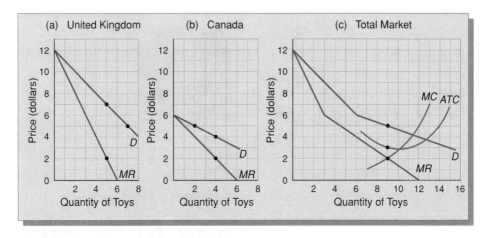

F I G U R E 6. 9 *International dumping schedules.*

graph paper, sketch Ecuador's demand and supply schedules of computers.

a. Assume that Hong Kong and Taiwan can supply computers to Ecuador at a per-unit price of $300 and $500, respectively. With free trade, how many computers does Ecuador import? From which nation does it import?

b. Suppose Ecuador and Hong Kong negotiate a voluntary export agreement in which Hong Kong imposes on its exporters a quota that limits shipments to Ecuador to 40 computers. Assume that Taiwan does not take advantage of the situation by exporting computers to Ecuador. Determine the quota-induced price increase and the reduction in consumer surplus for Ecuador. Determine the quota's redistribution effect, protective effect, consumption effect, and revenue effect. Because the export quota is administered by Hong Kong, its exporters will capture the quota's revenue effect. Determine the overall welfare loss to Ecuador as a result of the quota.

c. Again assume that Hong Kong imposes an export quota on its producers that restricts shipments to Ecuador to 40 computers, but now suppose that Taiwan, a nonrestrained exporter, ships an additional 20 computers to Ecuador. Ecuador thus imports 60 computers. Determine the overall welfare loss to Ecuador as a result of the quota.

d. In general, when increases in nonrestrained

supply offset part of the cutback in shipments that occur under an export quota, will the overall welfare loss for the importing country be greater or smaller than that which occurs in the absence of nonrestrained supply? Determine this amount in the Ecuador example.

18. Figure 6.9 illustrates the practice of international dumping by British Toys, Inc. (BTI). Figure 6.9(a) shows the domestic demand and marginal revenue schedules faced by BTI in the United Kingdom, and Figure 6.9(b) shows the demand and marginal revenue schedules faced by BTI in Canada. Figure 6.9(c) shows the combined demand and marginal revenue schedules for the two markets, as well as BTI's average total cost and marginal cost schedules.

a. In the absence of international dumping, BTI would charge a uniform price to U.K. and Canadian customers (ignoring transportation costs). Determine the firm's profit-maximizing output and price, as well as total profit. How much profit accrues to BTI on its U.K. sales and on its Canadian sales?

b. Suppose now that BTI engages in international dumping. Determine the price that BTI charges its U.K. buyers and the profits that accrue on U.K. sales. Also determine the price that BTI charges its Canadian buyers and the profits that accrue on Canadian sales. Does the practice of international dumping yield higher profits than the uniform pricing strategy? If so, by how much?

CHAPTER 7

Trade Regulations and Industrial Policies

Previous chapters have examined the benefits and costs of tariff and nontariff trade barriers. This chapter discusses the major trade regulations of the United States. It also considers the various industrial policies implemented by the United States, and other nations, to enhance the competitiveness of their producers.

THE SMOOT–HAWLEY ACT

As Table 7.1 makes clear, U.S. tariff history can be likened to a roller coaster. This was es-

pecially true until the early 1930s; since then, the overall trend of U.S. tariffs has been downward.

The high point of U.S. protectionism occurred with the passage of the **Smoot–Hawley Act** in 1930. Originally the bill was intended to give moderate protection to U.S. farmers, who faced stiff competition from foreign farmers. However, when the stock market crash of 1929 was followed by rapidly declining economic activity in the United States, protectionist pressures became so strong that average tariffs were raised to some 53 percent on protected imports!

TABLE 7. 1 / U.S. Tariff History:
Average Tariff Rates

Tariff Laws and Dates	Average Tariff Rate* (%)
McKinley Law, effective Oct. 6, 1890	48.4
Wilson Law, effective Aug. 28, 1894	41.3
Dingley Law, effective July 24, 1897	46.5
Payne–Aldrich Law, effective Aug. 6, 1909	40.8
Underwood Law, effective Oct. 4, 1913	27.0
Fordney–McCumber Law, effective Sept. 22, 1922	38.5
Smoot–Hawley Law, effective June 18, 1930	53.0
1930–1939	43.6
1940–1949	24.1
1950–1959	12.0
1960–1969	11.8
1970–1979	7.4
1980–1989	5.3
1990	5.0
1991	5.1

* Ratio of duties collected to FOB value on dutiable imports.

SOURCE: *Annual Report of the President of the United States on the Trade Agreements Program* (Washington, D.C.: Government Printing Office), various issues.

As the Smoot-Hawley bill moved through the U.S. Congress, formal protests from foreign nations flooded Washington, eventually adding up to a document of some 200 pages. Nevertheless, both the House of Representatives and the Senate approved the bill. Despite some 1,000 U.S. economists' beseeching President Hoover to veto the legislation, the tariff was signed into law on June 17, 1930.

The legislation provoked retaliation by 25 trading partners of the United States. Spain implemented the Wais tariff in reaction to tariffs on cork, oranges, and grapes. Protesting new tariffs on watches and shoes, Switzerland boycotted U.S. exports. Canada increased its tariffs threefold in reaction to U.S. tariffs on timber, logs, and many food products. Italy retaliated against tariffs on olive oil and hats with tariffs on U.S. automobiles. Mexico, France, Cuba, Australia, France, and New Zealand also participated in tariff wars. Such other beggarthy-neighbor policies as foreign-exchange controls and currency depreciations were also implemented. The effort by several nations to run a trade surplus by reducing imports led to a breakdown of the international trading system. Within two years following the Smoot–Hawley Act, U.S. exports decreased by nearly two-thirds.

How did Herbert Hoover fall into such a protectionist trap? The president felt compelled to honor the 1928 Republican platform calling for tariffs to aid the weakening farm economy. The stock market crash of 1929 and the imminent Great Depression further led to a crisis atmosphere. Republicans had been sympathetic to protectionism for decades. Now they viewed import tariffs as a method of fulfilling demands that government initiate positive steps to combat domestic unemployment.

President Hoover felt bound to tradition and to the platform of the Republican party. Henry Ford spent an evening with Hoover requesting a presidential veto of what he referred to as "economic stupidity." Other auto executives sided with Ford. However, tariff legislation had never before been vetoed by a president, and Hoover was not about to set a precedent. Hoover remarked that "with returning normal conditions, our foreign trade will continue to expand."

By 1932, U.S. trade with other nations had collapsed. Franklin Roosevelt denounced the trade legislation as ruinous. Hoover responded that Roosevelt would have U.S. workers compete with peasant labor overseas. Following Hoover's defeat in the presidential election of 1932, the Democrats dismantled the Smoot–Hawley legislation. But they used caution, relying on reciprocal trade agreements instead of across-the-board tariff concessions by the United States. Sam Rayburn, Speaker of the House of Representatives, insisted that any party member who wanted to be a member of the House Ways and Means Committee had to support trade reciprocity instead of protectionism. The Smoot–Hawley approach was discredited, and the United States pursued trade liberalization via reciprocal trade agreements.

THE RECIPROCAL TRADE AGREEMENTS ACT

The combined impact on U.S. exports of the Great Depression and the foreign retaliatory tariffs imposed in reaction to the Smoot–Hawley Act resulted in a reversal of U.S. trade policy. In 1934, Congress passed the **Reciprocal Trade Agreements Act**, which set the stage for a wave of *trade liberalization*. Specifically aimed at tariff reduction, the act contained two features: (1) negotiating authority and (2) generalized reductions.

Under this law, the president was given the unprecedented authority to negotiate tariff agreements with foreign governments. Without congressional approval, the president could lower tariffs by up to 50 percent of the existing level. Enactment of any tariff reductions was dependent on the willingness of other nations to reciprocally lower their tariffs against U.S. goods. From 1934 to 1947, the United States entered into 32 reciprocal tariff agreements, and over this period the average level of tariffs on protected products fell to about half of the 1934 levels.

The Reciprocal Trade Agreements Act also provided for generalized tariff reductions through the **most-favored-nation** (MFN) **clause**. This clause is an agreement between two nations to apply tariffs to each other at rates as low as those applied to any other nation. For example, if the United States extends MFN treatment to Brazil and then grants a low tariff on imports of machinery from France, the United States is obligated to provide the identical low-tariff treatment on imports of machinery from Brazil. Brazil thus receives the same treatment as the initially most favored nation, France. The advantage to Brazil of MFN status is that it can investigate all of the tariff policies of the United States concerning imported machinery to see if treatment to some nation is more favorable than that granted to it; if any more favorable terms are found, Brazil can call for equal treatment.

Granting MFN status or imposing differential tariffs has been used as an instrument of foreign policy. For example, a nation may punish unfriendly nations with high import tariffs on their goods and reward friendly nations with low tariffs. The United States has granted MFN status to most of the nations with which it trades. As of 1993, the United States did not grant MFN status to the following countries:

Afghanistan	Kampuchea	North Korea
Albania	Laos	Romania
Bulgaria	Latvia	Russia
Cuba	Lithuania	Vietnam
Estonia	Mongolia	

U.S. tariffs on imports from these countries are often three or four (or more) times as high as those on comparable imports from nations receiving MFN status, as seen in Table 7.2.

THE GENERAL AGREEMENT ON TARIFFS AND TRADE

Partly in response to the disruptions to international trade during the Great Depression, the

T A B L E   7. 2   /   *U.S. Tariffs on Imports from Nations Granted, and Not Granted,*
Most-Favored-Nation Status: Selected Examples

Product	Tariff	
	MFN Status	*Non-MFN Status*
Powdered milk	13.7 cents/kg	27.3 cents/kg
Cheese	10%	35%
Honey	2.2 cents/kg	6.6 cents/kg
Sweet potatoes	10%	50%
Wine	26.4 cents/liter	33 cents/liter
Writing paper	2.4%	28%
Cotton fabrics	6.5%	14.9%
Sewing thread	13%	55%
Women's suits	11%	90%
Men's overcoats	4.5%	35%
Track suits	7.8%	35%
Sports footwear	90 cents/pair + 20%	$1.58/pair + 35%
Drinking glasses	20%	60%
Wire	5.3%	35%

SOURCE: U.S. International Trade Commission, *Harmonized Tariff Schedule of the United States*, 1992.

United States and some of its trading partners sought to impose order on the flow of goods among nations after World War II. Plans called for the establishment of a *multilateral system* of world trade. Under the Reciprocal Trade Agreements Act, only bilateral negotiations could take place between the United States and its trading partners. The first major postwar step toward liberalization of world trade was the **General Agreement on Tariffs and Trade (GATT)** signed in 1947 by 23 countries, including the United States; today, GATT has more than 100 members.

GATT's purpose has been to stipulate a basic set of rules under which trade negotiations can occur. Participating nations agree to three basic principles: (1) nondiscrimination in trade through unconditional most-favored-nation treatment, (2) the reduction of tariffs by multilateral negotiations, and (3) elimination of most import quotas, with exceptions such as protec-

tion of domestic agriculture or safeguarding of a country's balance-of-payments position.

An important function of GATT is to furnish member nations a mechanism whereby disputes concerning trade policy can be settled. Suppose, for example, that Canada finds it necessary to raise tariffs on imported autos to protect its home industry—an action that harms Germany. Germany can issue a complaint, which is sent to member nations for review, discussion, and possible settlement. If an agreement cannot be reached, GATT will provide a conciliation panel to review the complaint and make recommendations. Canada, for example, may be encouraged to moderate its tariff barriers. Should this recommendation not be acknowledged, GATT has the authority to warrant Germany's enactment of retaliatory tariffs.

One of the most hotly contested trade disputes involving GATT was the so-called chicken war of 1963. During 1962, members of the European Community increased their import tariffs on poultry, triggering a decline in U.S. exports to Europe of more than 60 percent. After many rounds of accusations, the GATT conciliation panel ruled that U.S. exporters had suffered losses of more than $25 million. Although the ruling was accepted by both parties, the question of settlement was not resolved. In 1965, the United States levied retaliatory tariffs on selected imports from the European Community. Although the GATT forum did not completely settle the conflict, it was widely felt that it helped limit the possibility of a major trade war.

Despite GATT's success in liberalizing world trade relations, its operation has remained somewhat controversial. Many developing nations have refused to join GATT on the grounds that it is a rich nations' club. Their concern is that when wealthy industrial nations bargain with poor developing nations on a multilateral, nondiscriminatory basis, the latter will remain as producers of primary commodities instead of being able to industrialize. Developing nations sometimes argue that strict controls over imports for nonessential purposes are necessary if foreign currencies are to be available to finance domestic development programs. Another concern is that GATT has been only modestly successful in phasing out nontariff trade measures; nor has it significantly liberalized trade in agricultural commodities. GATT's future is directly tied to its finding solutions for these problems.

Let us consider two of the more recent rounds of multilateral trade negotiations sponsored by GATT.

The Tokyo Round

The Tokyo Round of Multilateral Trade Negotiations came to a conclusion in April 1979, following five years of intensive bargaining among 99 nations. Earlier rounds of trade negotiations were concerned only or primarily with reductions in tariffs. As average tariff rates in industrial nations became progressively lower during the postwar period, the importance of nontariff barriers increased. In response to these changes, negotiators shifted emphasis to the issue of

---

Fast-Track Approach for Negotiating Trade Agreements

If international trade agreements were subject to congressional amendments, achieving such pacts would be arduous, if not hopeless. The provisions that had been negotiated by the president would soon be modified by a deluge of congressional amendments, which would quickly meet the disapproval of the trading partner, or partners, that had accepted the original terms.

To prevent this scenario, the mechanism of **fast-track authority** was devised in 1974. Under this provision, the president must formally notify Congress of his/her intent to enter trade negotiations with another country. This notification starts a clock in which Congress has 60 legislative days to permit or deny "fast-track" authority. If fast-track authority is approved, the president has a limited time period in which to complete the trade negotiations; extensions of this time period are permissible with congressional approval. Once the negotiations are completed, their outcome is subject only to a straight up-or-down vote (without amendment) in both houses of Congress within 90 legislative days of submission. In return, the president agrees to consult actively with Congress and the private sector throughout the negotiation of the trade agreement.

nontariff distortions in international trade. The **Tokyo Round** was directed mainly at reducing or eliminating certain NTBs, although additional tariff cutting was also desired.

Under the Tokyo Round, the major industrial nations achieved significant reductions in tariffs. The average reductions for industrial products amounted to 31 percent for the United States, 27 percent for the European Community, 28 percent for Japan, and 34 percent for Canada. The most important tariff cuts came in nonelectrical machinery, wood products, chemicals, and transportation equipment. For agricultural products, the average tariff cut was 17 percent for the United States, 30 percent for the European Community, 4 percent for Japan, and 20 percent for Canada. Although the tariff reductions were substantial in percentage terms, they were not large in absolute terms because most tariffs were already fairly low.

A second accomplishment of the Tokyo Round was the agreement to remove or lessen the restrictive impact of a number of NTBs. Rules and guidelines were established that prevented otherwise reasonable domestic policies (such as environmental controls and promotion of domestic employment) from becoming hidden restraints on international trade. The rules and guidelines were specified in the form of several codes of conduct, the most important of which are discussed here.

Customs valuation. The customs valuation code is an agreement on how to value imported goods for the purpose of levying ad valorem duties. It is intended to promote a uniform standard whereby goods are neither undervalued nor overvalued. Exporters are thus able to predict accurately the valuation of their products and the import duties attached to them. The customs valuation code was seen as a way of preventing product values from being substantially inflated by arbitrary valuation methods, resulting in higher duty payments.

Product standards. In the post–World War II period, the number of product standards has

grown as governments have become increasingly involved in the protection of public health, the environment, and consumer welfare. Besides meeting these objectives, however, product standards have been structured to interfere with international trade. Product-certification systems have been manipulated to limit imports by denying certification to imported goods. Product-testing requirements have also been used to increase expenses for importers. The agreement on technical trade barriers outlaws discriminatory manipulations of product standards, product testing, and product-certification systems. The code is intended to ensure access to markets for both domestic and foreign suppliers.

Subsidies and countervailing duties. Recognizing that government subsidies can undermine competitive economic forces, the subsidies code attempts to reduce their impact on international trade flows. The use of export subsidies on manufactured goods and minerals is flatly prohibited, whereas greater discipline is encouraged in the use of export subsidies for agricultural, fishery, and forest products. Although the code acknowledges that domestic subsidies can be useful in promoting objectives of national policy (such as employment, research and development, or farm-income security), they are not to be used in ways that would injure the industries of other nations. Also specified are procedures whereby countervailing duties can be used to defend home producers from injurious, subsidized import competition in their domestic market.

Licensing. Governments issue import licenses to gather statistical information about imports and to administer certain import restrictions such as quotas. Internationally traded products have often been subject to needless bureaucratic delays as a result of import-licensing systems. Red tape involved in obtaining licenses can be expensive for importers. The import license code requires that the procedures importers must follow in obtaining a license be simplified and harmonized to the greatest extent possible. Governments must publish rules governing procedures for applying for import licenses and must permit any business, person, or institution to apply for a license. The code encourages governments to administer import licenses in a fair and neutral manner to prevent any distortions of international trade.

Government procurement.   In most nations, the government and its agencies are the largest purchasers of goods. Official discrimination in favor of domestic suppliers has resulted in trade barriers in products subject to government purchasing. The government procurement code prevents a government from discriminating against the products of foreign suppliers. The agreement's coverage extends to purchases of goods by central governments on contracts valued at approximately $200,000 or more. The code does not apply to purchases by state and local governments, national security items, construction contracts, or purchases from small and minority-owned businesses. By limiting favoritism toward domestic suppliers, the agreement is intended to promote competition in the government procurement market.

To eliminate discrimination against foreign products at all stages of the procurement process, the agreement includes detailed requirements as to how government purchasing is to be conducted. Governments must openly publish invitations to bid on all contracts, supply all documentation necessary to bid, apply the same qualification and selection criteria to both domestic and foreign businesses, and provide full information and explanation at every stage of the procurement process. Governments are permitted to purchase using one of two procedures: open tendering or selective tendering. Under *open tendering*, any interested business may bid. Under *selective tendering*, suppliers on a list of qualified bidders are invited to bid. In this case, all qualified bidders from signatories must be included on bidders' lists upon request, and selections from the bidders' lists must provide full opportunity for foreign bidders to compete.

The Uruguay Round

Although the Tokyo Round liberalized trade barriers among participating nations, many unresolved trading issues remained. By the mid-1980s, it was widely felt that the GATT trading system had become largely irrelevant to international businesspeople. Observers noted that many of GATT's rules were violated, that the system was often circumvented, and that large and growing sectors of international trade were not covered by GATT provisions. These concerns led to the initiation of the GATT trade negotiations of 1986–1993, known as the **Uruguay Round** after the South American country in which the negotiations began.

The Uruguay Round was the most ambitious of the GATT rounds of international trade negotiations. It went beyond traditional concerns such as tariffs and provided greater recognition to the links between trade and other economic policies. It covered areas that in the past had been largely neglected (such as agriculture) or relegated to special regimes (such as textiles and clothing) and explored new areas such as services. Moreover, discussions of issues pertaining to the operation of the GATT, including the dispute-settlement process, were a main focus of the negotiations. The overriding goal of the Uruguay Round was to create a liberal, durable, and nondiscriminatory multilateral trading system.

The Uruguay Round was scheduled to be completed by 1990, but disagreements, especially relating to protectionist policies in agriculture, led to a collapse of the talks. Additional negotiations led to the completion of the Uruguay Round in 1993, subject to ratification by the governments of participating nations. The most significant issues discussed in the Uruguay Round are summarized next.

Nontariff trade barriers. During the 1980s, NTBs proliferated. For example, nations such as Japan and the United States negotiated bilaterally for quantitative restrictions that protected domestic producers threatened by imports. These restrictions covered products ranging from steel and automobiles to semiconductors and kitchen utensils. Uruguay Round participants recognized that a reduction in NTBs by all participants was critical to the success of an international trading system.

Intellectual property protection. The United States, Japan, and Europe have wanted to combat the pirating of everything from movies to medicines to computer software. These nations have sought ways to retaliate against nations, mainly developing ones, that tolerate patent, copyright, and trademark infringement.

Services. It was maintained that GATT rules needed to be extended to services in many nations that have levied trade barriers. Six service sectors were identified: telecommunications, construction, transportation, tourism, financial services, and professional services.

Developing nations. The Uruguay Round attempted to formulate a system of codes that extended market-opening obligations to all participants and that increased participation by developing nations. A major reason for the limited participation of developing nations in prior negotiations had been the difficulty of reaching acceptable agreements with industrial nations. Developing nations maintained that industrial nations were not sensitive to their needs and vulnerabilities.

Agriculture. Agricultural policy reform became a priority for many nations in the Uruguay Round because domestic agriculture policies (such as subsidies) had become increasingly expensive and were an impediment to trade-policy liberalization. The central issue of reform was the European Community's agricultural support system that provides high price supports to bolster the income of European farmers and export subsidies that encourage foreign sale of European produce. The United States, backed by nations such as Argentina and Australia, insisted that the European Community slash its agricultural price supports and import barriers by 75 percent and cut export subsidies by 90 percent. Contending that such hefty cuts would force many of its farmers off the land, the European Community proposed a 30-percent reduction in its agricultural price supports and import barriers, with no change in its export subsidies. These vastly different positions led to an impasse and a breakdown of the Uruguay Round, with each side blaming the other for the failure. In 1992, the two parties reached a compromise on the agricultural support issue, which led to the completion of the Uruguay Round.

TRADE REMEDY LAWS

Is international competition unfair to U.S. exporters and import-competing firms? Does it impose excessive hardships on them? These are the concerns of the **trade remedy laws**. Their purpose is to redress hardships for U.S. firms resulting from the actions and policies of foreign firms and governments. The laws attempt to produce a "fair" trading environment for all parties engaging in international business. Table 7.3 summarizes the provisions of the U.S. trade remedy laws, which are discussed in the following sections.

The Escape Clause

The **escape clause** is intended to provide relief to U.S. firms and workers desiring protection from *fairly traded* imports. It allows the

TABLE 7.3 / *Trade Remedy Law Provisions*

Statute	Focus	Criteria for Action	Response
Fair trade (escape clause)	Increasing imports	Increasing imports are substantial cause of injury	Duties, quotas, tariff-rate quotas, orderly marketing arrangements, adjustment assistance
Subsidized imports (countervailing duty)	Manufacturing, production, or export subsidies	Material injury or threat of material injury	Duties
Dumped imports (antidumping duty)	Imports sold below cost of production or below foreign market price	Material injury or threat of material injury	Duties
Unfair trade (Section 301)	Foreign practices violating a trade agreement or injurious to U.S. trade	Unjustifiable, unreasonable, or discriminatory practices, burdensome to U.S. commerce	All appropriate and feasible action

SOURCE: Adapted from C. Coughlin, "U.S. Trade Remedy Laws: Do They Facilitate or Hinder Free Trade?" *Review,* Federal Reserve Bank of St. Louis, July/August 1991, p. 5.

president to terminate or make modifications in trade concessions granted foreign nations and levy restrictions on imports of any product that causes or threatens serious injury to the domestic industry manufacturing a like or directly competitive product. Relief provided by the escape clause is temporary: trade restrictions can be enacted for a five-year period and are to be phased down over this period in the transition to open markets.

An escape-clause action is usually initiated by a petition from an American industry to the U.S. International Trade Commission (ITC), which investigates and recommends to the president. All of the following conditions must be met for the ITC to recommend that import relief be extended:

1. Imports are *increasing,* either actually or relative to domestic production.
2. A domestic industry producing an article like or directly competitive with the

imported article is being *seriously injured* or threatened with such injury.
3. The increased imports are a *substantial cause* of serious injury or threat to the domestic industry producing a like or directly competitive article.

An affirmative decision by the ITC is reported to the president, who determines what remedy, if any, is in the national interest. Table 7.4 provides examples of relief granted to U.S. businesses under the escape clause.

An example of escape-clause relief occurred in 1983 when President Reagan increased tariffs and set import quotas on a variety of foreign-made steel products. The ruling was made following a recommendation by the ITC that U.S. producers of stainless steel products were being seriously injured by foreign competition. Under the program, tariffs of 8 to 10 percent were placed on stainless sheet, strip, and plate imports. After a period of four years,

T A B L E 7. 4 / Escape-Clause Relief: Selected Examples

Product	Type of Relief
Procelain-on-steel cooking ware	Additional duties imposed for four years of 20¢, 20¢, 15¢, and 10¢ per pound in the first, second, third, and fourth years, respectively
Prepared or preserved mushrooms	Additional duties imposed for three years of 20%, 15%, and 10% ad valorem in the first, second, and third years, respectively
Clothespins	Temporary global quota
Bolts, nuts, and large screws	Temporary duty increase
High-carbon ferrochromium	Temporary duty increase
Color TV receivers	Orderly marketing agreements with Taiwan and Korea
Footwear	Orderly marketing agreements with Taiwan and Korea

SOURCE: *Annual Report of the President of the United States on the Trade Agreements Program* (Washington, D.C.: Government Printing Office), various issues.

the tariffs would decrease to 4 percent. The program also set global tonnage quotas for bar, rod, and alloy tool steel. The purpose of the restrictions was to give U.S. steel firms temporary relief from import competition while they modernized and regained profitability.

Countervailing Duties

As consumers, we tend to appreciate the low prices of foreign subsidized steel. But foreign export subsidies are resented by import-competing producers, who must charge higher prices because they do not receive such subsidies. From their point of view, the export subsidies give foreign producers an unfair competitive advantage.

According to the General Agreement on Tariffs and Trade, export subsidies constitute unfair competition. Importing countries can retaliate by levying a **countervailing duty**. The size of the duty is limited to the amount of the foreign export subsidy. Its purpose is to increase the price of the imported good to its fair market value. Table 7.5 provides examples of countervailing duties imposed by the United States.

TABLE 7. 5 / Selected Countervailing Duty Orders

Country	Product	Duty Rate
Argentina	Woolen garments	3.23%
Australia	Butter	3 pence/lb
Belgium	Float glass	2.0%
Brazil	Footwear	1.0%
Canada	Radial tires	1.5%
India	Metal castings	13.3%
Israel	Fresh-cut roses	2.0%
Japan	Industrial fasteners	4.0%
Sweden	Rayon fiber	8.9%

SOURCE: *Annual Report of the President of the United States on the Trade Agreements Program* (Washington, D.C.: Government Printing Office), various issues.

Upon receipt of a petition by a U.S. industry or firm, the U.S. Department of Commerce conducts a preliminary investigation as to whether or not an export subsidy was given to a foreign supplier. If the preliminary investigation finds a reasonable indication of an export subsidy, U.S. importers must immediately pay a special tariff (equal to the estimated subsidy margin) on all imports of the product in question. The Commerce Department then conducts a final investigation to determine whether an export subsidy was in fact granted, as well as the amount of the subsidy. If it determines that there was no export subsidy, the special tariff is rebated to the U.S. importers. Otherwise, the case is investigated by the U.S. International Trade Commission, which determines if the import-competing industry suffered material injury as a result of the subsidy.[1] If both the Commerce Department and the International Trade Commission rule in favor of the subsidy petition, a permanent countervailing duty is imposed that equals the size of the subsidy margin calculated by the Commerce Department in its final investigation. Once the practice of export subsidization by the foreign nation is terminated, the countervailing duty is removed.

It can be argued, however, that preventing foreign subsidized goods from entering the domestic economy is *not* in the best interest of society. Economic theory suggests that if a nation is a net importer of a product subsidized by foreigners, the nation as a whole gains from the foreign subsidy. This is because the gains to domestic consumers of the subsidized good more than offset the losses to domestic producers of the import-competing goods.

Consider the trade situation illustrated in Figure 7.1. Let the price of steel produced by both U.S. and Japanese steelmakers be $400 per ton. Assume that, owing to a successful "Buy American" campaign initiated by the U.S. government, U.S. consumers purchase from U.S. producers all of their steel requirements, 9 million tons. U.S. consumer surplus is given by area *a*, whereas the producer surplus accruing to U.S. steelmakers equals area *b + e*.

Suppose now that the Japanese government, in order to penetrate the U.S. market, provides its steelmakers an export subsidy of $50 per ton of steel produced. This cost advantage permits Japan's supply schedule to shift from S_{J_0} to S_{J_1}. The resulting decrease in Japanese steel prices triggers a rise in U.S. consumption to 12 million tons and a fall in U.S. production to 6 million tons, with imports totaling 6 million tons. The subsidy has hurt U.S. steel firms; their producer surplus has decreased by area *b*. However, U.S. buyers find their consumer surplus rising by area *b + c + d*. The United States as a whole benefits from the foreign subsidy because the benefits to its consumers exceed the losses to its producers by area *c + d*.

Let us consider a countervailing duty case involving the U.S. lumber industry. In 1986, the Coalition for Fair Lumber Imports, a group of U.S. sawmill companies, filed a countervailing duty petition with the U.S. government charging that domestic producers were hurt by subsidized lumber exports from Canada. In its preliminary investigation, the Commerce Department determined that the margin of subsidies granted Canadian sawmills averaged 15-percent ad valorem. Before the Commerce Department made its final subsidy determination, the governments of the United States and Canada arrived at a settlement of the dispute regarding the existence and level of subsidies. Canada agreed to impose a 15-percent export tax on certain softwood lumber products, intended to drive up their market price and lessen their competitiveness in the United States. This tax could be reduced to the extent that the Canadian government decreased the subsidies granted to its sawmills. In exchange for Canada's agreement to collect an export tax, the U.S. lumber industry withdrew its countervailing duty petition, and the investigation was terminated.

In 1991, the Canadian government announced its intention to terminate collection of the lumber export taxes; the government apparently felt that it had eliminated its sawmill subsidies. The U.S. Commerce Department then self-initiated a countervailing duty investigation to determine whether Canadian softwood lumber was still being subsidized. In its final sub-

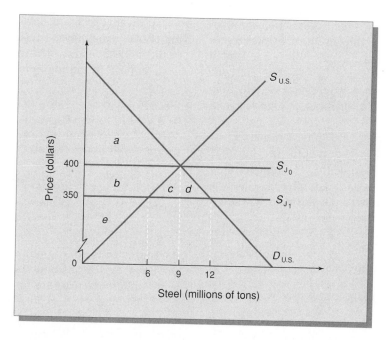

F I G U R E 7. 1 *Impact of Japanese export subsidy on U.S. welfare.*
A subsidy provided by a foreign government to its exporters permits them
to charge a lower price and increase shipments to the United States.
Although the subsidy leads to welfare losses for U.S. manufacturers, U.S.
consumers accrue welfare gains. The United States as a whole benefits from
the foreign subsidy because the welfare gains to its consumers exceed the
welfare losses to its producers.

sidy determination, the Commerce Department
found two countervailable practices: (1) stumpage (tree-cutting) fees and (2) log export restrictions. Together these programs were found to
convey a countrywide subsidy of 6.51 percent
(2.91 percent for stumpage and 3.60 percent
for log export restrictions) to Canadian
sawmills.

The stumpage decision stemmed from
complaints in the United States about the pricing system that Canadian provinces use in selling tree-cutting rights on provincial forest land
to private sawmill operators. In the United
States, companies bid years in advance for the
right to cut trees in government forests. Since
the tree-cutting fees are fixed, the companies
must forecast their prices accurately in order to

ensure profitability. By contrast, Canadian regulations permit provincial governments to
reduce their tree-cutting, or "stumpage," fees
when lumber prices decline so as to keep their
sawmills profitable. U.S. sawmill operators
maintained this amounts to subsidizing the
Canadian lumber mills.

In addition to stumpage, the Commerce
Department determined that Canadian log
export restrictions constituted a subsidy for
Canadian sawmills. Since the early 1900s, the
Canadian government has levied restrictions
(quotas) on the export of logs; such restrictions
encourage the retention of sawmill jobs for
Canadians. The effect of these restrictions is
that the supply of logs in Canada is artificially
high; this leads to relatively low log prices for

Canadian sawmills, a reduction in their production costs, and an improvement in their competitive position against sawmills in the United States. In the absence of these restrictions, the volume of log exports would increase which, in turn, would increase the price of logs to Canadian sawmills.

In 1992, the U.S. International Trade Commission ruled that imports of Canadian softwood lumber injured the U.S. lumber industry in terms of lost sales and profits. The decisions of the Commerce Department and International Trade Commission resulted in a countervailing duty of 6.51 percent, designed to offset the subsidy-induced price advantage for Canadian lumber imports.

Antidumping Duties

The objective of U.S. antidumping policy is to offset two unfair trading practices by foreign nations: (1) export sales in the United States at prices below the average total cost of production; and (2) price discrimination, in which foreign firms sell in the United States at a price less than that charged in the exporter's home market. Both practices can inflict economic hardship on U.S. import-competing producers; by reducing the price of the foreign export in the U.S. market, they encourage U.S. consumers to buy a smaller quantity of the domestically produced good.

Antidumping investigations are initiated upon a written request by the import-competing industry that includes evidence of (1) dumping; (2) material injury, such as lost sales, profits, and jobs; and (3) a casual link between the dumped imports and the alleged injury. Antidumping investigations commonly involve requests that foreign exporters and domestic importers fill out detailed questionnaires. Parties that elect not to complete questionnaires can be put at a disadvantage with respect to case decisions; findings are made on the best information available, which may simply be information supplied by the domestic industry in support of the dumping allegation.

If an investigation determines that dumping is occurring and is causing material injury to the domestic industry, then the U.S. response is to impose an **antidumping duty** (tariff) on dumped imports equal to the margin of dumping. The effect of the duty is to offset the extent to which the dumped goods' prices fall below average total cost, or below the price at which they are sold in the exporter's home market.

Section 301: Unfair Trading Practices

Section 301 of the Trade Act of 1974 gives the United States Trade Representative (USTR), subject to the approval of the president, authority and means to respond to unfair trading practices by foreign nations. Included among these unfair practices are foreign trade restrictions that hinder U.S. exports and foreign subsidies that hinder U.S. exports to third-country markets. The USTR responds when it determines that such practices result in "unreasonable" or "discriminatory" burdens on U.S. exporters. The legislation was primarily a congressional response to dissatisfaction with GATT's ineffectiveness in resolving trade disputes. Table 7.6 provides examples of Section 301 cases.

Section 301 investigations are usually initiated on the basis of petitions by adversely affected U.S. companies and labor unions; they also can be initiated by the president. If the investigation determines that a foreign nation is engaging in unfair trading practices, the USTR is empowered to (1) impose tariffs or other import restrictions on products and services and (2) deny the foreign country the benefits of trade-agreement concessions.

Although the ultimate sanction available to the United States is retaliatory import restrictions, the purpose of Section 301 is to obtain successful resolution of the conflict. In a large majority of cases, Section 301 has been used to convince foreign nations to modify or eliminate what the United States has considered to be unfair trading practices; only in a small minority of cases has the United States retaliated

T A B L E 7. 6 / Section 301 Investigations of Unfair Trading Practices: Selected Examples

U.S. Petitioner	Product	Unfair Trading Practice
Heilman Brewing Co.	Beer	Canadian import restrictions
Amtech Co.	Electronics	Norwegian government procurement code
Great Western Sugar Co.	Sugar	European Community subsidies
National Soybean Producers Association	Soybeans	Brazilian subsidies
Pharmaceutical Manufacturers Association	Drugs	Argentinian patent infringement
Association of American Vintners	Wine	South Korean import restrictions

SOURCE: U.S. International Trade Commission, *Operation of the Trade Agreements Program* (Washington, D.C.: Government Printing Office), various issues.

against foreign producers by means of tariffs or quotas. However, foreign nations have often likened Section 301 to a "crowbar" approach for resolving trade disputes, which invites retaliatory trade restrictions. At least two reasons have been advanced for the limitations of this approach to opening foreign markets to U.S. exports: (1) nationalism unites the people of a foreign nation against U.S. threats of trade restrictions; (2) the foreign nation reorients its economy toward trading partners other than the United States.

In 1989, the United States cited Japan for blocking U.S. sales of supercomputers, satellites, and wood products in that country; these unfair trade practices could have resulted in U.S. imposition of retaliatory protectionism under Section 301. By 1990, Japan granted the United States trade concessions on these and other products and agreed to address other, more subtle Japanese trade barriers. The United States subsequently removed Japan from its list of unfair traders. To Japan, Section 301 amounted to a vigilante trade policy in which the biggest kid on the block took matters into its own hands; Japan argued that the United States should have used traditional GATT mechanisms for resolving trade disputes.

Another Section 301 case involved semiconductors. In 1985, the U.S. Semiconductor Industry Association filed a petition alleging that the Japanese government had created a protective structure that acted as a major barrier to the sale of U.S. semiconductors in Japan. After investigating the matter, the USTR began discussions with Japan that led to an agreement under which Japan agreed to increase access for U.S. firms to the Japanese semiconductor market, and to help prevent dumping of semiconductors in the United States and other countries. In response to the failure of Japan to fulfill its obligations under the agreement, the U.S. government subsequently levied increased duties on imports of Japanese products including televisions, automatic data processing machines, and power hand tools. Later, Japan came into conformity with some of its obligations under the agreement; as a result, the United States terminated the increased duties.

PROTECTION OF INTELLECTUAL PROPERTY RIGHTS

In the 1800s, Charles Dickens criticized U.S. publishers for printing unauthorized versions of

*TABLE 7. 7   /   Intellectual Property
Right Violations*

Foreign Violator of U.S. Intellectual Property Rights	Products
Taiwan	Videos, chemicals
Mexico	Pharmaceuticals, software
South Korea	Publishing, videos
Brazil	Chemicals, pharmaceuticals
China	Publishing, software
Japan	High technology
Nigeria	Recordings
India	Pharmaceuticals
Thailand	Motion pictures

SOURCE: U.S. International Trade Commission, *Operation of the Trade Agreements Program,* various issues.

Intellectual property is an invention, idea, product, or process that has been registered with the government and that awards the inventor (or author) exclusive rights to use the invention for a given time period. Governments use several techniques to protect intellectual property. *Copyrights* are awarded to protect works of original authorship (for example, music compositions, textbooks); most nations issue copyright protection for the remainder of the author's life plus 50 years. *Trademarks* are awarded to manufacturers and provide exclusive rights to a distinguished name or symbol (for example, "Coca-Cola"). *Patents* secure to an inventor for a term, usually 15 years or more, the exclusive right to make, use, or sell the invention.

In spite of efforts to protect IPRs, competing firms sometimes infringe on the rights of others by making a cheaper imitation of the firm's product. In 1986, the courts ruled that Kodak had infringed on Polaroid's patents for instant cameras and awarded Polaroid more than $900 million in damages. Another infringement would occur if a company manufactured an instant camera similar to Polaroid's and labeled and marketed it as a Polaroid camera; this is an example of a counterfeit product.

The lack of effective international procedures for protecting IPRs becomes a problem when the expense of copying an innovation (including the cost of penalties if caught) is less than the cost of purchasing or leasing the technology. Suppose that Warner-Lambert Drug Co. develops a product that cures the common cold, called "Cold-Free," and that the firm plans to export it to Taiwan. If Cold-Free is not protected by a patent in Taiwan, either because Taiwan does not recognize IPRs or Warner-Lambert has not filed for protection, cheaper copies of Cold-Free could legally be developed and marketed. Also, if Warner-Lambert's trademark is not protected, counterfeit cold remedies that are indistinguishable from Cold-Free could be legally sold in Taiwan. These copies result in reduced sales and profits for Warner-Lambert. Moreover, if "Cold-Free" is a trademark that

his works without paying him one penny. But U.S. copyright protection did not apply to foreign (British) authors, so Dickens's popular fiction could be pirated without punishment. In recent years, it is U.S. companies whose profit expectations have been frustrated. Publishers in South Korea run off copies of bootlegged U.S. textbooks without providing royalty payments. U.S. research laboratories find themselves in legal tangles with Japanese electronic manufacturers concerning patent right infringement.

Certain industries and products are well-known targets of pirates, counterfeiters, and other infringers of **intellectual property rights** (IPRs). Counterfeiting has been widespread in industries such as automobile parts, jewelry, sporting goods, and watches. Piracy of audio- and videotapes, computer software, and publishing/printing has been widespread throughout the world. Industries in which product life cycles are shorter than the time necessary to obtain and enforce a patent are also subject to thievery; examples are photographic equipment and telecommunications. Table 7.7 provides examples of IPR violations.

consumers strongly associate with Warner-Lambert, a counterfeit product of noticeably inferior quality could adversely affect Warner-Lambert's reputation and thus detract from the sales of both Cold-Free and other Warner-Lambert products.

Although most nations have regulations protecting IPRs, there have been many problems associated with trade in products affected by IPRs. One problem is differing IPR regulations across nations. For example, the United States uses a first-to-invent rule when determining patent eligibility, whereas most other nations employ a first-to-file rule. Another problem is lack of enforcement of international IPR agreements. These problems stem largely from differing incentives to protect intellectual property, especially between nations that are innovating, technological exporters and those that are noninnovating, technological importers. Developing nations, lacking in research and development and patent innovation, sometimes pirate foreign technology and use it to produce goods at costs lower than could be achieved in the innovating country. Poorer developing nations often find it difficult to pay the higher prices that would prevail if innovated products (such as medical supplies) were provided patent protection. Thus, they have little incentive to provide patent protection to the products they need.

As long as the cost of pirating technology, including the probability and costs of being caught, is less than the profits captured by the firm doing the pirating, technology pirating tends to continue. Pirating, however, reduces the rate of profitability earned by firms in the innovating nations, which in turn deters them from investing in research and development. Over time, this leads to fewer products and welfare losses for the people of both nations.

The United States has faced many obstacles in trying to protect its intellectual property. Dozens of nations lack adequate legal structures to protect the patents of foreign firms. Others have consciously excluded products (such as chemicals) from protection to support their industries. Even in advanced countries, where legal safeguards exist, the fast pace of technological innovation often outruns the protection provided by the legal system.

In 1988, the U.S. government enacted the Omnibus Trade and Competitiveness Act, which addresses unfair trading practices including intellectual property infringement. Prior to the trade law's passage, even if a U.S. company could prove that a foreign competitor had violated a U.S. patent on a manufacturing process, it had to show that economic damage had resulted. Under the 1988 trade law, it is enough to prove that the patent has been violated.

TRADE ADJUSTMENT ASSISTANCE

According to the free-trade argument, in a dynamic economy in which trade proceeds according to the comparative-advantage principle, resources flow from uses with lower productivity to those with higher productivity. The result is a more efficient allocation of the world's resources over time. In the short run, however, painful adjustments may occur as less efficient companies go out of business and workers lose their jobs. These displacement costs can be quite severe to affected parties. Many industrial nations in recent years have enacted programs for giving **trade adjustment assistance** to those who incur short-run hardships because of displaced domestic production. The underlying rationale comes from the notion that if society in general enjoys welfare gains from the increased efficiency stemming from trade liberalization, some sort of compensation should be provided for those who are temporarily injured by import competition. As long as free trade generates significant gains to the nation, the winners can compensate the losers and still enjoy some of the gains from free trade.

Trade adjustment assistance was initially afforded U.S. workers and businesses with the passage of the 1962 Trade Expansion Act.

Whenever the U.S. Tariff Commission found that tariff concessions were resulting in severe import competition, it could recommend adjustment assistance. Injured workers were entitled to job-training programs, cash payments, and relocation allowances. To businesses, the program offered technical aid in moving into new lines of production, market research assistance, and low-interest loans.

The adjustment assistance program, however, did not live up to full expectations during the 1960s because eligibility requirements were very strict, with the result that labor and business became frustrated in not being able to obtain relief. In the 1970s, the eligibility requirements were loosened with the passage of the 1974 Trade Act. Either the secretary of labor or the secretary of commerce could determine whether aid should be extended to workers, businesses, and communities affected by increased imports. With the eligibility criteria liberalized, the number of grants has risen. In 1977, for example, relief was extended to displaced workers of such firms as Zenith, RCA, Youngstown Steel, General Motors, and U.S. Steel.

Enactment of adjustment assistance programs is considered a significant innovation in trade policy. Although it is often recognized that such programs are a political necessity in today's world, not all interested parties are enthusiastic about implementation of these programs. Adjustment assistance is intended to help domestic businesses become more competitive by switching to superior technologies and developing new products. But in practice, such programs can allegedly be manipulated to financially sustain a losing concern rather than help it become competitive. Proponents of adjustment assistance argue that it is preferable to help domestic labor and business become more productive or move into new occupations or product lines than to curb import competition through tariffs and quotas. In this way, the societal welfare gains arising from a competitive market are still attainable.

INDUSTRIAL POLICIES OF THE UNITED STATES

General recognition that the U.S. economy lost momentum during the 1970s and 1980s with respect to productivity, growth, and international competitiveness led to a variety of recommendations for remedial policy. In particular, it was argued that the United States should take a dose of the same medicine that had seemed to work elsewhere. This mixture was labeled **industrial policy**. As discussed in Chapter 4, such a policy involves government channeling of resources into specific, targeted industries that it views as important for future economic growth. Among the methods used to channel resources are tax incentives, loan guarantees, and low-interest loans.

The objectives of industrial policy can be summarized in several categories: (1) fostering industries that offer long-run comparative advantage; (2) supporting troubled industries if the difficulty is temporary, or if the industry represents an essential link to a larger industrial structure; (3) easing transitions for workers in declining industries and finding alternative uses for plant facilities; (4) improving the setting for industry, including communications and infrastructure.

In the United States, calls for an explicit industrial policy have contradicted the dominant free-market ideology that precludes active government direction of the economy. U.S. policymakers have traditionally been cautious about intervening in private-sector industrial matters and performing economic planning functions. This caution has been reinforced by theoretical support for the laissez-faire doctrine and the success of free enterprise in the United States.

Today, almost all nations implement some kinds of industrial policies. Although industrial policies are generally associated with formal, explicit efforts of governments (as in Japan and France) to enhance the development of specific industries (such as steel or electronics), other traditionally free-enterprise nations such as Germany and the United States also have less formal, implicit industrial policies.

Economic growth policies have deep roots in U.S. economic history. In the 19th century, the federal government backed the development of a transcontinental railroad by ceding huge tracts of land to get the job done. The government also sponsored a network of universities, extension services, and research to help U.S. farmers successfully reap the riches of a fertile land. During the 20th century, government financing nurtured industries such as airlines and electronics. In spite of these examples, the United States does not have a full-blown, comprehensive, and thought-through industrial policy; the policy has been de facto rather than de jure.

What has been the U.S. approach to industrial policy? Let us first consider what U.S. industrial policy has *not* included. Generally speaking, the U.S. government has not (1) formulated industry-specific economic policies designed to promote national champions, (2) nationalized basic industries such as steel and aircraft, (3) bailed out financially troubled firms with loan guarantees, (4) encouraged cartelization of industries, or (5) provided strong government support for exports. In short, the United States has developed and used very little explicit industrial policy, at least in the European or Japanese sense of the term. Those U.S. policies designed to affect industry have been piecemeal in nature and have occurred in response to particular problems, such as rising energy prices, declining exports, inflation, and dwindling investment. In general, the United States has maintained that government targeting of specific industries for subsidies is not desirable; commercial applications of technology are best left to the private sector.

What has U.S. industry policy included? The U.S. government has attempted to provide a favorable climate for business, given the social, environmental, and safety constraints imposed by modern society. Rather than formulating a coordinated industrial policy to affect particular industries, the U.S. government has generally emphasized macroeconomic policies (such as fiscal and monetary policies) aimed at such objectives as economic stability, growth, and the broad allocation of the gross domestic product.

In addition, tariff policy has been an element of U.S. industrial policy. Throughout most of the early development of the United States, policymakers implemented and maintained extremely high protective tariffs. In some cases, the United States has been willing to protect industries that have lost their historical comparative advantage (such as textiles and shoes). In a sense, these tariffs could be considered "support the loser" policies. In short, U.S. industrial assistance has generally encouraged a broad range of activity and has seldom been coordinated with other attempts to foster an individual industry.

There is no doubt, however, that the U.S. government uses a number of measures to shape the structure of the economy that would be called "industrial policies" in other nations. The most notable of these measures is agricultural policy. In agriculture, a farmer who initiates a major innovation can be imitated by many other farmers, who capture the benefits without sharing the risks. To rectify this problem, the U.S. government is involved in research in agricultural techniques and the dissemination of this information to farmers through its agricultural extension service, as well as the fostering of large-scale projects such as irrigation facilities. The U.S. government has also provided support for the shipping and shipbuilding industries, primarily on the grounds of national security.

Energy is another sector of the U.S. economy that has received government assistance. Subsidies have been provided for decades to promote development of the nuclear power industry. The extraction of oil from shale and sand has also received government support.

Subsidy critics contend that these industries have become expensive failures that serve as a warning to advocates of government targeting of specific industries for subsidies.

U.S. government defense spending is often cited as an industrial policy. As the world's largest market for military goods, it is no wonder that the United States dominates their production. U.S. spending on military goods supports domestic manufacturers and permits them to achieve large economies of scale. U.S. defense spending has provided spillover benefits to civilian industries, especially commercial aircraft, computers, and electronics. And military research and development provides U.S. companies with expertise that they can apply elsewhere. It has been argued, however, that defense spending has diverted talent and other resources to "noncompetitive" activities to an extent that more than offsets the gains associated with the spillover of defense spending to the civilian economy. Similar conclusions can be drawn regarding the U.S. space program.

In manufacturing, the U.S. government has provided assistance to financially troubled industries. In automobiles, for example, the government provided a $1.5-billion loan guarantee in 1979–1980 to bail out Chrysler Corporation. It also negotiated voluntary export restrictions on Japanese autos in the 1980s to ease the burden of import competition. In return, recipient firms and workers were expected to reduce labor costs and reorganize production. These measures had elements of industrial policy, but lacked an overt attempt on the part of the government to make public assistance conditional on the industry's performance. The steel and textile industries have also been major recipients of trade protection.

In the area of investment, the United States has no clearly formulated policy; in practice, however, many government policies exist. The Reagan tax cuts of the 1980s were aimed at increasing investment, which would result in expanding output and productivity; the tax cuts were not characterized as "industrial policy," however, because they were not targeted at specific civilian industries. The federal government has provided low-interest loans and loan guarantees that favor certain types of activity, such as rural electrification and small business. To encourage investment, state and local governments provide tax concessions, purchase commitments, cheap energy, and infrastructure; an example is the competition by state governments for auto assembly plants of domestic or foreign companies.

Export Promotion

Another element of U.S. industrial policy is export promotion. The U.S. government maintains a variety of export programs to encourage businesses to expand their sales overseas. A primary objective of these programs is to offset or minimize deficiencies in the market system. Because of high costs of obtaining information, for example, many foreign buyers might remain unaware of prospective U.S. sellers were it not for U.S. promotion programs. U.S. exporters might likewise remain ignorant of foreign sales possibilities through lack of knowledge about foreign markets and exporting procedures. The U.S. government furnishes exporters with marketing information and technical assistance, in addition to trade missions that help expose new exporters to foreign customers. The government also promotes exports by sponsoring exhibits of U.S. goods at international trade fairs and establishing overseas trade centers that enable U.S. businesses to exhibit and sell machinery and equipment.

Export Financing

In addition to direct promotion of exports, nations have used trade financing to increase foreign sales. Most industrial nations have developed extensive export-financing programs; in many cases, the availability of such credit or the extent of loan subsidization has determined export flows.

The maintenance of competitive credit terms for U.S. exporters is a function of the U.S.

T A B L E 7. 8 / Examples of Loans and Loan Guarantees Provided by Eximbank of the United States (in Millions of Dollars)

Foreign Borrower/U.S. Exporter	Purpose	Direct Loan	Loan Guarantee
Nippon Airways of Japan/Boeing Co.	Commercial jet	12.6	
Cement Col of India/Fuller International, Inc.	Cement plant	0.7	
National Bank of Mexico/Gulfstream Aerospace Co.	Small jet		10.6
South Korea Develop. Bank/The Badger Co.	Petroleum refining	35.7	
Dogus Construction (Turkey)/Caterpillar Co.	Construction equipment		11.6
Republic of Nigeria/General Electric Co.	Generators		93.5
Govt. of Indonesia/Bell Helicopter, Inc.	Helicopter components	18.3	
Republic of Colombia/Motorola, Inc.	Communications systems		4.3

SOURCE: Export-Import Bank of the United States, *Annual Report,* various issues.

Export-Import Bank and the Commodity Credit Corporation. The **Export-Import Bank** (Eximbank) is an independent agency of the U.S. government designed to finance U.S. exports. Direct loans are generally made to foreign buyers of U.S. high-technology products or capital equipment. Eximbank may even guarantee loans and provide insurance for loans made by private-sector commercial banks. Eximbank normally extends its financial assistance in cases in which the risks, maturity, and amounts involved are beyond the lending scope of the private sector. In offering competitive interest rates in financing exports, Eximbank has sometimes been criticized because part of its funds are borrowed from the U.S. Treasury. Critics question whether U.S. tax revenues should subsidize exports to foreign countries at interest rates lower than could be obtained from private institutions. To this extent, it is true that tax funds distort trade and redistribute income toward exporters. Table 7.8 provides examples of direct loans and loan guarantees made by Eximbank.

From an industrial policy viewpoint, it is interesting to see which U.S. industries have benefited most from Eximbank programs. Major beneficiaries have included aircraft, telecommunications, power-generating equipment, and energy developments. Firms such as Boeing, McDonnell Douglas, and Westinghouse have enjoyed substantial benefits from these programs.

Officially supported lending for U.S. exports is also provided by the **Commodity Credit Corporation** (CCC), a government-owned corporation administered by the U.S. Department of Agriculture. The CCC makes available export credit financing for eligible agricultural commodities. The interest rates charged by the CCC are usually slightly below prevailing rates charged from private financial institutions.

Other U.S. agencies active in overseas sales financing include the Agency for International Development, which makes available loans and grants to developing nations. A significant portion of each loan or grant is used to finance U.S. exports. The U.S. Overseas Private Investment Corporation encourages U.S. direct investments (such as factories) in developing nations through the provision of political-risk insurance and financing services. Many of these investment projects require the export of U.S. capital equipment and other products. For example, a flour mill may require continuing exports of

U.S. wheat. The U.S. Trade and Development Program finances planning services for major development projects. The program supports only those projects that offer a strong likelihood of future U.S. exports. The U.S. Small Business Administration encourages export expansion by providing credit to U.S. businesses for developing export markets and for financing labor and materials for preexport production. The U.S. government also provides tax benefits to U.S. exporters via the Foreign Sales Corporation Act of 1984.

Export Trade Associations

In the early 1900s, various exporters in the United States, led by the copper producers, urged the passage of legislation allowing businesses in a given industry to export through a single sales agency. The justification for such legislation was the existence of many selling and buying cartels in countries such as Germany and the United Kingdom. The U.S. exporters maintained that they should be allowed to combine in selling to match the market power of foreign cartels. Pressured by the efforts of organized exporters, in 1918 Congress passed the Export Trade Act, also called the Webb–Pomerene Act.

As a way of helping U.S. businesses trade in the world market on more equal terms with their organized competitors and buyers, the Export Trade Act of 1918 provides an exemption from U.S. antitrust laws for **export trade associations**—horizontal combinations of U.S. businesses, particularly small ones, engaged solely in export trade. Businesses have been permitted to form marketing associations that operate as individual sales agencies. Small businesses thus gain through combination the advantages large businesses enjoy when they sell abroad. The antitrust exemption has resulted in U.S. businesses' fixing prices and allocating customers in foreign markets. Associations have also attempted to reduce the costs of exporting by spreading overhead, eliminating

duplicate sales organizations, and obtaining lower rates on shipping and insurance. However, the antitrust exemption is limited in that export associations are prohibited from restraining trade within the United States; nor can they restrain exports of any U.S. business competing with the association.

There are some 30 export associations in the United States that market chemicals, dried fruit, motion pictures, wood chips, tire equipment, soybean oil, rice, and other commodities. At the peak of their popularity during the 1930s, U.S. export trade associations numbered 57 and accounted for 19 percent of U.S. exports. Today, the export trade associations have a minimal impact on U.S. sales overseas, accounting for less than 2 percent of U.S. exports. One reason for this modest impact is that small businesses are often reluctant to enter international trade. Also, it is not clear that export associations offer significant advantages over selling abroad through brokers and export merchants. Businesspeople have also questioned the certainty of the antitrust exemption, hesitating to become members of an association that, if challenged on legal grounds, could become involved in an expensive, long-term court case. Finally, the antitrust exemption does not include service industries (such as management consulting and architecture), which have become important contributors to U.S. exports.

Export Trading Companies

Compared to foreign firms, many U.S. firms have devoted only modest effort to export promotion. Apparently, U.S. businesses felt little need for a strong export orientation because the U.S. market offered sufficient opportunities for the sale of U.S.-produced goods and services. Moreover, many small- and medium-size U.S. businesses have not exported because of a lack of knowledge about foreign selling, difficulties of financing foreign sales, and the belief that exporting is too risky.

Pressured by organized business, in 1982 the U.S. government signed into law the Export Trading Company Act, aimed at giving U.S. businesses new tools to penetrate and expand overseas markets. This legislation encourages small- and medium-size companies to enter foreign markets for the first time. It permits producers of goods and services, banks, export marketing companies, and others to combine their resources into joint **export trading companies** (ETCs) to export their own products or to act as an export service for other producers. Banks are permitted to lend money to and invest in ETCs, which are given immunity from U.S. antitrust laws. ETCs are used widely by other industrial nations: two-thirds of Japan's exports are handled by ETCs; several Western European countries, Korea, and Hong Kong also use them.

Exporting through an ETC allows U.S. companies to enjoy various economies of scale associated with exporting. An ETC might pool the shipments of several U.S. companies, taking advantage of lower transportation costs. Exporting a large volume of products also permits lower per-unit costs of establishing overseas offices, insurance, and warehousing. ETCs also are intended to offer a wider range of products and services and to be equipped to better recognize potential overseas opportunities than individual exporters.

A number of ETCs have been established in the United States. The General Electric Trading Company serves GE business as well as external clients. Stressing industrial and technical goods, this trading company exports primarily to the high-growth developing nations. Other U.S. corporations initiating ETCs have been Sears, Rockwell, Control Data, and General Motors.

Knowledged-Based Growth Policy

Industrial-policy critics claim that government officials may not be able to consistently pick winners among products and firms, and thus encourage labor and capital to move into the industries with the highest growth prospects. This is because the development of commercially successful technology requires a knowledge of scientific possibilities, an awareness of market demand for new or improved products, and a good sense of timing. The critics feel that the free market is better than politicians and bureaucrats at picking winners.

Instead of targeting particular manufacturers for subsidization, an alternative is for government to sponsor the development of technologies that can be used by manufacturers to improve their competitiveness. For some years, the most competitive firms in the United States have been its brainiest, the ones producing cellular phones, supercomputers, synthetic drugs, and spreadsheets. These firms rely on ideas—ideas for raw materials, product designs, manufacturing processes, and ultimately, for commercial products. In this environment, knowledge counts more than capital and labor. A **knowledged-based growth policy** recognizes that knowledge is king in the world economy; those nations that excel at creating new knowledge and transforming it into new technologies and products will prosper in the years ahead.

Unlike industrial policies in manufacturing, a knowledge-based growth policy does not require government to pick winning and losing products and firms; it is the market that picks the winners and losers. The function of government is to support the development of technological breakthroughs that encourage economic growth. It is true that investment in plant and equipment raises the growth rate of real income. But throw in technological breakthroughs, such as a jet turbine or a new software program, and opportunities arise.

Proponents of a knowledge-based growth policy contend that the U.S. government should increase its research and development funding for civilian technologies. Science/technology institutes, such as the National Science Foundation and the National Institutes of Health (NIH) are often cited as worthy recipients of increased funding. The NIH, for example, supports research that has enhanced the development of knowledge about biology and disease, which in turn has spawned powerful drugs and an entirely new industry, biotechnology. Yet most of the commercial applications of this tax-payer-funded science were unforseen when basic research was being conducted. As of the early 1990s, the U.S. government was devoting modest amounts of funding to support commercial research and technology development for producers of supercomputers, software, high-speed trains, and electric cars. The government was also pushing national weapons laboratories, such as Los Alamos, to focus more on commercially relevant research.

In addition to funding R&D, a knowledge-based growth policy includes government diffusion of technical knowledge and new manufacturing techniques, especially to the nation's smaller manufacturers, who often lag behind in technological development. Numerous state governments (for example, Georgia, Pennsylvania) support technology extension centers to help smaller companies adopt up-to-date technologies and solve manufacturing problems. However, this support is paltry when compared to the support that Japan provides through its regional technology centers.

Knowledge-based growth policy advocates maintain that government financing of R&D is desirable because so many people across so many industries benefit from ideas that serve as building blocks for new technologies and products. Although investment in developing commercial applications of products in emerging industries may be adequately rewarded, R&D spending is not. Because the benefits are so widespread and the financial returns to R&D are low, such research requires government subsidies. Industry and government should thus be partners in economic growth.

In 1993, President Clinton announced a more activist role for government in support of American industry, as compared with the previous Bush administration. Clinton called for assistance in the form of high-technology research and electronic infrastructure. Government should not attempt to pick winners and losers among products and companies, but should choose basic industries with the potential to support high-wage jobs into the next century and support their technology at the pre-commercial stage. Clinton's goal was to shift the emphasis of federal agencies that worked on defense and energy to technology with commercial uses. Among the key technologies that Clinton wished to pursue were:

- The space station and the superconducting supercollider
- An electronic infrastructure based in information superhighways—wires that can carry such enormous quantities of data as to download the entire Encyclopedia Britannica in less than a second
- An electronic car that takes the automobile beyond the internal combustion engine
- Biotechnology as a long-term growth industry for the United States

INDUSTRIAL POLICIES OF OTHER NATIONS

Although the United States has generally not formulated explicit industrial policies to support specific industries, such policies are used elsewhere. The experiences of Japan and France indicate that government can successfully promote high-technology industries.

Japan

Japan has become a technological leader in the post–World War II era. During the 1950s, Japan's exports consisted primarily of textiles and other low-tech products. By the 1960s-1970s, its exports emphasized capital-intensive products such as autos, steel, and ships. By the 1980s–1990s, Japan had become a major world competitor in high-tech goods such as optical fibers and semiconductors.

Industrial policy advocates assert that government assistance for emerging industries has helped the Japanese economy transform from low-tech to heavy industry to high-tech. They claim that protection from imports, R&D subsidies, and the like fostered the development of Japanese industry. Clearly, the Japanese government provided assistance to shipbuilding and steel during the 1950s, to autos and machine tools during the 1960s, and to high-tech industries beginning in the early 1970s. Japanese industrial policy has had two distinct phases: From the 1950s to early 1970s, the Japanese government assumed strong control over the nation's resources and the direction of the economy's growth. Since the mid-1970s, the government's industrial policy has been more modest and subtle.

Japanese officials in charge of industrial policy maintain that, since the 1970s, Japan's comparative advantage in international trade has shifted from capital-intensive industries to high-tech industries. They argue that the free market does not generate sufficient incentives to invest in emerging, high-tech industries, for at least two reasons: (1) The risks of creating a new technology may be too great for competitive firms to absorb by themselves. (2) The benefits of new technologies to other firms and industries may be very widespread, so that the societal value of investing in emerging industries may be greater than the profits generated by the private firm undertaking the risks.

Japanese officials further contend that capital and labor do not flow smoothly out of declining industries any more than they flow smoothly into emerging industries; firms and workers are reluctant to abandon once profitable investments and careers for uncertain investments and careers in emerging industries. As a result, Japanese officials feel that government should assist declining industries in adapting to structural changes in their economy.

To implement its industrial policies in manufacturing, the Japanese government has created the **Ministry of International Trade and Industry** (MITI). The MITI attempts to facilitate the shifting of resources into high-tech industries by targeting specific industries for support. With the assistance of consultants from leading corporations, trade unions, banks, and universities, the MITI forms a consensus on the best policies to pursue. The next step of industrial policy is to increase domestic R&D, investment, and production. Targeted industries have received support in the form of trade protection, allocations of foreign exchange, R&D subsidies, loans at below-market interest rates, loans that must be repaid only if a firm becomes profitable, favorable tax treatment, and joint government–industry research projects intended to develop promising technologies.

Although government subsidies have enhanced Japanese industrial development, most of the funds for R&D projects and production facilities have come from private firms and commercial banks. The Japanese economy is very capitalistic and competitive, with none of the central planning that historically existed in Eastern Europe. Moreover, only a modest fraction of government subsidies go to emerging industries as compared to the subsidies granted to other sectors of the economy, such as agriculture, transportation, and the environment.

Without government support, it is improbable that Japanese semiconductor, telecommunications-equipment, fiber-optics, and machine-tool industries would be as competitive as they are. Not all Japanese industrial policies have been successful, however, as seen in the cases of computers, aluminum, and petrochemicals. Even industries in which Japan is competitive in world markets, such as shipbuilding and steel, have witnessed prolonged periods of excess capacity.

The extent to which industrial policy has contributed to Japan's economic growth in the post–World War II era is unclear. Japan has benefited from a high domestic savings rate, an educated and motivated labor force, good labor–management relations, a shift of labor from low-productivity sectors (such as agriculture) to high-productivity manufacturing, entrepreneurs willing to assume risks, and the like. These factors have enhanced Japan's transformation from a low-tech nation to a high-tech nation. It is debatable how rapidly this transformation would have occurred in the absence of an industrial policy. Although Japan has the most visible industrial policy of the industrial nations, its importance should not be exaggerated.

France

Another nation that has adopted an explicit industrial policy is France. The French have generally maintained that direct government involvement in the economy is necessary because (1) foreign competition from technological leaders is too powerful for less advanced French firms to overcome, (2) French firms are too risk-averse to take chances on investments in emerging industries, and (3) French capital markets are not sufficiently developed to permit investment funds to be channeled into new industries.

The element of French industrial policy that has been most visible is government support of French firms in technological competition with firms abroad. Believing that high-technology industries are important for future economic growth, French officials have targeted a number of industries for favorable treatment, including civilian aircraft, computers, telecommunications equipment, biotechnology, semiconductors, and nuclear energy. Although economic development policies have differed from industry to industry, the predominant approach has been to create a "national champion" by merging the strongest of the domestic firms. Government officials have contended that domestic firms in high-technology industries would be too small to compete with Japanese and U.S. firms in the absence of mergers.

To enhance the competitiveness of its national champions, the French government has subsidized their R&D projects and even their operating costs directly from its treasury. It has also directed government-owned banks to grant loans to targeted industries at favorable interest rates. To protect domestic producers of high-technology goods, French government agencies, and to a lesser extent government-owned companies, have refrained from purchasing high-technology imports.

In spite of large amounts of support and protection, French industrial policy has achieved only modest success in developing high-technology industries that are world-class competitors. The French government has not formulated the right policies for catching up with the technological leaders in Japan and the United States.

STRATEGIC TRADE POLICY

Beginning in the 1980s, a new argument for industrial policy gained prominence. Known as **strategic trade policy**, this argument asserts that government can assist domestic companies in capturing economic profits from foreign competitors.[2] Such assistance entails government support for certain "strategic" industries (such as high-technology) that are important to future domestic economic growth and that provide widespread benefits (externalities) to society.

Imperfect Competition and Government Subsidies

The essential notion underlying strategic trade policy is *imperfect competition*. Many industries participating in trade, the argument goes, are dominated by a small number of large companies—large enough for each company to significantly influence market price. Such market power gives these companies the potential to attain long-run economic profits. According to the strategic trade policy argument, government policy can alter the terms of competition to favor domestic companies over foreign companies and shift economic profits in imperfectly competitive markets from foreign to domestic companies.

T A B L E 7. 9 / Effects of a European Subsidy Granted to Airbus

Hypothetical Payoff Matrix: Millions of Dollars

Without Subsidy

Airbus

		Produces	Does Not Produce
Boeing	Produces	Airbus − 5 Boeing − 5	Airbus 0 Boeing 100
	Does Not Produce	Airbus 100 Boeing 0	Airbus 0 Boeing 0

With European Subsidy

Airbus

		Produces	Does Not Produce
Boeing	Produces	Airbus 5 Boeing − 5	Airbus 0 Boeing 100
	Does Not Produce	Airbus 110 Boeing 0	Airbus 0 Boeing 0

SOURCE: Adapted from Paul Krugman, "Is Free Trade Passé?" *Economic Perspectives* (Fall 1987), pp. 131–144.

A standard example is the aircraft industry. With high fixed costs of introducing a new aircraft and a significant learning curve in production that leads to decreasing unit production costs, this industry can support only a small number of manufacturers. It is also an industry that is closely associated with national prestige.

Assume that two competing manufacturers, Boeing and Airbus (representing the United States and Europe, respectively), are considering whether to construct a new aircraft. (Airbus is a consortium owned jointly by four European governments.) If *either* firm manufactures the aircraft by itself, it will attain *profits* of $100 million. If *both* firms manufacture the aircraft, they will each suffer a *loss* of $5 million.

Now assume the European government decides to subsidize Airbus production to the amount of $10 million. Even if both companies manufacture the new aircraft, Airbus is now certain of making a $5-million profit. But the point is this: Boeing will *cancel* its new aircraft project. The European subsidy thus ensures not only that Airbus will manufacture the new aircraft but also that Boeing will suffer a loss if it joins in. The result is that Airbus achieves a

profit of $110 million and can easily repay its subsidy to the European government. If we assume that the two manufacturers produce entirely for export, the subsidy of $10 million results in a transfer of $100 million in profits from the United States to Europe! Table 7.9 summarizes these results.

Consider another example. Suppose the electronics industry has just two companies, one in Japan and one in the United States. In this industry, learning-by-doing reduces unit production costs indefinitely with the expansion of output. Suppose the Japanese government considers its electronics industry to be "strategic" and imposes trade barriers that close its domestic market to the U.S. competitor; assume the United States keeps its electronics market open. The Japanese manufacturer can expand its output and thus reduce its unit cost. Over a period of time, this competitive advantage permits it to drive the U.S. manufacturer out of business. The profits that the U.S. company had extracted from U.S. buyers are transferred to the Japanese.

Advocates of strategic trade policy recognize that the classical argument for free trade considered externalities at length. The difference, they maintain, is that the classical theory was based on *perfect competition* and thus could not appreciate the most likely source of the externality, whereas modern theories based on *imperfect competition* can. The externality in question is the ability of companies to capture the fruits of expensive innovation. Classical theory based on perfect competition neglected this factor because large fixed costs are involved in innovation and research and development and such costs ensure that the number of competitors in an industry will be small.

The strategic trade policy concept has been criticized on several grounds. From a political perspective, there is danger that special-interest groups will dictate who will be the recipients of government support. Also, if a worldwide cycle of activist trade policy retaliation and counter-retaliation were to occur, all nations would be worse off. Moreover, governments lack the information to intervene intelligently in the marketplace. In our Boeing–Airbus example, the activist government must know how much profit would be achieved by proceeding with the new aircraft, both with and without foreign competition. Minor miscalculations could result in an intervention that makes the home economy worse off, instead of better off. Finally, the mere existence of imperfect competition does not guarantee that there is a strategic opportunity to be pursued, even by an omnipotent government. There must also be a continuing source of economic profits, with no potential competition to erase them. But *continuing* economic profits are probably less common than governments think.

The case of the European subsidization of aircraft during the 1970s provides an example of the benefits and costs encountered when applying the strategic trade policy concept. During the 1970s, Airbus received a government subsidy of $1.5 billion. The subsidy was intended to help Airbus offset the 20-percent cost disadvantage it faced on the production of its A300 aircraft compared to that of its main competitor, the Boeing 767. Did the subsidy help the European nations involved in the Airbus consortium? The evidence suggests no. Airbus itself lost money on its A300 plane and continued to face cost disadvantages relative to Boeing. There were benefits to European airlines and passengers because the subsidy kept Airbus prices lower; however, the amount of Airbus's losses roughly matched this gain. Because the costs of the subsidy had to be financed by higher taxes, Europe was probably worse off with the subsidy. The United States also lost, because Boeing's profits were smaller and were not fully offset by lower prices accruing to U.S. aircraft users; but the European subsidy did not drive Boeing out of the market. The only obvious gainers were other nations, whose airlines and passengers enjoyed benefits from lower Airbus prices at no cost to themselves.[3]

Welfare Effects

What are the effects on national welfare (of consumers, business firms, and taxpayers) of a strategic trade policy that targets a domestic industry for subsidies so as to help it capture monopoly profits on foreign sales? Note that strategic behavior by firms takes place in international markets in which the number of firms is small enough to permit some degree of market power. In designing a profit-maximizing strategy, a firm must take account of reactions of rival firms and their governments.

Let us consider the hypothetical case of high-definition television (HDTV), a sophisticated blend of video and computer technology that produces images as sharp as 35-millimeter film and sound worthy of compact-disc players.

Most analysts agree that HDTV fits the requirements for strategic trade policy. The HDTV industry is likely to be highly concentrated, with only a few dominant European and Japanese producers (imperfect competition). Also, the industry is expected to provide spillover benefits to a number of sectors of the economy. Its technology will not only enhance

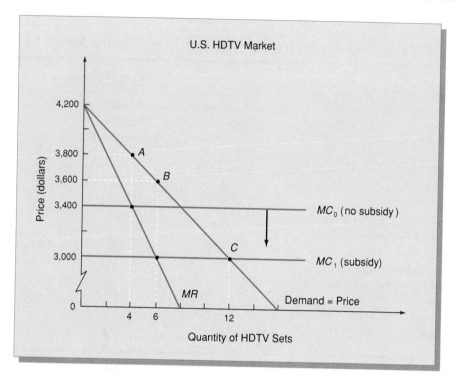

F I G U R E 7. 2 Welfare effects of strategic trade policy. A subsidy granted by the Japanese government to its HDTV exporters improves their competitiveness in the U.S. market; a sufficiently large Japanese subsidy will convince European exporters to retreat from the U.S. market, assuming that no retaliatory subsidies are granted by the European government. Japanese exporters thus enjoy increased export profits; however, Japanese taxpayers pick up the tab for the subsidy. If these export profits exceed the subsidy's cost to the Japanese taxpayer, Japan enjoys net gains. Consumers in the United States enjoy consumer surplus gains resulting from lower-priced HDTV sets due to the subsidy.

television for home use, but also computer memory, chip manufacturing, computer screen designs, and defense radar systems. The production of HDTV will provide a domestic market for other high-technology goods such as semiconductors. Moreover, the bulk of the cost of producing HDTV comes in the early research, development, and design stages. These costs occur irrespective of the number of television sets manufactured; the cost per set decreases substantially as more sets are manufactured, spreading the fixed costs over a larger number of units.

Suppose that Europe and Japan rival for monopoly profits in the U.S. HDTV market. Assume that these nations have government-sponsored R&D programs and antitrust laws that permit consortiums among their producers. Figure 7.2 illustrates several possible outcomes of the rivalry between these nations for monopoly profits. These outcomes depend on which producers first penetrate the U.S. market, how much government assistance is granted to producers, and the reaction of the producers' rivals.

Assume that a consortium of European firms is the first to develop and market HDTV

T A B L E   7. 10   /   *Welfare Effects of Strategic Trade Policy: High-Definition Television*

Situation	Gains (Losses)			
	European/ Japanese Consortium*	European/ Japanese Government	U.S. Consumer	World*
a. European consortium is the first to penetrate the U.S. market, and thus becomes a monopoly seller	$1,600	——	$ 800	$2,400
b. Japanese government grants a subsidy to its consortium, which now monopolizes the U.S. market	3,600	-$2,400	1,800	3,000
c. European and Japanese governments grant offsetting subsidies to their consortiums; both nations compete in the U.S. market	0	-4,800	7,200	2,400

* Minus fixed costs.

sets; this group of firms becomes a monopoly seller in the United States. Suppose these firms realize a constant marginal production cost of $3,400 per set, denoted by schedule MC_0.[4] As a monopoly, the European consortium maximizes profit by selling that output at which marginal revenue equals marginal cost; 4 sets are sold at a price of $3,800 per set. On those 4 sets, the consortium realizes a profit of $400 per set and a total profit of $1,600 (minus the fixed costs of becoming established in the United States). U.S. consumers also realize a consumer surplus of $800 (the area under the demand schedule down to the price of $3,800) from the availability of HDTV. World welfare thus rises by these amounts, as seen in Table 7.10a.

Suppose now that a consortium of Japanese firms develops HDTV and that its marginal costs are identical to those of the Europeans, $3,400 per set. To enhance international competitiveness, suppose the Japanese government grants a permanent subsidy of $400 on

each set manufactured by the Japanese consortium. The consortium's marginal costs now equal $3,400 less the $400 subsidy, or $3,000, as shown by MC_1. With the help of its government, the Japanese consortium is in a position to export to the United States even if the price of HDTV sets falls to low levels. If the subsidy policy convinces European producers that they can no longer compete with the Japanese, they will exit the U.S. market; the Japanese become the monopoly seller of HDTV sets in the United States. The subsidy thus facilitates the Japanese consortium's success in the U.S. market.

The Japanese consortium maximizes profits by selling 6 sets, where marginal revenue equals marginal cost, at a price of $3,600 per set. The consortium realizes a profit of $600 per set and a total profit of $3,600 on the 6 sets (minus fixed costs). Japanese taxpayers lose the $2,400 granted to the Japanese producers as a subsidy ($400 × 6 sets). However, Japan enjoys overall gains equal to the amount by which its export profits (less fixed costs) exceed the tax-payer cost of the subsidy, or $1,200. At the price of $3,600, U.S. consumers enjoy a consumer surplus of $1,800 from the availability of HDTV. The welfare gains to the world thus total $3,000, as seen in Table 7.10b.

This example assumes that if Japan provides a permanent subsidy to its producers, it will drive the European producers out of the U.S. market, thus capturing their sales and profits. Suppose, however, that Europe retaliates and provides a permanent subsidy to its producers. In this case, the welfare of Japan and Europe both tend to decrease, while U.S. welfare increases!

Assume that Japanese and European HDTV consortiums have identical marginal production costs of $3,400 and that each nation provides a $400 subsidy to its consortium; the subsidy-adjusted marginal costs are now $3,000. With government support, neither consortium will back down and exit the U.S. market. Open competition and intense price cutting result in the Japanese and European firms' reducing their prices to $3,000, at which 12 sets are sold and no profits are realized by either exporting nation.[5] The total cost of the subsidy to the Japanese and European governments is $4,800 ($400 × 12 sets). Japan and Europe are clearly worse off than in the case of no subsidies: their taxpayers bear the burdens of the subsidy, while their firms do not realize the profits that come with increased market share. On the other hand, the U.S. consumer realizes a consumer surplus of $7,200 (the area under the demand schedule down to the price of $3,000). To the extent that the gains to the U.S. consumer exceed the losses of Europe and Japan, the subsidy enhances world welfare. These results are summarized in Table 7.10c.

ECONOMIC SANCTIONS

Instead of promoting exports, governments may *restrict* exports for domestic and foreign policy objectives. **Economic sanctions** are government-mandated limitations placed on customary trade or financial relations among nations. They have been used to protect the domestic economy, reduce nuclear proliferation, set compensation for property expropriated by foreign governments, combat international terrorism, preserve national security, and protect human rights.

The nation initiating the economic sanctions, the *imposing nation,* hopes to impair the economic capabilities of the *target nation* to such an extent that the target nation will succumb to its objectives. The imposing nation can levy several types of economic sanctions. *Trade sanctions* involve boycotts on imposing-nation exports. The United States has used its role as a major producer of grain, military hardware, and high-technology goods as a lever to win overseas compliance with its foreign policy objectives. Trade sanctions may also include quotas on imposing-nation imports from the target nation. *Financial sanctions* can entail limitations on official lending or aid. During the late 1970s, the U.S. policy of freezing the financial assets of Iran was seen as a factor in the freeing of the U.S. hostages. Table 7.11 provides examples of economic sanctions levied by the United States for foreign policy objectives.

Welfare Effects

A country wishing to impose trade sanctions can impose either a quota on imports from the target nation or a quota on exports to the target nation. The *import quota* would directly reduce target-nation sales. Although this decrease might initially be absorbed out of profits, it ultimately forces a contraction of production and induces higher unemployment among target-nation workers. For the imposing nation, the quota results in higher consumer prices and lost consumer surplus. To the extent that imports are decreased, the import-competing industry enjoys higher sales, profits, and levels of employment. It is no wonder that the import-

T A B L E   7. 11   /   *Selected Economic Sanctions of the United States*

Year Initiated	Target Country	Objectives
1993	Haiti	Improve human rights
1992	Serbia	Terminate civil war in Bosnia-Herzegovina
1990	Iraq	Terminate Iraq's military takeover of Kuwait
1985	South Africa	Improve human rights
1983	Soviet Union	Retaliate for downing of Korean airliner
1981	Soviet Union	Terminate martial law in Poland; impair Soviet economic and military potential
1981	Nicaragua	Cease support for El Salvador rebels; destabilize Sandinista government
1979	Iran	Release U.S. hostages; settle expropriation claims

competing industry is usually most willing to support the "national interest" by calling for import sanctions.

The static welfare effects of an *export boycott* are illustrated in Figure 7.3, which represents the grain markets of the imposing nation and the target nation. Let the imposing-nation and target-nation demand schedules for grain be denoted by D_I and D_T, respectively. D_{I+T} denotes the sum of the imposing-nation and target-nation demand schedules, and S_I represents the supply schedule of imposing-nation grain farmers. Assume that all of the target nation's grain supply comes from the imposing nation. With free trade, the imposing nation's grain market achieves equilibrium at point *A*. The imposing nation produces 14 million bushels at a price of $4 per bushel. Of this quantity, 6 million bushels are purchased by imposing-nation buyers, and 8 million bushels are exported to the target nation at $4 per bushel. The export receipts of the imposing nation total $32 million.

Suppose the imposing nation imposes a *partial embargo* on grain exports to the target nation, equal to 4 million bushels. The export restriction results in a vertical target-nation supply schedule, $S_{Embargo}$, at the embargo quantity. Excess demand forces target-nation grain prices up to $6 per bushel. Compared with free-trade equilibrium, target-nation grain prices rise by $2 per bushel, while consumption decreases by 4 million bushels. Assuming that the exporters of the imposing nation behave as monopoly sellers, they will capture the price increase as improved terms of trade. The export receipts of the imposing nation total $24 million, down from the free-trade amount of $32 million. The $2 price increase results in a loss of target-nation consumer surplus equal to area *a* + *b*. Of this amount, area *a* is not redistributed to other sectors of the target-nation economy and constitutes a deadweight welfare loss (the consumption effect). Reflecting the higher price applied to a lower export volume, area *b* is captured by the imposing nation as export revenue. The overall welfare loss to the target nation resulting from the trade sanction consists of the sum of these effects.

For the imposing nation, the export restriction results in an improvement in its terms of trade (because the foreign price of its export good rises) and an increase in national welfare. But the export restriction reduces the volume of

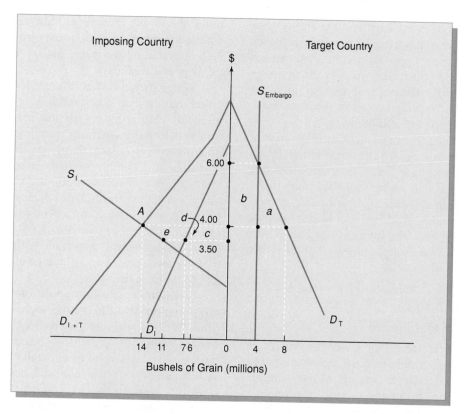

F I G U R E 7. 3 *Export quota levied against the target nation.* By reducing available supplies of a product, an export quota leads to rising prices in the target nation. Product scarcity and increasing prices cause reductions in consumer surplus and economic hardship in the target nation. For the imposing nation, the export quota leads to an improvement in its terms of trade.

trade and results in excess grain supply for the imposing nation totaling 4 million bushels, which causes the price of grain to fall to $3.50 per bushel. The price reduction leads to a rise in consumption from 6 million bushels to 7 million bushels and an increase in consumer surplus equal to area *c + d*. The price reduction also entails a decrease in production from 14 million bushels to 11 million bushels and a loss of producer surplus equal to area *c + d + e*. The imposing-nation economy faces a net welfare loss equal to area *e*, which represents the

amount by which the loss in producer surplus exceeds the increase in consumer surplus. To determine the overall welfare effect of an export sanction, we must compare the benefits of the improved terms of trade against the costs of a lower volume of exports.

Export sanctions also affect the imposing nation's level of employment in its export and export-supporting industries. If imposing-nation producers enjoy strong demand for their goods, a reduction in exports need not generate higher unemployment. But when imposing-nation producers face excess capacity, it is appropriate to assume that export sanctions induce higher unemployment. Imposing-nation employment may decrease still further as a result of fewer exports to other nations that are also imposing sanctions on the target nation, because those nations' exports are also declining.

Over time, export sanctions may cause a reduced growth rate for the target nation. Even if short-run welfare losses from sanctions are not large, they can appear in inefficiencies in the usage of labor and capital, deteriorating domestic expectations, and reductions in savings, investment, and employment. These effects result in a reduced output potential of the target nation.

Factors Influencing the Success of Sanctions

The historical record of economic sanctions provides some insight into the factors that govern their effectiveness. Among the most important determinants of the success of economic sanctions are (1) the number of nations imposing sanctions, (2) the degree to which the target nation has economic and political ties to the imposing nation(s), (3) the extent of political opposition in the target nation, and (4) cultural factors in the target nation. Table 7.12 summarizes the factors that increase or decrease the chances that sanctions will be successful.

Although unilateral sanctions may have some success in achieving intended results, it helps if sanctions are imposed by a large number of nations. Multilateral sanctions generally result in greater economic pressure on the target nation than unilateral measures. Multilateral measures also increase the probability of success by demonstrating that more than one nation disagrees with the target nation's behavior, thus enhancing the political legitimacy of the effort. International ostracism can have a significant psychological impact on the people of a target nation. Failure to get strong multilateral cooperation, however, can result in sanc-

tions' becoming counterproductive; disputes among the imposing nations over sanctions can be interpreted by the target nation as a sign of disarray and weakness.

Sanctions tend to be more effective if the target nation had substantial economic and political relationships with the imposing nation(s) before the sanctions were imposed. The potential costs to the target nation are very high if it does not comply with the wishes of the imposing nation(s). For example, the Western sanctions against South Africa during the 1980s helped convince the government to reform its apartheid system, in part because South Africa conducted four-fifths of its trade with six industrial Western nations and obtained almost all of its capital from the West.

Strength of political opposition within the target nation also affects the success of sanctions. When the target government faces substantial domestic opposition, economic sanctions can lead powerful business interests (such as companies with international ties) to pressure the government to conform with the imposing nation's wishes. Selected, moderate sanctions, with the threat of more severe measures to follow, inflict some economic hardship on domestic residents, while providing an incentive for them to lobby for compliance to forestall more severe sanctions; thus, the political advantage of levying graduated sanctions may outweigh the disadvantage of giving the target nation time to adjust its economy. If harsh, comprehensive sanctions are imposed immediately, domestic business interests have little incentive to pressure the target government to modify its policy; the economic damage has already been done.

When the people of the target nation have strong cultural ties to the imposing nation(s), they are likely to identify with the imposing nation's objectives, thus enhancing the effectiveness of sanctions. For example, South African whites have generally thought of themselves as part of the Western community. When economic sanctions were imposed on South

T A B L E 7. 12 / Factors Affecting the Possibility That Economic Sanctions Will Succeed

Sanctions	Factor Contributes to a Positive Outcome	Factor Reduces Chances for a Positive Outcome
Goals		
Compliance with sanctioning nation's political wishes	X	
Deterrence	X	
Punish target to uphold international norms		X
Support opposition groups in target	X	
Severity		
Harsh, comprehensive sanctions; severe economic damage		X
Moderate sanctions and threat of more severe measures as leverage	X	
Multilateral measures	X	
Attributes of target		
Target: friendly*	X	
Target: adversary*		X
Significant political opposition in the target	X	
Target's cultural norms: strict shame and honor code		X
Target's cultural norms: similar to sanctioning nation's	X	
Publicity		
Publicized threat of more severe sanctions after moderate measures imposed	X	
Publicized harsh, comprehensive sanctions (causing the "rally around the flag effect")		X

* A friendly (adversary) target nation is defined as having substantial (few) economic and political ties to the sanctioning country before sanctions are imposed.

SOURCE: J. McDermott and others, *Economic Sanctions: Effectiveness as Tools of Foreign Policy* (Washington, D.C.: U.S. Government Accounting Office, February 1992), p. 22.

Africa in the 1980s because of its apartheid practices, many liberal whites felt isolated and morally ostracized by the Western world; this encouraged them to lobby the South African government for political reforms.

Other cultural factors, however, may work against the effectiveness of sanctions. In nations where "face-saving" is important (that is, the culture has strong shame and honor codes), it may be hard for the target government to agree to the demands of the imposing nation(s) without appearing weak; this is especially true when the sanctions receive widespread publicity. Iraq's shame and honor have been cited as reasons for Saddam Hussein's reluctance to withdraw his military troops from Kuwait following his 1990 invasion, in spite of the economic damage that would surely be inflicted on Iraq.

South African Sanctions and Disinvestment

The economic sanctions and disinvestment movement against South Africa offer a prime example of the complexities of international restrictions in support of foreign policy goals.

In 1986, the U.S. Congress overrode a presidential veto and enacted the Comprehensive Anti-Apartheid Act, which (1) terminated new loans to the South African government and new investment in South Africa; (2) prohibited the export to South Africa of U.S. crude oil, petroleum products, and computers; (3) abolished the importation from South Africa of Krugerrands (gold coins), agricultural goods, iron, and steel; and (4) prohibited direct flights between airports in the United States and South Africa. Public pressure in the United States also resulted in a **disinvestment movement** in which many U.S. banks and corporations pulled out of South Africa; examples included General Motors, IBM, Xerox, and Eastman Kodak. Other nations that imposed sanctions on South Africa included Canada, Denmark, and France.

The stated objective of the economic sanctions and disinvestment movement was to pressure the South African government to eliminate racially discriminatory laws (apartheid) and grant blacks political franchise. Other supporters, who doubted that sanctions and disinvestment could produce such an ambitious result, contended that sanctions and disinvestment would at least provide a clear signal of U.S. dissatisfaction with South Africa's abuse of human rights.

Critics of the South African restrictions recalled that it took more than 15 years for economic sanctions and a civil war to convince Rhodesia (now Zimbabwe) to accept majority black rule. The Rhodesian example suggested that an embattled nation could adapt to foreign economic pressure. In the first decade after the sanctions were imposed on Rhodesia, the nation's industrial output almost doubled, and mining output increased by two-thirds. No

longer able to import many goods because of foreign sanctions, Rhodesia began producing everything from home appliances to shoes to nails. It was also able to obtain oil from maverick suppliers. Only the world recession of 1974 and a worsening civil war brought Rhodesia's economic growth to a halt, which led to the creation of black-ruled Zimbabwe.

Skeptics of South African sanctions argued that South Africa was better equipped to survive boycotts than was Rhodesia. South Africa was seen as a richer nation with a stronger industrial base and agricultural sector. South Africa also had business relationships with nations that did not honor the sanctions and who would supply needed products. Moreover, just because U.S. corporations left South Africa did not mean they would dismantle their factories and bring them home; many production units would likely be sold to white South Africans, who might eliminate costly "social responsibility" programs intended to help blacks. Finally, sanctions would result in the closing of some factories and mines, resulting in job losses for South African blacks as well as black workers in neighboring countries (such as Botswana) that were economically linked to South Africa. The foreign economic pressure on the South African government would thus exact a devastating price from the very people the sanctions were intended to help.

Indeed, some of these predictions proved to be accurate. South African businesses obtained licenses to produce computers that had formerly been imported. "South African" labels on textiles and citrus products were altered to "Mozambique" so these goods could be sold overseas. Even South African steel was obscured by the routing of exports to Western nations via Singapore. To combat bans on landing rights abroad, state-owned South African Airways repainted its jet liners and leased them to Swaziland.

Despite these maneuvers, the sanctions and disinvestment appeared to have some success in weakening South Africa's economy. In 1990, the South African government razed some of the pillars of apartheid when it ended a 30-year-old ban on the outlawed African National Congress and released black political prisoners, most notably Nelson Mandela. With agreement on a new constitution and multiracial elections, the sanctions were lifted in 1993.

Iraqi Sanctions

In August 1990, the Iraqi military crossed into Kuwait and within six hours occupied the whole country. Iraqi President Saddam Hussein maintained that his forces had been invited into Kuwait by a revolutionary government that had overthrown the Kuwaiti emir and his government.

In response to Iraq's aggression, a United Nations resolution resulted in economic sanctions against Iraq. Sanctions were applied by virtually the entire international community, with only a few hard-line Iraqi allies refusing to cooperate. Under the sanctions program, imposing nations placed embargoes on their exports to Iraq, froze Iraqi bank accounts, terminated purchases of Iraqi oil, and suspended credit granted to Iraq. To enforce the sanctions, the United States supplied naval forces to prevent ships from leaving or arriving in Iraq or occupied Kuwait. The sanctions were intended to convince Iraq that its aggression was costly and that its welfare would be enhanced if it withdrew from Kuwait. If Saddam Hussein could not be convinced to leave Kuwait, it was hoped the sanctions would pressure the Iraqi people or military into removing him from office.

Many observers felt that the Iraqi sanctions presented an ideal case to test whether sanctions could convince a nation to modify its political behavior. Iraq exported just one product, oil, which provided more than 95 percent of its export earnings; a boycott of Iraqi oil would leave Iraq starved for cash. Meanwhile, sanction-imposing nations were able to pur-

chase oil from non-Iraqi suppliers, albeit at high prices, and survive under the boycott. Also, Iraq relied on foreign imports for most of its industrial products and 60 to 70 percent of its food. Furthermore, the imposition of the sanctions was widespread in the international community; this is in contrast to past sanctions (as in the South African case), where just one or a few nations participated in the sanctions and the target nation could easily circumvent their restrictive impact.

The sanctions were intended to have both short- and long-run consequences for Iraq. By blocking Iraqi imports of foodstuffs, the sanctions forced Iraq to adopt food rationing within several weeks of their initiation; although Iraq is self-sufficient in fruits and vegetables, shortages of flour, rice, sugar, and milk developed immediately following the imposition of sanctions. Over the longer term, sanctions were intended to force Iraq to deindustrialize, interfering with its goal of becoming a regional economic power. With Iraqi financing drying up under the oil boycott, dams, petrochemical and fertilizer projects, power-generation facilities, water-treatment plants, and other projects essential to Iraq's transformation from an oil producer to a modern industrial state were expected to be mothballed or evolve into half-constructed "white elephants." Moreover, Iraq could not obtain foreign-manufactured spare parts for its machinery, and skilled foreign workers were fleeing the country. Although widespread industrial disruptions would not affect Iraq's ability to get along for some time, it was hoped that they would score a direct hit on the elite supporters of Saddam Hussein who controlled the economy and held key positions in the Iraqi military.

Despite the widespread application of sanctions against Iraq, it was widely felt that they would not bite hard enough to quickly destabilize the regime of Saddam Hussein. Over the short term, Iraq's ability to survive under the sanctions depended on how it rationed its existing stocks. One advantage Iraq had was a highly disciplined and authoritarian society and a people inured to shortages during its previous eight-year war with Iran; to enforce its rationing program, Saddam Hussein declared that black marketers would be executed. It was also widely believed that prior to the invasion of Kuwait, Saddam Hussein had spent some $3 billion from hidden funds to stockpile goods for domestic consumers. A plentiful agricultural harvest was also predicted for 1991.

Smuggled goods represented another potential source of supplies for Iraq. Although the United Nations pressured the governments of Jordan and Turkey (Iraq's neighbors) to comply with the sanctions, the potential rewards to smugglers increased as scarcities intensified and prices rose in Iraq. Reports indicated that families and tribes that straddled the Turkey–Iraq and Jordan–Iraq borders smuggled foodstuffs into Iraq. In addition, commodities flowed into Iraq from two of its traditional enemies, Iran and Syria. Such "leakages" detracted from the restrictive impact of the sanctions.

The sanctions also resulted in costs for the imposing nations. The closing down of the Iraqi and Kuwaiti oil trade removed some 5 million barrels of oil per day from the world marketplace, which led to price increases. From August to October 1990, oil prices jumped from $18 a barrel to $40 a barrel; oil prices subsequently decreased as other oil producers announced they would increase their production. In addition, nations dependent on Iraq for trade, especially neighboring countries, were hard hit by the embargoes. Turkey, for example, lost an estimated $2.7 billion in 1990 as a result of the embargoes. Jordan's economy, much smaller and more dependent on Iraq's, faced a crisis even more severe.

When the embargoes were initially imposed, most estimates suggested it would take three months to two years before they would force Iraq to alter its policies. Those predicting a quick Iraqi response appeared to assume that the Iraqi people or the military would remove

Saddam Hussein from office rather than suffer from shortages. Those who projected longer estimates, or believed the sanctions would fail, may have assumed that Iraq would shift its resources (plant potatoes, for example, to replace imported rice), that Iraq would control its supplies through rationing, that the embargo would "leak," or that spare-part shortages would not cause deindustrialization until later. The Bush administration concluded that sanctions would not succeed in the long run and instead decided to initiate a military strike against Iraq.

INTERNATIONAL SERVICES

Besides the exchange of tangible goods such as autos and oil, international trade has increasingly involved an exchange of *services*. Exports of services such as banking, transportation, motion pictures, tourism, insurance, advertising, engineering, construction, and computer services are gaining recognition as significant contributors to the foreign sales of many nations.

The rise of the service sector, now the dominant part of the U.S. economy, has become a global phenomenon. Most other industrial nations have experienced a pattern similar to that of the United States: the goods-producing sector (manufacturing, mining, agriculture) continues to grow, but is becoming a smaller portion of an expanding economy. Moreover, this trend has not escaped the developing nations. Singapore, for example, has a leading international airline, and South Korea is a major exporter of engineering and construction services.

The growth in the service sectors of the United States and other countries conforms to recent economic theory, which suggests that the evolution of industrial nations typically occurs through three developmental phases. The initial era is one of capital accumulation by means of savings generated from mineral extraction or agriculture. Next occurs a period of industrialization, during which the production of manufactured goods replaces agriculture and mining as the main source of domestic output. Finally, as the economy expands and income increases, services account for ever-increasing shares of national output, encroaching on the primacy of the manufacturing sector. It is often maintained that the United States has entered this third stage of development. Statistics showing services as a percentage of U.S. output tend to support this theory.

Service exports generate significant revenues for the United States. The importance of services lies not only in their growing volume but also in the role they play in support of exported U.S. goods. Growth of trade in services can promote growth of trade in goods. Service exports in such industries as construction and telecommunications have become a crucial factor in increasing U.S. exports of capital goods by generating additional demand for U.S. products. A strong link thus exists between goods and services trade.

The U.S. services sector has consistently been a *net exporter;* that is, the value of exports exceeds the value of imports. It may come as a surprise that Germany and Japan, two of the biggest foreign competitors of the United States in manufactured goods, have consistently been net importers of services.

How did the United States develop a competitive edge in service exports? As personal income increases, people tend to devote larger shares of income to services. The U.S. demand for services was strong in the post–World War II era, thanks to the high, and rising, incomes of U.S. workers. This demand led to specialization in the domestic services sector and greater efficiencies in production and delivery of services. The postwar era also saw rising income and increasing demand for services in other countries, providing the United States

with strong export markets. However, service-industry techniques and management practices can be learned and copied, just as in manufacturing, and U.S. service businesses have witnessed increasing competition from foreign companies.

U.S. service exports have increased in dollar value over the years but have remained at about 30 percent of the value of total exports. One reason for the apparent lagging performance of the services element within total U.S. exports is that most services are intrinsically nonexportable. Services such as auto repair and hairdressing, for example, have become sizable contributors to the nation's gross domestic product but are not important among U.S. exported services. Furthermore, U.S. exporters of services complain that U.S. government policies are formidable barriers to exports. These policies include taxation of U.S. workers overseas and the Foreign Corrupt Practices Act, which limits corporate payment of fees to obtain contracts abroad.

U.S. service exporters have also complained of foreign trade restrictions. As seen in Table 7.13, foreign barriers to service trade are numerous, ranging from government procurement programs to discriminatory tax policies.

The motion-picture industry offers an illustration of some of the barriers to service imports. The United States is the world's leading producer and exporter of motion pictures. Overseas markets account for about half of the industry's revenues through fees for rentals. In an attempt to protect their domestic motion-picture markets, foreign governments have imposed screen-time quotas requiring theaters and television stations to devote specified amounts of time to showing domestic films. Import quotas also restrict the number of films that can enter a country. Local work requirements reserve to domestic laboratories the manufacture of film prints. Discriminatory admissions taxes require local patrons to pay a premium to see foreign films.

T A B L E 7. 13 / Examples of Foreign Discrimination against U.S. Service Industries

Service, Country	Trade Restriction
Accounting, Brazil	All accountants must possess the requisite professional degree from a Brazilian university
Advertising, Australia	Radio and TV commercials produced outside the country are forbidden.
Air transport, Chile	National carriers are given preferential user (landing and other) rates, whereas foreign carriers are not.
Banking, Nigeria	Local incorporation of existing and new branches is mandatory.
Construction, Japan	A closed bidding system makes it difficult for foreign companies to participate in major construction projects.
Modeling, Germany	All models must be hired only through German agencies.
Motion pictures, Egypt	Imports must be made through state-owned commercial companies; no foreign films may be shown if Egyptian films are available.
Telecommunications, Germany	International leased lines are prohibited from being connected to German public networks unless the connection is made via a computer in Germany that carries out at least some processing.

SOURCE: Office of the U.S. Trade Representative, *Foreign Trade Barriers* (Washington, D.C.: Government Printing Office), various issues.

SUMMARY

1. The trade policies of the United States have reflected the motivations of many groups, including government officials, labor leaders, and business management.
2. U.S. tariff history has been marked by ups and downs. Many of the traditional arguments for tariffs (revenue, jobs, infant industry) have been incorporated into U.S. tariff legislation.
3. The Smoot–Hawley Act of 1930 raised U.S. tariffs to an all-time high. Passage of the Reciprocal Trade Act of 1934 resulted in generalized tariff reductions by the United States, as well as the enactment of most-favored-nation provisions.
4. The purpose of the General Agreement on Tariffs and Trade (GATT) has been to establish a set of rules under which trade negotiations can take place. Despite GATT's efforts in promoting trade liberalization, developing nations have often maintained that lowering tariffs on a multilateral, nondiscriminatory basis favors the advanced nations. The Tokyo Round and Uruguay Round of multilateral trade negotiations went beyond tariff reductions and attempted to liberalize various nontariff trade barriers.
5. Trade remedy laws can help protect domestic firms from stiff foreign competition. These laws include the escape clause, provisions for antidumping and countervailing duties, and Section 301 of the 1974 Trade Act, which addresses unfair trading practices of foreign nations.
6. The escape clause provides temporary protection to U.S. producers who desire relief from foreign imports that are fairly traded.
7. Countervailing duties are intended to offset any unfair competitive advantage that foreign producers might gain over domestic producers because of foreign subsidies.
8. Economic theory suggests that if a nation is a net importer of a product subsidized by foreigners, the nation as a whole gains from the foreign

subsidy. This is because the gains to domestic consumers of the subsidized good more than offset the losses to domestic producers of the import-competing goods.

9. U.S. antidumping duties are intended to neutralize two unfair trading practices: (1) export sales in the United States at prices below average total cost; and (2) international price discrimination, in which foreign firms sell in the United States at a price lower than that charged in the exporter's home market.

10. Section 301 of the 1974 Trade Act allows the U.S. government to levy trade restrictions against nations that are practicing unfair competition, if successful resolution of trade disagreements cannot be achieved.

11. Intellectual property includes copyrights, trademarks, and patents. Foreign counterfeiting of intellectual property has been a significant problem for many industrial nations.

12. Because foreign competition may displace import-competing businesses and workers, the United States and other nations have initiated programs of trade adjustment assistance involving government aid to adversely affected businesses, workers, and communities.

13. The United States has been reluctant to formulate an explicit industrial policy in which government picks winners and losers among products and firms. Instead, the U.S. government has generally taken a less activist approach in providing assistance to domestic producers (such as the Export-Import Bank and export trade associations). By the 1990s, the U.S. government was moving in the direction of supporting domestic producers through high-technology research and electronic infrastructure.

14. According to the strategic trade policy concept, government can assist firms in capturing economic profits from foreign competitors. The strategic trade policy concept applies to firms in imperfectly competitive markets.

15. Economic sanctions consist of trade and financial restraints imposed on foreign nations. They have been used to preserve national security, protect human rights, and combat international terrorism.

16. Trade in services has become increasingly important in the post–World War II era. However, many nations impose restrictions on service trade.

STUDY QUESTIONS

1. To what extent have the traditional arguments that justify protectionist barriers actually been incorporated into U.S. trade legislation?

2. At what stage in U.S. trade history did protectionism reach its high point?

3. What is meant by the most-favored-nation clause, and how does it relate to the tariff policies of the United States?

4. The GATT is intended to establish a basic set of rules for the commercial conduct of trading nations. Explain.

5. What are trade remedy laws? How do they attempt to protect U.S. firms from unfairly (fairly) traded goods?

6. What is intellectual property? Why has intellectual property become a major issue in recent rounds of international trade negotiations?

7. How does the trade adjustment assistance program attempt to help domestic firms and workers who are displaced as a result of import competition?

8. Under the Tokyo Round of trade negotiations, what were the major policies adopted concerning nontariff trade barriers? What about the Uruguay Round?

9. Describe the industrial policies adopted by the U.S. government. How have these policies differed from those adopted by Japan or France?

10. If the United States is a net importer of a product that is being subsidized by Japan, not only do U.S. consumers gain, but they gain more than U.S. producers lose from the Japanese subsidies. Explain why this is true.

11. What is the purpose of strategic trade policy?

12. What is the purpose of economic sanctions? What problems do they pose for the nation initiating the sanctions? When are sanctions most successful in achieving their goals?

13. Assume that the nation of Spain is "small," unable to influence the Brazilian (world) price of steel. Spain's supply and demand schedules are illustrated in Table 7.14. Assume Brazil's price to be $400 per ton. On graph paper, plot the demand and supply schedules of Spain and Brazil on the same figure.

   a. With free trade, how many tons of steel will

TABLE 7. 14 / *Steel Supply and Demand:*
Spain and Brazil

Price	Quantity Supplied	Quantity Demanded
$ 0	0	12
200	2	10
400	4	8
600	6	6
800	8	4
1000	10	2
1200	12	0

be produced, purchased, and imported by Spain? Calculate the dollar value of Spanish producer surplus and consumer surplus.

b. Suppose the Brazilian government grants its steel firms a production subsidy of $200 per ton. Plot Brazil's subsidy-adjusted supply schedule on the figure.

(1) What is the new market price of steel? At this price, how much steel will Spain produce, purchase, and import?

(2) The subsidy helps/hurts Spanish firms because their producer surplus rises/falls by $ ———; Spanish steel users realize a rise/fall in consumer surplus of $———. The Spanish economy as a whole bene-fits/suffers from the subsidy by an amount totaling $———.

Trade Policies for the Developing Nations

It is a commonly accepted practice to array all nations according to real income and then draw a dividing line between the advanced and the developing ones. Included in the category of **advanced nations** are those of North America and Western Europe, plus Australia, New Zealand, and Japan. Most nations of the world are classified as developing, or less developed, nations. The **developing nations** are most of those in Africa, Asia, Latin America, and the Middle East. Table 8.1 provides economic and social indicators for selected advanced nations and developing nations.

Although international trade can provide benefits to domestic producers and consumers, some economists maintain that the current international trading system hinders economic development in the developing nations. They believe that conventional international trade theory based on the principle of comparative advantage is irrelevant for these nations. This chapter examines the reasons some economists provide to explain their misgivings about the international trading system. The chapter also considers policies aimed at improving the economic conditions of the developing nations.

DEVELOPING-NATION TRADE CHARACTERISTICS

If we examine the characteristics of developing-nation trade, we find that developing nations are highly dependent on the advanced nations. A majority of developing-nation exports go to the advanced nations, and most developing-nation imports originate in the advanced

T A B L E   8. 1   /   Basic Economic and Social Indicators of Selected
Advanced Nations and Developing Nations, 1990

	Gross Domestic Product per Capita (dollars)	Life Expectancy (years)	Adult Illiteracy (percent)
High-Income Economies			
Switzerland	32,680	78	Under 5
Finland	26,040	76	"
Japan	25,430	79	"
Sweden	23,660	78	"
Norway	23,120	77	"
Germany	22,320	76	"
Denmark	22,080	75	"
United States	21,790	76	"
Canada	20,470	77	"
Middle-Income Economies			
Argentina	2,370	71	5
Malaysia	2,320	70	22
Algeria	2,060	65	43
Botswana	2,040	67	26
Panama	1,830	73	12
Turkey	1,500	67	19
Thailand	1,420	66	7
Peru	1,160	63	15
Cameroon	960	57	46
Low-Income Economies			
Togo	410	54	57
India	350	59	52
Nigeria	290	52	49
Zaire	220	52	28
Bangladesh	210	52	65
Chad	190	47	70
Nepal	170	52	74
Somalia	120	48	76
Mozambique	80	47	67

SOURCE: The World Bank, *World Development Report 1992*, pp. 218–219.

nations. Trade among the developing nations is relatively minor.

Another characteristic is the composition of developing-nation exports, with its emphasis on **primary products** (agricultural goods, raw materials, and fuels). Of the manufactured goods that are exported by the developing nations, many (such as textiles) are labor-

TABLE 8.2 / *Developing Economies' Merchandise Trade by Destination/Origin and Product, 1990 (Billions of Dollars)*

	Exports			Imports (f.o.b.)	
	World	Developed Countries	Developing Economies	World	Developing Economies
Food	221	171	39	237	57
Raw materials	70	55	11	75	15
Ores and minerals	31	25	5	40	13
Fuels	104	92	11	265	151
Nonferrous metals	52	44	7	58	10
Primary products	477	388	73	676	247
Iron and steel	86	63	18	74	7
Chemicals	254	195	49	211	11
Other semimanufactures	211	171	35	204	29
Machinery and transport equipment	1,033	801	201	900	91
Textiles	67	53	11	68	12
Clothing	48	44	4	96	43
Other consumer goods	232	192	35	249	45
Manufactures	1,931	1,518	354	1,803	238
Total	2,499	1,966	455	2,548	491

SOURCE: General Agreement on Tariffs and Trade, *International Trade 90–91*, Volume 2, p. 5.

intensive and include only modest amounts of technology in their production. Table 8.2 presents the developing economies' merchandise trade position for 1990.

It is significant, however, that in the past three decades the dominance of primary products in developing-nation trade has been diminishing. Developing nations have been able to increase their exports of manufactured goods relative to primary products. Compared with the advanced nations, however, the absolute value of manufactured goods produced by the developing nations is low. Note also that the rise in manufactured-goods exports has not accrued evenly to all developing nations. Instead, a handful of newly industrializing nations, such as South Korea and Hong Kong,

have accounted for much of the increase in manufactured-goods production by developing nations.

TRADE PROBLEMS OF THE DEVELOPING NATIONS

The theory of comparative advantage maintains that all nations can enjoy the benefits of free trade if they specialize in production of those goods in which they have a comparative advantage and exchange some of these goods for goods produced by other nations. Policymakers in the United States and many other advanced nations maintain that the market-oriented structure of the international trading system furnishes a setting in which the benefits of comparative advantage can be realized. They claim that the existing international trading system has provided widespread benefits and that the trading interests of all nations are best served by pragmatic, incremental changes in the existing system. Advanced nations also maintain that, to achieve trading success, they must administer their own domestic and international economic policies.

On the basis of their trading experience with the advanced nations, some developing nations have become dubious of the *distribution* of trade benefits between them and the advanced nations. They have argued that the protectionist trading policies of advanced nations hinder the industrialization of many developing nations. Accordingly, developing nations have sought a new international trading order with improved access to advanced nations' markets.

Among the problems that have plagued developing nations in their role as producers of primary products have been *unstable export markets* and *worsening terms of trade*.

Unstable Export Markets

One characteristic of many developing nations is that their exports are concentrated in a small number of primary products. This is apparent in Table 8.3, which illustrates the dependence of developing-nation export earnings on primary products. A poor harvest or a decrease in market demand that reduces export revenues can significantly disrupt domestic income and employment levels.

Many observers maintain that a key factor underlying the instability of primary-product prices and export receipts is the low price elasticity of the demand and supply schedules for products such as tin, copper, and coffee, as indicated in Table 8.4. Recall that the price elasticity of demand (supply) refers to the percentage change in quantity demanded (supplied) resulting from a 1-percent change in price. To the

TABLE 8. 3 / *Developing Nation Dependence on Primary Products*

Country	Major Export Product	Major Export Product as a Percentage of Total Exports
Saudi Arabia	Oil	87%
Zambia	Copper	85
Burundi	Coffee	79
Liberia	Iron ore	64
Rwanda	Coffee	57
Mauritania	Iron ore	42
Bolivia	Natural gas	36
Bangladesh	Jute goods	26
Guatemala	Coffee	26

SOURCE: *The Europa World Year Book* (London: Europa Publications Limited, 1992).

extent that commodity demand and supply schedules are relatively *inelastic*, suggesting that the percentage change in price exceeds the percentage change in quantity, a small shift in either schedule can induce a large change in price and export receipts.

Figure 8.1 illustrates the export market of Costa Rica, a producer of coffee. Once coffee has been planted, the quantity supplied is fixed for the following marketing period, irrespective of how the price of coffee may fluctuate. Let the supply of coffee be perfectly inelastic (vertical), as shown in the figure. As a result of changing preferences, suppose the world demand for coffee falls from D_0 to D_1. The decrease in demand causes the price of coffee to decline from $6 to $3 per pound; this price decrease is larger than would occur if Costa Rica's supply schedule was upward-sloping (that is, if it exhibited greater price elasticity). Because of the price decline, Costa Rica's export receipts fall from $240 to $120. Conversely, an increase in the

*T A B L E 8. 4 / Long-Run Price Elasticities of Supply
and Demand for Selected Commodities*

Commodity	Supply Elasticity (Developing Countries)	Demand Elasticity (Advanced Countries)
Coffee	0.3	0.2
Cocoa	0.3	0.3
Tea	0.2	0.1
Sugar	0.2	0.1
Wheat	0.6	0.5
Copper	0.1	0.4
Rubber	0.4	0.5
Bauxite	0.4	1.3
Iron ore	0.3	0.7

SOURCE: Jere R. Behrman, "International Commodity Agreements: An Evaluation of the UNCTAD Integrated Commodity Program," in William R. Cline, ed., *Policy Alternatives for a New International Economic Order* (New York: Praeger, 1979), pp. 118–121.

world demand for coffee would lead to higher prices and export receipts for Costa Rica. We conclude that export prices and earnings can be extremely volatile when supply is inelastic and there occurs a change in demand.

Not only do changes in demand induce wide fluctuations in price when supply is inelastic, but changes in supply induce wide fluctuations in price when demand is inelastic. The latter situation is illustrated in the two-period framework of Figure 8.2. The figure is based on the supply and demand conditions of coffee, Costa Rica's export product. Costa Rica's export supply schedule, S_0, is portrayed as perfectly inelastic, while the world demand schedule, D_0, is relatively price-inelastic. In equilibrium, the price of coffee equals $3 per pound, and Costa Rica's export receipts total $120.

In time period 1, suppose the world demand for coffee increases so that the demand schedule shifts from D_0 to D_1. This results in a substantial increase in price, from $3.00 to $5.25 per pound, and an increase in Costa

Rica's export receipts from $120 to $210. In response to the price increase, suppose Costa Rica growers plant additional coffee in the next time period, shifting the supply schedule from S_0 to S_1. Because of the relatively inelastic demand, the ensuing decrease in price will be substantial; the price of coffee falls from $5.25 to $1.50 per pound, and Costa Rica's export receipts fall to $90. Again we see that export prices and receipts can be very volatile when supply and demand conditions are price-inelastic.

Worsening Terms of Trade

How the gains from international trade are distributed among trading partners has been controversial, especially among developing nations whose exports are concentrated in primary products. These nations generally maintain that the benefits of international trade accrue disproportionately to the industrial nations.

Developing nations complain that their commodity terms of trade has deteriorated in

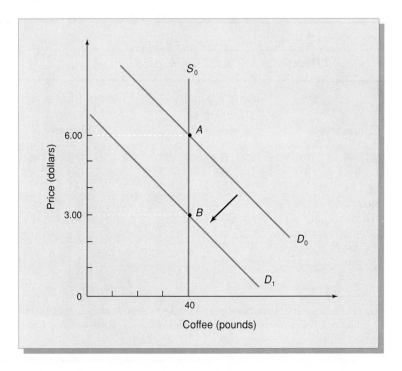

F I G U R E 8. 1   *Export price instability for a developing country: elasticity-of-supply effect.* When the supply of a commodity is highly price-inelastic, decreases (or increases) in demand will generate wide variations in price.

the past century or so, suggesting that the prices of their exports relative to their imports have fallen. Worsening terms of trade has been used to justify the refusal of many developing nations to participate in trade liberalization efforts, such as the Uruguay Round of multilateral trade negotiations. It also has underlain the developing nations' demands for preferential treatment in trade relations with the advanced nations.

Observers maintain that the monopoly power of manufacturers in the industrial nations results in continually rising prices. Gains in productivity accrue to manufacturers in the form of higher earnings rather than price reductions. Observers further contend that the export prices of the primary products of developing nations are determined in competitive markets. These prices fluctuate downward as well as upward. Gains in productivity are shared with foreign consumers in the form of lower prices. The developing nations maintain that market forces cause the prices they pay for imports to rise faster than the prices commanded by their exports, resulting in a deterioration in their commodity terms of trade.

The developing nations' assertion of worsening commodity terms of trade was supported by a United Nations study in 1949.[1] The study concluded that from the period 1876–1880 to 1946–1947, the prices of primary products compared with those of manufactured goods fell by 32 percent. However, because of data inadequacies and the problems of constructing price indexes, the UN study was hardly conclusive. Other studies led to opposite conclusions

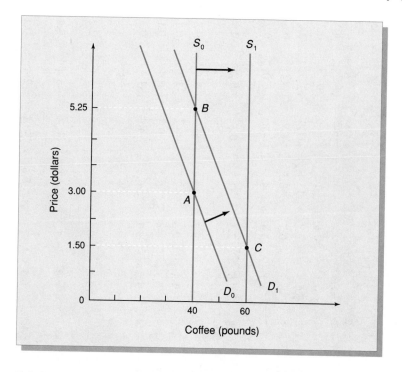

F I G U R E 8. 2 *Export price instability for a developing country: elasticity-of-demand-effect.* When the demand for a commodity is highly price-inelastic, increases (or decreases) in supply will generate wide variations in price.

about terms-of-trade movements. A 1983 study confirmed that the commodity terms of trade of developing nations deteriorated from 1870 to 1938, but much less so than previously maintained; by including data from the post–World War II era up to 1970, the study found no evidence of deterioration.[2] Consistent with these findings, a 1984 study concluded that the terms of trade of developing nations actually improved somewhat from 1952 to 1970.[3] Table 8.5 illustrates changes in the developing nations' commodity terms of trade during the period 1974–1992.

It is difficult to conclude whether the developing nations as a whole have experienced a deterioration or an improvement in their terms of trade. Conclusions about terms-of-trade movements become clouded by the choice of

the base year used in comparisons, by the problem of making allowances for changes in technology and productivity as well as for new products and product qualities, and by the methods used to value exports and imports and to weight the commodities used in the index.

CALL FOR A NEW INTERNATIONAL ECONOMIC ORDER

Dissatisfied with their economic performance and convinced that many of their problems are due to shortcomings of the existing international trading system, developing nations have pressed collective demands on the advanced nations for institutions and policies that improve the climate for economic development in

T A B L E 8. 5 / *Developing Nations' Commodity Terms of Trade (Annual Changes, in Percentages)*

	Average 1974–83	1984	1985	1986	1987	1988	1989	1990	1991	1992	1993
ALL DEVELOPING COUNTRIES	5.9	2.0	-2.2	-14.2	1.7	-3.9	1.7	2.1	-3.6	-1.8	0.2
By region											
Africa	3.1	4.7	-1.0	-20.9	1.4	-5.3	-0.9	3.9	-6.2	-6.3	-1.3
Asia	-1.0	1.3	-0.8	-3.5	1.8	0.1	0.6	-1.5	—	-0.7	-0.2
Middle East and Europe	13.9	0.9	-3.2	-30.7	8.2	-16.3	7.9	13.1	-11.3	-1.3	2.0
Western Hemisphere	1.5	4.1	-5.3	-9.6	-5.5	-0.5	0.5	-0.5	-4.7	-3.4	0.6
Sub-Saharan Africa	-1.5	10.0	-0.3	-9.1	-7.7	1.1	-3.4	-4.5	-4.8	-6.0	-0.2
Four newly industrializing Asian economies	-2.4	-0.1	1.1	4.1	1.8	0.8	2.1	-1.3	0.3	-0.2	-0.4
By predominant export											
Fuel	14.3	0.7	-4.3	-40.3	8.2	-17.0	9.2	14.4	-12.9	-3.3	0.8
Nonfuel exports	-2.0	3.2	-0.9	2.7	-0.7	1.1	-0.5	-2.5	-0.2	-1.2	-0.1
Manufactures	-3.2	1.3	0.1	5.0	-0.3	0.5	0.4	-2.1	0.5	-0.4	-0.1
Primary products	-1.5	6.3	-4.7	-2.4	-7.4	4.7	-4.1	-6.2	-4.4	-4.4	0.3
Agricultural products	-1.0	9.2	-4.6	-2.0	-11.1	-0.2	-6.2	-5.4	-4.6	-4.4	1.6
Minerals	-2.4	0.4	-5.3	-3.6	0.6	14.6	0.1	-7.0	-3.9	-4.4	-2.2
Services and private transfers	-0.3	4.5	1.8	1.4	-6.9	4.9	-1.2	-1.6	-1.3	-3.4	0.2
Diversified export base	-1.5	8.6	-2.7	-2.0	4.7	0.5	-1.4	-0.6	-0.1	-2.6	0.1

SOURCE: International Monetary Fund, *World Economic Outlook: World Economic and Financial Surveys* (Washington, D.C.: Author, October 1992).

the international trading system. The developing nations' call for a **new international economic order** (NIEO) led to the convening of the **United Nations Conference on Trade and Development** (UNCTAD) in 1964. UNCTAD has since become a permanent agency of the United Nations and conducts meetings every four years to address the trading relations of developing and advanced nations.

In its attempt to implement NIEO, UNCTAD has focused primarily on tariff preferences for developing-nation exports to advanced nations, international commodity agreements intended to stabilize prices of primary products, and advanced-nation aid to developing nations. But success in these areas has been modest. The foreign aid of advanced nations has remained at low levels, and efforts to stabilize commodity prices have often failed. Although advanced nations have reduced conventional tariff protection, they have raised other nontariff trade barriers (NTBs) applied to developing-nation products (such as quotas on agricultural products).

The effectiveness of UNCTAD has been limited partly because its resolutions are not binding on nations that do not concur. Although developing nations feel the NIEO proposals are justified, many advanced nations consider them a plea for massive redistribution of world income, which is not feasible. Advanced nations often argue that there is no quick fix for economic development; developing nations must pursue a gradual process of capital formation over many decades as did the advanced nations. This view has led to strained dialogues between advanced nations and developing nations at UNCTAD conferences.

By the late 1980s, attention was increasingly focused on the need for developing nations to initiate policies aimed at enhancing domestic economic growth. These would include *macroeconomic policies* designed to increase domestic savings, reduce inflation, and foster capital formation, as well as *structural policies* to allocate resources more efficiently. It has been widely argued that many developing nations need to make public enterprises more efficient or, otherwise, to proceed with privatization. They should also eliminate price distortions through more market-oriented pricing mechanisms and phase out administrative controls over goods, labor, and financial markets. Moreover, they should initiate tax reforms, including a broadening of the tax base and more effective enforcement, reduce government subsidies, extend the influence of markets over exchange rates, and eliminate exchange and trade restrictions.

STABILIZING COMMODITY PRICES

In an attempt to attain export market stability, developing nations have pressed for **international commodity agreements** (ICAs). ICAs are typically agreements between leading producing and consuming nations about matters such as stabilizing commodity prices, assuring adequate supplies to consumers, and promoting the economic development of producers.

Both producers and consumers desire *stable* commodity markets. For producers, volatile commodity prices may disrupt the flow of export earnings (needed to pay for imports) as well as create an unfavorable climate for investment in additional productive facilities. Consumers have also been motivated to form ICAs. During the 1970s, consuming nations were concerned by the sharp rise in commodity prices and by the questions raised about the longer-term availability of commodities. Consumers were also alarmed by the example of OPEC—that is, by the possibility that commodity supplies might be restricted through collusion among producing nations.

Table 8.6 gives examples of ICAs among producing and consuming nations. To promote stability in commodity markets, ICAs have

TABLE 8.6 / International Commodity Agreements

Agreement	Membership	Principal Stabilization Tools
International Cocoa Organization	26 consuming nations 18 producing nations	Buffer stock; export quota
International Tin Agreement	16 consuming nations 4 producing nations	Buffer stock; export controls
International Coffee Organization	24 consuming nations 43 producing nations	Export quota
International Sugar Organization	8 consuming nations 26 producing nations	Export quota; buffer stock
International Wheat Agreement	41 consuming nations 10 producing nations	Multilateral contract

SOURCE: *Annual Report of the President of the United States on the Trade Agreements Program* (Washington, D.C.: Government Printing Office), various issues.

relied on production and export controls, buffer stocks, and multilateral contracts.

Production and Export Controls

If an ICA accounts for a large share of total world output (or exports) of a commodity, its members may agree on **export controls** to stabilize export revenues. The idea behind such schemes is to offset a decrease in the market demand for the primary commodity by assigning cutbacks in the market supply. If successful, the rise in price due to the supply curtailment would be sufficient to compensate for the reduction in demand, so that total export earnings would remain at the original level.

Figure 8.3, which represents the market situation facing the International Coffee Agreement, illustrates the process by which export receipts can be maintained at target levels. Assume initial market equilibrium at point E. With the equilibrium price at $1 per pound and sales of 60 million pounds, the association's export receipts total $60 million. Let this figure be the target that the association wishes to maintain. Suppose now that, because of a global recession, the market demand for coffee

decreases from D_0 to D_1. The association's export revenues would thus fall below the target level. To prevent this from occurring, the coffee producers could artificially hold back the supply of coffee to S_1. Market equilibrium would be at point F, where 40 million pounds of coffee would be sold at a price of $1.50 per pound. Total export receipts would again be at $60 million, the association's target figure. This stabilization technique is contrary to what we might expect because it is based on efforts to increase prices during eras of worsening demand conditions.

In their efforts to stabilize export receipts, producers' associations have adopted export quotas to regulate market supply. Over the longer run, however, export quotas must be accompanied by **production controls** to be effective. If production is not controlled, expanding surpluses of the member nations will lead to a greater likelihood of price cutting and the eventual downfall of the association.

Buffer Stocks

Another technique for limiting commodity price swings is the **buffer stock**, in which a pro-

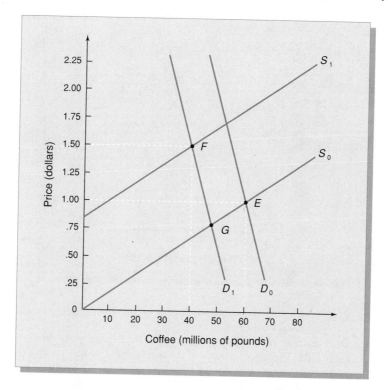

F I G U R E 8. 3 *Production and export controls.* Production controls and export restrictions attempt to offset decreases in market demand and increases in market supply so as to stabilize commodity prices. These restrictions, however, are often associated with cheating on the part of participating nations.

ducers' association (or international agency) is prepared to buy and sell a commodity in large amounts. The buffer stock consists of supplies of a commodity financed and held by the producers' association. The buffer stock manager buys from the market when supplies are abundant and prices are falling below acceptable levels, and sells from the buffer stock when supplies are tight and prices are high.

Perhaps the best-known case in which buffer stocks have been used to moderate commodity price fluctuations is the International Tin Agreement. Assume that the association sets a price range with floor ($3.27 per pound) and ceiling ($4.02 per pound) levels to guide the stabilization operations of the buffer stock

manager. Starting at equilibrium point *A* in Figure 8.4, suppose the buffer stock manager sees the demand for tin rising from D_0 to D_1. To defend the ceiling price of $4.02, the manager must be prepared to sell 20,000 pounds of tin to offset the excess demand for tin at the ceiling price. Conversely, starting at equilibrium point *E* in Figure 8.5, suppose the supply of tin rises from S_0 to S_1. To defend the floor price of $3.27, the buffer stock manager must purchase the 20,000-pound excess supply that exists at that price.

Proponents of buffer stocks contend that the scheme offers the primary producing nations several advantages. A well-run buffer stock can promote economic efficiency because

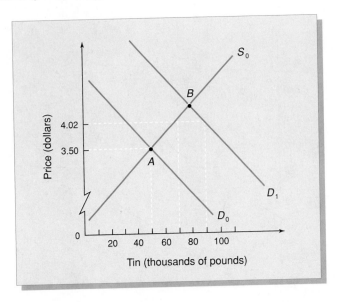

F I G U R E 8. 4   *Buffer stock: price ceiling in the face of rising demand.* During periods of rising tin demand, the buffer stock manager sells tin to prevent the price from rising above the ceiling level. Prolonged defense of the ceiling price, however, may result in depletion of the tin stockpile, undermining the effectiveness of this price-stabilization tool. This could lead to upward revision of the ceiling price.

primary producers can plan investment and expansion if they know that prices will not gyrate. It is also argued that soaring commodity prices invariably ratchet industrial prices upward, whereas commodity price decreases exert no comparable downward pressure. By stabilizing commodity prices, buffer stocks can moderate the price inflation of the industrialized nations. Buffer stocks in this context are viewed as a means of providing primary producers more stability than is provided by the free market.

But setting up and administering a buffer stock program is not without costs and problems. The basic difficulty in stabilizing prices with buffer stocks is agreeing on a target price that reflects long-term market trends. If the target price is set too low, the buffer stocks will become depleted as the stock manager sells the

commodity on the open market in an attempt to hold market prices in line with the target price. If the target price is set too high, the stock manager must purchase large quantities of the commodity in an effort to support market prices. The costs of holding the stocks tend to be high, for they include transportation expenses, insurance, and labor costs. In their choice of price targets, buffer stock officials have often made poor decisions. Rather than conduct massive stabilization operations, buffer stock officials will periodically revise target prices should they fall out of line with long-term price trends.

Multilateral Contracts

Another method of stabilizing commodity prices is the long-term contract that establishes

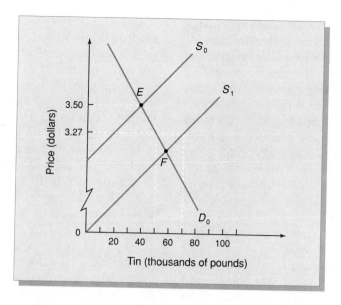

F I G U R E 8. 5 *Buffer stock: price support in the face of abundant supplies.* During periods of abundant tin supplies, the buffer stock manager purchases tin to prevent the price from falling below the floor level. Prolonged defense of the price floor may result in the buffer stock manager's running out of funds to purchase excess supplies of tin at the floor price. This could lead to downward revision of the floor price.

price and/or quantity. Such pacts generally stipulate a *minimum price* at which importers will purchase guaranteed quantities from the producing nations and a *maximum price* at which producing nations will sell guaranteed amounts to the importers. Such purchases and sales are designed to hold prices within a target range. Trading under a **multilateral contract** has often occurred among several exporters and several importing nations, as in the case of the International Sugar Agreement and the International Wheat Agreement.

One possible advantage of the multilateral contract as a price-stabilization device is that, in comparison with buffer stocks or export controls, it results in less distortion of the market mechanism and the allocation of resources. This is because the typical multilateral contract

does not involve output restraints and thus does not check the development of more efficient low-cost producers. But if target prices are not set near the long-term equilibrium price, discrepancies will occur between supply and demand. Excess demand would indicate a ceiling too low, whereas excess supply would suggest a floor too high. Multilateral contracts also tend to furnish only limited market stability, given the relative ease of withdrawal and entry by participating members.

COMMODITY AGREEMENT EXPERIENCE

Commodity-producing nations face the fact that imbalances between demand and supply on the commodity markets tend to trigger large fluctuations in prices. This is true for agricultural commodities as well as for metals and other raw materials. The desire to achieve orderly marketing during the 1920s and 1930s led to the establishment of producers' associations for tin, sugar, rubber, tea, and wheat. But it was not until after World War II that an international mechanism was formally initiated by the United Nations whereby commodity agreements, among both producers and consumers, could be implemented under the auspices of a world body.

Efforts to enact commodity agreements gained momentum following the stunning success of the Organization of Petroleum Exporting Countries (OPEC), which was able to raise prices fourfold in 1973–1974. The goals of the various commodity agreements have generally involved at least one of the following: (1) guarding against gyrating commodity prices, (2) stabilizing incomes or export revenues rather than prices, or (3) bidding prices significantly above their long-term trend. Part of the problem facing commodity agreements is that these objectives sometimes conflict with one another. The goal of stabilizing income, for example, may conflict with the goal of moderating price fluctuations for the pact nations. If a drought were to destroy part of the sugar crop, sales from a buffer stockpile might cushion price increases, but the result would be falling revenues for sugar exporters.

The International Tin Agreement is generally regarded as the commodity agreement with the best track record. Started in 1956, it used buffer stocks and export controls to limit price swings. The Tin Council periodically determined upper and lower price limits to guide the activities of the buffer stock manager. When the buffer stock operations could not moderate price decreases, they were sometimes supplemented by export controls.

When the International Tin Agreement went into operation in 1956, prices remained within the target limits set by the Tin Council.

Strong demand conditions forced the buffer stock manager to sell tin; by 1961 the stocks were exhausted, and prices pushed above the ceiling. In the face of strong demand, the upper and lower price limits were raised several times during the 1960s to keep pace with current market conditions. During the commodity boom of the 1970s, tin prices shot through the ceiling. However, during the early 1980s, the weakening of demand caused by recession led to a progressively lower price. In 1981, the price fell to the bottom of the target limit, triggering price-support actions by the buffer stock.

In 1982, the International Tin Agreement was extended for a five-year period. Consuming and producing nations agreed to set the target price range of tin equal to $5.67 per pound at the lower limit and $6.81 per pound at the upper limit. Defense of price floors and ceilings would be facilitated by export controls and a buffer stock. The nations participating in the pact accounted for 79 percent of the world tin output and 50 percent of tin consumption. The United States, however, chose not to sign the 1982 agreement, contending that the target price range benefited inefficient producers. Moreover, the U.S. government had a tin stockpile of 200,000 tons, equal to four years of domestic use.

In 1987, the International Tin Agreement collapsed. The pact's support of prices at artificially high levels encouraged increases in tin mining by nonmember nations, such as Brazil, which refused to honor production quotas. Meanwhile, consumers economized on the use of overpriced tin. Tin content was reduced in some products, and plastic and aluminum substitutes were designed (including the aluminum beverage can).

OTHER TRADE STRATEGIES

Besides attempting to stabilize commodity prices and export earnings through international commodity agreements, developing nations have pursued trade strategies of import substitution and export promotion. They also have attempted to win from the advanced nations trade concessions known as the generalized system of preferences.

Import Substitution versus Export Promotion

Developing nations realize that the most prosperous nations—with the exception of the wealthy oil-exporting states—are industrial nations. Distrusting the claims about gains from trade involving exports of primary products and imports of manufactured goods, many developing nations have pursued domestic industrialization. Industrialization is seen as yielding widespread benefits, including economic growth, employment, and self-reliance.

During the 1950s and 1960s, the trade strategy of **import substitution** became popular among developing nations such as Argentina, Brazil, and Mexico. Import substitution was seen as a way of promoting domestic industrialization, particularly in consumer goods (shoes, clothing, and household articles). Import-substitution policies restrict imports of manufactured goods so that the domestic market is preserved for domestic producers, who can thus take over markets already established in the country. Import substitution appears to have been beneficial, and Argentina and Brazil both found that their ratios of imports to total output decreased.

However, import substitution is no easy road to self-reliance. A developing nation's dependence on foreign manufacturers can increase for some time because reliance on foreign inputs (machinery and spare parts) often increases with the domestic production of finished goods. Also, the costs of import substitution become apparent when developing nations protect industries with no potential comparative advantage. In Chile, Peru, and Colombia, where local-content laws require that a high percentage of an auto's value be produced domestically, the cost of autos has run two to three times higher than the cost of similar autos produced abroad.[4]

Pessimistic about the merits of import-substitution strategies and disenchanted about exporting primary products, developing nations have pursued **export promotion** (export-led growth) as an industrialization strategy. Export promotion replaces commodity exports with nontraditional exports such as processed primary products, semimanufactures, and manufactures. Export promotion often results from multinational corporations' subcontracting the production of parts and components to developing nations to take advantage of favorable labor costs. Hong Kong, South Korea, and Singapore are examples of developing nations that have pursued export-led industrialization. Their major exports consist of footwear, textiles, clothing, and consumer goods; these exports are directed primarily to a few markets, including the United States, Japan, Germany, and the United Kingdom.

Compared with import-substitution policies, export promotion is *market-oriented*, placing greater emphasis on pricing incentives and on the comparative-advantage principle as a guide to resource allocation. Developing nations attempt to identify industries in which they have a potential comparative advantage. Although subsidies and other devices may be used to encourage development of these industries, it is expected that the industries will eventually produce and sell their goods at prices competitive with those of foreign producers.

South Korea is an example of a developing nation that has used export-promotion policies. During the 1960s, South Korea initiated measures encouraging exports of manufactures. Tariffs and quotas were eliminated on inputs imported for use in exported goods. Tax laws were modified to encourage foreign investment and to favor production that earned a profit on exports. The South Korean won was devalued.

Furthermore, the labor market was unregulated, with no labor unions and no minimum-wage laws. From 1963 to 1975, manufacturing employment in South Korea grew 10.7 percent per year. Exports as a percentage of South Korean gross national product rose from 3 percent in 1960 to 36 percent in 1977. Export growth accounted for 10 percent of South Korea's overall growth during 1955–1963; the figure was 22 percent in 1963–1970 and 56 percent in 1970–1973.[5]

Not everyone agrees with the implications of the South Korean example. Some maintain that import-substitution policies are necessary to lay the groundwork for export expansion. Others argue that although some developing nations have been able to penetrate the world market for manufactured goods, not all developing nations have the capability of doing so. Moreover, widespread penetration would trigger complaints of market disruption by importing nations and possibly protectionism by advanced nations.

Generalized System of Preferences

Gaining access to world markets is a problem that has plagued many developing nations. These nations have often found it difficult to become cost-efficient enough to compete in a wide range of products in world markets. Also, industrialized nations have typically levied low tariffs on raw materials and high tariffs on manufactured goods, discouraging industrial growth in developing nations.

To help developing nations strengthen their international competitiveness and expand their industrial base, many developed nations since the early 1970s have extended nonreciprocal tariff preferences to exports of developing nations. Under this **generalized system of preferences** (GSP), major industrial nations have temporarily reduced tariffs on designated imports from developing nations below the levels applied to developed-nation exports. The GSP does not constitute a uniform system, however, because it consists of many individual schemes that differ in the types of products covered and the extent of tariff reduction.

Since its origin in 1976, the U.S. GSP program has extended duty-free treatment to about 3,000 items. Beneficiaries of the U.S. program include some 140 developing nations and their dependent territories. Like the GSP programs of other developed nations, the U.S. program excludes certain import-sensitive products from preferential tariff treatment. These products include electronics items, glass, certain steel and iron products, watches, and some articles of footwear. Limits also exist on the amount of a particular product each beneficiary can export to the United States. Table 8.7 provides examples of U.S. imports under the GSP program.

NEWLY INDUSTRIALIZING COUNTRIES

The four **newly industrializing countries** (NICs) of East Asia—South Korea, Hong Kong, Taiwan, and Singapore—have been used as a model for emulation by other developing nations. Although the economies of the East Asian NICs are smaller than those of Japan and the advanced industrial nations of the West, these nations have excelled in growth rates of income and consumption per capita, in low unemployment and inflation rates, and in many social-welfare indicators such as literacy and life expectancy. These NICs have performed so well in the past 25 years that they are sometimes collectively referred to as the "Gang of Four" or the "Four Dragons."

Lacking abundant natural resources, the NICs have combined low-wage work forces, probusiness governments, and a Confucian ethic stressing education and hard work to establish strong manufacturing bases. In recent years, living standards have shot up, unemployment has remained low, and a middle class has emerged that seeks the finest in clothing, hous-

Import Substitution Laws Backfire on Brazil

Although import-substitution laws have often been used by developing nations in their industrialization efforts, they sometimes backfire. Let us consider the example of Brazil.

In 1991, Enrico Misasi was the president of the Brazilian unit of Italian computer maker Olivetti Inc., but he did not have an Olivetti computer. The computer behind his desk was instead manufactured by two Brazilian firms; it cost three times more than an Olivetti, and its quality was inferior. Rather than manufacturing computers in Brazil, Olivetti Inc. was permitted to manufacture only typewriters and calculators.

This anomaly was the result of import-substitution policies practiced by Brazil until 1991. From the 1970s until 1991, importing a foreign personal computer—or a microchip, a fax, or dozens of other electronics goods—was prohibited. Not only were electronic imports prohibited, but foreign firms willing to invest in Brazilian manufacturing plants were banned. Joint ventures were deterred by a law that kept foreign partners from owning more than 30 percent of a local business. These restrictions were intended to foster a home-grown electronics industry. Instead, even the law's proponents came to admit that the Brazilian electronics industry was uncompetitive and technologically outdated.

The costs of the import ban were clearly apparent by the early 1990s. Almost no Brazilian automobiles were equipped with electronic fuel injection or antiskid brake systems, both widespread throughout the world. Products such as Apple Computer's Macintosh computer were not permitted to be sold in Brazil. Brazil chose to allow Texas Instruments Inc. to shut down its Brazilian semiconductor plant, resulting in a loss of 250 jobs, rather than permit Texas Instruments to invest $133 million to modernize its product line. By adhering to its import-substitution policy, Brazil wound up a largely computer-unfriendly nation: by 1991, only 12 percent of small- and medium-size Brazilian companies were at least partially computerized, and only 0.5 percent of Brazil's classrooms were equipped with computers. Many Brazilian companies postponed modernization because computers available overseas were not manufactured in Brazil and could not be imported. Some Brazilian companies resorted to smuggling in computers and other electrical equipment; those companies that adhered to the rules wound up with outdated and overpriced equipment.

Realizing that the import-substitution policy had backfired on its computer industry, in 1991 the Brazilian government scrapped a cornerstone of its nationalistic approach by lifting the electronics import ban—though continuing to protect domestic industry with high import duties. The government also permitted foreign joint-venture partners to raise their ownership shares from 30 percent to 49 percent and to transfer technology into the Brazilian economy.

---

ing, and entertainment. The share of the NICs in the world market still is not large compared with Japan's in most products, but their growth rate has been strong. By the 1980s, Japan was losing to the NICs in some industries, notably steel and textiles. Another challenge to Japan's export supremacy is in autos; South Korea has now eliminated Japan's status as the only major Asian auto exporter.

The East Asian NICs' rapid economic growth rates over the past two decades have been associated with rapid expansion of exports. Increased exports contribute to economic growth for two reasons: (1) Exports generate a

T A B L E 8. 7 / *U.S. Imports for Consumption under the GSP from the Top Ten Beneficiaries, 1991*

Beneficiary	Total Imports (millions of dollars)	GSP Duty-Free Imports (millions of dollars)	Share of Total Imports (percentage)
Mexico	30,440	$3,838	12.6
Malaysia	6,073	1,922	31.7
Thailand	6,068	1,471	24.2
Brazil	6,733	1,303	19.4
Philippines	3,430	821	23.9
India	3,199	524	16.4
Israel	3,488	483	13.8
Argentina	1,250	363	29.1
Indonesia	3,465	351	10.1
Yugoslavia	665	251	37.7

SOURCE: U.S. International Trade Commission, *Operation of the Trade Agreements Program, 1991* (Washington, D.C.: Government Printing Office, August 1992).

source of demand for home-produced inputs and, through higher incomes, for domestic consumer goods. (2) Exports generate a source of foreign exchange, which helps finance imports of inputs and capital goods used in domestic production. Rapid economic growth has also been associated with high rates of domestic savings, which encourage expanded domestic investment. With comparative advantages tending to be in relatively labor-intensive products, export growth, coupled with an emphasis on education, has spurred higher employment and rising wages for NIC workers.

Although the East Asian NICs differ sharply in their attitudes toward government regulation of the economy, in varying degrees they have all adopted policies to promote exports. Export-promotion incentives have included unrestricted and tariff-free access to imported intermediate inputs used in export production, access to bank loans at favorable

interest rates for working capital needed for export activity, and periodic currency devaluations intended to keep exports competitive in international markets. Stable government policies and the elimination of bureaucratic obstacles to exports have enabled exporters to make plans for the future with confidence. Moreover, exporters have benefited from the creation of modern infrastructures including improvements in railways, roads, and ports.

The organization of trade unions has been discouraged in the East Asian NICs—whether by deliberate suppression (South Korea and Taiwan), by government paternalism (Singapore), or by a laissez-faire policy (Hong Kong). The outcome has been the prevention of minimum-wage legislation, as well as the maintenance of relatively free and competitive labor markets.

The stunning regional success of the East Asian NICs has created sensitive problems, however. The industrialize-at-all-costs emphasis has left the NICs with major pollution problems. Whopping trade surpluses have triggered a growing wave of protectionist sentiment overseas (especially in the United States, which sees the NICs depending heavily on the U.S. market for future export growth). Labor tensions have also become more common among NIC workers. For example, after two decades of economic growth based on relatively cheap but disciplined labor, South Korea has recently faced worker demands for higher wages and bonuses, better working conditions, and free, democratic unions.

THE OPEC OIL CARTEL

The **Organization of Petroleum Exporting Countries (OPEC)** is a group of nations that sells petroleum on the world market. The OPEC nations have attempted to support prices higher than would exist under more competitive conditions to maximize member-nation profits. After operating in obscurity throughout the 1960s, OPEC was able to capture control of petroleum pricing in 1973–1974, when the price of oil rose from approximately $3 to $12 per barrel. Oil prices were increased another 10 percent in 1975 and almost 15 percent from 1976 to early 1979. Triggered by the Iranian revolution in 1979, oil prices doubled from early 1979 to early 1980. By 1981, the price of oil averaged almost $36 per barrel. Largely because of world recession and falling demand, oil prices fell to $11 per barrel in 1986, only to rebound modestly thereafter.

Prior to OPEC, oil-producing nations behaved as *individual competitive sellers*. Each nation by itself was so unimportant relative to the overall market that changes in its export levels did not significantly affect international prices over a sustained period of time. By agreeing to restrict competition among themselves to exploit their joint market power, the oil-exporting nations found that they could exercise considerable control over world oil prices (as seen in the price hikes of the 1970s).

Maximizing Cartel Profits

The purpose of a **cartel** is to support prices higher than they would be under more competitive conditions, thus increasing profits of its members. Let us consider some of the difficulties encountered by a cartel in its quest for increased profits.

Assume that there are ten suppliers of oil, of equal size, in the world oil market and that oil is a standardized product. As a result of previous price wars, each supplier charges a price equal to minimum average cost. Each supplier is afraid to raise its price because it fears that the others will not do so and all of its sales will be lost.

Rather than engage in cutthroat price competition, suppose these suppliers decide to collude and form a cartel. How will a cartel go about maximizing the collective profits of its members? The answer is, by behaving like a profit-maximizing monopolist: restrict output and drive up price.

Figure 8.6 illustrates the demand and cost conditions of the ten oil suppliers as a group (left part of the figure) and the group's average supplier (right part of figure). Before the cartel is organized, the market price of oil under competition is $20 per barrel; because each supplier is able to achieve a price that just covers its minimum average cost, economic profit equals zero. Each supplier in the market produces 150 barrels per day; total industry output equals 1,500 barrels per day ($150 \times 10 = 1,500$).

Suppose the oil suppliers form a cartel whose objective is to maximize the collective profits of its members. To accomplish this objective, the cartel must first establish the profit-maximizing level of output; this output is where marginal revenue equals marginal cost. The cartel then divides up the cartel output

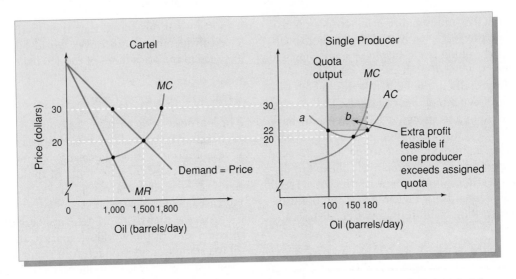

F I G U R E 8. 6   *Maximizing* OPEC *profits.* As a cartel, OPEC can increase the price of oil from $20 to $30 per barrel by assigning production quotas for its members. The quotas decrease output from 1,500 to 1,000 barrels per day and permit producers that were pricing oil at average cost to realize a profit. Each producer has the incentive to increase output beyond its assigned quota, to the point at which the OPEC price equals marginal cost. But if all producers increase output in this manner, there will be a surplus of oil at the cartel price, forcing the price of oil back to $20 per barrel.

among its members by setting up production quotas for each supplier.

In Figure 8.6, the cartel will maximize group profits by restricting output from 1,500 barrels per day to 1,000 barrels per day, as shown in the left part of the figure. This means that each member of the cartel must decrease its output from 150 barrels to 100 barrels per day, as shown in the right part of the figure. This production quota results in a rise in the market price of a barrel of oil from $20 to $30. Each member realizes a profit of $8 per barrel ($30 - $22 = $8) and a total profit of $800 on the 100 barrels of oil produced (area *a*).

The next step is to ensure that no cartel member sells more than its quota. This is a difficult task, because each supplier has the incentive to sell more than its assigned quota at the cartel price. But if all cartel members sell more than their quotas, the cartel price will fall toward the competitive level, and profits will

vanish. Cartels thus attempt to establish penalties for sellers that cheat on their assigned quotas.

Referring to the right part of Figure 8.6, each cartel member realizes economic profits of $800 by selling at the assigned quota of 100 barrels per day. However, an *individual supplier* knows that it can increase its profits if it sells more than this amount at the cartel price. Each individual supplier has the incentive to increase output to the level at which the cartel price, $30, equals the supplier's marginal cost; this occurs at 180 barrels per day. At this output level, the supplier would realize economic profits of $1,440, represented by area *a + b*. By cheating on its agreed-upon production quota, the supplier is able to realize an increase in profits of $640 ($1,440 - $800 = $640), denoted by area *b*. Note that this increase in profits occurs if the price of oil does not decrease as the supplier expands output; this would happen if the supplier's extra output is a negligible portion of the industry supply.

A single supplier may be able to get away with producing more than its quota without significantly decreasing the market price of oil. But if each member of the cartel increases its output to 180 barrels per day to earn more profits, total output will be 1,800 barrels (180 × 10 = 1,800). To maintain the price at $30, however, industry output must be held to only 1,000 barrels per day. The excess output of 800 barrels puts downward pressure on price, which causes economic profits to decline. If economic profits fall back to zero (the competitive level), the cartel will likely break up.

Besides the problem of cheating, there are several other obstacles to forming a cartel.

Number of sellers. Generally speaking, the larger the number of sellers, the more difficult it is to form a cartel. Coordination of price and output policies among three sellers that dominate the market is more easily achieved than when there are ten sellers each having 10 percent of the market.

Cost and demand differences. When cartel members' costs and product demands differ, it is more difficult to agree on price. Such differences result in a different profit-maximizing price for each member, so there is no single price that can be agreed upon by all members.

Potential competition. The increased profits that may occur under a cartel may attract new competitors. Their entry into the market triggers an increase in product supply, which leads to falling prices and profits. A successful cartel thus depends on its ability to block the market entry of new competitors.

Economic downturn. Economic downturn is generally problematic for cartels. As market sales dwindle in a weakening economy, profits fall. Cartel members may conclude that they can escape serious decreases in profits by reducing prices, in expectation of gaining sales at the expense of other cartel members.

OPEC as a Cartel

OPEC has generally disavowed the term *cartel*. But its organization is composed of a secretariat, a conference of ministers, a board of governors, and an economic commission. OPEC has repeatedly attempted to formulate plans for systematic production control among its members as a way of firming up oil prices. However, OPEC's production agreements have not always lived up to expectations because too many member nations have violated the agreements by producing more than their assigned quotas.

The burden of production cutbacks has not been shared equally among OPEC nations. Saudi Arabia has generally served as the dominant evener and adjuster in OPEC. Its eligibility for this role is based on its large oil reserves, small population, and limited need for oil revenues. This is not to say that OPEC has remained free from internal conflicts. For example, Saudi Arabia has sometimes increased output considerably to prevent other OPEC nations from achieving their goal of higher prices. During the world oil glut of 1982, Saudi Arabia was pressured by other OPEC nations to stop flooding the market with more oil than the market could absorb. Both Iran and Libya openly threatened to destroy the Saudis' oil fields or their government if the Saudis didn't lower production.

Most of the world's cartels have been short-lived. This is because the success of a cartel depends on several factors that are often difficult to achieve. Cartel members must control a very large share of the world market for their product and should agree on a common set of price and output policies. The length of time a cartel survives depends in part on the elasticity of supply of noncartel nations. If the noncartel supply is inelastic over the relevant price range, so that a significant increase in the cartel price calls forth only a small increase in output by noncartel nations, the cartel will face only minor competitive pressures. Similarly, the less elastic the demand for the cartel's product, the higher the cartel price can be raised without significantly reducing the amount demanded.

During the 1970s, OPEC was successful in increasing the revenues of its members. One reason is that the long-run price elasticity of oil supply in non-OPEC nations is inelastic. Estimates in the 1970s put the non-OPEC supply elasticity between 0.33 and 0.67, suggesting that a 1-percent increase in the OPEC price will induce only a 0.5-percent increase in non-OPEC output. The demand for gasoline in the United States was also estimated to be inelastic, having a long-run price elasticity coefficient of 0.8. Moreover, OPEC was able to dominate the world oil market, accounting for more than two-fifths of world production, two-thirds of world reserves, and more than four-fifths of world exports.

By the 1980s, however, OPEC increasingly faced the pressures that often lead to the demise of cartels. The OPEC price hikes had induced non-OPEC nations to develop new production techniques and initiate new discoveries. The result was a fall in the OPEC share of the world market from 56 percent in 1973 to 33 percent in 1986. The OPEC price hikes also led to decreases in demand owing to increased usage of smaller autos and insulation and the switch to substitute energy sources, including coal and nuclear power. Furthermore, the recession of 1981–1983 led to weakening demand and a glut of oil on the world market.

OPEC's response to weakening demand conditions, with the exception of a small price cut in 1982, was to make large reductions in output through production quotas assigned to each member nation. Although the cutbacks

TABLE 8. 8 / *OPEC Production Quotas, 1993**

Country	Production Quota (million barrels per day)
Saudi Arabia	8.0
Iran	3.3
Iraq	0.4
United Arab Emirates	2.2
Kuwait	1.6
Qatar	0.4
Nigeria	1.8
Libya	1.3
Algeria	0.7
Gabon	0.3
Venezuela	2.3
Indonesia	1.3
	23.6

* Second quarter.

Source: *Petroleum Intelligence Weekly,* February 8, 1993. See also U.S. Department of Energy, Energy Information Administration.

succeeded for a time in keeping oil prices relatively stable, they were unable to withstand the pressures of falling demand. By 1986, a global oil-price war had broken out, causing oil prices to fall to less than $11 per barrel. Again the OPEC cartel attempted to defy market forces by assigning production quotas that would stabilize oil prices at $18 per barrel, as seen in Table 8.8. In 1990, oil prices skyrocketed to more than $41 per barrel in response to Iraq's military invasion of Kuwait; this was followed by a moderation of oil prices as peace was restored in the Middle East.

SUMMARY

1. Developing nations have attempted to enact trade policies such as commodity agreements and cartels to increase their level of income and standard of living.
2. Among the alleged problems facing the developing nations are (a) unstable export markets and (b) worsening terms of trade.
3. International commodity agreements have been formed by producers and consumers of primary products to stabilize export receipts, production, and prices. The methods used to attain these objectives are buffer stocks, export controls, and multilateral contracts.
4. Past efforts to form viable international commodity agreements have suffered from a number of limitations. Because production is labor-intensive, output cutbacks are often socially unacceptable to workers. Agreeing on a target price that reflects existing economic conditions is also troublesome. Agricultural products often face high storage costs and are perishable. Stockpiles of commodities in importing nations can be used to offset production and export controls. Substitute products exist for many commodities.
5. Besides attempting to stabilize commodity prices, developing nations have promoted internal industrialization through import substitution and export-promotion policies.
6. To help developing nations gain access to world markets, many industrial nations offer assistance known as a generalized system of preferences.
7. The OPEC oil cartel was established in 1960 in reaction to the control that the major international oil companies exercised over the posted price of oil. OPEC has used production quotas to support prices and earnings above what could be achieved in more competitive conditions.
8. Compared with other commodities, oil enjoyed successful cartelization efforts, owing largely to the structural features of both the supply and demand sides of world oil markets. This was especially true during the 1970s and early 1980s. From the mid-1980s to the 1990s, however, the price of oil declined as supply and demand conditions became less favorable for OPEC.

STUDY QUESTIONS

1. What are the major reasons for the skepticism of many developing nations regarding the comparative-advantage principle and free trade?
2. Stabilizing commodity prices has been a major objective of many primary-product nations. What are the major methods used to achieve price stabilization?
3. What are some examples of international commodity agreements? Why have many of them broken down over time?
4. Why are the developing nations concerned with commodity-price stabilization?
5. How do import-substitution and export-promotion policies attempt to aid the industrialization of developing nations?
6. The generalized system of preferences is intended to help developing nations gain access to world markets. Explain.
7. The average person probably never heard of the Organization of Petroleum Exporting Countries until 1973 or 1974, when oil prices skyrocketed. In fact, OPEC was founded in 1960. Why is it that OPEC did not achieve worldwide prominence until the 1970s? What factors contributed to OPEC's downfall in the 1980s?
8. Why is cheating a typical problem for cartels?

CHAPTER 9

Preferential Trading Arrangements

A major ambivalence exists in the economic and political motivations of today's nations. Government leaders are often frustrated in their attempts to achieve national independence and self-reliance while striving to become more interdependent with the rest of the world. The movement toward integrated national economies has become more pronounced in the modern world. Finding a way to harmonize these two goals has been a major concern of government leaders.

In the post–World War II era, advanced nations have significantly lowered their tariff barriers, most notably on manufactured goods. Such trade liberalization has stemmed from two approaches. The first is a *reciprocal reduction of trade barriers* on a nondiscriminatory basis.

Under the General Agreement on Tariffs and Trade (GATT), for example, member nations acknowledge that tariff reductions agreed on by any two nations will be extended to all other members. Such an international approach encourages a gradual relaxation of tariffs throughout the world. A second approach toward trade liberalization occurs when a small group of nations, typically on a regional basis, forms a **preferential trading arrangement** whereby tariff reductions are limited to participating members only. Organizing a preferential trading arrangement that discriminates against outsiders involves what is commonly referred to as **economic integration**. This chapter investigates some of the theoretical and empirical aspects of preferential trading arrangements.

NATURE OF ECONOMIC INTEGRATION

Even though nations have constructed trade barriers, the underlying desire for free trade has been persistent. Since the mid-1950s, the term *economic integration* has become part of the vocabulary of economists. Economic integration is a process of eliminating restrictions on international trade, payments, and factor mobility. Economic integration thus results in the uniting of two or more national economies in a "preferential trade area." Before proceeding, let us distinguish the various forms of regional economic integration.

A **free trade area** is an association of trading nations whose members agree to remove all tariff and nontariff barriers among themselves. Each member, however, maintains its own set of trade restrictions against outsiders. An example of this stage of integration is the **European Free Trade Association** (EFTA), established in 1960.[1]

Like a free trade association, a **customs union** is an agreement among two or more trading partners to remove all tariff and nontariff trade barriers among themselves. In addition, however, each member nation imposes identical trade restrictions against nonparticipants. The effect of the common external trade policy is to permit free trade within the customs union, whereas all trade restrictions imposed against outsiders are equalized. A well-known example is Benelux (Belgium, the Netherlands, and Luxembourg), formed in 1948.

A **common market** is a group of trading nations that permits (1) the free movement of goods and services among member nations, (2) the initiation of common external trade restrictions against nonmembers, and (3) the free movement of factors of production across national borders within the economic bloc. The common market thus represents a more complete stage of integration than a free trade area or a customs union. The **European Community** (EC), sometimes called the Common Market, largely fits this definition.

Beyond these stages, economic integration could evolve to the stage of **economic union**, in which national, social, taxation, and fiscal policies are harmonized and administered by a supranational institution. Belgium and Luxembourg formed an economic union during the 1920s. The task of forming an economic union is much more ambitious than the other forms of integration. This is because a free trade area, customs union, or common market results primarily from the abolition of existing trade barriers, but an economic union requires an agreement to transfer economic sovereignty to a supranational authority. The ultimate degree of economic union would be the unification of national monetary policies and the acceptance of a common currency administered by a supranational monetary authority. The economic union would thus include the dimension of a **monetary union**.

EFFECTS OF PREFERENTIAL TRADING ARRANGEMENTS

What are the possible welfare implications of preferential trading arrangements? We can delineate the theoretical benefits and costs of such devices from two perspectives. First are the **static effects of economic integration** on productive efficiency and consumer welfare. Second are the **dynamic effects of economic integration**, which relate to member nations' long-run rates of growth. Because a small change in the growth rate can lead to a substantial cumulative effect on national output, the dynamic effects of trade policy changes can yield substantially larger magnitudes than those based on static models. Combined, these static and dynamic effects determine the overall welfare gains or losses associated with the formation of a preferential trading arrangement.

Static Effects

The static welfare effects of lowering tariff barriers among members of a trade area are illustrated in the following example. Assume a world composed of three countries: Luxembourg, Germany, and the United States. Suppose that Luxembourg and Germany decide to form a customs union, and the United States is a nonmember. The decision to form a customs union requires that Luxembourg and Germany abolish all tariff restrictions between themselves while maintaining a common tariff policy against the United States.

Referring to Figure 9.1, assume the supply and demand schedules of Luxembourg to be S_L and D_L. Assume also that Luxembourg is very small relative to Germany and to the United States. This means that Luxembourg cannot influence foreign prices, so that foreign supply schedules of grain are perfectly elastic. Let Germany's supply price be $3.25 per bushel and that of the United States, $3 per bushel. Note that the United States is assumed to be the most efficient supplier. Before the formation of the customs union, Luxembourg finds that under conditions of *free trade,* it purchases all of its import requirements from the United States. Germany does not participate in the market, because its supply price exceeds that of the United States. In free-trade equilibrium, Luxembourg's consumption equals 23 bushels, production equals 1 bushel, and imports equal 22 bushels. Suppose that Luxembourg levies a tariff equal to 50 cents on each bushel imported from the United States (or Germany). Luxembourg then finds its imports falling from 22 bushels to 10 bushels.

As part of a trade liberalization agreement, Luxembourg and Germany form a customs union. Luxembourg's import tariff against Germany is dropped, but it is still maintained on imports from nonmember United States. This means that Germany now becomes the low-price supplier. Luxembourg now purchases all of its imports, totaling 16 bushels, from Germany at $3.25 per bushel, while importing nothing from the United States.

The movement toward freer trade under a customs union affects world welfare in two opposing ways: a welfare-increasing *trade creation effect* and a welfare-reducing *trade diversion effect.* The overall consequence of a customs union on the welfare of its members, as well as on the world as a whole, depends on the relative strength of these two opposing forces.

The favorable trade creation effect consists of a *consumption effect* and a *production effect.* Before the formation of the customs union and under its tariff umbrella, Luxembourg imports from the United States at a price of $3.50 per bushel. Luxembourg's entry into the economic union results in its dropping all tariffs levied against Germany. Facing a lower price of $3.25, Luxembourg increases its consumption of grain by 3 bushels. The welfare gain associated with this increase in consumption equals triangle *b* in the figure.

The formation of the customs union also yields a production effect that results in a more efficient use of world resources. Eliminating the tariff barrier against Germany means that Luxembourg producers must now compete against lower-cost, more efficient German producers. Inefficient domestic producers drop out of the market, resulting in a decline in home output of 3 bushels. The reduction in the cost of obtaining this output equals triangle *a* in the figure. This represents the favorable production effect. The overall trade creation effect is thus given by the sum of triangles *a* and *b*.

Although a customs union may add to world welfare by way of trade creation, its trade diversion effect generally implies a welfare loss. Trade diversion occurs when imports from a low-cost supplier outside the union are replaced by purchases from a higher-cost supplier within the union. This suggests that world production is reorganized less efficiently. In the figure, although the total volume of trade increases under the customs union, part of this

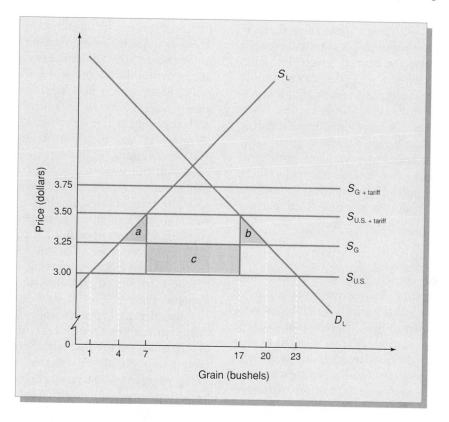

F I G U R E 9. 1 *Static welfare effects of a customs union.* The formation of a customs union leads to a welfare-increasing trade creation effect and a welfare-decreasing trade diversion effect. The overall effect of the customs union on the welfare of its members, as well as on the world as a whole, depends on the relative strength of these two opposing forces.

trade (10 bushels) has been diverted from a low-cost supplier, the United States, to a high-cost source, Germany. The increase in the cost of obtaining these 10 bushels of imported grain equals area *c*. This is the welfare loss to Luxembourg, as well as to the world as a whole. Our static analysis concludes that the formation of a customs union will increase the welfare of its members, as well as the rest of the world, if the positive trade creation effect more than offsets the negative trade diversion effect. Referring to the figure, this occurs if *a* + *b* exceeds *c*. The opposite also holds true.

This analysis illustrates that the success of a customs union depends on the factors contributing to trade creation and diversion. Several factors that bear on the relative size of these effects can be identified. One factor is the kinds of nations that tend to benefit from a customs union. Nations whose preunion economies are quite competitive are likely to benefit from trade creation, because the formation of the union offers greater opportunity for specialization in production. Also, the larger the size and the greater the number of nations in the union, the greater the gains are likely to be, because there is a greater possibility that the world's low-cost producers will be union members. In the extreme case in which the union consists of the entire world, there can exist only trade creation, not trade diversion. In addition, the scope for trade diversion is smaller when the customs union's common external tariff is lower rather than higher. Because a lower tariff allows greater trade to take place with non-member nations, there will be less replacement of cheaper imports from nonmember nations by relatively high-cost imports from partner nations.

Dynamic Effects

Not all welfare consequences of customs unions are static in nature. There may also be dynamic gains that influence member-nation growth rates over the long run. These dynamic gains stem from the creation of larger markets by the movement to freer trade under customs unions. The benefits associated with a customs union's dynamic gains may more than offset any unfavorable static effects. Dynamic gains include *economies of scale, greater competition*, and a *stimulus to investment*.

Perhaps the most noticeable result of a customs union is market enlargement. Being able to penetrate freely the domestic markets of other member nations, producers can take advantage of economies of scale that would not have occurred in smaller markets limited by trade restrictions. Larger markets may permit efficiencies attributable to greater specialization of workers and machinery, the use of the most efficient equipment, and the more complete use of by-products. There is evidence that significant economies of scale have been achieved by the EC in such products as steel, automobiles, footwear, and copper refining.

The European refrigerator industry provides an example of the dynamic effects of integration. Prior to the formation of the EC, each of the major European nations that produced refrigerators (Germany, Italy, and France) supported a small number of manufacturers that

produced primarily for the domestic market. These manufacturers enjoyed production runs of fewer than 100,000 units per year, a level too low to permit the adoption of automated equipment. Short production runs translated into high per-unit cost. The EC's formation resulted in the opening of European markets and paved the way for the adoption of large-scale production methods, including automated press lines and spot welding. By the late 1960s, the typical Italian refrigerator plant manufactured 850,000 refrigerators annually. This volume was more than sufficient to meet the minimum efficient scale of operation, estimated to be 800,000 units per year. The late 1960s also saw German and French manufacturers averaging 570,000 units and 290,000 units per year, respectively.[2]

Broader markets may also promote greater competition among producers within a customs union. It is often felt that trade restrictions promote monopoly power, whereby a small number of companies dominate a domestic market. Such companies may prefer to lead a quiet life, forming agreements not to compete on the basis of price. But with the movement to more open markets under a customs union, the potential for successful collusion is lessened as the number of competitors expands. With freer trade, domestic producers must compete or face the possibility of financial bankruptcy. To survive in expanded and more competitive markets, producers must undertake investments in new equipment, technologies, and product lines. This will have the effect of holding down costs and permitting expanded levels of output. Capital investment may also rise if nonmember nations decide to establish subsidiary operations inside the customs unions to avoid external tariff barriers.

EUROPEAN COMMUNITY

In the years immediately following World War II, the countries of Western Europe suffered balance-of-payments disturbances in response to reconstruction efforts. To deal with these problems, they initiated an elaborate network of tariff and exchange restrictions, quantitative controls, and state trading. In the 1950s, Western Europe began to dismantle its trade barriers in response to successful tariff negotiations under the auspices of GATT. Trade liberalization efforts within Western Europe were also aided by the establishment of the Organization of Economic Cooperation and Development and the European Payments Union. Convertibility for most European currencies had taken place by 1958, and most quantitative restrictions on trade within Western Europe had been eliminated.

It was against this background of trade liberalization that the European Community (EC) was created in 1957. The EC originally consisted of six nations: Belgium, France, Italy, Luxembourg, the Netherlands, and Germany. By 1973, the United Kingdom, Ireland, and Denmark had joined the community. Greece became the tenth member in 1981, and the entry of Spain and Portugal in 1987 raised EC membership to 12 nations. Table 9.1 gives an economic profile of the community members.

The primary objective of the EC has been to create an economic union in which trade and other transactions take place freely among member nations. According to the 1957 Treaty of Rome, member nations have agreed in principle to the following provisions:

1. Abolition of tariffs, quotas, and other trade restrictions among member nations
2. Imposition of a uniform external tariff on commodities coming from nonmember nations
3. Free movement within the community of capital, labor, and enterprise
4. Establishment of a common transport policy, a common agriculture policy, and a common policy toward competition and business conduct

5. Coordination and synchronization of member-nation monetary and fiscal policies

According to EC's timetable, member nations were to establish a free trade zone over a 12-year period. This was accomplished in 1968, by which time all trade restrictions on manufactured goods had been eliminated. During the 1958–1968 period, liberalization of trade within the community was accompanied by a nearly fivefold increase in the value of industrial trade—higher than that of world trade in general. By 1970, the EC had become a full-fledged customs union with a common external tariff system.

Several studies have been conducted on the overall impact of the EC on its members' welfare. In terms of static welfare benefits, one study concluded that trade creation was pronounced in machinery, transportation equipment, chemicals, and fuels, whereas trade diversion was apparent in agricultural commodities and raw materials.[3] Another study concluded that from 1965 to 1967 the trade creation effect of the EC for industrial products totaled $6.2 billion, whereas the trade diversion effect amounted to $2.2 billion.[4] In addition, it is widely presumed that the EC has enjoyed dynamic benefits from integration.

Pursuing Economic Integration

Although the EC achieved a customs union by 1970, little progress was made toward becoming a common market until 1985. The hostile economic climate (stagflation) of the 1970s led EC members to shield their people from external forces rather than dismantle trade restrictions. By the 1980s, however, EC members were increasingly frustrated with barriers that hindered transactions within the community. European officials also feared that the EC's competitiveness was lagging behind that of Japan and the United States.

In 1985, the EC announced a detailed program for attaining the common-market stage of

T A B L E   9. 1   /   *European Community: Economic Profile, 1990*

Country	Population (in millions)	Gross Domestic Product (in millions)	Per Capita Gross Domestic Product
Belgium	10.0	$ 154.7	$15,440
Denmark	5.1	113.5	22,090
France	56.4	1,099.8	19,480
Germany*	77.3	1,411.3	22,730
Greece	10.0	60.2	6,000
Ireland	3.5	33.5	9,550
Italy	57.6	970.6	16,850
Luxembourg	0.4	10.8	28,770
Netherlands	14.9	258.8	17,330
Portugal	10.4	50.1	4,890
Spain	39.3	429.4	10,920
United Kingdom	57.5	924.0	16,070
	342.4	5,516.7	

* Prior to reunification with East Germany.

Source: *The World Bank Atlas* (Washington, D.C.: The World Bank), 1991.

economic integration. Plans called for the elimination of remaining nontariff trade barriers by 1992. Examples of these barriers included border controls and customs red tape, divergent standards and technical regulations, conflicting business laws, and protectionist government procurement policies. The elimination of these barriers to intra-EC transactions would create a market of more than 325 million consumers. It would also turn the EC into the second largest economy in the world, almost as large as the U.S. economy.

The common market's completion was expected to trigger a supply-side shock to the EC as a whole, leading to cost decreases. Prices would fall under pressure of new rivals on previously protected markets. Falling prices would lead to increases in demand, thus allowing companies to expand output, use resources more efficiently, and become geared up for European and global competition. Four major benefits

were expected from removing the remaining nontariff barriers:

1. Cost reductions due to improved exploitation by companies of economies of scale in production and business organization
2. Improved efficiency within companies and an environment where prices fall toward production costs under the pressure of more competitive markets
3. Increased R&D and innovation fostered by the dynamics of an expanded internal market
4. New patterns of competition in which comparative advantages determine market success

Table 9.2 provides estimated microeconomic benefits of the completion of the EC internal market.

TABLE 9. 2 / *Potential Gains in Economic Welfare for the EC Resulting from Completion of the Common Market*

Source of Gain	Gain as a Percentage of GDP
Removal of barriers affecting intra-EEC trade	0.2–0.3
Removal of barriers to production	2.0–2.4
Economies of scale and intensified competition, reducing business inefficiencies and monopoly profits	2.1–3.7
	4.3–6.4

SOURCE: Paolo Cecchini, *The European Challenge: 1992* (Brookfield, Vt.: Gower, 1988), p. 84.

TABLE 9. 3 / *Economies of Scale in European Manufacturing Industries*

Industry	Cost Disadvantage at Half MES* (percent)
Motor vehicles	6–9%
Other means of transport	8–20
Chemicals	2.5–15
Fibers	5–10
Metals	Over 6
Office machinery	3–6
Mechanical engineering	3–10
Electrical engineering	5–15
Instrument engineering	5–15
Paper and publishing	8–36
Mineral products	Over 6
Rubber and plastics	3–6
Drink and tobacco	1–6
Food	3.5–21

* Minimum efficient scale (MES) refers to the minimum physical production capacity of plant required for lowest production costs.

SOURCE: D. Gowland and S. James, eds., *Economic Policy After 1992* (Brookfield, Vt.: Dartmouth Publishing Co., 1991), p. 27.

As previously noted, the advent of a larger European market would permit firms to take advantage of hitherto unexploited economies of scale, with resulting decreases in unit costs and expansion of output. The benefits from scale economies, however, were considered problematic. Significant economies of scale were expected to be concentrated in only a few European industries, as seen in Table 9.3. The realization of scale economies would also imply industries consisting of fewer but larger firms, which might conflict with the EC's objective of increased competition. Finally, economies of scale, at least at the manufacturing plant (technical) level, are often due to output standardization and long production runs. But output standardization, even at reduced prices, might increase consumer welfare less than would have occurred if a wider range of products were available. This product-diversity argument supported the view that national markets would remain distinctive after completion of the common market because of factors such as language and cultural differences.

The supply-side shock would also ripple through the European economy at large. The elimination of trade barriers and resulting intensified competition would increase productivity and reduce costs, shifting the aggregate supply curve to the right. Moreover, savings on spending as government procurement was opened up would decrease tax burdens and interest rates, the latter stimulating investment in productive capacity, further adding to the beneficial supply shift. The outcome would be

TABLE 9.4 / *Potential Macroeconomic Consequences for the EC of Forming a Common Market*

	Removal of Customs Formalities	Opening of Public Procurement	Liberalization of Financial Services	Supply-side Effects*
Change in GDP (%)	0.4	0.5	1.5	2.1
Change in consumer prices (%)	-1.0	-1.4	-1.4	-2.3
Change in employment (in thousands)	200	350	400	850

* Supply-side effects refer to the reduction in production costs due to the removal of trade restrictions.

SOURCE: Paolo Cecchini, *The European Challenge: 1992* (Brookfield, Vt.: Gower, 1988), p. 98.

increased output, reduced unemployment, and lower inflation. The estimated macroeconomic effects are summarized in Table 9.4.

While the EC was pursuing the common-market level of integration, its heads of state and government agreed to pursue much deeper levels of integration. At the **Maastricht Summit** of 1991, it was decided to pursue economic and monetary union (EMU) and European political union (EPU); for the treaty to take effect, however, it had to be ratified by each member nation.

EMU would be achieved in three stages. The EC had already entered stage one, which required members to dismantle controls on capital movements and to strengthen economic and monetary policy coordination. Stage two called for the establishment of a European Monetary Institute to further strengthen the coordination of national monetary policies. During the final stage, member nations would establish a European central bank and introduce a common currency. Eligibility of the member nations to join the common currency would be based on their ability to meet the convergence criteria, which established standards for exchange rates,

budget deficits, interest rates, and inflation. One of the main concerns was whether member nations could reform their economies to comply with the convergence criteria.

EPU encompasses several areas. Member nations agreed to a common defense policy, which would be compatible with the North Atlantic Treaty Organization (NATO), and a common foreign policy. They also agreed to a common visa policy, as well as a form of EC citizenship that would permit EC citizens to vote in local elections outside their native countries.

While the EC was deepening its internal integration, it was also initiating efforts to broaden its influence by concluding agreements with nations outside the community. The boldest of these efforts was an agreement to implement a **European Economic Area** (EEA), which was concluded with the European Free Trade Association (EFTA) in 1991. The EEA's purpose is to permit the free movement of goods, people, services, and capital among the EC and EFTA nations. Although the pact calls for the EFTA nations to be brought into compliance with the EC's single-market plan, both organizations would remain distinct entities. The pact is also seen as the first step for many EFTA nations toward full membership in the EC.

Agricultural Policy

Besides providing for free trade in industrial goods among its members, the EC has abolished restrictions on agricultural products traded internally. A **common agricultural policy** (CAP) has also replaced the agricultural stabilization policies of individual member nations, which had differed widely before the formation of the EC. A substantial element of CAP has been the support of prices received by farmers for their produce. Schemes involving deficiency payments, output controls, and direct income payments have been used for this purpose. In addition, CAP has supported EC farm prices through a system of variable levies, which applies tariffs to agricultural imports entering the EC. Exports of any surplus quantities of EC produce have been assured through the adoption of export subsidies.

One problem confronting the EC's price-support programs is that agricultural efficiencies differ among EC members. Consider the case of grains. German farmers, being high-cost producers, have sought high support prices to maintain themselves as going concerns. The more efficient French farmers do not need as high a level of support prices as the Germans to keep them in operation; nevertheless, French farmers have found it in their interest to lobby for high price supports. In recent years, high price supports have been applied to products such as beef, grains, and butter. CAP has thus encouraged inefficient farm production by EC farmers and restricted food imports from more efficient nonmember producers.

Figure 9.2 illustrates the operation of a system of variable levies and export subsidies. Assume that S_{EC_0} and D_{EC_0} represent the EC's supply and demand schedules for wheat and that the world price of wheat equals $3.50 per bushel. Suppose the EC wishes to guarantee its high-cost farmers a price of $4.50 per bushel. This price could not be sustained as long as imported wheat is allowed to enter the EC at the free market price of $3.50 per bushel. Suppose the EC, to validate the support price, initiates a variable levy. Given an import levy of $1 per bushel, EC farmers are permitted to produce 5 million bushels of wheat, as opposed to the 3 million bushels that would be produced under free trade. At the same time, EC imports total 2 million bushels instead of 6 million bushels.

Suppose now that, owing to increased productivity overseas, the world price of wheat falls to $2.50 per bushel. Under a variable levy system, the levy is determined daily and equals the difference between the lowest price on the world market and the support price. The sliding-scale nature of the variable levy results in the EC's increasing its import tariff to $2 per bushel. The support price of wheat is sustained at $4.50, and EC production and imports remain unchanged. EC farmers are thus insulated from the consequences of variations in foreign supply. Should EC wheat production decrease, the import levy could be reduced to encourage imports. EC consumers would be protected against rising wheat prices.

The variable import levy tends to be more restrictive than a fixed tariff. It discourages foreign producers from absorbing part of the tariff and cutting prices to maintain export sales. This would only trigger higher variable levies. For the same reason, variable levies discourage foreign producers from subsidizing their exports in order to penetrate domestic markets.

The EC has also used a system of export subsidies to ensure that any surplus agricultural output will be sold overseas. The high price supports of CAP have given EC farmers the incentive to increase production, often in surplus quantities. But the world price of agricultural commodities has generally been below the EC price. The EC pays its producers export subsidies so they can sell surplus produce

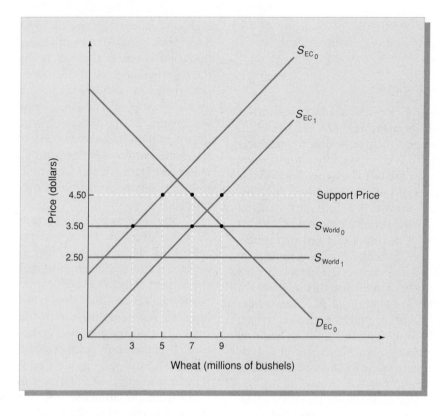

F I G U R E 9. 2 Variable levies and export subsidies. The CAP of the EC
includes the use of variable levies to protect EC farmers from low-cost foreign competition. During periods of falling world prices, the sliding-scale nature of the variable
levy results in automatic increases in the EC's import tariff. Export subsidies are also
used by the EC to make its agricultural products more competitive in world markets.

abroad at the low price but still receive the
higher support price.

Returning to Figure 9.2, let the world price
of wheat be $3.50 per bushel. Suppose that
improving technologies result in a shift in the
EC supply schedule from S_{EC_0} to S_{EC_1}. At the
internal support price of $4.50, EC production
exceeds EC consumption by 2 million bushels.
To facilitate the export of this surplus output,
the EC provides its producers an export subsidy
of $1 per bushel. EC wheat would be exported
at a price of $3.50, and EC producers would

receive a price (including the subsidy) of $4.50.
The EC export subsidies are also characterized
by a sliding scale. Should the world price of
wheat fall to $2.50, the $4.50 support price
would be maintained through the imposition of
a $2 export subsidy.

The EC's policy of assuring a high level of
income for its politically important farmers has
been costly. High support prices for products
including milk, butter, cheese, and meat have
led to high internal production and low consumption. The result has often been huge sur-

pluses (such as "milk lakes" and "butter mountains") that must be purchased by the EC to defend the support price.

To reduce these costs, the EC has been selling surplus produce in world markets at prices well below the cost of acquisition. These subsidized sales have met with resistance from farmers in other countries. For example, in response to U.S. farmer complaints about EC agricultural export subsidy programs in 1983, the U.S. government retaliated by subsidizing exports of wheat flour to Egypt. The subsidy, amounting to $100 per ton, enabled Egyptians to buy U.S. flour through commercial outlets at $155 per ton, well below the EC subsidized sales price of $175 per ton. The Europeans defended their subsidies by pointing out that the United States also uses subsidies to promote its agricultural sector; in 1982, for example, the United States subsidized the sale of 100,000 tons of butter to New Zealand to reduce the large U.S. dairy-product surplus. In addition, U.S. import restrictions on sugar and beef help support domestic farm prices without requiring government expenditures.

Virtually every developed country subsidizes its agricultural products. As seen in Table 9.5, government programs accounted for 48 percent of the value of agricultural products in the EC; this amount is even higher in certain countries, such as Japan and Switzerland, but it is much lower in others, including the United States, Australia, and New Zealand. Countries with relatively low agricultural subsidies have criticized the high-subsidy countries as being too protectionist. In 1992, the United States and the EC reached an agreement whereby internal subsidies and export subsidies were to be phased down over six years.

Government Procurement Policies

Governments are major purchasers of goods and services, ranging from off-the-shelf items such as paper and pencils to major projects such as nuclear power facilities and defense systems. Government procurement in the EC amounts to some 15 percent of the community's gross domestic product; it is especially concentrated in transport equipment, business services, telecommunications, building and civil engineering, and energy products. Public procurement has been used by EC nations to support national and regional firms and industries for several reasons: (1) national security (for example, aerospace); (2) compensation for local communities near environmentally damaging public industries (such as nuclear fuels); (3) support for emerging high-tech industries (for example, lasers); and (4) politics (as in assistance to highly visible industries such as automobiles).

There are, of course, sound justifications for purchasing locally, including lower transport costs, faster delivery, and more efficient after-sales service. By the 1980s, however, it was widely recognized that EC public procurement policies served as formidable barriers to foreign competitors; individual EC nations permitted only a minor fraction, often about 2 percent, of government contracts to be awarded to foreign suppliers. By downplaying intra-EC competition, governments paid more than they should for the products they needed and, in so doing, supported suboptimal producers within the community.

In its efforts to become a full-fledged common market, the EC has removed discrimination in government procurement by permitting all EC competitors to bid for public contracts. Government procurement liberalization applies to contracts with a value greater than ECU 200,000 (as of 1993, each European Currency Unit equaled $1.31) for supplies and services, and greater than ECU 5 million for capital projects. The criteria for awarding public contracts are specified as either the lowest price or the most economically advantageous tender that includes such factors as product quality, delivery dates, and reliability of supplies.

T A B L E 9. 5 / Government Support for Agriculture, 1990

Country	Producer-Subsidy Equivalents* as a Percentage of Total Value of Production
Australia	11%
Austria	46
Canada	41
European Community	48
Finland	72
Japan	68
New Zealand	5
Norway	77
Sweden	59
Switzerland	78
United States	30

* The producer-subsidy equivalent of an agricultural support policy is the estimated transfer needed to replace the support policy and leave the producer no worse off.

SOURCE: M. Kelly and A. McGuirk, *Issues and Developments in International Trade Policy* (Washington, D.C.: International Monetary Fund), 1992. See also Organization of Economic Cooperation and Development (OECD), *Agricultural Policies, Markets, and Trade, Monitoring and Outlook* (Paris), various issues.

It was believed that savings from a more competitive government procurement policy would come from three sources: (1) EC governments would be able to purchase from the cheapest foreign suppliers (static trade effect). (2) Increased competition would occur as domestic suppliers decreased prices to compete with foreign competitors that had previously been shut out of the home market (competition effect). (3) Industries would be restructured over the long run, permitting the surviving companies to achieve economies of scale (restructuring effect).

These three sources of savings are illustrated in Figure 9.3, which represents public procurement of computers. Suppose a liberalized procurement policy permits the British government to buy computers from the cheapest EC supplier, assumed to be Germany. The result is a reduction in average costs from $AC_{U.K.}$ to AC_G.

At the same time, increased competition results in falling prices and decreased profit margins. At an output of 10,000 computers, unit prices are reduced from $10,000 to $7,000, and profit margins from $Profit_0$ to $Profit_1$. What's more, exploitation of economies of scale gives rise to further decreases in unit costs and prices, as output expands from 10,000 to 25,000 computers along cost schedule AC_G.

It was estimated that liberalizing government procurement markets would generate long-run savings of 0.5 percent of EC gross domestic product, as seen in Table 9.6. In the process, some 350,000 additional jobs would be created. The price savings from open competition (trade and competition effects) were estimated at 40–50 percent for pharmaceuticals in Germany and the United Kingdom; 60–70 percent for telecommunications equipment in Germany and Belgium; and about 10 percent for

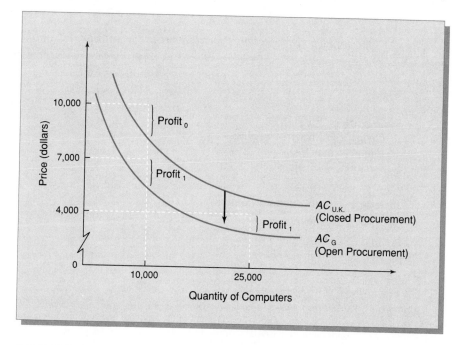

FIGURE 9.3 Opening up of government procurement. Procurement liberalization allows the U.K. government to import computers from Germany, the low-cost EC producer. Cost savings result from the trade effect, the competition effect, and the restructuring (economies-of-scale) effect.

automobiles in the United Kingdom and Italy. In sectors where companies were too small to compete internationally, additional savings could arise from mergers that resulted in a smaller number of EC companies able to exploit economies of scale. Examples included electric locomotives, turbine generators, and boilers, where decreases in units of costs of 12–20 percent were possible.

U.S. FREE TRADE AGREEMENTS

During the 1980s and early 1990s, the United States negotiated three free trade agreements (FTAs): (1) U.S.–Israel FTA of 1985; (2) U.S.-Canada FTA of 1989; (3) North American Free Trade Agreement (NAFTA) of 1993, whose members included Mexico, Canada, and the United States. Given the economic importance of Canada and Mexico to the United States, let us consider the latter two FTAs.

U.S.–Canada Free Trade Agreement

The concept of a U.S.–Canadian free trade area has a long tradition. During the 1800s and early 1900s, the two nations considered the free-trade issue several times. But because of the exigencies of nation building and apprehensions concerning political sovereignty, the nations maintained restrictionist stances. With the weakening of its position of world leadership by the 1980s, the United States appeared more willing to pursue bilateral trade negotiations with Canada. Moreover, Canada had grown increasingly dependent on the United States: by 1987, Canada exported more than 25 percent

T A B L E 9. 6 / *Opening Up Government Procurement in the European Community*

Effects	Billions of ECUs* (1989 prices)
Savings from:	
Buying from cheapest suppliers	5.5
Competitive pressure on prices	2.8
Economies-of-scale effects	8.9
	17.2
Increase in EC gross domestic product	+0.5%
Increase in EC employment	+350,000
Additional savings from opening up defense equipment markets	5.0

* In 1989, each European Currency Unit (ECU) equaled U.S. $1.20.

SOURCE: European Community, *Public Procurement: Regional and Social Aspects* (Brussels: Commission of the European Communities, July 1989). See also Keith Hartley, "Public Purchasing," in D. Gowland and S. James, eds., *Economic Policy After 1992* (Brookfield, Vt.: Dartmouth Publishing Co., 1991), pp. 114–125.

of its national output, and more than 73 percent of its exports were destined for the United States. Canadian business leaders also realized the difficulty of achieving economies of large-scale production without assured access to a large market.

These and other concerns led to the negotiation of the **U.S.–Canada Free Trade Agreement**, which became effective in 1989. The agreement, which fell short of establishing completely free trade between the United States and Canada, called for the elimination of all import tariffs and many NTBs over a ten-year period. The most controversial provision in the pact was the new mechanism it established for settling trade disputes between the two nations. In trade cases alleging unfair subsidies and dumping, a "binational" tribunal was created to hear final appeals instead of U.S. and Canadian courts. In summary, between 1989 and 1999, the FTA will

- Phase out all tariffs.
- Modify the 1965 U.S.–Canadian agree-

ment allowing for a form of free trade in cars and trucks.

- Give U.S. winegrowers greater access to the Canadian market.
- Remove some restrictions on cross-border investment.
- Guarantee the United States nondiscriminatory access to Canadian oil, natural gas, and uranium.
- Set up the first-ever rules governing trade in services.
- Create new procedures, including the establishment of a U.S.–Canadian tribunal, to settle trade disputes.
- Bring about additional talks on such difficult issues as trade subsidies in both nations and Canadian domestic-content rules for automobiles.[5]

Because trade between the two nations has been so much more important for Canada than for the United States, most of the theoretical work and empirical studies on the effects of a free trade agreement have been done on

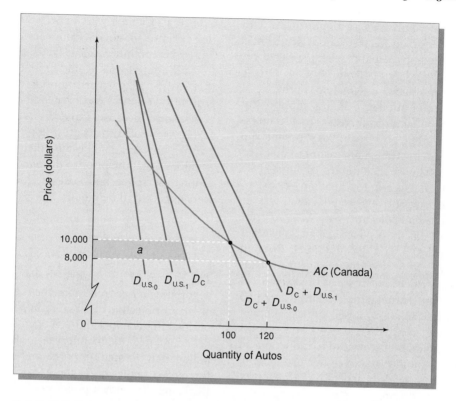

F I G U R E 9. 4 *Economies of scale in Canadian auto manufacturing: benefits to Canada of abolishing U.S. trade restrictions.* Bilateral free trade with the United States provides Canadian automakers a danger and an opportunity. The danger is that competing U.S. automakers may undercut Canadian manufacturers who maintain prices at $10,000. The opportunity is that longer production runs for Canadian manufacturers, made possible by the opening of the U.S. auto market, can result in cost reductions with economies of scale.

Canada. Proponents of the U.S.–Canada Free Trade Agreement generally cite economies of large-scale production as a major benefit to Canada, as illustrated in the following example.

Figure 9.4 represents the Canadian auto market, in which Canada is assumed to be a net exporter to the United States. Prior to the elimination of U.S. trade restrictions applied to Canada, assume that the U.S. demand for Canadian autos is $D_{U.S._0}$. Also assume that the Canadian auto demand is D_C. The overall demand schedule is thus denoted by $D_C + D_{U.S._0}$. Economies of scale are denoted in the

downward-sloping cost schedule *AC*. For simplicity, assume that Canadian manufacturers price their automobiles at average cost. In the absence of a free trade agreement, the total number of autos demanded is 100 units, and the price received by Canadian manufacturers is $10,000 per unit.

Under bilateral free trade with the United States, Canadian auto companies encounter a danger and an opportunity. The danger is that competing U.S. manufacturers may undercut Canadian companies who maintain prices at $10,000. But bilateral free trade also provides the Canadian companies an opportunity. The elimination of U.S. trade restrictions results in a shift in the export demand schedule faced by Canadian manufacturers from $D_{U.S._0}$ to $D_{U.S._1}$; thus, the overall demand schedule is now $D_C + D_{U.S._1}$. The total number of autos supplied by Canadian manufacturers increases to 120 units, and the resulting cost reductions permit the price charged by Canadian manufacturers to decrease to $8,000. Economies of large-scale production thus permit Canadian firms to adopt more competitive price policies.

For Canadian consumers, the $2,000 price reduction results in an increase in consumer surplus equal to area *a*, located under demand schedule D_C. Note that the gain to the Canadian consumer does *not* come at the expense of the Canadian manufacturer! The Canadian manufacturer can afford to sell autos at a lower price without any decrease in unit profits because economies of scale lead to reductions in unit costs. Economies of large-scale production, therefore, can provide benefits for *both* the producer *and* the consumer.

The U.S.–Canada Free Trade Agreement was described as a "win-win" situation, good for both nations. For Canada, bilateral free trade with the United States was expected to raise its real income in the range of 1–3 percent or more above existing levels. It was also estimated that Canadian production costs would decrease by an average of 2.1 percent because of the exploitation of economies of scale. With bilateral free trade, a number of Canadian industries were expected to expand, including forestry products, paper, and transportation equipment. Canadian industries likely to contract as a result of free trade included chemicals, electrical equipment, furniture, and miscellaneous manufacturing. The United States was expected to achieve modest economic gains from the free trade agreement; it was estimated that the gain in U.S. real income would be a small fraction of 1 percent.

Some *trade diversion* was expected to occur as a result of the free trade agreement. Canadian exports to the United States and U.S.

exports to Canada were expected to expand at the expense of goods from Germany, Japan, and other countries that faced trade restrictions. Welfare losses would exist to the degree that tariff-free partner exports replaced low-cost third-country exports encumbered by trade restrictions. Because Canada and the United States were each other's most important trading partner, however, and because their average tariff duties were low prior to the pact's implementation, the scope and cost of trade diversion were expected to be modest.[6]

North American Free Trade Agreement (NAFTA)

The notion of the United States and Mexico negotiating a free trade agreement evolved from a distant objective to a reality in a short period of time. In the mid-1980s, Mexico was mired in debt and tied to an interventionist economic policy that limited imports and discouraged foreign participation in the Mexican economy. Realizing that such a policy could not generate earnings of foreign exchange sufficient to pay its foreign debt and revitalize its economy, by the 1990s Mexico had reduced governmental intervention in the economy and opened its market to foreign goods, services, and investment. This paved the way for Presidents Bush and Salinas to endorse a comprehensive bilateral FTA as the best means to strengthen economic relations and meet the challenges of international competition.

Subsequently, Canada, which previously had an FTA with the United States, requested participation in the negotiations. Such trilateral negotiations would result in a **North American Free Trade Area (NAFTA)** that would rival the European Community, creating a $6-trillion market with more than 360 million consumers. Canada's benefits are mostly in the form of safeguards: maintaining its status in international trade, no loss of its current free-trade preferences in the U.S. market, and equal access to Mexico's market. Canada also desired to become part of any process that would eventually broaden market access to Central and South America. Although Canada hoped to benefit from trade with Mexico in the long run, most researchers predicted relatively small short-run gains because of the small amount of existing Canada–Mexico trade.

In 1993, NAFTA was approved by the governments of the United States, Mexico, and Canada. The pact went into effect on January 1, 1994.

The establishment of NAFTA was expected to provide each member nation better access to the others' markets, technology, labor, and expertise. In many respects, there were remarkable fits between the nations: the United States would benefit from Mexico's pool of cheap and increasingly skilled labor, while Mexico would benefit from U.S. investment and expertise. However, negotiating the FTA was difficult because it required meshing two large, advanced industrial economies (United States and Canada) with that of a sizable developing nation (Mexico). The huge living-standard gap between Mexico, with its miserable wage scale and booming population, and U.S./Canada was a politically sensitive issue.

U.S. labor unions were especially concerned that Mexico's low wage scale would encourage U.S. companies to locate in Mexico, resulting in job losses in the United States. Cities such as Muskegon, Michigan, which has thousands of workers cranking out such basic auto parts as piston rings, appeared especially vulnerable to low-wage Mexican competition. Indeed, the hourly manufacturing compensation for Mexican workers has been a small fraction of that paid to U.S. and Canadian workers, as seen in Table 9.7. While studies have shown that wages are not necessarily the driving factor in business location decisions, the huge disparity between U.S. and Mexican wages could not be ignored.

Another concern was Mexico's environmental regulations, criticized as being less stringent than those of the United States. U.S. labor and environmental activists feared that pollut-

TABLE 9. 7 / *Hourly Manufacturing Compensation Costs for Production Workers*

Year	United States	Canada	Mexico
1985	$13.01	$10.80	$1.60
1987	13.52	11.94	1.06
1989	14.31	14.81	1.59
1991	15.45	17.31	2.17
1992	16.17	17.02	2.35

SOURCE: U.S. Department of Labor, Bureau of Labor Statistics, *International Comparisons of Hourly Compensation Costs for Production Workers in Manufacturing*, various issues.

ing Mexican plants might cause plants in the United States, which are cleaner but more expensive to operate, to close down. Environmentalists also feared that increased Mexican growth would bring increased air and water pollution. However, NAFTA advocates countered that a more prosperous Mexico would be more able and more willing to enforce its environmental regulations; more economic openness is also associated with production closer to state-of-the-art technology, which tends to be cleaner.

NAFTA was also concerned about local content requirements (rules of origin). Recall that content requirements stipulate the minimum percentage of a product's value that must be produced or transformed domestically. The Big Three auto firms of the United States feared that Japanese companies would assemble Japanese-made parts in Mexico, which would be exported as finished autos to the United States duty free. To prevent this practice, NAFTA imposed local content requirements that ensured that a substantial portion of the value of each auto manufactured in Mexico and exported to the United States would involve North American production.

The common objectives of NAFTA were clear: to divert trade within the region, increase competitiveness, increase export penetration into other blocs, and use industrial complementarity as a major tool to improve productivity. To accomplish these goals, the three nations negotiated a gradual and comprehensive elimination of trade barriers over the course of 15 years, including (1) a full, phased elimination of import tariffs, (2) the elimination of many non-tariff trade barriers, (3) the establishment of clear, binding protection for intellectual property rights, and (4) fair and expeditious trade dispute settlement procedures. Following are the trade deal's key provisions, from the U.S. perspective.

Agriculture. Removes tariffs on half of U.S. farm exports to Mexico as soon as NAFTA takes effect. Remaining tariffs will be phased out entirely within 15 years.

Autos. Halves Mexican tariffs on autos to 10 percent immediately and to zero in ten years. Tariffs on most auto parts will be eliminated within five years. Cars must have 62.5-percent North American content to qualify for duty-free status; other vehicles and auto parts must have at least 60-percent North American content. After ten years, U.S. auto manufacturers would not have to produce in Mexico to sell there.

Energy. Lifts trade and investment curbs on most petrochemicals and permits Canadian and U.S. firms to sell goods to Pemex, the state oil monopoly, and Mexico's State Electricity Commission.

Financial services. Allows U.S. banks and securities firms to open wholly owned subsidiaries in Mexico. All restraints on services they can provide will be eliminated by the year 2000.

Transport. Allows U.S. trucking firms to carry international cargo into Mexican border states by 1995 and throughout Mexico by 1999. U.S. companies could buy majority stakes in Mexican truckers in the year 2000 and own them entirely in 2003.

Intellectual property. Boosts Mexico's protection for pharmaceutical patents to international standards and safeguards copyrights for North American movies, records, and computer software.

Rules of origin. Products manufactured with materials or labor from outside North America would qualify for NAFTA treatment only if they undergo substantial transformation within the United States, Canada, or Mexico.

Textiles and apparel. Stringent rules would eliminate tariffs only for goods manufactured from North American–spun yarn or from fabric made from North American fibers. Quotas could be reimposed temporarily if imports cause serious damage to industry.

NAFTA's benefits to Mexico would be proportionately much greater than for the United States and Canada, because Mexico would be integrating with economies many times larger than its own. Eliminating trade barriers would presumably lead to increases in the production of goods and services for which Mexico has a comparative advantage. Mexico's gains would especially come at the expense of other low-wage countries such as Korea, Taiwan, and Ireland. Generally, Mexico would produce more goods that benefit from a low-wage, low-skilled work force, such as fruits, vegetables, processed foods, sugar, tuna, and glass; labor-intensive manufactured exports, such as appliances and economy automobiles, would also increase. A free-trading Mexico, bordering on the world's largest and wealthiest market, would divert the flow of U.S. money and technology that previously had moved to low-cost havens in Asia and Eastern Europe. Rising investment spending in Mexico would increase wage incomes and employment, national output, and foreign exchange earnings; it would also facilitate the transfer of technology. Most studies suggested that Mexico's national output would rise between 3 percent and 10 percent as a result of the FTA. A richer Mexico would demand additional exports from the United States and Canada. However, many Mexicans feared a loss of national sovereignty that might occur by integrating with North American partners that dwarf its economy; they did not wish to become the 51st state of the United States!

NAFTA proponents maintained that the agreement would benefit the U.S. economy overall by expanding trade opportunities, reducing prices, increasing competition, and enhancing the ability of U.S. firms to attain economies of large-scale production. The United States would produce more goods that benefit from large amounts of physical capital and a highly skilled work force, including chemicals, plastics, cement, sophisticated electronics and communications gear, machine tools, and household appliances. U.S. insurance companies would also benefit from fewer restrictions on foreign insurers operating in Mexico. U.S. companies, particularly larger ones, would get better access to cheaper labor and parts. Moreover, the United States would benefit from a more reliable source of petroleum; less illegal Mexican immigration, as new jobs became available in Mexico and wages increased; and enhanced Mexican political stability as a result of the nation's increasing wealth.

There was an additional benefit of NAFTA for the United States: new rules that give trade benefits only to products with high percentages of North American–made parts would make it unprofitable for Japanese and European multinationals to assemble finished products in Mexico from foreign-made parts. That meant increased investment in U.S. manufacturing facilities by foreigners, creating jobs for U.S. workers. In spite of these benefits, the overall economic gains for the United States were esti-

mated to be modest, because the U.S. economy was 25 times the size of the Mexican economy and many U.S.–Mexico trade barriers had previously been dismantled. Most studies suggested that U.S. output would increase by no more than 0.1 or 0.2 percent under the FTA.

But even ardent proponents of NAFTA acknowledged that it would inflict pain on some segments of the U.S.–Mexico economy. On the business side, the most likely losers would be industries, such as citrus growing and sugar, that rely on trade barriers to limit imports of low-priced Mexican goods. Other major losers would be unskilled workers, such as those in the apparel industry, whose jobs are most vulnerable to competition from low-paid workers abroad. It was estimated that NAFTA would result in the creation of 240,000 new jobs in the United States; but the United States would lose 110,000 existing jobs as a result of increased Mexican competition. U.S. labor unions lobbied hard for the enactment of worker-displacement and job-retraining programs and assistance to compensate those who lost jobs as a result of NAFTA.

Proponents of NAFTA viewed it as an opportunity to create an enlarged productive base for the entire region through a new allocation of productive factors that would permit each nation to contribute to a larger pie. However, an increase in U.S./Canada trade with Mexico resulting from the reduction of trade barriers under an FTA would partly displace U.S./Canadian trade with other nations, including those in Central and South America, the Caribbean, and Asia. Some of this displacement would be expected to result in a loss of welfare associated with *trade diversion*—the shift from a lower-cost supplier to a higher-cost supplier. But since the displacement was expected to be small, it was projected to have only a minor negative effect on the U.S./Canadian economies.

In order to make the NAFTA treaty more agreeable to a skeptical U.S. Congress, the president negotiated side agreements with Mexico and Canada:

Environment. An agency would be established in Canada to investigate environmental abuses in any of the three countries. Fines or trade sanctions could be levied on countries that fail to enforce their own environmental laws.

Labor. An agency would be established in the United States to investigate labor abuses if two of the three countries agree. Fines or trade sanctions would be imposed only if countries fail to enforce minimum-wage standards, child-labor laws, or worker-safety rules.

The U.S. government also pledged to (1) spend up to $90 million to retrain and aid workers who lost their jobs because of NAFTA in the first 18 months, (2) establish a border environmental commission with Mexico that would spend up to $8 billion on various environmental cleanup projects, and (3) establish a development bank with Mexico that would lend up to $3 billion to aid communities hurt by NAFTA.

EAST–WEST TRADING ARRANGEMENTS

The concept of trade preferences has also been applied to commercial practices involving East–West trade. Prior to the recent economic reforms in the Eastern European nations, these nations were classified as nonmarket economies; the Western nations, including the United States, were classified as market economies. Let us consider the major features of these economic systems.

In a **market economy,** the commercial decisions of independent buyers and sellers acting in their own interest govern both domestic and international trade. Market-determined prices are used for valuing alternatives and allocating scarce resources. This means that prices play rationing and signaling roles so that the availability of goods is made consistent with buyer preferences and purchasing power.

In a **nonmarket economy** (one that is centrally planned), there is less regard to market considerations. Foreign and sometimes domestic trade is governed by state planning and control. The central plan often controls the prices and output of goods bought and sold, with minimal recognition given to considerations of cost and efficiency. The state fixes prices to ration arbitrary quantities among buyers, and these domestic prices are largely insulated from foreign-trade influences. Given these different pricing mechanisms, trade between market economies and centrally planned economies can be difficult.

The nonmarket nations of Eastern Europe and Asia historically have experienced only modest trade flows with the Western world. By the 1970s and 1980s, however, the nonmarket nations were increasingly looking to Western markets. In terms of the volume and composition of East–West trade, Western Europe has accounted for the largest share, whereas the U.S. share has been minor. Political considerations largely explain the relatively small amount of U.S. trade with the East. The United States historically has placed controls on exports of technology and goods of strategic importance to Communist countries and has also imposed restrictions on the credit terms extended to them.

What are some of the major issues currently affecting East–West trade? Among the most important are financing limitations and industrial cooperation, each of which will be discussed in turn.

Financing Limitations

Throughout the 1980s and 1990s, the Eastern European nations have run up significant trade deficits with the West. The basic problem has been that the Eastern European countries have not been able to increase their exports commensurate with the rise in their imports. Eastern European imports must be paid for either with hard currency generated from the exports of goods and services or by the accumulation of debt. Virtually all Eastern European deficits have been financed, in practice, by loans from Western banks and governments.

One major impediment that Eastern European countries face in obtaining financing for imports from the United States is the absence of U.S. government credit. Most lending has come from commercial banks instead of the government's export institutions—the Export-Import Bank and the Commodity Credit Corporation. Legal lending restrictions on the amount of commercial bank funds that can be used to finance exports also limits East–West trade. Another check is the Johnson Debt Default Act of 1934, which prevents U.S. institutions from making additional loans to foreign governments that are in default on debt obligations to the U.S. government. Finally, those Eastern European countries that have not been granted most-favored-nation status cannot receive credit from the U.S. government as long as they put restrictions on emigration, as provided by the Trade Act of 1974.

Industrial Cooperation

Until recently, East–West trade was carried out on a relatively simple basis. Exports to and imports from Eastern European countries were settled in hard currency or credit. But with the expansion of East–West trade has come **countertrade**, which establishes a greater degree of interdependence between the private corporations of Western economies and the state enterprises of the Eastern European countries.

Countertrade refers to all international trade in which goods are swapped for goods—a kind of barter. If swapping goods for goods sounds less efficient than using cash or credit, that's because it is. During tough economic times, however, shortages of hard currency and

tight credit can hinder East–West trade. Instead of facing the possibility of reduced foreign sales, Western producers have viewed countertrade as the next best alternative.

Many Western nations conduct countertrade with the Eastern European countries, as seen in Table 9.8. In the United States, General Motors, Sears, and General Electric have established trading companies that conduct countertrade. A simple form of countertrade occurs when a Eastern European country agrees to pay for the delivery of plant, machinery, or equipment with the goods produced by the plant. For example, Germany has sold Russia steel pipe in exchange for deliveries of natural gas; Austria has supplied Poland with technological expertise and equipment in exchange for diesel engines and truck components.

Industrial cooperation has also resulted in *coproduction agreements,* whereby Western companies establish production facilities in an Eastern European country. Because most Eastern European countries do not permit foreign ownership of such operations, an agreement is made whereby ownership is held by Eastern European nationals. Coproduction agreements are widely used in the areas of machine building, chemical products, electrical and electronic devices, and pharmaceutical goods.

Industrial cooperation may assume a number of other forms. Western companies have often made *joint R&D agreements* with Eastern European countries, particularly in industrial processes and technical areas. The findings of such activities are patented jointly, and license royalties are shared between the partners. Also popular are *contract manufacturing agreements,* whereby Western nations supply material inputs and design specifications to Eastern European enterprises, which produce the goods and ship them back to the Western nations.

The motivations for industrial cooperation are varied. For a Western company, such agreements get around the hard-currency scarcities of the Eastern European countries and permit

T A B L E 9. 8 / *Examples of Eastern European Countertrade Agreements with the West*

Western Country (Supplier)	Type of Eastern European Import	Type of Eastern European Export
West Germany*	Polyethylene plant Chemical plant	Polyethylene Methanol
Italy	Detergent plant	Organic chemicals
United States	Fertilizer plant	Ammonia
Japan	Car body-stamping assembly lines Forestry handling equipment	Chemicals Timber products
United Kingdom	Methanol plant	Methanol
France	Pulp paper plant	Wood pulp
Austria	Large-diameter pipe	Natural gas

* Prior to German reunification.

SOURCE: U.S. Department of Commerce, International Trade Administration.

access to the markets of Eastern Europe. Western companies may also be able to tap additional supplies of raw materials and intermediate goods, or possibly maximize revenues by selling obsolete equipment. The Eastern European partner typically views industrial cooperation as a means of obtaining new technologies and expanding industrial capacity with minimal sacrifices of hard currency.

Economic Reforms in Eastern Europe

After World War II, the Eastern European nations adopted the economic system that had previously been initiated in the Soviet Union. This included large-scale *nationalization* of the means of production and distribution and the institution of a *central planning system* to establish prices and wages and to allocate resources among enterprises. By the late 1980s, the relatively poor economic performance of the Eastern European nations was widely recognized. The income growth of these nations was steadily falling behind that of the industrial market economies as well as that of the newly industrializing countries in Asia.

Many factors contributed to the lagging economic performance of the Eastern European nations. Countries such as Poland and Hungary faced large buildups of external debt that had not been used, for the most part, to finance productive investment. Eastern European nations also emphasized a growth pattern that required massive increases in factor inputs rather than increases in productivity; such a pattern was unsustainable in the face of declines in the growth of labor input, as the sectoral migration from agriculture to manufacturing came to a halt. Moreover, political and social upheavals in the late 1980s led to deteriorating economic performance. The problems of central planning also became apparent. With no competition or profit maximization, Eastern European enterprises had little or no incentive to produce efficiently, develop new products or markets, innovate, and improve quality.

The poor economic performance of the Eastern European nations has provided the impetus for initiating *market-oriented reforms*. Of course, there is no simple blueprint for market-oriented reforms in these nations; the issues are nation-specific, and the economic reforms will evolve in different ways in the various nations. In general, however, the movement toward a market economy will involve a departure from the attempt to centrally plan and regulate economic activity at the microeconomic level. This suggests a phasing out of government price controls and allocative programs favoring heavy industry at the expense of agriculture, consumer goods, and housing. The system of microeconomic management of the economy will need to be replaced with a system of macroeconomic management operating through fiscal and monetary policies—a system that is largely nonexistent in Eastern Europe. It is also important to develop financial markets more fully and to privatize many, if not most, public enterprises. Unprofitable enterprises, whether private or public, will have to be permitted to go bankrupt. Government financing will have to be reformed so as to eliminate most

subsidies and to implement a tax system that enhances incentives to work, save, and establish new businesses by providing a "level playing field" on which private and public enterprises can compete on an equal footing.

The transition from a centrally planned to a market economy is not painless. Experience has shown that the elimination of microeconomic distortions through the removal of price controls and subsidies and the elimination of restrictions on the hiring and firing of labor initially may lead to higher inflation and unemployment. It is sometimes argued that a rapid transition to a market-oriented economy may be preferable to a gradual transition. The more rapid the economic reforms, the less those who benefited from the previous system will be able to block the reform process. What's more, public support of reform can perhaps be best maintained if tangible benefits of the reform become widely visible as soon as possible.

SUMMARY

1. Trade liberalization has assumed two main forms. One involves the reciprocal reduction in trade barriers on a nondiscriminatory basis, as seen in the operation of the General Agreement on Tariffs and Trade. The other approach is that used by the European Community, in which a group of nations on a regional basis establishes preferential trading arrangements among themselves.

2. The term *economic integration* refers to the process of eliminating restrictions to international trade, payments, and factor-input mobility. The stages of economic integration are (a) free trade area, (b) customs union, (c) common market, (d) economic union, and (e) monetary union.

3. The welfare implications of economic integration can be analyzed from two perspectives. First are the static welfare effects, resulting from trade creation and trade diversion. Second are the dynamic welfare effects that stem from greater competition, economies of scale, and the stimulus to investment spending that economic integration makes possible.

4. From a static perspective, the formation of a customs union yields net welfare gains if the consumption and production benefits of trade

creation more than offset the loss in world efficiency owing to trade diversion.

5. Several factors influence the extent of trade creation and trade diversion: (a) the degree of competitiveness that member-nation economies have prior to the customs union's formation, (b) the number and size of the customs union's members, and (c) the size of the customs union's external tariff against nonmembers.

6. The European Community was originally founded in 1957 by the Treaty of Rome. Today it consists of 12 members with a combined population approximately equal to that of the United States and a production output almost as large. By 1992, the EC had essentially reached the "common market" stage of integration. Empirical evidence suggests that the EC has enjoyed welfare benefits in trade creation that have outweighed the losses from trade diversion. One of the stumbling blocks confronting the EC has been its common agricultural policy, which has required large government subsidies to support European farmers.

7. In 1989, the United States and Canada successfully negotiated a free trade agreement under which free trade between the two nations would be phased in over a ten-year period. This

agreement was followed by negotiation of a North American Free Trade Agreement by the United States, Mexico, and Canada.

8. Among the important economic issues that affect East–West trading are financing limitations and industrial cooperation.

STUDY QUESTIONS

1. How can trade liberalization exist on a nondiscriminatory basis versus a discriminatory basis? What are some actual examples of each?
2. What is meant by the term *economic integration*? What are the various stages that economic integration can take?
3. How do the static welfare effects of trade creation and trade diversion relate to a nation's decision to form a customs union? Of what importance are the dynamic welfare effects to this decision?
4. Why has the so-called common agricultural policy been a controversial issue for the European Community?
5. What are the welfare effects of trade creation and trade diversion for the European Community, as determined by empirical studies?
6. Table 9.9 depicts the supply and demand schedules of gloves for Portugal, a small nation that is unable to affect the world price. On graph paper, draw the supply and demand schedules of gloves for Portugal.
   a. Assume that Germany and France can supply gloves to Portugal at a price of $2 and $3, respectively. With free trade, which nation exports gloves to Portugal? How many gloves does Portugal produce, consume, and import?
   b. Suppose Portugal levies a 100-percent nondiscriminatory tariff on its glove imports. Which nation exports gloves to Portugal? How many gloves will Portugal produce, consume, and import?

   c. Suppose Portugal forms a customs union with France. Determine the trade creation effect and the trade diversion effect of the customs union. What is the customs union's overall effect on the welfare of Portugal?
   d. Suppose instead that Portugal forms a customs union with Germany. Is this a trade-diverting or trade-creating customs union? By how much does the customs union increase or decrease the welfare of Portugal?

TABLE 9. 9 / *Supply and Demand for Gloves: Portugal*

Price ($)	Quantity Supplied	Quantity Demanded
0	0	18
1	2	16
2	4	14
3	6	12
4	8	10
5	10	8
6	12	6
7	14	4
8	16	2
9	18	0

International Factor Movements and Multinational Corporations

Our attention so far has been on international flows of goods and services. However, some of the most dramatic changes in the world economy have been due to international flows of factors of production, including labor and capital. In the 1800s, European capital and labor flowed to the United States and fostered its economic development. In the 1960s, the United States sent large amounts of investment capital to Canada and Western Europe; in the 1980s–1990s, investment flowed from Japan to the United States. Today, workers from southern Europe find employment in northern European factories, while Mexican workers migrate to the United States. The tearing down of the Berlin Wall in 1990 triggered a massive exodus of workers from East Germany to West Germany.

The economic forces underlying international movements in factors of production are virtually identical to those underlying international flows of goods and services. Productive factors move, when they are permitted to, from nations where they are abundant (low productivity) to nations where they are scarce (high productivity). Productive factors flow in response to differences in returns (such as wages and yields on capital) as long as these are large enough to more than outweigh the cost of moving from one country to another.

A nation in which labor is scarce can either import labor-intensive products or import labor itself; the same applies to capital. Thus, international trade in goods and services and flows of productive factors are *substitutes* for each other. One cannot conduct a satisfactory study of international trade without also analyzing the international mobility of labor and capital.

This chapter considers the role of international capital flows (investment) as a substitute for trade in capital-intensive products. Special attention is given to the multinational corporation that carries on the international reallocation of capital. The chapter also analyzes the international mobility of labor as a substitute for trade in labor-intensive products.

THE MULTINATIONAL CORPORATION

Although the term *corporation* can be precisely defined, there is no universal agreement on the exact definition of a **multinational corporation** (MNC). But a close look at some representative MNCs suggests that these businesses have a number of identifiable features. Operating in many host countries, the MNC often conducts research and development (R&D) activities in addition to manufacturing, mining, and extraction operations. The MNC cuts across national borders and is often directed from a corporate planning center that is distant from the host country. Both stock ownership and corporate management are typically multinational in character. A typical MNC has a high ratio of foreign sales to total sales, often 25 percent or more. Regardless of the lack of agreement as to what constitutes an MNC, there is no doubt that the multinational phenomenon is massive in size. Table 10.1 provides a glimpse of some U.S. MNCs.

MNCs may diversify their operations along vertical, horizontal, and conglomerate lines within the host and source countries. **Vertical integration** often occurs when the parent MNC decides to establish foreign subsidiaries to produce intermediate goods or inputs that go into the production of the finished good. For industries such as oil refining and steel, such *backward* integration may include the extraction and processing of raw materials. Most manufacturers tend to extend operations backward only to the production of component parts. The major international oil companies represent a classic case of backward vertical integration on a worldwide basis. Oil-production subsidiaries are located in areas such as the Middle East, whereas the refining and marketing operations occur in the industrial nations of the West. MNCs may also integrate *forward,* in the direction of the final consumer market. Automobile manufacturers, for example, may

establish foreign subsidiaries to market the finished goods of the parent company. In practice, most vertical foreign investment is backward. MNCs often wish to integrate their operations vertically to benefit from economies of scale and international specialization.

Horizontal integration occurs when a parent company producing a commodity in the source country sets up a subsidiary to produce the identical product in the host country. These subsidiaries are independent units in productive capacity and are established to produce and market the parent company's product in overseas markets. Coca-Cola and Pepsi-Cola, for example, are bottled not only in the United States but also throughout much of the world. MNCs sometimes locate production facilities overseas to avoid stiff foreign tariff barriers, which would place their products at a competitive disadvantage. Parent companies also like to locate close to their customers because differences in national preferences may require special designs for their products.

Besides making horizontal and vertical foreign investments, MNCs may diversify into nonrelated markets, in what is known as **conglomerate integration**. For example, in the 1980s the U.S. oil companies stepped up their nonenergy acquisitions in response to anticipated declines of future investment opportunities in oil and gas. Exxon acquired a foreign copper-mining subsidiary in Chile, and Tenneco bought a French company producing automotive exhaust systems.

To carry out their worldwide operations, MNCs rely on direct investment, which refers to the acquisition of a controlling interest in a company or facility. **Foreign direct investment** typically occurs when (1) the parent company obtains sufficient common stock in a foreign company to assume voting control (the U.S. Department of Commerce defines a company as directly foreign owned when a "foreign person" holds a 10-percent interest in the company); (2) the parent company acquires or con-

T A B L E 10. 1 / *U.S. Multinational Corporations: Selected Examples, 1991*

Company	Foreign Revenues (in billions of dollars)	Foreign Revenues as a Percentage of Total Revenues	Foreign Assets as a Percentage of Total Assets
Exxon	$78.1	75.9%	58.4%
IBM	40.4	62.3	54.3
General Motors	39.1	31.8	23.4
Mobil	38.8	68.1	56.6
Ford Motor	34.5	39.1	31.6
du Pont	17.1	44.8	39.8
Philip Morris	13.2	27.4	25.6
Xerox	8.6	44.3	27.3
Coca-Cola	7.4	64.0	46.8
Motorola	6.4	55.9	33.7
ITT	6.3	30.9	14.5
Goodyear Tire	4.7	42.9	40.2
PepsiCo	4.4	22.6	23.6
Woolworth	4.2	42.4	46.6
Monsanto	3.2	36.4	34.2
McDonald's	3.0	44.6	45.8

SOURCE: "The 100 Largest U.S. Multinationals," *Forbes* (July 20, 1992), pp. 298–300.

structs new plants and equipment overseas; (3) the parent company shifts funds abroad to finance an expansion of its foreign subsidiary; or (4) earnings of the parent company's foreign subsidiary are reinvested in plant expansion.

Table 10.2 summarizes the foreign direct investment position of the United States for 1991. Data are provided concerning U.S. direct investment abroad and foreign direct investment in the United States. In recent years, the majority of U.S. foreign direct investment has flowed to Europe and Canada, especially in the manufacturing sector. Most foreign direct investment in the United States has come from Europe, Japan, and Canada—areas that have invested heavily in U.S. manufacturing, petroleum, and wholesale trade facilities.

MOTIVES FOR DIRECT FOREIGN INVESTMENT

New MNCs do not pop up haphazardly in foreign nations. With the exception of the extractive industries, MNCs develop as a result of conscious planning by corporate managers. Both economic theory and empirical studies support the notion that direct foreign investment is conducted in anticipation of *future profits*. It is generally assumed that investment flows from regions of low anticipated profit to those of high anticipated profit, after allowing for risk. Although expected profits may ultimately explain the process of foreign direct investment, corporate management may emphasize a variety of other factors when asked

T A B L E 10. 2 / *Direct Investment Position of the United States, 1991 (Book Value)**

Country	U.S. Direct Investment Abroad		Foreign Direct Investment in U.S.	
	Amount (in billions of dollars)	Percentage	Amount (in billions of dollars)	Percentage
Canada	$68.5	15.2%	$ 30.0	7.4%
Europe	224.6	49.9	258.1	63.3
Japan	22.9	5.1	86.7	21.3
Other	134.2	29.8	32.8	8.0
	450.2	100.0	407.6	100.0

* Book value refers to the historical value of an investment; valuation is based on the time the investment occurred, with no adjustment for price changes.

SOURCE: U.S. Department of Commerce, *Survey of Current Business* (Washington, D.C.: Government Printing Office, August 1992).

about their investment motives. These factors include market demand conditions, trade restrictions, investment regulations, and labor-cost advantages. All these factors have a bearing on cost and revenue conditions, and hence on the level of profit.

Demand Factors

The quest for profits encourages MNCs to search for new markets and sources of demand. Some MNCs set up overseas subsidiaries to tap foreign markets that cannot be maintained adequately by export products. This sometimes occurs in response to dissatisfaction over distribution techniques abroad. Consequently, a business may set up a foreign marketing division and, later, manufacturing facilities. This incentive may be particularly strong when it is realized that local taste and design differences exist. A close familiarity with local conditions is of utmost importance to a successful marketing program.

The location of foreign manufacturing facilities may be influenced by the fact that some

parent companies find their productive capacity already sufficient to meet domestic demands. If they wish to enjoy growth rates that exceed the expansion of domestic demand, they must either export or establish foreign production operations. General Motors, for example, has felt that the markets of such countries as Britain, France, and Brazil are strong enough to permit the survival of GM manufacturing subsidiaries. But Boeing Aircraft has centralized its manufacturing operations in the United States and exports abroad because an efficient production plant for jet planes is a large investment relative to the size of most foreign markets.

Market competition may also influence a firm's decision to set up foreign facilities. Corporate strategies may be defensive in nature if they are directed at preserving market shares from actual or potential competition. The most certain method of preventing foreign competition from becoming a strong force is to acquire foreign businesses. For the United States, the 1960s and early 1970s witnessed a tremendous surge in acquisition of foreign businesses. Approximately half of the foreign subsidiaries operated by U.S. MNCs were originally acquired through purchase of already existing concerns during this era. Once again, General Motors exemplifies this practice, purchasing and setting up auto producers around the globe. GM has been successful in gaining control of many larger foreign-made models, including Monarch (GM Canada) and Opel (GM Germany). It did not acquire smaller-model firms such as Toyota, Datsun, and Volkswagen, all of which have become significant competitors for General Motors.

Cost Factors

MNCs often seek to increase profit levels through reductions in production costs. Such cost-reducing foreign direct investments may take a number of forms. The pursuit of essential raw materials may underlie a company's intent to go multinational. This is particularly true of the extractive industries and certain agricultural commodities. United Fruit, for example, has established banana-producing facilities in Honduras to take advantage of the natural trade advantages afforded by the weather and growing conditions. Similar types of natural trade advantages explain why Anaconda has set up mining operations in Bolivia and why Shell produces and refines oil in Indonesia. Natural supply advantages such as resource endowments or climatic conditions may indeed influence a company's decision to invest abroad.

Production costs include factors other than material inputs, notably labor. *Labor costs* tend to differ among national economies. MNCs may be able to hold costs down by locating part or all of their productive facilities abroad. Many U.S. electronics firms, for instance, have had their products produced or at least assembled abroad to take advantage of cheap foreign labor. (The mere fact that the United States pays higher wages than those prevailing abroad does not necessarily indicate higher costs. High wages may result from U.S. workers' being

more productive than their foreign counterparts. Only when high U.S. wages are not offset by superior U.S. labor productivity will foreign labor become relatively more attractive.)

Government policies may also lead to foreign direct investment. Some nations seeking to lure foreign manufacturers to set up employment-generating facilities in their countries may grant subsidies, such as preferential tax treatment or free factory buildings, to MNCs. More commonly, direct investment may be a way of circumventing import tariff barriers. The very high tariffs that Brazil levies on auto imports mean that foreign auto producers wishing to sell in the Brazilian market must locate production facilities in that country. Another example is the response of U.S. business to the formation of the European Community, which imposed common external tariffs against outsiders while reducing trade barriers among member nations. U.S. companies were induced to circumvent these barriers by setting up subsidiaries in the member nations. Another example is Japanese businesses that apparently located additional auto-assembly plants in the United States in the 1980s and 1990s to defuse mounting protectionist pressures.

SUPPLYING PRODUCTS TO FOREIGN BUYERS: WHETHER TO PRODUCE DOMESTICALLY OR ABROAD

Once a firm knows that foreign demand for its goods exists, it must ascertain the least-cost method of supplying these goods abroad. Suppose Anheuser-Busch Inc. (A-B) of the United States wants to sell its Budweiser beer in Canada. A-B can do this one of three ways: (1) brew Bud in the United States and export it to Canada (direct exporting); (2) license the rights to a Canadian brewery to produce and market Bud in Canada; or (3) establish its own production subsidiary in Canada (foreign direct investment). The method A-B chooses depends on the extent of economies of scale, transportation and distribution costs, and international trade barriers. These considerations are discussed in the following sections.

Direct Exporting versus Foreign Direct Investment/Licensing

Let us consider A-B's decision to supply Bud to Canada via direct exports versus foreign direct investment/licensing. We will first analyze the influence of economies of scale on A-B's decision. One would expect economies of scale to encourage A-B to *export* Bud to Canada when the quantity of beer demanded in Canada is relatively *small* and to encourage *Canadian production,* via either licensing agreements or foreign direct investment, when a relatively *large* quantity of beer is demanded in Canada.

To illustrate this principle, assume that A-B, a Canadian brewery, and a Canadian subsidiary of A-B have identical production functions exhibiting economies of scale and that the firms pay the same price for their inputs. As illustrated in Figure 10.1, their average cost schedules are identical and are denoted by *AC*.

Suppose U.S. consumers demand 200 cases per year of Bud at the going price. Producing this output permits A-B to realize economies of scale and a cost of $8 per case. Suppose that Canadians demand a smaller quantity of Bud, say 100 cases. Because this quantity is too small to permit efficient production in Canada, the Canadian brewery or A-B's production subsidiary realizes a higher cost of $11 per case. A-B thus minimizes cost by increasing its U.S. production to meet the additional Canadian demand. By brewing 300 cases, A-B achieves a longer production run and the resulting economies of scale, so that costs fall to $6 per case. Canadian consumers are thus supplied 100 cases of Bud via direct export. As long as the cost of transporting Bud from the United States to Canada is less than $5 a case, A-B increases its profit by exporting beer to Canada.

If the quantity of Bud demanded by Canadians is 300 cases or more, it may be more profitable for A-B to locate production in Canada, either by licensing production technology to a Canadian brewery or by investing in a production subsidiary. Referring to Figure 10.1, suppose Canadians demand 400 cases of Bud while Bud sales in the United States remain at 200 cases. With economies of scale exhausted at 300 cases, the larger Canadian demand does not permit A-B to brew Bud at a cost lower than $6 per case. By increasing output from 100 to 400 cases, however, the Canadian brewery or production subsidiary of A-B could match A-B's efficiency since they realize the least possible cost of $6 per case. Given equal production costs, A-B minimizes total cost by avoiding the additional costs of transporting beer to Canada. A-B thus increases profits by either licensing its beer technology to a Canadian brewer or investing in a production subsidiary in Canada. Similar to transportation costs, trade restrictions can neutralize production-cost advantages. If Canada has high import tariffs, production-cost advantages in the United States may be offset, so that foreign direct investment or licensing is the only feasible way of penetrating the Canadian market.

Foreign Direct Investment versus Licensing

Once a firm chooses foreign production as a method of supplying goods abroad, it must decide whether it is more efficient to establish a foreign production subsidiary or license the technology to a foreign firm to produce its goods. In the United Kingdom, there are Kentucky Fried Chicken establishments that are owned and run by local residents. The parent U.S. organization merely provides its name and operating procedures in return for royalty fees paid by the local establishments. Although licensing is widely used in practice, it presupposes that local firms are capable of adapting their operations to the production process or technology of the parent organization.

Figure 10.2 portrays the hypothetical cost conditions confronting A-B as it contemplates

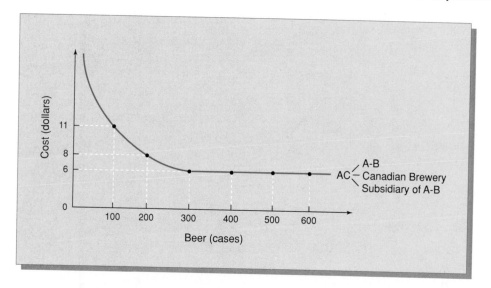

FIGURE 10. 1   *The choice between direct exporting and foreign direct investment/ licensing.* When the Canadian market's size is large enough to permit efficient production in Canada, a U.S. firm increases profits by establishing a Canadian production subsidiary or licensing the rights to a Canadian firm to produce/market its product in Canada. The U.S. firm increases profits by exporting its product to Canada when the Canadian market is too small to permit efficient production.

whether to license Bud production technology to a Canadian brewery or invest in a Canadian production subsidiary. Curve $AVC_{Subsidiary}$ represents the average variable cost (such as labor and materials) of A-B's production subsidiary, and AVC_{Canada} represents the average variable cost of a Canadian brewery. The establishment of a foreign production subsidiary also entails fixed costs denoted by curve $AFC_{Subsidiary}$. These include expenses of coordinating the subsidiary with the parent organization and the sunk costs of assessing the market potential of the foreign country. The total unit costs that A-B faces when establishing a foreign subsidiary are given by $ATC_{Subsidiary}$.

Comparing $ATC_{Subsidiary}$ with AVC_{Canada}, for a relatively small market of less than 400 cases of beer the Canadian brewery has an absolute cost advantage. Licensing Bud production technology to a Canadian brewery in this case is more profitable for A-B. But if the Canadian market for Bud exceeds 400 cases, A-B's production subsidiary has an absolute cost advantage; A-B increases profits by supplying beer to Canadians via foreign direct investment.

Several factors influence the output level at which A-B's production subsidiary begins to realize an absolute cost advantage vis-à-vis the Canadian brewery (400 cases in Figure 10.2). To the extent that production is capital-intensive and A-B's production subsidiary can acquire capital at a lower cost than that paid by the Canadian brewery, the variable cost advantage of the subsidiary is greater. This neutralizes the influence of a fixed-cost disadvantage for the subsidiary at a lower level of output. The amount of the production subsidiary's fixed costs also has a bearing on this minimum output level. Smaller fixed costs lower the subsidiary's average total costs, again resulting in a smaller output at which the subsidiary first begins to have an absolute cost advantage.

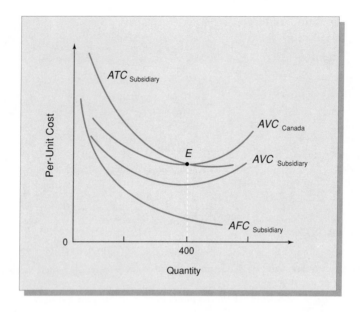

F I G U R E 10. 2 The choice between foreign direct invest-ment and licensing. The decision to establish foreign operations through direct investment or licensing depends on (1) the extent to which capital is used in the production process, (2) the size of the foreign market, and (3) the amount of fixed cost a business must bear when establishing an overseas facility.

As noted, international business decisions are influenced by such factors as production costs, fixed costs of locating overseas, the relative importance of labor and capital in the production process, and the size of the foreign market. Another factor is the element of risk and uncertainty. Management is concerned with possibilities such as currency fluctuations and subsidiary expropriations when determining where to locate production operations.

IS FOREIGN DIRECT INVESTMENT A THREAT TO THE UNITED STATES?

On a daily basis, many people in the United States use the products of foreign-owned U.S. businesses. If, for example, you drank Hills Brothers coffee this morning, used a dab of Vaseline Intensive Care hand lotion, ran a Hamilton Beach appliance, used a Scripto or Bic pen to write your international economics notes, or read the comics in the *Boston Herald*, you were using the output of foreign-owned U.S. businesses.

When listening to the evening news, one might conclude that most foreign direct investment in the United States comes from Japan. There have been widely publicized Japanese investments in American landmarks such as the Rockefeller Center, Algonquin Hotel, CBS Records, and Columbia Pictures. But in the past decade, the largest supplier of direct investment in the United States has been the United Kingdom.

Direct investment patterns between Japan and the United States in the 1980s provide a classic example of the effects of capital flows between a *high-saving* nation and a *low-saving* nation. During the 1980s, the Japanese savings rate was two to three times higher than that of the United States, depending on how savings are measured. The United States was a low-saving nation primarily because of a low domestic savings rate among households and large federal budget deficits. In the early 1980s, a combination of high real interest rates in the United States and a strengthening dollar caused investors in Japan and elsewhere to sharply increase their purchases of U.S. assets. As the 1980s continued, large-scale Japanese investments were attracted to the United States by a strong and growing U.S. economy.

The upward trend in foreign direct investment throughout the 1980s coincided with a surge of mergers and acquisitions in the United States. During this period, acquisitions of existing companies played an expanding role as a vehicle for foreign direct investment. The United States has been one of the most attractive nations in which to invest, due in part to the sheer size and scope of its markets. As the world economy became more integrated, it was hardly surprising that foreign companies would be, with increasing frequency, the highest bidders for U.S. corporate assets.

Foreign-owned companies operating in the United States receive *national treatment*; they must operate under the same antitrust, environmental, and other regulations as domestically owned companies. Although the precise tax treatment may be affected by tax regulations in their home country, they are liable for U.S. taxes and are subject to international tax treaties. They hire from the same pool of labor as U.S. businesses. Foreign-owned companies therefore behave similarly to their U.S. counterparts in such business decisions as R&D expenditures and compensation of employees.

The United States has traditionally recognized that a free flow of investment capital across borders benefits both investor and recipient nations. The United States generally provides foreign investors nondiscriminatory treatment under U.S. laws and regulations, maintaining that it is in the best interests of U.S. investors, workers, and consumers to foster an open policy. National security considerations, however, have been a longstanding exception to an open investment policy. Like other industrial nations, the United States maintains barriers on foreign direct investment in sensitive military areas (such as supercomputers).

The implications of foreign direct investment for the welfare of the recipient nation is a matter of controversy. Proponents of direct investment laud it for transferring to the recipient nation not merely capital but also managerial skills and technology. But critics of direct investment maintain that it exploits the recipient nation's market, decreases its sovereignty, and frustrates its economic policies. Critics of Japanese direct investment in the United States have contended that Japanese ownership of U.S. assets carries the risk that policy decisions will shift to Tokyo.

Although many people in the United States during the 1980s grumbled about the increasing Japanese presence, by 1990 Japan was reducing its new investments in the United States. Wary of a weak U.S. economy, Japanese investors bought fewer hotels and office towers. They also curbed purchases of U.S. corporate stocks and bonds as well as Treasury securities. Japanese banks became more conservative in the loans they granted to U.S. borrowers. One casualty was the city of Philadelphia, which had to scuttle a $375-million note sale when it failed to obtain a letter of credit from Japanese banks to guarantee the borrowing.

Why did the Japanese reduce their investments in the United States in the early 1990s? Climbing interest rates in Japan and Europe, relative to the United States, attracted Japanese investors and diminished the attractiveness of U.S. securities. The decline in the dollar's exchange value against the yen reduced the worth of U.S. assets to Japanese investors. Poor performance of some previous Japanese investments in the United States (such as real estate and leveraged buyouts), coupled with a wave of U.S. anti-Japan sentiment, may have dampened some of the investment optimism. Japanese investors also became increasingly interested in Europe, with the headline events surrounding implementation of the European Common Market and German unification.

JAPANESE TRANSPLANTS IN THE U.S. AUTOMOBILE INDUSTRY

During the 1980s, the growth of Japanese direct investment in the U.S. auto industry was widely publicized. From 1980 to 1990, Japanese automakers invested more than $5 billion in U.S.-based assembly facilities, known as **transplants.** Eight Japanese-affiliated auto manufacturers and more than 100 Japanese parts suppliers operated or constructed facilities in the United States. By 1990, Japanese transplants built more than 15 percent of the passenger cars produced in the United States. Table 10.3 provides examples of Japanese transplant automakers in the United States.

Establishing transplants in the United States provided a number of benefits to Japanese automakers, including opportunities to

- Silence critics who insist that autos sold in the United States be built there.
- Avoid export restraints imposed by the Japanese government and potential import barriers of the United States.
- Gain access to an expanding market at a time when the Japanese market was nearing saturation.
- Provide a hedge against fluctuations in the yen-dollar exchange rate.

The rapid growth of Japanese investment in the U.S. auto industry led to concerns over the future of U.S.-owned auto-manufacturing and parts-supplier industries. Proponents of foreign direct investment maintained that it would foster improvement in the overall competitive position of the domestic auto-assembly and parts industries. They also argued that foreign investment generates jobs and provides consumers with a wider product choice at lower prices than would otherwise be available.

However, the United Auto Workers (UAW) union maintained that this foreign investment would result in job losses in the auto-assembly and parts-supplier industries. They and other critics felt that Japanese transplants would decrease the market share for U.S. automakers and parts suppliers and contribute to excess capacity at both the automaker and parts-supplier levels. Data Resources, Inc./McGraw-Hill predicted that every three autos made by the transplants would displace one import and two Detroit vehicles.

A study by the U.S. General Accounting Office (GAO) analyzed the likely effects of the growing Japanese presence in the U.S. auto industry. As summarized in Table 10.4, the study concluded that U.S. auto-related employment would be substantially smaller in 1990 than it was in 1985 because of increases in worker productivity, rising usage of foreign parts by U.S. auto companies, and expanded imports. The operations of Japanese transplants in the United States would likely result in even more losses because they hire fewer workers and use more foreign content than U.S. auto companies.

One factor that influences the number of workers hired is a company's *job classifications,* which stipulate the scope of work each employee performs. As the number of job classifications increases, the scope of work decreases, along with the flexibility of using available employees; this can lead to falling worker productivity and rising production costs.

Japanese-affiliated auto companies tend to use significantly fewer job classifications than traditional U.S. auto companies. Japanese transplants use work teams, and each team member is trained to do all the operations performed by the team. A typical Japanese-affiliated assembly plant has three to four job

T A B L E 10. 3 / *Japanese Auto Plants in the United States*

Plant Name/Parent Company	Location/Date Open
Honda of America, Inc. (Honda)	Marysville, Ohio (1982) East Liberty, Ohio (1989)
Nissan Motor Manufacturing Corp. (Nissan)	Smyrna, Tennessee (1983)
New United Motor Manufacturing, Inc. (Toyota/General Motors)	Fremont, California (1984)
Toyota Motor Manufacturing USA, Inc. (Toyota)	Georgetown, Kentucky (1988, 1993)
Mazda Motor Manufacturing, USA, Inc. (Mazda)	Flat Rock, Michigan (1987)
Diamond-Star Motors Corp. (Mitsubishi/Chrysler)	Normal, Illinois (1988)
Ford Motor Co. (Nissan/Ford)	Avon Lake, Ohio (1991)

T A B L E 10. 4 / *U.S. Auto Industry: Net Auto-Related Job Losses, 1985–1990, by Cause*

Contributing Factor	Estimated Job Losses	Percentage of Total
Labor productivity gains	132,000	35.7
Increased use of foreign content by U.S. automakers	44,000	11.9
Increased imports	137,000	37.0
Increased U.S. production of Japanese-affiliated automakers	57,000	15.4
	370,000	100.0

SOURCE: U.S. General Accounting Office, *Foreign Investment: Growing Japanese Presence in the U.S. Auto Industry* (Washington, D.C.: Government Printing Office, March 1988).

classifications: one team leader, one production technician, and one or two maintenance technicians. Often, jobs are rotated among team members. In contrast, traditional U.S. auto plants have more than 90 different job classifications, and employees generally perform only those operations specifically permitted for their classification. These trends have contributed to the superior labor productivity of Japanese transplants compared to the Big Three. Although powerful forces within the Big Three have resisted change, international competition has forced U.S. automakers to slowly dismantle U.S. management and production methods and remake them along Japanese lines.

Japanese transplants in the United States also import a large part of their automobile components from Japan or buy from nonunion Japanese suppliers that have relocated in the United States. The GAO put the domestic content of an average vehicle produced by the transplants in 1988 at 38 percent, against 88 percent for the Big Three. That difference cost U.S. workers their jobs. It also helped the transplants to control prices and quality and to achieve an average $700 per-auto cost advantage over the Big Three plants.

For policymakers, the broader issue is whether the Japanese transplants have lived up to expectations. When the Japanese initiated investment in U.S. auto-manufacturing facilities in the 1980s, many Americans viewed them as models for a revitalized U.S. auto industry and new customers for U.S. auto-part suppliers. Transplants were seen as a way of providing jobs for U.S. autoworkers whose jobs were dwindling as imports increased. When the transplant factories were announced, Americans anticipated that transplant production would be based primarily on American parts, material, and labor; transplant production would displace imports in the U.S. market while transferring new management techniques and technology to the United States.

Certainly, the transplant factories boosted the economies in the regions where they located. And there is no doubt that the transplants helped to transfer Japanese quality control, just-in-time delivery, and other production techniques to the United States. However, the original expectations of the transplants were only partially fulfilled.

Skeptics maintained that transplant automobiles were mostly collections of Japanese parts handled by Americans but designed, engineered, and fabricated in Japan. As seen in Table 10.5, the estimated North American content of the 1992 Honda Accord, produced in the United States at a Honda transplant factory, was about 38 percent; in contrast, the average North American content of a Big Three car was about 88 percent. Those transplant parts provided by U.S.-owned suppliers were generally low-margin components, while the more lucrative parts came from Japan or from Japanese suppliers who set up shop in the United States.

Skeptics also contended that Japanese manufacturing operations were twice as likely to import parts for assembly in the United States as the average foreign company; and they were four times as likely to import parts as the average U.S. company. Extensive use of imported parts by Japanese transplants would contribute to a U.S. automotive trade deficit with Japan and would result in fewer jobs for U.S. autoworkers.

How competitive are Japanese transplants relative to other U.S. auto manufacturers? Table 10.6a compares U.S. and transplant production costs for a small car as of 1992. At that time, Ford was estimated to be the low-cost producer, although the average transplant's costs were lower than the average U.S. firm's costs. The transplants' competitiveness was due primarily to low labor costs, which resulted from relatively high worker productivity, low wage scales, and low fringe-benefit payments to nonunion workers. Low capital costs in Japan also enhanced transplant competitiveness. As seen in Table 10.6b, the transplants would have realized even lower costs if they had purchased more parts and materials from U.S. suppliers; instead, they adopted the unusual strategy of sourcing more expensive parts and components heavily from Japan.

INTERNATIONAL JOINT VENTURES

In a trend that accelerated during the 1980s, companies have begun to link up with former rivals in a vast array of joint ventures. A *joint venture* is a business organization established by two or more companies that combines their

T A B L E   1 0 . 5   /   *Transplant Local Content: North American Content of the Honda Accord*

	Total	North American Sourced	Japan Sourced
Imported parts	$ 3,820	$0	$3,820
Transplant parts			
U.S. content (32.4%)	850	850	0
Japanese content (67.6%)	1,775	0	1,775
Total transplant parts	2,625	850	1,775
Parts from U.S. suppliers	1,585	1,585	0
Labor, depreciation, and overhead	2,000	1,369	631
Total manufacturing cost	10,030	3,804	6,226
Assembly profit	213	213	0
Ex-factory price	10,243	4,017	6,226
Distributor margin	1,668	1,668	0
Wholesale price	11,911	5,685	6,226
U.S. content as a percent of:			
Manufacturing cost	38%		
Ex-factory price	39%		
Wholesale price	48%		

SOURCE: C. Prestowitz and P. Wilen, *The Future of the Auto Industry: It Can Compete, Can It Survive?* (Washington, D.C.: Economic Strategy Institute, 1992), p. 37.

skills and assets. It may have a limited objective (such as research or production) and be short-lived. It may also be multinational in character, involving cooperation among several domestic and foreign companies. Joint ventures differ from mergers in that they involve the creation of a *new* business firm, rather than the union of two existing companies. Table 10.7 provides examples of recent joint ventures between U.S. and foreign companies.

There are three types of **international joint ventures.** The first is a joint venture formed by two businesses that conduct business in a third country. For example, a U.S. oil firm and a British oil firm may form a joint venture for oil exploration in the Middle East. Next is the formation of a joint venture with local private

interests. Honeywell Information Systems, Inc., of Japan was formed by Honeywell, Inc., of the United States and Mitsubishi Office Machinery Company of Japan to sell information systems equipment to the Japanese. The third type of joint venture includes local government participation. Bechtel Company of the United States, Messerschmitt-Boelkow-Blom of West Germany, and National Iranian Oil Company (representing the government of Iran) formed Iran Oil Investment Company for oil extraction in Iran.

Several reasons have been advanced to justify the creation of joint ventures. Some functions, such as R&D, can involve costs too large for any one company to absorb by itself. Many of the world's largest copper deposits have been

T A B L E 10. 6 /   Comparison of U.S. and Japanese
Production Costs for a Small Car, 1992

	Average U.S. Firm	Average Japanese Transplant
a. Based on the sourcing of parts and materials that actually occurred in 1992		
Labor costs		
Wage rate/hour	$18.76	$18.00
Benefits/hour	13.22	5.00
Total compensation/hour	31.98	23.00
Labor hours per car	64	42
Total labor costs*	$2,047	$966
Purchased components and materials	$4,202	$4,818
Other manufacturing costs	798	665
Nonmanufacturing costs	379	760
Total production costs	$7,426	$7,209
b. Assuming that Japanese producers took full advantage of lower U.S. parts and materials costs		
Labor costs		
Wage rate	$18.76	$18.00
Benefits	13.22	5.00
Total compensation	31.98	23.00
Labor hours per car	64	42
Total labor costs*	$2,047	$966
Purchased components and materials	$4,202	$3,434
Other manufacturing costs	798	665
Nonmanufacturing costs	379	760
Total production costs	$7,426	$5,825

* The product of labor hours per car times total compensation per hour.

SOURCE: C. Prestowitz and P. Wilen, *The Future of the Auto Industry: It Can Compete, Can It Survive?* (Washington D.C.: Economic Strategy Institute, 1992), pp. 82–83.

owned and mined jointly by the largest copper companies on the grounds that joint financing is required to raise enough capital. The exploitation of oil deposits is often done by a consortium of several oil companies. Exploratory drilling projects typically involve several companies united in a joint venture, and several refining companies traditionally own long-distance crude-oil pipelines. Oil refineries in foreign countries may be co-owned by several large U.S. and foreign oil companies.

Another factor that encourages the formation of international joint ventures is the restrictions some governments place on foreign own-

T A B L E 10. 7 / *Joint Ventures between U.S. and Foreign Companies*

Joint Venture	U.S. Partner	Foreign Partner	Products
New United Motor Manufacturing	General Motors	Toyota (Japan)	Subcompact cars
National Steel	National Intergroup	Nippon Kokan	Steel
Siecor	Corning Glass Works	Siemens (Germany)	Optical cable
Honeywell/Ericsson Development	Honeywell	L. M. Ericsson (Sweden)	PBX systems
Himont	Hercules	Montedison (Italy)	Polypropylene resin
GMFanuc Robotics	General Motors	Fanuc (Japan)	Robots
International Aero Engines	United Technologies	Rolls-Royce (Britain)	Aircraft engines
Tokyo Disneyland	Walt Disney Productions	Oriental Land Company	Entertainment

ership of local businesses. Governments in developing nations often close their borders to foreign companies unless they are willing to take on local partners. Mexico, India, and Peru require that their own national companies represent a major interest in any foreign company conducting business within their boundaries. The foreign investor is forced to either accept local equity participation or forgo operation in the country. Such government policies are defended on the grounds that joint ventures result in the transfer of managerial techniques and know-how to the developing nation. Joint ventures may also prevent the possibility of excessive political influence on the part of foreign investors. Finally, joint ventures help minimize dividend transfers abroad and thus strengthen the developing nation's balance of payments.

International joint ventures are also viewed as a means of forestalling protectionism against imports. Apparently motivated by fear that rising protectionism would restrict their access to U.S. markets, Japanese manufacturers (such as Toyota Motor Corporation) increasingly formed joint ventures with U.S. corporations in the 1980s. Such ventures typically resulted in U.S. workers' assembling Japanese components, with the finished goods sold to U.S. consumers. Not only did this process permit Japanese production to enter the U.S. market, but it also blurred the distinction between U.S. and Japanese production. Just who is us? And who is them? The rationale for protecting domestic output and jobs from foreign competition is thus lessened.

There are, however, disadvantages to forming an international joint venture. A joint venture is a cumbersome organization compared with a single organization. Control is divided, creating problems of "two masters." Success or failure depends on how well companies with different objectives, corporate cultures, and ways of doing things can work together. The action of corporate chemistry is difficult to predict, but it is critical because joint venture agreements usually provide both partners an ongoing role in management. When joint venture ownership is divided equally, as often occurs, deadlocks in decision making can take place. If balance is to be preserved between different economic interests, negotiation must establish a hierarchical command. Even when negotiated balance is achieved, it can be upset by changing corporate goals or personnel.

Welfare Effects

International joint ventures can yield both welfare-increasing effects and welfare-decreasing effects for the domestic economy. Joint ventures lead to *welfare gains* when (1) the newly established business adds to preexisting productive capacity and fosters additional competition, (2) the newly established business is able to enter new markets that neither parent could have entered individually, or (3) the business yields cost reductions that would have been unavailable if each parent performed the same function separately. However, the formation of a joint venture may also result in *welfare losses*. For instance, it may give rise to increased market power, suggesting greater ability to influence market output and price. This is especially likely to occur when the joint venture is formed in markets in which the parents conduct business. Under such circumstances, the parents, through their representatives in the joint venture, agree on prices and output in the very market that they themselves operate. Such coordination of activities limits competition, reinforces upward pressure on prices, and lowers the level of domestic welfare.

Let's consider an example that contrasts two situations: (1) Two competing companies sell autos in the domestic market. (2) The two competitors form a joint venture that operates as a single seller (a monopoly) in the domestic market. We would expect to see a higher price and smaller quantity when the joint venture behaves as a monopoly. This will always occur as long as the marginal cost curve for the joint venture is identical to the horizontal sum of the marginal cost curves of the individual competitors. The result of this *market-power effect* is a deadweight welfare loss for the domestic economy—a reduction in consumer surplus that is not offset by a corresponding gain to produc-

ers. If, however, the formation of the joint venture entails *productivity gains* that neither parent could realize prior to its formation, domestic welfare may increase. This is because a smaller amount of the domestic economy's resources is now required to produce any given output. Whether domestic welfare rises or falls because of the joint venture depends on the magnitudes of these two opposing forces.

Figure 10.3 illustrates the welfare effects of two parent companies that form a joint venture in the market in which they operate.[1] Assume that Sony Auto Company of Japan and American Auto Company of the United States are the only two firms producing autos for sale in the U.S. market. Suppose each company realizes constant long-run costs, suggesting that average total cost equals marginal cost at each level of output. Let the cost schedules of each company prior to the formation of the joint venture be $MC_0 = ATC_0$, which equals \$10,000. $MC_0 = ATC_0$ thus becomes the long-run market supply schedule of autos.

Assume that Sony Auto Company and American Auto Company initially operate as competitors, charging a price equal to marginal cost. In Figure 10.3, market equilibrium exists at point *A*, where 100 autos are sold at a price of \$10,000 per unit. Consumer surplus totals area $a + b + c$. Producer surplus does not exist, given the horizontal supply schedule of autos (recall that producer surplus equals the sum of the differences between the market price and each of the minimum prices indicated on the supply schedule for quantities between zero and the market output). Now suppose that the two competitors announce the formation of a joint venture known as JV Company, which manufactures autos for sale in the United States. The autos sold by JV replace the autos sold by the two parents in the United States.

Suppose the formation of JV Company entails new production efficiencies that result in cost reductions. Let JV's new cost schedule, $MC_1 = ATC_1$, be located at \$7,000. As a monopoly, JV maximizes profit by equating

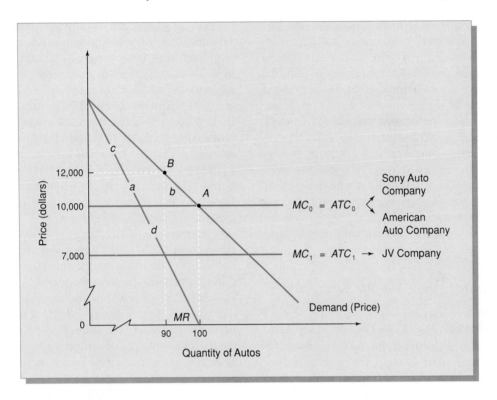

F I G U R E 10. 3 *Welfare effects of an international joint venture.* An international joint venture can yield a welfare-decreasing market-power effect and a welfare-increasing cost-reduction effect. The source of the cost-reduction effect may be lower resource prices or improvements in technology/productivity. The joint venture leads to improvements in national welfare if its cost-reduction effect is due to improvements in technology/productivity and if it more than offsets the market-power effect.

marginal revenue with marginal cost. Market equilibrium exists at point *B*, where 90 autos are sold at a price of $12,000 per unit. The price increase leads to a reduction in consumer surplus equal to area *a* + *b*. Of this amount, area *a* is transferred to JV as producer surplus. Area *b* represents the loss of consumer surplus *not* transferred to JV and becomes a deadweight welfare loss for the U.S. economy (the consumption effect). Against this deadweight welfare loss lies the efficiency effect of JV Company: a decrease in unit costs from $10,000 to $7,000 per auto. JV can produce its profit-max-

imizing output, 90 autos, at a cost reduction equal to area *d* as compared with the costs that would exist if the parent companies produced the same output. Area *d* thus represents additional producer surplus, which is a welfare gain for the U.S. economy. Our analysis concludes that, for the United States, the formation of JV Company is desirable if area *d* exceeds area *b*.

It has been assumed that JV Company achieves cost reductions that are unavailable to either parent as a stand-alone company. Whether the cost reductions benefit the overall U.S. economy depends on their *source*. If they result from *productivity improvements* (for example, new work rules leading to higher output per worker), a welfare gain exists for the economy because fewer resources are required to produce a given number of autos and the excess can be shifted to other industries. However, the cost reductions stemming from JV Company's formation may be *monetary* in nature. Being a newly formed company, JV may be able to negotiate wage concessions from domestic workers that could not be achieved by American Auto Company. Such a cost reduction represents a transfer of dollars from domestic workers to JV profits and does not constitute an overall welfare gain for the economy.

New United Motor Manufacturing, Inc.

A widely publicized international joint venture was announced in 1983 by General Motors and Toyota Motor Corporation, the first- and third-largest auto companies in the world, respectively. The Federal Trade Commission allowed the two competitors to form a new separate corporation, called **New United Motor Manufacturing, Inc.** (NUMMI), for a 12-year period. General Motors and Toyota each own half of NUMMI.

Located at a formerly idle GM plant in Fremont, California, NUMMI manufactures approximately 250,000 subcompacts a year. NUMMI's first subcompact, the Nova, copied the design of the Toyota Corolla and did not represent a new car developed for the U.S. market. Novas were sold to GM for distribution through its dealers. GM contributed the plant, the land, the dealer network, and $20 million. Toyota, contributing $150 million and a subcompact, was largely responsible for plant production and management. The subcompact's advanced components, such as its engine and transmission, were manufactured in Japan; the Fremont plant performed stamping and assembling. As years passed, NUMMI dropped the Nova from its product line and added the Geoprism and the Toyota Corolla.

GM's announced goal was to learn the Japanese art of management and small-car manufacturing by getting a firsthand look at how Toyota organizes its operations, motivates its workers, and locates machines and materials. GM maintained that if it learned how to build lower-cost cars, it would transfer those cost-saving methods to its other plants. It was estimated that GM would save as much as $1,000 per car because it did not have to design a new subcompact from the ground up. Use of Japanese-made components was estimated to save an additional $700 per car.

Another potential area of cost savings stems from NUMMI's simpler and more flexible job classifications, work rules, and procedures, which are different from those common at other U.S. auto plants and are intended to increase labor productivity. NUMMI uses only four job classifications; some GM plants have more than 90 classifications. On Fremont assembly lines, employees work in teams of eight to ten, with each person performing up to 15 separate jobs. NUMMI management thus has greater flexibility in assigning jobs, and fewer assemblers and quality inspectors are needed. In return for these concessions from the UAW, NUMMI agreed to pay Fremont workers prevailing wage and benefit rates for new hires in the industry. NUMMI also agreed that Fremont workers would not lose jobs because of automation.

For Toyota, NUMMI represented a relatively low-cost opportunity to test the transferability of its production techniques overseas. It provided Toyota a quick way to learn how to operate in the United States with a partner who knew the U.S. auto market. Toyota also viewed a manufacturing foothold in the United States as insurance against rising protectionism.

Critics of NUMMI maintained that the joint venture would result in overall job losses for U.S. workers. At the Fremont plant, up to 3,000 new jobs would be generated. However, only 50 percent of NUMMI's Nova was sourced in the United States, with the remainder representing Japanese production. Because the NUMMI vehicle was to replace GM's Chevette, which had almost 100-percent U.S. content, the result would be an overall decrease in jobs for U.S. workers. Moreover, most of the sophisticated systems and components for the NUMMI vehicle would be produced in Japan, providing highly skilled jobs for the Japanese. U.S. workers would merely put the final pieces together, working in low-skilled jobs that would become increasingly automated in the years ahead.

Operating in a refurbished GM plant, NUMMI has used equipment rather conventional by international standards. The level of automation in the NUMMI plant has been below that of GM's most recently retooled high-technology plants. Moreover, NUMMI's work force has consisted mainly of the same UAW employees who were on the payroll when the plant was under GM management.

The improvement in the Fremont plant's efficiency under NUMMI's management has been remarkable. Table 10.8 compares NUMMI's productivity with typical high-technology and low-technology GM plants and NUMMI's cousin Toyota plant in Japan (which produced an identical product) as of 1987. Compared to GM's older low-technology plants, NUMMI eliminated more than 40 percent of the labor hours involved in the manufacturing of an automobile. Of greater significance is that NUMMI used 30-percent less labor and vastly cheaper process machinery than GM's state-of-the-art manufacturing plants.

MULTINATIONAL CORPORATIONS AS A SOURCE OF CONFLICT

The advocates of MNCs often point out the benefits these corporations can provide for the nations they affect, including both the source country where the parent organization is located and the host country where subsidiary firms are established. Benefits allegedly exist in

TABLE 10. 8 / *Labor Productivity Comparisons of Three Auto Companies: NUMMI, General Motors, Toyota of Japan*

Auto Company/ year	Labor Hours per Vehicle	Percentage Difference from NUMMI
NUMMI (1986)	19.0	—
General Motors (1987)		
Low-technology plant	33.4	76
High-technology plant	27.0	42
Toyota Takaoka (1986)	15.7	-17

SOURCE: J. P. Womack, "Multinational Joint Ventures in Motor Vehicles," in D. Mowery, *International Collaborative Ventures in U.S. Manufacturing* (Cambridge, Mass.: Ballinger, 1988), chap. 9.

the forms of additional levels of investment and capital, creation of new jobs, and development of technologies and production processes. But critics contend that MNCs often create trade restraints, conflict with national economic and political objectives, and have adverse effects on a nation's balance of payments. The differences between these arguments perhaps explain why some nations frown on direct investment while others welcome it. This section examines some of the more controversial issues involving the multinationals. The frame of reference is the U.S. MNC, although the same issues apply no matter where the parent organization is based.

Employment

One of the most hotly debated issues surrounding the MNC is its effects on *employment* in both the host and source countries. MNCs often contend that their direct foreign investment yields favorable benefits to the labor force of the recipient nation. Setting up a new multinational automobile manufacturing plant in Canada creates more jobs for Canadian workers. But the MNC's effect on jobs varies from business to business. One source of controversy arises when the direct investment spending of foreign-based MNCs is used to purchase already existing local businesses rather than to establish new ones. In this case, the investment spending may not result in additional production capacity; nor may it have noticeable effects on employment in the host country. Another problem arises when MNCs bring in foreign managers and other top executives to run the subsidiary in the host country. In the U.S. oil companies locating in Saudi Arabia, the Saudis are increasingly demanding that their own people be employed in higher-level positions.

As for the source country, the issues of runaway jobs and cheap foreign labor are of vital concern to home workers. Because labor unions are confined to individual countries, the multinational nature of these businesses permits them to escape much of the collective-bargaining influence of domestic unions. It is also pointed out that MNCs can seek out those countries where labor has minimal market power.

The ultimate impact that MNCs have on employment in the host and source countries seems to depend, in part, on the time scale. In the short run, the source country will likely experience an employment decline when production is shifted overseas. But other industries in the source country may find foreign sales rising over time. This is because foreign labor consumes as well as produces and tends to purchase more as employment and income increase as a result of increased investment. Perhaps the main source of controversy stems from the fact that the MNCs are involved in rapid changes in technology and in the transmission of productive enterprise to host countries. Although such efforts may promote global welfare in the long run, the potential short-run adjustment problems facing source-country labor cannot be ignored.

National Sovereignty

Another controversial issue involving the conduct of MNCs is their effect on the *economic and political policies* of the host and source governments. There is a suspicion in many nations that the presence of MNCs in a given country results in a loss of its national sovereignty. For example, MNCs may resist government attempts to redistribute national income through taxation. By using accounting techniques that shift profits overseas, an MNC may be able to evade taxes of a host country. An MNC could accomplish this by raising prices on goods from its subsidiaries in nations with modest tax rates to reduce profits on its operations in a high-tax nation where most of its business actually takes place.

The political influence of MNCs is also questioned by many, as illustrated by the case of Chile. For years, U.S. businesses had pursued direct investments in Chile, largely in copper mining. When Salvador Allende was in the process of winning the presidency, he was opposed by U.S. businesses fearing that their Chilean operations would be expropriated by the host government. International Telephone and Telegraph tried to prevent the election of Allende and attempted to promote civil disturbances that would lead to his fall from power. Another case of MNCs' meddling in host-country affairs is that of United Brands, the MNC engaged in food-product sales. In 1974, the company paid a $1.25-million bribe to the president of Honduras in return for an export-tax reduction applied to bananas. When the payoff was revealed, the president was removed from office.

There are other areas of controversy. Suppose a Canadian subsidiary of a U.S.-based MNC conducts trade with a country subject to U.S. trade embargoes. Should U.S. policymakers outlaw such activities? The Canadian subsidiary may be pressured by the parent organization to comply with U.S. foreign policy. During international crises, MNCs may move funds rapidly from one financial center to another to avoid losses (make profits) from changes in exchange rates. This conduct makes it difficult for national governments to stabilize their economies.

In a world where national economies are interdependent and factors of production are mobile, the possible loss of national sovereignty is often viewed as a necessary cost whenever direct investment results in control of foreign production facilities. Whether the welfare gains accruing from the international division of labor and specialization outweigh the potential diminution of national independence involves value judgments by policymakers and interested citizens.

Balance of Payments

The United States offers a good example of how an MNC can affect a nation's balance of payments. In brief, the *balance of payments* is an account of the value of goods and services, capital movements including direct foreign investment, and other items that flow into or out of a country. Items that make a positive contribution to a nation's payments position include exports of goods and services and capital inflows (foreign investment entering the home country), whereas the opposite flows would weaken the payments position. At first glance, we might conclude that when U.S. MNCs make direct foreign investments, it represents an outflow of capital from the United States and hence a negative factor on the U.S. payments position. Although this view may be true in the short run, it ignores the positive effects on trade flows and earnings that direct investment provides in the long run.

When a U.S. MNC sets up a subsidiary overseas, it generally purchases U.S. capital equipment and materials needed to run the subsidiary. Once in operation, the subsidiary tends to purchase additional capital equipment and other material inputs from the United States.

Both of these factors stimulate U.S. exports, strengthening its payments position.

Another long-run impact that U.S. direct foreign investment has on its balance of payments is the return inflow of income that overseas operations generate. Such income includes earnings of overseas affiliates, interest and dividends, and fees and royalties. These items generate inflows of revenues for the economy and strengthen the balance-of-payments position.

Multinational Corporation Taxation

One of the most controversial issues involving MNCs for U.S. policymakers is the taxation of income stemming from direct foreign investment. Labor unions and other groups often contend that U.S. tax laws provide a disincentive to invest at home that results from tax concessions offered by the U.S. government on direct foreign investment. These concessions include *foreign tax credits* and *tax deferrals*.

According to U.S. tax law, an MNC headquartered in the United States is permitted credits against its U.S. income-tax liabilities in an amount equal to the income taxes it pays to foreign governments. Assuming that a Canadian subsidiary earns $100,000 taxable income and that Canada's income-tax rate is 25 percent, it would pay the Canadian government $25,000. But if that income were applied to the parent organization in the United States, the tax owed to the U.S. government would be $48,000, given an income-tax rate of 48 percent. Under the tax credit system, the parent organization would pay the U.S. government only $23,000 ($48,000 - $25,000 = $23,000). The rationale of the foreign tax credit is to allow MNCs headquartered in the United States to avoid double taxation, whereby the same income would be subject to comparable taxes in two countries. The foreign tax credit is designed to prevent the combined tax rates of the foreign host and domestic source governments from exceeding the higher of the two national rates. In this example, should Canada's income tax rate be 48 percent, the parent organization would not pay any taxes in the United States on the income of its Canadian subsidiary.

Under U.S. tax laws, U.S.-based MNCs also enjoy a tax-deferral advantage. The parent organization has the option of deferring U.S. taxes paid on its foreign subsidiary income as long as that income is retained overseas rather than repatriated to the United States. This system amounts to an interest-free loan extended by the U.S. government to the parent for as long as the income is maintained abroad. Retained earnings of an overseas subsidiary can be reinvested abroad without being subject to U.S. taxes. No similar provisions apply to domestic investments. Such discriminatory tax treatment encourages foreign direct investment over domestic investment.

Transfer Pricing

Another device that MNCs utilize in their effort to decrease their overall tax burden is **transfer pricing**. Using this technique, an MNC reports most of its profits in a low-tax country, even though the profits are earned in a high-tax country. For example, if corporate profit taxes are higher in the parent country than in the host country, and if the parent firm is exporting to its subsidiary in the host country, the MNC can lower its overall tax burden by *underpricing* its exports to its host-country subsidiary, thus shifting profits from the parent to the subsidiary, as illustrated in Figure 10.4. Profits are thus "transferred" from the branch in the high-tax country to the branch in the low-tax country. Conversely, if the host-country subsidiary is exporting to the parent and the parent country has high tax levels, it would be in the interest of the subsidiary to *overprice* its exports, thus decreasing taxable profits in the parent country. The result is lower overall taxes for the MNC in question.

Both foreign governments and the U.S. government are interested in the part that transfer prices play in the realization of corporate profits. Abuses in pricing across national bor-

ders are illegal if they can be proved. According to U.S. Internal Revenue Service (IRS) regulations, corporations dealing with their own subsidiaries are required to set prices at "arms length," just as they would for unrelated customers. However, proving that the prices that one subsidiary charges another are far from market prices is very difficult.

There's no question that transfer pricing abuses can be enormous. It is estimated that foreign-based multinationals dodge more than $20 billion in U.S. taxes each year, while U.S. multinationals account for an additional $5 billion in lost U.S. taxes on profits dubiously allocated to foreign tax havens. In its biggest known tax-abuse victory, the IRS argued that Toyota Inc. of Japan had systematically overcharged its U.S. subsidiary for years on most of the automobiles, trucks, and parts sold in the United States. What would have been taxable profits from the United States were shifted back to Japan. Although Toyota denied improprieties, it agreed to a $1-billion settlement with the IRS, paid in part with tax rebates from the Japanese government.

MAQUILADORAS

The ships sail east from South Korea and Japan to the Mexican port of Guaymas. There, rolls of steel are transferred to trains and shipped to Ford Motor Company's assembly plant in Hermosillo, Sonora. Ford stamps and assembles the steel into Mercury auto bodies, puts in Japanese engines, and transports the autos to the United States. Manufacturers such as Ford not only have changed the methods by which autos are produced but also have brought industry to Mexico's north, turning cow towns like Hermosillo into manufacturing centers.

Mexico's north, once a desert buffer between the capital in Mexico City and the United States, has been the recipient of direct investment by foreign companies who have set up manufacturing facilities from the beaches

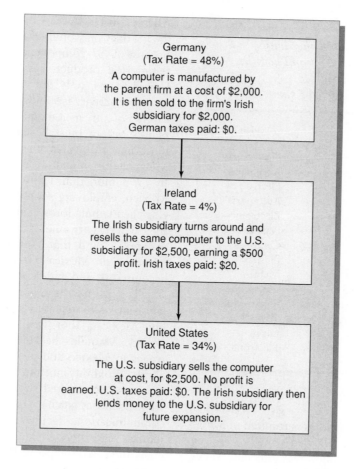

F I G U R E 10. 4 *Transfer pricing.* This hypothetical example illustrates how MNCs can shift profits to countries with low corporate tax rates and thus get away with a smaller total tax bite. The MNC is headquartered in Germany (high-tax country) and has subsidiaries in Ireland (low-tax country) and in the United States. The bottom line is that the MNC pays no taxes either in Germany or in the United States!

south of San Diego to the Gulf Coast dunes beyond Brownsville, Texas. Mexico's **maquiladoras,** or industrial parks, typically refer to an assemblage of U.S.-owned companies that combine U.S. parts and supplies and Mexican assembly to manufacture goods that are exported to the United States. The mix of maquiladora products has traditionally been dominated by electronics (such as televisions) and automobiles. The largest concentration of maquiladora plants is in the border cities, including Ciudad Juárez, Tijuana, and Mexicali. Table 10.9 provides examples of companies that have located production facilities in Mexico.

The maquiladora program was developed in response to the cancellation of the U.S. bracero program. During World War II, a

TABLE 10. 9 / *Companies with Production Facilities in Mexico: Selected Examples*

Company	Product
Unisys	Electronics
Borg Warner	Auto parts
Motorola	Electronics
Honda	Auto parts
General Instruments	Electronics
Efka Plastics	Plastics
Lasting	Ceramics
Calmar Inc.	Plastics
Carrier	Metal
Emerson Electric	Electronics
American Electric	Electronics
Mattel	Toys
Sentek	Glass
Digital Power	Electronics

shortage of U.S. farmworkers resulted in Mexican workers' being allowed to work in the United States; the policy was officially sanctioned in the 1950s. As a result, many Mexicans moved to the country's northern border so they could be hired as seasonal bracero workers in the United States. Because of political pressure from U.S. labor groups, the United States abolished the program in 1964.

The Mexican and U.S. governments devised the maquiladora scheme in 1965 to help develop both sides of the impoverished border region. The maquiladora program encourages U.S. companies to open plants in Mexico that use U.S.-made parts and Mexican assembly; today, foreigners can own 100 percent of a *maquila,* a plant in a maquiladora. Imports of finished industrial products into Mexico pay exorbitant duties; but parts and supplies for a maquila are waved through at the border and enter duty-free. In turn, the maquila's products

when exported to the United States are subject to U.S. duty only on the value added in Mexico. Because U.S. components embedded in the reimported products return duty-free to the United States, only the value of the Mexican assembly activity is subject to tariff.

To qualify as a maquila, 80 percent of the plant's output must be exported. In practice, most maquilas have not sold any output in Mexico, shipping all of it to the United States. By 1993, more than 1,300 maquilas operated in Mexico, employing some half a million workers. The maquiladoras' managers point out that their workers are among the most highly skilled in Mexico and that they have trained large numbers of Mexican technicians, engineers, accountants, and middle managers.

The maquiladoras are engaged primarily in labor-intensive assembly operations that combine Mexican labor with U.S. capital and technology. Maquilas benefit from relatively low wages in Mexico and proximity to the United States. Proximity not only reduces transportation costs, compared with more distant low-wage countries (such as Taiwan), but also eases communication, facilitates supervision, and reduces lead times for delivery. After the debt crisis and peso collapse in 1982, cheap Mexican wages triggered a maquiladora explosion; the number of maquilas doubled between 1982 and 1989.

The maquiladoras have drawn a considerable amount of capital to Mexico's northern border region, providing jobs and earning much-needed foreign exchange. But they have generated much controversy in both Mexico and the United States.

Opposition in the United States has come mainly from labor unions that maintain that maquiladora investment by U.S. companies results in "runaway jobs." Proponents of the maquiladoras counter that northern Mexico is actually competing with other countries for labor-intensive factories and that jobs "lost" to the maquilas would eventually have been lost to other low-wage countries. Without the maquilas, many small- and medium-size U.S. companies would be driven out of business by foreign low-wage competitors in South Korea, Taiwan, and elsewhere. Having their unskilled jobs performed just across the border allows these companies to maintain the jobs of their skilled workers in the United States. They also contend that when U.S. jobs migrate to the border, a large amount of employment is generated in U.S. border communities and elsewhere in the United States because border production requires large quantities of U.S. inputs. Moreover, if it were not for the maquiladoras, additional Mexicans would likely be living in the United States as illegal immigrants.

In Mexico, critics of the maquiladoras contend that they make poor models for Mexican development. They assert that the maquilas exploit Mexican workers: in 1991, U.S. employers paid Mexican workers about half of what Mexican companies paid them. Also, U.S. employers have relied on the most vulnerable and cheapest workers—young women and girls, who represent two-thirds of the maquiladora labor force. It is also maintained that a negligible fraction of the components used in the assembly of maquiladora output comes from Mexican suppliers. And the work itself is low-skilled, so workers receive minimal training. Because the maquiladoras do not transfer technology, there is little linkage between the maquiladoras and the rest of the Mexican economy, and few secondary benefits are generated. Maquiladoras tend to make Mexico more dependent on the rest of the world because important economic decisions are made outside of Mexico.

INTERNATIONAL TRADE THEORY AND MULTINATIONAL ENTERPRISE

Perhaps the main explanation of the development of MNCs lies in the strategies of corporate management. The reasons for engaging in international business can be outlined in terms of the comparative-advantage principle. Corporate managers see advantages they can exploit in the forms of access to factor inputs, new technologies and products, and managerial know-how. Organizations establish overseas subsidiaries largely because profit prospects are best enhanced by foreign production. From a trade-theory perspective, the multinational-enterprise analysis is fundamentally in agreement with the predictions of the comparative-advantage principle. Both approaches contend that a given commodity will be produced in the low-cost country. The major difference between the multinational-enterprise analysis and the conventional trade model is that the former stresses the international movement of factor inputs, whereas the latter is based on the movement of merchandise among nations.

International trade theory suggests that the aggregate welfare of both the source and host countries is enhanced when MNCs make foreign direct investments for their own benefit. The presumption is that if businesses can earn a higher return on overseas investments than on those at home, resources are transferred from lower to higher productive uses, and on balance an improvement in the world allocation of resources will occur. Thus, analysis of MNCs is essentially the same as conventional trade theory, which rests on the movement of products among nations.

Despite the basic agreement between conventional trade theory and the multinational-enterprise analysis, there are some notable differences. The conventional model presupposes that goods are exchanged between interdependent organizations on international markets at competitively determined prices. But MNCs are generally vertically integrated companies whose subsidiaries manufacture intermediate goods as well as finished goods. In an MNC, sales become *intrafirm* when goods are transferred from subsidiary to subsidiary. Although such sales are part of international trade, their value may be determined by factors other than a competitive pricing system.

TABLE 10. 10 / *U.S. Immigration,*
1820–1990
(in Thousands)

Period	Number
1820–1830	152
1831–1840	599
1841–1850	1,713
1851–1860	2,598
1861–1870	2,315
1871–1880	2,812
1881–1890	5,247
1891–1900	3,688
1901–1910	8,795
1911–1920	5,736
1921–1930	4,107
1931–1940	528
1941–1950	1,035
1951–1960	2,515
1961–1970	3,322
1971–1980	4,493
1981–1990	7,338

SOURCE: U.S. Department of Commerce, Bureau of the Census, *Statistical Abstracts of the United States* (Washington, D.C.: Government Printing Office, 1992).

INTERNATIONAL LABOR MOBILITY: MIGRATION

Historically, the United States has been a favorite target for international **migration.** Because of the vast inflow of migrants, the United States has been described as the "melting pot" of the world. Table 10.10 indicates the total number of immigrants to the United States, by decade, from 1820 to 1990. Western Europe was a major source of migrants during this era, with Germany, Italy, and the United Kingdom among the largest contributors. In recent years, large numbers of Mexicans have migrated to the United States, as well as people from Asia. Migrants have been motivated by better economic opportunities and by noneconomic factors such as politics, war, and religion.

Although international labor movements can enhance the world economy's efficiency, they are often restricted by government controls. The United States, like most countries, limits immigration. Following waves of immigration at the turn of the century, the Immigration Act of 1924 was enacted. Besides restricting the overall flow of immigrants to the United States, the act implemented a quota that limited the number of immigrants from each foreign country. Because the quotas were based on the number of U.S. citizens who had previously emigrated from those countries, the allocation system favored emigrants from northern Europe relative to southern Europe. In the late 1960s, the quota formula was modified, which led to increasing numbers of Asian immigrants to the United States.

Figure 10.5 illustrates the economics of labor migration. Suppose the world consists of two countries, the United States and Mexico, that are initially in isolation. The horizontal axes of the figure denote the total quantity of labor in the United States and Mexico, and the vertical axes depict the wages paid to labor. For each country, the demand schedule for labor is designated by the value of the marginal product (*VMP*) of labor.[2] Also assume a fixed labor supply of 7 workers in the United States, denoted by S_0, and 7 workers in Mexico, denoted by S^*_0.

The equilibrium wage in each country is determined at the point of intersection of the supply and demand schedules for labor. In the United States, the equilibrium wage is $9, and total labor income is $63; this amount is represented by the area $a + b$ under the U.S. demand schedule at point A. The remaining area under the labor demand schedule is area c, which equals $24.50; this represents the share of the nation's income accruing to owners of capital.[3] In Mexico, the equilibrium wage is $3; labor income totals $21, represented by area $a^* + b^*$; capital owners enjoy incomes equaling area $c^* + d^* + e^*$, or $24.50.

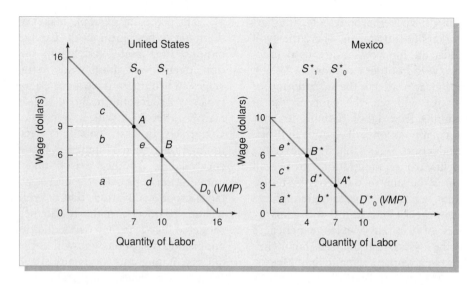

F I G U R E 10. 5 *Effects of labor migration from Mexico to the United States.* Prior to migration, the wage rate in the United States exceeds that of Mexico. Responding to the wage differential, Mexican workers immigrate to the United States; this leads to a reduction in the Mexican labor supply and an increase in the U.S. labor supply. Wage rates continue to fall in Mexico and rise in the United States until they eventually equalize. The labor migration hurts native U.S. workers but helps U.S. owners of capital; the opposite occurs in Mexico. Because migrant workers flow from uses of lower productivity to higher productivity, world output expands.

Suppose labor can move freely between Mexico and the United States and that migration is costless and occurs solely in response to wage differentials. Because U.S. wage rates are relatively high, there is an incentive for Mexican workers to migrate to the United States and compete in the U.S. labor market; this process will continue until the wage differential is eliminated. Suppose three workers migrate from Mexico to the United States. In the United States, the new labor supply schedule becomes S_1; the excess supply of labor at the $9 wage rate causes the wage rate to fall to $6. In Mexico, the labor emigration results in a new labor supply schedule at S^*_1; the excess demand for labor at wage rate $3 causes the wage rate to rise to $6. The effect of **labor mobility** is thus to equalize wage rates in the two countries.[4]

Our next job is to assess how labor migration in response to wage differentials affects the world economy's efficiency. Does *world output* expand or contract with open migration? For the United States, migration increases the labor supply from S_0 to S_1. This leads to an expansion of output; the value of the additional output is denoted by area $d + e$ ($22.50). For Mexico, the decrease in labor supply from S^*_0 to S^*_1 results in a contraction in output; the value of the lost output is represented by area $b^* + d^*$ ($13.50). The result is a net gain of $9 in world output as a result of labor migration. This is because the *VMP* of labor in the United States exceeds that of Mexico throughout the range S_0-S_1 and $S^*_0-S^*_1$. Workers are attracted to the United States by the higher wages paid. These higher wages signal to Mexican labor the higher value of worker productivity, thus attracting workers to those areas where they will be most efficient. As workers are used more productively, world output expands.

Migration also affects the *distribution of income*. As we will see, the gains in world income resulting from labor mobility are not distributed equally among all nations and factors of production. The United States as a whole benefits from immigration; its overall income gain is the sum of the losses by native U.S. workers, gains by Mexican immigrants now living in the United States, and gains by U.S. owners of capital. Mexico experiences overall income losses as a result of its labor emigration; however, workers remaining in Mexico gain relative to Mexican owners of capital. As previously suggested, the Mexican immigrants gain from their relocation to the United States.

For the United States, the gain in income as a result of immigration is denoted by area $d + e$ ($22.50) in Figure 10.5. Of this amount, Mexican immigrants capture area d ($18), while area e ($4.50) is the extra income accruing to U.S. owners of capital thanks to the availability of additional labor to use with the capital. However, immigration forces wage rates down from $9 to $6. The earnings of the native U.S. workers fall by area b ($21); this amount is transferred to U.S. owners of capital.

As for Mexico, its labor emigration results in a decrease in output equal to $b^* + d^*$ ($13.50); this represents a transfer from Mexico to the United States. The remaining workers in Mexico gain area c ($12) as a result of higher wages. However, Mexican capital owners lose because less labor is available for use with their capital.

We can conclude that the effect of labor mobility is to increase overall world income and to redistribute income from labor to capital in the United States and from capital to labor in Mexico. Migration has an impact on the distribution of income similar to an increase in exports of labor-intensive goods from Mexico to the United States.

The preceding example makes it clear why domestic labor groups in capital-abundant nations often prefer restrictions on immigration; open immigration tends to reduce their wages. When migrant workers are unskilled, as typically occurs, the negative effect on wages mainly affects unskilled domestic workers. Conversely, domestic manufacturers will tend to favor unrestricted immigration as a source of cheap labor. Another reason underlying the immigration controversy concerns public assistance programs. Nations that provide generous welfare payments to the economically disadvantaged may fear they will induce an influx of nonproductive people who will not produce, as did the immigrants of Figure 10.5, but will enjoy welfare benefits at the expense of domestic residents and working immigrants. Developing nations have sometimes feared open immigration policies because they can result in a **brain drain**—the emigration of highly educated and skilled people from developing nations to industrial nations, thus limiting the growth potential of the developing nations. The brain drain has been encouraged by national immigration laws, as in the United States and other industrial nations, that permit the immigration of skilled persons while restricting that of unskilled workers.

In the previous labor-migration example, we implicitly assumed that the Mexican workers' migration decision was more or less permanent. In practice, much labor migration is temporary, especially in the European Community. That is, a country such as France will allow the immigration of foreign workers on a temporary basis when needed; these workers are known as **guest workers**. During periods of business recession, France will refuse to issue work permits when foreign workers are no longer needed. Such a practice tends to insulate the French economy from labor shortages during business expansions and labor surpluses during business recessions. However, the labor adjustment problem is shifted to the labor-emigrating countries.

There is also the problem of illegal migration. In the United States, this has become a political "hot potato" in which millions of illegal immigrants find employment in the so-called underground economy at below-minimum wages. Some 3 to 15 million illegal immigrants are estimated to be in the United States. Many of these people have come from Mexico. For the United States, and especially the southwestern states, immigration of Mexican workers has provided a cheap supply of agricultural and less skilled workers. For Mexico, it has been a major source of foreign exchange and a safety cushion against domestic unemployment. Illegal immigration also affects the distribution of income for U.S. natives because it tends to reduce the income of low-skilled U.S. workers. It is no wonder that Cesar Chavez of the United Farm Workers has been critical of letting in large numbers of new Mexican farmworkers.

IMMIGRATION AND THE U.S. LABOR MARKET

By the 1970s and 1980s, immigration and trade had become increasingly significant for the U.S. labor market. The number of legal and illegal immigrants to the United States grew, modifying the size and composition of the work force and increasing the immigrant share of labor in "gateway" cities such as Los Angeles, New York, and Miami. The national origins of immigrants to the United States changed from primarily European to Mexican, Latin American, and Asian.

For native workers whose skills compete with those of new immigrants, immigration can adversely affect wages and employment, making their economic well-being a central issue in immigration policy. If certain segments of the native labor force, such as the low-wage workers for whom immigrants may be good substitutes, undergo sizable reductions in employment and earning opportunities, then the case

for immigration controls to aid these workers is strengthened. Conversely, if the labor market can easily absorb additional immigrants without serious distributional impacts on native workers, allowing increasing numbers of immigrants seems more reasonable.

Critics of U.S. liberal trade and immigration policies maintain they have depressed U.S. wages. In 1991, the National Bureau of Economic Research (NBER) analyzed this issue by considering the widening gap in earnings between lesser-educated and higher-educated U.S. workers during the 1980s.[5] This was a period in which college graduates' wages increased in inflationary-adjusted terms while inflationary-adjusted earnings of lesser-educated workers either failed to rise or actually decreased.

According to the NBER study, both trade and immigration augmented the effective U.S. supply of workers during the 1980s. The large U.S. trade deficits in manufacturers increased the "implicit" labor supply by some 6 percent annually during this period; the immigration flow increased the share of the U.S. work force that was foreign-born from 6.9 percent in 1980 to 9.3 percent in 1988. Moreover, trade and immigration augmented the supply of less-skilled workers more than they augmented the supply of more-skilled workers. This was because the largest portion of the U.S. trade deficit was concentrated in industries that intensively employed high-school dropouts, while the wave of new immigrants during the 1980s included many poorly educated workers. Many of these immigrants were non-English-speaking, sometimes barely literate in their own native languages, less able and less willing to adapt to American culture, and more of a burden on social services.

The NBER estimated that by 1988, the combination of the trade deficit and continued high immigration had increased the effective supply of high-school dropouts by approximately 30 percent. These two factors accounted for some 30 to 50 percent of the 10 percentage-point decline in dropout wages relative to those of high-school and college graduates during the 1980–1988 period. In short, by increasing the effective supply of less-educated workers in the 1980s, imports and increased immigration depressed wages and thus widened the earnings gap between less-skilled and more-skilled Americans. By the 1990s, many Americans were expressing concerns that immigrants harmed the country by taking away jobs, driving down wages, and using too many government services.

The infusion of foreigners into the United States during the 1980s–1990s, however, did not include only people with minimal skills and minimal education. Enjoying the benefits of a foreign "brain drain," the United States reaped a bonanza of highly educated newcomers who enhanced the competitiveness of its companies.

America's high-tech industries, from biotechnology to semiconductors, increasingly depended on immigrant scientists, engineers, and entrepreneurs to remain competitive; in Silicon Valley, the jewel of U.S. high-tech centers, much of the work force is foreign-born. With their bilingual skills, family ties, and knowledge of how things get done overseas, immigrants also contributed to the export of Made-in-USA goods and services. Moreover, they helped revitalize America by establishing new businesses and generating jobs, profits, and taxes to pay for social services. The infusion of new people into the United States thus helped improve the globally competitive top half of its economy. These benefits must be weighed against the economic disruptions caused by the infusion of less-educated and less capable people into the nation.

SUMMARY

1. Today the world economy is characterized by the international movement of factor inputs. The multinational corporation plays a central part in this process.

2. There is no single agreed-on definition of what constitutes an MNC. Some of the most identifiable characteristics of multinationals are the following: (a) Stock ownership and management are multinational in character. (b) Corporate headquarters are far removed from where a particular activity occurs. (c) Foreign sales represent a high proportion of total sales.

3. MNCs have diversified their operations along vertical, horizontal, and conglomerate lines.

4. Among the major factors that influence decisions to undertake direct foreign investment are (a) market demand, (b) trade restrictions, (c) investment regulations, and (d) labor productivity and costs.

5. In planning to set up overseas operations, a business must decide whether to construct (purchase) plants abroad or extend licenses to foreign businesses to produce its goods.

6. In recent years, companies have increasingly linked up with former rivals in a vast array of joint ventures. International joint ventures can yield welfare-increasing effects as well as market-power effects.

7. Some of the more controversial issues involving MNCs are (a) employment, (b) national sovereignty, (c) balance of payments, and (d) taxation.

8. The theory of multinational enterprise essentially agrees with the predictions of the comparative-advantage principle.

9. There are major differences between the theory of multinational enterprise and conventional trade theory. The conventional model assumes that commodities are traded between independent, competitive businesses. However, MNCs are often vertically integrated businesses with substantial intrafirm sales. Also, MNCs may use transfer pricing to maximize overall company profits instead of the profits of any single subsidiary.

10. Mexico's maquiladoras are assemblages of foreign-owned companies that use foreign parts and Mexican assembly to produce goods that are exported to the United States. Maquiladora products have traditionally emphasized electronics and automobiles.

11. International labor migration occurs for economic and noneconomic reasons. Migration increases output and decreases wages in the country of immigration while decreasing output and increasing wages in the country of emigration. For the world as a whole, migration leads to net increases in output.

STUDY QUESTIONS

1. Multinational corporations may diversify their operations along vertical, horizontal, and conglomerate lines within the host and source countries. Distinguish among these diversification approaches.

2. What are the major foreign industries in which U.S. businesses have chosen to place direct investments? What are the major industries in the United States in which foreigners place direct investments?

3. Why is it that the rate of return on U.S. direct investments in the developing nations often exceeds the rate of return on its investments in industrial nations?

4. What are the most important motives behind a corporation's decision to undertake direct foreign investment?

5. What is meant by the term *multinational corporation?*

6. Under what conditions would a business wish to enter foreign markets by extending licenses or franchises to local businesses to produce its goods?

7. What are the major issues involving multinational corporations as a source of conflict for source and host countries?

8. Is the theory of multinational enterprise essentially consistent or inconsistent with the traditional model of comparative advantage?

9. What are some examples of welfare gains and welfare losses that can result from the formation of international joint ventures among competing businesses?

10. What effects does labor migration have on the country of immigration? The country of emigration? The world as a whole?

11. Table 10.11 illustrates the revenue conditions facing ABC, Inc., and XYZ, Inc., which operate as competitors in the U.S. calculator market. Each firm realizes constant long-run costs ($MC = AC$) of $4 per unit. On graph paper, plot the corporations' demand, marginal revenue, and $MC = AC$ schedules. On the basis of this information, answer the following questions.

    a. With ABC and XYZ behaving as competitors, the equilibrium price is $_____ and output, is _____. At the equilibrium price, U.S. households attain $_____ of consumer surplus, while company profits total $_____.

    b. Suppose the two organizations jointly form a new one, JV, Inc., whose calculators replace the output sold by the parent com-

TABLE 10. 11 / Price and Marginal Revenue: Calculators

Quantity	Price ($)	Marginal Revenue ($)
0	9	—
1	8	8
2	7	6
3	6	4
4	5	2
5	4	0
6	3	-2
7	2	-4

panies in the U.S. market. Assuming that JV operates as a monopoly and that its costs ($MC = AC$) equal $4 per unit, the company's output would be _____ at a price of $_____, and total profit would be $_____. Compared to the market equilibrium position achieved by ABC and XYZ as competitors, JV as a monopoly leads to a deadweight loss of consumer surplus equal to $_____.

    c. Assume now that the formation of JV yields technological advances that result in a per-unit cost of only $2; sketch the new $MC = AC$ schedule in the figure. Realizing that JV results in a deadweight loss of consumer surplus, as described in *b*, the net effect of the formation of JV on U.S. welfare is a gain/loss of $_____. If JV's cost reduction was due to wage concessions of JV's U.S. employees, the net welfare gain/loss for the United States would equal $_____. If JV's cost reductions resulted from changes in work rules leading to higher worker productivity, the net welfare gain/loss for the United States would equal $_____.

12. Table 10.12 illustrates the hypothetical demand and supply schedules of labor in the United States. Assume that labor and capital are the only two factors of production. On graph paper, plot these schedules.

    a. Without immigration, suppose the labor force in the United States is denoted by schedule S_0. The equilibrium wage rate is

TABLE 10. 12   /   *Demand and Supply*
of Labor

Wage ($)	Quantity Demanded	Quantity Supplied$_0$	Quantity Supplied$_1$
8	0	2	4
6	2	2	4
4	4	2	4
2	6	2	4
0	8	2	4

$\_\_\_$; payments to native U.S. workers total $\$\_\_\_$, while payments to U.S. capital owners equal $\$\_\_\_$.

b. Suppose immigration from Hong Kong results in an overall increase in the U.S. labor force to S_1. Wages would rise/fall to $\$\_\_\_$, payments to native U.S. workers would total $\$\_\_\_$, and payments to Hong Kong immigrants would total $\$\_\_\_$. U.S. owners of capital would receive payments of $\$\_\_\_$.

c. Which U.S. factor of production would gain from expanded immigration? $\_\_\_$ Which U.S. factor of production would likely resist policies permitting Hong Kong workers to freely migrate to the United States? $\_\_\_$

Part Two

International Monetary Relations

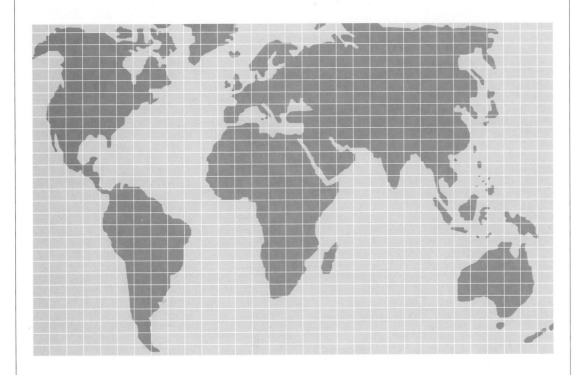

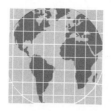

The Balance of Payments

Previous chapters have emphasized international trade flows and commercial policies. In this chapter, we examine the monetary aspects of international trade by considering the nature and significance of a nation's balance of payments.

THE BALANCE OF PAYMENTS

Over the course of a year, the residents of one country engage in a variety of transactions with residents abroad. These include payments for goods and services, loans, investments, and gifts. To analyze the economic importance of these transactions, it is necessary to classify and aggregate them into a summary statement. The **balance of payments** is a record of the economic transactions between the residents of one coun-

try and the rest of the world. Because the balance of payments is calculated over the course of a one-year period (or one quarter), it is interpreted as a *flow* concept.

An *international transaction* refers to the exchange of goods, services, and assets between residents of one country and those abroad. But what is meant by the term *resident*? Residents include businesses, individuals, and government agencies that make the country in question their legal domicile. Although a corporation is considered to be a resident of the country in which it is incorporated, its overseas branch or subsidiary is not. Military personnel, government diplomats, tourists, and workers who emigrate temporarily are considered residents of the country in which they hold citizenship.

DOUBLE-ENTRY ACCOUNTING

The arrangement of international transactions into a balance-of-payments account requires that each transaction be entered as a credit or a debit. A **credit transaction** is one that results in a *receipt* of a payment from foreigners. A **debit transaction** is one that leads to a *payment* to foreigners. This distinction is clarified when we assume that transactions take place between U.S. residents and foreigners and that all payments are financed in dollars.

From the U.S. perspective, what types of transactions are credits, leading to the receipt of dollars from foreigners?

- Merchandise exports
- Transportation and travel receipts
- Income received from investments abroad
- Gifts received from foreign residents
- Aid received from foreign governments
- Investments in the United States by overseas residents

Conversely, the following transactions are debits from the U.S. viewpoint because they involve payments to foreigners:

- Merchandise imports
- Transportation and travel expenditures
- Income paid on investments of foreigners
- Gifts to foreign residents
- Aid given by the U.S. government
- Overseas investment by U.S. residents

Although we speak in terms of credit transactions and debit transactions, every international transaction involves an exchange of assets and so has both a credit and a debit side. Each credit entry is balanced by a debit entry, and vice versa. The recording of any international transaction, therefore, leads to two offsetting entries. This means that the balance-of-payments accounts utilize a double-entry bookkeeping system.

Even though the entire balance of payments by definition must numerically balance, it does *not* necessarily hold that any single subaccount or subaccounts of the statement must balance. For instance, merchandise exports may or may not be in balance with merchandise imports. **Double-entry accounting** assumes only that the total of all the entries on the left-hand side of the statement matches the total of the entries on the right-hand side. The following two examples illustrate the double-entry technique.

1. IBM sells $25 million worth of computers to a German importer. Payment is made by a bill of exchange, which increases the balances of New York banks on their Bonn correspondents. Because the export involves a transfer of U.S. assets abroad for which payment is to be received, it is entered in the U.S. balance of payments as a credit transaction. IBM's receipt of payment held in the German bank is classified a short-term capital movement because the financial claims of the United States against the German bank have increased. The entries on the U.S. balance of payments would appear as follows:

	Credits (+)	Debits (-)
Merchandise exports	$25 million	
Short-term capital movement		$25 million

2. A U.S. resident who owns bonds issued by a Japanese company receives interest payments of $10,000. With payment, the balances owned by New York banks at their Tokyo affiliate are increased. The impact of this transaction on the U.S. balance of payments would be as follows:

	Credits (+)	Debits (-)
Service exports	$10,000	
Short-term capital movement		$10,000

In short, double-entry accouting in balance-of-payments analysis results in the equality of total debits and credits.

BALANCE-OF-PAYMENTS STRUCTURE

Besides classifying a country's international transactions according to the direction of payment involved, the balance of payments identifies transactions along functional lines. Balance-of-payments transactions are grouped into two categories: the current account and the capital account.

Current Account

The **current account** of the balance of payments refers to the overall accounting of the monetary value of international flows associated with transactions in goods, services, and unilateral transfers.

The goods and services component of the current account shows the monetary value of all of the goods and services a nation exports or imports. It is not difficult to identify exports and imports of *merchandise* because these transactions involve physical goods that cross a country's boundaries. The dollar value of exports is recorded as a plus (credit), and the dollar value of imports is recorded as a minus (debit). Merchandise trade normally represents the major component of the **goods and services account**.

As for exports and imports of *services,* a variety of items are covered here. Should U.S. ships carry foreign products or should foreign tourists spend money at U.S. restaurants and motels, valuable services are being provided by U.S. residents, who must be compensated. Such services are considered exports and are recorded as credit items on the goods and services account. Conversely, when foreign ships carry U.S. products or when U.S. tourists spend money at hotels and restaurants abroad, then foreign residents are providing services that require compensation. Because U.S. residents are in effect importing these services, the services are recorded as debit items. Insurance and banking services are explained in the same way.

Perhaps somewhat surprisingly, dividends and interest from investments are thought of as service exports and imports. The value to U.S. residents of investment income earned on foreign government securities or stock in foreign corporations reflects the export of the services of U.S. capital. In return for the value of the services that U.S. capital invested abroad gives foreign residents, the U.S. investors expect payment. The value of this service rendered is taken to be a credit item on the U.S. goods and services account. In like manner, the amount of investment income paid by U.S. residents to foreigners represents the value of the services rendered by foreign capital in the United States. This results in a debit entry in the U.S. goods and services account.

Just what does a surplus or deficit balance appearing on the U.S. goods and services account indicate? Should the goods and services account show a surplus, the United States has transferred more resources (goods and services) to foreigners than it has received from them over the period of one year. Besides measuring the value of the *net transfer of resources,* the goods and services balance also furnishes information about the status of a nation's gross domestic product (GDP). This is because the balance on the goods and services account is defined essentially the same way as the *net export of goods and services,* which constitutes part of a nation's GDP.

For a nation's GDP, the balance on the goods and services account can be interpreted as follows. A positive balance on the account indicates an excess of exports over imports, and this difference must be added to the GDP. When the account is in deficit, the excess of imports over exports must be subtracted from the GDP. Should a nation's exports of goods and services

International Payments Process

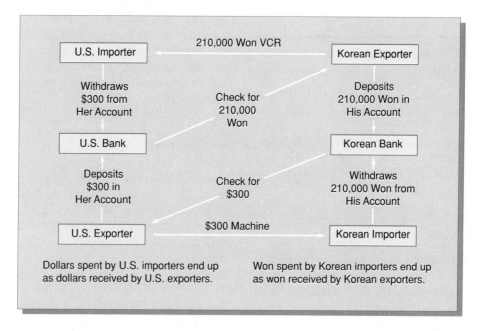

Dollars spent by U.S. importers end up as dollars received by U.S. exporters.

Won spent by Korean importers end up as won received by Korean exporters.

When residents in different countries contemplate selling or buying products, they must consider how payments will occur. Assume that you, as a resident of the United States, buy a VCR directly from a producer in South Korea. How, when, and where will the South Korean producer obtain his won so that he can spend the money in South Korea?

Initially, you would write a check for $300, which your U.S. bank would convert to 210,000 won (assuming an exchange rate of 700 won per dollar). When the South Korean producer receives your payment in won, he deposits the funds in his bank. The bank in South Korea thus holds a check from a U.S. bank that promises to pay a stipulated amount of won.

Assume that at the same time you paid for your VCR, a buyer in South Korea paid a U.S. producer $300 for machinery. The flowchart denotes the path of both transactions.

When trade is in balance, money of different countries does not actually change hands across the oceans. In this example, the value of South Korea's exports to the United States equals the value of South Korea's imports from the United States; the won that South Korean importers use to purchase dollars to pay for U.S. goods are equal to the won that South Korean exporters receive in payment for the products they ship to the United States. The dollars that would flow, in effect, from U.S. importers to U.S. exporters follows a similar equality.

In theory, importers in a country pay the exporters in that same country in the national currency. In reality, however, importers and exporters in a given country do not deal directly with one another; to facilitate payments, banks carry out these transactions.

equal its imports, the account would have a net imbalance of zero and would not affect the status of the GDP. Therefore, depending on the relative value of exports and imports, the balance on the goods and services account contributes to the level of a nation's national product.

Unilateral transfers refer to transactions that are *one-sided*, reflecting the movement of goods and services in one direction without corresponding payments in the other direction. These one-way transactions represent gifts and transfer payments between the United States and the rest of the world. *Private transfer payments* refer to gifts made by individuals and nongovernment institutions to foreigners. These might include a remittance from an immigrant living in the United States to relatives back home or a contribution by a U.S. resident to a relief fund for underdeveloped nations. *Government transfers* refer to gifts or grants made by one government to foreign residents or foreign governments. The U.S. government makes transfers in the form of money and capital goods to underdeveloped nations, military aid to foreign governments, and remittances such as retirement pensions to foreign workers who have moved back home. In some cases, U.S. government transfers represent payments associated with foreign assistance programs that can be used by foreign governments to finance trade with the United States. It should be noted that many U.S. transfer (foreign aid) programs are tied to the purchase of U.S. exports (such as military equipment or farm exports) and thus represent a subsidy to U.S. exporters.

Capital Account

Capital transactions in the balance of payments include all international purchases or sales of assets. The term *assets* is broadly defined to include items such as titles to real estate, corporation stocks and bonds, government securities, and ordinary commercial bank deposits. The

capital account includes both private-sector and official (central bank) transactions. The following are examples of private-sector capital transactions:

- *Direct investment*. Direct investment occurs when residents of one country acquire a controlling interest (stock ownership of 10 percent or more) in a business enterprise in another country.
- *Securities*. Securities are private-sector purchases of short- and long-term debt securities such as Treasury bills, Treasury notes, Treasury bonds, and securities of private enterprises.
- *Bank claims and liabilities*. Bank claims consist of loans, overseas deposits, acceptances, foreign commercial paper, claims on affiliated banks abroad, and foreign government obligations. Bank liabilities include demand deposits and NOW (negotiable order of withdrawl) accounts, passbook savings deposits, certificates of deposit, and liabilities to affiliated banks abroad.

Capital transactions are recorded in the balance-of-payments statement by applying a plus sign (credit) to capital inflows and a minus sign (debit) to capital outflows. For the United States, a *capital inflow* might occur under the following circumstances: (1) U.S. liabilities to foreigners rise (for example, a French resident purchases securities of IBM); (2) U.S. claims on foreigners decrease (Citibank receives repayment for a loan it made to a Mexican enterprise); (3) foreign-held assets in the United States rise (Toyota builds an auto-assembly plant in the United States); (4) U.S. assets overseas decrease (Coca-Cola sells one of its Japanese bottling plants to a Japanese buyer). A *capital outflow* would imply the opposite.

The following rule may be helpful in appreciating the fundamental difference between credit and debit transactions that make up the capital account. Any transaction that leads to

TABLE 11. 1 / *U.S. Reserve Assets, February 1993*

Type	Amount (in billions of dollars)
Gold stock*	11.1
Convertible foreign currencies	41.1
Special drawing rights	8.7
Reserve positions in the International Monetary Fund	12.0
Total	72.9

* Gold is valued at $42.22 per fine troy ounce.

SOURCE: *Federal Reserve Bulletin*, May 1993, p. A-54.

the home country's receiving payments from foreigners can be regarded as a credit. A capital inflow can be likened to the *export* of goods and services. Conversely, any transaction that leads to foreigners' receiving payment from the home country is considered a debit. A capital outflow is similar in effect to the *import* of goods and services.

Besides including private-sector transactions, the capital account includes **official settlements transactions** of the home country's central bank. Official settlements transactions refer to the movement of financial assets among official holders (for example, the U.S. Federal Reserve and the Bank of England). These financial assets fall into two categories: official reserve assets (U.S. government assets abroad) and liabilities to foreign official agencies (foreign official assets in the United States).

Table 11.1 summarizes the **official reserve assets** position of the United States as of 1993. One such asset is the stock of gold reserves held by the U.S. government. Next are convertible currencies, such as the German mark, that are readily acceptable as payment for international

transactions and can be easily exchanged for one another. Another reserve asset is the special drawing right (SDR), described in Chapter 18. Last is the reserve position that the United States maintains in the International Monetary Fund, also described in Chapter 18. Central banks often buy or sell international reserve assets in private-sector markets to affect their currencies' exchange rates, as will be discussed in a later chapter.

Official settlements transactions also include liabilities to foreign official holders. These liabilities refer to foreign official holdings with U.S. commercial banks and official holdings of U.S. Treasury securities. Foreign governments often wish to hold such assets because of the interest earnings they provide. Table 11.2 illustrates the U.S. liabilities to foreign official holders as of 1993.

Financing the Current Account

The current account and the capital account are not unrelated; they are essentially reflections of one another. Because the balance of payments is a double-entry accounting system, total debits will always equal total credits. It follows that if the current account registers a deficit (debits outweigh credits), the capital account must register a surplus, or net capital inflow (credits outweigh debits). Conversely, if the current account registers a surplus, the capital account must register a deficit, or net capital outflow.

To better understand this notion, assume that in a particular year your spending is greater than your income. How will you finance your "deficit"? The answer is by borrowing or by selling some of your assets. You might liquidate some real assets (for example, sell your personal computer) or perhaps some financial assets (sell a U.S. government security that you own). In like manner, when a nation experiences a current account deficit, its expenditures for foreign goods and services are greater than the income received from the international sales of its own goods and services, after making

T A B L E   11. 2 / Selected U.S. Liabilities to Foreign Official Institutions, February 1993

Liabilities	Amount (in billions of dollars)
BY TYPE	
Liabilities reported by U.S. banks*	63.6
U.S. Treasury bills and certificates	111.5
U.S. Treasury bonds and notes	207.6
Other U.S. securities	28.9
Total	411.6
BY AREA	
Western Europe	196.1
Canada	8.3
Latin America/Caribbean	41.4
Asia	156.2
Africa	3.7
Other	5.9
Total	411.6

* Includes demand deposits, time deposits, bank acceptances, commercial paper, negotiable time certificates of deposit, and borrowings under repurchase agreements.

SOURCE: *Federal Reserve Bulletin,* May 1993, p. A-57.

allowances for gifts to and from foreigners. The nation must somehow finance its current account deficit. But how? The answer lies in selling assets and borrowing. In other words, a nation's current account deficit (debits outweigh credits) is financed essentially by a net inflow of capital (credits outweigh debits) in its capital account.

The current account balance is thus synonymous with **net foreign investment** in national income accounting. A *current account surplus* means an excess of exports over imports of goods, services, and unilateral transfers. This permits a net receipt of financial claims for home-nation residents. These funds can be used by the home nation to build up its financial assets or to reduce its liabilities to the rest of the world, improving its net foreign investment position (its net worth vis-à-vis the rest of the world). Conversely, a *current account deficit* implies an excess of imports over exports of goods, services, and unilateral transfers. This leads to an increase in net foreign claims upon the home nation. The home nation becomes a net demander of funds from abroad, the demand being met through borrowing from other nations or liquidating foreign assets. The result is a worsening of the home nation's net foreign investment position.

Statistical Discrepancy: Errors and Omissions

The data-collection process that underlies the published balance-of-payments figures is far from perfect. The cost of collecting balance-of-payments statistics is high, and a perfectly accurate collection system would be prohibitively costly. Government statisticians thus base their figures partly on information collected and partly on estimates. Probably the most reliable information consists in merchandise trade data, which are collected mainly from customs records. Capital account information is derived from reports by financial institutions indicating changes in their liabilities and claims to foreigners; these data are not matched with specific current account transactions. Because statisticians do not have a system whereby they can simultaneously record the credit side and debit side of each transaction, such information for any particular transaction tends to come from different sources. Large numbers of transactions fail to get recorded.

When statisticians sum the credits and debits, it is not surprising when the two totals do not match. Because total debits must equal total credits in principle, statisticians insert a *residual* to make them equal. This correcting entry is known as **statistical discrepancy,** or errors and omissions. In the balance-of-payments statement, statistical discrepancy is treated as part of the capital account because short-term capital transactions are generally the most frequent source of error.

THE U.S. BALANCE OF PAYMENTS

For the United States, the method the U.S. Department of Commerce uses in presenting balance-of-payments statistics is shown in Table 11.3. This format groups specific transactions together along functional lines to provide analysts with information about the impact of international transactions on the domestic economy. The *partial balances* published on a regular basis include the merchandise trade balance, the balance on goods and services, the current account balance, and information about capital account transactions.

The **merchandise trade balance,** commonly referred to as the **trade balance** by the news media, is derived by computing the net exports (imports) in the merchandise accounts. Owing to its narrow focus on traded goods, the merchandise trade balance offers limited policy insight. The popularity of the merchandise trade balance is largely due to its availability on a monthly basis. Merchandise trade data can be rapidly gathered and reported, whereas measuring trade in services requires time-consuming questionnaires.

As seen in Table 11.3, the United States had a merchandise trade deficit of $96.3 billion in 1992, resulting from the difference between U.S. merchandise exports ($439.3 billion) and U.S. merchandise imports ($535.6 billion). The United States was thus a net importer of merchandise. Table 11.4 shows that the United States has consistently faced merchandise trade deficits throughout the 1970s–1990s. This situation contrasts with the 1950s–1960s, when merchandise trade surpluses were common for the United States.

Trade deficits generally are not popular with domestic residents and policymakers because they tend to exert adverse consequences on the home nation's terms of trade and employment levels, as well as on the stability of the international money markets. For the United States, economists' concerns over persistent trade deficits have often focused on their possible effects on the terms at which the United States trades with other nations. With a trade deficit, the value of the dollar may fall in international currency markets as dollar outpayments exceed dollar inpayments. Foreign currencies would become more expensive in terms of dollars, so that imports would become more costly to U.S. residents. A trade deficit that induces a decrease in the dollar's international value imposes a real cost on U.S. residents in the form of higher import costs.

Another potentially harmful consequence of a trade deficit is its impact on local employment levels. A worsening trade balance may injure domestic labor, not only by the number of jobs lost to foreign workers who produce our imports but also by the employment losses due to deteriorating export sales. It is no wonder

T A B L E   11. 3   /   U.S. Balance of Payments, 1992

Item	Amount* (in billions of dollars)
CURRENT ACCOUNT	-62.4
Merchandise trade	
Exports	439.3
Imports	-535.6
Net	-96.3
Services	
Investment income, net	10.1
Military transactions, net	-2.5
Other services, net	57.6
All services, net	65.2
Balance on goods and services	-31.1
Unilateral transfers	
U.S. government grants	-13.8
U.S. government pensions and other transfers	-3.7
Private remittances and other transfers	-13.8
All transfers, net	-31.3
Balance on current account	-62.4
CAPITAL ACCOUNT	
Changes in U.S. assets abroad, net†	
U.S. official reserve assets	3.9
Other U.S. government assets	0.1
U.S. private assets	-47.8
All changes, net	-43.8
Changes in foreign assets in the United States, net‡	
Foreign official assets	40.1
Foreign private assets	80.0
All changes, net	120.1
Allocations of SDRs	0
Statistical discrepancy	-13.9

* Credits (+), debits (-).

†Increase/capital outflow (-).

‡Increase/capital inflow (+).

SOURCE: *Federal Reserve Bulletin*, May 1993, p. A-52.

T A B L E 11. 4 / *U.S. Balance of Payments: Selected Accounts* (in Billions of Dollars)

Year	Merchandise Trade Balance	Services Balance	Goods and Services Balance	Unilateral Transfers Balance	Current Account Balance
1970	2.1	1.5	3.6	-3.1	0.5
1972	-7.0	1.0	-6.0	-3.8	-9.8
1974	-5.4	9.0	3.6	-7.2	-3.6
1976	-9.4	18.7	9.3	-5.0	4.3
1978	-34.1	23.2	-10.9	-5.1	-16.0
1980	-25.3	33.6	8.3	-6.8	1.5
1982	-36.3	36.1	-0.2	-7.9	-8.1
1984	-112.5	18.2	-94.3	-12.2	-106.5
1986	-147.7	22.3	-125.4	-15.2	-140.6
1988	-127.2	15.3	-111.9	-14.6	-126.5
1990	-108.9	51.3	-57.6	-32.8	-90.4
1992	-96.3	65.2	-31.1	-31.3	-62.4

SOURCE: *Federal Reserve Bulletin*, various issues.

that home-nation unions often raise the most vocal arguments about the evils of trade deficits for the domestic economy.

Discussion of U.S. competitiveness in merchandise trade often gives the impression that the United States has consistently performed poorly relative to other industrial nations. However, the merchandise trade deficit is a narrow concept, because goods are only part of what the world trades. Another part of trade is services. A better indication of the nation's international payments position is the *goods and services balance*. Table 11.3 shows that in 1992, the United States generated a surplus of $65.2 billion on service transactions. Combining this surplus with the merchandise trade deficit of $96.3 billion yields a deficit on the goods and services balance of $31.1 billion. This means that the United States transferred fewer resources (goods and services) to other nations than it received from them during 1992.

In recent decades, the United States has generated a surplus in its services account, as seen in Table 11.4. The United States has been very competitive in the "other services" category, including construction, engineering, brokers' commissions, and certain health-care services. The United States also has traditionally registered large net receipts from transactions involving proprietary rights—fees, royalties, and other receipts derived mostly from long-established relationships between U.S.-based parent companies and their affiliates abroad. Moreover, the United States has traditionally enjoyed net inflows of investment income; by the late 1980s, however, this surplus diminished as foreign investors accumulated large holdings of U.S. government securities and other U.S. assets.

As Table 11.3 shows, the United States had a *current account* deficit of $62.4 billion in 1992. This meant that an excess of imports over exports—of goods, services, and unilateral transfers—resulted in decreasing net foreign investment for the United States. We should *not* become unduly preoccupied with the current account balance by itself, for it ignores capital account transactions. If foreigners purchase more U.S. assets in the United States (such as land, buildings, and bonds), then the United States can afford to import more goods and services from abroad. To look at one aspect of a nation's international payment position without considering the others is misleading.

Taken as a whole, U.S. international transactions always balance. This means that any force leading to an increase or decrease in one balance-of-payments account sets in motion a process leading to exactly offsetting changes in the balances of other accounts. As seen in Table 11.3, the United States had a current account deficit in 1992 of $62.4 billion. Offsetting this deficit was a combined surplus of $62.4 billion in the remaining capital accounts, as follows: (1) U.S. assets abroad, deficit of $43.8 billion; (2) foreign assets in the United States, surplus of $120.1 billion; (3) SDR allocation, no change; (4) statistical discrepancy, $13.9 billion outflow.

BALANCE OF INTERNATIONAL INDEBTEDNESS

A main feature of the U.S. balance of payments is that it measures the economic transactions of the United States over the period of one year. The balance of payments is thus a *flow concept*. But at any particular moment, a nation will have a fixed stock of assets and liabilities against the rest of the world. The statement that summarizes this situation is known as the **balance of international indebtedness**. Because the balance of international indebtedness is a record of the international position of the United States at a particular time (year-end data), it is a *stock concept*.

The U.S. balance of international indebtedness indicates the international investment position of the United States, reflecting the value of U.S. investments abroad as opposed to foreign investments in the United States. The United States is considered a **net creditor** to the rest of the world when U.S. claims on foreigners

exceed foreign claims on the United States at a particular time. When the reverse occurs, the United States assumes a **net debtor** position.

The terms *net creditor* and *net debtor* in themselves are not particularly meaningful. We need additional information about the specific types of claims and liabilities involved. The balance of international indebtedness therefore looks at the short- and long-term investment positions of both the private and government sectors of the economy. Table 11.5 summarizes the U.S. balance of international indebtedness.

Of what use is the balance of international indebtedness? Perhaps of greatest significance is that it breaks down international investment holdings into several categories so that policy implications can be drawn from each separate category about the *liquidity status* of the nation. For the short-term investment position, the strategic factor is the amount of short-term liabilities (bank deposits and government securities) held by foreigners. This is because these holdings potentially can be withdrawn at very short notice, resulting in a disruption of domestic financial markets. The balance of official monetary holdings is also significant. Assume that this balance is negative from the U.S. viewpoint. Should foreign monetary authorities decide to liquidate their holdings of U.S. government securities and have them converted into official reserve assets, the financial strength of the dollar would be reduced. As for a nation's long-term investment position, it is of less importance for the U.S. liquidity position because long-term investments generally respond to basic economic trends and are not subject to erratic withdrawals.

THE UNITED STATES AS A DEBTOR NATION

In the early stages of its industrial development, the United States was a net international debtor. Relying heavily on foreign capital, the United States built up its industries by mortgaging part

T A B L E   11. 5   /   U.S. Balance of International Indebtedness (in Billions of Dollars)

Type of Investment*	1983	1987	1991
U.S. assets abroad	1,169	1,565	1,960
U.S. government assets	203	252	238
U.S. private assets	966	1,313	1,722
Foreign assets in the United States	832	1,591	2,322
Foreign official assets	195	283	397
Other foreign assets	637	1,308	1,925
Net international investment position	337	-26	-362

* At current cost.

SOURCE: U.S. Department of Commerce, *Survey of Current Business*, various June issues.

of its wealth to foreigners. Following World War I, the United States became a net international creditor. The U.S. international investment position evolved steadily from a net creditor position of $6 billion in 1919 to a position of $337 billion in 1983. After 1983, however, the long-term increase in the U.S. net investment position reversed dramatically. By 1987, the United States became a net international debtor, in the amount of $26 billion, for the first time since World War I; it has been an international debtor ever since.

How did this turnabout occur so rapidly? The reason was that foreign investors placed more funds in the United States than U.S. residents invested abroad. The United States was considered attractive to investors from other countries because of its rapid economic recovery from the recession of the early 1980s, its political stability, and its relatively high interest rates. U.S. investments overseas fell because of sluggish loan demand in Europe, a desire by commercial banks to reduce their overseas exposure as a reaction to the debt-repayment problems of Latin American countries, and decreases in credit demand by oil-importing developing nations as the result of declining oil prices. Of the foreign investment funds in the United States, less than one-fourth went to

direct ownership of U.S. real estate and business. Most of the funds were in financial assets such as bank deposits, stocks, and bonds.

For the typical U.S. resident, the transition from net creditor to net debtor went unnoticed. However, the net debtor status of the United States raised an issue of impropriety. To many observers, it seemed inappropriate for the United States, one of the richest nations in the world, to be borrowing on a massive scale from the rest of the world.

What were the consequences of the deterioration of the U.S. net international investment position? In the short run, the net investment inflow provided positive effects for the U.S. economy. The inflow increased the pool of savings in the U.S. economy, thus helping to finance the capital needs of the private sector for business investment and of the U.S. government for its budget deficits. By adding to the pool of money available for borrowing, the investment inflow helped slow the rise of U.S. interest rates and enabled the U.S. economy to grow faster than it would have otherwise. Without such an inflow, U.S. budget deficits would have led to even higher interest rates, which would have "crowded out" private investment much more severely. Foreigners' desire to hold U.S. assets promoted a rise in the

Views Concerning U.S. International Indebtedness

In the decades following World War II, the United States became the world's largest lender, helping to finance economic growth overseas. By the late 1980s, however, the United States had become the world's largest debtor. There has been much controversy concerning the effects of foreign indebtedness for the economic future of the United States. Some economists maintain that the United States has borrowed to consume beyond its means and that the U.S. standard of living will deteriorate when the bills become due. Others argue that foreign investment inflows are favorable for the United States because they facilitate increasing economic growth and prosperity.

The significance of investment to debtors is the same for nations, businesses, and households: successful investment generates income. Assume that a nation uses borrowed funds to finance the construction of an auto-assembly plant and this plant provides more than enough income to pay the interest on the loan. The excess income fosters a higher living standard for the nation. In contrast, assume that a nation finances rising consumption by means of reduced domestic investment and increased funds borrowed from overseas. With slower accumulation of capital, the growth in domestic income will slow. Moreover, some of the income must be used for interest payments on the debt. These two effects could lead to reductions in the domestic living standard.

The experience of the United States in the 1880s demonstrates the significance of investment to debtors. This was a period of large investment inflows and increasing indebtedness for the United States. This influx of funds permitted rapid industrialization and construction of railroads, which led to increases in U.S. output of some 10 percent per year. Favorable opportunities for investment motivated foreigners to shift capital to the United States, which fostered rising industrial output and living standards for U.S. residents.

Some economists have argued that the recent experience of the United States is similar to the events of a century ago. They contend that during the 1980s, the United States experienced improving business opportunities as the economy climbed out of recession and gained control of its inflation rate. These opportunities contributed to a strong demand for funds needed to finance investment, some of which were supplied by foreigners. The investment inflows meant that U.S. borrowers had to pay larger amounts

(continued)

dollar's value against other currencies (see Chapter 12) during the early 1980s. A strong dollar helped keep a lid on U.S. inflation by lowering prices for imports and spurring cost cutting by U.S. companies that competed against foreign companies.

But continued heavy borrowing from overseas has its costs. A highly valued dollar, resulting from investment inflows, increases imports by making foreign goods cheaper and reduces exports by increasing prices foreigners must pay for U.S. goods. The result is merchandise trade deficits, which ballooned during the 1980s. Over the long run, continued heavy borrowing by the United States results in greater interest and dividend payments to foreigners and a corresponding drain on U.S. economic resources. What's more, the positive impact of net investment inflows on the U.S. economy had a negative counterpart as far as other nations were concerned. By draining the world pool of savings to finance U.S. business expansion and government budget deficits, the investment inflow led to higher interest rates abroad, retarding investment and growth worldwide.

Views Concerning U.S. International Indebtedness

(continued)

of interest and dividends to foreigners. But they also helped finance increased amounts of physical capital (such as factories) that generated more than enough income to pay the foreigners. That income was in addition to the income that U.S. residents would otherwise have earned. The foreign investment inflow was thus seen as of benefit to U.S. residents who, as a result, worked with a larger capital stock that provided higher productivity and real incomes.

This contention is strongly debated by other economists, who predict future austerity as a result of U.S. indebtedness. These economists maintain that in the 1980s the United States reduced saving for the future in favor of consuming in the present. The savings reductions led to greater competition among borrowers for funds, which drove interest rates upward. Although higher interest rates attracted foreign investment to the United States, they squeezed some borrowers out of the market and reduced U.S. investment.

It is also noted that the recent situation of the United States is in direct contrast to the U.S. experience a century ago when U.S. indebtedness led to rising standards of living. During the 1880s, the United States invested at record rates. The federal government's budget was in surplus, and the nation's saving rate was high. In the 1980s, U.S. government budget deficits were larger in relation to income than during any prior peacetime expansion. The U.S. private saving rate was also low by historical standards. Moreover, the U.S. government did not invest what it borrowed.

The crux of the debate is whether U.S. investment was strong or weak in the 1980s. Some studies conclude that U.S. investment was weak during this period and that the combination of weak investment and strong growth of foreign indebtedness threatens future U.S. living standards. Other studies assert that an investment boom in the United States occurred after the recession of the early 1980s. Unfortunately, there is no clear answer because the opposing camps measure investment differently (such as gross versus net investment) and use different standards when assessing whether investment is strong or weak.

SOURCE: Jon Faust, "U.S. Foreign Indebtedness: Are We Investing What We Borrow?" *Economic Review,* Federal Reserve Bank of Kansas City (July–August 1989).

SUMMARY

1. The balance of payments is a record of a nation's economic transactions with all other nations for a given year. A credit transaction is one that results in a receipt of payments from foreigners, whereas a debit transaction leads to a payment abroad. Owing to double-entry bookkeeping, a nation's balance of payments will always balance.

2. From a functional viewpoint, the balance of payments identifies economic transactions as (a) current account transactions and (b) capital account transactions.

3. The balance on goods and services is important to policymakers because it indicates the net transfer of real resources overseas. It also measures the extent to which a nation's exports and imports are part of its gross national product.

4. The capital account of the balance of payments shows the international movement of loans and investments. Capital inflows (outflows) are analogous to exports (imports) of goods and services because they result in the receipt (payment) of funds from (to) other nations.

5. Official reserves consist of a nation's financial assets: (a) monetary gold holdings, (b) convertible currencies, (c) special drawing rights, and (d) drawing positions on the International Monetary Fund.

6. The current method employed by the Department of Commerce in presenting the U.S. international payments position makes use of a functional format emphasizing the following *partial* balances: (a) merchandise trade balance, (b) balance on goods and services, and (c) current account balance.

7. The international investment position of the United States at a particular time is measured by the balance of international indebtedness. Unlike the balance of payments, which is a flow concept, the balance of international indebtedness is a stock concept.

STUDY QUESTIONS

1. What is meant by the balance of payments?
2. What economic transactions give rise to the receipt of dollars from foreigners? What transactions give rise to payments to foreigners?
3. Why does the balance-of-payments statement "balance"?
4. From a functional viewpoint, a nation's balance of payments can be grouped into several categories. What are these categories?
5. What financial assets are categorized as official reserve assets for the United States?
6. What is the meaning of a surplus (deficit) on the (a) merchandise trade balance, (b) goods and services balance, and (c) current account balance?
7. Why has the goods and services balance sometimes shown a surplus while the merchandise trade balance shows a deficit?
8. What does the balance of international indebtedness measure? How does this statement differ from the balance of payments?
9. Indicate whether each of the following transactions is a *debit* or a *credit* on the U.S. balance of payments:
   a. A U.S. importer purchases a shipload of French wine.
   b. A Japanese automobile firm builds an assembly plant in Seattle.
   c. A British manufacturer exports machinery to Taiwan on a U.S. vessel.
   d. A U.S. college student spends a year studying in Switzerland.
   e. U.S. charities donate food to people in drought-plagued Africa.
   f. Japanese investors collect interest income on their holdings of U.S. government securities.
   g. Remittance from a German resident to her relatives in the United States.
   h. Lloyds of London sells an insurance policy to a U.S. business firm.
   i. A Swiss resident receives dividends on her IBM stock.

10. The following hypothetical transactions, in billions of U.S. dollars, took place during a year:

Merchandise imports	450
U.S. government grants	-10
Allocation of SDRs	15
Investment income, net	5
Statistical discrepancy	40
Changes in U.S. assets abroad, net	-150
Remittances, pensions, etc.	-10
Merchandise exports	375
Other services, net	50
Military transactions, net	-15

   a. Calculate the U.S. merchandise trade balance, services balance, goods and services balance, unilateral transfers balance, and current account balance.
   b. Which of these balances pertains to the net foreign investment position of the United States? How would you describe that position?

11. Given the following items, in billions of U.S. dollars, determine the international investment position of the United States. Is the United States a *net creditor* nation or a *net debtor* nation?

Foreign official assets in the U.S.	25
Other foreign assets in the U.S.	225
U.S. government assets abroad	150
U.S. private assets abroad	75

CHAPTER *12*

Foreign Exchange

KEY CONCEPTS AND TERMS

Appreciation
Arbitrage
Bid rate
Call option
Covered interest
   arbitrage
Cross exchange rate
Currency swaps
Depreciation
Destabilizing
   speculation
Discount
Effective exchange rate
Exchange arbitrage
Exchange-rate
   determination
Foreign currency
   options
Foreign exchange
   market
Forward market
Forward rate
Forward transaction
Futures market
Hedging

Interbank market
Interest arbitrage
International Monetary
   Market
Long position
Nominal effective
   exchange rate
Offer rate
Premium
Put option
Real effective exchange
   rate
Short position
Speculation
Spot market
Spot transactions
Spread
Stabilizing speculation
Strike price
Three-point arbitrage
Trade-weighted dollar
Two-point arbitrage
Uncovered interest
   arbitrage

Among the factors that make international economics a distinct subject is the existence of different national monetary units of account. In the United States, prices and money are measured in terms of the dollar. The Deutsche mark represents Germany's unit of account, whereas the franc and yen signify the units of account of France and Japan, respectively.

A typical international transaction requires two distinct purchases. First, the foreign currency is bought; second, the foreign currency is used to facilitate the international transaction. For example, before French importers can purchase commodities from, say, U.S. exporters, they must first purchase dollars to meet their international obligation. Some institutional arrangements are required that provide an efficient mechanism whereby monetary claims can be settled with a minimum of inconvenience to both parties. Such a mechanism exists in the form of the foreign exchange market.[1]

FOREIGN EXCHANGE MARKET

The **foreign exchange market** refers to the organizational setting within which individuals, businesses, governments, and banks buy and sell foreign currencies and other debt instruments. Only a small fraction of daily transactions in foreign exchange actually involve trading of currency (for example, the Canadian dollar bill). Most foreign exchange transactions involve the transfer of bank deposits. Major U.S. banks, such as Citibank, maintain inventories of foreign exchange in the form of foreign-denominated deposits held in branch or correspondent banks in foreign cities. Americans can obtain this foreign exchange from hometown banks that, in turn, purchase it from Citibank.

Unlike stock or commodity exchanges, the foreign exchange market is not an organized structure. It has no centralized meeting place and no formal requirements for participation. Nor is the foreign exchange market limited to any one country. For any currency, such as the U.S. dollar, the foreign exchange market consists of all locations where dollars are exchanged for other national currencies. Three of the largest foreign exchange markets in the world are located in London, New York, and Tokyo. A dozen or so other market centers also exist around the world, such as Paris and Zurich. Because foreign exchange dealers are in constant telephone and computer contact, the market is very competitive; in effect, it functions no differently from a centralized market.

The foreign exchange market opens on Monday morning in Hong Kong, which is still Sunday evening in New York. As the day progresses, markets open in Tokyo, Frankfurt, London, New York, Chicago, San Francisco, and elsewhere. As the West Coast markets of the United States close, Hong Kong is only one hour away from opening for Tuesday business.

Indeed, the foreign exchange market is a round-the-clock operation!

A typical foreign exchange market functions at three levels: (1) in transactions between commercial banks and their commercial customers, who are the ultimate demanders and suppliers of foreign exchange, (2) in the domestic interbank market conducted through brokers, and (3) in active trading in foreign exchange with banks overseas.

Exporters, importers, investors, and tourists buy and sell foreign exchange from and to commercial banks rather than each other. As an example, consider the import of German autos by a U.S. dealer. The dealer is billed for each car it imports at the rate of 50,000 Deutsche marks (the German currency) per car. The U.S. dealer cannot write a check for this amount because it does not have a checking account denominated in marks. Instead, the dealer goes to the foreign exchange department of, say, Chase Manhattan Bank to arrange payment. If the exchange rate is 2 marks = \$1, the auto dealer writes a check to Chase Manhattan Bank for \$25,000 (50,000/2 = 25,000) per car. Chase Manhattan will then pay the German manufacturer 50,000 marks per car in Germany. Chase Manhattan is able to do this because it has a checking deposit in marks at its branch in Bonn.

The major banks who trade foreign exchange generally do not deal directly with one another but instead use the services of *foreign exchange brokers*. The purpose of a broker is to permit the trading banks to maintain desired foreign exchange balances. If at a particular moment a bank does not have the proper foreign exchange balances, it can turn to a broker to buy additional foreign currency or sell the surplus. Brokers thus provide a wholesale, interbank market in which trading banks can buy and sell foreign exchange. Brokers are paid a commission for their services by the selling bank. Table 12.1 provides examples of U.S. foreign exchange brokers.

The third tier of the foreign exchange market consists of the transactions between the trad-

---

TABLE 12. 1   /   *U.S. Currency Brokers*

Berisford Capital Markets, Inc.
Bierbaum-Martin Inc.
Chapdelaine Foreign Exchange
Debeausse and Company
Fulton Prebon Money Brokers
GFI Group Inc.
Harlow Butler Currency Options
Harlow, Meyer and Savage
Intercontinental Exchange Partners
Laasser Marshall Inc.
Noonan, Astley and Pearce
Rada Foreign Exchange Corporation
Transforex
Tradition Financial Services
Tullet and Tokyo Forex
Wallich and Matthes

---

ing banks and their overseas branches or foreign correspondents. Although several dozen U.S. banks trade in foreign exchange, it is the major New York banks that usually carry out transactions with foreign banks. The other, inland trading banks meet their foreign exchange needs by maintaining correspondent relationships with the New York banks. Trading with foreign banks permits the matching of supply and demand of foreign exchange in the New York market. These international transactions are carried out primarily by telephone and computers.

TYPES OF FOREIGN EXCHANGE TRANSACTIONS

When conducting purchases and sales of foreign currencies, banks promise to pay a stipulated amount of currency to another bank or customer on an agreed-upon date. Banks typically engage in three types of foreign exchange transactions: spot, forward, and swap.

For currency trading among banks, **spot transactions** are the most widely used. Spot transactions refer to outright purchase and sale of foreign currency for cash settlement not more than two business days after the date the transactions are recorded as spot deals. The two-day period, known as *immediate delivery,* allows time for the two parties to forward instructions to debit and credit bank accounts at home and abroad.

In many cases, a business or financial institution knows it will be receiving or paying an amount of foreign currency on a specific date in the future. For example, in August a U.S. importer may arrange for a special Christmas-season shipment of Japanese radios to arrive in October. The agreement with the Japanese manufacturer may call for payment in yen on October 20. To guard against the possibility of the yen's becoming more expensive in terms of the dollar, the importer may contract with a bank to buy yen at a stipulated price, but not actually receive them until October 20 when they are needed. When the contract matures, the U.S. importer pays for the yen with a known amount of dollars. This is known as a **forward transaction**.

Forward transactions differ from spot transactions in that their maturity date is more than two business days in the future. A forward exchange contract's maturity date can be a few months, or even years, in the future. The exchange rate is fixed when the contract is initially made.

Trading foreign currencies among banks also involves **currency swaps**. *Swap transactions* entail the conversion of one currency to another currency at one point, with an agreement to reconvert it back to the original currency at some point in the future. The rates of both exchanges are agreed to in advance. Swaps provide an efficient mechanism through which banks can meet their foreign exchange needs over a period of time. Banks are able to use a currency for a period in exchange for another currency that is not needed during that time.

For example, Chase Manhattan Bank may have excess balances of dollars but needs pounds to meet the requirements of its corporate clients. At the same time, Royal Bank of Scotland may have excess balances of pounds and insufficient amounts of dollars. The banks could negotiate a swap agreement in which Chase Manhattan Bank agrees to exchange dollars for pounds today and pounds for dollars in the future. The key aspect is that the two banks arrange the swap as a single transaction in which they agree to pay and receive stipulated amounts of currencies at specified rates.

INTERBANK TRADING

In the foreign exchange market, currencies are actively traded around the clock and throughout the world. Banks are linked by telecommunications equipment that permits instantaneous communication. A relatively small number of money center banks carry out most of the foreign exchange transactions in the United States. Virtually all the big New York banks have active currency trading operations, as do their counterparts in London, Tokyo, Hong Kong, Frankfurt, and other financial centers. Large banks in cities such as Los Angeles, Chicago, San Francisco, and Detroit also have active currency trading operations. For most U.S. banks, currency transactions are not a large part of their business; these banks have ties to correspondent banks in New York and elsewhere to conduct currency transactions.

All these banks are prepared to purchase or sell foreign currencies for their customers. Bank purchases from and sales to consumers are classified as *retail transactions* when the amount involved is less than 1 million currency units. *Wholesale transactions*, involving more than 1 million currency units, generally occur between banks or with large corporate customers. Bank transactions with each other constitute the **interbank market**. It is in this market that most foreign exchange trading occurs.

Table 12.2 illustrates the distribution of foreign exchange transactions by U.S. banking institutions in 1992. The average daily amount of foreign exchange transactions was estimated

TABLE 12. 2 / *Distribution of Foreign Exchange Transactions by U.S. Banks, 1992*

Transactions	Percentage
BY TYPE	
Spot	51
Swap	33
Options/futures	10
Forward	6
	100
BY FOREIGN CURRENCY	
German mark	34
Japanese yen	23
British pound	9
Swiss franc	8
French franc	3
Canadian dollar	3
Australian dollar	2
Other	18
	100

SOURCE: Federal Reserve Bank of New York, *U.S. Foreign Exchange Market Survey,* April 1992.

at $258 billion, of which $192 billion involved banks and $66 billion involved brokers. About half of all trading activity was in spot contracts. The U.S. dollar was by far the most important currency traded in foreign exchange markets, being involved in about 89 percent of all transactions. The next four most widely traded currencies were the German mark, Japanese yen, British pound, and Swiss franc. Among currency pairs, dollar-mark and dollar-yen were the most widely traded, accounting for 34 percent and 23 percent of all transactions among banks, respectively. The average deal size for foreign exchange transactions was $6 million for banks and $7 million for brokers.

Foreign exchange departments of major commercial banks typically serve as profit centers. A bank's foreign exchange dealers are in constant contact with other dealers to buy and sell currencies. In most large banks, dealers specialize in one or more foreign currencies. The chief dealer establishes the overall trading policy and direction of trading, trying to service the foreign exchange needs of the bank's customers and make a profit for the bank. Currency trading is conducted on a 24-hour basis, and exchange rates may fluctuate at any moment. Bank dealers must be light sleepers, ready to react to a nighttime phone call that indicates exchange rates are moving sharply in foreign markets. Banks often allow senior dealers to conduct exchange trading at home in response to such developments.

With the latest electronic equipment, currency exchanges are negotiated on computer terminals; a push of a button confirms a trade. Dealers use electronic trading boards that permit them to instantly register transactions and verify their bank's positions. Besides trading currencies during daytime hours, major banks have established night trading desks to capitalize on foreign exchange fluctuations during the evening and to accommodate corporate requests for currency trades. In the interbank market, currencies are traded in amounts involving at least 1 million units of a specific foreign currency. Table 12.3 provides examples of leading banks that trade in the foreign exchange market.

How do banks, such as Bank of America or Citibank, earn profits in foreign exchange transactions? Banks that regularly deal in the interbank market quote both a bid and an offer rate to other banks. The **bid rate** refers to the price that the bank is willing to pay for a unit of foreign currency; the **offer rate** is the price at which the bank is willing to sell a unit of foreign currency. The difference between the bid and the offer rate is the **spread**. At any given time, a bank's bid quote for a foreign currency will be less than its offer quote. The spread is intended to cover the bank's costs of implementing the exchange of currencies. The large trading banks are prepared to "make a market" in a currency by providing bid and offer rates on request.

TABLE 12. 3 / *Customers' Favorite Banks That Trade Foreign Exchange

Bank	Country
Citibank	United States
Chemical	United States
Barclays	United Kingdom
BankAmerica	United States
Midland	United Kingdom
JP Morgan	United States
Union Bank of Switzerland	Switzerland
NatWest	United Kingdom
Bankers Trust	United States
Hong Kong Bank	Hong Kong
Lloyds	United Kingdom
Chase Manhattan	United States
Deutsche Bank	Germany
First Chicago	United States
Swiss Bank Corporation	Switzerland

* Ranked by *Euromoney* survey of over 3,000 users of foreign exchange. This survey is updated annually.

SOURCE: "Citibank Sweeps the Board," *Euromoney*, May 1992, pp. 63–70.

Foreign exchange dealers who simultaneously purchase and sell foreign currency earn the spread as profit. For example, Citibank might quote bid and offer rates for the German mark at $.5851/.5854. The bid rate is $.5851 per mark. At this price, Citibank would be prepared to buy 1 million marks for $585,100. The offer rate is $.5854 per mark. Citibank would be willing to sell 1 million marks for $585,400. If Citibank is able to simultaneously buy and sell 1 million marks, it will earn $300 on the transaction. This profit equals the spread ($.0003) multiplied by the amount of the transaction (1 million marks).

Table 12.4 illustrates the bid/offer spreads at the close of business on April 14, 1993, in London. When the London currency market closed, the (French) franc price that a bank

TABLE 12. 4 / *Closing Spreads on London Market, April 14, 1993*

Country	Spread
United Kingdom*	1.5520–1.5530
Ireland*	1.5320–1.5330
Canada	1.2630–1.2640
Netherlands	1.7860–1.7870
Belgium	32.70–32.80
Denmark	6.0950–6.1000
Germany	1.5910–1.5920
Portugal	147.15–147.25
Spain	114.70–114.80
Italy	1539.25–1539.75
Norway	6.7400–6.7450
France	5.3750–5.3800
Sweden	7.4000–7.4050
Japan	113.90–114.00
Austria	11.2025–11.2075
Switzerland	1.4555–1.4565
ECU*	1.2240–1.2250

* Exchange-rate quotes for the United Kingdom, Ireland, and the European Currency Unit are in terms of U.S. dollars per British pound, Irish punt, and ECU. All other exchange-rate quotes are in terms of domestic currency units per U.S. dollar.

SOURCE: *Financial Times*, April 15, 1993.

attempt to profit by anticipating correctly the future direction of currency movements. Suppose a Citibank dealer expects the German mark to *appreciate* (strengthen) against the U.S. dollar. The dealer will likely *raise* both bid and offer rates, attempting to persuade other dealers to sell marks to Citibank and dissuade other dealers from purchasing marks from Citibank. The bank dealer thus purchases more marks than are sold. If the mark appreciates against the dollar as predicted, the Citibank dealer can sell the marks at a higher rate and earn profit. Conversely, should the Citibank dealer anticipate that the mark is about to *depreciate* (weaken) against the dollar, the dealer will *lower* the bid and offer rates. Such action encourages sales and discourages purchases; the dealer thus sells more marks than are bought. If the mark depreciates as expected, the dealer can purchase marks back at a lower price to make a profit.

If exchange rates move in the desired direction, foreign exchange traders earn profits. However, losses accrue if exchange rates move in the opposite, unexpected direction. To limit possible losses on exchange market transactions, banks impose financial restrictions on their dealers' trading volume. Dealers are subject to *position limits* that stipulate the amount of buying and selling that can be conducted in a given currency. Although banks maintain formal restrictions, they have sometimes absorbed substantial losses from unauthorized trading activity beyond position limits. Because foreign exchange departments are considered by bank management to be profit centers, dealers feel pressure to generate an acceptable rate of return on the bank's funds invested in this operation.

would pay for the dollar was 5.3750 francs per dollar. Dollars would be sold for francs by the bank at 5.3800 francs per dollar. The spread thus equals (5.3800 − 5.3750) / 5.3800 = .0009. Tiny spreads, often less than one-tenth of 1 percent, are common in currency markets. For a particular currency, the spread varies according to the individual currency trader and the overall attitude of the trading bank concerning future market conditions. The spread that is quoted is generally larger for currencies that are traded in smaller quantities or when the trading bank views trading in a particular currency to be risky.

Besides earning profits from a currency's bid/offer spread, foreign exchange dealers

READING FOREIGN EXCHANGE QUOTATIONS

Most daily newspapers in the United States and other countries give foreign exchange quotations for major currencies. Table 12.5 lists the rates taken from the *Wall Street Journal* for April 14, 1993.

In columns 2 and 3 (*U.S. dollar equivalent*) of the upper portion of Table 12.5, the selling prices of foreign currencies are listed in dollars. The columns state how many dollars are required to purchase one unit of a given foreign currency. For example, the quote for the Austrian schilling for Wednesday was .08913. This means that $0.08913 was required to purchase 1 schilling. Columns 4 and 5 (*currency per U.S. dollar*) show the foreign exchange rates from the opposite perspective, telling how many units of a foreign currency are required to buy a U.S. dollar. Again referring to Wednesday, it would take 11.22 Austrian schillings to purchase 1 U.S. dollar.

The term *selling rate* in the table's caption refers to the price at which a New York bank will sell foreign exchange, in amounts of $1 million and more, to another bank. The table caption also states at what time during the day the quotation was made, because currency prices fluctuate throughout the day in response to changing supply and demand conditions. The *Wall Street Journal* customarily quotes the rates at the closing of trading, 3 P.M. Eastern time. Next-day readers of the newspaper are thus offered the most recent currency prices. Retail foreign exchange transactions, in amounts under $1 million, carry an additional service charge and are thus made at a different exchange rate.

Most tables of exchange-rate quotations express currency values relative to the U.S. dollar, regardless of the country where the quote is provided. Yet there are many instances in which the U.S. dollar is not part of a foreign exchange transaction. In such cases, the people involved need to obtain an exchange quote between two nondollar currencies. As an example, if a British importer needs francs to purchase Swiss watches, the exchange rate of interest is the value of the Swiss franc relative to the British pound. The exchange rate between any two currencies (such as the franc and the pound) can be derived from the rates of these two currencies in terms of a third currency (the dollar).

The resulting rate is called the **cross exchange rate**.

Referring to the New York foreign exchange market quotations in the upper portion of Table 12.5, we see that, as of Wednesday, the dollar value of the British pound is $1.5515 and the dollar value of the Swiss franc is $0.6845. We can then calculate the value of the British pound relative to the Swiss franc as follows:

$$\frac{\$ \text{ value of British pound}}{\$ \text{ value of Swiss franc}} = \frac{\$1.55515}{\$0.6845} = 2.26$$

Thus, each British pound buys about 2.26 Swiss francs; this is the cross exchange rate between the pound and the franc. In similar fashion, cross exchange rates can be calculated between any other two nondollar currencies in Table 12.5.

The lower portion of Table 12.5 gives the cross exchange rates for several leading currencies. Here, to find the value of the British pound relative to the Swiss franc, we simply locate the intersection of the Pound column and the Switzerland row. The cross rate is given as 2.2644. In like manner, the cross exchange rates of other key currencies can be read directly from the table.

FORWARD AND FUTURES MARKETS

Foreign exchange can be bought and sold for delivery immediately (the **spot market**) or for future delivery (the **forward market**). Forward contracts are normally made by those who will receive or make payment in foreign exchange in the weeks or months ahead. As seen in Table 12.5, the New York foreign exchange market is a spot market for most currencies of the world. Regular forward markets, however, exist only for the more widely traded currencies. Exporters and importers, whose foreign exchange receipts and payments are in the future, are the

T A B L E 12. 5 / *Foreign Exchange Quotations*

EXCHANGE RATES
Wednesday, April 14, 1993

The New York foreign exchange selling rates below apply to trading among banks in amounts of $1 million and more, as quoted at 3 p.m. Eastern time by Bankers Trust Co., Telerate and other sources. Retail transactions provide fewer units of foreign currency per dollar.

Country	U.S. $ equiv. Wed.	Tues.	Currency per U.S. $ Wed.	Tues.
Argentina (Peso)	1.01	1.01	.99	.99
Australia (Dollar)	.7217	.7173	1.3856	1.3941
Austria (Schilling)	.08913	.08989	11.22	11.13
Bahrain (Dinar)	2.6522	2.6522	.3771	.3771
Belgium (Franc)	.03048	.03068	32.81	32.59
Brazil (Cruzeiro)	.0000375	.0000380	26694.00	26341.02
Britain (Pound)	1.5515	1.5580	.6445	.6418
30-Day Forward	1.5478	1.5543	.6461	.6434
90-Day Forward	1.5410	1.5477	.6489	.6461
180-Day Forward	1.5311	1.5384	.6531	.6500
Canada (Dollar)	.7918	.7929	1.2630	1.2612
30-Day Forward	.7906	.7917	1.2649	1.2631
90-Day Forward	.7878	.7890	1.2693	1.2675
180-Day Forward	.7828	.7839	1.2775	1.2757
Czech. Republic (Koruna)				
Commercial rate	.0358295	.0355745	27.9100	28.1100
Chile (Peso)	.002581	.002578	387.39	387.97
China (Renminbi)	.174856	.174856	5.7190	5.7190
Colombia (Peso)	.001530	.001536	653.65	651.10
Denmark (Krone)	.1635	.1648	6.1157	6.0671
Ecuador (Sucre)				
Floating rate	.000547	.000547	1829.02	1829.02
Finland (Markka)	.18052	.17780	5.5395	5.6244
France (Franc)	.18544	.18702	5.3925	5.3470
30-Day Forward	.18444	.18601	5.4218	5.3760
90-Day Forward	.18278	.18435	5.4710	5.4245
180-Day Forward	.18059	.18220	5.5375	5.4885
Germany (Mark)	.6272	.6325	1.5945	1.5810
30-Day Forward	.6244	.6296	1.6016	1.5882
90-Day Forward	.6197	.6251	1.6136	1.5998
180-Day Forward	.6139	.6193	1.6289	1.6148
Greece (Drachma)	.004587	.004629	218.00	216.05
Hong Kong (Dollar)	.12937	.12935	7.7300	7.7312
Hungary (Forint)	.0116306	.0115701	85.9600	86.4300
India (Rupee)	.03228	.03228	30.98	30.98
Indonesia (Rupiah)	.0004833	.0004833	2069.02	2069.02
Ireland (Punt)	1.5290	1.5457	.6540	.6470

Country	U.S. $ equiv. Wed.	Tues.	Currency per U.S. $ Wed.	Tues.
Israel (Shekel)	.3723	.3701	2.6858	2.7022
Italy (Lira)	.0006479	.0006561	1543.50	1524.09
Japan (Yen)	.008776	.008828	113.95	113.28
30-Day Forward	.008775	.008828	113.96	113.28
90-Day Forward	.008775	.008828	113.96	113.28
180-Day Forward	.008775	.008828	113.95	113.28
Jordan (Dinar)	1.4874	1.4874	.6723	.6723
Kuwait (Dinar)	3.3135	3.3135	.3018	.3018
Lebanon (Pound)	.000574	.000574	1742.00	1742.00
Malaysia (Ringgit)	.3874	.3878	2.5815	2.5785
Malta (Lira)	2.6954	2.6954	.3710	.3710
Mexico (Peso)				
Floating Rate	.3227889	.3227889	3.0980	3.0980
Netherland (Guilder)	.5581	.5628	1.7919	1.7768
New Zealand (Dollar)	.5431	.5421	1.8413	1.8447
Norway (Krone)	.1480	.1488	6.7581	6.7208
Pakistan (Rupee)	.0377	.0377	26.53	26.53
Peru (New Sol)	.5456	.5499	1.83	1.82
Phillippines (Peso)	.03914	.03914	25.55	25.55
Poland (Zloty)	.00006383	.00006348	15666.00	15729.99
Portugal (Escudo)	.006758	.006805	147.97	146.95
Saudi Arabia (Rival)	.26702	.26702	3.7450	3.7450
Singapore (Dollar)	.6144	.6164	1.6275	1.6223
Slovak Rep. (Koruna)	.0358295	.0355745	27.9100	28.1100
South Africa (Rand)				
Commercial rate	.3161	.3164	3.1633	3.1603
Financial rate	.2068	.2096	4.8350	4.7700
South Korea (Won)	.0012564	.0012564	795.90	795.90
Spain (Peseta)	.008692	.008776	115.04	113.94
Sweden (Krona)	.1346	.1346	7.4304	7.4307
Switzerland (Franc)	.6845	.6912	1.4610	1.4467
30-Day Forward	.6832	.6899	1.4637	1.4494
90-Day Forward	.6812	.6880	1.4680	1.4535
180-Day Forward	.6792	.6860	1.4723	1.4577
Taiwan (Dollar)	.038775	.038835	25.79	25.75
Thailand (Baht)	.03956	.03956	25.28	25.28
Turkey (Lira)	.0001057	.0001055	9462.00	9476.01
United Arab (Dirham)	.2723	.2723	3.6725	3.6725
Uruguay (New Peso)				
Financial	.000260	.000260	3852.01	3852.01
Venezuela (Bolivar)				
Floating rate	.01193	.01194	83.82	83.72
SDR	1.41291	1.41211	.70776	.70816
ECU	1.22090	1.23160	....	....

Special Drawing Rights (SDR) are based on exchange rates for the U.S., German, British, French and Japanese currencies. Source: International Monetary Fund.

European Currency Unit (ECU) is based on a basket of community currencies.

Key Currency Cross Rates Late New York Trading Apr. 14, 1993

	Dollar	Pound	SFranc	Guilder	Yen	Lira	D-Mark	FFranc	CdnDlr
Canada	1.2633	1.9606	.86587	.70544	.01109	.00082	.79278	.23444	....
France	5.3885	8.363	3.6933	3.0090	.04732	.00349	3.3816	....	4.2654
Germany	1.5935	2.4731	1.0922	.88983	.01399	.00103	....	.29572	1.2614
Italy	1543.3	2395.2	1057.80	861.81	13.552	....	968.52	286.41	1221.7
Japan	113.88	176.74	78.053	63.592	....	.07379	71.465	21.134	90.14
Netherlands	1.7908	2.7793	1.2274	....	.01573	.00116	1.1238	.33234	1.4176
Switzerland	1.4590	2.2644	....	.81472	.01281	.00095	.91559	.27076	1.1549
U.K.	.64433	....	.44162	.35980	.00566	.00042	.40435	.11958	.51004
U.S.	....	1.5520	.68540	.55841	.00878	.00065	.62755	.18558	.79158

Source: Telerate

T A B L E   12. 6   /   *Forward Contract versus Futures Contract*

	Forward Contract	Futures Contract
Issuer	Commercial bank	International Monetary Market (IMM) of the Chicago Mercantile Exchange and other foreign exchanges such as the Tokyo International Financial Futures Exchange
Trading	"Over the counter" by telephone	On the IMM's market floor
Contract size	Tailored to the needs of the exporter/importer/investor; no set size	Standardized in round lots
Date of delivery	Negotiable	Only on particular dates
Contract costs	Based on the bid/offer spread	Brokerage fees for sell and buy orders
Settlement	On expiration date only, at prearranged price	Profits or losses paid daily at close of trading

primary participants in the forward market. The forward quotations for the British pound, Canadian dollar, French franc, German mark, Japanese yen, and Swiss franc are for delivery 30, 90, or 180 days from the date indicated in the table's caption (April 14, 1993).

Trading in foreign exchange can also be done in the **futures market**. In this market, contracting parties agree to future exchanges of currencies and set applicable exchange rates in advance. The futures market is distinguished from the forward market in that only several currencies are traded; moreover, trading takes place in standardized contract amounts and in a specific geographic location. Table 12.6 summarizes the major differences between the forward market and futures market.

One such futures market is the **International Monetary Market** (IMM) of the Chicago Mercantile Exchange. Founded in 1972, the IMM is an extension of the commodity futures markets in which specific quantities of wheat, corn, and other commodities are bought and sold for future delivery at specific dates. The IMM provides trading facilities for the purchase and sale for future delivery of financial instruments (such as foreign currencies) and precious metals (such as gold). The IMM is especially popular with smaller banks and companies. Also, the IMM is one of the few places where individuals can speculate on changes in exchange rates.

Foreign exchange trading on the IMM is limited to major currencies. Contracts are set for delivery on the third Wednesday of March, June, September, and December. Price quotations are in terms of U.S. dollars per unit of foreign currency, but futures contracts are for a fixed amount (for example, 62,500 British pounds).

Here is how to read the IMM's futures prices, illustrated in Table 12.7. Column 1 gives the months for which delivery of the currency may be obtained. The next three columns give the opening, highest, and lowest prices of the day. Column 5 gives the settlement price, which approximates the last price of the day.[2] Column 6, "Change," shows the difference between the latest settlement price and the one for the previous day. The next two columns give the highest

T A B L E 12. 7 / International Monetary Market (Chicago Mercantile Exchange): Currency Futures

	Open	High	Low	Settle	Change	Lifetime High	Lifetime Low	Open Interest
JAPAN YEN (CME) — 12.5 million yen; $ per yen (.00)								
June	.8817	.8837	.8774	.8781	− .0045	.8882	.7745	74,455
Sept	.8826	.8826	.8776	.8780	− .0046	.8875	.7945	2,969
Dec	.8798	.8798	.8798	.8784	− .0048	.8873	.7970	669
Est vol 16,092; vol Tues 22,419; open int 78,095, −433.								
DEUTSCHEMARK (CME) — 125,000 marks; $ per mark								
June	.6267	.6280	.6215	.6219	− .0052	.6920	.5890	111,524
Sept	.6188	.6192	.6157	.6157	− .0053	.6720	.5863	6,530
Dec	....	....	....	.6112	− .0054	.6650	.5830	199
Est vol 41,689; vol Tues 57,575; open int 118,261, +2,812.								
CANADIAN DOLLAR (CME) — 100,000 dlrs.; $ per Can $								
June	.7901	.7901	.7878	.7891	− .0011	.8360	.7532	18,934
Sept	.7840	.7847	.7837	.7846	− .0011	.8335	.7515	1,672
Dec	.7795	.7795	.7790	.7796	− .0011	.8310	.7470	802
Mr94	....	....	....	.7750	− .0011	.7860	.7550	782
Est vol 2,327; vol Tues 1,517; open int 22,199, −129.								
BRITISH POUND (CME) — 62,500 pds.; $ per pound								
June	1.5482	1.5522	1.5428	1.5438	− .0068	1.9100	1.4020	37,628
Sept	1.5430	1.5430	1.5330	1.5340	− .0074	1.5580	1.3980	780
Est vol 10,436; vol Tues 16,109; open int 38,474, +1,192.								
SWISS FRANC (CME) — 125,000 francs; $ per franc								
June	.6886	.6889	.6817	.6821	− .0070	.8070	.6405	42,403
Sept	.6840	.6845	.6790	.6798	− .0070	.7100	.6380	1,230
Dec	.6825	.6830	.6780	.6786	− .0070	.6730	.6400	223
Est vol 21,851; vol Tues 29,475; open int 43,856, +658.								
AUSTRALIAN DOLLAR (CME) — 100,000 dlrs., $ per A.$								
June	.7200	.7210	.7182	.7200	+ .0032	.7210	.6590	2,592
Est vol 562; vol Tues 1,020; open int 2,612, +202								
U.S. DOLLAR INDEX (FINEX) — 1,000 times USDX								
June	90.82	91.49	90.90	91.44	+ .59	97.20	82.55	7,002
Sept	91.90	92.47	92.10	92.54	+ .61	97.10	91.75	1,193
Est vol 3,100; vol Tues 2,341; open int 8,200, +273.								
The index: High 90.62; Low 89.95; CLose 90.61 + .60								

* SOURCE: *The Wall Street Journal*, April 15, 1993.

and lowest prices at which each contract has ever traded. The last column, "Open Interest," shows the number of contracts outstanding and is a measure of public interest in a contract.

FOREIGN CURRENCY OPTIONS

During the 1980s, a new feature of the foreign exchange market was developed: the option market. An *option* is simply an agreement between a holder (buyer) and a writer (seller) that gives the holder the *right,* but not the obligation, to buy or sell financial instruments at any time through a specified date. Having a throwaway feature, options are a unique type of financial contract in that you only use the contract if you want to. By contrast, forward contracts *obligate* a person to carry out a transaction at a specified price, even if the market has changed and the person would rather not.

Foreign currency options provide an options holder the right to buy or sell a fixed amount of foreign currency at a prearranged price, within a few days to a couple of years. The options holder can choose the exchange rate she wants to guarantee, as well as the length of the contract. Foreign currency options have been used by companies seeking to hedge against exchange-rate risk as well as by speculators in foreign currencies.

There are two types of foreign currency options. A **call option** gives the holder the right to *buy* foreign currency at a specified price, whereas a **put option** gives the holder the right to *sell* foreign currency at a specified price. The price at which the option can be exercised (that is, the price at which the foreign currency is bought or sold) is called the **strike price**. The holder of a foreign currency option has the right to exercise the contract but may wish not to do so if it turns out to be unprofitable. The writer of the options contract (for example, Bank of America, Citibank, Merrill Lynch International Bank) must deliver the foreign currency if called on by a call-holder or must buy foreign currency if it is put to them by a put-holder. For this obligation, the writer of the options contract receives a *premium*, or fee (the option price). Financial institutions have been willing to write foreign currency options because they generate substantial premium income (the fee income on a $5-million deal can run $100,000 or more). However, writing currency options is a risky business because the writer takes chances on tricky pricing and hedging.

Foreign currency options are traded in a variety of currencies in Europe and the United States. The bank market for foreign currency options consists of large U.S. banks that write options for their corporate customers. In addition, the Amsterdam, Montreal, and Philadelphia exchanges provide centralized trading floors devoted to foreign currency option trading.

In 1984, the IMM introduced a new option instrument to compete with the currency options issued by the major banks and exchanges: an *option on a foreign currency futures contract*. This option provides the holder the right to buy or sell a futures contract for Swiss francs instead of the francs themselves. The options holder has the right to buy or sell a stipulated number of standardized futures contracts on a stipulated currency at a stipulated price up to a stipulated date. When the options holder exercises the right to buy or sell the foreign currency futures, he buys or sells futures contracts that are actually executed at maturity.

A first impression might be that an option on a foreign currency futures contract is an unnecessarily cumbersome instrument. But this instrument is especially attractive to small traders who desire to make large trades and who find it difficult to deal in the spot or forward markets. In trading spot currencies with a bank, small traders typically must pay retail prices that are higher than the wholesale prices that are charged on large currency transactions. Moreover, banks often hesitate to make forward contracts that are large compared to the financial resources of small traders. In contrast, small traders can readily arrange with the IMM for a large futures contract to make delivery under an option. Two examples will illustrate the advantages of trading in options.

CASE 1

Sale of Boeing aircraft to Japan

To see how exporters can use foreign currency options to cope with exchange-rate risk, consider the hypothetical case of Boeing, Inc., which submits a bid for the sale of jet planes to an airline company in Japan. Boeing must deal not only with the uncertainty of winning the bid but also with exchange-rate risk. If Boeing wins the bid, it will receive yen in the future. But what if the yen depreciates in the interim from, say, 115 yen = $1 to 120 yen = $1? Boeing's yen holdings would convert into fewer dollars, thus eroding the profitability of the jet sale.

Because Boeing wants to sell yen in exchange for dollars, it can offset this exchange-market risk by purchasing put options giving the company the right to sell yen for dollars at a specified price. Having obtained a put option, if Boeing wins the bid it has limited the exchange-rate risk. On the other hand, if the bid is lost, Boeing's losses are limited to the cost of the option. Foreign currency options thus provide a worst-case rate of exchange for companies conducting international business. The maximum amount the company can lose by covering its exchange-rate risk is the amount of the option price.

CASE 2

Speculating on future currency values

Foreign currency options are also appealing to international speculators because of their high leverage and limited price risk. The buyer of a foreign currency option can realize sizable returns on an investment through her ability to control a futures contract with a modest premium outlay. Meanwhile, the option buyer's risk is strictly limited to the option's price plus any other transaction costs.

For example, a U.S. speculator who purchases a call option on foreign currency expects the foreign currency to strengthen (appreciate) in relation to the dollar. Through the call option, the option holder has the right to buy a futures contract for foreign currency at the stated strike price. The call-holder can make a profit if the foreign currency rises in price but limits her losses to the option's cost if the price of foreign currency goes down. Conversely, a speculator would buy a put option on a foreign currency if he expected it to weaken (depreciate) against the dollar.

The prices of futures options (Chicago Mercantile Exchange) and foreign currency options (Philadelphia Exchange) are published daily in the financial press. Table 12.8 illustrates the prices for April 14, 1993, as listed in the *Wall Street Journal* on the following day.

Referring to the futures options of the Chicago Mercantile Exchange, let's look at the call options for the Swiss franc. These are the rights to buy franc futures at a specified price—

the strike price. For example, consider the call option at the strike price 6700. This means that one can purchase an option to buy 125,000-franc May futures up to the May settlement date at 67 cents per franc. The price one pays to purchase the option (the premium of the option's writer) is 1.67 cents per franc, or $2,088 (125,000 × 1.67 cents), plus brokerage fees. The June option to buy June futures at 67 cents per franc will cost 2.07 cents per franc, or $2588 (125,000 × 2.07 cents), plus brokerage fees.

Now refer to the Philadelphia Exchange quotations in Table 12.8. The Philadelphia Exchange deals with options for standardized bundles of currencies on the spot market. When a call option is exercised, foreign currency is thus obtained immediately. The only difference in the presentation of the foreign currency option prices, as compared with the futures options of the Chicago Mercantile Exchange, is that the spot price is stated instead of the futures price. Referring to the Philadelphia Exchange, we see that call options on April 62,500 Swiss francs at the strike price of 66 1/2 cents per franc cost 2.3 cents per franc, or $1,438 (2.3 cents × 62,500), plus brokerage fees.

EXCHANGE-RATE DETERMINATION

What determines the equilibrium exchange rate in a free market? Let us consider the exchange rate from the perspective of the United States—in dollars per unit of foreign currency. Because an exchange rate is a price, it would be expected to change over time. An increase in the U.S. exchange rate from $2 = £1 (pound) to $2.25 = £1 suggests that the dollar has *depreciated* against the pound (the pound has appreciated relative to the dollar). This is because more dollars are needed to purchase 1 pound. Conversely, a decrease in the U.S. exchange rate from $2 = £1 to $1.75 = £1 means the dollar has *appreciated* against the pound (the pound has depreciated relative to the dollar). Like other prices, the exchange rate in a free market

T A B L E   12. 8   /   *Prices of Futures Options and Foreign Currency Options, April 14, 1993*

Futures Options:
Chicago Mercantile Exchange

SWISS FRANC (CME)
125,000 francs; cents per franc

Strike Price	Calls – Settle			Puts – Settle		
	May	Jun	Jly	May	Jun	Jly
6700	1.67	2.07	....	0.46	0.87	....
6750	1.34	1.78	....	0.63	....	....
6800	1.05	1.51	....	0.84	1.30	....
6850	0.82	1.27	....	1.11	1.66	....
6900	0.62	1.05	....	1.41	1.84	....
6950	0.46	0.87	....	....	....	....

Est. vol. 4,202;
Tues vol. 3,075 calls; 1,085 puts
Op. int. Tues 10,256 calls; 12,373 puts

Foreign Currency Options:
Philadelphia Exchange

Option & Underlying*	Strike Price	Calls–Last			Puts–Last		
		Apr	May	Jun	Apr	May	Jun
62,500 Swiss Francs-cents per unit.							
SFranc	64½	r	r	r	r	0.08	r
68.42	65	r	r	r	r	0.10	r
68.42	66	r	r	3.14	r	0.25	0.53
68.42	66½	2.30	r	r	r	r	r
68.42	67	r	r	2.40	r	r	r
68.42	67½	r	r	r	r	r	1.13
68.42	68	0.90	r	r	r	r	1.20
68.42	68½	0.42	1.25	r	r	1.07	r
68.42	69	r	0.91	1.44	0.48	r	r
68.42	70	r	0.60	r	r	r	r
68.42	72	r	r	0.44	3.26	r	r
68.42	73	r	r	0.28	r	r	r
68.42	76	s	s	r	s	s	7.44

* The closing spot price of the Swiss franc that day, for comparison.

SOURCE: *The Wall Street Journal,* April 15, 1993.

is determined by both supply and demand conditions.

Demand for Foreign Exchange

A nation's *demand for foreign exchange* is derived from, or corresponds to, the *debit* items on its balance of payments. For example, the U.S. demand for pounds may stem from its desire to import British goods and services, to make investments in Britain, or to make transfer payments to residents in Britain.

Like most demand schedules, the U.S. demand for pounds varies inversely with its price; that is, fewer pounds are demanded at higher prices than at lower prices. This relationship is depicted by line *DD* in Figure 12.1. As the dollar depreciates against the pound (the dollar price of the pound rises), British goods and services become more expensive to U.S. importers. This is because more dollars are

required to purchase each pound needed to finance the import purchases. The higher exchange rate reduces the number of imports bought, lowering the number of pounds demanded by U.S. residents. In like manner, an appreciation of the U.S. dollar relative to the pound would be expected to induce larger import purchases and more pounds demanded by U.S. residents. The U.S. demand for pounds is based on the assumption that all relevant factors other than the exchange rate are given and constant. These other factors include changes in income, prices, interest rates, costs, and tastes and preferences, all of which can induce changes in the debit items of the balance of payments.

Supply of Foreign Exchange

The *supply of foreign exchange* refers to the amount of foreign exchange that will be offered to the market at various exchange rates, all

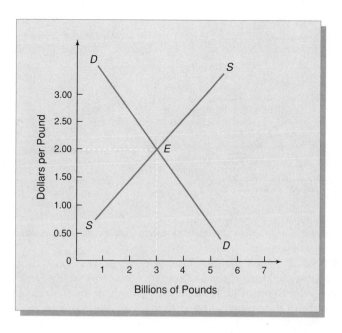

F I G U R E 12. 1 *Exchange-rate determination.* The equilibrium exchange rate is established at the point of intersection of the supply and demand schedules of foreign exchange. The demand for foreign exchange corresponds to the debit items on a nation's balance-of-payments statement; the supply of foreign exchange corresponds to the credit items.

other factors held constant. The supply of pounds, for example, is generated by the desire of British residents and businesses to import U.S. goods and services, to lend funds and make investments in the United States, to repay debts owed to U.S. lenders, and to extend transfer payments to U.S. residents. In each of these cases, the British offer pounds in the foreign exchange market to obtain the dollars they need to make payments to U.S. residents. Note that the supply of pounds results from transactions that appear on the *credit* side of the U.S. balance of payments; thus, one can make a connection between the balance of payments and the foreign exchange market.

The supply of pounds is denoted by schedule *SS* in Figure 12.1. The schedule represents the number of pounds offered by the British to obtain dollars with which to buy U.S. goods, services, and assets. It is depicted in the figure as a positive function of the U.S. exchange rate. As the dollar depreciates against the pound (dollar price of the pound rises), the British will be inclined to buy more U.S. goods. The reason, of course, is that, at higher and higher dollar prices of pounds, the British can get more U.S. dollars and hence more U.S. goods per pound. U.S. goods thus become cheaper to the British, who are induced to purchase additional quantities. These purchases result in more pounds being offered in the foreign exchange market to buy dollars with which to pay U.S. exporters.

Can we be assured that the supply of pounds is always upward sloping? Not necessarily. In the foreign exchange market, the demand for dollars *implies* supply of pounds.

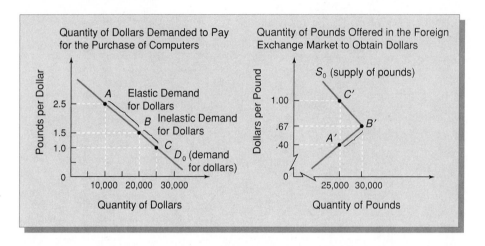

F I G U R E 12. 2   *Supply schedule of foreign exchange.* The supply schedule of pounds has a positive (upward) sloping region and a negative (backward) sloping region. The positive-sloping region corresponds to the elastic region on the British demand schedule for dollars; the negative-sloping region corresponds to the inelastic region on the British demand schedule for dollars.

This idea is illustrated in Figure 12.2, which shows the British demand for dollars in the left panel transformed into the supply of pounds in the right panel.

Let's look at an example, based on the following assumptions: (1) British residents buy computers from U.S. firms, with payment being made in dollars; (2) the exchange rate is £2.5 = $1, equivalent to 40 cents per pound; (3) the price of each computer equals $1,000 in the United States and remains constant. In terms of the pound, each computer costs £2,500.

Assuming that the British demand 10 computers at this price, they must obtain $10,000 from the foreign exchange market with which to pay the U.S. computer company. This quantity of dollars is indicated by point A on the British demand schedule for dollars, shown in the left panel of Figure 12.2. Purchasing this sum of dollars requires an outlay of £25,000, which equals the area under the demand schedule at point A. This establishes point A' on the supply-of-pounds schedule S_0 in the right panel

of the figure. Note that the quantity of pounds offered in the foreign exchange market is recorded on the horizontal axis of the supply-of-pounds figure. At an exchange rate of £1.50 per dollar (equivalent to 67 cents per pound), the $1,000 computer costs the British £1,500. Assuming that the price reduction results in the British buying 20 computers, British payments to the U.S. company total $20,000. Obtaining this sum of dollars in the foreign exchange market requires an outlay of £30,000, equal to the area under the demand schedule for dollars at point B. This establishes point B' on the supply-of-pounds schedule.

At an exchange rate of £1 per dollar (equivalent to $1 per pound), the $1,000 computer costs the British £1,000. If this price reduction leads to the British demanding 25 computers, British payments to the U.S. exporter total $25,000. Obtaining this quantity of dollars in the foreign exchange market requires an outlay of £25,000, which equals the area under the British demand schedule for dollars at point *C*. This establishes point *C'* on the supply-of-pounds schedule.

This example illustrates how the British demand for dollars is transformed into the supply of pounds offered in the foreign exchange market. The quantity of pounds supplied at each exchange rate equals the area *under* the British demand schedule for dollars. In Figure 12.2, note that the supply-of-pounds schedule is *upward-sloping* between points *A'* and *B'*, whereas the supply-of-pounds schedule is *backward-sloping* between points *B'* and *C'*. Why does the supply-of-pounds schedule assume this appearance? The answer lies in the *elasticity of the British demand for dollars*.

The elasticity of demand for dollars indicates the relationship between the percentage change in the quantity of dollars demanded and the percentage change in the pound price of dollars. Between any two points along the demand schedule, the average elasticity of demand (Ed) can be determined as follows:

$$Ed = \frac{\% \text{ change in \$ quantity}}{\% \text{ change in \$ price}}$$

$$= \frac{\text{change in quantity/average quantity}}{\text{change in price/average price}}$$

Demand is said to be *elastic* if the percentage change in quantity exceeds the percentage change in price (Ed > 1). If the percentage change in price exceeds the percentage change in quantity, demand is said to be *inelastic* (Ed < 1).

Applying the elasticity formula to the pairs of points on the British demand schedule for dollars in Figure 12.2 yields the elasticities of demand. Between points *A* and *B*, Ed = 1.34; demand is elastic. Over this range on the demand schedule, a 1-percent *decrease* in the pound price of the dollar causes a 1.34-percent *increase* in the quantity of dollars demanded. The net effect of the price reduction is a *greater* number of pounds being offered in the foreign exchange market to purchase dollars. The supply-of-pounds schedule is thus *upward-*

sloping when the British demand for dollars is in its elastic range.

Between points *B* and *C* on the British demand schedule for dollars, Ed = 0.56; demand is inelastic. Over this range on the demand schedule, a 1-percent *decrease* in the pound price of the dollar results in a 0.56-percent *increase* in the quantity of dollars demanded. The net effect is a *decrease* in the number of pounds offered in payment for dollars. The supply-of-pounds schedule is thus *backward-sloping* when the British demand schedule for dollars is in its inelastic range.

Like the demand schedule for foreign exchange, the supply schedule of foreign exchange is based on the assumption that factors other than the exchange rate are held constant. These factors include domestic inflation rates, tastes and preferences, interest rates, and income levels.

Equilibrium Rate of Exchange

As long as monetary authorities do not attempt to stabilize exchange rates or moderate their movements, the *equilibrium exchange* rate is determined by the market forces of supply and demand. In Figure 12.1, exchange market equilibrium occurs at point *E*, where *SS* and *DD* intersect. Three billion pounds will be traded at a price of $2 per pound. The foreign exchange market is precisely cleared, leaving neither an excess supply nor an excess demand for pounds.

Given the supply and demand schedules of Figure 12.1, there is no reason for the exchange rate to deviate from the equilibrium level. But, in practice, it is unlikely that the equilibrium exchange rate will remain very long at the existing level. This is because the forces that underlie the location of the supply and demand schedules tend to change over time, causing shifts in the schedules. Should the *demand* for pounds shift *rightward* (an increase in demand), the dollar will *depreciate* against the pound; *leftward* shifts in the demand for pounds (a decrease in demand) cause the dollar to *appreciate*. On the other hand, a *rightward* shift in the *supply* of pounds (increase in supply) causes the dollar to *appreciate* against the pound; a *leftward* shift in the supply of pounds (decrease in supply) results in a *depreciation* of the dollar. But what causes shifts in these schedules? This topic will be considered in Chapter 13.

EFFECTIVE EXCHANGE RATE: THE TRADE-WEIGHTED DOLLAR

Since 1973, the value of the U.S. dollar in terms of foreign currencies has changed daily. In this environment of market-determined exchange rates, measuring the international value of the dollar is a confusing task. Financial pages of newspapers may headline a **depreciation** in the value of the dollar relative to some currencies while at the same time reporting its **appreciation** relative to others. Such events may leave the general public confused as to the actual value of the dollar.

Suppose the U.S. dollar appreciates 10 percent relative to the yen and depreciates 5 percent against the pound. The change in the dollar's international value is some weighted average of the changes of these two bilateral exchange rates. Throughout the day, the value of the dollar may change relative to the values of any number of currencies under market-determined exchange rates. Direct comparison of the dollar's exchange rate over time thus requires a *weighted average* of all the bilateral changes. This average is referred to as the dollar's **effective exchange rate** or the **trade-weighted dollar**.

The effective exchange rate is a weighted average of the exchange rates between the domestic currency and the nation's most important trading partners, with weights given by relative importance of the nation's trade with each of these trade partners. One popular index of effective exchange rates is constructed by the U.S. Federal Reserve Board of Governors. This

TABLE 12. 9   /   *Trade-Weighted Value of the U.S. Dollar* (March 1973 = 100)

Year	Effective Exchange Rate*	
	Nominal	*Real*
1973 (March)	100.0	100.0
1980	87.4	84.8
1982	116.6	111.7
1984	138.3	128.5
1986	112.0	103.4
1988	92.7	88.0
1990	89.1	86.0
1992	86.6	83.3

* The nations included in the construction of the index are Germany, Japan, Canada, France, United Kingdom, Italy, Netherlands, Belgium, Sweden, and Switzerland.

SOURCE: *Economic Report of the President* and *Federal Reserve Bulletin,* various issues.

index reflects the impact of changes in the dollar's exchange rate on U.S. exports and imports with ten industrial nations. The base period of the index is March 1973, when the major industrial nations adopted market-determined exchange rates.

Table 12.9 illustrates the trade-weighted value of the U.S. dollar. An *increase* in the dollar's nominal effective exchange rate indicates a dollar *appreciation* relative to the currencies of the ten other nations in the index and a *loss* of price competitiveness for the United States. Conversely, a *decrease* in the dollar's nominal effective exchange rate implies a dollar *depreciation* relative to the other currencies and an *improvement* in U.S. international price competitiveness.

The trade-weighted dollar mentioned so far is based on the **nominal effective exchange rate,** which does not take into account differences between domestic and foreign inflation rates. It is widely maintained, however, that international trade patterns depend on inflation-adjusted exchange rates, rather than on the purely nominal exchange value of currencies. The **real effective exchange rate** of the U.S. dollar, also shown in Table 12.9, is derived by adjusting the nominal exchange rate for the differential between the U.S. inflation rate and the weighted average of the inflation rates in the ten other nations in the index. If the real value of the trade-weighted dollar rises, the dollar appreciates relative to other currencies, and vice versa.

ARBITRAGE

We have seen how the supply and demand for foreign exchange can set the market exchange rate. This analysis was from the perspective of the U.S. (New York) foreign exchange market. But what about the relationship between the exchange rate in the U.S. market and that in other nations? When restrictions do not modify the ability of the foreign exchange market to operate efficiently, normal market forces result in a *consistent relationship* among the market exchange rates of all currencies. That is to say, if £1 = $2 in New York, then $1 = 0.5 pound in London. The prices for the same currency in different world locations will be identical.

The factor underlying the consistency of the exchange rates is called **exchange arbitrage**. Exchange arbitrage refers to the *simultaneous* purchase and sale of a currency in different foreign exchange markets in order to profit from exchange-rate differentials in the two locations. This process brings about an *identical price* for the same currency in different locations and thus results in one market.

Suppose that the dollar/pound exchange rate is £1 = $2 in New York but £1 = $2.01 in London. Foreign exchange traders would find it profitable to purchase pounds in New York at $2 per pound and immediately resell them in London for $2.01. A profit of 1 cent would be made on each pound sold, less the cost of the

bank transfer and the interest charge on the money tied up during the arbitrage process. This return may appear to be insignificant, but on a $1-million arbitrage transaction it would generate a profit of approximately $5,000—not bad for a few minutes' work! As the demand for pounds increases in New York, the dollar price of a pound will rise above $2. This arbitrage process will continue until the exchange rate between the dollar and pound in New York is approximately the same as it is in London. Arbitrage between the two currencies thus unifies the foreign exchange markets.

The preceding example illustrates **two-point arbitrage**, in which two currencies are traded between two financial centers. A more intricate form of arbitrage, involving three currencies and three financial centers, is known as **three-point arbitrage**, or triangular arbitrage. Three-point arbitrage involves switching funds among three currencies in order to profit from exchange-rate inconsistencies, as seen in the following example.

Consider three currencies—the U.S. dollar ($), the Deutsche mark (DM), and the British pound (£)—all of which are traded in New York, Frankfurt, and London. Assume that the rates of exchange that prevail in all three financial centers are as follows: £1 pound = $1.50, £1 = DM 4, DM 1 = $0.50. Because the same exchange rates (prices) prevail in all three financial centers, two-point arbitrage is not profitable. However, these quoted exchange rates are mutually inconsistent. Thus, an arbitrager with $1.5 million could make a profit as follows:

1. Sell $1.5 million for 1 million pounds.
2. Simultaneously, sell 1 million pounds for 4 million marks.
3. At the same time, sell 4 million marks for $2 million. The arbitrager has just made a risk-free profit of $500,000 ($2 million - $1.5 million) before transaction costs!

These transactions tend to cause shifts in all three exchange rates that would bring them into proper alignment and eliminate the profitability of arbitrage. From a practical standpoint, opportunities for such profitable currency arbitrage have decreased in recent years, given the large number of currency traders—aided by sophisticated computer information systems—who monitor currency quotes in all financial markets. The result of this activity is that currency exchange rates tend to be consistent throughout the world, with only minimal deviations due to transactions costs.

THE FORWARD MARKET

Foreign exchange markets, as we have seen, may be spot or forward. In the *spot market*, currencies are bought and sold for immediate delivery (generally two business days after the conclusion of the deal). In the *forward market*, currencies are bought and sold now for future delivery, typically 30, 90, or 180 days from the date of the transaction. The exchange rate is agreed on at the time of the contract, but payment is not made until the future delivery actually takes place. Only the most widely traded currencies are included in the regular forward market, but individual forward contracts can be negotiated for most national currencies.

The Forward Rate

The rate of exchange used in the settlement of forward transactions is called the **forward rate**. This rate is quoted in the same way as the spot rate: the price of one currency in terms of another currency. Table 12.10 provides examples of forward rates as of March 28, 1990. Thus, under the Wednesday quotations, the selling price of 30-day British pounds is $1.6182 per pound, the selling price of 90-day pounds is $1.6013 per pound, and for 180-day pounds it is $1.5772 per pound.

It is customary for a currency's forward rate to be stated in relation to its spot rate.

When a foreign currency is worth more in the forward market than in the spot market, it is said to be at a **premium**; conversely, when the currency is worth less in the forward market than in the spot market, it is said to be at a **discount**. The per-annum percentage premium (discount) in forward quotations is computed by the following formula:

$$\text{Premium (discount)} = \frac{\text{forward rate - spot rate}}{\text{spot rate}}$$
$$\times \frac{12}{\text{no. of months forward}}$$

If the result is a negative forward premium, it means that the currency is at a forward discount.

According to Table 12.10, on Wednesday the 30-day forward German mark was selling at $0.5853, whereas the spot price of the mark was $0.5851. Because the forward price of the mark exceeded the spot price, the mark was at a 30-day forward premium of 0.02 cents, or at a 0.4-percent forward premium per annum against the dollar:

$$\text{Premium} = \frac{\$0.5853 - \$0.5851}{\$0.5851} \times \frac{12}{1} = 0.004$$

Similarly, the mark was at a 90-day premium of 0.03 cents, or at a 0.2-percent forward premium per annum against the dollar:

$$\text{Premium} = \frac{\$0.5854 - \$0.5851}{\$0.5851} \times \frac{12}{3} = 0.002$$

As for the French franc, the 180-day forward franc was at a discount of 1.9 percent per annum against the dollar:

$$\text{Discount} = \frac{\$0.17253 - \$0.17419}{\$0.17419} \times \frac{12}{6} = -0.019$$

What determines the forward rate? Why might it be at a premium or discount compared to the spot rate? The forward rate is generally

T A B L E 12. 10 / Forward Exchange Rates

Country	U.S. $ equiv.		Currency per U.S. $	
	Wed.	Tues.	Wed.	Tues.
Britain (Pound)	1.6270	1.6240	.6146	.6158
30-Day Forward	1.6182	1.6150	.6180	.6192
90-Day Forward	1.6013	1.5977	.6245	.6259
180-Day Forward	1.5772	1.5740	.6340	.6363
Canada (Dollar)	.8503	.8500	1.1760	1.1765
30-Day Forward	.8467	.8464	1.1810	1.1815
90-Day Forward	.8402	.8398	1.1902	1.1907
180-Day Forward	.8312	.8313	1.2031	1.2030
France (Franc)	.17419	.17369	5.7410	5.7575
30-Day Forward	.17391	.17340	5.7500	5.7670
90-Day Forward	.17334	.17255	5.7690	5.7955
180-Day Forward	.17253	.17204	5.7960	5.8125
Germany (Mark)	.5851	.5846	1.7090	1.7105
30-Day Forward	.5853	.5848	1.7084	1.7099
90-Day Forward	.5854	.5849	1.7081	1.7096
180-Day Forward	.5851	.5847	1.7090	1.7103
Switzerland (Franc) ..	.6598	.6590	1.5155	1.5175
30-Day Forward	.6592	.6585	1.5169	1.5187
90-Day Forward	.6585	.6578	1.5185	1.5203
180-Day Forward	.6577	.6572	1.5205	1.5215
Japan (Yen)	.006289	.006357	159.00	157.30
30-Day Forward	.006294	.006362	158.89	157.18
90-Day Forward	.006304	.006373	158.63	156.90
180-Day Forward	006319	.006388	158.25	156.55

* SOURCE: *The Wall Street Journal*, April 29, 1990.

regarded as the exchange market's consensus forecast (average expectation) of what will happen to the spot rate over the period of the forward contract. If you desire to know the informed opinion of the market concerning what the pound will be worth in 30 days' time, you can look up the 30-day forward rate. For instance, if the spot rate of the pound is $1.60 and the 30-day forward rate is $1.56, the market's consensus is that the pound's spot rate will depreciate by 4 cents during the next 30 days. To use a sports analogy, the forward rate is like the point spread on a baseball game—the number of runs by which the average gambler believes that the superior team will win.

Forward Market Functions

The forward market can be used to protect international traders and investors from the risks involved in fluctuations of the spot rate. The process of avoiding or covering a foreign exchange risk is known as **hedging**. People who expect to make or receive payments in a foreign currency at a future date are concerned that if the spot rate changes, they will have to make a greater payment or will receive less in terms of the domestic currency than expected. This could wipe out anticipated profit levels. The solution is for such traders and investors to eliminate the element of uncertainty of the foreign exchange rate. Consider the following examples.

C A S E 1

U.S. importer hedges against a dollar depreciation

Assume Sears Roebuck and Co. owes 1 million francs to a Swiss watch manufacturer in three

Exchange-Rate Risk: The Hazard of Investing Abroad

Return on a 3-Month German Investment in 1992

	Deutsche Mark Return	Percent Change in $/DM Exchange Rate	Dollar Return
May 27–August 26	2.4%	16.6%	19.0%
September 30–December 30	2.3	-12.5	-10.0

Exchange-rate fluctuations can substantially change the returns on assets denominated in a foreign currency. A real-world demonstration follows.

Throughout 1992, short-term interest rates in Germany were significantly higher than those in the United States; however, an American choosing between a dollar-denominated and mark-denominated certificate of deposit (CD) with similar liquidities and default risks would not necessarily have earned a higher return on the German CD.

On May 27, 1992, an American saver with $10,000 to invest had the choice between a 3-month CD with an annual interest rate of 3.85 percent from an American bank and a 3-month CD with an annual interest rate of 9.65 percent (approximately 2.4 percent for 3 months) from a German bank. After 3 months, the U.S. CD was worth $10,096 and the German CD was worth $11,900 after exchanging the marks for dollars. As the table shows, the substantially larger value of the German CD was due primarily to a 16.6-percent appreciation of the mark against the dollar from May 27 to August 26.

Now consider the choice facing our investor on September 30, 1992: a 3-month U.S. CD offer-

ing an annual interest rate of 3.09 percent, and a comparable German investment offering an annual interest rate of 9.1 percent (approximately 2.3 percent for 3 months). After 3 months, the U.S. CD was worth $10,077. If the investor purchased the German CD, however, she would have had only $8,964 at the end of the three months—$1,036 less than the purchase price. This loss resulted from the 12.5-percent appreciation of the dollar against the mark between September and December 1992. With hindsight, the American saver would have preferred the U.S. CD to the German CD, even though the German interest rate was higher.

These examples provide a clear message. Even though interest rates play a key role in determining the relative attractiveness of assets denominated in domestic and foreign currencies, the effects of exchange-rate changes can swamp the effects of interest-rate differentials. Such large differences in returns illustrate why many investors choose to hedge against exchange-rate changes.

SOURCE: Patricia S. Pollard, "Exchange Rate Risk: The Hazard of Investing Abroad," *International Economic Conditions*, Federal Reserve Bank of St. Louis, February 1993, p. 1.

months' time. During this period, Sears is in an exposed or *uncovered* position. Sears bears the risk that the dollar price of the franc might rise in three months (the dollar depreciates against the franc), say, from $0.60 to $0.70 per franc; if

so, purchasing 1 million francs would require an extra $100,000!

To cover itself against this risk, Sears could immediately buy 1 million francs in the spot market, but this would immobilize its funds for three months. Alternatively, Sears could contract to purchase 1 million francs in the forward market, at today's forward rate, for delivery in three months. In three months, Sears would purchase francs with dollars, at the contracted price, and use the francs to pay the Swiss exporter. Sears has thus hedged against the possibility of francs' becoming more expensive in three months. Note that hedging in the forward market does not require Sears to tie up its own funds for three months.

CASE 2

U.S. exporter hedges against a dollar appreciation

Assume that Microsoft Corporation anticipates receiving 1 million marks in three months from its exports of computer software to a German retailer. During this period, Microsoft is in an *uncovered* position. If the dollar price of the mark falls (the dollar appreciates against the mark), say, from $0.50 to $0.40 per mark, Microsoft's receipts will be worth $100,000 less when the 1 million marks are converted into dollars!

To avoid this foreign exchange risk, Microsoft can contract to sell its expected mark receipts in the forward market at today's forward rate. By locking into a set forward exchange rate, Microsoft is guaranteed that the value of its mark receipts will be maintained in terms of the dollar, even if the value of the mark should happen to fall.

The forward market thus eliminates the uncertainty of fluctuating spot rates from international transactions. Exporters can hedge against the possibility that the domestic currency will appreciate against the foreign currency, and importers can hedge against the possibility that the domestic currency will depreciate against the foreign currency. Hedging is not limited to exporters and importers. It applies to anyone who is obligated to make a foreign currency payment or who will enjoy foreign currency receipts at a future time. Inter-national investors, for example, also make use of the forward market for hedging purposes.

INTEREST ARBITRAGE

Investors make their financial decisions by comparing the rates of return of foreign investment with those of domestic investment. If rates of return from foreign investment are larger, they will desire to shift their funds abroad. **Interest arbitrage** refers to the process of moving funds into foreign currencies to take advantage of higher investment yields abroad. But investors assume a risk when they have foreign investments: when the investment's proceeds are converted back into the home currency, their value may fall because of a change in the exchange rate. Investors can eliminate this exchange risk by obtaining "cover" in the forward market.

Uncovered Interest Arbitrage

Uncovered interest arbitrage occurs when an investor does not obtain exchange market cover to protect investment proceeds from foreign currency fluctuations. Although this practice is rarely used, it is a good pedagogical starting point.

Suppose the interest rate on 3-month Treasury bills is 6 percent (per annum) in New York and 10 percent (per annum) in London, and that the current spot rate is $2 per pound. A U.S. investor would seek to profit from this opportunity by exchanging dollars for pounds at the rate of $2 per pound and using these pounds to purchase 3-month British Treasury bills in London. The investor would earn 4 percent more per year, or 1 percent more for the 3 months, than if the same dollars had been used to buy 3-month Treasury bills in New York. These results are summarized in Table 12.11.

However, it is *not* necessarily true that our U.S. investor realizes an extra 1-percent rate of return (per 3 months) by moving funds to London. This amount will be realized only if the exchange value of the pound remains constant

TABLE 12. 11   /   *Uncovered Interest Arbitrage: An Example*

	Rate per Year	Rate per 3 Months
U.K. 3-month Treasury bill interest rate	10%	2.5%
U.S. 3-month Treasury bill interest rate	6%	1.5%
Uncovered interest-rate differential favoring the U.K.	4%	1.0%

over the investment period. If the pound *depreciates* against the dollar, the investor makes *less*; if the pound *appreciates* against the dollar, the investor makes *more!*

Suppose our investor earns an extra 1 percent by purchasing 3-month British Treasury bills rather than U.S. Treasury bills. Over the same period, suppose the dollar price of the pound falls from $2.00 to $1.99 (the pound *depreciates* against the dollar). When the proceeds are converted back into dollars, the investor *loses* 0.5 percent [($2.00 - $1.99) / $2.00 = 0.005]. The investor thus earns only 0.5 percent more (1 percent minus 0.5 percent) than if the funds had been placed in U.S. Treasury bills. The reader can verify that if the dollar price of the pound fell from $2 to $1.98 over the investment period, the U.S. investor would earn nothing extra by investing in British Treasury bills.

Alternatively, suppose that in three months the pound rises from $2 to $2.02, a 1-percent *appreciation* against the dollar. This time, in addition to the extra 1-percent return on British Treasury bills, our investor realizes a return of 1 percent from the appreciation of the pound. The reason? When she bought pounds to finance her purchase of British Treasury bills, she paid $2 per pound; when she converted her

investment proceeds back into dollars, she received $2.02 per pound [($2.02 - $2.00) / $2.00 = .01]. Because the pound's appreciation adds to her investment's profitability, she earns 2 percent more than if she had purchased U.S. treasury bills.

In summary, a U.S. investor's extra rate of return on an investment in the United Kingdom, as compared to the United States, equals the interest-rate differential adjusted for any change in the value of the pound, as follows:

Extra return = (U.K. interest rate - U.S. interest rate) - % depreciation of the pound

or

Extra return = (U.K. interest rate - U.S. interest rate) + % appreciation of the pound

Covered Interest Arbitrage

Investing funds in a foreign financial center involves an exchange rate risk. Because investors typically desire to avoid this risk, interest arbitrage is usually covered.

Covered interest arbitrage involves two basic steps: (1) An investor exchanges domestic currency for foreign currency, at the current spot rate, and uses the foreign currency to finance a foreign investment. (2) At the same time, the investor contracts in the forward market to sell the amount of foreign currency that will be received as the proceeds from the investment, with a delivery date to coincide with the maturity of the investment. It pays for the investor to make the foreign investment if the positive interest-rate differential in favor of the foreign investment more than offsets the cost of obtaining the forward cover.

Suppose the interest rate on 3-month treasury bills is 12 percent (per annum) in London and 8 percent (per annum) in New York; the interest differential in favor of London is 4 percent per annum, or 1 percent for 3 months. Suppose also that the current spot rate for the pound is $2, while the 3-month forward pound sells for $1.99. This means that the 3-month

TABLE 12. 12 / *Covered Interest Arbitrage: An Example*

	Rate per Year	Rate per 3 Months
U.K. 3-month Treasury bill interest rate	12%	3%
U.S. 3-month Treasury bill interest rate	8%	2%
Uncovered interest-rate differential favoring the U.K.	4%	1%
Forward discount on the 3-month pound		-0.5%
Covered interest-rate differential favoring the U.K.		0.5%

forward pound is at a 0.5-percent *discount* [($1.99 - $2.00) / $2.00 = -.005].

By purchasing 3-month Treasury bills in London, a U.S. investor could earn 1 percent more for the 3 months than if he bought 3-month Treasury bills in New York. To eliminate the uncertainty over how many dollars will be received when the pounds are converted into dollars, the investor sells enough pounds on the 3-month forward market to coincide with the anticipated proceeds of the investment. The cost of the forward cover equals the difference between the spot rate and the contracted 3-month forward rate; this difference is the discount on the forward pound, or 0.5 percent. Subtracting this 0.5 percent from the interest-rate differential of 1 percent, the investor is able to realize a net rate of return that is 0.5 percent higher than if he had bought U.S. Treasury bills. These results are summarized in Table 12.12.

This investment opportunity will not last long, because the net profit margin will soon disappear. As U.S. investors purchase spot pounds, the spot rate will rise. Concurrently, the sale of forward pounds will push the forward rate downward. The result is a *widening* of the discount on the forward pounds, which means that the cost of covering the exchange-rate risk increases. This arbitraging process will continue until the forward discount on the pound widens to 1 percent, at which point the extra profitability of the foreign investment vanishes. The discount on the pound now equals the interest-rate differential between New York and London:

Pound forward discount = U.K. interest rate
- U.S. interest rate

In short, the theory of foreign exchange suggests that the forward discount or premium on one currency against another reflects the difference in the short-term interest rates between the two nations. The currency of the *higher* interest-rate nation should be at a forward *discount*, while the currency of the *lower* interest-rate nation should be at a forward *premium*.

International differences in interest rates do exert a major influence on the relationship between the spot and forward rates. But on any particular day, one would hardly expect the spread on short-term interest rates between financial centers to precisely equal the discount or premium on foreign exchange, for several reasons. First, changes in interest-rate differentials do not always induce an immediate investor response necessary to eliminate the investment profits. Second, investors sometimes transfer funds on an uncovered basis; such transfers do not have an effect on the forward rate. Third, factors such as governmental exchange controls and speculation may weaken the connection between the interest-rate differential and the spot and forward rates.

FOREIGN EXCHANGE MARKET SPECULATION

Besides being used for the financing of commercial transactions and investments, the foreign exchange market is also used for exchange-rate speculation. **Speculation** is the attempt to profit by trading on expectations about prices in the future. Some speculators are traders acting for financial institutions or firms; others are individuals. In either case, speculators buy currencies that they expect to go up in value and sell currencies that they expect to go down in value.

Note the difference between arbitrage and speculation. With arbitrage, a currency trader *simultaneously* buys a currency at a low price and sells that currency at a high price, thus making a riskless profit. A speculator's goal is to buy a currency at one moment (such as today) and sell that currency at a higher price in the future (such as tomorrow). Speculation thus implies the deliberate assumption of exchange risk: if the price of the currency falls between today and tomorrow, the speculator loses money.

Speculating in the Spot Market

Imagine that you are a currency speculator in New York, willing to risk money on your own opinion about future prices of a foreign currency—say, the German mark. Consider the following scenarios.

C A S E   1

Speculating on a German mark appreciation

GIVEN

Today's spot price is $0.40 per mark.

ASSUMPTION

In 3 months, the spot price of the mark will rise to $0.50.

PROCEDURE

1. Purchase marks at today's spot price of $0.40 and deposit them in a bank to earn interest.
2. In 3 months, sell the marks at the prevailing spot price of $0.50 per mark.

OUTCOME

If assumption is right, profit = $0.10 per mark.

If assumption is wrong and the spot price of the mark falls instead, you incur a loss, reselling marks at a price lower than the purchase price.

C A S E   2

Speculating on a German mark depreciation

GIVEN

Today's spot price is $0.40 per mark.

ASSUMPTION

In 3 months, the spot price of the mark will fall to $0.25.

PROCEDURE

1. Borrow marks today, exchange them for dollars at the prevailing spot price of $0.40 per mark, and deposit the dollars in a bank to earn interest.
2. In 3 months, buy marks at the prevailing spot price of $0.25 per mark and use them to pay back the loan.

OUTCOME

If assumption is right, profit = $0.15 per mark. (This return is reduced by the interest paid on borrowed money, but increased by the interest received on the bank savings account.)

If assumption is wrong and the spot price of the mark rises instead, you will incur a loss, buying marks at a higher price than the initial selling price.

Speculating in the Forward Market

Although speculation on the spot market can lead to profits, it has a serious drawback: the speculator must have a large amount of idle cash or borrowing privileges, which require interest payments. Speculation in the forward market, however, does not require cash or credit facilities. All the speculator needs to do is sign a forward contract with a bank to either purchase or sell a specified amount of foreign currency at a specified future date. The bank may impose a *margin requirement,* requiring the speculator to put up, say, 10 percent of the value of the foreign contract as security. In practice, most speculation is done in the forward market.

Forward market speculation occurs when a speculator believes that a currency's spot price at some future date will differ from today's forward price for that same date. For example, suppose the 30-day forward pound is selling at a 10-percent discount; this discount is the market's consensus (average expectation) that in 30 days the spot rate of the pound will be 10-percent lower than it is today. As a speculator, however, you feel you have better information than the market. You believe that in 30 days the pound's spot rate will be only 5-percent lower (or maybe 15-percent higher) than it is today. You are willing to bet your money that the market consensus is wrong. Your gains or losses will equal the difference between the current forward rate and the spot rate 30 days from now. Consider the following scenarios.

C A S E   1

Speculating that the spot rate of the German mark in 3 months will be higher *than its current 3-month forward rate*

GIVEN

The current price of the 3-month forward mark is $0.40.

ASSUMPTION

In 3 months, the prevailing spot price of the mark will be $0.50.

PROCEDURE

1. Contract to purchase a specified amount of marks in the forward market, at $0.40 per mark, for 3-month delivery.
2. After receiving delivery of the marks in 3 months, resell them in the spot market at the prevailing price of $0.50 per mark.

OUTCOME

If assumption is right, profit = $0.10 per mark.

If assumption is wrong and the prevailing spot price in 3 months is lower than $0.40 per mark, you incur a loss.

C A S E   2

Speculating that the spot rate of the German mark in 3 months will be lower *than its current 3-month forward rate*

GIVEN

The current price of the 3-month forward mark is $0.40.

ASSUMPTION

In 3 months, the prevailing spot price of the mark will be $0.30.

PROCEDURE

1. Contract to sell a specified amount of marks (which you do not currently have) for delivery in 3 months at the forward price of $0.40 per mark.
2. In 3 months, purchase an identical amount of marks in the spot market at $0.30 per mark and deliver them to fulfill the forward contract.

OUTCOME

If assumption is right, profit = $0.10 per mark.

If assumption is wrong and the prevailing spot price in 3 months is higher than $0.40 per mark, you incur a loss.

When speculators purchase foreign currency on the spot or forward market with the anticipation of selling it at a higher future spot price, they are said to take a **long position** in the currency. But when speculators borrow or sell forward a foreign currency with the anticipation of purchasing it at a future lower price to repay the foreign exchange loan or fulfill the forward sale contract, they are said to take a **short position** (that is, they are selling what they do not presently have).

Other Forms of Speculation

Besides speculation in the spot and forward markets, there are other ways of capitalizing on expectations of currency movements. One way is to *purchase securities* denominated in a foreign currency. A U.S. speculator who anticipates that the German mark's spot rate will significantly appreciate in the near future might purchase bonds issued by German corporations and expressed in marks. The bonds are paid for in marks, which are purchased by converting dollars into marks at the prevailing spot rate. If the mark goes up, the speculator gets not only the accrued interest from the bond but also its appreciated value in dollars. The catch is that, in all likelihood, others have the same expectations. The overall demand for the bonds may be sufficient to force up the bond price, resulting in a lower interest rate. For the speculator to win, the mark's appreciation must exceed the loss of interest income. In many cases, the exchange-rate changes are not large enough to make such investments worthwhile.

Rather than investing in foreign securities, some speculators choose to *purchase stocks* of foreign corporations, denominated in foreign currencies. The speculator in this case is trying to predict the trend of not only the foreign currency but also its stock market. The speculator must be highly knowledgeable about both financial and economic affairs in the foreign country.

For investors who expect that the spot rate of a foreign currency will soon rise, the answer lies in a *savings account* denominated in a foreign currency. For example, a U.S. investor may contact a major New York bank or a U.S. branch of a foreign bank and take out an interest-bearing certificate of deposit expressed in a foreign currency. An advantage of such a savings account is that the investor is guaranteed a fixed interest rate. An investor who has guessed correctly also enjoys the gains stemming from the foreign currency's appreciation. However, the investor must be aware of the possibility that governments might tax or shut off such deposits or interfere with the investor's freedom to hold another nation's currency.

SPECULATION AND EXCHANGE MARKET STABILITY

An exchange market speculator deliberately assumes foreign exchange risk on the expectation of profiting from future changes in the spot exchange rate. Such activity can exert either a stabilizing or a destabilizing influence on the foreign exchange market.

Stabilizing speculation goes against market forces by *moderating* or *reversing* a rise or fall in a currency's exchange rate. It occurs when a speculator buys foreign currency with domestic currency when the domestic price of the foreign currency falls, or depreciates. The hope is that the domestic price of the foreign currency will soon increase, leading to a profit. Such purchases increase the demand for the foreign currency, which moderates its depreciation. Stabilizing speculation also occurs when a speculator sells foreign currency when the domestic price of the foreign currency rises, or appreciates, in the hope that the price will soon fall. Such sales moderate the appreciation of the foreign currency. Stabilizing speculation performs a useful function for bankers and businesspeople, who desire stable exchange rates.

Destabilizing speculation goes with market forces by *reinforcing* fluctuations in a currency's exchange rate. It occurs when a speculator sells a foreign currency when it depreciates, on the expectation that it will depreciate further in the future. Such sales depress the foreign currency's value. It also occurs when speculators buy a foreign currency when its exchange rate appreciates, on the expectation that it will appreciate even further in the future. Such purchases increase the foreign currency's value. Destabilizing speculation reinforces exchange-rate fluctuations and can disrupt international trade and investment.

Should destabilizing speculation against a currency be sufficiently large, it may induce sizable forward discounts on the currency. If speculators view a currency as particularly weak, they may anticipate a significant decline in its value. Immediately they would begin selling the currency forward for future delivery, in the hope of fulfilling their futures contracts at lower spot rates. These sales tend to further weaken the forward rate, causing the forward discount to become larger. When there is a sizable forward discount on a currency, the ability of interest-rate differentials to promote order in the exchange market may be limited.

Destabilizing speculation can disrupt international transactions in several ways. Because of the uncertainty of financing exports and imports, the cost of hedging may become so high that international trade is impeded. What

is more, unstable exchange rates may disrupt international investment activity. This is because the cost of obtaining forward cover for international capital transactions may rise significantly as foreign exchange risk intensifies.

A slight variation of the concept of foreign market speculation is that of *capital flight*. This is motivated not by the expectation of profit but rather by the fear of exchange market loss. Capital flight may be induced by fear of currency devaluation, political instability, or government restrictions on foreign exchange movements. Such short-run monetary flows, sometimes referred to as *hot money*, created marked disruptions in the international monetary system during the late 1960s and early 1970s. Major capital flights out of the overvalued U.S. dollar in 1971 and 1973 touched off not only the termination of the dollar's gold convertibility but also the collapse of the historic Bretton Woods monetary system.

SUMMARY

1. The foreign exchange market provides the institutional framework within which individuals, businesses, and financial institutions purchase and sell foreign exchange. Two of the world's largest foreign exchange markets are located in New York and London.

2. The exchange rate is the price of one unit of foreign currency in terms of the domestic currency. From a U.S. viewpoint, the exchange rate might refer to the number of dollars necessary to buy a German mark. A dollar depreciation (appreciation) is an increase (decrease) in the number of dollars required to buy a unit of foreign exchange.

3. In the foreign exchange market, currencies are traded around the clock and throughout the world. Most foreign exchange trading is in the interbank market. Banks typically engage in three types of foreign exchange transactions: spot, forward, and swap.

4. The *Wall Street Journal*'s foreign exchange quotations include those of the New York foreign exchange market and the International Monetary Market located in Chicago. Both spot quotations and forward quotations are provided.

5. The equilibrium rate of exchange in a free market is determined by the intersection of the supply and demand schedules of foreign exchange. These schedules are derived from the credit and debit items in a nation's balance of payments.

6. Whereas the demand schedule for foreign exchange is normally drawn as downward-sloping, the supply schedule may be positively sloped or negatively sloped.

7. Exchange arbitrage permits the rates of exchange in different parts of the world to be kept the same. This is achieved by selling a currency when its price is high and purchasing when the price is low.

8. Foreign traders and investors often deal in the forward market for protection from possible exchange-rate fluctuations. However, speculators also buy and sell currencies in the futures markets in anticipation of sizable profits. In general, interest arbitrage determines the relationship between the spot rate and the forward rate.

9. Speculation in the foreign exchange markets may be either stabilizing or destablizing in nature.

STUDY QUESTIONS

1. What is meant by the foreign exchange market? Where is it located?
2. What is meant by the forward market? How does this differ from the spot market?
3. The supply and demand for foreign exchange are considered to be derived schedules. Explain.
4. Explain how the supply of foreign exchange may be upward-sloping and backward-sloping at various exchange rates.
5. What factors cause shifts in the supply and demand schedules of foreign exchange?
6. Explain why exchange-rate quotations stated in different financial centers tend to be consistent with each other.
7. Who are the participants in the forward exchange market? What advantages does this market afford these participants?
8. What explains the relationship between the spot rate and the forward rate?
9. What is the strategy of speculating in the forward market? In what other ways can one speculate on exchange-rate changes?
10. Distinguish between stabilizing speculation and destabilizing speculation.
11. If the exchange rate changes from $1.70 = £1 to $1.68 = £1, what does this mean for the dollar? For the pound? What if the exchange rate changes from $1.70 = £1 to $1.72 = £1?
12. Suppose $1.69 = £1 in New York and $1.71 = £1 in London. How can foreign exchange arbitragers profit from these exchange rates? Explain how foreign exchange arbitrage results in the same dollar/pound exchange rate in New York and London.
13. Table 12.13 shows supply and demand schedules for the British pound. Assume that exchange rates are flexible.
    a. The equilibrium exchange rate equals _____. At this exchange rate, how many pounds will be purchased, and at what cost in terms of dollars?
    b. Suppose the exchange rate is $2.00 per pound. At this exchange rate, there is an excess (supply/demand) of pounds. This imbalance causes (an increase/a decrease) in the dollar price of the pound, which leads to (a/an) _____ in the quantity of pounds supplied and (a/an) _____ in the quantity of pounds demanded.
    c. Suppose the exchange rate is $1.00 per pound. At this exchange rate, there is an excess (supply/demand) for pounds. This

TABLE 12. 13 / *Supply and Demand of British Pounds*

Quantity of Pounds Supplied	Dollars per Pound	Quantity of Pounds Demanded
50	$2.50	10
40	2.00	20
30	1.50	30
20	1.00	40
10	.50	50

imbalance causes (an increase/a decrease) in the price of the pound, which leads to (a/an) _____ in the quantity of pounds supplied and (a/an) _____ in the quantity of pounds demanded.

14. Suppose the spot rate of the pound today is $1.70 and the 3-month forward rate is $1.75.
    a. How can a U.S. importer who has to pay $20,000 pounds in 3 months hedge her foreign exchange risk?
    b. What occurs if the U.S. importer does not hedge and the spot rate of the pound in 3 months is $1.80?
15. Suppose the interest rate (on an annual basis) on 3-month treasury bills is 10 percent in London and 6 percent in New York, and the spot rate of the pound is $2.00.
    a. How can a U.S. investor profit from uncovered interest arbitrage?
    b. If the price of the 3-month forward pound is $1.99, will a U.S. investor benefit from covered interest arbitrage? If so, by how much?
16. Table 12.14 gives hypothetical dollar/mark exchange values for Wednesday, May 1, 1993.
    a. Fill in the last two columns of the table with the reciprocal price of the dollar in terms of the mark.
    b. On Wednesday, the spot price of the two currencies was _____ dollars per mark, or _____ marks per dollar.
    c. From Tuesday to Wednesday, in the spot market the dollar (appreciated/depreciated) against the mark; the mark (appreciated/depreciated) against the dollar.

T A B L E 12. 14   /   Dollar/Mark Exchange Values

	U.S. $ equiv.		Currency per U.S. $	
	Wed.	Tues.	Wed.	Tues.
German (Mark)	.5851	.5846		
30-Day Forward	.5853	.5848		
90-Day Forward	.5854	.5849		
180-Day Forward	.5851	.5847		

d. In Wednesday's spot market, the cost of buying 100 marks was $_____; the cost of buying $100 was _____ marks.

e. On Wednesday, the 30-day forward mark was at a (premium/discount) of _____ dollars, which equaled _____ percent on an annual basis. What about the 90-day forward mark?

17. Assume a speculator anticipates that the spot rate of the mark in 3 months will be lower than today's 3-month forward rate of the mark, $0.50 = 1 mark.

a. How can this speculator use her $1 million to speculate in the forward market?

b. What occurs if the mark's spot rate in 3 months is $0.40? $0.60? $0.50?

18. You are given the following spot exchange rates: $1 = 3 marks, $1 = 4 francs, and 1 mark = 2 francs. Ignoring transaction costs, how much profit could a person make via three-point arbitrage?

Exchange-Rate Determination

Since the introduction of market-determined exchange rates by the major industrial nations in the 1970s, wide shifts in exchange rates have been observed. From 1980 to 1985, for example, the U.S. dollar appreciated more than 47 percent on a trade-weighted basis against the currencies of its major trading partners—only to be followed by subsequent depreciations in its value, as seen in Figure 13.1. What underlies the exchange value of a currency?

To state simply that demand and supply underlie exchange rates in a free market is at once to say everything and to say nothing. If we are to understand why some exchange rates depreciate and others appreciate, we must investigate the factors that cause supply and demand to move. Although professional traders and scholars agree on some of the fundamentals of exchange-rate determination, they admit that their understanding and forecasting ability are limited. In developing theories of exchange-rate behavior, economists consider *long-run move-*

ments (over several years) in exchange rates as well as *short-run fluctuations* that occur on a day-to-day basis.

This chapter investigates the factors that determine exchange rates in markets in which they are allowed to fluctuate according to the forces of supply and demand. It is possible to identify several theories of **exchange-rate determination**: (1) the balance-of-payments approach, (2) the purchasing-power-parity approach, (3) the monetary approach, (4) the expectations approach, and (5) the asset-markets approach. Table 13.1 summarizes the major factors that affect a currency's exchange value, as discussed throughout this chapter.

BALANCE-OF-PAYMENTS APPROACH

The **balance-of-payments approach** to exchange-rate determination shows how changes in the equilibrium exchange rate are brought about by

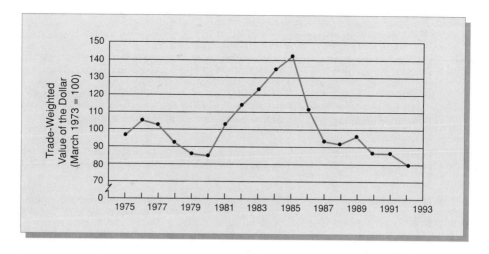

F I G U R E *13. 1 The dance of the U.S. dollar.* From the end of World War II until the late 1960s, the U.S. dollar was universally recognized as the world's key currency. During the 1970s, however, the exchange value of the dollar fell relative to most leading currencies, hitting its low point in 1978. During the first half of the 1980s, the dollar's exchange value steadily rose, only to be followed by a decline in the dollar's exchange rate toward the end of the 1980s. The depreciation of the dollar in 1985–1990 wiped out almost all of the 1980–1985 appreciation. (SOURCE: *Federal Reserve Bulletin,* various issues.)

forces that shift the supply and demand schedules of foreign exchange. These forces include anything (other than the exchange rate itself) that induces changes in purchases of goods, services, or assets by foreign residents. The demand for foreign exchange involves all *debit* transactions that appear in a nation's balance of payments, whereas the supply of foreign exchange involves all *credit* transactions. The balance-of-payments approach emphasizes the *flows* of goods, services, and investment capital that respond gradually to fundamental or real economic factors (such as income).

Goods and Services Transactions

Shifts in the supply and demand for foreign exchange reflect changes in the domestic demand for foreign goods and services and in the foreign demand for domestic goods and services. The supply and demand schedules of goods and services, in turn, are influenced by macroeconomic conditions at home and abroad, the major ones being (1) relative prices of domestic and foreign goods and (2) the level of real income within countries. Other factors that affect the supply and demand of foreign and home goods include consumer tastes, technological change, resource accumulation, harvest conditions, strikes, market structure, and trade policy.

Let's consider how changes in U.S. *real income* affect the exchange rate between the dollar and the pound. Figure 13.2 illustrates the foreign exchange market. The demand and supply schedules of pounds are denoted by D_0 and S_0, respectively, and the equilibrium exchange rate is $1.50 per pound. Suppose there occurs an increase in the growth rate of the U.S. economy that results in higher real incomes for U.S. households. As the economy grows, U.S. consumers buy more domestically produced goods and also more foreign goods. If the U.S. economy is expanding rapidly and the British economy is stagnant, U.S. imports of

T A B L E 13. 1 / *Factors Influencing the Dollar's Exchange Value*

Factor	Change	Effect on the Dollar's Exchange Value
Foreign demand for U.S. exports	Decrease Increase	Depreciation Appreciation
Foreign demand for U.S. assets (stocks, bonds, bank deposits)	Decrease Increase	Depreciation Appreciation
U.S. demand for foreign imports	Decrease Increase	Appreciation Depreciation
U.S. demand for foreign assets	Decrease Increase	Appreciation Depreciation
U.S. price level relative to foreign price level	Decrease Increase	Appreciation Depreciation
U.S. interest rates relative to foreign interest rates	Decrease Increase	Depreciation Appreciation
U.S. income relative to foreign income	Decrease Increase	Appreciation Depreciation

British goods will increase. The demand for pounds thus increases from D_0 to D_1 in the figure. Given supply-of-pounds schedule S_0, the dollar depreciates to $2 per pound.

Because consumer spending rises with an increase in income and falls when income falls, the same is likely to occur with spending on imported goods. When the U.S. rate of economic growth increases, U.S. imports will gradually rise, thus leading to a depreciation in the dollar's value. But if economic growth also occurs in the United Kingdom, British households will buy more U.S. goods, and the supply of pounds will shift outward to the right. Whether the dollar depreciates or appreciates against the pound depends on whether U.S. imports from the United Kingdom are rising faster than U.S. exports to the United Kingdom.

The general rule is that a nation experiencing *faster* economic growth than the rest of the world tends to find its currency's exchange value *depreciating!* This is because its imports rise faster than its exports, and thus its demand for foreign currency rises more rapidly than its supply of foreign currency.

The exchange rate between the U.S. dollar and the German mark provides an example of this tendency. During the rebound from global recession in 1974–1976, the U.S. economy experienced faster growth than the German economy. This is one reason why the dollar depreciated against the mark from late 1976 to late 1978.

International Capital Movements

Although economic growth is an important determinant of exchange rates over the longer run, other factors influence exchange rates in the short run. One such factor is *short-term interest-rate differentials* between nations, which influence **international capital movements**.

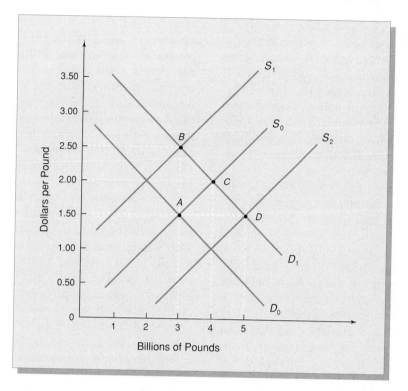

FIGURE 13. 2 *Changes in the equilibrium exchange rate.* In a free market, changes in the equilibrium exchange rate occur in response to shifts in the supply and demand schedules of foreign exchange. Shifts in these schedules can be caused by changes in inflation, interest rates, income levels, market expectations, money supply, money demand, consumer tastes, and technology/productivity.

Recall that the capital account of the balance of payments is a measure of the total domestic currency value of financial transactions between domestic residents and the rest of the world over a period of time. It involves financial transactions associated not only with international trade but also with portfolio shifts involving the purchase of foreign stocks, bonds, and bank deposits.

A common view is that easy credit and relatively low short-term interest rates lead to exchange-rate depreciation for a nation, whereas tight credit and relatively high short-term interest rates cause a nation's currency to appreciate. These conclusions are based on the assumption that short-term interest-rate differentials between any two nations are a key determinant of international capital movements, as seen in the following example.

Referring to Figure 13.2, suppose the equilibrium exchange rate for the dollar and pound is $1.50 per pound, determined at the point of intersection of schedules S_0 and D_0. Assume that an expansionary monetary policy of the U.S. Federal Reserve results in a fall in U.S. short-term interest rates to 8 percent, while interest rates in the United Kingdom equal 10 percent. U.S. investors will be attracted by the relatively high interest rates in the United Kingdom and will demand more pounds to buy

British securities. The demand for pounds thus rises to D_1 in the figure. Concurrently, the British will find investing in the United States less attractive than before, so fewer pounds will be offered to buy dollars for purchases of U.S. securities. The supply of pounds thus shifts to S_1 in the figure. The combined effect of these two shifts is to move the market equilibrium from point A to point B, and the dollar depreciates to $2.50 per pound.

Observers point to the U.S. dollar during 1981–1985 as an example of currency appreciation caused by high interest rates. During 1983 and 1984, the U.S. economy enjoyed rapid recovery from the global recession while sluggish economic growth plagued its trading partners. The result was a decrease in the value of U.S. exports relative to the value of U.S. imports. This situation by itself would have caused the dollar to depreciate. That the dollar continued to appreciate suggested that the downward pressure of a worsening trade deficit was being more than offset by the upward pressure of an increasing demand for dollars by international investors.

Things may not always be so simple, though, concerning the relationship between interest rates and exchange rates. It is important to distinguish between the **nominal (money) interest rate** and the **real interest rate** (the nominal interest rate minus the inflation rate). For international investors, it is relative changes in the real interest rate that matter.

If a rise in the nominal interest rate in the United States is accompanied by an *equal* rise in the U.S. inflation rate, the real interest rate remains *constant*. In this case, higher nominal interest rates do not make dollar-denominated securities more attractive to British investors. This is because rising U.S. inflation will encourage U.S. buyers to seek out low-priced British goods, which will increase the demand for pounds and cause the dollar to depreciate. British investors will expect the exchange rate of the dollar, in terms of the pound, to depreciate along with the declining purchasing power of the dollar. The higher nominal return on U.S.

securities will thus be offset by the expectation of a lower future exchange rate, leaving the motivation for increased British investment in the United States unaffected. Only if higher nominal interest rates in the United States signal an *increase* in the real interest rate would the dollar *appreciate*. If they signal rising inflationary expectations and a *falling* real interest rate, the dollar will *depreciate*. Table 13.2 provides examples of short-term real interest rates for various nations.

One explanation of U.S. experience prior to October 1979 was that inflationary expectations were dominant in U.S. financial markets. Increases in nominal interest rates were linked to falling real rates and future dollar depreciation. In October 1979, the Federal Reserve changed its operating procedure by lessening its control over interest rates and adopting tight control of the money supply. The policy prevailed for three years and succeeded in breaking inflationary expectations. As a result, increases in nominal interest rates became associated with rising real rates, which led to added demand for the dollar and an appreciation in its exchange rate.

In sum, the balance-of-payments approach is recognized by economists as a general statement of exchange-rate determination. It predicts exchange rate *depreciation* for nations with *deficits* in their international transactions and *appreciation* for nations with *surpluses*. A major problem in using the balance-of-payments approach to forecast exchange-rate movements is that it is difficult to define unambiguously what constitutes balance in a nation's international payments. Consequently, nations have resorted to classifications of their international transactions into the trade account, the current account, and various arbitrary breakdowns of the capital account (discussed in Chapter 11). None of these accounts alone can predict exchange-rate fluctuations.

Because the balance-of-payments approach emphasizes flows of funds that adjust gradually over a period of time, it has difficulty in explaining short-run volatility of exchange

Interest Rates and the Dollar's Exchange Value

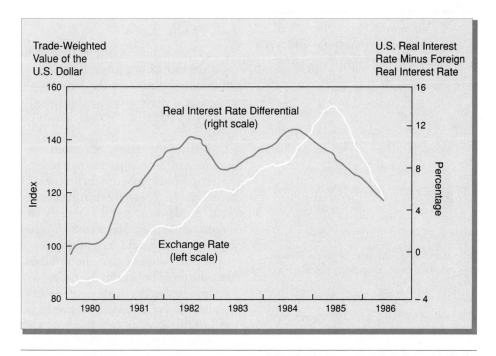

SOURCE: Craig Hakkio, "Interest Rates and Exchange Rates: What Is the Relationship?" *Economic Review*, Federal Reserve Bank of Kansas City (November 1986).

The theory of flexible exchange rates helps explain the behavior of the dollar in the 1980s. When real interest rates in the United States are increasing relative to real interest rates overseas, the U.S. dollar should appreciate as investors seek to locate their funds in the United States.

The figure shows the real interest-rate differential between the United States and other industrial nations in the 1980s. Over the period 1980–1984, the real interest rate rose in the United States relative to the other nations. This attracted investment funds into the United States and promoted a steady appreciation in the dollar's value until early 1985. Subsequently, the dollar's exchange value decreased sharply as the real interest-rate differential moved lower.

rates. The failure to explain this volatility, which has been so widespread throughout 1970s–1990s, is one reason why the balance-of-payments approach is no longer so popular.

As discussed later in this chapter, the asset-markets approach to exchange-rate determination attempts to explain why exchange rates can exhibit large swings from day to day.

TABLE 13. 2 / *Short-Term Nominal and Real Interest Rates, 1992*

Country	Nominal Interest Rate*	Inflation Rate†	Real Interest Rate
Italy	13.9%	5.0%	8.9%
France	10.1	2.8	7.3
United Kingdom	9.6	3.7	5.9
Germany	9.4	3.9	5.5
Belgium	9.3	2.4	6.9
Netherlands	9.3	3.7	5.6
Switzerland	7.7	4.1	3.6
Canada	6.8	1.5	5.3
Japan	4.4	2.1	2.3
United States	3.5	3.3	0.2

* Rates are for 3-month interbank loans, with the following exceptions: Canada, finance company paper; Belgium, 3-month Treasury bills; Japan, CD rate.

†Measured by the consumer price index.

SOURCE: *Federal Reserve Bulletin*, April 1993, and *International Financial Statistics*, March 1993.

PURCHASING-POWER-PARITY APPROACH

Determining the long-run equilibrium value of an exchange rate (the value toward which the actual rate tends to move, given current economic conditions and policies) is important for successful exchange-rate management. For example, if a nation's exchange rate rises above the level warranted by economic conditions, so that its currency becomes *overvalued,* the nation's costs will no longer be competitive and a trade *deficit* will likely occur. An *undervalued* currency tends to lead to a trade *surplus.* National authorities have tried to forecast the long-run equilibrium rate and initiate exchange-rate adjustments to keep the actual rate in line with the forecasted rate. The **purchasing-power-**parity approach can be used to make predictions about exchange rates.

Law of One Price

The simplest concept of purchasing-power-parity is the **law of one price**. It asserts that identical goods should cost the same in all nations, assuming it is costless to ship goods between nations and there are no barriers to trade (such as tariffs).

Before the costs of goods in different nations can be compared, prices must first be converted into a common currency. Once converted at the going market exchange rate, the prices of identical goods from any two nations should be identical. After converting marks into dollars, for example, machine tools purchased in Germany should cost the same as identical machine tools bought in the United States.

In theory, the pursuit of profits tends to equalize the price of identical products in different nations. Assume that machine tools bought in Germany are cheaper than the same machine tools bought in the United States, after converting marks into dollars. German exporters could realize a profit by purchasing machine tools in Germany at a low price and selling them in the United States at a high price. Such transactions would force prices up in Germany and force prices down in the United States until the price of the machine tools would eventually equalize in both nations, whether prices are expressed in marks or dollars. As a result, the law of one price would prevail.

In practice, however, the law of one price does not always prevail. International trade is more complicated than suggested by simple theories. For example, tariffs and other trade barriers tend to drive a wedge between prices of identical products in different nations. Moreover, the cost of transporting goods from one nation to another restricts the potential profit from buying and selling identical products with different prices.

Inflation Rates and the Dollar's Exchange Value

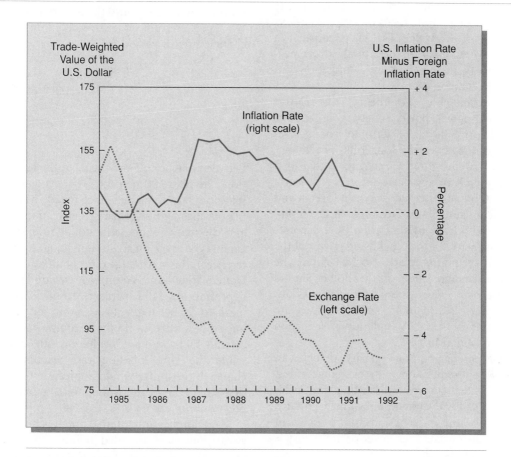

SOURCE: Federal Reserve Bank of St. Louis, *International Economic Conditions* (February 1992), p. 41.

The purchasing-power-parity theory helps explain the behavior of a currency's exchange value. According to this theory, changes in relative national price levels determine changes in exchange rates over the long run. A currency would be expected to depreciate by an amount equal to the excess of domestic inflation over foreign inflation; it would appreciate by an amount equal to the excess of foreign inflation over domestic inflation.

During the late 1980s and early 1990s, the U.S. inflation rate exceeded the average inflation rate of its major trading partners, as seen in the figure. The relatively high U.S. inflation rate contributed to a depreciation in the dollar's exchange value against the trade-weighted average of their currencies.

Relative Purchasing-Power Parity

Rather than focusing on a particular good when applying the purchasing-power-parity concept, most analysts focus on market baskets consisting of many goods. They consider a nation's overall inflation (deflation) rate as measured by, say, the producer price index or consumer price index.

According to the theory of **relative purchasing-power parity**, changes in relative national price levels determine changes in exchange rates over the long run. The theory predicts that the foreign exchange value of a currency tends to appreciate or depreciate at a rate equal to the difference between foreign and domestic inflation. As an example, if U.S. inflation exceeds Germany's inflation by 4 percentage points per year, the purchasing power of the dollar falls 4 points relative to the mark. The foreign exchange value of the dollar should therefore depreciate 4 percent per year. Conversely, the U.S. dollar should appreciate against the mark if U.S. inflation is less than Germany's inflation.

The purchasing-power-parity theory can be used to predict long-run exchange rates. We'll consider an example using the price indexes (P) of the United States and Germany. Letting 0 be the base period and 1 represent period 1, the purchasing-power-parity theory is given in symbols as[1]

$$S_1 = S_0 \frac{P_{U.S._1} / P_{U.S._0}}{P_{G_1} / P_{G_0}}.$$

where S_0 equals the equilibrium exchange rate existing in the base period and S_1 equals the estimated target at which the actual rate should be in the future.

For example, let the price indexes of the United States and Germany and the equilibrium exchange rate be as follows:

$$P_{U.S._0} = 100$$
$$P_{U.S._1} = 200$$
$$P_{G_0} = 100$$

$$P_{G_1} = 100$$
$$S_0 = \$0.50$$

Putting these figures into the previous equation, we can determine the new equilibrium exchange rate for period 1:

$$S_1 = \$0.50 \times \frac{200/100}{100/100}$$

$$= \$0.50 \times 2$$
$$= \$1.00$$

Between one period and the next, the U.S. inflation rate rose 100 percent, whereas Germany's inflation rate remained unchanged. Maintaining purchasing-power parity between the dollar and the mark requires the dollar to depreciate against the mark by an amount equal to the difference in the percentage rates of inflation in the United States and Germany. The dollar must depreciate by 100 percent, from $0.50 per mark to $1 per mark, to maintain its purchasing-power parity. If the example assumed instead that Germany's inflation rate doubled while the U.S. inflation rate remained unchanged, the dollar would appreciate to a level of $0.25 per mark, according to the purchasing-power-parity theory.

An application of the purchasing-power-parity concept is provided in Table 13.3, which gives the dollar/peso exchange rate over the period 1985–1989, during which time Mexico experienced high inflation. From 1985 to 1989, U.S. prices rose by about 15 percent, whereas Mexico's prices skyrocketed some 1100 percent. Applying the purchasing-power-parity formula to these figures, we would expect the dollar to appreciate against the peso, from $0.0039 per peso to $0.0004 per peso, owing to the relative decline in the peso's domestic purchasing power. Actually, the dollar appreciated to $0.0004 per peso! Purchasing-power parity can be illustrated in terms of the supply and demand for foreign exchange. In Figure 13.2 (page 353), D_0 and S_0 represent the demand and supply schedules of

T A B L E 13. 3 / Purchasing-Power Parity in Action, 1985–1989

Year	U.S. Consumer Price Index	Mexican Consumer Price Index	Actual Exchange Rate: Dollars/Peso	Forecasted Exchange Rate: Dollars/Peso
1985	100.0	100.0	0.0039	—
1987	105.7	431.7	0.0007	0.0010
1989	115.2	1,109.6	0.0004	0.0004

SOURCE: International Monetary Fund, *IMF Financial Statistics* (Washington, D.C.: Author, May 1990).

pounds, and the equilibrium exchange rate is $1.50 per pound. Suppose the domestic price level increases rapidly in the United States and remains constant in the United Kingdom. U.S. consumers will desire relatively low-priced British goods. The demand for pounds thus increases to D_1 in the figure. Conversely, the British will be less interested in purchasing relatively high-priced U.S. goods, thus reducing the supply of pounds to S_1. The increase in the demand for pounds and the decrease in the supply of pounds result in a depreciation of the dollar to $2.50 per pound.

Although the purchasing-power-parity theory can be helpful in forecasting appropriate levels to which currency values should be adjusted, it is *not* an infallible guide to exchange-rate determination. For instance, the theory overlooks the fact that exchange-rate movements may be influenced by capital flows. The theory also faces the problems of choosing the appropriate price index to be used in price calculations (for example, consumer prices or producer prices) and of determining the equilibrium period to use as a base. Moreover, government policy may interfere with the operation of the theory (for example, trade restrictions that disrupt the flow of exports and imports among nations).

Evidence concerning the validity of the purchasing-power-parity theory is mixed. The theory appears roughly valid as a guide to exchange-rate determination when inflation is

extreme. Over the period from 1982 to 1985, Israel's annual inflation rate was in the triple-digit range. The Israeli shekel depreciated against the U.S. dollar in an amount that approximated the excess of Israeli inflation over U.S. inflation. The currencies of Latin American countries, such as Argentina and Mexico, also tend to follow this rule. However, where inflation differentials are *small,* factors other than price comparisons can become more important in the determination of exchange rates. The purchasing-power-parity theory also does not appear to hold as well when tests are conducted over relatively short (such as year-to-year) time periods, because of lags in the balance-of-payments adjustment process, government interference, and so on.

For many years, the purchasing-power-parity theory appeared to operate reasonably well. Although precise exchange-rate predictions based on purchasing-power-parity calculations were not always accurate, nations having higher inflation rates did at least experience depreciating currencies. In the early 1980s, however, even this broke down. For example, between 1980 and 1983 the U.S. inflation rate was much *higher* than Japan's and modestly *higher* than Germany's. Nevertheless, the dollar *appreciated* against both the yen and the mark during this period.

Observers maintain that exchange-rate movements are often caused by news that, by its very nature, is unpredictable. Foreign exchange rates have been viewed to behave similarly to asset markets (such as stock markets), which incorporate new information quickly and adjust their prices continuously. However, purchasing-power-parity calculations are based on commodity prices (such as the consumer price index), which respond sluggishly to changing economic circumstances. To the extent that exchange rates respond quickly to new information and commodity prices respond slowly, departures from the purchasing-power-parity theory will occur. Most economists maintain that other factors are much more important than relative price levels for exchange-rate determination in the short run.

Although the purchasing-power-parity theory is of limited value in the short run, over a sufficiently long period it is possible that economic forces work to maintain purchasing-power-parity levels. One study used annual data over the period 1869–1984 to estimate the degree to which the dollar/pound exchange rate returns to purchasing-power-parity equilibrium. Over the course of this period, the estimated speed of adjustment to purchasing-power parity was 14 percent per year. This means that 50 percent of the adjustment toward purchasing-power parity occurs after 4.5 years and 90 percent of the adjustment occurs by the end of 15 years. These results suggest that the purchasing-power-parity theory provides a rough approximation of the long-run exchange rate if the adjustment process is analyzed over many years. A time horizon of such length, however, is of little relevance to decision makers.[2]

THE MONETARY APPROACH

A growing number of economists find fault with the balance-of-payments approach to exchange-rate determination considered earlier in this chapter. They view its reliance on the relative supply and demand of goods, services, and capital flows as indirect at best—and theoretically misleading at worst—as an explanation of exchange rates. Unlike the balance-of-payments approach, which discusses exchange-rate determination in terms of the *flow* of funds in the foreign exchange market over a period of time, the **monetary approach** views exchange rates as determined by the responses to changes in the *stock* (or total) demands and supplies of national currencies.

The monetary approach emphasizes the fact that the foreign exchange market is a monetary phenomenon, where monies are traded for monies. The money supply and money demand at home and abroad are thus used to explain a nation's exchange-rate trend. Because money supplies can be controlled by central banks, the monetary approach emphasizes a nation's demand for money and its determinants.

According to the monetary approach, the aggregate demand for money in a nation depends on the level of *real income, prices,* and *interest rates.* As the economy grows and real income rises, the public's demand for money increases in order to finance rising transactions. If prices rise, the public will demand more money to cover their economic transactions. The interest rate represents the opportunity cost of holding money. Lower interest rates induce the public to hold more money because the opportunity cost of holding cash balances is decreased. In other words, the public has less incentive to shift away from money balances, which pay no interest, to interest-bearing financial assets during eras of low interest rates. Conversely, as these determinants change in the opposite direction, the demand for money decreases.

The following example illustrates how an *increase* in the domestic money *supply* causes the home currency's exchange rate to *depreciate,* according to the monetary approach. Given an initial equilibrium in the domestic money market and foreign exchange market, suppose the Federal Reserve increases the U.S. money supply. The monetary expansion makes it easier for individuals and companies to borrow money. A rise in domestic spending and income thus occurs, leading to increased imports and a

The "Big Mac" Index

The Price of a Big Mac, April 13, 1993

Country	Prices in Local Currency	U.S. Equivalent (in dollars)	Local Currency Overvaluation (+) or Undervaluation (-)
United States	$2.28	$2.28	——
Denmark	25.75 krone	4.25	+86%
Switzerland	5.70 francs	3.94	+72
Argentina	3.60 pesos	3.60	+58
Japan	391 yen	3.45	+51
Sweden	25.50 kronar	3.43	+50
Belgium	109 francs	3.36	+47
Italy	4500 lira	2.95	+30
Ireland	1.48 punt	2.29	0
Mexico	7.09 pesos	2.29	0
Canada	$2.76 Canadian	2.19	-4
Thailand	48 baht	1.91	-16
Australia	$2.45 Australian	1.76	-23

SOURCE: Data taken from "Big MacCurrencies," *The Economist*, April 17, 1993.

(continued)

rise in the demand for foreign currency. The monetary expansion also results in lower interest rates, assuming the absence of inflationary expectations. Lower domestic interest rates motivate U.S. investment overseas, again increasing the demand for foreign currency. With the demand for foreign currency now exceeding the supply, the dollar depreciates in value under market-determined exchange rates. The dollar depreciation induces higher prices for imports and a greater demand for exports, leading to higher domestic prices. Higher-priced transactions result in an increase in the demand for money. The adjustment process continues until the excess supply of money is eliminated. According to the monetary approach, the depreciation of the U.S. dollar and the appreciation of the German mark during the 1970s were attributable to excessive monetary growth in the United States and to a much smaller rate of monetary growth in Germany than in the rest of the world.

Similar reasoning can be used to determine how an *increase* in the *demand* for money leads to an *appreciation* in the nation's exchange rate. Given initial equilibrium in the domestic money market and foreign exchange market, suppose Egypt's real income increases following the discovery of new oil reserves. Because additional oil sales lead to a larger money value of goods exchanged in the economy, a larger amount of money will be needed to negotiate these

The "Big Mac" Index

(continued)

The "Big Mac" hamburger sandwich sold by McDonalds has been viewed as an international monetary standard. Although economists generally prefer vast indexes based on thousands of commodities and prices to measure purchasing power, playful ones have opted for hamburger sandwiches. After all, the amount you pay for a Big Mac is a reflection of everything from sesame-seed prices to labor costs.

The so-called Big Mac Index is a popular stand-in for a much more serious concept, the purchasing-power-parity theory. Based solely on the price of a Big Mac, the index is used to roughly assess which currencies are *overvalued* and which are *undervalued* relative to the U.S. dollar. The *Economist* magazine publishes Big Mac updates each year.

Consistent with the purchasing-power-parity doctrine, the Big Mac Index suggests that the exchange rate between the dollar and the yen is in equilibrium (that is, at purchasing-power parity) when it equates the prices of hamburger sandwiches in the United States and Japan. Big Macs should thus cost the same in each country when the prices are converted to the dollar. When Big Macs do not cost the same, the yen is said to be overvalued or undervalued compared to the dollar.

The table shows what a Big Mac cost in different countries as of April 13, 1993. The U.S. equivalent prices denote which currencies are overvalued and which are undervalued relative to the dollar. In the United States (New York), a Big Mac cost $2.28. In Denmark, the dollar equivalent price of a Big Mac was $4.25. Compared to the dollar, the krone was *overvalued* by 86 percent (4.25 / 2.28 = 1.86). The Big Mac was a bargain in Australia, however, where the U.S. dollar equivalent price was $1.76; the Australian dollar was *undervalued* by 23 percent (1.76 / 2.28 = 0.77).

To be sure, the Big Mac Index is primitive and has many flaws. However, it is widely understood by noneconomists and serves as an approximation of which currencies are too weak or strong, and by how much.

transactions. The demand for Egypt's pound as a currency thus increases. But this demand cannot be fulfilled by the existing money supply (recall the initial assumption that money supply equals money demand in the domestic market). Efforts to get additional pounds, say, by exporting Egyptian goods, result in foreign nations' needing pounds to pay Egyptian exporters. The demand for the pound thus rises, which leads to an increase in its value.

The monetary approach emphasizes that under a system of market-determined exchange rates, movements in currency values play a primary role in restoring equilibrium between money demand and money supply. Table 13.4 summarizes the impact of changes in the money supply and money demand on domestic currency values according to the monetary approach. (The monetary approach to the balance of payments under a system of *fixed* exchange rates will be considered in the following chapter.)

The monetary approach to exchange-rate determination has made a significant contribution to economic theory by counteracting the tendency to ignore the importance of money and to focus exclusively on real variables. However, some theorists have criticized the monetary approach as being too extreme in stressing monetary variables to the almost total exclusion of other factors. These critics also maintain that the monetary approach cannot be a full substitute for the traditional approaches exchange-rate determination. The numerous

T A B L E 13. 4 / *Changes in Money Supply and Money Demand under Market-Determined Exchange Rates: Impact on the Exchange Rate According to the Monetary Approach*

Change*	Impact
Increase in money supply	Depreciate
Decrease in money supply	Appreciate
Increase in money demand	Appreciate
Decrease in money demand	Depreciate

* Starting from the point of equilibrium between money supply and money demand.

tests that have been conducted on the monetary approach so far have produced mixed results and provide no clear-cut empirical support for the theory.

EXPECTATIONS AND EXCHANGE RATES

According to the monetary approach to exchange-rate determination, if we can forecast money demands and money supplies, we should be able to forecast long-run movements in exchange rates. However, discrepancies from this pattern on a day-to-day or week-to-week basis are harder to predict. These short-run movements in exchange rates are often due to changes in people's *expectations* of the future.

A fairly good parallel exists between the foreign exchange markets and the stock markets. In each, the exchange rate (or price) responds quickly as new information reaches the market. Elections, wars, or personnel changes at the Federal Reserve may signal changes in future monetary policy. These or similar events—or simply rumors about them—can affect exchange rates in the same manner as they affect daily stock prices.

Suppose it is widely expected that the U.S. economy will (1) grow faster than the Japanese economy, (2) have lower future interest rates than Japan, (3) experience more rapid inflation than Japan, and (4) have a greater growth in its money supply than Japan. All these expectations suggest that the dollar in the future will *depreciate* against the yen. To avoid the exchange-market loss resulting from this projected dollar depreciation, holders of dollars will try to convert them into yen, thus increasing the demand for the yen. This conversion leads to an appreciation in the yen and a depreciation in the dollar.

Figure 13.2 (page 353) can be used to illustrate how expectations of future inflation can affect exchange rates. Exchange market equilibrium initially exists at point A, where $S_0 = D_0$, and the equilibrium exchange rate is $1.50 per pound. Suppose that an unanticipated rise in the growth rate of the U.S. money supply is interpreted as a signal that the U.S. inflation rate will rise, which in turn signals a possible *depreciation* in the dollar's exchange rate. This set of expectations causes U.S. buyers who intend to make purchases in the United Kingdom to obtain pounds prior to the anticipated depreciation of the dollar (when the pound would become more expensive in dollars). Accordingly, the demand for pounds rises in the foreign exchange market, say, to D_1. Concurrently, the British, who hold the same set of expectations, will be less willing to give up pounds in exchange for dollars that will soon decrease in value. The supply of pounds offered in the foreign exchange market thus shifts to the left, say, to S_1. The shifts in these schedules result in a *depreciation* of the dollar to $2.50 per pound at equilibrium point *B*. As we have seen, future expectations of a dollar depreciation can be self-fulfilling. More will be said about the role of market expectations in the next section.

THE ASSET-MARKETS APPROACH

As noted earlier, the monetary approach to exchange-rate determination emphasizes the influence of domestic demand and supply of money on the exchange rate over the long run. This section extends the monetary approach to include financial assets other than domestic money. The **asset-markets** (or portfolio-balance) **approach** considers domestic currencies to be one among an entire spectrum of financial assets that residents of a nation may desire to hold. That is, an individual may choose to hold financial wealth in some combination of domestic currency, domestic securities, foreign securities denominated in a foreign currency, or even foreign currency.

The asset-markets approach recognizes that short-term capital movements among nations can have both a continuing-flow component and a stock-adjustment component. The *continuing-flow* component (the investment flows discussed under "Balance-of-Payments Approach") entails investors' shifting a growing supply of funds among assets in different nations as their wealth expands. The *stock-adjustment* component involves the reallocation of an existing stock of wealth among assets in various nations. It is the stock-adjustment component of international capital movements that the asset-markets approach emphasizes.

According to the asset-markets approach, stock adjustments among financial assets are a key determinant of *short-run* movements in exchange rates. Recall that the balance-of-payments approach emphasized the effect on exchange rates of flows in import and export purchases. The asset-markets approach does not emphasize such flows because they tend to be minor compared with the holdings of domestic and foreign assets at a particular time. Stock adjustments among financial assets are guided by the profit motive—the opportunity to gain from the expected return on one financial asset compared with the expected return on another asset. The asset-markets approach maintains that it is mainly through the medium of market expectations of future returns that exchange rates are affected in the short run; other variables, such as the current account balance or the growth rate in the money supply, affect the exchange rate primarily to the extent that they influence market expectations.

Concerning the *demand* for financial assets, an individual's desire to hold domestic or foreign securities is based on the income they are expected to generate. In addition, foreign securities may be desired because they enable domestic investors to spread their risks. Such investments, however, carry the risk of possible default and variations in their market values over time. For foreign securities denominated in a foreign currency, there is the additional risk that the foreign currency may depreciate. Investors also desire to maintain a portion of their financial wealth in currency in order to make business payments. Although holding domestic currency is riskless, it provides no interest income. The opportunity cost of holding domestic currency is the interest income sacrificed by not holding securities.

Suppose the United States is the home country and U.S. assets are denominated in dollars; the United Kingdom represents the foreign country. The asset-markets approach contends that the most important factor influencing the demand for dollar-denominated assets is the anticipated return on these assets relative to the anticipated return on British assets. If the anticipated return on dollar-denominated assets is high compared with that of British assets, there is a larger demand for dollar-denominated assets, and vice versa. This expected return depends on (1) the interest rate payable in dollars on U.S. securities, (2) the interest rate payable in pounds on British securities, and (3) the expected changes in the dollar's exchange rate against the pound.

Consider a U.S. or British resident's decision to hold dollar-denominated assets versus pound-denominated assets. If the annual interest rate on dollar-denominated assets is 10 percent and the dollar is anticipated to *appreciate* by 5 percent per year against the pound, the expected return on the dollar-denominated assets is 15 percent in terms of the pound. Conversely, if the annual interest rate on the dollar-denominated assets is 10 percent and the dollar is anticipated to *depreciate* by 5 percent per year against the pound, the anticipated return on dollar-denominated assets would be only 5 percent (the 10-percent interest less the 5-percent anticipated depreciation). In general, we can conclude that a U.S. or British resident would demand more dollar-denominated assets if the interest rate on these assets increases relative to the *interest rate* on British-denominated assets, assuming exchange-rate expectations are constant. More dollar-denominated assets would also be demanded if the *expected rate of appreciation* in the dollar increases, assuming the interest rate is constant.

Figure 13.3 illustrates the foreign exchange market according to the asset-markets approach. Demand schedule D_0 denotes the quantity of dollar-denominated financial assets demanded at various current pound/dollar exchange rates by all potential holders, both domestic and foreign. The demand for dollar-denominated financial assets (dollars) is *inversely* related to the value of the U.S. dollar; that is, as the current exchange rate (pounds/dollar) rises, fewer exchange market participants are willing to trade an increasing quantity of pounds for dollars, assuming that no change in the exchange rate is anticipated.[3] The supply schedule of dollar-denominated assets

in the international exchange market is ultimately fixed by the total quantity of assets in the U.S. economy (S_0). Exchange market equilibrium exists at point A, where the quantity of dollar-denominated assets equals the quantity supplied.

We know that the demand for dollar-denominated assets is directly related to the anticipated return on dollar assets relative to the anticipated return on British assets. This return depends on the interest rate payable in dollars on U.S. securities, the interest rate payable in pounds on British securities, and the expected change in the dollar's exchange rate against the pound. As we have seen, *movements along* the demand schedule for dollar-denominated assets are caused by changes in the *current* pound/dollar exchange rate. *Shifts* in the demand schedule are caused by changes in interest rates and in future exchange-rate expectations. Let's see how the asset-markets approach explains short-run fluctuations in exchange rates.

Figure 13.4 illustrates the exchange market equilibrium for dollar-denominated financial assets. Referring to Figure 13.4(a), assume that exchange market equilibrium exists at point A, where $S_0 = D_0$, and the equilibrium exchange rate is 1 pound per dollar. Suppose now that U.S. real interest rates *rise*, all else being equal. Residents will want to take advantage of the higher expected return on U.S. financial assets. This leads to a shift in the demand schedule for dollar assets to D_1 and an *appreciation* in the dollar's value to 1.5 pounds per dollar at equilibrium point B. Should U.S. real interest rates *fall*, the demand for dollar assets decreases, and the dollar *depreciates* in value. Conversely, suppose that British real interest rates rise. The expected return on British assets thus increases relative to dollar-denominated assets. The quantity of dollar assets demanded falls, and the dollar depreciates against the pound. A fall in British real interest rates leads to an increased demand for dollar-denominated assets and a rise in the dollar's value. This

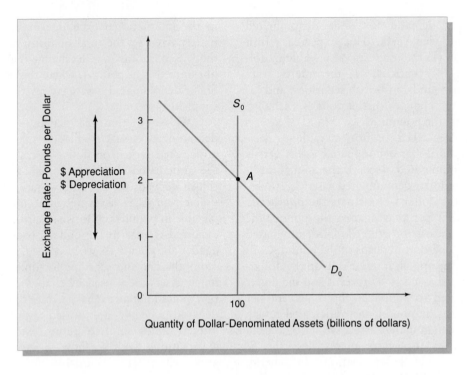

F I G U R E 13. 3   *Exchange market equilibrium according to the asset-markets approach.* Unlike previous illustrations of the foreign exchange market, in which the exchange rate was given in terms of dollars per pound, this illustration expresses the exchange rate in terms of pounds per dollar.

analysis applies to *expected,* as well as actual, interest-rate changes. The reader is left to determine how factors that influence the expected future pound/dollar exchange rate (such as tariffs expected to be levied by the U.S. government) affect the demand for dollar assets and the pound/dollar exchange rate.

Now refer to Figure 13.4(b), which illustrates shifts in the supply schedule of dollar-denominated assets. Suppose the U.S. Federal Reserve *purchases* $5 billion of its currency in the foreign exchange market, using its international currency reserves to do so. This action causes the overall *supply* of U.S. dollar assets to *fall*. The supply schedule of dollar assets thus shifts to S_1, and the dollar *appreciates* against the pound. Conversely, if the Federal Reserve *sells* $5 billion of its currency in the foreign

exchange market, increasing its international reserves, this means a *rise* in the overall supply of dollar assets. The supply schedule shifts to S_2, which results in a *depreciation* in the dollar's value. Obviously, central banks can have a major impact on exchange rates by intervening in the foreign exchange market.[4]

The asset-markets approach can be used to explain the volatility of exchange rates, as occurred in the 1980s. Although variables such as the current account balance or the rate of monetary growth affect exchange rates over the long run, changes in short-run exchange rates are most likely to reflect the effect of adjustments in financial assets and expectations. Whenever changes occur in expectations of variables (such as monetary policy), there tends to be an immediate impact on exchange rates.

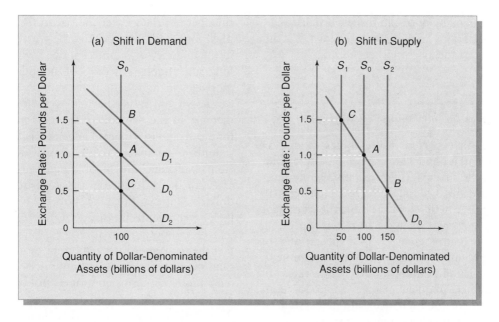

F I G U R E 13. 4 *Short-run exchange rates and the asset-markets approach.* The asset-markets model can be used to explain changes in exchange rates that occur in the short run. The model views exchange-rate determination as similar to the stock market, in which prices are volatile and future expectations are important.

The asset-markets model thus views exchange-rate determination as similar to the stock market, in which future expectations are important and prices are volatile.

As we have seen, the asset-markets approach emphasizes the influence on exchange rates of expected returns on investments. Such was the case with the appreciation of the U.S. dollar from 1980 to February 1985, as discussed earlier in this chapter. According to the asset-markets approach, most of the dollar appreciation probably stemmed from portfolio shifts into U.S. dollar assets because of increased expected returns relative to assets denominated in other currencies. In 1980, real (inflation-adjusted) interest rates paid on long-term U.S. government securities were approximately 2 percentage points *below* those paid on a weighted average of similar securities among U.S. trading partners. By 1985, the real interest rate on U.S. securities was some 3 percentage

points *above* that on securities of U.S. trading partners. According to the asset-markets approach, this 5-percentage-point swing in real interest rates in favor of the United States motivated investors to channel funds into dollar-denominated assets. This added to the demand for the dollar and reinforced its appreciation in the foreign exchange market.

In general, tests of the asset-markets approach have produced mixed or inconclusive results concerning its empirical validity. What's more, such tests are hampered because data on currencies in private holdings of foreign assets are usually not available. It is clear, however, that asset managers working for commercial banks, investment banks, pension funds, and insurance companies do use portfolio theory in determining where and how to invest their funds. A reasonable guess is that short-term exchange-rate movements that occur in practice between major currencies tend to approximate those implied by portfolio theory. Because market expectations are not readily known, it is difficult to test the asset-markets approach.

EXCHANGE-RATE OVERSHOOTING

Changes in expected future values of market fundamentals contribute to exchange-rate volatility in the short run. For example, announcements by the Federal Reserve of changes in monetary-growth targets or by the president and Congress of changes in tax or spending programs cause changes in expectations of future exchange rates that can lead to immediate changes in equilibrium exchange rates. In this manner, frequent changes in policy contribute to volatile exchange rates in a system of market-determined exchange rates.

The volatility of exchange rates is further intensified by the phenomenon of **overshooting**. An exchange rate is said to overshoot when its short-run response (depreciation or appreciation) to a change in market fundamentals is *greater* than its long-run response. Changes in market fundamentals thus exert a disproportionately large *short-run* impact on exchange rates. Exchange-rate overshooting is an important phenomenon because it helps explain why exchange rates depreciate or appreciate so sharply from day to day.

Exchange-rate overshooting can be explained by the tendency of elasticities to be smaller in the short run than in the long run. Referring to Figure 13.5, the short-run supply schedule and demand schedule of the British pound are denoted by S_0 and D_0, respectively, and the equilibrium exchange rate is $2 per pound. If the demand for pounds increases to D_1, the dollar depreciates to $2.20 per pound in the short run. Because of the dollar depreciation, there occurs a decrease in the British price of U.S. exports, an increase in the quantity of U.S. exports demanded, and thus an increase in the quantity of pounds supplied. The longer the

time period, the greater the rise in the quantity of exports is likely to be, and the greater the rise in the quantity of pounds supplied will be. The long-run supply schedule of pounds is thus more elastic than the short-run supply schedule, as shown by S_1 in the figure. Following the increase in the demand for pounds to D_1, the long-run equilibrium exchange rate is $2.10 per pound, as compared to the short-run equilibrium exchange rate of $2.20 per pound. Because of the difference in these elasticities, the dollar's depreciation in the short run overshoots its long-run depreciation.

Overshooting can also be explained by the fact that exchange rates tend to be more flexible than many other prices. Many prices are written into long-term contracts (for example, workers' wages) and do not respond immediately to changes in market fundamentals. Exchange rates, however, tend to be highly sensitive to current demand and supply conditions. Exchange rates often depreciate or appreciate more in the short run than in the long run so as to compensate for other prices that are slower to adjust to their long-run equilibrium levels. As the general price level slowly gravitates to its new equilibrium level, the amount of exchange-rate overshooting *dissipates,* and the exchange rate moves toward its long-run equilibrium level.

To illustrate the overshooting process, suppose the Federal Reserve unexpectedly increases the money supply. Assuming that goods prices (P) are inflexible in the short run, the increase in the nominal money supply (M) leads to an increase in the real money supply (M/P). Interest rates decrease to restore balance between money supply and money demand. Lower U.S. interest rates, in turn, cause domestic and foreign investors to pull funds out of the United States, which leads to a depreciation in the dollar's exchange value. Because goods prices are assumed to not adjust immediately to a higher equilibrium level, the dollar's exchange value compensates by depreciating to a level lower

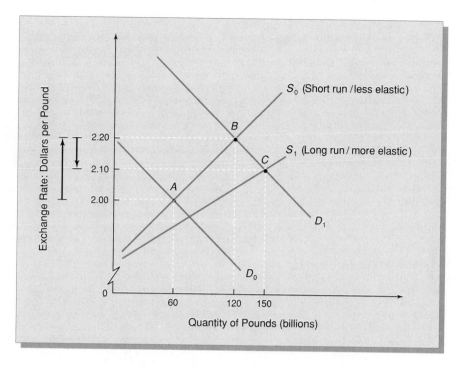

F I G U R E 13. 5 *Short-run/long-run equilibrium exchange-rates: exchange-rate overshooting.* Given the short-run supply of pounds (S_0), if the demand for pounds increases from D_0 to D_1, the dollar depreciates from $2 per pound to a short-run equilibrium of $2.20 per pound. In the long run, the supply of pounds is more elastic (S_1), and the equilibrium exchange rate is lower, at $2.10 per pound. Because of the difference in these elasticities, the short-run depreciation of the dollar overshoots its long-run depreciation.

than its long-run equilibrium value. Over time, the depreciation of the dollar and lower interest rates stimulate U.S. and foreign demand for domestically produced goods, which leads to higher prices. As the price level slowly increases, the real money supply (M/P) slowly falls, which promotes higher U.S. interest rates, investment flows into the United States, and an appreciation in the dollar's exchange value. The dollar's exchange value thus rises to its long-run equilibrium level. In long-run equilibrium, the dollar's exchange value is *lower* than it was prior to the increase in the money supply but *higher* than the trough it hit during the over-

shoot. Even though the long-run equilibrium value of the dollar tends to depreciate by the *same* proportion as the money-supply increase, its short-term equilibrium exchange value depreciates *more than* proportionately.

Figure 13.6(a) indicates how the U.S. price level and exchange value of the dollar would respond to an unexpected 10-percent increase in the money supply if goods prices were totally *flexible.* Following the money supply increase, the general price level immediately rises by 10 percent to its new long-run equilibrium level. The real money supply (M/P) thus remains constant, as do domestic interest rates. The dollar's

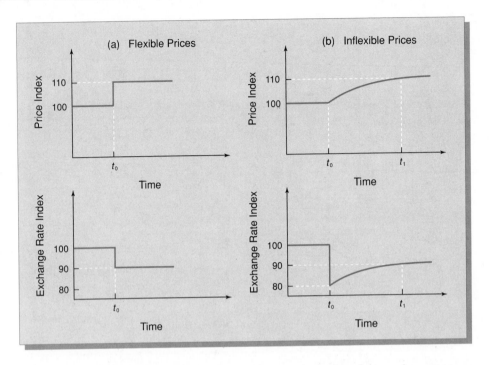

F I G U R E 13. 6   *Exchange-rate overshooting.* At t_0, domestic money supply unexpectedly rises 10 percent. With flexible prices (a), this leads to an immediate 10-percent decline in the dollar's exchange value. When prices are inflexible (b), the monetary expansion leads initially to a dollar depreciation that exceeds 10 percent, followed by a gradual appreciation of the dollar. In long-run equilibrium, the dollar's exchange value is 10-percent below its initial level.

exchange value thus drops right away, by 10 percent, to its new long-run equilibrium level and stays there—no overshooting occurs.

In contrast, the adjustment is more protracted when prices are *inflexible,* as shown in Figure 13.6(b). With no change in domestic prices immediately following the monetary expansion, the dollar's exchange value initially overshoots its new, lower, long-run equilibrium level. Subsequently, the dollar's value appreciates as domestic prices gradually increase. Because of both the initial overshooting and the subsequent rebounding toward long-run equilibrium, the effect of changes in market fundamentals on exchange-rate volatility is magnified.

FORECASTING FOREIGN EXCHANGE RATES

The first part of this chapter has examined various economic theories that claim to determine exchange-rate movements. It should be clear that no single theory as yet can be said to have solved the problem. Over time, all these economic theories contain elements of truth. But past experience suggests that many exchange-rate theories often lead to opposite conclusions. Because no single theory has an unblemished track record when it comes to forecasting, especially in the short-run (less than one year), it is not surprising that few market participants place great reliance on any one of them.

A major issue, as far as business is concerned, however, is whether **forecasting exchange rates** is feasible and, if so, how to do it. Because the future is unclear, participants in international financial markets are unsure what the spot rate will be in the months ahead. Exchange-rate forecasts are required by exporters, importers, investors, bankers, and foreign-exchange dealers.

Multinational corporations (MNCs) need short-term currency price forecasts for a variety of reasons. For example, corporations often have for brief periods large amounts of cash, which is used to make bank deposits in various currencies. Choosing a currency in which to make deposits requires some idea of what the currency's exchange rate will be in the future. Long-term corporate planning, especially concerning foreign investment decisions, necessitates an awareness of where exchange rates will move over an extended time period—hence the need for long-term forecasts. For MNCs, short-term forecasting tends to be more widespread than long-term forecasting. Most corporations revise their currency forecasts at least every quarter.

The need of MNCs and investors for forecasted currency values has resulted in the emergence of *consulting firms,* including Predex, Goldman Sachs, and Wharton Econometric Forecasting Associates. In addition, large banks such as Chase Manhattan Bank, Chemical Bank, and Citibank have provided free currency forecasts to corporate clients. Customers of consulting firms often pay fees ranging up to $25,000 per year or more for expert opinions. Consulting firms provide forecast-services ranging from video screens to "listening-post" interviews with forecast-service employees who provide their predictions of exchange-rate movements and respond to specific questions from the client. It has become customary for corporate managers to use home or hotel telephones to connect portable terminals to advisory services that make available foreign exchange forecasts.

Most exchange-rate forecasting methods use accepted economic relationships to formulate a model that is then refined through statistical analysis of past data. The forecasts generated by the models are usually tempered by the additional insights or intuition of the forecaster before being offered to the final user.

In the current system of market-determined exchange rates, currency values fluctuate almost instantaneously in response to new information regarding changes in interest rates, inflation rates, money supplies, trade balances, and the like. To successfully forecast exchange-rate movements, it is necessary to estimate the future values of these economic variables and determine the relationship between them and future exchange rates. Even the most sophisticated analysis, however, can be rendered worthless by unexpected exchange-rate fluctuations due to changes in government policy, market psychology, and so forth. Indeed, people who deal in the currency markets on a daily basis have come to feel that market psychology is a dominant influence on future exchange rates. Despite these problems, exchange-rate forecasters are in current demand. Their forecasting approaches are classified as judgmental, technical, and fundamental (econometric). Table 13.5 provides examples of exchange-rate forecasting organizations and their methodologies.

Judgmental Forecasts

Judgmental forecasts are sometimes known as subjective or commonsense models. They require the gathering of a wide array of political and economic data and the interpretation of these data in terms of the timing, direction, and magnitude of exchange-rate changes. Judgmental forecasters formulate projections based on a thorough examination of individual nations.

T A B L E 13. 5   /   *Exchange-Rate Forecasters*

Forecasting Organization	Methodology	Horizon
Chase Econometrics	Econometric	8 quarters
Chase Manhattan Bank	Judgmental	Under 12 months
Predex-Forecast	Econometric	7 quarters
Predex–Short Term Forecast	Technical	1–3 months ahead
Wharton Econometric Forecasting Associates	Econometric	24 months ahead
Goldman Sachs	Technical	Under 12 months
	Econometric	Over 12 months
Phillips & Drew	Judgmental/econometric	6, 12 months ahead
Data Resources	Econometric	6 quarters
Exchange Rate Outlook	Judgmental	12 months ahead

SOURCE: *Euromoney,* various issues.

They consider economic indicators such as inflation rates and trade data, political factors such as a future national election, technical factors such as potential intervention by a central bank in the foreign exchange market, and psychological factors that relate to one's "feel for the market."

Technical Forecasts

Technical analysis involves the use of historical exchange-rate data to estimate future values. The approach is "technical" in that it extrapolates from past exchange-rate trends while ignoring economic and political determinants of exchange-rate movements. Technical analysts look for specific exchange-rate patterns. Once the beginning of a particular pattern has been determined, it automatically implies what the short-run behavior of the exchange rate will be.

Technical analysts use computer-based statistical programs to find recurring exchange-rate patterns and then issue sell or buy instructions if exchange rates deviate from their past pattern. For example, time-series models are used to analyze moving averages of exchange rates. They permit a forecaster to formulate some rule, such as "the franc tends to rise in value after a fall in the franc's average over four consecutive periods." Generally, consultants who adopt such an approach will not disclose their particular rules for forecasting. If they did, their potential customers might use the rules themselves instead of purchasing the consultants' forecasts.

Because technical analysis follows the market closely, it is used to forecast exchange-rate movements in the *very near future*. Determining an exchange-rate pattern is useful only as long as the market continues to consistently follow that pattern. No pattern, however, can be relied on to continue more than a few days, perhaps weeks. A client must therefore respond quickly to a technical recommendation to buy or sell a currency. This is why clients require immediate communication of technical recommendations via computer terminals or telex so as to make timely financial decisions.

Fundamental Analysis

Fundamental analysis is the opposite of technical analysis. It involves consideration of macroeconomic variables and policies that are likely to affect a currency's value. Fundamental analysis uses computer-based econometric models, which are statistical estimations of economic theories. To generate forecasts, econometricians develop models for individual nations that attempt to incorporate the fundamental variables that underlie exchange-rate movements: trade and investment flows, industrial activity, inflation rates, income levels, and the like.

Econometricians assume that changes in key economic variables will induce changes in future exchange rates in approximately the same patterns as in the past. The formulation of an econometric model requires specifying *independent variables* (for example, previous quarterly percentage changes in interest rates or inflation rates) that influence the *dependent variable* (for example, quarterly percentage change in a currency's value). The econometrician must also identify the nature of the functional relationship (for example, linear, exponential) that best explains the dependent variable. The econometric model determines the direction and degree to which a currency's exchange rate is affected by each independent variable.

Econometric models used to forecast exchange rates, however, face limitations. They often rely on predictions of key independent variables, such as inflation rates or interest rates, that influence exchange rates; obtaining reliable information, however, can be difficult. Moreover, there are always factors affecting exchange rates that cannot easily be quantified (such as central bank intervention in currency markets). Also, the precise timing of some factors on a currency's exchange rate are unclear. For example, inflation-rate changes may not have their full impact on a currency's value until 3 or 6 months in the future. Because econometric models may not always generate accurate forecasts, econometricians must exercise judgment when the results of their equations appear to be questionable. Moreover, users of econometric forecasts must allow for a margin of error and recognize the potential for error when applying forecasts to financial decision making.

Econometric models are best suited for forecasting *long-term* exchange-rate trends. This is because exchange rates in the short run are influenced by many factors that change on a day-to-day basis (for example, the release of information concerning the nation's inflation rate), resulting in considerable short-term volatility.

Econometric models are also best suited for forecasting by way of averages over a period of time instead of predicting exchange rates at a particular time. If one asks an econometric forecaster for a currency forecast for, say, March 1 of next year, she will likely respond by giving a range. The critic might conclude that she is improving her odds of getting the forecast right. Although there may be some truth in this, the critic should also recognize that because she is forecasting an average, there is no way she can accurately forecast an exchange rate for a particular moment. Despite a wide range, the actual exchange rate may lie outside, and yet the average forecast may still be accurate.

Forecast Performance of Advisory Services

To be successful, a forecasting model should provide better information about future exchange rates than is available to the market in general. Successful forecasters are those who can consistently profit from their forecasting activities by predicting *more accurately* than the rest of the market.

In evaluating the performance of forecasters, it is important to determine what a naive forecast would be in the absence of any specific model or information. Assuming efficient foreign exchange markets, in which prices reflect all available information, what exchange-rate prediction is implicit in market quotations? As discussed in Chapter 12, the *forward exchange rate* (the spot rate plus the interest-rate differential) is the rational approximation of the market's expectation of the spot rate that will exist at the end of the forward period. This means that the forward *premium* or *discount* on a currency serves as a rough benchmark of the expected rate of appreciation or depreciation of a currency. A successful forecaster should thus be able to predict spot rates better than what is implied by the forward rate.

When evaluating a consulting firm, one might compare its currency forecasts to the forward rates, which are quoted in newspapers and magazines. Although forward rates provide simple and easy-to-use currency forecasts, several studies have shown that forward rates are *not* reliable predictors of future spot rates. It appears that unanticipated news and the market's expectations of future policies can have a frequent and noticeable impact on spot rates, making them inherently volatile and unpredictable in the short run. *Caution* must be exercised when attempting to interpret forward exchange rates.

Consulting firms are not always successful in forecasting currency values. One study compared the forward rate to the forecasts of several consulting firms concerning nine different currencies. Of all the consulting firms and all currencies forecasted, only 5 percent of the forecasts for 1 month ahead were more accurate than the forward rate; only 14 percent of forecasts for 3 months ahead were more accurate. These results can be discouraging to clients who pay thousands of dollars for advisory services.[5]

SUMMARY

1. Economists generally agree that the major determinants of exchange-rate fluctuations are different in the long run than in the short run.
2. The balance-of-payments approach to exchange-rate determination emphasizes the flows of goods, services, and investment capital that respond gradually to real economic factors. It predicts exchange-rate depreciation for nations with deficits in their international transactions and appreciation for nations with surpluses.
3. According to the balance-of-payments approach, trade in goods and services is primarily underlain by relative prices of domestic and foreign goods and the level of real income within nations. Other determinants include consumer tastes, technological change, resource accumulation, market structure, and trade policy.
4. Short-term interest-rate differentials between any two nations are an important determinant of international investment flows and short-term exchange rates. More important, international investors are concerned about relative changes in the real interest rate, which is the nominal rate adjusted for inflation.
5. According to the purchasing-power-parity theory, changes in relative national price levels determine changes in exchange rates over the long run. A currency maintains its purchasing-power parity if it depreciates (appreciates) by an amount equal to the excess of domestic (foreign) inflation over foreign (domestic) inflation.
6. The monetary approach suggests that an increase in the domestic money supply causes the home currency's exchange rate to depreciate, and vice versa. It also maintains that an increase in the domestic demand for money leads to an appreciation in the home country's exchange rate. The monetary approach appears to be most valid as a predictor of exchange-rate movements over the long run.

7. In the short run, market expectations influence exchange-rate movements. Future expectations of rapid domestic economic growth, falling domestic interest rates, and high domestic inflation rates tend to cause the domestic currency to depreciate.

8. The asset-markets approach contends that stock adjustments among financial assets are a key determinant of short-run movements in exchange rates. The demand for domestic assets is primarily determined by the interest rate payable in domestic currency on domestic securities, the interest rate payable in foreign currency on foreign securities, and expected changes in the domestic currency's exchange rate.

9. Exchange-rate volatility is intensified by the phenomenon of overshooting. An exchange rate is said to overshoot when its short-run response to a change in market fundamentals is greater than its long-run response.

10. Currency forecasters use several methods to predict future exchange-rate movements: (a) judgmental forecasts, (b) technical analysis, and (c) fundamental analysis.

STUDY QUESTIONS

1. Which approaches best apply to exchange-rate determination (a) in the long run and (b) in the short run?

2. How does the balance-of-payments approach explain changes in currency values?

3. Why are international investors especially concerned about the real interest rate as opposed to the nominal rate?

4. What predictions does the purchasing-power-parity theory make concerning the impact of domestic inflation on the home country's exchange rate? What are some limitations of the purchasing-power-parity theory?

5. If a currency becomes overvalued in the foreign exchange market, what will be the likely impact on the home country's trade balance? What if the home currency becomes undervalued?

6. What is meant by the monetary approach to exchange-rate determination? What are its major predictions concerning exchange-rate movements?

7. How does the asset-markets approach attempt to improve on the monetary approach in the determination of exchange rates?

8. Explain how the following factors affect the dollar's exchange rate under a system of market-determined exchange rates: (a) a rise in the U.S. price level, with the foreign price level held constant; (b) tariffs and quotas placed on U.S. imports; (c) decreased demand for U.S. exports and increased U.S. demand for imports; (d) rising productivity in the United States relative to other countries; (e) rising real interest rates overseas, relative to U.S. rates; (f) an increase in U.S. money growth; (g) an increase in U.S. money demand.

9. What is meant by exchange-rate overshooting? Why does it occur?

10. What methods do currency forecasters use to predict future changes in exchange rates?

11. Assuming market-determined exchange rates, use supply and demand schedules for pounds to analyze the effect on the exchange rate (dollars per pound) between the U.S. dollar and the British pounds under each of the following circumstances:

   a. Voter polls suggest that Britain's conservative government will be replaced by radicals who pledge to nationalize all foreign-owned assets.

   b. The British economy and U.S. economy slide into recession, but the British recession is less severe than the U.S. recession.

   c. The Federal Reserve adopts a tight monetary policy that dramatically increases U.S. interest rates.

   d. Britain's oil production in the North Sea decreases, which results in falling exports to the United States.

   e. The United States unilaterally reduces tariffs on British products.

   f. Britain encounters severe inflation while price stability exists in the United States.

   g. Fears of terrorism reduce U.S. tourism in Britain.

   h. The British government invites U.S. firms to invest in British oil fields.

   i. The rate of productivity growth in Britain decreases sharply.

   j. An economic boom occurs in Britain, which induces the British to purchase more U.S.-made autos, trucks, and computers.

k. Ten-percent inflation occurs in both Britain and the United States.

12. Explain why you agree or disagree with each of the following statements:
   a. "A nation's currency will depreciate if its inflation rate is less than that of its trading partners."
   b. "A nation whose interest rate falls more rapidly than that of other nations can expect the exchange value of its currency to depreciate."
   c. "A nation whose economy grows more slowly than its major trading partners can expect the exchange value of its currency to appreciate."
   d. "A nation's currency will depreciate if its interest rate falls relative to that of its trading partners and its income level rises relative to that of its trading partners."

13. The appreciation in the dollar's exchange value from 1980 to 1985 made U.S. products (less, more) _____ expensive and foreign products (less, more) _____ expensive, (decreased, increased) _____ U.S. imports, and (decreased, increased) _____ U.S. exports.

14. Suppose the dollar/mark exchange rate equals $0.50 per mark. According to the purchasing-power-parity theory, what will happen to the dollar's exchange value under each of the following circumstances?
   a. The U.S. price level increases by 10 percent and the price level in Germany stays constant.
   b. The U.S. price level increases by 10 percent and the price level in Germany increases by 20 percent.
   c. The U.S. price level decreases by 10 percent and the price level in Germany increases by 5 percent.
   d. The U.S. price level decreases by 10 percent and the price level in Germany decreases by 15 percent.

15. Suppose that the nominal interest rate on 3-month Treasury bills is 8 percent in the United States and 6 percent in the United Kingdom, and the rate of inflation is 10 percent in the United States and 4 percent in the United Kingdom.
   a. What is the real interest rate in each nation?
   b. In which direction would international investment flow in response to these real interest rates?
   c. What impact would these investment flows have on the dollar's exchange value?

KEY CONCEPTS AND TERMS

Adjustment mechanism
Automatic adjustment
Foreign repercussion
  effect
Foreign trade multiplier
Gold standard
Income adjustments
Income determination

Interest-rate
  adjustments
Monetary adjustments
Price adjustments
Quantity theory of
  money
Rules of the game

Balance-of-Payments Adjustments under Fixed Exchange Rates

Chapter 11 examined the meaning of a balance-of-payments deficit and surplus. Recall that, owing to double-entry bookkeeping, total inpayments (credits) always equal total outpayments (debits) when all balance-of-payments accounts are considered. A deficit refers to an excess of outpayments over inpayments for selected accounts grouped along functional lines. For example, a current account deficit suggests an excess of imports over exports of goods, services, and unilateral transfers. A current account surplus implies the opposite.

A nation finances or covers a current account deficit out of its international reserves or by attracting investment (such as purchases of factories or securities) from its trading partners. However, the capacity of a *deficit nation* to cover the excess of outpayments over inpayments is limited by its stocks of international reserves and the willingness of its trading partners to invest in the deficit nation. For a surplus nation, once it believes that its stocks of international reserves or overseas investments are adequate—although

history shows that this belief may be a long time in coming—it will be reluctant to run prolonged surpluses. In general, the incentive for reducing a payments surplus is not so direct and immediate as that for a payments deficit.

The **adjustment mechanism** works for the return to equilibrium after the initial equilibrium has been disrupted. The process of payments adjustment takes two different forms. First, under certain conditions, there are adjustment factors that automatically promote equilibrium. Second, should the automatic adjustments be unable to restore equilibrium, discretionary government policies may be adopted to achieve this objective.

This chapter emphasizes the **automatic adjustment** of the balance-of-payments process that occurs under a fixed exchange-rate system.[1] The adjustment variables that we will examine include prices, interest rates, and income. The impact of money on the balance of payments is also considered. Subsequent chapters discuss the adjustment mechanism under flexible exchange rates and the role of government policy in promoting payments adjustment.

Although the various automatic adjustment approaches have their contemporary advocates, each was formulated during a particular period and reflects a different philosophical climate. That the balance of payments could be adjusted by prices and interest rates stemmed from the *classical* economic thinking of the 1800s and early 1900s. The classical approach was geared toward the existing gold standard associated with fixed exchange rates. That income changes could promote balance-of-payments adjustments reflected the *Keynesian* theory of income determination that grew out of the Great Depression era of the 1930s. That money plays a crucial role in the long run as a disturbance and adjustment in the nation's balance of payments is an extension of domestic monetarism. This approach originated during the late 1960s and is associated with the *Chicago school* of thought.

PRICE ADJUSTMENTS

The original theory of balance-of-payments adjustment is credited to David Hume (1711–1776), noted English philosopher and economist.[2] Hume's theory arose from his concern with the prevailing mercantilist view that advocated government controls to ensure a continuous favorable balance of payments. According to Hume, this strategy was self-defeating over the long run because a nation's balance of payments tends *automatically* to move toward equilibrium. Hume's theory stresses the role that adjustments in national *price levels* play in promoting balance-of-payments equilibrium.

Gold Standard

The classical **gold standard** that existed from the late 1800s to the early 1900s was characterized by the following conditions: (1) Each member nation's money supply consisted of gold or paper money backed by gold. (2) Each member nation defined the official price of gold in terms of its national currency and was prepared to buy and sell gold at that price. (3) Free import and export of gold was permitted by member nations. These conditions resulted in a nation's money supply being directly tied to its balance of payments. A nation with a balance-of-payments surplus would acquire gold, directly expanding its money supply. Conversely, the money supply of a deficit nation would decline as the result of a gold outflow.

The balance of payments can also be directly tied to a nation's money supply under a modified gold standard, which requires that the nation's stock of money be fractionally backed by gold at a constant ratio. It would also apply to a fixed exchange-rate system in which payments disequilibria are financed by some acceptable international reserve asset, assuming that a constant ratio between the nation's international reserves and its money supply is maintained.

Quantity Theory of Money

The essence of the classical price-adjustment mechanism is embodied in the **quantity theory of money.** Consider the *equation of exchange*:

$$MV = PQ$$

M refers to a nation's money supply. V refers to the velocity of money—that is, the number of times per year the average currency unit is spent on final goods. The expression MV corresponds to the aggregate demand, or total monetary expenditures on final goods. Alternatively, the monetary expenditures on any year's output can be interpreted as the physical volume of all final goods produced (Q) multiplied by the average price at which each of the final goods is sold (P). As a result, $MV = PQ$.

This equation is an identity. It says that total monetary expenditures on final goods equals the monetary value of the final goods sold; the amount spent on final goods equals the amount received from selling them.

The classical economists made two additional assumptions. First, they took the volume of final output (Q) to be fixed at the full employment level in the long run. Second, they assumed that the velocity of money (V) was constant, depending on institutional, structural, and physical factors that rarely changed. With V and Q relatively stable, a change in M must induce a *direct and proportionate change* in P. The model linking changes in M to changes in P became known as the quantity theory of money.

Balance-of-Payments Adjustment

The preceding analysis showed how, under the classical gold standard, the balance of payments is linked to a nation's money supply, which is linked to its domestic price level. This section illustrates how the price level is linked to the balance of payments. Referring to Figure 14.1, suppose that, under the classical gold standard, a nation finds itself located at point C, where its balance of payments ($X - M$) shows a $40-billion deficit. The deficit nation would experience a gold outflow, which would reduce its money supply and thus its price level. The nation's international competitiveness would be enhanced, so that its exports would rise and imports fall. This process would continue until its price index had fallen from 180 to 120; $X = M$ would thus be achieved at point B. Conversely, a nation located at point A would find its $40-billion surplus being eliminated by a persistent gold inflow and an increase in its money supply, until its price index had risen from 60 to 120; $X = M$ is again achieved at point B. These two examples stress how the opposite price-adjustment process would occur at the same time in each trading partner.

The price-adjustment mechanism as devised by Hume illustrated the impossibility of the mercantilist notion of maintaining a continuous favorable balance of payments. The linkages (balance of payments–money supply–price, level–balance of payments) demonstrated to Hume that, over time, balance-of-payments equilibrium tends to be achieved automatically.

Critique of the Price-Adjustment Mechanism

With the advent of Hume's price-adjustment mechanism, classical economists had a very powerful and influential theory. It was not until the Keynesian revolution in economic thinking during the 1930s that this theory was effectively challenged. Even today, the price-adjustment mechanism is a hotly debated issue. A brief discussion of some of the major criticisms against the price-adjustment mechanism is in order.

The classical linkage between changes in a nation's gold supply and changes in its money supply no longer holds. Central bankers can easily offset a gold outflow (or inflow) by adopting an expansionary (or contractionary) monetary policy. The experience of the gold standard of the late 1800s and early 1900s indicates these offsetting monetary policies often occurred. The classical view that full employment always exists has also been challenged. When an economy is far below its full employment level, there is a smaller chance that prices in general will rise in response to an increase in the money supply than if the economy is at full employment. It has also been pointed out that, in a modern industrial world, prices and wages are inflexible in a downward direction. If prices are inflexible downward, then changes in M will affect not P but rather Q. A deficit nation's falling money supply would bring about a fall in output and employment. Furthermore, the stability and predictability of V have been questioned. Should a gold inflow that results in an increase in M be offset by a decline in V, total spending (MV) and PQ would remain unchanged.

These issues are part of the current debate over the price-adjustment mechanism's relevance. They have caused sufficient doubts

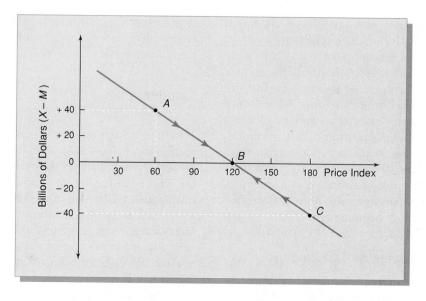

F I G U R E 14. 1   *Price-adjustment mechanism.* According to the price-adjustment mechanism, flexible prices lead to trade equilibrium. A nation with a trade surplus experiences price inflation, which detracts from its competitive position and reduces its surplus. A trade-deficit nation experiences price deflation, which enhances its competitive position and reduces its deficit.

among economists to warrant a search for additional balance-of-payments adjustment explanations. The most notable include the effect of interest-rate changes on capital movements and the effect of changing incomes on trade flows.

INTEREST-RATE ADJUSTMENTS

Under the classical gold standard, the price-adjustment mechanism was not the only vehicle that served to restore equilibrium in the balance of payments. Another monetary effect of a payments surplus or deficit lay in its impact on *short-term interest rates* and hence on short-term private capital flows.

Consider a world of two countries—nation A enjoying a surplus and nation B facing a deficit. The inflow of gold from the deficit to the surplus nation automatically results in an increase in nation A's money supply and a decline in the money supply of nation B. Given

a constant demand for money, the increase in nation A's money supply would lower domestic interest rates. At the same time, nation B's gold outflow and declining money supply would bid up interest rates. In response to falling domestic interest rates and rising foreign interest rates, the investors of nation A would find it attractive to send additional investment funds abroad. Conversely, nation-B investors would not only be discouraged from sending money overseas, but might find it beneficial to liquidate foreign investment holdings and put the funds into domestic assets.

This process facilitates the automatic restoration of payments equilibrium in both nations. Because of the induced changes in interest rates, stabilizing capital movements automatically flow from the surplus to the deficit nation, thereby reducing the payment imbalances of both nations. Although this induced short-term capital movement is of a temporary rather than continuous nature, it nevertheless facilitates the automatic balance-of-payments adjustment process.

During the actual operation of the gold standard, however, central bankers were not totally passive to these automatic adjustments. They instead agreed to reinforce and speed up the interest-rate adjustment mechanism by adhering to the so-called **rules of the game**. This required central bankers in a *surplus* nation to *expand* credit, leading to lower interest rates; central bankers in *deficit* nations would *tighten* credit, bidding interest rates upward. Private short-term capital presumably would flow from the surplus nation to the deficit nation. Not only would the deficit nation's ability to finance its payments imbalance be strengthened, but also the surplus nation's gold inflows would be checked.

CAPITAL FLOWS AND THE BALANCE OF PAYMENTS

The classical economists were aware of the impact of changes in interest rates on international capital movements, even though this factor was not the central focus of their balance-of-payments adjustment theory. With national financial systems closely integrated today, it is recognized that interest-rate fluctuations can induce significant changes in a nation's capital account and balance-of-payments position.

Recall that the capital account of the balance of payments records net changes in a nation's international financial assets and liabilities, excluding changes in official reserves, over a one-year period. Its size depends on all the factors that cause financial assets to move across national borders. The most important of these factors is interest rates in domestic and foreign markets. However, other factors are important too, such as investment profitability, national tax policies, and political stability.

Figure 14.2 shows hypothetical capital account schedules for the United States. Capital account *surpluses* (net capital inflows) and

deficits (net capital outflows) are measured on the vertical axis. Capital flows between the United States and the rest of the world are assumed to respond to *interest-rate differentials* between the two areas (U.S. interest rate minus foreign interest rate) for a particular set of economic conditions in the United States and abroad.

Referring to capital account schedules CA_0, the U.S. capital account is in *balance* (zero net capital flow) at point *A*, where the U.S. interest rate is equal to that abroad. Should the United States reduce its monetary growth, the scarcity of money would tend to raise interest rates in the United States compared with the rest of the world. Suppose U.S. interest rates rise 1 percent above those overseas. Investors, seeing higher U.S. interest rates, will tend to sell foreign securities to purchase U.S. securities that offer a higher yield. The 1-percent interest-rate differential leads to *net capital inflows* of $5 billion for the United States, which thus moves to point *B* on schedule CA_0. Conversely, should foreign interest rates rise above those in the United States, the United States will face *net capital outflows* as investors sell U.S. securities to purchase foreign securities offering a higher yield.

Figure 14.2 assumes that interest-rate differentials are the basic determinant of capital flows for the United States. Movements along a given capital account schedule are caused by changes in the interest rate in the United States relative to that in the rest of the world. However, there are certain determinants other than interest-rate differentials that might cause the United States to import (or export) more or less capital at each possible interest-rate differential and thereby change the location of the capital account schedule.

To illustrate, assume the United States is located along capital account schedule CA_0 at point *A*. Suppose that rising U.S. income leads to higher sales and increased profits. Direct investment (in an auto-assembly plant, for example) becomes more profitable in the

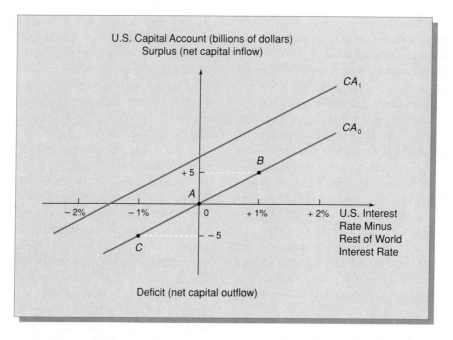

F I G U R E 14. 2   Capital account schedule for the United States. Interest-rate differentials between the United States and the rest of the world induce movements along the U.S. capital account schedule. Relatively high (low) U.S. interest rates trigger net capital inflows (outflows) and an upward (downward) movement along the capital account schedule. The capital account schedule shifts upward/downward in response to changes in non-interest-rate determinants such as investment profitability, tax policies, and political stability.

United States. Nations such as Japan will invest more in their U.S. subsidiaries, whereas General Motors will invest less overseas. The higher profitability of direct investment leads to more capital flowing into the United States at each possible interest-rate differential and an upward shift in the capital account schedule (illustrated by schedule CA_1).

Suppose the U.S. government levies an *interest equalization tax,* as it did from 1964 to 1974. This tax was intended to help reverse the large capital outflows that the United States faced when European interest rates exceeded those in the United States. By taxing U.S. investors on dividend and interest income from foreign securities, the tax reduced the net profitability (that is, the after-tax yield) of foreign

securities. At the same time, the U.S. government enacted a foreign credit-restraint program, which placed direct restrictions on foreign lending by U.S. banks and financial institutions and later on foreign lending of non-financial corporations. By discouraging capital outflows from the United States to Europe, these policies resulted in an upward shift in the U.S. capital account schedule in terms of Figure 14.2, suggesting that less capital would flow out of the United States in response to higher interest rates overseas.

Although the emphasis of this chapter is on balance-of-payments adjustment under a system of fixed exchange rates, the reader may recognize that expectations of future exchange-rate movements can also influence international capital flows. It is possible that capital could flow between two nations in response to *exchange-rate expectations,* even though the nations' interest rates are identical.

As an example, suppose a U.S. investor with $1 million is considering whether to use the funds to purchase securities issued by the U.S. government or similar securities issued by Great Britain. To reach a decision, what factors would this investor consider? The investor would compare the maturities and interest rates of the two securities. Suppose the rates of interest on British and U.S. securities are identical at 10 percent per year and that both securities mature in one year's time. What other factors should be considered in the investment decision? The investor would also want to consider any change that might be expected to occur in exchange rates between the time the securities are purchased and their maturity date.

Assume that today's exchange rate is $1 per pound, but our investor anticipates that the dollar will *depreciate* in one year's time to $2 per pound. If the investor trades her $1 million for pounds today, she can obtain £1 million worth of British securities. In one year's time, when the securities mature, the investor will have £1.1 million, including the accumulated interest. By then, however, if the dollar depreciates to $2 per pound as anticipated, she will be able to exchange her £1.1 million for $2.2 million. This is clearly preferable to the $1.1 million she would have received if she had invested in U.S. securities. This example illustrates that when interest rates are identical in two countries, one should *avoid* the securities of the country whose currency is expected to *depreciate.*

Suppose instead that today's exchange rate is $2 per pound, but our investor anticipates that the dollar will *appreciate* against the pound in the next year, to $1 per pound. Suppose she decides to purchase £500,000 worth of securities with her $1 million. In one year's time, the investment will be worth £550,000, including interest. If the dollar really does appreciate to $1 per pound, these pounds can

be exchanged for $550,000—clearly less than the $1.1 million that could have been obtained by investing in U.S. securities. This example illustrates that, given identical interest rates in two countries, one should *invest* in the securities of the country whose currency is expected to *appreciate* in value.

If one is a *borrower,* these conclusions apply in *reverse.* Given identical interest rates in two countries, it is advantageous to borrow from the country where the exchange rate is expected to depreciate. If it does, the borrower can pay the loan back in "cheaper" pounds (or dollars) when it comes due.

These examples can be illustrated in the capital account analysis of Figure 14.2. Suppose the United States is located at point *A* along capital account schedule CA_0. At this point, the interest rates of the United States and the rest of the world (United Kingdom) are identical, and the United States experiences zero capital flows. Given the expectation of a *dollar appreciation,* investors will want to switch their pound-denominated securities into dollar-denominated securities, which would lead to capital inflows for the United States. Concurrently, borrowers who anticipate that the dollar will appreciate over the life of their loan will look abroad for their borrowing sources, resulting in less capital outflow from the United States. These actions lead to an increase in the net quantity of dollars demanded on the capital account. The U.S. capital account schedule thus shifts upward in the figure, suggesting that a greater amount of capital will flow into the United States at each possible interest-rate differential.

INCOME ADJUSTMENTS

The classical balance-of-payments adjustment theory relied primarily on the price-adjustment mechanism, while delegating a secondary role to the effects of interest rates on private short-term capital movements. A main criticism of the classical theory was that it almost completely neglected the effect of **income adjustments**. The classical economists were aware that the income, or purchasing power, of a surplus nation rose relative to that of the deficit nation. This would have an impact on the level of imports in each nation. But the income effect was viewed as an accompaniment of price changes. Largely because the gold movements of the 19th century exerted only minor impacts on price and interest-rate levels, economic theorists began to look for alternate balance-of-payments adjustment explanations under a fixed exchange-rate system. The theory of **income determination** developed by John Maynard Keynes in the 1930s provided such an explanation.[3]

The Keynesian theory suggests that, under a system of fixed exchange rates, the influence of income changes in surplus and deficit nations will *automatically* help restore payments equilibrium. Given a persistent payments imbalance, a surplus nation will experience rising income, and its imports will increase. Conversely, a deficit nation will experience a fall in income, resulting in a decline in imports. These effects of income changes on import levels will reverse the disequilibrium in the balance of payments.

Income Determination in a Closed Economy

Begin by assuming a *closed economy* with no foreign trade, with price and interest-rate levels constant. In this simple Keynesian model, national income (Y) is the sum of consumption expenditures (C) plus savings (S):

$$Y = C + S$$

Total expenditures on national product are C plus business investment (I). This relationship is given by

$$Y = C + I$$

The upper part of Figure 14.3 represents the familiar income-determination model found in introductory economics textbooks. Consumption is assumed to be functionally dependent on income, whereas investment spending is autonomous—that is, independent of the level of income. The economy is in equilibrium when the level of planned expenditures equals income. This occurs at Y_E, where the 45°-line intersects the ($C + I$) schedule. At any level of income lower (or higher) than Y_E, planned expenditure would exceed (or fall below) income and income would rise (or fall).

Combining these relationships yields the following:

$$Y = C + S = C + I$$

The basic equilibrium condition can be stated as

$$S = I$$

or

$$S - I = 0$$

This equivalent condition for equilibrium income is illustrated in the lower part of Figure 14.3. Like consumption, saving is assumed to be functionally related to income. Given a constant level of investment, the ($S - I$) schedule is upward-sloping. Savings can be regarded as a leakage from the income stream, whereas investment is an injection into the income stream. At income levels below Y_E, I exceeds S, and the level of income rises. The opposite holds equally true. The economy is thus in equilibrium where $S = I$ (or $S - I = 0$). The lower part of Figure 14.3 will be used later to illustrate income determination in an open economy.

Suppose an economy that is initially in equilibrium experiences some disturbance, say, an increase in investment spending. This would bid up the level of equilibrium income. This result comes about through a *multiple process;*

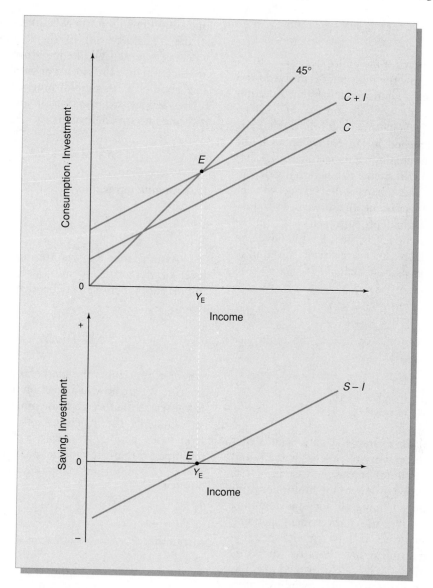

F I G U R E 14. 3 *Income determination in a closed economy.* In an economy not exposed to international trade, equilibrium income occurs where the level of planned expenditures (consumption plus investment) equals income: $Y = C + I$. An equivalent condition for equilibrium income is planned saving equals planned investment: $S = I$, or $S - I = 0$.

that is, the initial investment sets off a chain reaction that results in greater levels of spending, so that income increases by some multiple of the initial investment. Given an autonomous injection of investment spending into the economy, the induced increase in income is given by

$$\Delta Y = k\Delta I$$

where k represents some multiplier.

Let's see how the multiplier is derived for a closed economy. First remember that, in equilibrium, an economy will find planned saving equal to planned investment. It follows that any I must be matched by an equivalent S if the economy is to remain in balance. Because it has been assumed that saving is functionally dependent on income, changes in saving will be related to changes in income. If we use s to represent the marginal propensity to save out of additional income levels, then $S = sY$. Given an autonomous increase in investment, the equilibrium condition suggests that

$$\Delta I = \Delta S = s\Delta Y$$

From the preceding expression, the multiplier can be derived as

$$\Delta Y = \frac{1}{s} \Delta I$$

Suppose, for example, a nation finds that its marginal propensity to save (s) is 0.25, and there occurs an autonomous increase in investment of $100. According to the multiplier principle, the induced change in income stemming from the initial increase in investment spending equals the increase in investment spending times the multiplier (k). Because the s is assumed to equal 0.25, $k = 1/s = 1/0.25 = 4$. The $100 increase in investment expenditure ultimately results in a $400 increase in the level of income.

Income Determination in an Open Economy

Now assume an *open economy* subject to international trade. The condition for equilibrium income, as well as the formulation of the spending multiplier, must both be modified. In an open economy, imports (M), like savings, constitute a leakage out of the income stream, whereas exports (X), like investment, represent an injection into the stream of national income. The condition for equilibrium income, which relates leakages to injections in an open economy's income stream, becomes

$$S + M = I + X$$

Rearranging terms, this becomes

$$S - I = X - M$$

Assume that exports are unrelated to the level of domestic income. Also assume that imports are functionally dependent on domestic income—that is,

$$\Delta M = m\Delta Y$$

where m represents the marginal propensity to import. We are now in a position to derive what is known as the **foreign trade multiplier**.

First, let the injections into and leakages from the income stream rise by the same amount, so that the induced change in income will be of equilibrium magnitude. This yields

$$\Delta S + \Delta M = \Delta I + \Delta X$$

Given that

$$\Delta S = s\Delta Y$$

and

$$\Delta M = m\Delta Y$$

the induced change in income stemming from the changes in injections and leakages can be shown as follows:

$$(s + m) \Delta Y = \Delta I + \Delta X$$

Holding exports constant, the induced change in income is equal to the change in investment times the foreign trade multiplier, or

$$\Delta Y = \frac{1}{s+m} \times \Delta I$$

The preceding expression states that *the foreign trade multiplier equals the reciprocal of the sum of the marginal propensities to save and to import*. In this formulation, an autonomous change in exports, investment remaining fixed, would have an impact on domestic income identical to that of an equivalent change in investment.

Implications of the Foreign Trade Multiplier

To show the adjustment implications of the foreign trade multiplier concept, we construct a diagram based on the framework of Figure 14.3. Remember that the $(S - I)$ schedule is positively sloped. This is because changes in savings are assumed to be directly related to changes in income, investment being unaffected. Subtracting investment from saving yields an upward-sloping $(S - I)$ schedule, as shown in Figure 14.4. Similarly, it has been assumed that changes in imports are directly related to changes in income, exports remaining constant. When imports are subtracted from exports, the result is a downward-sloping $(X - M)$ schedule. As before, the equilibrium condition of an open economy with no government is $(X - M) = (S - I)$.

Starting at equilibrium income level $1,000 in Figure 14.4, suppose a disturbance results in an autonomous increase in exports by, say, $200. This is shown by shifting the $(X - M)$ schedule upward by $200, resulting in the new schedule $(X' - M)$. The level of income rises, generating increases in imports and savings. Domestic equilibrium is established at income level $1,400, where $(S - I) = (X' - M)$. The trade account is no longer in balance; there is a surplus of $100. This trade surplus is less than the initial $200 rise in exports because part of the surplus is offset by increases in imports induced by the rise in income from $1,000 to $1,400.

In this example, we can use the foreign trade multiplier concept to determine the effect of the increase in exports on the home economy. Inspection of the $(S - I)$ schedule in Figure 14.4 reveals that the slope of the schedule, which represents the marginal propensity to save, equals 0.25. The slope of the $(X - M)$ schedule indicates that the marginal propensity to import also equals 0.25. The foreign trade multiplier is the reciprocal of the sum of the marginal propensities to save and to import—that is, 1/0.50, or 2. An autonomous increase in exports of $200 thus generates a twofold increase in domestic income, and equilibrium income rises from $1,000 to $1,400.

As for the trade-account effect, the $400 rise in domestic income induces a $100 increase in imports, given a marginal propensity to import of 0.25. Part of the initial export-led surplus is thus neutralized, lowering it from $200 to $100. Over time, the increase in imports generated by increased domestic expenditures will tend to reduce the trade surplus, but not enough to restore balance-of-payments equilibrium.

Consider another case that illustrates the national-income and balance-of-payments effects of a change in expenditures. Assume that, owing to improved profit expectations, domestic investment rises autonomously by $200. Starting at equilibrium level $1,000 in Figure 14.5, the increase in investment will displace the $(S - I)$ schedule downward by $200 because the negative term is increased. This gives us the new schedule $(S - I')$. Domestic income rises from $1,000 to $1,400, which stimulates a rise in imports, producing a trade deficit of $100. Unlike the previous case of export-led expansion, an autonomous increase in domestic investment spending (or government expenditures) increases domestic income but at the expense of a balance-of-payments deficit. This

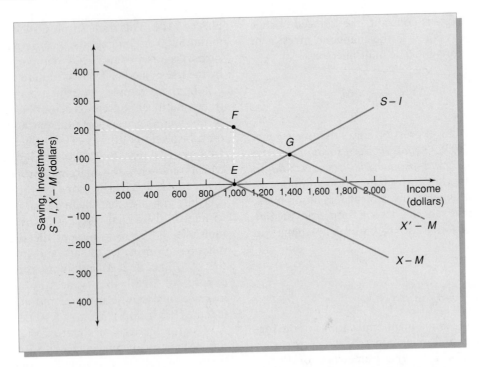

F I G U R E 14. 4 *Domestic-income and trade-balance effects of an increase in exports.*
Starting at equilibrium income, an autonomous increase in domestic exports leads to a rise in
domestic income, which promotes an increase in imports and savings. Because of the multiplier effect, the induced increase in income tends to be larger than the initial increase in
exports. The trade account moves into surplus because the induced increase in imports tends
to be less than the initial increase in exports.

should serve as a reminder to economic policymakers that, under a system of fixed exchange
rates, the impact of domestic policies on the
balance of payments cannot be overlooked.

Foreign Repercussions

The preceding income-adjustment analysis
needs to be modified to include the impact that
changes in domestic expenditures and income
levels have on foreign economies. This process
is referred to as the **foreign repercussion effect**.

Assume a two-country world, the United
States and Canada, in which there initially

exists balance-of-payments equilibrium. Owing
to changing consumer preferences, suppose the
United States faces an autonomous increase in
imports from Canada. This results in an
increase in Canada's exports. According to the
multiplier principle, U.S. income will fall, and
Canada's income will rise. The fall in U.S.
income induces a fall in the level of U.S. imports
(and a fall in Canada's exports). At the same
time, the rise in Canada's income induces a rise
in Canada's imports (and a rise in U.S. exports).
This feedback process is repeated again and
again.

The consequence of this process is that
both the rise in income of the surplus nation

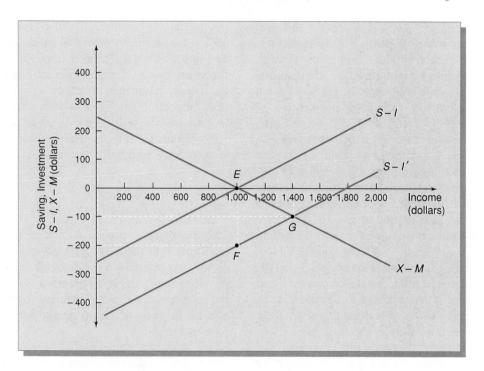

F I G U R E 14. 5 *Domestic-income and trade-balance effects of an increase in investment.* Starting at equilibrium income, an autonomous increase in domestic investment generates an increase in income, which promotes additional savings and imports. Because of the multiplier effect, the increase in investment generates a magnified increase in income. As the increase in income induces a rise in imports, a trade deficit appears.

(Canada) and the fall in income of the deficit nation (United States) are dampened. This is because the autonomous increase in U.S. imports (and Canada's exports) will cause U.S. income to decrease as imports are substituted for home-produced goods. Given the marginal propensity to import, the decline in U.S. income will generate a reduction in its imports. Because U.S. imports are Canada's exports, the result will be to moderate the rise in Canada's income. From the perspective of the United States, the decline in its income will be cushioned by an increase in exports to Canada stemming from a rise in Canada's income.

The importance of the foreign repercussion effect depends in part on the economic size of a country as far as international trade is concerned. A small nation that increases its imports from a large nation will have little impact on the large nation's income level. But for major trading nations, the foreign repercussion effect is likely to be significant and must be taken into account when the income-adjustment mechanism is being considered.

Disadvantages of Automatic Adjustment Mechanisms

The preceding sections have considered automatic balance-of-payments adjustment mechanisms under a system of fixed exchange rates.

According to the classical school of thought, adjustments occur as prices and interest rates respond to international gold movements. Keynesian theory emphasized another adjustment process, the effect of changes in national income on a nation's balance of payments.

Although elements of price, interest-rate, and income adjustments may operate in the real world, these adjustment mechanisms have a major shortcoming. The problem is that an efficient adjustment mechanism requires central bankers to forgo their use of monetary policy to promote the goal of full employment without inflation. Each nation must therefore be willing to accept *inflation* or *recession* when balance-of-payments adjustment requires it. Take the case of a nation that faces a deficit caused by an autonomous increase in imports or decrease in exports. For income adjustments to reverse the deficit, monetary authorities must permit domestic income to decrease and not undertake policies to offset its decline. The opposite applies equally to a nation with a balance-of-payments surplus.

To the classical economists, the abandonment of an independent monetary policy would not be considered a disadvantage. This is because classical thought envisioned a system that would automatically move toward full employment over time, as well as placing a high priority on balance-of-payments adjustment. In today's world, *unemployment* is often the norm, and its elimination is generally given priority over balance-of-payments equilibrium. Modern nations are thus reluctant to make significant internal sacrifices for the sake of external equilibrium. The result is that reliance on an automatic payments-adjustment process is politically unacceptable.

MONETARY ADJUSTMENTS

The previous sections have examined how changes in national price, interest-rate, and income levels automatically lead to balance-of-payments adjustment. During the 1960s–1970s, a new theory emerged, called the *monetary approach* to the balance of payments.[4] The monetary approach views disequilibrium in the balance of payments primarily as a monetary phenomenon. Money acts as both a *disturbance* and an *adjustment* to the balance of payments. Adjustment in the balance of payments is viewed as an automatic process.

Payments Imbalances under Fixed Exchange Rates

The monetary approach emphasizes that disequilibrium in the balance of payments reflects an imbalance between the demand and the supply of money. A first assumption is that, over the long run, the nation's demand for money is a stable function of real income, prices, and the interest rate.

The quantity of nominal money balances demanded is *directly* related to income and prices. Increases in income and/or prices trigger increases in the value of transactions and an increased need for money to finance the transactions, and vice versa. The quantity of money demanded is *inversely* related to the interest rate. Whenever money is held rather than used to make an investment, the money holder sacrifices interest that could have been earned. If interest rates are high, people will try to keep as little money on hand as possible, putting the rest into interest-earning investments. Conversely, a decline in interest rates increases the quantity of money demanded.

The nation's *money supply* is a multiple of the monetary base that includes two components. The *domestic component* refers to credit created by the nation's monetary authorities (such as Federal Reserve liabilities for the United States). The *international component* refers to the foreign exchange reserves of a nation, which can be increased or decreased as the result of balance-of-payments disequilibrium.

The monetary approach maintains that all payments *deficits* are the result of an *excess in*

T A B L E 14. 1 / *Changes in the Supply of Money and Demand for Money Under Fixed Exchange Rates: Impact on the Balance of Payments According to the Monetary Approach*

Change*	Impact
Increase in money supply	Deficit
Decrease in money supply	Surplus
Increase in money demand	Surplus
Decrease in money demand	Deficit

*Starting from a position at which the nation's money demand equals the money supply and its balance of payments is in equilibrium.

the supply of money over the demand for money in the home country. Under a fixed exchange-rate system, the excess supply of money results in foreign exchange reserves' flowing overseas, thus reducing the domestic money supply. Conversely, an *excess demand for money* in the home country leads to a payments *surplus*, resulting in the inflow of foreign exchange reserves from overseas and an increase in the domestic money supply. Balance in the nation's payments position is restored when the excess supply of money, or the excess demand for money, has fallen enough to restore the equilibrium condition: money supply equals money demand. Table 14.1 summarizes the conclusions of the monetary approach, given a system of fixed exchange rates.

Assume that, to finance a budget deficit, the Canadian government creates additional money. Considering this money to be in excess of desired levels (excess money supply), Canadian residents choose to increase their spending on goods and services instead of holding extra cash balances. Given a fixed exchange-rate system, the rise in home spending will push up the prices of Canadian goods and services relative to those abroad. Canadian buyers will be induced to decrease purchases of Canadian-produced goods and services, as will foreign

buyers. Conversely, Canadian sellers will offer more goods at home and fewer abroad, whereas foreign sellers will try to increase sales to Canada. By encouraging a rise in imports and a fall in exports, these forces tend to worsen the Canadian payments position. As Canada finances its deficit by transferring international reserves to foreign nations, the Canadian money supply will fall back toward desired levels. This, in turn, will reduce Canadian spending and demand for imports, restoring payments balance.

The monetary approach views balance-of-payments adjustment as an automatic process. Any payments imbalance reflects a disparity between actual and desired money balances that tends to be eliminated by inflows or outflows of foreign exchange reserves, which lead to increases or decreases in the domestic money supply. This self-correcting process requires time. Except for implying that the adjustment process takes place over the long run, the monetary approach does not consider the time period needed to achieve equilibrium. The monetary approach thus emphasizes the economy's final, long-run equilibrium position.

The monetary approach assumes that flows in foreign exchange reserves associated with payments imbalances do exert an influence on the domestic money supply. This is true as long as central banks do not use monetary policies to neutralize the impact of flows in foreign exchange reserves on the domestic money supply. If they do neutralize such flows, payments imbalances will continue, according to the monetary approach.

Policy Implications

What implications does the monetary approach have for domestic economic policies? The approach suggests that economic policy affects the balance of payments through its impact on the domestic demand for and supply of money. Policies that increase the supply of money relative to the demand for money will lead to a payments deficit, an outflow of foreign exchange reserves, and a reduction in the domestic money supply. Policies that increase the demand for money relative to the supply of money will trigger a payments surplus, an inflow of foreign exchange reserves, and an increase in the domestic money supply.

The monetary approach also suggests that nonmonetary policies that attempt to influence a nation's balance of payments (such as tariffs, quotas, or currency devaluation) are unnecessary because payments disequilibria are self-correcting over time. However, in the short run, such policies may speed up the adjustment process by reducing excesses in the supply of money or the demand for money.

For example, given an initial equilibrium, suppose the Canadian government creates money in excess of that demanded by the economy, leading to a payments deficit. The monetary approach maintains that, in the long run, foreign exchange reserves will flow out of Canada and the Canadian money supply will decrease. This automatic adjustment process will continue until the money supply decreases enough to restore the equilibrium condition: money supply equals money demand. Suppose Canada, to speed the return to equilibrium, imposes a tariff on imports. The tariff increases the price of imports as well as the prices of non-traded goods (goods produced exclusively for the domestic market, which face no competition from imports), owing to interproduct substitution. Higher Canadian prices trigger an increase in the quantity of money demanded, because Canadians now require additional funds to finance higher-priced purchases. The increase in the quantity of money demanded absorbs part of the excess money supply. The tariff therefore results in a more speedy elimination of the excess money supply and payments deficit than would occur under an automatic adjustment mechanism.[5]

The monetary approach also has policy implications for the growth of the economy. Starting from the point of equilibrium, as the nation's output and real income expand, so do the number of transactions and the quantity of money demanded. If the government does not increase the domestic component of the money supply commensurate with the increase in the quantity of money demanded, the excess demand will induce an inflow of funds from abroad and a payments surplus. This explanation is often advanced for the German payments surpluses that occurred during the late 1960s and early 1970s, a period when the growth in German national output and money demand surpassed the growth in the domestic component of the German money supply.

SUMMARY

1. Because persistent balance-of-payments disequilibrium—whether surplus or deficit—tends to have adverse economic consequences, there exists a need for adjustment.

2. Balance-of-payments adjustment may be classified as automatic or discretionary. Under a system of fixed exchange rates, automatic adjustments may occur through variations in prices,

interest rates, and incomes. The demand for and supply of money can also influence the adjustment process.

3. David Hume's theory provided an explanation of the automatic adjustment process that occurs under the gold standard. Starting from a condition of payments balance, any surplus or deficit would automatically be eliminated by changes in domestic price levels. Hume's theory relied heavily on the quantity theory of money.

4. Another important consequence of international gold movements under the classical theory was their impact on short-term interest rates. A deficit nation suffering gold losses would face a shrinking money supply, which would force up interest rates, promoting capital inflows and payments equilibrium. The opposite held true for a surplus nation. Rather than relying on automatic adjustments in interest rates to restore payments balance, central bankers often resorted to monetary policies designed to reinforce the adjustment mechanism during the gold-standard era.

5. With the advent of Keynesian economics during the 1930s, greater adjustment emphasis was put on the income effects of trade.

6. The foreign repercussion effect refers to a situation in which a change in one nation's macroeconomic variables relative to another nation will induce a chain reaction in both nations' economies.

7. An automatic balance-of-payments adjustment mechanism has several disadvantages. Nations must be willing to accept adverse changes in the domestic economy when required for balance-of-payments adjustment. Policymakers must forgo using discretionary economic policy to promote domestic equilibrium.

8. The monetary approach to the balance of payments is presented as an alternative, rather than a supplement, to traditional adjustment theories. It maintains that, over the long run, payments disequilibria are rooted in the relationship between the demand for and the supply of money. Adjustment in the balance of payments is viewed as an automatic process.

STUDY QUESTIONS

1. What is meant by the term *balance-of-payments adjustment*? Why does a deficit nation have an incentive to undergo adjustment? What about a surplus nation?

2. Under a fixed exchange-rate system, what automatic adjustments promote payments equilibrium?

3. What is meant by the quantity theory of money? How did it relate to the classical price-adjustment mechanism?

4. How can adjustments in domestic interest rates help promote payments balance?

5. In the gold-standard era, there existed the so-called rules of the game. What were these rules? Were they followed in practice?

6. Keynesian theory suggests that, under a system of fixed exchange rates, the influence of income changes in surplus and deficit nations helps promote balance-of-payments equilibrium. Explain.

7. When analyzing the income-adjustment mechanism, one must account for the foreign repercussion effect. Explain.

8. What are some major disadvantages of the automatic adjustment mechanism under a system of fixed exchange rates?

9. According to the monetary approach, balance in a nation's payments position is restored when the excess supply of money or the excess demand for money has fallen to restore the equilibrium condition: money supply equals money demand. Explain.

10. What implications does the monetary approach have for domestic economic policies?

CHAPTER 15

Exchange-Rate Adjustments and the Balance of Payments

The previous chapter demonstrated that balance-of-payments disequilibria tend to be reversed by automatic adjustments in prices, interest rates, and incomes. If these adjustments are allowed to operate, however, reversing balance-of-payments disequilibria may come at the expense of domestic recession or price inflation. The cure may be perceived as worse than the disease.

Instead of relying on adjustments in prices, interest rates, and incomes to counteract payments imbalances, governments permit alterations in exchange rates. By adopting a floating exchange-rate system, a nation permits its currency to depreciate or appreciate in a free market in response to shifts in either the demand for or supply of the currency. Under a fixed exchange-rate system, rates are set by government in the short run. However, if the official exchange rate becomes overvalued over a period of time, a government may initiate policies to *devalue* its currency. Currency devaluation causes a depreciation of a currency's exchange value; it is initiated by government policy rather than free-market forces of supply and demand. When a nation's currency is undervalued, it may

be *revalued* by the government; this policy causes the currency's exchange value to appreciate. Currency devaluation and revaluation will be discussed further in the next chapter.

In this chapter, we examine the impact of exchange-rate adjustments on the balance of payments. We will learn under what conditions currency depreciation (devaluation) and appreciation (revaluation) will improve/worsen a nation's payments position.

EFFECTS OF EXCHANGE-RATE CHANGES ON COSTS AND PRICES

Industries that compete with foreign producers, or that rely on imported inputs in production, can be noticeably affected by exchange-rate fluctuations. Changing exchange rates influence the international competitiveness of a nation's industries through their influence on relative costs. In 1990, for example, the U.S. steel industry's cost advantage compared to German manufacturers was about $79 per ton. By 1991, a 16-percent appreciation of the dollar against the German mark had eroded this margin and production costs were about equal.

TABLE 15. 1 / Effects of a Dollar Appreciation on a U.S. Steel Firm's Production Costs When All Costs Are Dollar-Denominated

	Cost of Producing a Ton of Steel			
	Period 1 50 cents per mark (2 marks = $1)		Period 2 25 cents per mark (4 marks = $1)	
	Dollar Cost	Mark Equivalent	Dollar Cost	Mark Equivalent
Labor	$160	DM 320	$160	DM 640
Materials (iron/coal)	300	600	300	1,200
Other costs (energy)	40	80	40	160
Total	$500	DM 1,000	$500	DM 2,000
Percentage change	——	——	——	100%

How do exchange-rate fluctuations affect relative costs? The answer depends on the extent to which a firm's costs are denominated in terms of the home currency or foreign currency.

CASE 1

No foreign sourcing: all costs are denominated in dollars

Table 15.1 illustrates the hypothetical production costs of Bethlehem Steel Inc., a U.S. manufacturer. Assume that in its production of steel, Bethlehem utilizes U.S. labor, coal, iron, and other inputs whose costs are denominated in dollars. In period 1, the exchange value of the dollar is assumed to be 50 cents per mark (2 marks per dollar). Assume that the firm's cost of producing a ton of steel is $500, which is equivalent to 1,000 marks at this exchange rate.

Suppose that in period 2, because of changing market conditions, the dollar's exchange

value *appreciates* from 50 cents per mark to 25 cents per mark, a 100-percent appreciation (the mark depreciates from 2 to 4 marks per dollar). With the dollar appreciation, Bethlehem's labor, iron, coal, and other input costs remain constant in dollar terms. In terms of the mark, however, these costs rise from 1,000 to 2,000 marks per ton, a 100-percent increase. The 100-percent dollar appreciation induces a 100-percent increase in Bethlehem's mark-denominated production cost. The international competitiveness of Bethlehem is thus reduced.

The previous example assumed that all of a firm's inputs were acquired domestically and their costs were denominated in the domestic currency. In many industries, however, some of a firm's inputs are purchased in foreign markets (foreign sourcing), and these input costs are denominated in a foreign currency. What impact does a change in the home currency's exchange value have on a firm's costs in this situation?

T A B L E   15. 2   /   *Effects of a Dollar Appreciation on a U.S. Steel Firm's*
Production Costs When Some Costs Are Dollar-Denominated
and Other Costs Are Mark-Denominated

	Cost of Producing a Ton of Steel			
	Period 1 50 cents per mark (2 marks = $1)		Period 2 25 cents per mark (4 marks = $1)	
	Dollar Cost	Mark Equivalent	Dollar Cost	Mark Equivalent
Labor	$160	DM 320	$160	DM 640
Materials Dollar-denominated (iron/coal)	120	240	120	480
Mark-denominated (scrap iron)	180	360	90	360
Total	300	600	210	840
Other costs (energy)	40	80	40	160
Total cost	$500	DM 1,000	$410	DM 1,640
Percentage change	——	——	-18%	+64%

C A S E   2

Foreign sourcing: some costs denominated in
dollars and some costs denominated in marks

Table 15.2 again illustrates the hypothetical
production costs of Bethlehem Steel Inc., whose
costs of labor, iron, coal, and certain other
inputs are assumed to be denominated in dollars. However, suppose Bethlehem acquires
scrap iron from German suppliers (foreign
sourcing), and these costs are denominated in
marks. Once again, assume that the dollar's
exchange value appreciates from 50 cents per
mark to 25 cents per mark. As before, the
mark cost of Bethlehem's labor, iron, coal, and
certain other inputs rise by 100 percent following the dollar appreciation; however, the mark

cost of scrap iron remains constant. As can be
seen in the table, Bethlehem's mark cost per ton
of steel rises from 1,000 to 1,640 marks—an
increase of only 64 percent. Thus, the dollar
appreciation worsens Bethlehem's international
competitiveness, but not as much as in the previous example.

In addition to influencing Bethlehem's
mark-denominated cost of steel, a dollar appreciation affects the firm's dollar cost when mark-
denominated inputs are involved. Because
scrap-iron costs are denominated in marks, they
remain at 360 marks after the dollar appreciation; however, the dollar-equivalent scrap-iron
cost falls from $180 to $90. Since the costs of
Bethlehem's other inputs are denominated in
dollars and do not change following the dollar

appreciation, the firm's total dollar cost falls from $500 to $410 per ton—a decrease of 18 percent. This cost reduction offsets some of the cost disadvantage that Bethlehem incurs relative to German exporters as a result of the dollar appreciation (mark depreciation).

The preceding examples suggest the following generalization: as mark-denominated costs become a *larger* portion of Bethlehem's total costs, a dollar appreciation (depreciation) leads to a *smaller increase (decrease)* in the mark cost of Bethlehem steel and a *larger decrease (increase)* in the dollar cost of Bethlehem steel compared to the cost changes that occur when all input costs are dollar-denominated. As mark-denominated costs become a smaller portion of total costs, the opposite conclusions apply. These conclusions are especially significant for the world trading system during the 1980s–1990s, as industries (such as autos and computers) have become increasingly internationalized and utilize increasing amounts of imported inputs in the production process.

Changes in relative costs due to exchange rate fluctuations also influence relative prices and the volume of goods traded among nations. By increasing relative U.S. production costs, a dollar *appreciation* tends to *raise* U.S. export prices in foreign currency terms, which induces a decrease in the quantity of U.S. goods sold abroad; similarly, the dollar appreciation leads to an increase in U.S. imports. By decreasing relative U.S. production costs, a dollar *depreciation* tends to *lower* U.S. export prices in foreign currency terms, which induces an increase in the quantity of U.S. goods sold abroad; similarly, the dollar depreciation leads to a decrease in U.S. imports.

Several factors govern the extent by which exchange-rate movements lead to relative price changes among nations. Some U.S. exporters may able to offset the price-increasing effects of an appreciation in the dollar's exchange value by reducing profit margins to maintain competitiveness. Perceptions concerning long-term

TABLE 15. 3 / *Estimated Effects of a 1-Percent Dollar Appreciation on Prices of U.S. Steel Imports and Exports*

	Price Change (%)
IMPORT PRICE	
Hot-rolled sheet	-0.78
Cold-rolled sheet	-0.36
EXPORT PRICE	
Hot-rolled sheet	0.22
Cold-rolled sheet	0.52

SOURCE: U.S. International Trade Commission, *Steel Industry Annual Report* (Washington, D.C., September 1991), Appendix G.

trends in exchange rates also promote price rigidity: U.S. exporters may be less willing to raise prices if the dollar's appreciation is viewed as temporary. The extent to which industries implement pricing strategies depends significantly on the substitutability of their product: the greater the degree of product differentiation (as in quality or service), the greater control producers can exercise over prices; the pricing policies of such producers are somewhat insulated from exchange-rate movements.

The U.S. International Trade Commission (USITC) has estimated the effect of exchange-rate changes on prices of U.S. imports and exports of selected steel products over the period 1981–1989. Table 15.3 summarizes their findings for two products, hot-rolled sheet steel and cold-rolled sheet steel. According to the USITC's estimates, a 1-percent appreciation in the dollar's exchange value induces a much smaller percentage change in steel import and export prices; moreover, most of the induced price changes do not occur until after 9–12 months. These results are not surprising given the lead time required to order, produce, and ship steel and the fact that steel export pricing tends to be especially sensitive to foreign steel consumption levels and domestic costs.

Is there any way in which companies can offset the impact of currency swings on their competitiveness? Suppose the exchange value of the Japanese yen appreciates against other currencies, which results in Japanese goods' becoming less competitive in world markets. To insulate themselves from the squeeze on profits caused by the rising yen, Japanese companies could move production to affiliates located in countries whose currencies have depreciated against the yen. This would be most likely to occur if the yen's appreciation was sizable and was regarded as being permanent; even if the yen's appreciation was not permanent, shifting production offshore could help reduce the uncertainties associated with currency swings. Indeed, Japanese companies have resorted to offshore production to protect themselves from an appreciating yen. Following the Plaza Accord of 1985, which sent the yen soaring against the dollar, Japanese makers of autos, machinery, and electronics pumped billions of dollars into global production networks, giving them remarkable flexibility.

REQUIREMENTS FOR A SUCCESSFUL DEPRECIATION (DEVALUATION)

The previous section concluded that currency depreciation tends to improve a nation's competitiveness by reducing its costs and prices, while currency appreciation implies the opposite. When will currency depreciation (devaluation) succeed in reducing a payments deficit?

Several approaches to currency depreciation (devaluation) must be considered, and each of them will be dealt with in a separate section. The **elasticity approach** emphasizes the relative *price effects* of depreciation and suggests that depreciation works best when demand elasticities are high. The **absorption approach** deals

with the *income effects* of depreciation; the implication is that a decrease in domestic expenditure relative to income must occur for depreciation to promote payments equilibrium. The **monetary approach** stresses the effects depreciation has on the *purchasing power of money* and the resulting impact on domestic expenditure levels.

The Elasticity Approach to Exchange-Rate Adjustment

Currency devaluation (depreciation) affects a country's *balance of trade* through changes in the relative prices of goods and services internationally. A trade-deficit nation may be able to reverse its imbalance by lowering its relative prices, so that exports increase while imports decrease. The nation can lower its relative prices by permitting its exchange rate to depreciate in a free market or formally devaluing its currency under a system of fixed exchange rates. The ultimate outcome of currency depreciation (devaluation) depends on the price elasticity of demand for a nation's imports and the price elasticity of demand for its exports.

Recall that *elasticity of demand* refers to the responsiveness of buyers to changes in price. It indicates the percentage change in the quantity demanded stemming from a 1-percent change in price. Mathematically, elasticity is the ratio of the percentage change in the quantity demanded to the percentage change in price. This may be symbolized as

$$Elasticity = \frac{\Delta Q/Q}{\Delta P/P}$$

The elasticity coefficient is stated numerically, without regard to the algebraic sign. If the preceding ratio exceeds 1, a given percentage change in price results in a larger percentage change in quantity demanded; this is referred to as relatively *elastic* demand. If the ratio is less than 1, demand is said to be relatively *inelastic*, because the percentage change in quantity demanded is less than the percentage change in

T A B L E 15. 4 / *British Devaluation: Improved Trade Balance*

Sector	Trade-Balance Effect		
	Change in Pound Price (%)	Change in Quantity Demanded (%)	Net Effect (in pounds)
Import	+10	-25	-15% outpayments
Export	0	+15	+15% inpayments

Assumptions
British demand elasticity for imports = 2.5 ⎫
Demand elasticity for British exports = 1.5 ⎬ Sum = 4.0
Pound devaluation = 10% ⎭

price. A ratio precisely equal to 1 denotes *unitary elastic* demand, meaning that the percentage change in quantity demanded just matches the percentage change in price.

The following analysis investigates the effects of a currency depreciation (devaluation) on a nation's balance of trade—that is, the value of its exports minus imports. Suppose the British monetary authorities decide to devalue the pound by 10 percent to correct a trade deficit with the United States. Whether the British trade balance will be improved depends on what happens to the dollar inpayments for Britain's exports as opposed to the dollar outpayments for its imports. This, in turn, depends on whether the U.S. demand for British exports is elastic or inelastic and whether the British demand for imports is elastic or inelastic.

Depending on the size of the demand elasticities for British exports and imports, Britain's trade balance may improve, worsen, or remain unchanged in response to the pound devaluation. The general rule that determines the actual outcome is the so-called **Marshall–Lerner condition**. The Marshall–Lerner condition states: (1) Devaluation (depreciation) will *improve* the trade balance if the devaluing nation's demand elasticity for imports plus the foreign demand elasticity for the nation's exports exceeds 1.

(2) If the sum of the demand elasticities is less than 1, devaluation will *worsen* the trade balance. (3) The trade balance will be *neither helped nor hurt* if the sum of the demand elasticities equals 1. The Marshall–Lerner condition may be stated in terms of the currency of either the nation undergoing a devaluation or its trading partner, but it cannot be expressed in terms of both currencies simultaneously. Our discussion is confined to the currency of the devaluing country, Great Britain.

C A S E   1
Improved trade balance

Referring to Table 15.4, assume that the British demand elasticity for imports equals 2.5 and the U.S. demand elasticity for British exports equals 1.5; the sum of the elasticities is 4.0. To improve its payments position, Britain officially devalues the pound by 10 percent, which leads to a depreciation of the pound against the dollar by the same amount. An assessment of the overall impact of the devaluation on Britain's payments position requires identification of the devaluation's impact on import expenditures and export receipts.

If prices of imports remain constant in terms of foreign currency, then a devaluation

TABLE 15. 5 / *British Devaluation: Worsened Trade Balance*

Sector	Trade-Balance Effect		
	Change in Pound Price (%)	Change in Quantity Demanded (%)	Net Effect (in pounds)
Import	+10	-2	+8% outpayments
Export	0	+1	+1% inpayments

Assumptions
British demand elasticity for imports = 0.2 ⎤
Demand elasticity for British exports = 0.1 ⎦   Sum = 0.3
* Pound devaluation = 10%

increases the home-currency price of goods imported. Because of the devaluation, the pound price of British imports rises 10 percent. British consumers would thus be expected to reduce their purchases from abroad. Given an import demand elasticity of 2.5, the devaluation triggers a 25-percent decline in the quantity of imports demanded. The 10-percent price increase in conjunction with a 25-percent quantity reduction results in approximately a 15-percent decrease in British outpayments in pounds. This cutback in import purchases actually reduces import expenditures, which reduces the British deficit.

What about British export receipts? The pound price of the exports remains constant, but after devaluation of the pound, consumers in the United States find British exports costing 10-percent less in terms of dollars. Given a U.S. demand elasticity of 1.5 for British exports, the 10-percent British devaluation will stimulate foreign sales by 15 percent, so that export receipts in pounds will increase by approximately 15 percent. This strengthens the British payments position. The 15-percent reduction in import expenditures coupled with a 15-percent rise in export receipts means that the pound devaluation will reduce the British payments deficit. With the sum of the elasticities exceed-

ing 1, the devaluation *strengthens* Britain's trade position.

CASE 2

Worsened trade balance

In Table 15.5, the British demand elasticity for imports is 0.2 and the U.S. demand elasticity for British exports is 0.1; the sum of the elasticities is 0.3. The 10-percent British devaluation raises the pound price of imports by 10 percent, inducing a 2-percent reduction in the quantity of imports demanded. In contrast to the previous case, under relatively inelastic conditions the devaluation contributes to an *increase*, rather than a decrease, in import expenditures of some 8 percent. As before, the pound price of British exports is unaffected by the devaluation, whereas the dollar price of exports falls 10 percent. U.S. purchases from abroad increase by 1 percent, resulting in an increase in pound receipts of about 1 percent. With expenditures on imports rising 8 percent while export receipts increase only 1 percent, the British deficit will tend to *worsen*. The Marshall–Lerner condition holds that *devaluation will cause a deterioration in a nation's trade position if the sum of the elasticities is less than 1*. The reader is left to verify that a nation's trade balance remains unaffected by devaluation if the sum of the demand elasticities equals 1.

Although the Marshall–Lerner condition provides a general rule as to when a currency devaluation (depreciation) will be successful in restoring payments equilibrium, it depends on some simplifying assumptions. For one, it is assumed that a nation's trade balance is in equilibrium when the devaluation occurs. If there is initially a very large trade deficit, with imports exceeding exports, then a devaluation might cause import expenditures to change more than export receipts, even though the sum of the demand elasticities exceeds 1. The analysis also assumes no change in the sellers' prices in their own currency. But this may not always be true. To protect their competitive position, foreign sellers may lower their prices in response to a home-country devaluation; or domestic sellers may raise home-currency prices so that the devaluation's effects are not fully transmitted into lower foreign exchange prices for their goods. However, neither of these assumptions invalidates the Marshall–Lerner condition's spirit, which suggests that devaluations work best when demand elasticities are high.

Empirical Measurement: Import/Export Demand Elasticities

The Marshall–Lerner condition illustrates the price effects of a nation's depreciation (devaluation) on its trade balance. The extent to which price changes affect the volume of goods traded depends on the elasticity of demand for imports. If the elasticities were known in advance, it would be possible to determine the proper exchange-rate policy to restore payments equilibrium. Without such knowledge, nations often have been reluctant to change the par values of their currencies.

During the 1940s and 1950s, there was considerable debate among economists concerning the empirical measurement of demand elasticities. Several early studies suggested low

demand elasticities, close to unity or even less. Those findings led to the formation of the *elasticity pessimist* school of thought, which contended that currency devaluations and revaluations would be largely ineffectual in promoting changes in a nation's trade balance. By the 1960s, most economists considered themselves *elasticity optimists,* estimating the demand elasticities for most nations to be rather high. Table 15.6 shows estimated price elasticities of demand for total imports and exports by country.

Time Path of Depreciation (Devaluation)

Empirical estimates of price elasticities in international trade suggest that, according to the Marshall–Lerner condition, devaluation (depreciation) is likely to improve a nation's trade balance. A basic problem in measuring world price elasticities, however, is that there tends to be a *time lag* between changes in exchange rates and their ultimate effect on real trade. One popular description of the time path of trade flows is the so-called **J-curve effect.** This view suggests that, in the very short run, a currency devaluation will lead to a worsening of a nation's trade balance. But as time passes, the trade balance will likely improve. This is because it takes time for new information about the price effects of devaluation to be disseminated throughout the economy and for economic units to adjust their behavior accordingly.

J-curve effect. A currency devaluation (depreciation) affects a nation's trade balance through its net impact on export receipts and import expenditures. Export receipts and import expenditures are calculated by multiplying the commodity's per-unit price times the quantity being demanded. Figure 15.1 illustrates the process by which devaluation influences export receipts and import expenditures.

The immediate effect of devaluation is a change in relative prices. If a nation devalues its currency by 10 percent, it means that import prices initially increase 10 percent in terms of

T A B L E 15. 6 / Price Elasticities of Demand for Total Imports and Exports of Selected Countries

Country	Import Price Elasticity	Export Price Elasticity	Sum of Import and Export Elasticities
United States	0.92	0.99	1.91
United Kingdom	0.47	0.44	0.91
Germany	0.60	0.66	1.26
Japan	0.93	0.93	1.86
Canada	1.02	0.83	1.85
Other developed countries	0.49	0.83	1.32
Less developed countries	0.81	0.63	1.44
OPEC	1.14	0.57	1.71

SOURCE: Jaime Marques, "Bilateral Trade Elasticities," *Review of Economics and Statistics* 72, no. 1 (February 1990), pp. 75–76.

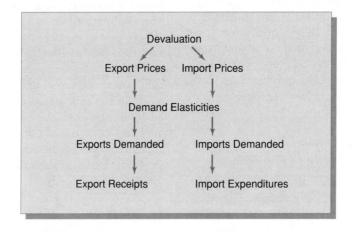

F I G U R E 15. 1   Devaluation flowchart.

the home currency. The quantity of imports demanded will then fall according to home demand elasticities. At the same time, exporters will initially receive 10 percent more in home currency for each unit of foreign currency they earn. This means they can become more competitive and lower their export prices measured in terms of foreign currencies. Export sales will then rise in accordance with foreign demand elasticities. The problem with this process is that, for devaluation to take effect, time is required for the pricing mechanism to induce changes in the volume of exports and imports.

The time path of the response of trade flows to a devaluation can be described in terms of the J-curve effect—so called because the trade balance continues to get worse for a while after devaluation (sliding down the hook of the J) and then gets better (moving up the stem of the J). This effect occurs because the initial effect of devaluation is an increase in import expenditures: the home-currency price of imports has risen, but the volume is unchanged owing to prior commitments. As time passes, the quantity adjustment period becomes relevant: import volume is depressed, while exports become more attractive to foreign buyers.

Advocates of the J-curve effect use the 1967 devaluation of the British pound as an example. As seen in Figure 15.2, the British balance of payments showed a $1.3-billion deficit in 1967. To improve its payments position, Britain devalued the pound by 14.3 percent in November 1967. The initial impact of the devaluation was negative: in 1968, the British balance of payments showed a $3-billion deficit. After a lag, however, the British balance of payments improved, with a reduction in the growth of imports and a rise in the growth of exports. By 1969, the British balance of payments showed a $1-billion surplus; by 1971, the surplus was $6.5 billion.

What factors might explain the time lags in a devaluation's adjustment process? The types of lags that may occur between changes in relative prices and the quantities of goods traded include the following:

1. *Recognition lags* of changing competitive conditions
2. *Decision lags* in forming new business connections and placing new orders
3. *Delivery lags* between the time new orders are placed and their impact on trade and payment flows is felt
4. *Replacement lags* in using up inventories and wearing out existing machinery before placing new orders
5. *Production lags* involved in increasing the output of commodities for which demand has increased

Empirical evidence suggests that the trade-balance effects of devaluation do not materialize until years afterward. Adjustment lags may be four years or more, although the major portion of adjustment takes place in about two years. One study made the following estimates of the lags in the devaluation adjustment process for trade in manufactured goods: (1) The response of trade flows to relative price changes stretches out over a period of some four to five years. (2) Following a price change, almost 50 percent of the full trade-flow response occurs within the first three years, and about 90 percent takes place during the first five years.[1]

The experience of the United States during the 1980s is consistent with the idea of time lags in the market adjustment to changes in the exchange rate. Figure 15.3 illustrates the trade-weighted value of the dollar on the right axis and the U.S. current-account balance on the left axis. The figure shows that the dollar appreciated by almost 60 percent, against the currencies of the major industrial nations, from the second quarter of 1980 to the first quarter of 1985; however, the U.S. current account did not begin to deteriorate until first quarter of 1983. The figure also indicates that the dollar continued to depreciate from the first quarter of 1985 through the end of 1990; however, the U.S. current-account balance did not start to improve until the third quarter of 1987. Consistent with the J-curve concept, the U.S. current-account balance during the 1980s appeared to respond to exchange-rate movements only after a lengthy time lag.

Currency pass-through. The J-curve analysis assumes that a given change in the exchange rate brings about a proportionate change in import prices. In practice, this relationship may be *less than proportionate,* thus weakening the influence of a change in the exchange rate on the volume of trade.

The extent to which changing currency values lead to changes in import and export prices is known as the **currency pass-through** relationship. Pass-through is important because buyers have incentives to alter their purchases of foreign goods only to the extent that the

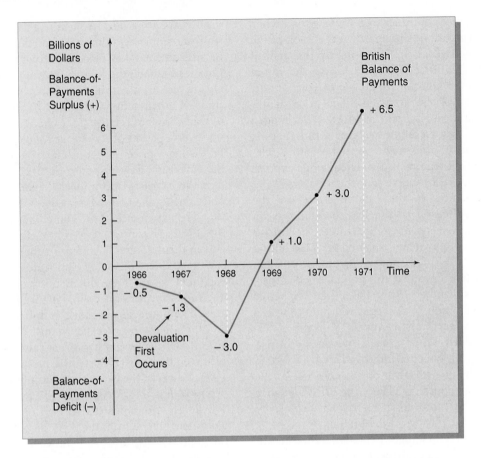

F I G U R E 15. 2 *Time path of British balance of payments in response to pound devaluation.* According to the J-curve effect, currency devaluation (depreciation) initially promotes trade deficit for the devaluing nation because the price effects of devaluation occur before the quantity effects. After a period of time, the quantities of exports and imports demanded adjust to the devaluation-induced price changes, and the trade balance moves in the direction of surplus. (SOURCE: U.S. Department of Commerce, *International Economic Indicators*, February 1975).

prices of these goods change in terms of their domestic currency following a change in the exchange rate. This depends on the willingness of exporters to permit the change in the exchange rate to affect the prices they charge for their goods, measured in terms of the buyer's currency.

Assume that Toyota of Japan exports autos to the United States and that the prices of Toyota are fixed in terms of the yen. Suppose the dollar's value depreciates 10 percent relative to the yen. Assuming no offsetting actions by Toyota, U.S. import prices will rise 10 percent. This is because 10-percent more dollars are needed to purchase the yen that are used in payment of the import purchases. *Complete pass-through* thus exists, because import prices in dollars rise by the full proportion of the dollar depreciation.

To illustrate the calculation of complete currency pass-through, assume that Caterpillar

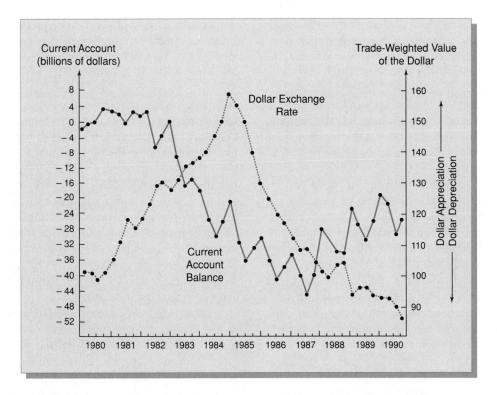

F I G U R E 15. 3   Time path of U.S. current-account balance in response to dollar appreciation and depreciation. The U.S. dollar began to appreciate in the second quarter of 1980; however, the U.S. current-account balance did not begin to deteriorate until the first quarter of 1983. Moreover, the dollar began to depreciate in the first quarter of 1985; but the U.S. current-account balance did not begin to improve until the third quarter of 1987.

Inc. charges $50,000 for a tractor exported to Japan. If the exchange rate is 150 yen per U.S. dollar, the price paid by the Japanese buyer will be 7,500,000 yen. Assuming the dollar price of the tractor remains constant, a 10-percent appreciation in the dollar's exchange value will increase the tractor's yen price 10 percent, to 8,250,000 yen ($165 \times 50,000 = 8,250,000$). Conversely, if the dollar depreciates by 10 percent, the yen price of the tractor will fall by 10 percent, to 6,750,000. So long as Caterpillar keeps the dollar price of its tractor constant, changes in the dollar's exchange rate will be fully reflected in changes in the foreign currency price of exports. The ratio of changes in the foreign currency price to changes in the exchange rate will be 100 percent, implying complete currency pass-through.

Empirical evidence suggests, however, that currency pass-through generally is *partial*, with significant time lags. Concerning the United States, it is estimated that for every 10-percent change in the value of the dollar, both import prices and export prices change about 6 percent. Moreover, exchange-rate changes tend to be absorbed by profit margins for as long as two years or more before affecting product prices. These lags depend on the length of time before dollar-denominated contracts expire as well as on the extent to which businesses view exchange-rate changes to be permanent rather than temporary.

The dollar depreciation of the mid-1980s provides an example of partial currency pass-through. Following a five-year rise in value, the dollar began to depreciate in 1985. By 1986, the value of the dollar had fallen more than 25 percent against the currencies of the major U.S. trading partners on a trade-weighted basis and more than 47 percent against the Japanese yen. Other things being equal, the dollar depreciation should have led to higher U.S. exports and lower U.S. imports. But other things were not equal. Foreign manufacturers, particularly the Japanese, were not willing to sacrifice their share of the U.S. market without a struggle.

Rather than permit increases in the prices of their goods sold in the United States, Japanese firms absorbed the dollar depreciation in reduced profits—and even losses—which triggered accusations of dumping by their U.S. competitors. But Japanese companies could not cut profits or absorb losses indefinitely. So, many concerns attempted to reduce manufacturing costs, either by leaving Japan for lower-cost sites such as South Korea or by overhauling products and factories in Japan. The result was only a partial pass-through of the dollar depreciation into retail price increases in the United States.

Prior to the dollar depreciation, Japanese automakers enjoyed an estimated 12-percent profit margin on their exports to the United States—nearly double that of U.S. companies. As a way of compensating for the depreciating dollar, throughout 1986 Japanese automakers pared profits by some $518 per vehicle. Yet foreign businesses could not persistently operate on razor-thin profit margins because they would lack money for product development and sales promotion. Eventually the businesses would have to reduce their emphasis on market share, and the U.S. trade deficit would shrink. However, it was estimated that if foreigners kept profit margins thin, they could preserve their market share for two years or longer.

U.S. imports also remained strong because of pricing policies of U.S. companies. As foreign prices inched upward as a result of the dollar depreciation, many U.S. businesses followed the price increases, although at a slower rate. In April 1986, General Motors surprised the auto industry with price increases, which were matched by Ford in July. It was argued that such price hikes would result in U.S. companies' frittering away a chance to increase market share and close the U.S. trade deficit.

Currency pass-through also had implications for U.S. exporters. A factor that contributed to sluggish U.S. exports was that U.S. prices in foreign markets did not fall proportionate to the dollar depreciation, implying partial pass-through. Throughout 1986, many U.S. exporters sought to restore profit margins, which had deteriorated when the dollar was so strong in the early 1980s, by maintaining or even increasing export prices.

Other U.S. exporters passed through the dollar depreciation into price reductions, only to have these reductions offset; that is, foreign intermediaries along the distribution network pocketed the price cuts instead of passing them through to customers. A survey of Japan's Ministry of International Trade and Industry found that only 10 to 15 percent of the savings from the dollar's depreciation were passed through to Japanese customers via price cuts in 1986. Moreover, some U.S. companies that cut export prices in 1986 were hampered by the aggressive price cuts of foreign competitors intent on maintaining market share.

THE ABSORPTION APPROACH TO EXCHANGE-RATE ADJUSTMENT

According to the elasticities approach, currency devaluation offers a price incentive to reduce imports and increase exports. But even if elasticity conditions are favorable, whether the home country's trade balance will actually improve may depend on how the economy reacts to the devaluation. The *absorption approach*[2] provides insights into this question by considering the impact of devaluation on the spending behavior of the domestic economy and the influence of domestic spending on the trade balance.

The absorption approach starts with the idea that the value of total domestic output (Y) equals the level of total spending. Total spending consists of consumption (C), investment (I), government expenditures (G), and net exports ($X - M$). This can be written as

$$Y = C + I + G + (X - M)$$

The absorption approach then consolidates $C + I + G$ into a single term A, which is referred to as absorption, while letting net exports ($X - M$) be designated as B. Total domestic output thus equals the sum of absorption plus the level of net exports, or

$$Y = A + B$$

This can be rewritten as

$$B = Y - A$$

This expression suggests that the balance of trade (B) equals the difference between total domestic output (Y) and the level of absorption (A). If national output exceeds domestic absorption, the economy's trade balance will be positive. Conversely, a negative trade balance suggests that an economy is spending beyond its ability to produce.

The absorption approach predicts that, if a currency devaluation is to improve an economy's trade balance, national output must *rise* relative to absorption. This means that a country must increase its total output, reduce its absorption, or do some combination of the two. The following examples illustrate these possibilities.

Assume that an economy faces *unemployment* as well as a *trade deficit*. With the economy operating below maximum capacity, the price incentives of devaluation would tend to direct idle resources into the production of goods for export, in addition to diverting spending away from imports to domestically

produced substitutes. The impact of the devaluation is thus to expand domestic output as well as to improve the trade balance. It is no wonder that policymakers tend to view currency devaluation as an effective tool when an economy faces unemployment with a trade deficit!

In the case of an economy operating at *full employment,* however, there are no unutilized resources available for additional production. National output is at a fixed level. The only way in which devaluation can improve the trade balance is for the economy to somehow cut domestic absorption, freeing resources needed to produce additional export goods and import substitutes. For example, domestic policymakers could decrease absorption by adopting restrictive fiscal and monetary policies in the face of higher prices resulting from the devaluation. But this would result in sacrifice on the part of those who bear the burden of such measures. Devaluation may thus be considered *inappropriate* when an economy is operating at maximum capacity.

The absorption approach goes beyond the elasticity approach, which views the economy's trade balance as distinct from the rest of the economy. Instead, devaluation is viewed in relation to the economy's utilization of its resources and level of production. The two approaches are therefore complementary.

THE MONETARY APPROACH TO EXCHANGE-RATE ADJUSTMENT

A survey of the traditional approaches to devaluation reveals a major shortcoming. According to the elasticities and absorption approaches, monetary consequences are not associated with balance-of-payments adjustment; or, to the extent that such consequences exist, they can be neutralized by domestic monetary authorities. The elasticities and absorption approaches apply only to the trade account of the balance of payments, neglecting the implications of capital movements. The *monetary approach* to devaluation addresses this shortcoming.[3]

According to the monetary approach, currency devaluation may induce a *temporary* improvement in a nation's balance-of-payments position. For example, assume that equilibrium initially exists in the home country's money market. A devaluation of the home currency would increase the price level (that is, the domestic currency prices of potential imports and exports). This increases the demand for money, because larger amounts of money are needed for transactions. If that increased demand is not fulfilled from domestic sources, an inflow of money from overseas occurs. This inflow results in a balance-of-payments surplus and a rise in international reserves.

But the surplus does not last forever. By adding to the international component of the home-country money supply, the devaluation leads to an increase in spending (absorption), which reduces the surplus. The surplus eventually disappears when equilibrium is restored in the home country's money market. The effects of devaluation on real economic variables are thus temporary. Over the long run, currency devaluation merely raises the domestic price level.

SUMMARY

1. Currency depreciation or devaluation may affect a nation's trade position through its impact on relative prices, incomes, and purchasing power of money balances.

2. When all of a firm's inputs are acquired domestically and their costs are denominated in the domestic currency, an appreciation in the domestic currency's exchange value tends to increase the firm's costs by the same proportion, in terms of the foreign currency. Conversely, a depreciation of the domestic currency's exchange value tends to reduce the firm's costs by the same proportion in terms of the foreign currency.

3. Manufacturers often obtain inputs from abroad (foreign sourcing) whose costs are denominated in terms of a foreign currency. As foreign-currency-denominated costs become a larger portion of a producer's total costs, an appreciation of the domestic currency's exchange value leads to a smaller increase in the foreign-currency cost of the firm's output and a larger decrease in the domestic cost of the firm's output—compared to the cost changes that occur when all input costs are denominated in the domestic currency. The opposite applies for currency depreciation.

4. By increasing (decreasing) relative U.S. production costs, a dollar appreciation (depreciation) tends to raise (lower) U.S. export prices in terms of a foreign currency, which induces a decrease (increase) in the quantity of U.S. goods sold abroad; similarly, a dollar appreciation (depreciation) tends to raise (lower) the amount of U.S. imports.

5. According to the elasticities approach, currency depreciation or devaluation lead to the greatest improvement in a country's trade position when demand elasticities are high. Recent empirical studies indicate that the estimated demand elasticities for most nations are quite high.

6. The time path of currency depreciation or devaluation can be explained in terms of the J-curve effect. According to this concept, the response of trade flows to changes in relative prices increases with the passage of time. Currency depreciation tends to worsen a country's trade balance in the short run, only to be followed by an improvement in the long run (assuming favorable elasticities).

7. The extent to which exchange-rate changes lead to changes in import prices and export prices is known as the pass-through relationship. Complete (partial) pass-through occurs when a change in the exchange rate brings about a proportionate (less than proportionate) change in export prices and import prices. Empirical evidence suggests that pass-through tends to be partial rather than complete.

8. The absorption approach emphasizes the income effects of currency devaluation. According to this view, a devaluation may initially stimulate a nation's exports and production of import-competing goods. But this will promote excess domestic spending unless real output can be expanded or domestic absorption reduced. The result would be a return to a payments deficit.

9. The monetary approach to devaluation emphasizes the effect that devaluation has on the pur-

chasing power of money balances and the resulting impacts on domestic expenditures and import levels. According to the monetary approach,

the influence of currency devaluation on real output is temporary; over the long run, devaluation merely raises the domestic price level.

STUDY QUESTIONS

1. How does a currency depreciation or devaluation affect a nation's balance of trade?
2. Three major approaches to analyzing the economic impact of currency depreciation or devaluation are: (a) the elasticities approach, (b) the absorption approach, and (c) the monetary approach. Distinguish among the three.
3. What implications does currency pass-through have for a nation whose currency depreciates or is devalued?
4. What is meant by the Marshall–Lerner condition? Do recent empirical studies suggest that world elasticity conditions are sufficiently high to permit successful depreciations or devaluations?
5. How does the J-curve effect relate to the time path of currency depreciation or devaluation?
6. According to the absorption approach, does it make any difference whether a nation devalues its currency when the economy is operating at less than full capacity versus at full capacity?
7. How can devaluation-induced changes in household money balances promote payments equilibrium?
8. Suppose ABC Inc., a U.S. auto manufacturer, obtains all of its auto components in the United States and that their costs are denominated in dollars. Assume the dollar's exchange value appreciates by 50 percent against the Mexican peso. What impact does the dollar appreciation have on the firm's international competitiveness? What about a dollar depreciation?
9. Suppose ABC Inc., a U.S. auto manufacturer, obtains some of its auto components in Mexico

and that the cost of these components are denominated in pesos; the cost of the remaining components are denominated in dollars. Assume the dollar's exchange value appreciates by 50 percent against the peso. Compared to your answer in study question 8, what impact will the dollar appreciation have on the firm's international competitiveness? What about a dollar depreciation?

10. Assume the United States exports 1,000 computers at a price of $3,000 each and imports 150 British autos at a price of 10,000 pounds each. Assume that the dollar/pound exchange rate is $2 per pound.
    a. Calculate, in dollar terms, the U.S. export receipts, import payments, and trade balance prior to a depreciation of the dollar's exchange value.
    b. Suppose the dollar's exchange value depreciates by 10 percent. Assuming that the price elasticity of demand for U.S. exports equals 3.0 and the price elasticity of demand for U.S. imports equal 2.0, calculate the U.S. export receipts, import payments, and trade balance. Does the dollar depreciation improve or worsen the U.S. trade balance? Why?
    c. Now assume that the price elasticity of demand for U.S. exports equals 0.3 and the price elasticity of demand for U.S. imports equals 0.2. Does this change the outcome? Why?

Exchange-Rate Systems

During the quarter-century following World War II, the Western nations operated under a largely uniform system of fixed exchange rates for their currencies. During the 1960s–1970s, there occurred a series of crises in the foreign exchange market that disrupted the confidence of international traders and investors in fixed exchange rates. This led to reforms in the international monetary system that permitted nations to choose the exchange-rate system most compatible with their own economic objectives.

In choosing an exchange-rate system, a nation must decide whether to allow its currency to be determined by free market forces (floating rate) or to be fixed (pegged) against some standard of value. If a nation adopts floating rates, it must decide whether to float independently, to float in unison with a group of other currencies, or to crawl according to a predetermined formula such as relative inflation rates. The decision to peg a currency includes the options of pegging to a single currency, to a basket of currencies, or to gold. Since 1971, however, the technique of expressing official exchange rates in terms of gold has not been used; gold has been phased out of the international monetary system.

This chapter considers the major present and historic exchange-rate practices that have been used during the post–World War II era.

The discussion focuses on the nature and operation of actual exchange-rate systems and identifies economic factors that influence the choice of alternative exchange-rate systems.

EXCHANGE-RATE PRACTICES

Since the termination of fixed exchange rates in 1973, members of the International Monetary Fund (IMF) have been free to follow any exchange-rate policy that conforms to three principles: (1) Exchange rates should not be manipulated to prevent effective balance-of-payments adjustments or to gain unfair competitive advantage over other members. (2) Members should act to counter short-term, disorderly conditions in exchange markets. (3) When members intervene in exchange markets, they should take into account the interests of other members.

As seen in Table 16.1, 76 members of the IMF chose to peg their currencies in some manner in 1992, out of a total of 154 member nations. The remaining members permitted greater exchange-rate flexibility, such as independently floating rates or managed floating rates.

Fixed (pegged) **exchange rates** are used primarily by small, developing nations that maintain pegs to a **key currency** such as the U.S. dollar or the French franc. A key currency is one that is widely traded on world money markets, has demonstrated relatively stable values over time, and has been widely accepted as a means of international settlement. Table 16.2 identifies the major key currencies of the world.

One reason why developing nations choose to tie their currencies to a key currency is that it is used as a means of international settlement. Consider a Norwegian importer who wants to purchase Argentinean beef over the next year. If the Argentine exporter is unsure of what the Norwegian krone will purchase in one year, he might reject the krone in settlement. Similarly, the Norwegian importer might doubt the value of Argentina's peso. One solution is for the contract to be written in terms of a key currency such as the U.S. dollar. Generally speaking, smaller nations with relatively undiversified economies and large foreign trade sectors have been inclined to peg their currencies to one of the key currencies.

Maintaining pegs to a key currency provides several benefits for developing nations. First, the prices of many developing nations' traded products are determined primarily in the markets of industrialized nations such as the United States; by pegging, say, to the dollar, these nations can stabilize the domestic currency prices of their imports and exports. Second, many nations with high inflation have pegged to the dollar (the United States has relatively low inflation) in order to exert restraint on domestic policies and reduce inflation. By making the commitment to stabilize their exchange rates against the dollar, governments hope to convince their citizens that they are willing to adopt the responsible monetary policies necessary to achieve low inflation. Pegging the exchange rate may thus lessen inflationary expectations, leading to lower interest rates, a lessening of the loss of output due to disinflation, and a moderation of price pressures.

In maintaining fixed exchange rates, nations must decide whether to peg their currencies to another currency or to a currency basket. Pegging to a *single currency* is generally done by developing nations whose trade and financial relationships are mainly with a single industrial-country partner. For example, Ivory Coast, which trades primarily with France, pegs its currency to the French franc.

Developing nations with more than one major trading partner often peg their currencies to a group or *basket of currencies*. The basket is composed of prescribed quantities of foreign currencies in proportion to the amount of trade done with the nation pegging its currency. Once the basket has been selected, the currency value of the nation is computed using the exchange rates of the foreign currencies in the basket. Pegging the domestic currency value of the basket enables a nation to average out fluctuations in

T A B L E 16. 1 / Exchange-Rate Arrangements of IMF Members, December 31, 1992

Pegged				
Single Currency			Currency Composite	
U.S. Dollar	French Franc	Other	SDR	Other
Angola	Benin	Bhutan	Burundi	Albania
Antigua and	Burkina Faso	(Indian	Iran, Islamic Republic of	Algeria
Barbuda	Cameroon	rupee)	Libyan Arab Jamahirya	Austria
Argentina	Central African	Lesotho	Myanmar	Bangladesh
Bahamas, The	Republic	(South	Rwanda	Botswana
Barbados	Chad	African	Seychelles	Cape Verde
Belize	Comoros	rand)		Cyprus
Djibouti	Congo	Swaziland		Czechoslovakia
Dominica	Côte d'Ivoire	(South		Fiji
Ethiopia	Equatorial Guinea	African		Finland
Grenada	Gabon	rand)		Hungary
Iraq	Mali	Yugoslavia		Iceland
Liberia	Niger	(Deutsche		Jordan
Mongolia	Senegal	mark)		Kenya
Nicaragua	Togo			Kuwait
Oman				Malawi
Panama				Malaysia
St. Kitts and Nevis				Malta
St. Lucia				Mauritius
St. Vincent and the				Morocco
Grenadines				Nepal
Suriname				Norway
Syrian Arab				Papua New
Republic				Guinea
Trinidad and				Solomon Islands
Tobago				Sweden
Yemen				Tanzania
				Thailand
				Tonga
				Vanuatu
				Western Samoa
				Zimbabwe

SOURCE: International Monetary Fund, *Annual Report*, 1992, p. 113.

Flexibility Limited against a Single Currency or Group of Currencies		*More Flexible*		
Single Currency	*Cooperative Arrangements*	*Adjusted According to a Set of Indicators*	*Other Managed Floating*	*Independently Floating*
Bahrain	Belgium	Chile	China	Afghanistan
Qatar	Denmark	Colombia	Ecuador	Australia
Saudi Arabia	France	Madagascar	Egypt	Costa Rica
United Arab Emirates	Germany	Mozambique	Greece	Bolivia
	Ireland	Zambia	Guinea	Brazil
	Italy		Guinea-Bissau	Bulgaria
	Luxembourg		India	Canada
	Netherlands		Indonesia	Dominican Republic
	Spain		Israel	El Salvador
	United Kingdom		Korea	Gambia, The
			Lao People's Democratic Republic	Ghana
			Maldives	Guatemala
			Mauritania	Guyana
			Mexico	Haiti
			Pakistan	Honduras
			Poland	Jamaica
			Portugal	Japan
			Romania	Kiribati
			Sao Tome and Principe	Lebanon
			Singapore	Namibia
			Somalia	New Zealand
			Sri Lanka	Nigeria
			Tunisia	Paraguay
			Turkey	Peru
			Uruguay	Philippines
			Viet Nam	Sierra Leone
				South Africa
				Sudan
				Uganda
				United States
				Venezuela
				Zaïre

TABLE 16. 2 / *Key Currencies:*
Share of National
Currencies in Total
Identified Official Holdings
of Foreign Exchange, 1991

ALL COUNTRIES	
U.S dollar	56.2%
Pound sterling	3.8
Deutsche mark	17.3
French franc	3.6
Swiss franc	1.4
Netherlands guilder	1.2
Japanese yen	9.9
Other	6.6
	100.0
INDUSTRIAL COUNTRIES	
U.S. dollar	51.6%
Pound sterling	2.1
Deutsche mark	21.2
French franc	4.6
Swiss franc	0.9
Netherlands guilder	1.4
Japanese yen	11.3
Other	6.9
	100.0
DEVELOPING COUNTRIES	
U.S. dollar	63.8%
Pound sterling	6.6
Deutsche mark	10.7
French franc	1.9
Swiss franc	2.3
Netherlands guilder	0.8
Japanese yen	7.6
Other	6.3
	100.0

SOURCE: International Monetary Fund, *Annual Report*, 1992, p. 92.

TABLE 16. 3 / *Special Drawing Right*
Basket of Currencies, 1993

Currency	Amount	Percentage Weight
U.S. dollar	0.572	40%
Deutsche mark	0.453	21
Japanese yen	31.8	17
French franc	0.800	11
Pound sterling	0.0812	11

export or import prices caused by exchange-rate movements. The effects of exchange-rate changes on the domestic economy are thus reduced.

Rather than constructing their own currency basket, many nations peg the value of their currencies to the **special drawing right** (SDR), a basket of five currencies established by the IMF. The IMF requires that the valuation of the SDR basket be reviewed every five years; the basket is to include, in proportional amounts, the currencies of the members having the largest exports of goods and services during the previous five years. The currencies comprising the basket as of 1993, along with their amounts and percentage weights, are listed in Table 16.3.

The idea behind the SDR basket valuation method is to make the SDR's value more stable than the foreign currency value of any single national currency. The SDR is valued according to an index based on the moving average of those currencies in the basket. Should the values of the basket currencies either depreciate or appreciate against one another, the SDR's value would remain in the center. The SDR would depreciate against those currencies that are rising in value and appreciate against the currencies whose values are falling. Nations desiring exchange-rate stability are attracted to the SDR as a currency basket against which to peg their currency values.

FIXED EXCHANGE-RATE SYSTEM

Few nations have allowed their currencies' exchange values to be determined solely by the forces of supply and demand in a free market. Until the industrialized nations adopted managed floating exchange rates in the 1970s, the practice generally was to maintain a pattern of relatively fixed (pegged) exchange rates among national currencies. Changes in national exchange rates presumably were to be initiated by domestic monetary authorities when long-term market forces warranted it.

Par Value and Official Exchange Rate

Under a fixed exchange-rate system, governments assign their currencies a **par value** in terms of gold or other key currencies. By comparing the par values of two currencies, we can determine their **official exchange rate**. For example, the official exchange rate between the U.S. dollar and the British pound was $2.80 = £1 as long as the United States bought and sold gold at a fixed price of $35 per ounce and Britain bought and sold gold at £12.50 per ounce (35.00 / 12.50 = 2.80). The major industrial nations set their currencies' par values in terms of gold until gold was phased out of the international monetary system in the early 1970s.

Today, many developing nations choose to define their par values in terms of certain key currencies such as the U.S. dollar. Under this arrangement, the monetary authority first defines its official exchange rate in terms of the key currency. It then defends the fixed parity by purchasing and selling its currency for the key currency at that rate. Assume, for example, that Bolivian central bankers fix their peso at 20 pesos = $1 U.S., whereas Ecuador's sucre is set at 10 sucres = $1 U.S. The official exchange rate between the peso and sucre becomes 1 peso = 0.50 sucre.

Exchange-Rate Stabilization

A first requirement for a nation participating in a fixed exchange-rate system is to determine an official exchange rate for its currency. The next step is to set up an **exchange stabilization fund** to defend the official rate. Through purchases and sales of foreign currencies, the exchange stabilization fund attempts to ensure that the market exchange rate does not move above or below the official exchange rate.

In Figure 16.1, assume that the market exchange rate equals $2.80 per pound, seen at the intersection of the demand and supply schedules of British pounds, D_0 and S_0. Also assume that the official exchange rate is defined as $2.80 per pound. Now suppose that rising interest rates in Britain result in U.S. investors' demanding additional pounds to finance the purchase of British securities; let the demand for pounds rise from D_0 to D_1 in the figure. Under free market conditions, the dollar would depreciate from $2.80 per pound to $2.90 per pound. But under a fixed exchange-rate system, the monetary authority will attempt to defend the official rate of $2.80 per pound. At this rate, there exists an excess demand for pounds equal to £40 billion; this means that the British face an excess supply of dollars by the same amount. To keep the market exchange rate from depreciating beyond $2.80 per pound, the U.S. exchange stabilization fund would purchase the excess supply of dollars for an equivalent number of pounds. The supply of pounds thus rises from S_0 to S_1, resulting in a stabilization of the market exchange rate at $2.80 per pound. Conversely, during times of a dollar shortage, the stabilization process would require the U.S. stabilization fund to purchase foreign currency with dollars.

This example illustrates how an exchange stabilization fund undertakes its pegging operations to offset short-term fluctuations in the market exchange rate. Over the long run, however, the official exchange rate and the market

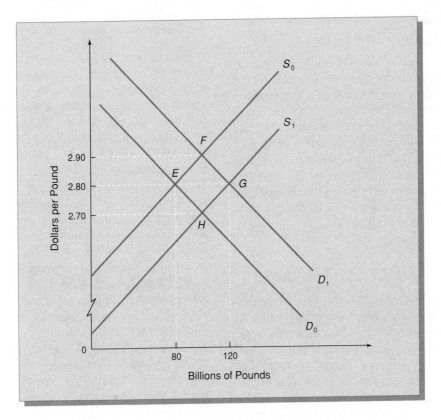

F I G U R E 16. 1 Exchange-rate stabilization under a fixed exchange rate system. To defend the official exchange rate of $2.80 per pound, the central bank must supply all of the nation's currency that is demanded at the official rate and demand all of the nation's currency that is supplied to it at the official rate. To prevent a dollar depreciation, the central bank must purchase the excess supply of dollars with an equivalent amount of pounds. To prevent a dollar appreciation, the central bank must purchase the excess supply of pounds with an equivalent amount of dollars.

exchange rate may move apart, reflecting changes in fundamental economic conditions—income levels, tastes and preferences, and technological factors. In the case of a **fundamental disequilibrium,** the cost of defending the existing official rate may become prohibitive.

Consider the case of a deficit nation that finds its currency depreciating in the exchange market. Maintaining the official rate may require the exchange stabilization fund to purchase sizable quantities of its currency with for-

eign currencies or other reserve assets. This may impose a severe drain on the deficit nation's stock of international reserves. Although the deficit nation may be able to borrow reserves from other nations or from the International Monetary Fund to continue the defense of its exchange rate, such borrowing privileges are generally of limited magnitude. At the same time, the deficit nation will be undergoing internal adjustments to curb the disequilibrium. These measures will likely be aimed at controlling inflationary pressures and raising interest rates to promote capital inflows and discourage imports. If the imbalance is persistent, the deficit nation may view such internal adjustments as too costly in terms of falling income and employment levels. Rather than continually resorting to such measures, the deficit nation may decide that the reversal of the disequilibrium calls for an adjustment in the exchange rate itself. Under a system of pegged exchange rates, a chronic imbalance may be counteracted by a currency devaluation or revaluation.

Devaluation and Revaluation

Under a fixed exchange-rate system, a nation's monetary authority may decide to pursue balance-of-payments equilibrium by devaluing or revaluing its currency. The purpose of **devaluation** is to cause the home currency's exchange value to *depreciate,* thus counteracting a payments *deficit*. The purpose of currency **revaluation** is to cause the home currency's exchange value to *appreciate,* thus counteracting a payments *surplus*.

The terms *devaluation* and *revaluation* refer to a legal redefinition of a currency's par value under a system of fixed exchange rates. The terms *depreciation* and *appreciation* refer to the actual impact on the market exchange rate caused by a redefinition of a par value, or to changes in an exchange rate stemming from changes in the supply of or demand for foreign exchange.

Devaluation and revaluation policies are considered to be *expenditure-switching instruments* because they work on relative prices to divert domestic and foreign expenditures between home and foreign goods. By raising the home price of the foreign currency, a devaluation makes the home country's exports cheaper to foreigners in terms of the foreign currency while making the home country's imports more expensive in terms of the home currency. Expenditures are diverted from foreign to home goods as home exports rise and imports fall. In like manner, a revaluation discourages the home country's exports and encourages its imports, diverting expenditures from home goods to foreign goods.

Before implementing a devaluation or revaluation, the monetary authority must decide (1) if an adjustment in the official exchange rate is necessary to correct a payments disequilibrium, (2) when the adjustment will occur, and (3) how large the adjustment should be. Exchange-rate decisions of government officials may be incorrect—that is, ill timed and of improper magnitude. In making the decision to undergo a devaluation or revaluation, monetary authorities generally attempt to hide behind a veil of secrecy. Just hours before the decision is to become effective, public denials of any such policies by official government representatives are common. This is to discourage currency speculators, who try to profit by shifting funds from a currency falling in value to one rising in value. Given the destabilizing impact that massive speculation can exert on financial markets, it is hard to criticize monetary authorities for being secretive in their actions. However, the need for devaluation tends to be obvious to outsiders as well as to government officials and in the past has nearly always resulted in heavy speculative pressures.

Legal versus Economic Implications

Currency devaluations and revaluations are used in conjunction with a fixed exchange-rate system. The monetary authority changes a currency's exchange rate by decree, usually by a sizable amount at one time. How is such a policy implemented?

Recall that under a fixed exchange-rate system, the home currency is assigned a par value by the nation's monetary authorities. The par value is the amount of a nation's currency that is required to purchase a fixed amount of gold, a key currency, or the SDR. These assets represent the legal *numeraire,* or the unit of contractual obligations. By comparing various national currency prices of the numeraire, monetary authorities determine the official rate of exchange for the currencies.

In the *legal* sense, a devaluation or revaluation occurs when the home country redefines its currency price of the official numeraire, changing the par value. The *economic* effect of the par value's redefinition is the impact on the market rate of exchange. Assuming that other trading nations retain their existing par values, one would expect (1) a devaluation to result in a depreciation in the currency's exchange value; (2) a revaluation to result in an appreciation in the currency's exchange value.

Figure 16.2 illustrates the legal and economic implications of devaluation/revaluation policies. Assume that the special drawing right (SDR) serves as the numeraire by which the value of individual currencies—Burundi's franc and Uganda's shilling—can be defined relative to each other. The diagram's vertical axis denotes the shilling price of an SDR, and the horizontal axis depicts the franc's price of an SDR. Three price ratios are illustrated by each point in the figure: (1) the shilling price of the SDR, (2) the franc price of the SDR, and (3) the shilling price of the franc, indicated by the slope of a ray connecting the origin with any point in the figure.

Suppose Uganda sets its par value at 700 shillings per SDR, whereas Burundi's par value equals 350 francs per SDR. Connecting these two prices yields point *A* in the diagram. Relative to each other, the official exchange rate between the shilling and the franc is 2 shillings = 1 franc, denoted by the slope of the ray 0*A* (700 / 350 = 2.0).

Assume that Uganda wishes to devalue the shilling by, say, 10 percent to correct a payments deficit. Starting at point *A,* Uganda would raise the shilling price of the SDR to from 700 to 770 shillings per SDR, a 10-percent increase. This results in a movement from point *A* to point *B* in the figure. Corre-

sponding to the slope of ray 0*B,* the new exchange rate is 2.2 shillings = 1 franc (770 / 350 = 2.2). Uganda's devaluation results in the shilling's exchange value depreciating from 2 shillings = 1 franc to 2.2 shillings = 1 franc, a 10-percent change. Conversely, suppose that Uganda revalues the shilling by 10 percent to reverse a payments surplus. Starting at point *A* in the figure, Uganda would lower the official price of the SDR from 700 shillings to 630 shillings, a 10-percent decrease. The exchange value of the shilling would increase from 2 shillings = 1 franc to 1.8 shillings = 1 franc, a 10-percent change.

To change the shilling/franc exchange rate, it is not sufficient for Uganda to redefine the shilling's par value. It is also necessary that the par value of the Burundi franc remain constant or be altered by a smaller fraction. In Figure 16.2, a change in the shilling/franc exchange rate requires a change in the *slope* of ray 0*A.* Acting by itself, Uganda can establish only the vertical position in the diagram. Because Burundi determines the horizontal position, any redefinition of Uganda's par value can be neutralized by an equivalent change in Burundi's par value. In other words, Burundi can offset any change in the slope of the ray that Uganda may wish to undertake.

Let us start again at point *A* in the figure, where the exchange rate is set at 2 shillings = 1 franc. Facing a payments deficit, suppose Uganda devalues the shilling 10 percent by increasing the official price of the SDR from 700 to 770 shillings. This would cause a movement from point *A* to point *B,* where the exchange rate is 2.2 shillings = 1 franc. But what if Burundi determines that the shilling's devaluation gives Uganda an unfair competitive advantage? Suppose Burundi retaliates by devaluing the franc 10 percent, thus increasing the official price of the SDR from 350 to 385 francs. A movement from point *B* to point *C* in the diagram would result. Although both currencies have been officially devalued by 10 percent, the exchange rate between them remains

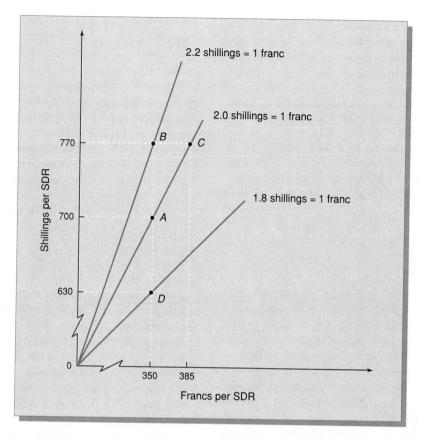

F I G U R E   16. 2   Devaluation/revaluation: legal versus economic implications. Starting at the official exchange rate of 2 Uganda shillings per Burundi franc, a 10-percent devaluation of the shilling results in the shilling's depreciating 10 percent against the franc, to 2.2 shillings per franc. Such a policy enhances the competitiveness of Uganda producers. Should Burundi retaliate and devalue its franc by 10 percent, the exchange rate will revert back to 2 shillings per franc. Policy coordination among governments is necessary for successful currency realignments.

constant at 2 shillings = 1 franc. The conclusion is that a devaluation in the legal sense does not necessarily ensure a devaluation in the economic sense—a depreciation in the exchange rate. This occurs only if other nations do not retaliate by initiating offsetting devaluations of their own.

Currency devaluations do have foreign repercussions similar to those of domestic economic policies. The larger and more significant the devaluing nation, the greater the economic effects transmitted abroad. A nation that devalues to initiate an export-led economic recovery may be the cause of recession in its trading partners. This was often the case during the Great Depression of the 1930s, when competitive devaluations were widespread. It is no wonder that when currency realignments involving devaluations and revaluations are called for, they usually require intense negotiations and the harmonization of economic interests among participating nations.

FLOATING EXCHANGE RATES

Instead of utilizing fixed exchange rates, some nations allow their currencies to float in the foreign exchange market. By **floating** (or flexible) **exchange rates**, we mean currency prices that are established daily in the foreign exchange market, without restrictions imposed by government policy on the extent to which the prices can move. With floating rates, there is an equilibrium exchange rate that equates the demand for and supply of the home currency. Changes in the exchange rate will ideally correct a payments imbalance by bringing about shifts in imports and exports of goods, services, and short-term capital movements. The exchange rate depends on relative money supplies, income levels, interest rates, prices, and other factors discussed in Chapter 13.

Unlike fixed exchange rates, floating exchange rates are not characterized by par values and official exchange rates; they are determined by market supply and demand conditions rather than central bankers. Although floating rates do not have an exchange stabilization fund to maintain existing rates, it does not necessarily follow that floating rates must fluctuate erratically. They will do so if the underlying market forces become unstable. Because there is no exchange stabilization fund under floating rates, any holdings of international reserves serve as working balances rather than to maintain a given exchange rate for any currency.

Achieving Market Equilibrium

How do floating exchange rates promote payments equilibrium for a nation? Consider Figure 16.3, which illustrates the foreign exchange (German marks) market for the United States. The intersection of supply schedule S_0 and demand schedule D_0 determines the equilibrium exchange rate of $0.50 per mark.

Suppose a rise in real income causes U.S. residents to demand more German products, and therefore more marks; let the demand for marks rise from D_0 to D_1. Initially the market is in disequilibrium, because the quantity of marks demanded (50 marks) exceeds the quantity supplied (30 marks) at the exchange rate of $0.50 per mark. The excess demand for marks leads to an increase in the exchange rate from $0.50 to $0.55 per mark; the dollar thus falls in value, or depreciates, against the mark while the mark rises in value, or appreciates, against the dollar. The higher value of the mark prompts German residents to increase the quantity of marks supplied on the foreign exchange market to purchase more U.S. goods, which are now cheaper in terms of the mark; at the same time, it dampens U.S. demand for more expensive German goods. Market equilibrium is restored at the exchange rate of $0.55 per mark, at which the quantity of marks supplied and demanded are equated.

Supposed instead that real income in the United States falls, which causes U.S. residents to demand fewer German products, and therefore fewer marks. In Figure 16.3, let the demand for marks fall from D_0 to D_2. The market is initially in disequilibrium, because the quantity of marks supplied (30 marks) exceeds the quantity demanded (10 marks) at the exchange rate $0.50 per mark. The excess supply of marks causes the exchange rate to fall from $0.50 to $0.45 per mark; the dollar thus appreciates against the mark, while the mark depreciates against the dollar. Market equilibrium is restored at the exchange rate of $0.45 per mark, at which the quantity of marks supplied and demanded are equated.

This example illustrates one argument in favor of floating rates: when the exchange rate is permitted to adjust freely in response to market forces, market equilibrium will be established at a point where the quantities of foreign exchange supplied and demanded are equated. If the

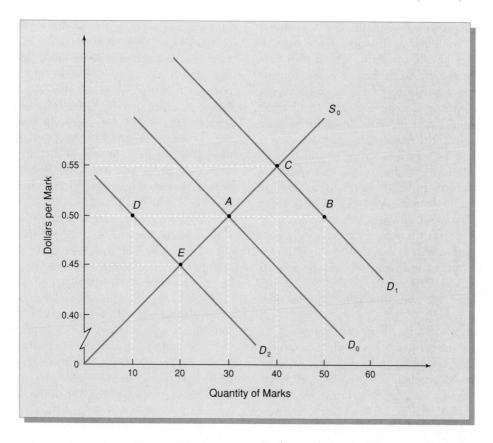

F I G U R E 16. 3   *Market adjustment under floating exchange rates.* Under a floating exchange-rate system, continuous changes in currency values restore payments equilibrium at which the quantity supplied and quantity demanded of a currency are equated.

exchange rate promotes market equilibrium, monetary authorities will not need international reserves for the purpose of intervening in the market to maintain exchange rates at their par value. Presumably, these resources can be used more productively elsewhere in the economy.

Arguments for and against Floating Rates

One advantage claimed for floating rates is their simplicity. Floating rates allegedly respond quickly to changing supply and demand conditions, clearing the market of shortages or surpluses of a given currency. Instead of having

formal rules of conduct among central bankers governing exchange-rate movements, floating rates are market-determined. They operate under simplified institutional arrangements that are relatively easy to enact. Because floating rates fluctuate throughout the day, they permit continuous adjustment in the balance of payments. The adverse effects of prolonged disequilibria that tend to occur under fixed exchange rates are minimized under floating rates. It is also argued that floating rates partially insulate the home economy from external forces. This means that governments will not have to restore payments equilibrium through painful inflationary or deflationary adjustment policies. Switching to floating rates frees a nation from having to adopt policies that perpetuate domestic disequilibrium as the price of maintaining a satisfactory balance-of-payments position. Nations thus have greater freedom to pursue policies that promote domestic balance than they do under fixed exchange rates.

Although there are strong arguments in favor of floating exchange rates, this system is often considered to be of limited usefulness for bankers and businesspeople. Critics of floating rates maintain that an unregulated market may lead to wide fluctuations in currency values, discouraging foreign trade and investment. Although traders and investors may be able to hedge exchange-rate risk by dealing in the forward market, the cost of hedging may become prohibitively high.

Floating rates in theory are supposed to allow governments to set independent monetary and fiscal policies. But this flexibility may cause a problem of another sort: *inflationary bias.* Under a system of floating rates, monetary authorities may lack the sense of financial discipline required by a fixed exchange-rate system. Suppose a nation faces relatively high rates of inflation compared with the rest of the world. This domestic inflation will have no negative impact on the nation's trade balance under floating rates because its currency will automatically depreciate in the exchange market. However, a protracted depreciation of the currency would result in persistently increasing import prices and a rising price level, making inflation self-perpetuating and the depreciation continuous. Because there is greater freedom for domestic financial management under floating rates, there may be less resistance to overspending and to its subsequent pressure on wages and prices.

ADJUSTABLE PEGGED RATES

In 1944, delegates from 44 member nations of the United Nations met at Bretton Woods, New Hampshire, to create a new international monetary system. They were aware of the unsatisfactory monetary experience of the 1930s, during which the international gold standard collapsed as the result of the economic and financial crises of the Great Depression and nations experimented unsuccessfully with floating exchange rates and exchange controls. The delegates wanted to establish international monetary order and avoid the instability and nationalistic practices that had occurred during the pre–World War II era.

The international monetary system that was created became known as the **Bretton Woods system**. The founders felt that neither completely fixed exchange rates nor floating rates were optimal; instead, they adopted a kind of managed exchange-rate system known as **adjustable pegged exchange rates**. The Bretton Woods system lasted from 1944 until 1973.

The main feature of the adjustable peg system is that currencies are tied to each other to provide stable exchange rates for commercial and financial transactions. When the balance of payments moves away from its long-run equilibrium position, a nation can repeg its exchange rate via devaluation or revaluation policies. Member nations agreed in principle to defend existing par values as long as possible in times of balance-of-payments disequilibrium. They were expected to use fiscal and monetary policies first to correct payments imbalances. But if reversing a persistent payments imbalance would mean severe disruption to the domestic economy in terms of inflation or unemployment, member nations could correct this *fundamental disequilibrium* by repegging their currencies up to 10 percent without permission from the International Monetary Fund.

Under the Bretton Woods system, each member nation set the par value of its currency in terms of gold or, alternatively, the gold content of the U.S. dollar in 1944. Market exchange rates were almost but not completely fixed, being kept within a band of 1 percent on either side of parity for a total spread of 2 per-

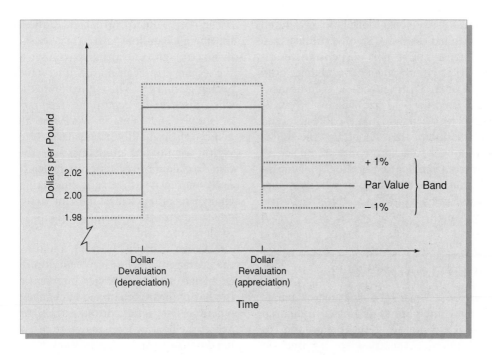

F I G U R E 16. 4 *Adjustable pegged exchange rates.* Market exchange rates are almost completely fixed, being maintained within a narrow band around the currency's official exchange rate. When a nation experiences a fundamental disequilibrium, it can devalue (revalue) its currency to restore payments balance.

cent, as illustrated in Figure 16.4. National exchange stabilization funds were used to maintain the band limits. In 1971, the exchange support margins were widened to 2.25 percent on either side of parity to eliminate payments imbalances by setting in motion corrective trade and capital movements. As seen in Figure 16.4, devaluations or revaluations could be used to adjust the par value of currency when it became overvalued or undervalued.

Although adjustable pegged rates are intended to promote a viable balance-of-payments adjustment mechanism, they have been plagued with operational problems. In the Bretton Woods system, adjustments in prices and incomes often conflicted with domestic stabilization objectives. Also, currency devaluation was considered undesirable because it seemed to indicate a failure of domestic policies and a

loss of international prestige. Conversely, revaluations were unacceptable to exporters whose livelihoods were vulnerable to such policies. Repegging exchange rates only as a last resort often meant that when adjustments did occur, they were sizable. Moreover, adjustable pegged rates posed difficulties in estimating the equilibrium rate to which a currency should be repegged. Finally, once the market exchange rate reached the margin of the permissible band around parity, it in effect became a rigid fixed rate that presented speculators with a one-way bet. Given persistent weakening pressure, for example, at the band's outer limit speculators had the incentive to move out of a weakening currency that was expected to depreciate further in value as the result of official devaluation.

These problems reached a climax in the early 1970s. Faced with continuing and growing balance-of-payments deficits, the United States suspended the dollar's convertibility into gold in August 1971. This suspension terminated the U.S. commitment to exchange gold for dollars at $35 per ounce—a commitment that had existed for 37 years. This policy abolished the tie between gold and the international value of the dollar, thus "floating" the dollar and permitting its exchange rate to be set by market forces. The floating of the dollar terminated U.S. support of the Bretton Woods system of adjustable pegged rates and led to the demise of that system.

MANAGED FLOATING RATES

The adoption of managed floating exchange rates by the United States and other industrial nations in 1973 followed the breakdown of the international monetary system based on adjustable pegged rates. Before the 1970s, only a handful of economists gave serious consideration to a general system of floating rates. Because of defects in the decision-making process caused by procedural difficulties and political biases, however, adjustments of par values under the Bretton Woods system were often delayed and discontinuous. It was recognized that exchange rates should be adjusted more promptly and in small but continuous amounts in response to evolving market forces. In 1973, a **managed floating system** was adopted, under which informal guidelines were established by the IMF for coordination of national exchange-rate policies.

The motivation for the formulation of guidelines for floating arose from two concerns. The first was that nations might intervene in the exchange markets to avoid exchange-rate alterations that would weaken their competitive position. When the United States suspended its gold-convertibility pledge and allowed its overvalued dollar to float in the exchange markets, it hoped that a free market adjustment would result in a depreciation of the dollar against

other, undervalued currencies. Rather than permitting a **clean float** (a free market solution) to occur, foreign central banks refused to permit the dollar depreciation by intervening in the exchange market. The United States considered this a **dirty float**, because the free market forces of supply and demand were not allowed to achieve their equilibrating role. A second motivation for floating guidelines was the concern that free floats over time might lead to disorderly markets with erratic fluctuations in exchange rates. Such destabilizing activity could create an uncertain business climate and reduce the level of world trade.

Under managed floating, a nation can alter the degree to which it intervenes on the foreign exchange market. Heavier intervention moves the nation nearer the fixed exchange-rate case, whereas less intervention moves the nation nearer the floating exchange-rate case. Concerning day-to-day and week-to-week exchange-rate movements, a main objective of the floating guidelines has been to prevent the emergence of erratic fluctuations. Member nations should intervene on the foreign exchange market as necessary to prevent sharp and disruptive exchange-rate fluctuations from day to day and week to week. Such a policy is known as **leaning against the wind**—intervening to reduce short-term fluctuations in exchange rates without attempting to adhere to any particular rate over the long run. Members should also not act aggressively with respect to their currency exchange rates; that is, they should not enhance the value when it is appreciating or depress the value when it is depreciating.

Under the managed float, some nations choose *target exchange rates* and intervene to support them. Target exchange rates are intended to reflect long-term economic forces that underlie exchange-rate movements. One way for managed floaters to estimate a target exchange rate is to follow statistical indicators that respond to the same economic forces as the exchange-rate trend. Then, when the values of indicators change, the exchange-rate target can

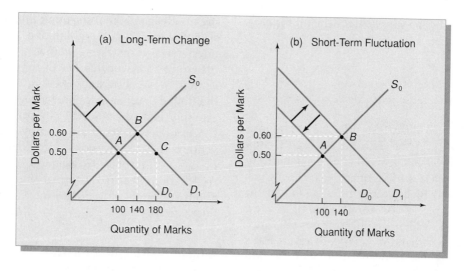

F I G U R E 16. 5 *Managed floating exchange rates.* Under this system, central bank intervention is used to stabilize exchange rates in the short run; in the long run, market forces are permitted to determine exchange rates.

be adjusted accordingly. Among these indicators are rates of inflation in different nations, levels of official foreign reserves, and persistent imbalances in international payments accounts.

Managed Floating Rates in the Short Run and Long Run

Managed floating exchange rates attempt to combine market-determined exchange rates with foreign exchange market intervention in order to take advantage of the best features of floating exchange rates and fixed exchange rates. Under a managed float, market intervention is used to stabilize exchange rates in the short run; in the long run, a managed float allows market forces to determine exchange rates.

Figure 16.5 illustrates the theory of a managed float in a two-country framework, Germany and the United States. The supply and demand schedules for marks are denoted by S_0 and D_0, respectively; the equilibrium exchange rate, at which the quantity of marks supplied equals the quantity demanded, is $0.50 per mark. Consider the following cases.

CASE 1

Permanent increase in the demand for marks

Suppose there occurs a permanent increase in U.S. real income, which results in U.S. residents' demanding additional marks to purchase more German products. Let the demand for marks rise from D_0 to D_1, as shown in Figure 16.5(a). Because this increase in demand is the result of long-run market forces, a managed float permits supply and demand conditions to determine the exchange rate. With the increase in the demand for marks, the quantity of marks demanded (180 marks) exceeds the quantity supplied (100 marks) at the exchange rate of $0.50 per mark. The excess demand results in a rise in the exchange rate to $0.60 per mark, at which the quantity of marks supplied and the quantity demanded are equal. In this manner, long-run movements in exchange rates are determined by the supply and demand for various currencies.

Temporary increase in the demand for marks

Figure 16.5(b) illustrates the case of a short-term increase in the demand for marks. Suppose U.S. investors demand additional marks to finance purchases of German securities, which pay relatively high interest rates; again, let the demand for marks rise from D_0 to D_1. In a few weeks, suppose German interest rates fall, causing the U.S. demand for marks to revert to its original level, D_0. Under floating rates, the dollar price of the mark would rise from $0.50 per mark to $0.60 per mark and then fall back to $0.50 per mark. This type of exchange-rate irascibility is widely considered to be a disadvantage of floating rates, because it leads to uncertainty regarding the profitability of international trade and financial transactions; as a result, the pattern of trade and finance may be disrupted.

Under managed floating rates, the response to this temporary disturbance is exchange-rate intervention by the Federal Reserve to keep the exchange rate at its long-term equilibrium level of $0.50 per mark. During the time period in which demand was at D_1, the central bank would sell marks to meet the excess demand. As soon as the disturbance was over and demand reverted back to D_0, exchange market intervention would no longer be needed. In short, central bank intervention is used to offset temporary fluctuations in exchange rates that contribute to uncertainty of carrying out transactions in international trade and finance.

Since the advent of managed floating rates in 1973, the frequency and size of U.S. foreign exchange interventions have varied, as seen in Figure 16.6. Intervention was substantial during 1977–1979, when the dollar's exchange value was considered to be unacceptably low. U.S. stabilization operations were minimal dur-ing the Reagan administration's first term, consistent with its goal of limiting government interference in markets; they were directed at offsetting short-run market disruptions. Intervention was substantial again in 1985, when the dollar's exchange value was deemed unacceptably high, hurting the competitiveness of U.S. producers. The most extensive U.S. intervention operations took place following the Louvre Accord of 1987, when the major industrial nations reached informal understandings about the limits of tolerance for exchange-rate fluctuations.

Exchange-Rate Stabilization and Monetary Policy

We have seen how central banks can buy and sell foreign currencies to stabilize their values under a system of managed floating exchange rates. Another stabilization technique involves a nation's *monetary policy*. As we shall see, stabilizing a currency's exchange value requires the central bank to adopt (1) an *expansionary* monetary policy to offset currency *appreciation*; (2) a *contractionary* monetary policy to offset currency *depreciation*.

Figure 16.7 illustrates the foreign exchange market for the United States. Assume the supply schedule of British pounds is denoted by S_0 and the demand schedule of pounds is denoted by D_0. The equilibrium exchange rate, at which the quantity of pounds supplied and the quantity demanded are equalized, is $2 per pound. Considering the following examples.

Offsetting a dollar appreciation with an expansionary monetary policy

Suppose production shutdowns in Britain, caused by labor strikes, result in U.S. residents' purchasing fewer British products and therefore demanding fewer pounds. Let the demand for pounds decrease from D_0 to D_1 in Figure

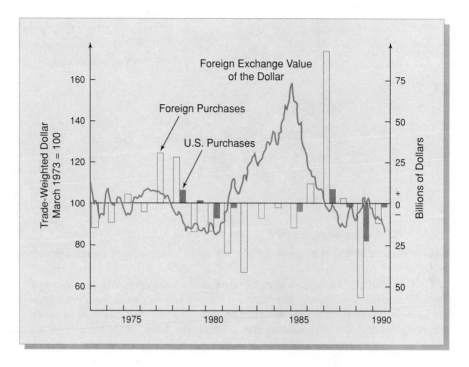

F I G U R E 16. 6 *Exchange market intervention under the managed float.* The figure shows the net official foreign purchases of dollars by 13 major foreign nations. (SOURCE: *Federal Reserve Bulletin,* November 1990.)

16.7(a). In the absence of central bank intervention, the dollar price of the pound falls from $2.00 to $1.80; the dollar thus appreciates against the pound.

To offset the appreciation of the dollar, the Federal Reserve can increase the supply of money in the United States, which will decrease domestic interest rates in the short run. The reduced interest rates will cause the foreign demand for U.S. securities to decline. Fewer pounds will thus be supplied to the foreign exchange market to buy dollars with which to purchase U.S. securities. As the supply of pounds shifts leftward to S_1, the dollar's exchange value reverts to $2 per pound. In this manner, the expansionary monetary policy has offset the dollar's appreciation.

C A S E 2

Offsetting a dollar depreciation with a contractionary monetary policy

Referring to Figure 16.7(b), suppose a temporary surge in British interest rates causes U.S. investors to demand additional pounds with which to purchase additional British securities. Let the demand for pounds rise from D_0 to D_1. In the absence of central bank intervention, the dollar's exchange value rises from $2.00 to $2.20 per pound; the dollar has depreciated against the pound.

To offset this dollar depreciation, the Federal Reserve can decrease the supply of money in the United States, which will increase domestic interest rates and attract British investment.

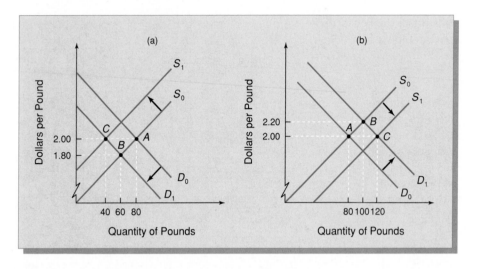

F I G U R E 16. 7 *Exchange-rate stabilization and monetary policy.* In the absence of
international policy coordination, stabilizing a currency's exchange value requires a central
bank to initiate (a) an expansionary monetary policy to offset an appreciation of its currency;
(b) a contractionary monetary policy to offset a depreciation of its currency.

More pounds will be supplied to the foreign
exchange market to purchase dollars with
which to buy U.S. securities. As the supply of
pounds increases from S_0 to S_1, the dollar's
exchange value reverts to $2 per pound. The
contractionary monetary policy thus helps offset the dollar depreciation.

The preceding cases illustrate how domestic
monetary policies can be used to stabilize currency values. These policies are not without
costs, however, as seen in the following example.

Suppose the U.S. government increases federal spending that is not matched by tax increases. To finance the resulting budget deficit,
assume the government borrows funds from the
money market, which raises domestic interest
rates. High U.S. interest rates enhance the
attractiveness of dollar-denominated securities,
leading to increased foreign purchases of these
assets, an increased demand for dollars, and an
appreciation in the dollar's exchange value. The

appreciating dollar makes U.S. goods more
expensive overseas and foreign goods less
expensive in the United States, thus causing the
U.S. trade account to fall into deficit.

Now suppose the Federal Reserve intervenes and adopts an expansionary monetary
policy. The resulting increase in the supply of
money dampens the rise in U.S. interest rates
and the dollar's appreciation. By restraining the
increase in the dollar's exchange value, the expansionary monetary policy enhances the competitiveness of U.S. businesses and keeps the
U.S. trade account in balance.

However, the favorable effects of the
expansionary monetary policy on the domestic
economy are temporary. When pursued indefinitely (over the long run), a policy of increasing
the domestic money supply leads to a *weakening* in the U.S. trade position because the monetary expansion required to offset the dollar's
appreciation eventually promotes higher prices
in the United States. The higher prices of

domestic goods offset the benefits to U.S. competitiveness that initially occur under the monetary expansion. U.S. spending eventually shifts back to foreign products and away from domestically produced goods, causing the U.S. trade account to fall into deficit!

This example shows how monetary policy can be used to stabilize the dollar's exchange value in the short run. But when monetary expansion occurs on a sustained, long-run basis, it brings with it eventual price increases that nullify the initial gains in domestic competitiveness. The long-run effectiveness of using monetary policy to stabilize the dollar's exchange value is limited because the increase in the money supply to offset the dollar's appreciation does not permanently correct the underlying cause of the trade deficit—the increase in domestic spending.

THE EUROPEAN MONETARY SYSTEM

Besides individual nations independently floating their currencies, the international monetary system has been characterized by blocs of currencies that float in unison. Under a system of **joint floating**, currencies are linked by limits placed on the range of exchange-rate fluctuations between any two currencies in the bloc; currencies thus float together, rising or falling as a group.

Such an arrangement has been used by the **European Monetary System** (EMS), which was established in 1979 and includes members of the European Community. A primary objective of the EMS is the establishment of a zone of monetary stability for Europe. To accomplish this goal, European currencies are linked by virtually fixed exchange rates that float as a group (joint float) against the dollar.

To facilitate linkage of the member currencies, the EMS established the **European Currency Unit** (ECU). This asset serves as the numeraire of the EMS exchange-rate mechanism and as a means of settlement among member central banks. The ECU's value is a weighted average, reflecting the values of the EMS member currencies as a group.

Under the exchange-rate mechanism of the EMS, most member nations are required to maintain their exchange rates within 2.25 percent of *central rates* (par values) established between their currency and each of the other members' currencies. When an exchange rate between two members' currencies moves 2.25 percent above or below its central rate (that is, to the edge of the exchange-rate band), the central banks of both nations are required to intervene to prevent the exchange rate from moving outside the band. Realignments of each nation's central rate are permitted via devaluation and revaluation policies. The EMS thus provides for the exchange rates of member currencies' remaining within a narrow band.

Figure 16.8 illustrates the operation of the EMS exchange-rate band for France and Germany. Suppose the central rate of these nations' currencies is 3 francs per mark. Because the upper and lower intervention limits are 2.25 percent on each side of the central rate, intervention occurs when the exchange value of the franc rises to 3.07 francs per mark or falls to 2.93 francs per mark. Suppose that, because of a weakening payments position for France, at time t_0 the franc is devalued from 3 francs per mark to 4 francs per mark. The band moves with the central-rate realignment; central bankers are now obligated to keep the exchange rate between 4.09 francs per mark and 3.91 francs per mark.

When the EMS was created, it was expected that central rates would be changed quite often, in small increments, to promote balance-of-payments adjustment for member nations. In fact, this has occurred. High-inflation nations, such as France and Italy, have needed to periodically devalue their currencies in order to maintain competitiveness relative to

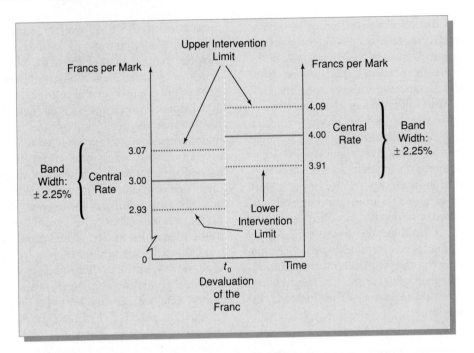

FIGURE 16. 8 *The European Monetary System.* Central bankers intervene to prevent the market exchange rate from moving outside a narrow band around the central rate. Sometimes the central rate is changed, via devaluation (revaluation) policies, moving the band with it.

low-inflation nations such as the Netherlands and Germany.

The Maastricht Treaty

In the **Maastricht Treaty** of 1991, members of the European Community agreed to further integration of Europe's monetary system. The treaty was a blueprint for replacement of the EMS by an **Economic and Monetary Union** (EMU) with a single currency and a European central bank overseeing a single monetary policy. With a common central bank, the central bank of each nation would conduct operations similar to those of the 12 regional Federal Reserve banks in the United States.

The Maastricht Treaty stipulates high standards that nations must meet if they are to become members of the monetary union: (1) The domestic inflation rate must not be more than 1.5 percentage points above the average of the three European Community nations with the lowest inflation. (2) Interest rates on long-term government bonds cannot exceed those of the three members with the lowest inflation by more than 2 percent. (3) The nation's budget deficit must not exceed 3 percent of its gross domestic product, and outstanding government debt must not exceed 60 percent of its gross domestic product. Moreover, a nation's currency must have remained within its EMS band for at least two years without realignment. As of 1994, only three nations of the European

Community met all of these conditions: France, Luxembourg, and Denmark. Nations that met none of the conditions included Portugal, Italy, and Greece. Observers noted that the conditions would likely have to be relaxed for most nations to meet the 1999 target date.

Progress toward monetary unification in Europe was apparently slowed by the partial collapse of the EMS in 1992. The immediate cause of the collapse was tension over the monetary-policy stance of Germany and other nations in the EMS. High German interest rates were blamed for limiting the prospects for economic recovery in Europe by forcing other members to keep their own rates high in order to maintain the value of their currencies against the German mark. Market speculation against the central rates set by the EMS resulted in the devaluation of several currencies against the mark, as well as the withdrawal of the United Kingdom and Italy from the EMS. Although the currency crisis forced exchange-rate parities to reflect more accurately the economic fundamentals, it appeared to slow the creation of a single currency and a unified monetary policy for all European Community members. Observers suggested that a two-tier process might develop in attempting to meet the monetary union timetable. Those nations with the strongest currencies, such as Germany and the Netherlands, might link their currencies and monetary policies more tightly and move ahead, perhaps on the 1999 timetable. Other nations with weaker currencies, such as Spain and Italy, would retain more monetary independence to focus on domestic economic conditions.

The European Currency Crises of 1992–1993

The cut in short-term interest rates by Germany's central bank, the Bundesbank, in 1992 illustrated that the world is not a loosely connected collection of national economies; the only closed economy is the global economy. It also illustrated the need for policy coordination among European governments.

Following the reuniting of the two Germanys in 1990, western Germany embarked on an expansionist spending spree that involved huge borrowing to finance the reconstruction of eastern Germany. Fears of large budget deficits alarmed inflation fighters at the Bundesbank. As a result, the Bundesbank adopted a restrictive monetary policy that drove short-term interest rates up to 9.75 percent, the highest level since World War II. These high short-term interest rates triggered investment flows into Germany, an increased demand for the mark, and an appreciation in the mark's exchange value.

Because European currencies were tied together under the rules of the European Monetary System, high interest rates in Germany forced other European nations to maintain high interest rates, which weakened their economies. Critics maintained that the Germans were selfishly hurting the rest of Europe and fueling rising unemployment by keeping their interest rates high; the rest of Europe felt it was being forced to suffer economic slowdown to pay for German reunification. With their economies hurting, European nations demanded fewer U.S.-made goods, which weakened the current account of the U.S. balance of payments.

Instead of keeping their interest rates high in accordance with those of Germany, other European nations had an alternative: devaluation against the mark. But past experience indicated that European governments that tried it—especially the French government in the 1980s—found it counterproductive. Inevitably they were forced to raise, not lower, their interest rates to ward off a currency crisis and looming inflation, and any competitive gains were quickly eliminated. As a result, a European consensus emerged: an anti-inflation stance closely linked to Germany's, even if it meant painfully high interest rates at a time of slow or nonexistent growth, was preferable to a deval-ued currency.

High German interest rates also had impli-cations for U.S. monetary policy. Throughout 1991 and 1992, the Federal Reserve repeatedly reduced short-term interest rates to jumpstart a sluggish U.S. economy. It was widely recog-nized that further interest-rate reductions would be needed to stimulate economic activity. But with short-term U.S. interest rates at low levels (3 percent) and German interest rates at high levels (9.75 percent), the discrepancy was causing investment funds to flow out of the United States to Germany. This led to a decline in the dollar's exchange value. Fears of trigger-ing a free-fall of the dollar's exchange value, which would greatly disrupt the world financial system, prevented the Federal Reserve from adopting further policies to lower short-term interest rates.

Throughout 1992, governments in Europe and the United States pressed Germany to ease its short-term interest rates. Tensions reached their high point when Sweden raised interest rates to a staggering 75 percent in order to defend the krona and maintain its value against other European currencies. After several weeks of turbulence on foreign exchange markets, in September 1992 the Bundesbank agreed to cut interest rates by a quarter of a percent, relieving a European currency crisis and cheering finan-cial markets around the world. Critics, how-ever, maintained that the reduction was proba-bly too small for what ailed the world economy.

The Bundesbank move was part of a coor-dinated effort among European governments that resulted in interest-rate cuts in the Nether-lands, Belgium, Austria, and Sweden. More-over, the Italian lira was devalued by 7 percent. In the United States, the German rate cuts were welcomed. By buoying the dollar, the cuts did remove a possible obstacle to further Federal Reserve action; they also lessened the chances of a serious dollar panic.

By 1993, the European Monetary System again found itself in turmoil. The efforts to enforce economic harmony through close cur-rency links centered on the German mark were failing; to stay abreast of the strong mark, other European Community countries were forced to maintain their currencies through painfully high interest rates that pushed them into recession. Such costs proved to be unbear-able for nations such as Britain, Italy, and France, which chose the pragmatic goal of jobs for their people over the abstract goal of cur-rency stability. These nations abandoned the rigid currency bands of the EMS and thus per-mitted their currencies to float; as a result, they were free to reduce interest rates so as to jump-start their sluggish economies. These actions led observers to question whether the Maas-tricht Treaty goal of monetary union would ever become a reality.

THE CRAWLING PEG

Since 1968, the Brazilian government has announced a change in the par value of the cruzeiro several times a year. The frequent adjustments in Brazil's exchange rate occur in response to the following indicators: (1) the movement in prices in Brazil relative to those of its main trading partners, (2) the level of foreign exchange reserves, (3) export performance, and (4) the overall balance-of-payments position. These exchange-rate adjustments are an appli-cation of a mechanism dubbed the **crawling peg.** Not only has Brazil adopted this system, but it also has been used by such nations as Argentina, Chile, Israel, and Peru.

The crawling-peg system, a compromise between fixed and floating rates, means that a nation makes small, frequent changes in the par value of its currency to correct balance-of-payments disequilibria. Deficit and surplus nations both keep adjusting until the desired exchange-rate level is attained. The term *crawl-ing peg* reflects the fact that par-value changes are implemented in a large number of small steps to make the process of exchange-rate adjustment continuous for all practical purposes. The peg thus crawls from one par value to another.

The crawling-peg mechanism has been used primarily by nations having high inflation rates. Some developing nations, mostly South American, have recognized that a pegging system can operate in an inflationary environment only if there is provision for frequent changes in the par values. Associating national inflation rates with international competitiveness, these nations have generally used price indicators as a basis for adjusting crawling pegged rates. In these nations, the primary concern is the criterion that governs exchange-rate movements, rather than the currency or basket of currencies against which the peg is defined.

The crawling peg differs from the system of adjustable pegged rates. Under the adjustable peg, currencies are presumably tied to a par value that changes infrequently (perhaps once every several years) but suddenly, usually in large jumps. The idea behind the crawling peg is that a nation can make small, frequent (perhaps several times a year) changes in par values so that they creep along slowly in response to evolving market conditions.

Supporters of the crawling peg argue that the system combines the flexibility of floating rates with the stability usually associated with fixed rates. They contend that a system providing continuous, steady adjustments is more responsive to changing competitive conditions and avoids a main problem of adjustable pegged rates—that changes in par values are frequently wide of the mark. Moreover, small, frequent changes in par values made at random intervals frustrate speculators with their irregularity.

In recent years, the crawling-peg formula has been used by developing nations facing rapid and persistent inflation. But the IMF has generally contended that such a system would not be in the best interests of nations such as the United States or Germany, which bear responsibilities for international currency levels. The IMF has felt that it would be hard to apply such a system to the industrialized nations, whose currencies serve as a source of international liquidity. Although even the most ardent proponents of the crawling peg admit that the time for its widespread adoption has not yet come, the debate over its potential merits is bound to continue.

EXCHANGE CONTROLS

The exchange-rate mechanisms discussed so far all have one important characteristic in common: they are all based on the principle of a free exchange market and automatic market forces. It is true that monetary authorities may modify the exchange-rate outcome by purchasing and selling national currencies, but the foreign exchange transactions conducted among private exporters and importers are free from government regulation; a private foreign exchange market thus exists. A government that does *not* wish to permit a free foreign exchange market can set up a system of exchange measures to keep its balance of payments under control when the exchange rate moves away from its equilibrium level. Among the devices that have been used to achieve this objective are direct control over balance-of-payments transactions and multiple exchange rates.

Exchange controls achieved prominence during the economic crises of the late 1930s and immediately following World War II. It was not until the late 1950s that the industrialized nations of Western Europe considered themselves financially stable enough so that most controls could be dismantled and a high degree of freedom provided for many international transactions. Exchange controls are still widespread today in the less developed nations of Africa, South America, the Far East, and the Near East.

At one extreme, a government may seek to gain control over its payments position by directly circumventing market forces through the imposition of direct controls on international transactions. For example, a government that has a virtual monopoly over foreign exchange dealings may require that all foreign exchange earnings be turned over to authorized dealers. The government then allocates foreign exchange among domestic traders and investors at government-set prices. The advantage of such a system is that the government can influence its payments position by regulating the amount of foreign exchange allocated to imports or capital outflows, limiting the extent of these transactions. Exchange controls also permit the government to encourage or discourage certain transactions by offering different rates for foreign currency for different purposes. Furthermore, exchange controls may give domestic monetary and fiscal policies greater freedom in their stabilization roles. By controlling the balance of payments through exchange controls, a government can pursue its domestic economic policies without fear of balance-of-payments repercussions.

A related method of gaining control of the balance of payments is the practice of **multiple exchange rates.** Used primarily by the developing nations, multiple exchange rates attempt to ensure that necessary goods are imported and less essential goods are discouraged. Essential imports, such as raw materials or capital goods, are subsidized when the government sets a low exchange rate for these commodities, resulting in lower prices to domestic buyers. For less desirable imports, such as luxury products, a higher price will be set when the government makes foreign exchange available only at a high rate. Multiple exchange rates can thus be used to subsidize or tax import purchases so that a nation's scarce supply of foreign exchange will be rationed among only the most essential commodities. Obviously, the implementation of such a mechanism requires an elaborate classification system, as well as strict penalties against smuggling. Table 16.4 illustrates the multiple exchange rates used by Chile during the early 1970s.

TABLE 16. 4   /   *Chile's Multiple Exchange-Rate System, 1972*

Foreign Exchange Usage	Exchange Rate: Chilean Escudos per U.S. Dollar
Residential travel	130
Luxury imports	80
Tourism (to Chile)	46
Machinery imports	40
Student expenses	36
Specified exports	30
Raw material imports	25
General trade	25
Special trade	20
Essential imports	20
Banking transactions	12

SOURCE: *Pick's Currency Yearbook 1977–1979* (New York: Pick Publishing Co., 1979), p. 150.

DUAL EXCHANGE RATES

The operation of the world financial system has sometimes been disrupted by international capital flows. Short-term capital tends to move across national borders in response to anticipated changes in exchange rates and interest-rate differentials. Such movements may prevent monetary authorities from pursuing policies insulated from balance-of-payments considerations or even from defending official exchange rates. One method of controlling international capital movements is for a nation to adopt a system of **dual** (two-tier) **exchange rates.** Such a mechanism has been used not only in the less developed nations, but also in such industrial nations as Belgium, France, and Italy.

Dual exchange rates attempt to insulate a nation from the balance-of-payments effects of capital flows while providing a stable business climate for commercial (current-account) transactions involving merchandise trade and services. This is accomplished by having separate exchange rates for commercial and capital transactions. *Commercial* transactions must be conducted in a market where exchange rates are officially *pegged* by national monetary authorities, whereas *capital* transactions occur in a financial market in which exchange rates are *floating*. Although history gives no example of a dual exchange-rate system in which complete segregation of commercial and capital transactions has been achieved, the experiences of Belgium, France, and Italy have approximated such a mechanism.

To carry out the segregation of commercial and capital transactions, the system must be able to distinguish between these activities. For example, the Belgian dual exchange-rate system required that all current transactions involving the export and import of goods and services pass through the commercial market. All financial transactions had to pass through the capital market. The French system, however, permitted several types of current-account transactions—those relating to tourism, profit, and interest—to pass through the financial market. The point is that the distinction between the markets does not require a uniform classification system for all nations; the market eligibility of any given transaction depends on the objectives of a particular nation. With dual rates, the capital account is always in balance; any balance-of-payments disequilibrium will stem from commercial transactions. Although dual exchange-rate systems have recently been used by nations whose financial structures are particularly sensitive to short-term capital flows, several factors limit dual rates as a cushion.

One problem of dual rates is the disruptive effect on trade and capital flows when the commercial and financial rates split apart. Should the demand for a nation's currency in the financial market continually decline, its financial rate might depreciate enough to fall below its commercial rate. Administration of the commercial rate would become increasingly difficult as fraudulent intermarket transfers of funds became more profitable. Also, investor expectations concerning the future financial rate would govern the extent to which equilibrating capital flows would respond to exchange-rate changes. Should speculators interpret a nation's financial rate falling below its commercial rate as indicating a further decline in the financial rate, they might continue selling the weakening currency. This would put greater downward pressure on the financial rate and disrupt the exchange markets.

Dual rates are also unable to cope with a type of speculation known as **commercial leads and lags**. Traders sometimes speed up import payments and delay export receipts in anticipation of a currency depreciation; the opposite holds for an expected currency appreciation. Dual rates are designed to moderate speculative flows of capital in the financial market. In times of speculative pressure, traders of goods may attempt to change the timing of their basic transactions or payments to gain extra profits from changes in the price of foreign exchange. Under these conditions, dual rates would be unable to cope with exchange-market speculation.

The experience of dual exchange rates also indicates that such nations do not have much more independence in their monetary policies than they would under a single-rate, pegged system. This is because a divergence of the commercial and financial rates might occur if a nation attempted to determine its interest rates independently of other nations. Should a dual-rate nation attempt to set its interest rates higher than those of its trading partners, there would be an inducement for capital flows into the country, and this would likely lead to an appreciation of the financial rate above the commercial rate. Belgium's decision to adopt a monetary policy that maintains its interest rates consistent with those abroad apparently reflects concern over the disruptive consequences that diverging rates have for a dual-rate system.

Probably the main benefit of dual exchange rates for a single nation is that they may provide a temporary cushion against the destabilizing effects of speculative capital flows on the balance of payments. However, dual rates cannot cope with the speculative activity of commercial leads and lags. If speculation persists, the maintenance of dual rates may require monetary intervention or other direct controls to prevent the two rates from significantly splitting apart. Thus, dual rates have not been widely adopted by trading nations.

SUMMARY

1. Most nations maintain neither completely fixed nor floating exchange rates. Contemporary exchange-rate systems generally embody some features of each of these standards.

2. Small, developing nations often peg their currencies to a single currency or a currency basket. Pegging to a single currency is generally used by small nations whose trade and financial relationships are mainly with a single trading partner. Small nations with more than one major trading partner often peg their currencies to a basket of currencies.

3. The special drawing right is a currency basket composed of five currencies of International Monetary Fund members. The basket valuation technique attempts to make the SDR's value more stable than the foreign currency value of any single currency in the basket. Developing nations often choose to peg their exchange rates to the SDR.

4. Under a fixed exchange-rate system, a government defines the official exchange rate for its currency. It then establishes an exchange stabilization fund, which buys and sells foreign currencies to prevent the market exchange rate from moving above or below the official rate.

5. Under a fixed exchange-rate system, nations may officially devalue/revalue their currencies to restore trade equilibrium. The purpose of devaluation is to promote a depreciation in the home currency's exchange value, which helps reduce a trade deficit. The purpose of revaluation is to promote an appreciation in the home currency's exchange value, which helps reduce a trade surplus.

6. Under floating exchange-rates, market forces of supply and demand determine currency values. Among the major arguments for floating rates are (a) simplicity, (b) continuous adjustment, (c) independent domestic policies, and (d) reduced need for international reserves. Arguments against floating rates stress (a) disorderly exchange markets, (b) reckless financial policies on the part of governments, and (c) conduciveness to price inflation.

7. The adjustable pegged exchange-rate system resulted from the Bretton Woods Agreement of 1944. The idea was to provide participating nations with stable but flexible exchange rates. In the short run, nations would use exchange stabilization funds to maintain fixed exchange rates; in the long run, currency devaluations and revaluations would be used to help reverse persistent payment imbalances.

8. With the breakdown of the Bretton Woods system, the major industrial nations adopted a system of managed floating exchange rates. Under this system, central bank intervention in the foreign exchange market is intended to prevent disorderly market conditions in the short run. In the long run, exchange rates are permitted to float in accordance with changing supply and demand conditions.

9. To offset a depreciation in the home currency's exchange value, a central bank can: (1) use its international reserves to purchase quantities of that currency on the foreign exchange market; (2) initiate a contractionary monetary policy, which leads to higher domestic interest rates, increased investment inflows, and increased demand for the home currency. To offset an appreciation in the home currency's exchange value, a central bank can sell additional quantities of its currency on the foreign exchange market or initiate an expansionary monetary policy.

10. As part of their efforts to achieve monetary union, members of the European Community established the European Monetary System in 1979. Under the EMS, member nations agree to maintain their exchange rates within a band of plus/minus 2.25 percent around the central exchange rate. In the Maastricht Treaty of

1991, member nations agreed to replace the EMS by an Economic and Monetary Union with a single currency and a European central bank.

11. Under a crawling-peg exchange-rate system, a nation makes frequent devaluations (or revaluations) of its currency to restore payments balance. Developing nations suffering from high inflation rates have been major users of this mechanism.

12. Exchange controls are sometimes used by governments in an attempt to gain control of the balance of payments. The government may ration foreign exchange to domestic traders and investors to limit imports. Multiple exchange rates are sometimes used in an attempt to ensure that only necessary goods will be imported.

13. Nations such as Belgium have resorted to dual exchange rates to insulate the balance of payments from short-term capital movements while providing exchange-rate stability for commercial transactions.

STUDY QUESTIONS

1. What factors underlie a nation's decision to adopt floating exchange rates or fixed exchange rates?

2. How do managed floating exchange rates operate? Why were they adopted by the industrialized nations in 1973?

3. Of what significance is a joint float for members of the European Monetary System?

4. Discuss the philosophy and operation of the Bretton Woods system of adjustable pegged exchange rates.

5. Why have nations such as Brazil adopted a crawling-peg exchange-rate system?

6. What is the purpose of exchange controls? Are they still being used today?

7. How do dual exchange rates attempt to provide a steady environment for commercial transactions while insulating the balance of payments from destabilizing capital movements?

8. Why do small nations adopt currency baskets against which to peg their exchange rates?

9. What advantage does the SDR offer to small nations seeking to peg their exchange rates?

10. Present the case for and the case against a system of floating exchange rates.

11. What techniques can a central bank use to stabilize the exchange value of its currency?

12. What is the purpose of a currency devaluation? What about a currency revaluation?

CHAPTER **17**

International Economic Policy

KEY CONCEPTS AND TERMS

Bank for International
    Settlements
Bonn Summit
    Agreement
Demand-pull inflation
Direct controls
Expenditure-changing
    policies
Expenditure-switching
    policies
External balance
Fiscal policy
Group of Five
Group of Seven
Institutional constraints

Internal balance
International economic
    policy
International economic
    policy coordination
Leaning with the wind
Louvre Accord
Monetary policy
Operation Twist
Overall balance
Plaza Agreement
Policy agreement
Policy conflict
Wage and price
    controls

A nation with a closed economy can select its economic policies in view of its own goals. In an open world economy, however, consequences of a nation's activities are felt by its trading partners. The result is a need for economic policy cooperation among nations. This chapter examines government policies designed to achieve full employment with price stability and equilibrium in the balance of payments. The importance of international economic policy cooperation is emphasized throughout the discussion.

ECONOMIC POLICY IN AN OPEN ECONOMY

International economic policy refers to activities of national governments that affect the movement of trade and factor inputs among nations.

Included are not only the obvious measures such as import tariffs and quotas, but also domestic measures such as monetary policy and fiscal policy. Policies that are undertaken to improve the conditions of one sector in a nation tend to have repercussions that spill over into other sectors. Since an economy's *internal* (domestic) sector is tied to its *external* (foreign) sector, one cannot designate economic policies as purely domestic or purely foreign. Rather, the effects of economic policy should be viewed as being located on a continuum between two poles—an internal-effects pole and an external-effects pole. While the primary impact of an import restriction is on a nation's trade balance, for example, there are secondary effects on national output, employment, and income. Most economic policies are located between the external and internal poles rather than falling directly on either one.

ECONOMIC OBJECTIVES OF NATIONS

What are the basic objectives of economic policies? Since the Great Depression of the 1930s, governments have actively pursued the goal of economic stability at full employment. Known as **internal balance**, this objective has two dimensions: (1) a fully employed economy; (2) no inflation—or, more realistically, a "reasonable" amount of inflation. Nations traditionally have considered internal balance to be of primary importance and have formulated economic policies to attain this goal.

Policymakers are also aware of a nation's balance-of-payments (BOP) position. A nation is said to be in **external balance** when it realizes neither BOP deficits nor BOP surpluses.[1] In practice, policymakers usually express external balance in terms of a BOP subaccount, such as the current account. In this context, external balance occurs when the current account is neither so deeply in deficit that the home nation is incapable of repaying its foreign debts in the future nor so strongly in surplus that foreign nations cannot repay their debts to it. Although nations usually consider internal balance as the highest priority, they are sometimes forced to modify priorities when confronted with large and persistent external imbalances.

Figure 17.1 illustrates these two basic policy dimensions. The vertical axis of the diagram depicts the size of a nation's BOP deficit or surplus. *External balance* is reached at the diagram's origin, with neither BOP surplus nor BOP deficit. The horizontal axis indicates the extent of domestic recession or inflation. Full employment (zero recession without inflation, or *internal balance,* is also achieved at the diagram's origin. An economy reaches **overall balance** when it attains internal balance and external balance.

Nations have economic targets other than internal balance and external balance, such as long-run economic development and a reasonably equitable distribution of national income.

Although these and other commitments may influence international economic policies, the discussion in this chapter is confined to the pursuit of internal balance and external balance.

POLICY INSTRUMENTS

To attain the objectives of external balance and internal balance, policymakers enact expenditure-changing policies, expenditure-switching policies, and direct controls.

Expenditure-changing policies alter the level of aggregate demand for goods and services, including those produced domestically and those imported. They include **fiscal policy**, which refers to changes in government spending and taxes, and **monetary policy**, which refers to changes in the money supply by a nation's central bank (such as the Federal Reserve). Depending on the direction of change, expenditure-changing policies are either expenditure increasing or expenditure reducing.

If *inflation* is a problem, it is likely to be because the level of aggregate demand (total spending) is too high for the level of output that can be sustained by the nation's resources at constant prices. The standard recommendation in this case is for policymakers to reduce aggregate demand by implementing *expenditure-decreasing* policies, such as government expenditure reductions, tax increases, or decreases in the money supply; these policies offset the upward pressure on prices due to excess aggregate demand. If *unemployment* is excessive, the standard recommendation is for policymakers to increase aggregate demand for goods and services by initiating *expenditure-increasing* policies.

Expenditure-switching policies modify the direction of demand, shifting it between domestic output and imports. Under a system of fixed exchange rates, a trade-deficit nation could devalue its currency to increase the international competitiveness of its industries, thus

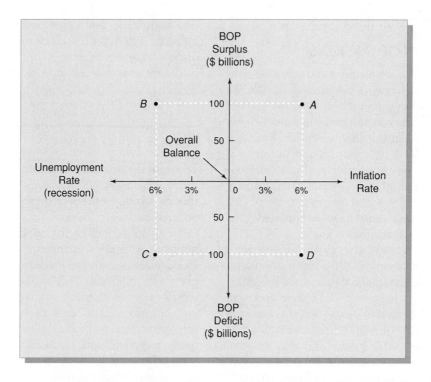

F I G U R E 17. 1   *Economic objectives and macroeconomic policy.* A nation attains overall balance when it simultaneously achieves internal balance and external balance. When overall balance is not realized, nations can implement expenditure-switching policies (such as currency devaluation/revaluation) or expenditure-changing policies (such as monetary/fiscal policy) to help eliminate internal and/or external disequilibrium, thus pushing the economy toward overall balance.

diverting spending from foreign goods to domestic goods. To increase its competitiveness under a managed floating exchange-rate system, the nation could purchase other currencies with its currency, thereby causing the exchange value of its currency to depreciate. The success of these policies in promoting trade balance largely depends on switching demand in the proper direction and amount, as well as on the capacity of the home economy to meet the additional demand by supplying more goods. Exchange-rate adjustments are general switching policies that influence the balance of pay-

ments indirectly, through their effects on the price mechanism and national income.

Direct controls consist of government restrictions on the market economy. They are selective expenditure-switching policies whose objective is to control particular items in the balance of payments. Direct controls, such as automobile tariffs and dairy quotas, are levied on imports in an attempt to switch domestic spending away from foreign goods to domestic goods. Similarly, the object of an export subsidy is to enhance exports by switching foreign spending to domestic output. When a government wishes to limit the volume of its overseas sales, it may impose an export quota (such as Japan's automobile export quotas of the 1980s). Direct controls may also be levied on capital flows so as to either restrain excessive capital outflows or stimulate capital inflows.

Economic policy formation is subject to **institutional constraints** that involve considerations of fairness and equity.[2] Policymakers are aware of the needs of groups they represent, such as labor and business, especially when pursuing conflicting economic objectives. For example, to what extent are policymakers willing to permit reductions in national income, output, and employment as the cost of restoring BOP equilibrium? The outcry of adversely affected groups within the nation may be more than sufficient to convince policymakers not to pursue external balance as a goal. During election years, government officials tend to be especially sensitive to domestic economic problems. Reflecting perceptions of fairness and equity, policy formation tends to be characterized by negotiation and compromise.

EXCHANGE-RATE POLICIES AND OVERALL BALANCE

As noted previously, expenditure-switching policies can help a nation attain overall balance. Although these measures are designed primarily to influence the nation's external sector, they have secondary impacts on its internal sector. Let us examine one expenditure-switching instrument, the exchange rate, and see its impact on a nation's external sector and internal sector.

Referring to Figure 17.1, suppose a nation is located in the disequilibrium zone of *BOP deficit with recession*, indicated by point *C* in the figure. A *depreciation* (devaluation) of the nation's currency increases the international competitiveness of its goods; this leads to rising exports and a reduction in the BOP deficit.

Additional export sales provide an injection of spending into the economy, which encourages additional production and thus reduces the level of unemployment. In terms of the figure, the currency depreciation induces movement in a *northeasterly* direction, promoting both internal balance and external balance.

Conversely, suppose that a nation experiences *BOP surplus with inflation*, indicated by point *A* in Figure 17.1. If this nation permits an *appreciation* (revaluation) of its currency, the international competitiveness of its goods will decline, causing exports to fall. Falling export sales decrease the level of spending in the economy, thus reducing its inflation rate. By promoting internal balance and external balance, the currency appreciation induces a *southwesterly* movement in the figure.

As these examples suggest, the ability to implement exchange-rate policies is subject to international policy cooperation for several reasons. A *depreciation* of one nation's currency implies an *appreciation* for its trading partners. If the dollar depreciates by 30 percent, this can be equivalent to a 30-percent subsidy on U.S. exports and a 30-percent tax on U.S. imports! Furthermore, changes in the exchange rate influence the external sectors and internal sectors of both the home country and its trading partners. In a global system, one nation cannot achieve overall balance single-handedly via its own policy tools. Other nations can implement retaliatory policies—such as tariffs and currency devaluations—that offset the nation's pursuit of overall balance, as occurred during the Great Depression of the 1930s .

MONETARY POLICY AND FISCAL POLICY: EFFECTS ON INTERNAL BALANCE

The previous section suggested that exchange-rate policies primarily affect the economy's external sector, while having secondary effects

T A B L E 17. 1 / *The Effectiveness of Fiscal Policy and Monetary Policy in Promoting Internal Balance* *

Exchange-Rate Regime	Monetary Policy	Fiscal Policy
Floating exchange rates	Effective	Ineffective
Fixed exchange rates	Ineffective	Effective

* Assuming a high degree of capital mobility.

on its internal sector. Let us now consider monetary policy and fiscal policy as stabilization tools. These tools are generally used to stabilize the economy's internal sector, while having secondary effects on its external sector. How successful are monetary policy and fiscal policy in achieving full employment and price stability?

Let us assume that international capital mobility is high. This suggests that a small change in the relative interest rate across nations induces a large international flow of capital (investment funds). This assumption is consistent with capital movements among many industrial nations, such as the United States and Germany, and the conclusions of many analysts that capital mobility is increasing as national financial markets have become internationalized.

Two conclusions will emerge from our discussion: (1) Under a fixed exchange-rate system, fiscal policy is successful in promoting internal balance, whereas monetary policy is unsuccessful. (2) Under a floating rate system, monetary policy is successful in promoting internal balance, whereas fiscal policy is unsuccessful. These conclusions are summarized in Table 17.1.

In practice, most industrial nations maintain neither rigidly fixed exchange rates nor freely floating exchange rates. Rather, they maintain managed floating exchange rates in which central banks buy and sell currencies in

an attempt to prevent exchange-rate movements from becoming disorderly. Heavier exchange-rate intervention moves a nation closer to our fixed exchange-rate conclusions for monetary and fiscal policy; less intervention moves a nation closer to our floating exchange-rate conclusions.

Fiscal Policy with Fixed Exchange Rates and Floating Exchange Rates

Assume that a nation operates under a fixed exchange-rate system and experiences high unemployment. Let us follow the case of an expansionary fiscal policy—say, an increase in government purchases of goods and services. The rise in government spending increases aggregate demand, which leads to higher output, employment, and income, as seen in the upper portion of Figure 17.2(a).

Now refer to the lower portion of Figure 17.2(a). As total spending rises, so does the demand for money. Given the supply of money, interest rates increase; this encourages foreigners to invest more in the home nation and discourages its residents from investing abroad. The resulting net capital inflows push the nation's capital account into surplus. Concurrently, the increase in spending results in higher imports and a trade deficit. If investment flows are highly mobile, it is likely that the capital-

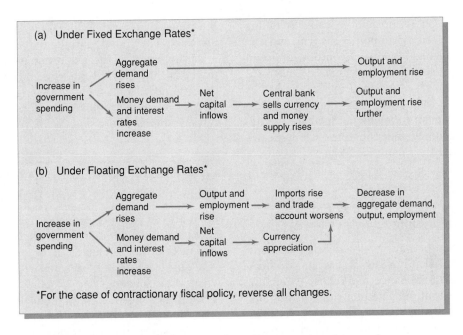

F I G U R E   17. 2   *Fiscal policy: short-run effects on a nation's internal sector.*
(a) Under fixed exchange rates, an expansionary (contractionary) fiscal policy helps correct
the problem of recession (inflation). (b) Under floating exchange rates, an expansionary
(contractionary) fiscal policy is unsuccessful in correcting the problem of recession
(inflation).

account surplus will exceed the trade-account deficit; the overall BOP thus moves into surplus. Because the nation is committed to fixed exchange rates, its central bank buys foreign currency, thus preventing an appreciation of the home currency. This increases the German money supply, which leads to additional spending, output, and employment. In this manner, the expansionary fiscal policy promotes internal balance.

If capital mobility is low, however, the trade-account deficit may more than offset the capital-account surplus, pulling the overall BOP into deficit. To prevent the home currency from depreciating, central bankers would purchase it on the foreign exchange market. This would cause a decrease in the money supply, an increase in interest rates, a decline in investment

spending, and a decrease in output. The attempt to use expansionary fiscal policy to jump-start the economy could backfire!

The result is different if the country has floating exchange rates. As before, fiscal expansion leads to higher output and income as well as higher interest rates. Higher income induces rising imports, which push the trade account into deficit. Higher interest rates lead to net investment inflows and a surplus in the capital account. With highly mobile capital, it is likely that the surplus in the capital account exceeds the deficit in the trade account, so that the overall BOP moves into surplus. This leads to an appreciation in the home currency's exchange value. With a floating exchange-rate system, however, the central bank does nothing to offset this appreciation. By making the nation less competitive, the appreciation leads to falling exports and rising imports; the ensuing decrease in aggregate demand, output, and employment offsets the initial gains of the fiscal expansion. The expansionary fiscal policy is thus unable to mitigate the economy's recession. Adjustment following an increase in government spending under floating exchange rates is summarized in Figure 17.2(b).

Monetary Policy with Fixed Exchange Rates and Floating Exchange Rates

Suppose that a nation experiences domestic recession and that it allows its currency to float in the foreign exchange market. To stimulate domestic output, assume that the central bank adopts an expansionary monetary policy. By increasing the supply of money relative to the money demand, the monetary policy leads to lower interest rates, which stimulate aggregate demand and output. Lower interest rates also discourage foreigners from investing in the home country and encourage its residents to invest abroad. The resulting net capital outflows induce a depreciation of the nation's currency and an improvement in its international competitiveness. The subsequent rise in exports and fall in imports lead to further increases in output and employment; the expansionary monetary policy thus promotes internal balance. Adjustment following an expansionary monetary policy under floating exchange rates is summarized in Figure 17.3(a).

Contrast this outcome with the effects of monetary policy under a system of fixed exchange rates. The monetary expansion reduces interest rates, leading to rising aggregate demand, output, and employment. Lower interest rates result in net capital outflows and a depreciation in the currency's exchange value. To maintain a fixed exchange rate, however, the central bank intervenes on the foreign exchange market and purchases the home currency with foreign currency. This decreases the money supply and offsets the initial money supply increase. The initial output and employment expansion due to the expansionary monetary policy is thus blunted, and internal balance is not attained. Adjustment following an expansionary monetary policy under fixed exchange rates is summarized in Figure 17.3(b).

MONETARY AND FISCAL POLICY: EFFECTS ON EXTERNAL BALANCE

What are the effects of monetary policy and fiscal policy on a nation's external balance? We assume that the exchange rate is fixed, because BOP surpluses or BOP deficits are issues only when the exchange rate is fixed; recall that floating exchange rates automatically adjust to promote BOP equilibrium.

The short-run effects of monetary policy on the BOP are definite: an expansion in the money supply worsens the BOP; a contraction in the money supply improves the BOP. These effects are illustrated in Figure 17.4.

To illustrate, assume the central bank increases the money supply, relative to the money demand, which pushes interest rates downward. Falling interest rates encourage additional investment spending, which leads to an increase in aggregate demand, output, and income. The rise in income, in turn, increases imports and worsens the trade balance. At the same time, falling interest rates induce net investment outflows and a deterioration in the capital account. By worsening the trade balance and the capital-account balance, the monetary expansion worsens overall BOP. In the long run, the overseas investments will be repaid with interest, resulting in a positive feedback into the BOP, but the negative effect on the trade balance will persist.

The short-run effects on the BOP of expansionary fiscal policy are not as clear as those of monetary policy. Assume the government increases its purchases of goods and services, leading to increases in aggregate demand, out-

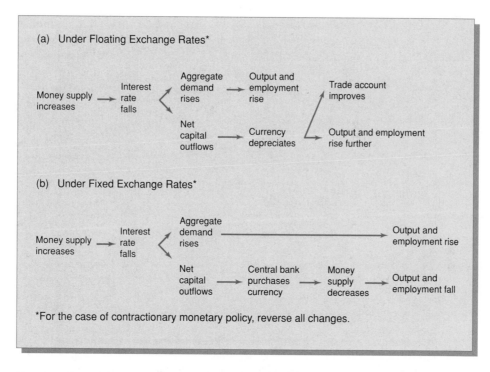

F I G U R E 17. 3   *Monetary policy: short-run effects on a nation's internal sector.* (a) Under floating exchange rates, an expansionary (contractionary) monetary policy is successful in correcting the problem of recession (inflation). (b) Under fixed exchange rates, an expansionary (contractionary) monetary policy is unsuccessful in correcting the problem of recession (inflation).

put, and income. Rising income, in turn, induces rising imports and a worsening trade balance. Meanwhile, increased government spending leads to increased money demand and rising interest rates. The higher interest rates, in turn, induce net investment inflows and an improvement in the capital account. If capital mobility is sufficiently high, the improvement in the capital account more than offsets the trade-account deterioration, and the overall BOP improves. In the long run, however, foreign investors must be repaid with interest, and this more than offsets the investment inflows caused by higher interest rates. As a result, the fiscal expansion probably worsens the overall BOP in the long run, albeit improving it in the short run

if enough investment inflows occur in response to higher interest rates.

MONETARY POLICY AND FISCAL POLICY: POLICY AGREEMENT AND POLICY CONFLICT

With fixed exchange rates, let us consider monetary policy and fiscal policy and see what effects they have on a nation's internal balance and external balance.

Consider monetary policy first. Referring to Figure 17.1, suppose that a nation experiences *unemployment with BOP surplus,* shown by point B. The previous section suggested that

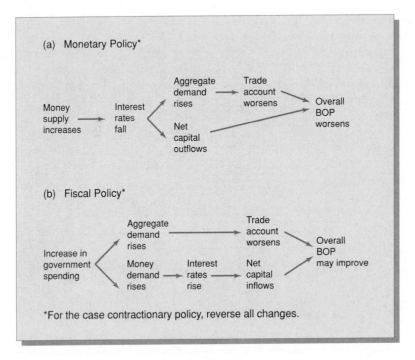

(a) Monetary Policy*

(b) Fiscal Policy*

*For the case contractionary policy, reverse all changes.

F I G U R E 17. 4   *Monetary policy and fiscal policy under fixed exchange rates: short-run effects on a nation's external sector.* (a) An expansionary (contractionary) monetary policy leads to a worsening (improving) trade account and capital account, thus worsening (improving) the overall balance of payments. (b) An expansionary (contractionary) fiscal policy leads to a worsening (improving) trade account and an improving (worsening) capital account. The overall balance of payments improves (worsens) depending on the relative strength of these two opposing forces.

if the central bank increases the money supply, which leads to rising aggregate demand, unemployment will fall and the BOP surplus will decrease. In this case, the expansionary monetary policy clearly promotes overall balance. Alternately, suppose that a country experiences *inflation with BOP deficit,* shown by point *D* in Figure 17.1. A reduction in the money supply, which reduces aggregate demand, decreases the inflation rate as well as the BOP deficit, thus promoting overall balance. These two disequilibrium zones illustrate **policy agreement** for monetary policy: changes in the money supply move the economy toward both internal balance and external balance.

Not all disequilibrium zones, however, are as favorable for monetary policy. Suppose now that a nation experiences *unemployment with BOP deficit,* shown by point *C* in Figure 17.1. The previous section suggested that an expansionary monetary policy, which raises aggregate demand, will reduce unemployment—but at the cost of a larger BOP deficit (southeast from point *C*)! If a country experiences *inflation with BOP surplus,* shown by point *A* in Figure 17.1, a contractionary monetary policy leads to less inflation but increased BOP surplus (northwest from point *A*). These disequilibrium zones imply **policy conflict** for monetary policy: although changes in the money supply improve one economic objective, they detract from another objective. A dilemma thus exists for monetary authorities concerning which objective to pursue.

Instead of utilizing monetary policy in policy-conflict zones, suppose a nation resorts to fiscal policy. Assume, for example, that a country experiences *unemployment and BOP deficit,* as shown by point *C* in Figure 17.1. Recall that an expansionary fiscal policy, which raises aggregate demand, promotes full employment; however, it reduces a nation's BOP deficit only if the ensuing improvement in the capital account more than offsets the deterioration in the trade account. If a country experiences *inflation and BOP surplus,* shown by point *A* in Figure 17.1, a contractionary fiscal policy lessens inflation; whether the BOP surplus rises or falls depends on whether the worsening of its capital account more than offsets the improvement of its trade account. It is thus not clear whether fiscal policy is able to promote overall balance for a nation situated in one of these policy-conflict zones.

When a nation finds itself in a policy-conflict zone, fiscal policy or monetary policy alone will not necessarily restore both internal and external balance. A combination of policies is generally needed. Suppose, for example, that a nation experiences *unemployment with BOP deficit,* shown by point *C* in Figure 17.1. An expansionary monetary policy to combat unemployment might be accompanied by tariffs or quotas, or possibly currency devaluation, to reduce imports and improve the BOP. Each economic objective is matched with an appropriate policy instrument so that both objectives can be attained at the same time.

In U.S. history, the Federal Reserve has attempted to line up policy instruments with targets during conflict situations. During the early 1960s, the conflict was *domestic recession with BOP deficit.* The Federal Reserve attempted to match instruments with targets by manipulating the structure of domestic interest rates in a program called **Operation Twist.**

Under this program, the U.S. interest-rate structure was modified so that short-term rates were used primarily to promote external balance while long-term rates were used primarily for internal balance. By keeping short-term interest rates high, the United States would presumably experience net investment inflows, thereby improving its BOP position. Low long-term rates would presumably stimulate domestic investment, output, and employment, thus correcting the recession. At best, Operation Twist was only partially successful in promoting overall balance. The policy was initially successful in keeping short-term rates above long-term rates; as time passed, however, the differential between them disappeared as inflation pushed both short-term and long-term rates upward, thus moderating the program's success.

INFLATION WITH UNEMPLOYMENT

The analysis so far has looked at internal balance under special circumstances. It has been assumed that as the economy advances to full employment, domestic prices remain unchanged until full employment is reached. Once the nation's capacity to produce has been achieved, further increases in aggregate demand pull prices upward. This type of inflation is known as **demand-pull inflation.** Under these conditions, internal balance (full employment with stable prices) can be viewed as a single target that requires but one policy instrument: reductions in aggregate demand via monetary policy or fiscal policy.

A more troublesome problem is the appropriate policy to implement when a nation experiences *inflation with unemployment.* Here the problem is that internal balance cannot be achieved just by manipulating aggregate demand. To decrease inflation, a reduction in aggregate demand is required; to decrease unemployment, an expansion in aggregate demand is required. The objectives of full employment and stable prices thus cannot be

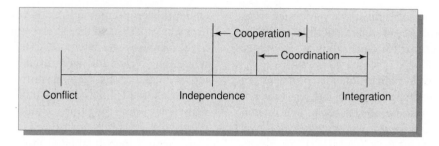

FIGURE 17.5 *Relations among national governments.* Relations among national governments can be visualized along a spectrum ranging from policy conflict to policy integration. Between these extremes are a variety of forms of cooperation and coordination. This figure is adapted from W. Dobson, *Economic Policy Coordination: Requiem or Prologue?* (Washington, D.C.: Institute for International Economics, 1991), p. 3.

considered as one and the same target. Attainment of full employment and attainment of price stability are instead recognized as two independent targets, requiring two distinct policy instruments. Achieving overall balance thus involves three separate targets: (1) BOP equilibrium, (2) full employment, and (3) price stability. A third policy instrument may be needed to ensure that all three objectives can be achieved simultaneously.

Inflation with unemployment has been a problem for the United States. In 1971, for example, the U.S. economy experienced *inflation with recession and BOP deficit*. Increasing aggregate demand to achieve full employment would presumably intensify inflationary pressures. The president therefore implemented a comprehensive system of **wage and price controls** to remove the inflationary constraint. Later the same year, the United States entered into the Smithsonian exchange-rate realignments that resulted in a depreciation of the dollar by 12 percent against the trade-weighted value of other major currencies. The dollar depreciation was intended to help the United States reverse its BOP deficit. In short, it was the president's view that the internal and external problems of the United States could not be

eliminated through expenditure-changing policies alone.

INTERNATIONAL ECONOMIC POLICY COORDINATION

Policymakers have long been aware that the welfare of their economies is linked to that of the world economy. Because of the international mobility of goods, services, capital, and labor, economic policies of one nation have spillover effects on others. This spillover is especially true for the larger industrial economies, but even here, the linkages are stronger among some nations, such as those within Western Europe, than for others. Recognizing these spillover effects, governments have often made attempts to coordinate their economic policies.

Economic relations among nations can be visualized along a spectrum, illustrated in Figure 17.5, ranging from *open conflict* to *integration*, where nations implement policies jointly in a supranational forum to which they have ceded a large degree of authority (such as the European Community). At the spectrum's midpoint lies *policy independence*: nations take the actions of other nations as a given; they do not attempt to influence those actions or be influenced by them. Between independence and integration lie various forms of policy coordination and cooperation.

Cooperative policymaking can take many forms, but in general it occurs whenever officials from different nations meet to evaluate world economic conditions. During these meetings, policymakers may present briefings on their individual economies and discuss current policies. Such meetings represent a simple form of cooperation. A more involved format might consist of economists' studies on a particular subject, combined with an in-depth discussion of possible solutions. True policy coordination, however, goes beyond these two forms of cooperation. Policy coordination is a formal agreement among nations to initiate particular policies.

International economic policy coordination is the attempt to significantly modify national policies (monetary policy, fiscal policy, exchange-rate policy) in recognition of international economic interdependence. Policy coordination does not necessarily imply that nations give precedence to international over domestic concerns. It does recognize, however, that the policies of one nation can spill over to influence the objectives of others; nations should therefore communicate with one another and attempt to coordinate their policies so as to take these linkages into account. Presumably, they will be better off than if they had acted independently.

There are many examples of international economic policy coordination. The Smithsonian Agreement of 1971 was a coordinated attempt by the major industrial nations to realign the exchange values of their currencies using currency devaluations and revaluations. The 1978 Bonn Summit resulted in the enactment by Germany and Japan of expansionary fiscal and monetary policies to stimulate their demand for U.S. goods and reduce the U.S. trade deficit; in return, the United States raised its price of oil to the world level. In the Plaza Accord of 1985, Germany and Japan agreed to adopt stimulative fiscal policies to promote imports from the United States and to intervene in foreign currency markets to further a depreciation in the dollar's exchange value.

To facilitate policy coordination, economic officials of the major governments talk with each other frequently in the context of the International Monetary Fund (IMF) and the Organization for Economic Cooperation and Development (OECD). Also, central bank senior officials meet monthly at the Basel meetings of the **Bank for International Settlements** (BIS). Since 1975, government officials of the seven largest industrial economies (United States, Canada, Japan, United Kingdom, Germany, France, and Italy), known as the **Group of Seven** (G-7), have met in annual economic summits to discuss economic issues of common concern. Not only do the G-7 nations initiate dialogues concerning economic objectives and policy, but they also devise economic indicators that provide a framework for multilateral surveillance of their economies and help monitor the international consequences of domestic policies.

Policy Coordination in Theory

If economic policies in each of two nations affect the other, then the case for policy coordination would appear to be obvious. Policy coordination is considered important in the modern world because economic disruptions are transmitted rapidly from one nation to another. Without policy coordination, national economic policies can destabilize other economies. The logic of policy coordination is illustrated in the following basketball spectator problem.[3]

Suppose you are attending a basketball game between the Seattle Supersonics and Portland Trail Blazers. If everyone is sitting, someone who stands has a superior view. Spectators usually can see well if everyone sits or if everyone stands. Sitting in seats is more comfortable than standing. When there is no cooperation, everyone stands; each spectator does what is best for herself/himself given the actions of other spectators. If all spectators sit, someone, taking what the others will do as a given, will stand. If all spectators are standing, then it is best to remain standing. With spectator cooperation, the solution is for everyone to sit. The problem is that each spectator may be tempted to get a better view by standing. The cooperative solution will not be attained, therefore, without an outright agreement on coordination—in this situation, everyone remains seated.

Consider the following economic example. Suppose the world consists of just two nations, Germany and Japan. Although these nations freely trade goods with each other, they desire to pursue their own domestic economic priorities. Germany wants to avoid trade deficits with Japan, while achieving full employment for its economy; Japan desires full employment for its economy, while avoiding trade deficits with Germany. Assume that both nations achieve balanced trade with each other, but each nation's economy operates below full employment. Germany and Japan contemplate enacting expansionary government spending policies that would stimulate demand, output, and employment. But each nation rejects the idea, recognizing the policy's adverse impact on the trade balance. Germany and Japan realize that bolstering domestic income to increase jobs has the side effect of stimulating the demand for imports, thus pushing the trade account into deficit.

The preceding situation is favorable for successful policy coordination. If Germany and Japan agree to simultaneously expand their government spending, then output, employment, and incomes will rise concurrently. While higher German income promotes increased imports from Japan, higher Japanese income promotes increased imports from Germany. An appropriate increase in government spending results in each nation's increased demand for imports being offset by an increased demand for exports, which leads to balanced trade between Germany and Japan. In our example of mutual implementation of expansionary fiscal policies, policy coordination permits each nation to achieve full employment and balanced trade.

This is an optimistic portrayal of international economic policy coordination. The synchronization of policies appears simple because there are only two economies and two objectives. In the real world, however, policy coordination generally involves many countries and many diverse objectives, such as low inflation, high employment, economic growth, and trade balance.

If the benefits of international economic policy coordination are really so obvious, it may seem odd that agreements do not occur more often than they do. Several obstacles hinder successful policy coordination. Even if national economic objectives are harmonious, there is no guarantee that governments can design and implement coordinated policies. Policymakers in the real world do not always have sufficient information to understand the nature of the economic problem or how their policies will affect economies. Implementing appropriate policies when governments disagree about economic fundamentals is difficult.

Policy coordination is also complicated by different national starting points:[4]

1. *Different economic objectives.* Some nations give higher priority to price stability, for instance, or to full employment, than others.
2. *Different national institutions.* Some nations have a stronger legislature, or weaker trade unions, than others.
3. *Different national political climates.* The party pendulums in different nations, for example, shift with elections occurring in different years.

4. *Different phases in the business cycle.* One nation may experience economic recession while another nation experiences rapid inflation.

Although the theoretical advantages of international economic policy coordination are fairly clearly established, attempts to quantify their gains are rare. Skeptics point out that in practice, the gains from policy coordination are smaller than what is often suggested. Let us consider several examples of international economic policy coordination.

Bonn Summit Agreement of 1978

The **Bonn Summit Agreement** of 1978 is widely recognized as a rare instance in which the leading Western nations were able to achieve international economic policy coordination. During the early 1970s, economic performance in the industrial nations was suboptimal. Rising inflation and unemployment plagued the industrial economies. After the 1973 skyrocketing of oil prices, policy priorities emphasized dealing with the escalating price of oil and the need to avoid beggar-thy-neighbor trade policies. Expansionary fiscal policy was a favored instrument to help economies move toward full employment.

Current-account (balance-of-payments) deficits and inflation constraints, however, made it clear that nations acting on their own could not achieve overall balance. Although the U.S. economy recovered from the 1974–1975 recession, following a tax cut, its recovery contributed to a U.S. current-account deficit and a depreciation in the dollar's exchange value. Part of the reason for the current-account deficit was the U.S. policy of maintaining the domestic price of oil below the world price, which prevented any reduction in domestic demand for oil, reduced domestic supply, and thus promoted imports of large quantities of oil. U.S. trading partners maintained that the United States should initiate further efforts to promote energy conservation.

Germany, meanwhile, was concerned about its prospects for economic growth. Moreover, Germany and Japan were running current-account surpluses. The United States felt that these conditions warranted the enactment of expansionary fiscal and monetary policies by Germany and Japan. Such policies, it was hoped, would increase the demand for U.S. goods, thereby helping reduce the U.S. current-account deficit and strengthen the dollar. Germany and Japan would be "locomotives" that would pull the U.S. economy out of its current-account deficit. The elements of a policy coordination package seemed to exist.

At the 1978 Bonn Summit, the United States, Germany, and Japan addressed the problems of unemployment and oil-import dependence. An agreement was reached in which Germany and Japan would add a dose of fiscal stimulus (tax cuts or government spending increases) to their economies in exchange for a commitment by the United States to raise domestic oil prices to world levels and reduce inflationary pressures. Proponents of the Bonn Summit Agreement maintained that it represented a coordinated package in which actions were pledged by each nation in return for specific undertakings by others.

Although the Bonn Summit Agreement provides an example of international economic policy coordination, it is now widely believed to have been a failure in substantive terms. As the German and Japanese policies of fiscal stimulus were having their effect, the OPEC nations engineered a sharp increase in crude-oil prices in 1979, fueling inflationary fears in Germany. Despite efforts to reduce the U.S. current-account imbalance, the dollar continued to weaken into 1979. The United States attempted to persuade Germany to intervene in the foreign exchange markets, while the Germans called for further adjustments in U.S. policy. The onset of unexpected inflation and conflicts over continued adjustment of policies led to abandonment of the agreement.

Plaza Agreement of 1985 and Louvre Accord of 1987

By early 1984, the U.S. economy was recovering from the recession of 1981–1983; domestic output was rising and unemployment was falling. While an expansionary fiscal policy contributed to economic recovery, growing U.S. government budget deficits were causing concern about the stability of the world financial system. Equally problematic was the appreciation in the dollar's exchange value, which encouraged U.S. consumers to purchase cheaper imports and resulted in large U.S. trade deficits. By 1985, it was estimated that the dollar was overvalued by about 30–35 percent. As the U.S. recovery slowed, protectionist pressures skyrocketed in the U.S. Congress.

U.S. trading partners were also exasperated by the hands-off approach of the Reagan administration. During the early 1980s, they had pleaded for a reduction in the U.S. budget deficits and a depreciation in the dollar's exchange value, but to no avail. The exchange values of the industrial nations' currencies oscillated, straining the world trading system. Trade wars, both between the United States and Western Europe and between the United States and Japan, seemed a possibility. This was the environment that led to the **Plaza Agreement** of 1985.

Fearing a disaster in the world trading system, government officials of the **Group of Five** (G-5) nations—the United States, Japan, Germany, Great Britain, and France—met at New York's Plaza Hotel in September 1985. There was widespread agreement that the dollar was overvalued and that the twin U.S. deficits (trade and federal budget) were too large. The Plaza strategy was threefold: (1) to combat protectionism in the U.S. Congress, a short-term strategy; (2) to promote world economic expansion by stimulating demand in Germany and Japan, a medium-term strategy; and (3) to ease the burden of the U.S. debt service, a long-term strategy.

The Plaza strategy was presented as a comprehensive package that included monetary, fiscal, and exchange-rate policies. To stimulate demand, German and Japanese officials agreed to more expansionary fiscal policies—accelerating planned tax cuts and expanding spending programs, respectively. For its part, the United States agreed to attempt to bring down its budget deficit. Moreover, all participants agreed to intervene in the currency markets, when necessary, to further the dollar's orderly decline. The Plaza Agreement represented an abrupt change in policy for the Reagan administration, a reversal of its opposition to foreign-exchange intervention.

Prior to the 1985 Plaza meeting, some participants were skeptical that concerted intervention could push the U.S. dollar down sufficiently to dampen protectionist sentiments in the U.S. Congress. Nevertheless, concerted intervention was decided upon, and the operation succeeded beyond expectations. The objective of intervention was to **lean with the wind**, accelerating the downward pace of the already depreciating U.S. dollar. Large-scale intervention occurred in the month after the Plaza Agreement; the dollar's trade-weighted exchange value fell sharply after the agreement and continued to fall through the spring of 1986. At that time, central bankers began to indicate reservations about the dollar's continued depreciation, and central bankers in the non-U.S. industrial countries intervened heavily to support the dollar's value.

The Plaza Agreement complicated the Federal Reserve's mission of pursuing both domestic and international objectives. To lower the dollar's exchange value, the Federal Reserve would have to adopt an expansionary monetary policy that would force down domestic interest rates; this would induce investment outflows, a lower demand for the dollar, and a depreciation in the dollar's value. The Federal Reserve's concern, however, was that such a policy would intensify U.S. inflation. It would then have to decide whether to give higher priority to fighting inflation, which would call for a restrictive monetary policy, or to promoting a dollar depreciation, which would call for an expansionary monetary policy. It turned out that 1985 was a year of modest inflation, and the Federal Reserve was able to give higher priority to international objectives.

The Plaza Agreement was generally viewed as a success, though not an unqualified one. In 1987, citing increased inflationary pressures, German officials were cautious in approaching implementation of the coordinated fiscal policy expansion agreed to in the Plaza accord. This development did not set well with the United States, which disagreed over the extent to which accelerating inflation was a problem in West Germany. The slow progress on reducing the federal budget deficit in the United States, especially during the second half of 1987, also strained the pact. Other nations were understandably reluctant to enact stimulative policies without evidence of fiscal restraint in the United States. The agreement, however, survived numerous attacks, with the participating nations repeatedly expressing their support for it.

By early 1987, the dollar's exchange value had become a topic of disagreement among the G-5 nations. The United States continued to pressure foreign governments for further dollar depreciation to help restore current-account balance. Officials of other G-5 nations, however, maintained that appreciation of their currencies against the dollar had gone far enough. In February 1987, the G-5 nations plus Canada meet at the Louvre in Paris. In the **Louvre Accord**, these six nations agreed to stabilize exchange rates around levels then prevailing, which officials considered as generally harmonious with underlying economic fundamentals.

SUMMARY

1. International economic policy refers to various government activities that influence trade patterns among nations, including (a) monetary and fiscal policies, (b) exchange-rate adjustments, (c) tariff and nontariff trade barriers, (d) foreign-exchange controls and investment controls, and (5) export-promotion measures.

2. Since the 1930s, nations have actively pursued internal balance (full employment without inflation) as a primary economic objective. Nations also consider external balance (balance-of-payments equilibrium) as an economic objective. A nation realizes overall balance when it attains internal balance and external balance.

3. To achieve overall balance, nations implement expenditure-changing policies (monetary and fiscal policies), expenditure-switching policies (exchange-rate adjustments), and direct controls (price and wage controls).

4. Although exchange-rate adjustments primarily influence a nation's BOP position, they have secondary impacts on the domestic economy. A nation with a BOP deficit and high unemployment could devalue its currency to resolve these problems; a nation with a BOP surplus and inflation could revalue its currency. Such policies are dependent upon the willingness of other nations to refrain from implementing offsetting exchange-rate adjustments. International economic policy cooperation is thus essential when nations are economically interdependent.

5. Under a fixed exchange-rate system, fiscal policy is successful in promoting internal balance, whereas monetary policy is unsuccessful. Under a floating exchange-rate system, monetary policy is successful in promoting internal balance, whereas fiscal policy is unsuccessful.

6. Given a fixed exchange-rate system, in the short run, an expansionary monetary policy worsens the BOP position and a contractionary monetary policy improves the BOP position. An expansionary fiscal policy leads to a worsening of the trade account and an improvement in the capital account; the impact on the overall BOP depends on the relative strength of these opposing forces.

7. Policy agreement occurs when an economic policy helps eliminate internal disequilibrium and external disequilibrium, thus promoting overall balance for the nation. Policy conflict occurs when an economic policy helps eliminate one economic problem (such as internal disequilibrium), but aggravates another economic problem (such as external disequilibrium).

8. Given a fixed exchange-rate system, for monetary policy the disequilibrium zones of unemployment-with-BOP-surplus and inflation-with-BOP-deficit are zones of policy agreement. The disequilibrium zones of unemployment-with-BOP-deficit and inflation-with-BOP-surplus are zones of policy conflict; a dilemma exists for monetary authorities concerning which objective to pursue. A combination of policies may be needed to resolve these economic problems.

9. When a nation experiences inflation and unemployment (stagflation), achieving overall balance involves three separate targets: BOP equilibrium, full employment, and price stability. Three policy instruments may be needed to achieve these targets.

10. International economic policy coordination is the attempt to significantly modify national policies in recognition of international economic interdependence. Nations regularly consult with each other in the context of the IMF, OECD, Bank for International Settlements, and Group of Seven. The Bonn Summit Agreement, Plaza Accord, and Louvre Accord are examples of international economic policy coordination.

11. Several problems confront international economic policy coordination: (a) different national economic objectives, (b) different national institutions, (c) different national political climates, and (d) different phases in the business cycle. Moreover, there is no guarantee that governments can design and implement policies that are capable of achieving the intended results.

STUDY QUESTIONS

1. Distinguish among external balance, internal balance, and overall balance.

2. What are the most important instruments of international economic policy?

3. What is meant by the terms *expenditure-changing policy* and *expenditure-switching policy*? Give some examples of each.

4. What institutional constraints bear on the formation of economic policies?

5. Assume that a nation faces a BOP deficit with high unemployment. What exchange-rate adjustment can be made to resolve these problems? What if the nation experiences a BOP surplus with inflation?

6. Under a system of fixed exchange rates, is monetary policy or fiscal policy better suited for promoting internal balance? Why?

7. Under a system of floating exchange rates, is monetary policy or fiscal policy better suited for promoting internal balance? Why?

8. With fixed exchange rates, what impact does an expansionary monetary policy have on the nation's BOP? What about a contractionary monetary policy?

9. With fixed exchange rates, when does an expansionary fiscal policy improve the nation's BOP? When does it worsen the BOP?

10. What is meant by the terms *policy agreement* and *policy conflict*?

11. Given a system of fixed exchange rates, for monetary policy, is unemployment-with-BOP-surplus a zone of policy agreement or policy conflict? What about inflation-with-BOP-deficit, unemployment-with-BOP-deficit, or inflation-with-BOP-surplus?

12. What are some obstacles to successful international economic policy coordination?

International Banking: Reserves, Debt, and Risk

Commercial banks (such as Citicorp) and *central banks* (such as the International Monetary Fund) play a vital role in facilitating international transactions. They help finance trade and investment and provide loans to international borrowers. This chapter concentrates on the role that banks play in world financial markets, the risks associated with international banking, and strategies employed to deal with these risks.

We'll begin with an investigation of the nature of international reserves and their importance for the world financial system. This is followed by a discussion of central banks and commercial banks as international lenders and the problems associated with international debt.

NATURE OF INTERNATIONAL RESERVES

A central bank's need for international reserves is similar to a householder's desire to hold cash balances (currency and checkable deposits). At both levels, monetary reserves are intended to bridge the gap between monetary receipts and monetary payments.

Suppose that a householder receives income in equal installments every minute of the day and that expenditures for goods and services are likewise evenly spaced over time. The householder will require only a minimum cash reserve to finance purchases, because no significant imbalances between cash receipts and cash disbursements will arise. In reality, however, most householders purchase goods and services on a fairly regular basis from day to day, but receive paychecks only at weekly or longer intervals. A certain amount of cash is therefore required to finance the discrepancy that arises between monetary receipts and payments.

When a householder initially receives a paycheck, cash balances are high. But as time progresses, these holdings of cash may fall to virtually zero just before the next paycheck is received. Householders are thus concerned with the amount of cash balances that, on average, are necessary to keep them going until the next paycheck arrives. Although householders desire cash balances primarily to fill the gap between monetary receipts and payments, this desire is influenced by a number of other factors. The need for cash balances may become more acute if the absolute dollar volume of transactions increases, because larger imbalances may result between receipts and payments. Conversely, to the extent that householders can finance their transactions on credit, they require less cash in hand.

Just as an individual householder desires to hold cash balances, national governments have a need for **international reserves**. The chief purpose of international reserves is to enable nations to finance disequilibria in their balance-of-payments positions. When a nation finds its monetary receipts falling short of its monetary payments, the deficit is settled by international reserves. Eventually, the deficit must be eliminated, because central banks tend to have limited stocks of reserves. The advantage of international reserves from a policy perspective is that they enable nations to sustain *temporary* balance-of-payments deficits until acceptable adjustment measures can operate to correct the disequilibrium. Holdings of international reserves facilitate effective policy formation

because corrective adjustment measures need not be implemented prematurely. Should a deficit nation possess abundant stocks of reserve balances, however, it may be able to resist unpopular adjustment measures, making eventual adjustments even more troublesome.

DEMAND FOR INTERNATIONAL RESERVES

When a nation's international monetary payments exceed its international monetary receipts, some means of settlement is required to finance its payments deficit. Settlement ultimately consists of transfers of international reserves among nations. Both the magnitude and the longevity of a balance-of-payments deficit that can be sustained in the absence of equilibrating adjustments are limited by a nation's stock of international reserves. On a global basis, the **demand for international reserves** depends on two related factors: (1) the monetary value of international transactions and (2) the disequilibria that can arise in balance-of-payments positions. The demand for international reserves is also contingent on such things as the speed and strength of the balance-of-payments adjustment mechanism and the overall institutional framework of the world economy.

Exchange-Rate Flexibility

One determinant of the demand for international reserves is the degree of *exchange-rate flexibility* of the international monetary system. This is because exchange-rate flexibility in part underlies the efficiency of the balance-of-payments adjustment process.

Figure 18.1 represents the exchange-market position of the United States in trade with Great Britain. Starting at equilibrium point *E*, suppose that an increase in imports increases the U.S. demand for pounds from D_0 to D_1. The prevailing exchange-rate system will determine the quantity of international reserves

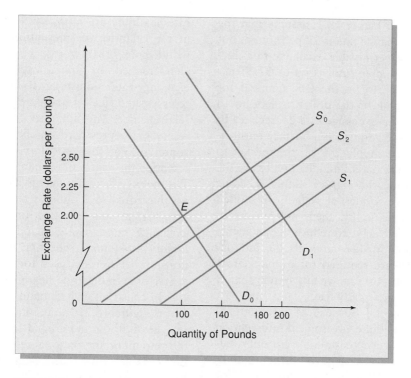

F I G U R E 18. 1 *The demand for international reserves and exchange-rate flexibility.* When exchange rates are fixed (pegged) by monetary authorities, international reserves are necessary for the financing of payments imbalances and the stabilization of exchange rates. With floating exchange rates, payments imbalances tend to be corrected by market-induced fluctuations in the exchange rate; the need for exchange-rate stabilization and international reserves disappears.

needed to bridge the gap between the number of pounds demanded and the number supplied.

If exchange rates are fixed or pegged by the monetary authorities, international reserves play a crucial role in the exchange-rate stabilization process. In Figure 18.1, suppose the exchange rate is pegged at $2 per pound. Given a rise in the demand for pounds from D_0 to D_1, the United States would face an excess demand for pounds equal to £100 at the pegged rate. If the U.S. dollar is not to depreciate beyond the pegged rate, the monetary authorities must enter the market to supply pounds (in exchange for dollars) in an amount necessary to eliminate the disequilibrium. In the figure, the pegged rate

of $2 per pound can be maintained if the monetary authorities supply £100 on the market. Coupled with the existing supply schedule S_0, the added supply will result in a new supply schedule at S_1. Market equilibrium is restored at the pegged rate.

Rather than operating under a rigidly pegged system, suppose a nation makes an agreement to foster some automatic adjustments by allowing market rates to float within a narrow band around the official exchange rate. This limited exchange-rate flexibility would be aimed at correcting minor payments imbalances, whereas large and persistent disequilibria would require other adjustment measures.

Referring to Figure 18.1, assume that the U.S. official exchange rate is $2 per pound, but with a band of permissible exchange-rate fluctuations whose upper limit is set at $2.25 per pound. Given a rise in the U.S. demand for pounds, the value of the dollar will begin to decline. Once the exchange rate depreciates to $2.25 per pound, domestic monetary authorities will need to supply £40 on the market to defend the band's outer limit. This will have the effect of shifting the market supply schedule from S_0 to S_2. Under a system of limited exchange-rate flexibility, then, movements in the exchange rate serve to reduce the payments disequilibrium. Smaller amounts of international reserves are required for exchange-rate stabilization purposes under this system than if exchange rates are rigidly fixed.

A fundamental purpose of international reserves is to facilitate government intervention in exchange markets to stabilize currency values. The more active a government's stabilization activities, the greater is the need for reserves. Most exchange-rate standards today involve some stabilization operations and require international reserves. However, if exchange rates were allowed to float freely without government interference, theoretically there would be no need for reserves. This is because a floating rate would serve to eliminate an incipient payments imbalance, negating the need for stabilization operations. Referring again to Figure 18.1, suppose the exchange market is initially in equilibrium at a rate of $2 per pound. Given an increase in the demand for foreign exchange from D_0 to D_1, the home currency would begin to depreciate. It would continue to weaken until it reached an exchange value of $2.50 per pound, at which point market equilibrium would be restored. The need for international reserves would thus be nonexistent under freely floating rates.

Other Determinants

The lesson to be learned from the previous section is that changes in the degree of exchange-rate flexibility are *inversely related* to changes in the quantity of international reserves demanded. In other words, a monetary system characterized by more rapid and flexible exchange-rate adjustments requires smaller reserves, and vice versa. Figure 18.2 depicts this relationship. The quantity of international reserves is represented on the diagram's horizontal axis; on the vertical axis is an index representing the degree of exchange-rate flexibility. The index of flexibility would have, as its limits, a value equal to 1 under a floating exchange-rate system and a value of 0 under fixed exchange rates. The demand for reserves is *downward-sloping*, reflecting the inverse relationship between the need for reserves and the degree of exchange-rate flexibility.

In constructing a demand schedule such as D_0 in Figure 18.2, we assume that exchange-rate flexibility is the crucial factor underlying the amount of international reserves demanded. But variables other than exchange-rate flexibility can and do exert an influence on the desire for reserves. A given demand schedule assumes that these other factors are held constant. When these determinants undergo changes, the demand schedule will shift outward to the right or inward to the left.

What are the major determinants of the demand for international reserves, other than the exchange rate? Among the most important are (1) automatic adjustment mechanisms that respond to payments disequilibria, (2) economic policies used to bring about payments equilibrium, and (3) the international coordination of economic policies. Our earlier analysis has shown that adjustment mechanisms involving prices, interest rates, incomes, and monetary flows automatically tend to correct balance-of-payments disequilibria. A payments deficit or surplus initiates changes in each of these variables. The more efficient each of these adjustment mechanisms is, the smaller and more short-lived market imbalances will be and the fewer reserves will be needed. The demand for international reserves therefore tends to be

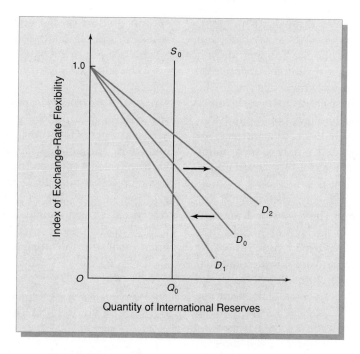

F I G U R E 18. 2 *International reserves: supply and demand.*
Besides being governed by the degree of exchange-rate flexibility, the
demand for international reserves is influenced by (1) automatic
adjustment mechanisms (prices, interest rates, income) that respond
to payments disequilibria, (2) domestic economic policies that promote payments equilibrium, and (3) international coordination of
economic policies.

smaller (shifts leftward in Figure 18.2) with
speedier and more complete automatic adjustment mechanisms.

The demand for international reserves is
also influenced by the choice and effectiveness
of government policies adopted to correct payments imbalances. Unlike automatic adjustment mechanisms, which rely on the free market to identify industries and labor groups that
must bear the adjustment burden, the use of
government policies involves political decisions.
All else being equal, the greater a nation's
propensity to apply commercial policies (including tariffs, quotas, and subsidies) to key
sectors, the less will be its need for international
reserves. This assumes, of course, that the poli-

cies are effective in reducing payments disequilibria. Because of uncertainties about the nature
and timing of payments disturbances, however,
nations are often slow to initiate such trade
policies and find themselves requiring international reserves to weather periods of payments
disequilibria.

The international coordination of economic policies is another determinant of the
demand for international reserves. A primary
goal of economic cooperation among finance
ministers is to reduce the frequency and extent
of payments imbalances and hence the demand
for international reserves. Since the end of
World War II, nations have moved toward the
harmonization of national economic objectives

by establishing programs through such organizations as the International Monetary Fund and the Organization of Economic Cooperation and Development. Another example of international economic organization has been the European Community, whose goal is to achieve a common macroeconomic policy and full monetary union. By reducing the intensity of disturbances to payments balance, such policy coordination reduces the need for international reserves.

Other factors influence the demand for international reserves. The quantity demanded is positively related to the level of world prices and income. One would expect rising price levels to inflate the market value of international transactions, and therefore to increase the potential demand for reserves. The need for reserves would also be expected to rise with the level of global income and trade activity.

In summary, central banks need international reserves to cover possible or expected excess payments to other nations at some future time. The quantity of international reserves demanded is directly related to the size and duration of these payment gaps. If a nation with a payments deficit is willing and able to initiate quick actions to increase receipts or decrease payments, the amount of reserves needed will be relatively small. Conversely, the demand for reserves will be relatively large if nations initiate no actions to correct payments imbalances or adopt policies that prolong such disequilibria.

SUPPLY OF INTERNATIONAL RESERVES

The analysis so far has emphasized the demand for international reserves. But what about the **supply of international reserves?** For simplicity, assume that the quantity of reserves is given and constant at Q_0 in Figure 18.2. The supply schedule of reserves is denoted by the vertical line S_0 in the figure. This assumption corresponds well to reality if there are reserve assets, such as gold or special drawing rights (SDRs), whose sources are independent of the monetary system's degree of exchange-rate flexibility.

The total supply of international reserves consists of two distinct categories, *owned reserves* and *borrowed reserves*. Reserve assets such as gold, acceptable foreign currencies, and SDRs are generally considered to be directly owned by the holding nations. But if nations with payments deficits find their stocks of owned reserves falling to unacceptably low levels, they may be able to borrow international reserves as a cushioning device. Lenders may be foreign nations with excess reserves, foreign financial institutions, or international agencies such as the IMF.

FOREIGN CURRENCIES

International reserves are a means of payment used in financing foreign transactions. As long as they are generally acceptable to foreign payees, reserve assets can be an effective medium of exchange. One such asset is holdings of *national currencies* (foreign exchange). As seen in Table 18.1, the largest share of international reserves today consists of national currency holdings.

Over the course of the 1800s–1900s, two national currencies in particular have gained prominence as means of financing international transactions. These currencies, the U.S. dollar and the British pound, have been considered *reserve (key) currencies* because trading nations have traditionally been willing to hold them along with gold as international reserve assets. Since World War II, the U.S. dollar has been the dominant reserve currency. Other reserve currencies are the British pound, German mark, French franc, Japanese yen, and a few other currencies that are acceptable in payment for international transactions.

The role of the pound as a reserve currency is due largely to circumstances of the late 1800s and early 1900s. Not only did Britain at that time play a dominant role in world trade, but

The International Monetary Fund

The International Monetary Fund (IMF) was one of two international institutions established near the end of World War II to ease the transition from a wartime to a peacetime environment and to help prevent a recurrence of the turbulent economic conditions of the Great Depression era. The IMF and the World Bank (the International Bank for Reconstruction and Development) were established at the United Nations Monetary and Financial Conference held at Bretton Woods, New Hampshire, in July 1944. The World Bank's main purpose is to make long-term development and reconstruction loans, whereas the IMF provides short-term balance-of-payments adjustment loans.

Today, the IMF includes more than 150 nations. The goals of the IMF are (1) to promote international cooperation by providing the means for members to consult on international monetary issues; (2) to facilitate the growth of international trade and foster a multilateral system of international payments; (3) to promote stability of exchange rates and seek the elimination of exchange restrictions that disrupt international trade; and (4) to make short-term financial resources available to member nations on a temporary basis so as to allow them to correct payments disequilibria without resorting to measures that would destroy national prosperity.

The IMF can be thought of as a large group of nations that come together and combine resources. Over a given time period, some nations will face balance-of-payments surpluses while others will face deficits. Nations experiencing payments deficits initially draw on their stock of international reserves (such as the dollar) that are accepted in payment by other nations. However, the deficit nation will sometimes have insufficient amounts of international reserves. That is when other nations, via the IMF, can provide assistance. By making available international reserves to the IMF, the surplus nations channel funds to nations with temporary payments deficits. Over the long run, payments deficits must be corrected, and the IMF attempts to ensure that this adjustment will be as prompt and orderly as possible.

The IMF's loanable resources come from two major sources: quotas and loans. Quotas (or subscriptions), which are pooled funds of member nations, generate most of the IMF's loanable funds.

(continued)

the efficiency of London as an international money market was widely recognized. This was the golden age of the gold standard, and the pound was freely convertible into gold. Traders and investors felt confident financing their transactions with pounds. With the demise of the gold standard and the onset of the Great Depression during the 1930s, Britain's commercial and financial status began to deteriorate, and the pound lost some of its international luster. Today, the pound still serves as an important international reserve asset, but its status as the most prestigious reserve currency has been replaced by the U.S. dollar.

The emergence of the U.S. dollar as a reserve currency stems from a different set of circumstances. Emerging from World War II, the U.S. economy was not only unharmed but actually stronger. Because of the vast inflows of gold into the United States during the 1930s and 1940s, the dollar was in a better position than the pound to assume the role of a reserve currency.

The mechanism that supplied the world with dollar balances was the balance-of-payments deficits of the United States. These deficits stemmed largely from U.S. foreign aid granted to Europe immediately following

The International Monetary Fund

(continued)

The size of a member's quota depends on its economic and financial importance in the world; nations with larger economic importance have larger quotas. The quotas are increased periodically as a means of boosting the IMF's resources. The IMF also obtains loanable resources through loans from member nations. The IMF has "lines of credit" with major industrial nations as well as with Saudi Arabia. Interest and other terms on IMF borrowing arrangements vary considerably. Frequently, interest is charged according to a floating rate, and loans are repaid within five to seven years.

Member nations can draw against the IMF's pooled and borrowed funds to finance temporary balance-of-payments deficits. Deficit nations borrow from the IMF by purchasing the currencies of other member nations (typically, dollars or other major currencies) or SDRs with their own currencies. The IMF's resources are available for limited periods, and members that purchase foreign currencies from the IMF must subsequently repurchase their own currencies, thus repaying the loan.

All IMF loans are subject to some degree of *conditionality*. This means that, to obtain a loan, a deficit nation must agree to implement economic and financial policies as stipulated by the IMF. These policies are intended to correct the member's balance-of-payments deficit and promote non-inflationary economic growth. However, the conditionality attachment to IMF lending has often met strong resistance among deficit nations. The IMF has sometimes demanded that deficit nations undergo austerity programs, including the slashing of public spending and private consumption and the reduction of imports, in order to live within their means.

The IMF makes its assistance available through a number of different programs, which vary with international economic conditions (for example, buffer stock facility or oil facility). The IMF generally finances only part of a member's payments deficit. In addition, IMF assistance is sometimes made in loose connection with World Bank lending, a portion of which can be used for balance-of-payments adjustment loans.

World War II, as well as from the flow of private investment funds abroad from U.S. residents. The early 1950s were characterized as a *dollar-shortage* era when the massive development programs of the European nations resulted in an excess demand for the dollars used to finance such efforts. As the United States began to run modest payments deficits during the early 1950s, the dollar outflow was appreciated by the recipient nations.

By the late 1950s, the U.S. payments deficits had become larger. As foreign nations began to accumulate larger dollar balances than they were accustomed to, the dollar-shortage era gave way to a *dollar glut*. Throughout the 1960s, the United States continued to provide reserves to the world through its payments deficits. However, the persistently weak position of the U.S. balance of payments increasingly led foreigners to question the soundness of the dollar as a reserve currency. By 1970, the amount of dollar liabilities in the hands of foreigners was several times as large as U.S. reserve assets. Lack of confidence in the soundness of the dollar inspired several European nations to exercise their rights to demand that the U.S. Treasury convert their dollar holdings into gold, which in turn led the United States to sus-

TABLE 18. 1 / International Reserves, 1992, All Countries (in Billions of SDRs*)

Item	Amount	Percentage
Gold†	33.0	4.5
Foreign exchange	648.9	89.2
IMF reserve positions	25.5	3.5
SDRs	20.6	2.8
Total	728.0	100.0

* For 1992, 1 SDR = $1.43.

†At 35 SDRs per ounce.

SOURCE: International Monetary Fund, *International Financial Statistics,* December 1992, pp. 20–31.

pend its gold convertibility pledge to the rest of the world in 1971.

Using the dollar as a reserve currency meant that the supply of international reserves varied with the payments position of the United States. During the 1960s, this situation gave rise to the so-called **liquidity problem,** which involved the following dilemma. To preserve confidence in the dollar as a reserve currency, the United States had to strengthen its payments position by eliminating its deficits. But correction of the U.S. deficits would mean elimination of additional dollars as a source of reserves for the international monetary system. The creation in 1970 of SDRs as reserve assets and their subsequent allocations have been intended as a solution for this problem.

GOLD

The historical importance of gold as an international reserve asset should not be underemphasized. At one time, gold served as the key monetary asset of the international payments mechanism; it also constituted the basis of

many nations' money supplies. As an international money, gold fulfilled several important functions. Under the historic **gold standard,** gold served directly as an international means of payments. It also provided a unit of account against which commodity prices as well as the parities of national currencies were quoted. Although gold holdings do not yield interest income, gold has generally served as a viable store of value despite inflation, wars, and revolutions. Perhaps the greatest advantage of gold as a monetary asset is its overall acceptability, especially when compared with other forms of international monies.

Today, the role of gold as an international reserve asset has declined. Over the past 30 years, gold has fallen from nearly 70 percent to about 5 percent of world reserves. Private individuals rarely use gold as a medium of payment and virtually never as a unit of account. Nor do central banks currently use gold as an official unit of account for stating the parities of national currencies. The monetary role of gold is currently recognized by only a few nations, mostly in the Middle East. In most nations outside the United States, private residents have long been able to buy and sell gold as they would any other commodity. On December 31, 1974, the U.S. government revoked a 41-year ban on U.S. citizens' ownership of gold. The monetary role of gold today is only that of a glittering ghost haunting efforts to reform the international monetary system.

International Gold Standard

Under the international gold standard, which reached its golden age during the 1880–1914 period, the values of most national currencies were anchored in gold. Gold coins circulated within these countries as well as across national boundaries as generally accepted means of payment. Monetary authorities were concerned about maintaining the public's confidence in the paper currencies that supplemented gold's role as money. To maintain the integrity of paper currencies, governments agreed to convert them into gold at a fixed rate. This requirement was supposed to prevent monetary authorities from producing excessive amounts of paper money. The so-called *discipline* of the gold standard was achieved by having the money supply bear a fixed relation to the monetary stock of gold. Given the cost of producing gold relative to the cost of other commodities, a monetary price of gold could be established to produce growth in monetary gold—and thus in the money supply—at a rate that corresponded to the growth in real national output.

Over the course of the gold standard's era, the importance of gold began to decline, whereas both paper money and demand deposits showed marked increases. From 1815 to 1913, gold as a share of the aggregate money supply of the United States, France, and Britain fell from about 33 percent to 10 percent. At the same time, the proportion of bank deposits skyrocketed from a modest 6 percent to about 68 percent. By 1913, paper monies plus demand deposits accounted for approximately 90 percent of the U.S. money supply.

After World War I, popular sentiment favored a return to the discipline of the gold standard, in part because of the inflation that gripped many economies during the war years. The United States was the first to return to the gold standard, followed by several European nations. Efforts to restore the prewar gold standard, however, ended in complete collapse during the 1930s. In response to the economic strains of the Great Depression, nations one by one announced that they could no longer maintain the gold standard.

As for the United States, the Great Depression brought an important modification of the gold standard. In 1934, the Gold Reserve Act gave the U.S. government title to all monetary gold, and citizens turned in their private holdings to the U.S. Treasury. This was done because the government wanted to end the pressure on U.S. commercial banks to convert their liabilities into gold. The U.S. dollar was also devalued in 1934, when the official price of gold was raised from $20.67 to $35 per ounce. The dollar devaluation was not specifically aimed at defending the U.S. trade balance. The rationale was that a rise in the domestic price of gold would encourage gold production, adding to the money supply and the level of economic activity. The Great Depression would be solved! In retrospect, the devaluation may have had some minor economic effects, but there is no indication that it did anything to lift the economy out of its depressed condition.

Gold Exchange Standard

Emerging from the discussions among the world powers during World War II was a new international monetary organization, the International Monetary Fund. A main objective of the fund was to reestablish a system of fixed exchange rates, with gold serving as the primary reserve asset. Gold became an international unit of account when member nations officially agreed to state the par values of their currencies in terms of gold or, alternatively, the gold content of the U.S. dollar. The post–World War II international monetary system as formulated by the fund nations was nominally a **gold exchange standard**. The idea was to economize on monetary gold stocks as international reserves, because they could not expand as fast as international trade was growing. This required the United States, which emerged from the war with a dominant economy in terms of productive capacity and national wealth, to assume the role of world banker. The dollar was to become the international monetary system's chief reserve currency. The coexistence of both dollars and gold as international reserve assets led to this system's being dubbed the *dollar-gold system.*

As a world banker, the United States assumed responsibility for buying and selling gold at a fixed price to foreign official holders of dollars. The dollar was the only currency that was made convertible into gold; other national currencies were pegged to the dollar. The dollar was therefore regarded as a reserve currency that was as good as gold because it was thought that the dollar would retain its value relative to other currencies and remain convertible into gold. As long as the monetary gold stocks of the United States were large relative to outstanding dollar liabilities abroad, confidence in the dollar as a viable reserve currency remained intact. Immediately following World War II, the U.S. monetary gold stocks peaked at $24 billion, about two-thirds of the world total. But as time passed, the amount of foreign dollar holdings rose significantly because of the U.S. payments deficits, whereas the U.S. monetary gold stock dwindled as some of the dollars were turned back to the U.S. Treasury for gold. By 1965, the total supply of foreign-held dollars exceeded the U.S. stock of monetary gold. With the United States unable to redeem all outstanding dollars for gold at $35 per ounce, its ability as a world banker to deliver on demand was questioned.

These circumstances led to speculation that the United States might attempt to solve its gold-shortage problem by devaluing the dollar. By increasing the official price of gold, a dollar devaluation would lead to a rise in the value of U.S. monetary gold stocks. To prevent speculative profits from any rise in the official price of gold, the United States along with several other nations in 1968 established a *two-tier gold system*. This consisted of an *official tier,* in which central banks could buy and sell gold for monetary purposes at the official price of $35 per ounce, and a *private market,* where gold as a commodity could be traded at the free market price. By separating the official gold market from the private gold market, the two-tier system was a step toward the complete demonetization of gold.

Demonetization of Gold

The formation of the two-tier gold system was a remedy that could only delay the inevitable collapse of the gold exchange standard. By 1971, the U.S. stock of monetary gold had declined to $11 billion, only a fraction of U.S. dollar liabilities to foreign central banks. The U.S. balance-of-payments position was also deteriorating dramatically. In August 1971, President Nixon announced that the United States was suspending its commitment to buy and sell gold at $35 per ounce. The closing of the gold window to foreign official holders brought an end to the gold exchange standard, and the last functional link between the dollar and monetary gold was severed.

It took several years for the world's monetary authorities to formalize the **demonetization of gold** as an international reserve asset. On January 1, 1975, the official price of gold was abolished as the unit of account for the international monetary system. National monetary authorities could enter into gold transactions at market-determined prices, and the use of gold was terminated by the IMF. It was agreed that one-sixth of the fund's gold would be auctioned at prevailing prices and the profits distributed to the less developed nations.

As for the United States, the 41-year ban on gold ownership for U.S. residents ended on January 1, 1975. Within a few weeks, the U.S. Treasury was auctioning a portion of its gold on the commodity markets. These actions were a signal by the United States that it would treat gold in the same way it treats any other commodity.

SPECIAL DRAWING RIGHTS

The liquidity and confidence problems of the gold exchange standard that resulted from reliance on the dollar and gold as international monies led in 1970 to the creation by the IMF of a new reserve asset, termed **special drawing rights (SDRs)**. The objective was to introduce into the payments mechanism a *new* reserve asset, in addition to the dollar and gold, that could be transferred among participating nations in settlement of payments deficits. With the IMF managing the stock of SDRs, world reserves would presumably grow in line with world commerce.

SDRs are unconditional rights to draw currencies of other nations. When the fund creates a certain number of SDRs, they are allocated to the member nations in proportion to the relative size of their fund quotas. Nations can then draw on their SDR balances in financing their payments deficits. The key point is that certain surplus nations are designated by the fund to trade their currencies for an equivalent amount in SDRs to deficit nations in need of foreign exchange reserves. Nations whose currencies are acquired as foreign exchange are not required to accept more than three times their initial SDR allotments. SDRs pay interest to surplus nations on their net holdings (the amount by which a nation's SDR balance exceeds its allocation as determined by its fund quota). Interest payments come from deficit nations that draw their SDR balances below their original allotments. The SDR interest rate is adjusted periodically in line with the short-term interest rates in world money markets. It is reviewed quarterly and adjusted on the basis of a formula that takes into account the short-term interest rates of the United States, the United Kingdom, Germany, France, and Japan.

When the SDR was initially adopted, it was agreed that its value should be maintained at a fixed tie to the U.S. dollar's par value, which was then expressed in terms of gold. The value of the SDR was originally set at $1 U.S. But this linkage became unacceptable following several monetary developments. With the suspension of U.S. gold convertibility in 1971, it was doubted whether the gold value of the dollar should serve as the official unit of account for international transactions. The United States was also making it known at that time that it wished to phase out gold as an international monetary instrument. Furthermore, the dollar's exchange rate against gold fell twice as the result of U.S. devaluations in 1971 and 1973. Finally, under the system of managed floating exchange rates adopted by

the industrialized nations in 1973, it became possible for the SDR's value to fluctuate against other currencies while still bearing a fixed tie to the dollar's value. In view of these problems, in 1974, a new method of SDR valuation was initiated—the **basket valuation**.

Basket valuation is intended to provide stability for the SDR's value under a system of fluctuating exchange rates, making the SDR more attractive as an international reserve asset. The SDR is called a basket currency because it is based on the value of five currencies—the U.S. dollar, German mark, Japanese yen, French franc, and British pound. An appreciation, or increase in value, of any one currency in the basket in terms of all other currencies will raise the value of the SDR in terms of each of the other currencies. Conversely, a depreciation, or decline in value, of any one currency will lower the value of the SDR in terms of each of the other currencies. Because the movements of some currencies can be offset or moderated by the movements of other currencies, the value of the SDR in terms of a group of currencies is likely to be relatively stable.

Besides helping nations finance balance-of-payments deficits, SDRs have a number of other uses. Some of the fund's member nations peg their currency values to the SDR. The SDR is the unit of account for IMF transactions and is used as a unit of account for individuals (such as exporters, importers, or investors) who desire protection against the risk of fluctuating exchange rates.

For example, several major banks in London offer certificates of deposit (CDs) denominated in SDRs. The major attraction of SDR-denominated CDs is that they offer investors a financial instrument that is less susceptible to exchange-rate fluctuations than financial assets denominated in any single currency. Although the SDR-denominated CDs are sold for and repaid in dollars, their dollar value at (or any time before) maturity depends on the dollar/SDR exchange rate. Because the dollar/SDR rate is a weighted average of the dollar exchange rates relative to other currencies in the

SDR basket, the exchange-rate gains or losses over the term of the deposit will be less than those for any one of the currencies making up the SDR. Therefore, by purchasing SDR-indexed CDs, investors can reduce their overall exchange-rate risk, because any losses on one currency may be offset by gains on another in the SDR basket.

Since its adoption in 1970, the SDR has gained in importance as an acceptable international reserve asset. Today, SDRs possess all the qualities of a genuine money and represent a net addition to international reserves as useful as dollars and gold. With the monetary future of gold in doubt, SDRs have become enhanced as a primary reserve asset because of the following attractive features.

The creation of SDRs has represented a first major step in providing a means of internationally controlled reserves for the world. The SDR is unlike the dollar, whose supply stemmed from the balance-of-payments deficits of the United States under the gold exchange standard. Nor is it like gold, the supply of which has often fluctuated owing to speculative and technological factors. Unlike gold, SDRs as bookkeeping entries are virtually costless to produce. Moreover, SDRs benefit the world in terms of the resources saved in bypassing gold production.

The use of SDRs also gives the world a more equitable method of distributing resources than does either the dollar or gold. When money is widely accepted as a means of payment, the issuer of money may benefit from what is referred to as **seigniorage**. This represents the value of resources that accrue to the issuer of money by virtue of the fact that money's face value exceeds the cost of producing it. Under the gold exchange standard, the United States as the principal issuer of international money (dollars) was widely criticized for enjoying an exorbitant financial privilege. The United States could attain considerable seigniorage benefits by running persistent deficits in its balance of payments. Under a pure gold standard, seigniorage gains accrued to gold-producing nations to the degree that the cost of producing gold was less than its official price. In contrast, the seigniorage gains of SDR creation have been distributed to participating nations in compliance with internationally determined standards.

FACILITIES FOR BORROWING RESERVES

The discussion so far has considered the different types of *owned reserves*—national currencies, gold, and SDRs. Various facilities for *borrowing reserves* have also been implemented for nations with weak balance-of-payments positions. Borrowed reserves do not eliminate the need for owned reserves, but they do add to the flexibility of the international monetary system by increasing the time available for nations to correct payments disequilibria. Let's examine the major forms of international credit.

IMF Drawings

One of the original purposes of the IMF was to help member nations finance balance-of-payments deficits. The fund has furnished a pool of revolving credit for nations in need of reserves. Temporary loans of foreign currency are made to deficit nations, which are expected to repay them within a stipulated time. The transactions by which the fund makes foreign currency loans available are called **IMF drawings**.

Deficit nations do not borrow from the fund. Instead they "purchase" with their own currency the foreign currency required to help finance deficits. When the nation's balance-of-payments position improves, it is expected to reverse the transaction and make repayment by repurchasing its currency from the fund. The fund currently allows members to purchase other currencies at their own option up to the first 50 percent of their fund quotas, which are based on the nation's economic size. Special permission must be granted by the fund if a nation is to purchase foreign currencies in excess of this figure. The fund extends such permission once it is convinced the deficit nation has enacted reasonable measures to restore payments equilibrium.

Since the early 1950s, the fund has also fostered liberal exchange-rate policies by entering into *standby arrangements* with interested member nations. These agreements guarantee that a member nation may draw specified amounts of foreign currencies from the fund over given time periods. The advantage is that participating nations can count on credit from the fund should it be needed. It also saves the drawing nation from administrative time delays when the loans are actually made.

General Arrangements to Borrow

During the early 1960s, the question was raised whether the IMF had sufficient amounts of foreign currencies to meet the exchange stabilization needs of its deficit member nations. Owing to the possibility that large drawings by major nations might exhaust the fund's stocks of foreign currencies, the **General Arrangements to Borrow** were initiated in 1962. Ten leading industrial nations, called the Group of Ten, originally agreed to lend the fund up to a maximum of $6 billion. In 1964, the membership expanded when Switzerland joined the group. By serving as an intermediary and guarantor, the fund could use these reserves to offer compensatory financial assistance to one or more of the participating nations. Such credit arrangements presumably would be used only when the deficit nation's borrowing needs exceeded the amount of assistance that could be provided under the fund's own drawing facilities.

The General Arrangements to Borrow do *not* provide a permanent increase in the supply of world reserves once the loans are repaid and world reserves revert back to their original levels. However, these arrangements have made world reserves more flexible and adaptable to the needs of deficit nations.

Swap Arrangements

During the early 1960s, there occurred a wave of speculative attacks against the U.S. dollar, which was expected by many to be devalued in terms of other currencies. To help offset the flow of short-term capital out of the dollar into stronger foreign currencies, the U.S. Federal Reserve agreed with several European central banks in 1962 to initiate reciprocal currency arrangements, commonly referred to as **swap arrangements.** Today, the swap network on which the United States depends to finance its interventions in the foreign exchange market includes the central banks of 14 other nations and the Bank for International Settlements. Table 18.2 illustrates the Federal Reserve's swap network as of 1993.

Swap arrangements are bilateral agreements between central banks. Each government provides for an exchange, or swap, of currencies to help finance temporary payments disequilibria. If the United States, for example, is short of marks, it can ask the German Federal Bank to supply them in exchange for dollars; conversely, the German Federal Bank can ask for dollars. A drawing on the swap network is usually initiated by telephone, followed by an exchange of wire messages specifying terms and conditions. The actual swap is in the form of a foreign exchange contract calling for the sale of dollars by the Federal Reserve for the currency of a foreign central bank. The nation requesting the swap presumably will use the funds to help ease its payments deficits and discourage speculative capital outflows. Swaps are to be repaid (reversed) within a stipulated period of time, normally within 3 to 12 months.

A number of factors have enhanced swaps as credit instruments compared with the fund's drawing facilities. Not only are fund drawings relatively costly for borrowing nations, but gaining aid from the fund is quite visible to the public. A large drawing from the fund may signal economic weakness and touch off adverse speculative activity. Swap transactions are also made on an unconditional basis, whereas bor-

T A B L E 18. 2 / Federal Reserve Reciprocal Currency Arrangements, January 31, 1993

Institution	Amount of Facility (millions of dollars)
Austrian National Bank	250
National Bank of Belgium	1,000
Bank of Canada	2,000
National Bank of Denmark	250
Bank of England	3,000
Bank of France	2,000
Deutsche Bundesbank	6,000
Bank of Italy	3,000
Bank of Japan	5,000
Bank of Mexico	700
Netherlands Bank	500
Bank of Norway	250
Bank of Sweden	300
Swiss National Bank	4,000
Bank for International Settlements	
Dollars against Swiss francs	600
Dollars against other authorized European currencies	1,250
Total	30,100

SOURCE: *Federal Reserve Bulletin*, April 1993, p. 269.

rowing from the fund (in excess of 50 percent of a nation's quota) may require substantial justification. Finally, swap operations involve minimal administrative lags and can be executed on extremely short notice.

Compensatory Financing for Exports

In 1963, the IMF approved a special credit facility to aid the less developed nations. The idea was to extend the fund's balance-of-payments assistance to member nations suffering from fluctuations in receipts from exports of primary products owing to circumstances beyond their control. Borrowings from the so-called **compensatory financing facility** are separate from and in addition to a nation's regular borrowing privileges from the fund. A nation facing temporary declines in its commodity export earnings can, under this facility, borrow an amount up to 50 percent of its fund quota.

Oil Facility

In 1974, the IMF established a special facility to help member nations cushion the impact on their balance of payments of the skyrocketing costs of oil imports generated by the OPEC price increases of 1973–1974. Under the **oil facility**, fund resources are made available to members as a supplement to other fund-drawing arrangements. Although the oil facility has been used primarily by the less developed nations, industrialized nations including Italy and the United Kingdom have borrowed reserves under these arrangements.

Buffer Stock Financing Facility

A major concern of the less developed nations has been erratic fluctuations in their commodity export prices. To correct such disturbances, commodity producers have often banded together and formulated price-stabilization schemes based on buffer stocks, as discussed in Chapter 8.

Consistent with the IMF's support of commodity-price stabilization for the less developed nations, in 1969 the fund established a facility to aid members in financing their contributions to buffer stocks. Under this scheme, a member nation with a balance-of-payments need can obtain financial assistance from the fund in amounts up to the value of the nation's buffer stocks calculated at the floor price of the agreement or at the average market price of these stocks should the market price fall below the floor price. Borrowing under the **buffer stock facility** cannot exceed 50 percent of a member's fund quota. Like the fund's compensatory financing facility, buffer stock arrangements are separate from and additional to normal fund facilities for dealing with balance-of-payments difficulties. The borrowings are generally expected to be repaid within a period of three to five years after the date of the loan.

The preceding sections have analyzed the nature of international reserves and the role of central banks in the international monetary system. Let us now consider *commercial banks* as international lenders and the problems associated with international debt.

INTERNATIONAL LENDING RISK

In many respects, the principles that apply to international lending are similar to those of domestic lending: the lender needs to determine the credit risk that the borrower will default. When making international loans, however, bankers face two additional risks: country risk and currency risk. Each of these three risks will be discussed in turn.

Credit (financial) **risk** refers to the probability that part or all of the interest or principal of a loan will not be repaid. The larger the potential for default on a loan, the higher the interest rate that the bank must charge the borrower. Assessing credit risk on international loans tends to be more difficult than on domestic loans. U.S. banks are often less familiar with foreign business practices and economic conditions than those in the United States. Obtaining reliable information to evaluate foreign credit risk can be time-consuming and costly. Many U.S. banks, therefore, confine their international lending to major multinational corporations or financial institutions. To attract lending by U.S. banks, a foreign government may provide assurances against default by a local private borrower, thus reducing the credit risk of the loan.

Country (political) **risk** is closely related to political developments in a country, especially the government's views concerning international investments and loans. Some governments encourage the inflow of foreign funds to foster domestic economic development. Fearing loss of national sovereignty, other governments may discourage such inflows by enacting additional taxes, profit restrictions, and wage/price controls that can hinder the ability of local borrowers to repay loans. In the extreme, foreign governments can expropriate the assets of foreign investors or make foreign loan repayments illegal.

Currency (economic) **risk** is associated with currency depreciations and appreciations as well as exchange controls. Some loans of U.S. banks are denominated in foreign currency instead of dollars. If the currency in which the loan is made depreciates against the dollar during the period of the loan, the repayment will be worth fewer dollars. If the foreign currency has a well-developed forward market, the loan may be hedged. But many foreign currencies, especially of the developing nations, do not have such markets, and loans denominated in these currencies cannot always be hedged to decrease this type of currency risk. Another type of currency risk arises from exchange controls, which are common in developing nations. Exchange controls restrict the movement of funds across national borders or limit a currency's convertibility into dollars for repayment, thus adding to the risk of international lenders.

When lending overseas, bankers must evaluate credit risk, country risk, and currency risk. Evaluating risks in foreign lending often results in detailed analyses, compiled by a bank's research department, that are based on a nation's financial, economic, and political conditions. When international lenders consider detailed analyses too expensive, they often use reports and statistical indicators to help them determine the risk of lending.

Analyses of international lending risk have been conducted by several organizations, one of which is International Reports Inc. Each month this organization publishes the *International Country Risk Guide*. The guide provides individual ratings on more than 120 nations for political, financial, and economic risk, plus a composite rating for a nation's overall risk. The ratings are based on a number of risk factors, weighted to reflect current conditions. The breakdown of factors is shown in Table 18.3.

Table 18.4 shows the *International Country Risk Guide* ratings for selected nations. In assessing a nation's composite risk, a higher score (100-point maximum) indicates a lower overall risk; a lower score indicates a higher overall risk. The composite risk rating of a particular nation can be estimated using the following fairly broad categories: (1) low risk, 85–100 points; (2) moderate risk, 60–84 points; (3) high risk, 0–59 points.

THE INTERNATIONAL DEBT PROBLEM

Much concern has been voiced over the volume of international lending in recent years. At times, the concern has been that international lending was insufficient. Such was the case following the oil shocks in 1974–1975 and 1979–1980, when it was feared that some oil-importing developing nations might not be able to obtain loans to finance trade deficits resulting from the huge increases in the price of oil. It so happened that many oil-importing nations were able to borrow dollars from commercial banks. They paid the dollars to OPEC nations, who redeposited the money in commercial banks, which then re-lent the money to oil importers, and so on. In the 1970s, the banks were part of the solution; if they had not lent large sums to the developing nations, the oil shocks would have done far more damage to the world economy.

By the 1980s, however, commercial banks were viewed as part of an international debt problem because they had lent so much to developing nations. Flush with OPEC money after the oil price increases of the 1970s, the banks actively sought borrowers and had no trouble finding them among the developing nations. Some nations borrowed to prop up consumption because their living standards were already low and hit hard by oil price hikes. Most nations borrowed to avoid cuts in developmental programs and to invest in energy projects. It was generally recognized that banks were successful in recycling their OPEC deposits to developing nations following the first round of oil price hikes in 1974–1975. But the international lending mechanism encountered increasing difficulties beginning with the global recession of the early 1980s. In particular, some developing nations were unable to pay their external debts on schedule.

Table 18.5 summarizes the magnitude of the international debt problem of the developing nations. From 1978 to 1993, the external

T A B L E   18. 3   /   *International Lending Risk:*
Political, Financial, and Economic Indicators

Political Risk Indicators (100 points possible)	Financial Risk Indicators (50 points possible)	Economic Risk Indicators (50 points possible)
Economic expectations versus reality	Loan default or unfavorable loan restructuring	Inflation
Law and order tradition	Delayed payment of suppliers' credits	Debt service as a percentage of exports
Economic planning failures	Repudiation of contracts by governments	International liquidity
Racial and nationality tensions	Losses from exchange controls	Collection experience
Political leadership	Expropriation of private investments	Current account deficit as a percentage of exports
Political terrorism		Foreign exchange market factors
External conflict risk		
Civil war risks		
Corruption in government		
Political party development		
Military in politics		
Organized religion in politics		
Bureaucracy quality		

debt of the non-oil-developing nations rose from $328 billion to almost $1,500 billion. Much of that debt was incurred by a few Latin American nations such as Mexico and Brazil. As a percentage of the gross domestic product of developing nations, external debt rose from about 25 percent in the 1970s to as high as 37 percent in 1987, only to be followed by a decrease to 27 percent by 1993.

Most of the external debt of the developing nations is denominated in U.S. dollars. Repayment of this debt thus requires developing nations to earn foreign exchange via exports of goods and services to industrial nations. One measure of a nation's debt burden is its external debt relative to its current export earnings. Changes in this **debt-to-export ratio** indicate whether a nation's debt burden is rising or falling in relation to its ability to pay. From the late 1970s to 1987, the ratio of developing-nation external debt-to-export revenues rose

from 133 percent to 161 percent. This suggests that the external debt exceeded and grew more rapidly than export revenues over this period. By 1993, the debt-to-export ratio had moderated to 113.4 percent.

Another indicator of debt burden is the **debt service/export ratio**, which refers to scheduled interest and principal payments as a percentage of export earnings. From 1978 to 1987, the debt service/export ratio of the non-oil-developing nations rose from 17 percent to 19 percent, dropping off to 14.3 percent in 1993. The debt service/export ratio permits one to focus on two key indicators of whether a reduction in the debt burden is possible in the short run: (1) the interest rate that the nation pays on its external debt and (2) the growth in its exports of goods and services. All else being constant, a rise in the interest rate increases the debt service/export ratio, while a rise in exports decreases the ratio. It is a well-known rule of

T A B L E 18. 4 / International Lending Risk: Selected Country Ratings, January 1992

	Composite Risk Rating (100 points possible)*	Political Risk Rating (100 points possible)	Financial Risk Rating (50 points possible)	Economic Risk Rating (50 points possible)
Switzerland	92.0	93.0	50.0	40.5
Luxembourg	90.0	93.0	49.0	38.0
Austria	89.0	90.0	48.0	39.5
Norway	87.5	84.0	47.0	43.5
Germany, FR	86.5	84.0	50.0	39.0
Denmark	85.5	87.0	46.0	38.0
Japan	84.5	78.0	50.0	40.5
Sweden	84.0	83.0	47.0	38.0
Canada	83.5	81.0	48.0	37.5
United Kingdom	83.0	79.0	50.0	37.0
United States	82.5	77.0	49.0	39.0
South Korea	79.5	75.0	47.0	46.5
Saudi Arabia	77.0	70.0	41.0	42.5
Mexico	72.0	72.0	41.0	31.0
Israel	69.0	70.0	39.0	28.5
Poland	65.5	64.0	33.0	34.0
Brazil	64.0	66.0	36.0	25.5
China, PR	63.5	59.0	27.0	40.5
Kenya	53.0	54.0	26.0	25.5
India	49.0	43.0	29.0	25.5
Bangladesh	43.5	34.0	21.0	32.0
Yugoslavia	34.5	30.0	20.0	18.5
Iraq	28.5	26.0	4.0	26.5
Liberia	13.0	11.0	8.0	7.0

* The composite risk rating is based on a 200-point scale in which 100 points are assigned to political risk (PR) indicators, 50 points are assigned to financial risk (FR) indicators, and 50 points are assigned to economic risk (ER) indicators. In the calculation of the composite risk rating for a particular nation, the 200-point scale was adjusted to a 100-point scale according to the following formula: Composite risk = 0.5 (PR + FR + ER).

SOURCE: International Reports: A Division of IBC USA (Publications) Inc., *International Country Risk Guide,* January 1992, pp. S3–S11.

international finance that a nation's debt burden rises if the interest rate on the debt exceeds the rate of growth of exports.

By the 1980s, it was apparent that many developing nations were encountering increasing difficulties in servicing their debt. The major borrowers in difficulty included Argentina, Brazil, and Mexico. A nation may experience debt-servicing problems for a number of reasons: (1) it may have pursued improper macroeconomic policies that contribute to large balance-of-payments deficits; (2) it may have borrowed excessively or on unfavorable terms; or (3) it may have been

T A B L E 18. 5 / Developing Nations' External Debt

	1984	1989	1993*
Outstanding debt (billions)	$873.6	$1,206.5	$1,473.5
Outstanding debt by area (billions)			
Africa	$129.6	$207.7	$239.8
Asia	223.0	337.6	478.5
Middle East/Europe	161.1	251.4	285.8
Western Hemisphere	359.9	409.8	469.4
Ratio of external debt to gross domestic product	33.8%	32.9%	27.2%
Ratio of external debt to exports of goods and services	136.0%	132.8%	113.4%
Debt service/export ratio	19.3%	16.1%	14.3%

* Estimated.

SOURCE: International Monetary Fund, *World Economic Outlook*, October 1992, pp. 157–164.

affected by adverse economic events that it could not control.

Although there are marked differences among the developing nations, a common set of factors appears to have been behind the debt-servicing problems of the developing nations. The world recession of the early 1980s was one cause. Because of stagnant or declining demand, the prices of the developing nations' exports declined—and declined more rapidly than the less flexible prices of the goods they import. The recession thus made it more difficult for developing nations to obtain the foreign exchange required to service their debt. The sharp rise in interest rates also made it more costly for developing nations to borrow funds. Moreover, the rise in the value of the U.S. dollar during the early 1980s resulted in increased costs of debt repayment because most developing-nation debt is denominated in dollars. These factors resulted in commercial banks' losing confidence that their loans would be repaid promptly.

A nation facing debt-servicing difficulties has several options. First, it can cease repayments on its debt. Such an action, however, undermines confidence in the nation, making it

difficult (if not impossible) for it to borrow in the future. Furthermore, there is a possibility of the nation's being declared in default, in which case its assets (such as ships and aircraft) may be confiscated and sold to discharge the debt. As a group, however, developing nations in debt may have considerable leverage in winning concessions from their lenders. A second option is for the nation to try to service its debt at all costs. To do so may require the restriction of other foreign exchange expenditures, a step that may be viewed as socially unacceptable. Finally, a nation may seek debt rescheduling, which generally involves a stretching out of the original payment schedule of the debt. There is a cost because the debtor nation must pay interest on the amount outstanding until the debt has been repaid.

When a nation faces debt-servicing problems, its creditors seek to reduce their exposure by collecting all interest and principal payments as they come due, while granting no new credit. But there is an old adage that goes as follows: When a man owes a bank $1,000, the bank owns him; but when a man owes the bank $1 million, he owns the bank. Banks with large amounts of international loans find it in their best interest to help the debtor recover financially. To deal with debt-servicing problems, therefore, debtor nations and their creditors generally attempt to negotiate rescheduling agreements. That is, creditors agree to lengthen the time period for repayment of the principal and sometimes part of the interest on existing loans. Banks have little option but to accommodate demands for debt rescheduling because they do not want the debtor to officially default on the loan. A default would result in the bank's assets becoming nonperforming and subject to markdowns by government regulators. This could lead to possible withdrawals of deposits and bank insolvency.

Besides rescheduling debt with commercial banks, developing nations may obtain emergency loans from the IMF. The IMF provides loans to nations experiencing balance-of-payments difficulties provided that the borrowers initiated programs to correct these difficulties.

By insisting on **conditionality**, the IMF asks borrowers to adopt austerity programs to shore up their economies and put their muddled finances in order. Such measures have resulted in the slashing of public spending, private consumption, and, in some cases, capital investment. Borrowers also must cut imports and expand exports. The IMF views austerity programs as a necessity because with a sovereign debtor there is no other way to make it pay back its loans. The IMF faces a difficult situation in deciding how tough to get with borrowers. If it goes soft and offers money on easier terms, it sets a precedent for other debtor nations. But if it miscalculates and requires excessive austerity measures, it risks triggering political turmoil and possibly a declaration of default.

The IMF has been criticized, notably by developing nations, for demanding austerity policies that excessively emphasize short-term improvements in the balance of payments rather than fostering long-run economic growth. Developing nations also contend that the IMF austerity programs promote downward pressure on economic activity in nations that are already exposed to recessionary forces. The crucial issue faced by the IMF is how to resolve the economic problems of the debtor nations in a manner most advantageous to them, to their creditors, and to the world as a whole. The mutually advantageous solution is one that enables these nations to achieve sustainable, noninflationary economic growth, thus assuring creditors of repayment and benefiting the world economy through expansion of trade and economic activity.

At the 1985 annual meetings of the IMF and World Bank, the Reagan administration proposed that the international debt problem could best be solved via economic growth in the debtor nations. It was argued that the World Bank should make large loans, co-financed by commercial banks, that permit debtor nations to resume investment and capital formation. The Reagan proposal called for a larger role for the World Bank and a smaller role for the austerity measures of the IMF. These measures were incorporated into a 1986 loan accord reached by Mexico and its creditors.

The Mexican Debt Crisis

The debt experience of Mexico provides an example of the costs that can be inflicted on an economy when it neglects its balance of payments and borrows heavily from other nations. Mexico's financial and economic problems of the 1980s were the results of the discovery of an estimated 72 billion barrels of oil reserves in 1977. The oil discovery raised the hope that oil exports would generate additional revenues, encouraging rapid economic development and raising the nation's living standard. The goals of the Mexican government were optimistic: an economic growth rate of 8 percent per year, increased government spending, expansion of the private sector, and rapid development of the petroleum sector.

To obtain the funds to finance its free-spending policies, Mexico borrowed heavily from commercial banks, including Citicorp, Bank of America, and Manufacturers Hanover.

By 1983, some 92 percent of Mexico's loans were from private commercial banks, while debt from official lenders fell to a low of 8 percent. As Mexico relied more on private lenders, the terms of borrowing changed. Floating interest rates, which escalated with rises in market rates, were increasingly applied to Mexican loans by commercial banks. By 1982, some 82 percent of the loans to Mexico were based on floating rates, compared with 47 percent in the mid-1970s.

A result of Mexico's free-spending policies was inflation, which was running at close to 30 percent by 1981. The global recession in 1981, combined with falling oil prices and increasing interest rates, dealt the economy another blow. Rising interest rates led to increased debt service costs, while decreasing oil prices induced falling export revenues. By 1986, Mexico's oil export revenues were about $6 billion, down from $20 billion in 1981. The resulting balance-of-payments deficit led the Mexican government to devalue the peso in 1982 as a way of improving its competitive position. The policy failed.

By 1986, it was clear that Mexico could not meet its debt obligations. At that point, a comprehensive new loan package was configured by Mexico, various commercial banks, the IMF, the World Bank, the Inter-American Development Bank, and the U.S. government.

The Mexican accord marked the start of a new chapter in the handling of the international debt problem. Previously, the IMF and other creditors had insisted that debtor nations adopt rigid austerity programs to put their economic houses in order. But with the Mexican accord, the creditors indicated a willingness to be more flexible, emphasizing that the debt crisis could be resolved only through sustained growth and that austerity policies by themselves would be self-defeating over time.

To promote economic growth, the Mexican accord called for programs of economic reform and structural adjustment, including export promotion and trade liberalization, policies to increase domestic investment, reduction of government subsidies and price controls, and increased reliance on the private sector. The program also called on private commercial banks and multilateral institutions to increase their loans to Mexico for a two-year period. As seen in Table 18.6, commercial banks were to provide about $6 billion in new loans to Mexico; an additional $6.2 billion would come from the IMF, the World Bank, and other government agencies.

Another feature of the accord was a $1.5-billion contingency fund agreed to by the United States to help safeguard Mexico's finances until loans could be disbursed by other agencies. The contingency fund was designed to make up for lost oil revenues due to falling prices. Under the plan, the United States would make money available automatically any time oil prices fell to between $5 and $9 a barrel for 90 days or more during the first nine months of the accord. After nine months, Mexico would have to absorb the burden of decreasing oil prices. Furthermore, if oil prices increased above $14, Mexico would have to repay some of its loans.

Reducing Bank Exposure to Developing-Nation Debt

When it became clear in the early 1980s that Mexico could not meet its debt obligation to foreign commercial banks, the stability of the international financial system was thrown into question. With a significant share of their loan portfolios in developing-nation debt and their exposure concentrated in the largest problem debtors, major banks in the United States and other nations would have been threatened by large losses on their foreign loans. U.S. commercial banks gradually improved their financial positions by increasing their capital base, setting aside reserves to cover losses, and reducing new loans to debtor nations.

Banks have used additional means to improve their loan portfolios. One method is to liquidate developing-nation debt by engaging in outright *loan sales* to other banks in the sec-

T A B L E   18. 6 /   Mexican Loan Package, 1986–1987 (in Millions of Dollars)

	1986	1987	Total
IMF	700	900	1,600
World Bank	900	1,000	1,900
Inter-American Development Bank	200	200	400
Commercial banks	2,500	3,500	6,000
International export credits	500	1,000	1,500
U.S. farm credits	200	600	800
Total	5,000	7,200	12,200

SOURCE: U.S. Treasury, June 22, 1986. See also "Mexico—IMF Pact Is Seen Easing Cash Crunch, Altering Economy," *Wall Street Journal* (23 July 1986).

ondary market. But if there occurs an unexpected increase in the default risk of such loans, their market value will be less than their face value. The selling bank thus absorbs costs because its loans must be sold at a discount. Following the sale, the bank must adjust its balance sheet to take account of any previously unrecorded difference between the face value of the loans and their market value. Many small- and medium-size U.S. banks, eager to dump their bad loans in the 1980s, were willing to sell them in the secondary market at discounts as high as 70 percent, or 30 cents on the dollar. But many banks could not afford such huge discounts. Even worse, if the banks all rushed to sell bad loans at once, prices would fall further. Sales of loans in the secondary market were often viewed as a last-resort measure.

Another debt-reduction technique is the *debt buyback,* in which the government of the debtor nation buys the loans from the commercial bank at a discount. Banks have also engaged in *debt-for-debt swaps,* in which a bank exchanges its loans for securities issued by the debtor nation's government at a lower interest rate or discount.

Cutting losses on developing-nation loans has sometimes involved banks in **debt-equity swaps.** Under this approach, a commercial bank sells its loans at a discount to the developing-nation government for local currency, which it then uses to finance an equity investment in the debtor nation. In the late 1980s, Citicorp converted some of its Chilean loans into pesos, which were used to purchase ownership shares in Chilean gold mines and pulp mills. Citicorp maintained that it could get better value by selling and swapping the loans without using the secondary market. In Chile, Citicorp typically converted debt at about 87 cents worth of local currency for each $1 of debt. Although debt-equity swaps enhance a bank's chances of selling developing-nation debt, they do not necessarily decrease its risk. Some equity investments in developing nations may be just as risky as the loans that were swapped for local factories or land. Moreover, banks that acquire an equity interest in developing-nation assets may not have the knowledge to manage those assets. Debtor nations also worry that debt-equity swaps allow major companies to fall into foreign hands.

Debt Reduction and Debt Forgiveness

Although coordinated international response to the problem in the mid-1980s helped stabilize

How a Debt-Equity Swap Works

Brazil owes Manufacturers Hanover Trust (of New York) $1 billion. Manufacturers Hanover decides to swap some of the debt for ownership shares in Companhia Suzano del Papel e Celulose, a pulp-and-paper company. Here is what occurs:

- Manufacturers Hanover takes $115 million in Brazilian government-guaranteed loans to a Brazilian broker. The broker takes the loans to the Brazilian central bank's monthly debt auction, where they are valued at an average of 87 cents on the dollar.

- Through the broker, Manufacturers Hanover exchanges the loans at the central bank for $100 million worth of Brazilian cruzados. The broker is paid a commission, and the central bank retires the loans.
- With its cruzados, Manufacturers Hanover purchases 12 percent of Suzano's stock, and Suzano uses the bank's funds to increase capacity and exports.

---

financial markets, many developing nations encountered high-level indebtedness and default risk. This led to pleas for debt reduction and/or debt forgiveness on the part of lending nations.

Debt reduction refers to any voluntary scheme that lessens the burden on the debtor nation to service its external debt. Debt reduction is accomplished through two main approaches. The first is through negotiated modifications in the terms and conditions of the contracted debt, such as debt reschedulings, retiming of interest payments, and improved borrowing terms. Debt reduction may also be achieved through measures such as debt-equity swaps and debt buybacks. The purpose of debt reduction is to foster comprehensive policies for economic growth by easing the ability of the debtor nation to service its debt, thus freeing resources that will be used for investment.

An example of a debt-reduction proposal is the Brady Initiative of 1989, named after U.S. Treasury Secretary Nicholas Brady. During the late 1980s, the persistence of serious problems in the debtor economies and concern over the economic hardships sustained by their populations resulted in the Brady Initiative. This pro-

posal called for the mobilization of private-sector financing to generate growth in debtor nations. The major innovation of the initiative is that it emphasized debt reduction by commercial banks. It also called for IMF and World Bank financial support for debt reduction to those nations enacting effective economic reform policies.

Some proponents of debt relief maintain that the lending nations should permit **debt forgiveness**. Debt forgiveness refers to any arrangement that reduces the value of contractual obligations of the debtor nation; it includes schemes such as markdowns or write-offs of developing-nation debt or the abrogation of existing obligations to pay interest.

Debt-forgiveness advocates maintain that the most heavily indebted developing nations are unable to service their external debt and maintain an acceptable rate of per capita income growth because their debt burden is overwhelming. They contend that if some of this debt is forgiven, a debtor nation could use the freed-up foreign exchange resources to increase its imports and invest domestically, thus increasing domestic economic growth rates. The release of the limitation on foreign exchange would provide the debtor nation additional incentive to invest because it would not have to share as much of the benefits of its increased growth and investment with its creditors in the form of interest payments. Moreover, debt forgiveness would allow the debtor nation to service its debt more easily; this would reduce the debt-load burden of a debtor nation and could potentially lead to greater inflows of foreign investment.

Debt-forgiveness critics question whether the amount of debt is a major limitation on developing-nation growth and whether growth would in fact resume if a large portion of that debt were forgiven. They contend that nations such as Indonesia and South Korea have experienced large amounts of external debt relative to national output but have not faced debt-servicing problems. Also, debt forgiveness does not guarantee that the freed-up foreign exchange resources will be used productively—that is, invested in sectors that will ultimately generate additional foreign exchange.

THE EUROCURRENCY MARKET

One of the most widely misunderstood topics in international finance is the nature and operation of the **Eurocurrency market**. To the non-practitioner, this market may seem like a financial "black box" into which goes the money of U.S. and other foreign residents and from which comes credits for foreigners. Even academic economists disagree about the market's operation and its economic impact. This section discusses what the Eurocurrency market is and how it operates.

Eurocurrencies are deposits, denominated and payable in dollars and other foreign currencies (such as the German mark and Swiss franc), in banks outside the United States, primarily in London, the market's center. The term *Eurocurrency market* is something of a misnomer, because much Eurocurrency trading occurs in non-European centers such as Hong Kong and Singapore. Dollar deposits located in banks outside the United States are known as *Eurodollars*, and banks that conduct trading in the markets for Eurocurrencies (including the dollar) are designated *Eurobanks*.

Eurocurrency depositors may be foreign exporters who have sold products in the United States and have received dollars in payment. They may also be U.S. residents who have withdrawn funds from their accounts in the United States and put them in a bank overseas. Foreign-currency deposits in overseas banks are generally for a specified time period and bear a stated yield, because most Eurocurrency deposits are held for investment rather than as transaction balances.

Borrowers go to Eurocurrency banks for a variety of purposes. When the market was first developed, borrowers were primarily corporations that required financing for international trade. But other lending opportunities have evolved with the market's development. Borrowers currently include the British government and U.S. banks.

The purpose of the Eurocurrency market is to operate as a financial intermediary, bringing together lenders and borrowers. It serves as one of the most important tools for moving short-term funds across national borders. When the Eurocurrency market first came into existence in the 1950s, its volume was estimated to be approximately $1 billion. The size of the Eurocurrency market in the early 1990s was estimated to be more than $5,000 billion.

Eurocurrency Market Development

Although several hundred banks currently issue Eurocurrency deposits on investor demand, it was not until the late 1950s and early 1960s that the market began to gain prominence as a major source of short-term capital. Several factors contributed to the Eurocurrency market's growth.

One factor was fear that deposits held in the United States would be frozen by the government in the event of an international conflict. The Eastern European countries, notably Russia, were among the first depositors of dollars in European banks because during World War II the United States had impounded Russian dollar holdings located in U.S. banks. Russia was thus motivated to maintain dollar holdings free from U.S. regulation.

Ceilings on interest rates that U.S. banks could pay on time deposits provided another reason for the Eurocurrency market's growth. These ceilings limited the U.S. banks in competing with foreign banks for deposits. During the 1930s, the Federal Reserve system under Regulation Q established ceiling rates to prevent banks from paying excessive interest rates on savings accounts and thus being forced to make risky loans to generate high earnings. By the late 1950s, when London was paying interest rates on dollar deposits that exceeded the levels set by Regulation Q, it was profitable for U.S. residents and foreigners to transfer their dollar balances to London. Large U.S. banks directed their foreign branches to bid for dollars by offering higher interest rates than those allowed in the United States. The parent offices then borrowed the money from their overseas branches. To limit such activity, the Federal Reserve in 1969 established high reserve requirements on head-office borrowings from abroad. In 1973, the Federal Reserve system made large-denomination certificates of deposit exempt from Regulation Q ceilings, further reducing the incentive to borrow funds from overseas branches.

Throughout the 1970s, 1980s, and 1990s, the Eurocurrency market has continued to grow. A major factor behind the sustained high growth of the market has been the risk-adjusted interest-rate advantage of Eurocurrency deposits relative to domestic deposits, reflecting increases in the level of dollar interest rates and reductions in the perceived riskiness of Euromarket deposits.

Financial Implications

Eurocurrencies have significant implications for international finance. By increasing the financial interdependence of nations involved in the market, Eurocurrencies facilitate the financing of international trade and investment. They may also reduce the need for official reserve financing, because a given quantity of dollars can support a large volume of international transactions. On the other hand, it is argued that Eurocurrencies may undermine a nation's efforts to implement its monetary policy. Volatile movements of these balances into and out of a nation's banking system complicate a central bank's attempt to hit a monetary target.

Another concern is that the Eurocurrency market does not face the same financial regulations as do the domestic banking systems of most industrialized nations. Should the Eurocurrency banks not maintain sound reserve requirements or enact responsible policies, the pyramid of Eurocurrency credit might collapse. Such fears became widespread in 1974 with the failure of the Franklin National Bank in the United States and the Bankus Herstatt of Germany, both of which lost huge sums speculating in the foreign exchange market.

SUMMARY

1. The purpose of international reserves is to permit nations to bridge the gap between monetary receipts and payments. Deficit nations can use international reserves to buy time in order to postpone adjustment measures.

2. The demand for international reserves depends on two major factors: (a) the monetary value of international transactions and (b) the size and duration of balance-of-payments disequilibria.

3. The need for international reserves tends to

become less acute under a system of floating exchange rates than under a system of fixed rates. The more efficient the international adjustment mechanism and the greater the extent of international policy coordination, the smaller the need for international reserves.

4. The supply of international reserves consists of owned and borrowed reserves. Among the major sources of reserves are the following: (a) foreign currencies, (b) monetary gold stocks, (c) special drawing rights, (d) IMF drawing positions, (e) the General Arrangements to Borrow, and (f) swap arrangements.

5. When making international loans, bankers face credit risk, country risk, and currency risk.

6. Among the indicators used to analyze a nation's external debt position are its debt-to-export ratio and debt service/export ratio.

7. A nation experiencing debt-servicing difficulties has several options: (a) cease repayment on its debt; (b) service its debt at all costs; or (c) reschedule its debt. Debt rescheduling has been widely used by borrowing nations in recent years.

8. A bank can reduce its exposure to developing-nation debt through outright loan sales in the secondary market, debt buybacks, debt-for-debt swaps, and debt-equity swaps.

9. Eurocurrencies are deposits, denominated and payable in dollars and other foreign currencies, in banks outside the United States. Dollar deposits located in banks outside the United States are called Eurodollars, and banks that conduct trading in markets for Eurocurrencies are known as Eurobanks.

STUDY QUESTIONS

1. A nation's need for international reserves is similar to a householder's desire to hold cash balances. Explain.

2. What are the major factors that determine a nation's demand for international reserves?

3. The total supply of international reserves consists of two categories: (a) owned reserves and (b) borrowed reserves. What do these categories include?

4. In terms of volume, which component of world reserves is currently most important? Which is currently least important?

5. What is meant by a reserve currency? Historically, which currencies have assumed this role?

6. What was the so-called liquidity problem that plagued the operation of the Bretton Woods system?

7. What is the current role of gold in the international monetary system?

8. What advantages does a gold exchange standard have over a pure gold standard?

9. What are special drawing rights? Why were they created? How is their value determined?

10. What facilities exist for trading nations that wish to borrow international reserves?

11. What caused the international debt problem of the developing nations in the 1980s? Why did this debt problem threaten the stability of the international banking system?

12. What is a Eurocurrency? How did the Eurocurrency market develop?

13. What risks do bankers assume when making loans to foreign borrowers?

14. Distinguish between debt-to-export ratio and debt service/export ratio.

15. What options are available to a nation experiencing debt-servicing difficulties? What limitations apply to each option?

16. What methods do banks use to reduce their exposure to developing-nation debt?

17. How can debt-equity swaps help banks reduce losses on developing-nation loans?

Notes

Chapter 1

1. Robert Reich has served as a professor of political economy at Harvard University and as U.S. Secretary of Labor. This section is based on his article "Who Is Us?" *Harvard Business Review* (January–February 1990), pp. 53–64.

2. The definitions of the eight competitiveness categories of Table 1.6 are as follows. *Domestic economic strength* is an overall evaluation of the domestic economy of a nation. *Internationalization* describes the degree to which a nation participates in international trade and investment flows. *Government* describes the degree to which government policies promote competitiveness. *Finance* evaluates the performance of capital markets and the quality of financial services. *Infrastructure* describes the degree to which resources and systems are adequate to serve the basic needs of business. *Management* describes the degree to which firms are managed in an innovative, profitable, and responsible fashion. *Science and technology* evaluates scientific and technological capacity, combined with the success of basic and applied research. *People* evaluates the availability and qualifications of human resources.

Chapter 2

1. See E. A. J. Johnson, *Predecessors of Adam Smith* (New York: Prentice-Hall, 1937).

2. David Hume, "Of Money," *Essays* (London: Green and Co., 1912), vol. 1, p. 319. Hume's writings are also available in Eugene Rotwein, *The Economic Writings of David Hume* (Edinburgh: Nelson, 1955).

3. Adam Smith, *The Wealth of Nations* (New York: Modern Library, 1937), pp. 424–426. For a discussion concerning the logical possibility of the absolute-advantage concept, see Royall Brandis, "The Myth of Absolute Advantage," *American Economic Review* (March 1967).

4. David Ricardo, *The Principles of Political Economy and Taxation* (London: Cambridge University Press, 1966), chap. 7.

5. See Gottfried Haberler, *The Theory of International Trade* (New York: Macmillan, 1950), chap. 10.

6. G. D. A. MacDougall, "British and American Exports: A Study Suggested by the Theory of Comparative Costs," *Economic Journal* 61 (1951).

7. B. Balassa, "An Empirical Demonstration of Classical Comparative Cost Theory," *Review of Economics and Statistics,* August 1963, pp. 231–238. See also R. Stern, "British and American Productivity and Comparative Costs in International Trade," *Oxford Economic Papers,* October 1962.

Chapter 3

1. John Stuart Mill, *Principles of Political Economy* (New York: Longmans, Green, 1921), pp. 584–585.

2. The case of immiserizing growth is most likely to occur when (a) the nation's economic growth is biased toward its export sector; (b) the country is large relative to the world market, so that its export price falls when domestic output expands; (c) the foreign demand for the nation's export product is highly price-inelastic, which implies a large decrease in price in response to an increase in export supply; and (d) the nation is heavily engaged in international trade, so that the negative effects of the terms-of-trade deterioration more than offset the positive effects of increased production.

3. Other difficulties encountered when interpreting the commodity terms of trade include (a) allowing for changes in product quality and for

new products, (b) determining methods of valuing exports and imports, and (c) determining methods to weight the products included in the price indexes.

4. Other terms-of-trade measures include the *income terms of trade,* the *single-factorial terms of trade,* and the *double-factorial terms of trade.* A fuller discussion of terms-of-trade measurement can be found in J. Viner, *Studies in Theory of International Trade* (New York: Harper & Brothers, 1937). See also G. Meier, *The International Economics of Development* (New York: Harper & Row, 1968), chap. 3.

Chapter 4

1. Eli Heckscher's explanation of the factor endowment theory is outlined in his article "The Effects of Foreign Trade on the Distribution of Income," *Economisk Tidskrift,* 21 (1919), pp. 497–512. Bertil Ohlin's account is summarized in his *Interregional and International Trade* (Cambridge, Mass.: Harvard University Press, 1933).

2. See Paul A. Samuelson, "International Trade and Equalization of Factor Prices," *Economic Journal* (June 1948), pp. 163–184, and "International Factor-Price Equalization Once Again," *Economic Journal* (June 1949), pp. 181–197.

3. Wassily W. Leontief, "Domestic Production and Foreign Trade: The American Capital Position Reexamined," *Proceedings of the American Philosophical Society* 97 (September 1953).

4. The value of marginal product (VMP) refers to the price of a product (P) times the marginal product of labor (MP). The VMP schedule is the labor demand schedule. This is because a business hiring under competitive conditions finds it most profitable to hire labor up to the point at which the price of labor (wage rate) equals its VMP. The VMP schedule is downward sloping because of the law of diminishing returns: as extra units of labor are added to capital, beyond some point the marginal product attributable to each additional unit of labor will decrease. Because $VMP = P \times MP$, falling MP means that VMP decreases as more units of labor are hired.

5. Because $VMP = P \times MP$, a 100-percent rise in computer prices (P) leads to a 100-percent increase in VMP. As a result, the labor demand schedule shifts upward by 100 percent from $D_{L(C)}$ to $D_{L'(C)}$ following the price increase. To visualize this shift, compare point A and point C along the two demand schedules. After the increase in demand, computer firms will be willing to hire a given amount of labor, say 14 workers, at a wage rate of up to $30 instead of $15, a 100-percent increase. In like manner, all points along $D_{L'(C)}$ are located at a wage rate that is 100-percent greater than the corresponding wage rate along $D_{L(C)}$.

6. Not only do the real incomes of steel capital owners fall, but so do their nominal incomes. Trade results in a decrease in their VMP due to a decline in their MP, even if the price of steel remains the same.

7. Staffan B. Linder, *An Essay on Trade and Transformation* (New York: Wiley, 1961), chap. 3.

8. See Raymond Vernon, "International Investment and International Trade in the Product Life Cycle," *Quarterly Journal of Economics* 80 (May 1966), pp. 190–207.

9. J. P. Kalt, "The Impact of Domestic Environmental Regulatory Policies on U.S. International Competitiveness," in A. M. Spence and H. A. Hazard, eds., *International Competitiveness* (Cambridge, Mass.: MIT Press, 1988), pp. 261–262. See also J. D. Richardson and J. H. Mutti, "Industrial Displacement Through Environmental Controls: The International Competitive Aspect," in I. Walter, ed., *Studies in International Environmental Economics* (New York: Wiley, 1976), pp. 71–75.

10. The U.S. Commerce Department describes business services as those provided to facilitate merchandise trade (such as insurance and transportation) and other business services (such as tourism and passenger transportation). Business services do not include services provided directly by governments nor international income from interest payments and dividends. See U.S. Department of Commerce, *U.S. Trade Performance in 1988,* p. 80.

Chapter 5

1. The effective tariff is a measure that applies to a single nation. In a world of floating exchange rates, if all nominal or effective tariff rates rose, the effect would be offset by a change in the exchange rate.

2. This section assumes that the U.S. elasticity of supply of imports (CB radios and motorcycles) is infinite and that increasing cost conditions prevail in the U.S. market. Because the United States can import as much of the product as it desires without affecting import price, it is considered a small nation. Although this assumption does not reflect the reality of the CB radio

and motorcycle industries for the United States, it does correspond to the assumptions underlying the empirical estimates of the welfare costs of tariff restrictions presented in this section. Because the precise character of real-world demand and supply schedules is unknown, the statements of the welfare effects of tariffs are at best merely estimates, and often very rough estimates. This also applies to the welfare estimates of nontariff trade barriers that are presented in subsequent chapters.

3. Daniel Klein, "Taking America for a Ride: The Politics of Motorcycle Tariffs," *Cato Institute Policy Analysis,* No. 32 (January 1984). See also U.S. International Trade Commission, *Heavyweight Motorcycles, and Engines and Power Train Subassemblies Therefor* (Washington, D.C.: Government Printing Office, February 1983); and Peter Reid, *Well Made in America* (New York: McGraw-Hill, 1989).

Chapter 6

1. The VER with the European Community did not apply to Spain and Portugal, whose steel imports were restricted by separate agreements that remained in force after they joined the EC in 1986. Other countries covered by the VERs were Australia, Austria, Brazil, Czechoslovakia, East Germany, Finland, Hungary, Japan, Mexico, People's Republic of China, Poland, Romania, South Africa, South Korea, Trinidad and Tobago, Venezuela, and Yugoslavia. Canada was the only major steel-producing country that successfully resisted U.S. government pressure to limit steel exports.

2. John Kline, *State Government Influence in U.S. International Economic Policy* (Lexington, Mass.: Heath, 1983), pp. 87–91.

Chapter 7

1. For those nations that are signatories to the GATT Subsidy Code, the International Trade Commission must determine that their export subsidies have injured U.S. producers before countervailing duties are imposed. The export subsidies of nonsignatory nations are subject to countervailing duties immediately following the Commerce Department's determination of their occurrence; the International Trade Commission does not have to make an injury determination.

2. The argument for strategic trade policy was first presented in J. Brander and B. Spencer, "International R&D Rivalry and Industrial Strategy," *Review of Economic Studies,* 50 (1983), pp.

707–722. See also P. Krugman, ed., *Strategic Trade Policy and the New International Economics* (Cambridge, Mass.: MIT Press, 1986).

3. R. Baldwin and P. Krugman, "Industrial Policy and International Competition in Wide-Bodied Jet Aircraft," in R. Baldwin, ed., *Trade Policy Issues and Empirical Analysis* (Chicago: University of Chicago Press, 1988), pp. 45–77.

4. For production with constant marginal cost, average variable cost and marginal cost are identical. Marginal cost always lies below average total cost for such processes. The average total cost schedule is downsloping because of the declining average fixed cost.

5. Because the European and Japanese consortiums compete with each other, each must accept a price no higher than marginal cost. Both consortiums lose the fixed costs of becoming established in the United States. Over time, one or both consortiums may go bankrupt.

Chapter 8

1. United Nations Commission for Latin America, *The Economic Development of Latin America and Its Principal Problems, 1950.*

2. J. Sporas, *Equalizing Trade?* (Oxford, England: Clarendon Press, 1983).

3. M. Michaely, *Trade Income Levels and Dependence* (Amsterdam: North-Holland, 1984).

4. Bernard Munk, "The Colombian Automobile Industry: The Welfare Consequences of Import Substitution," *Economic and Business Bulletin* (Fall 1970), pp. 6–22.

5. Joel Bergsman, "Growth: A Tale of Two Nations—Korea and Argentina," *Report: News and Views from the World Bank* (May–June 1980), p. 2.

6. Brook Ezriel and Euzo Grilli, "Commodity Price Stabilization and the Developing World," *Finance and Development* (March 1977), p. 11.

Chapter 9

1. Founded in 1960, the EFTA is a free trade area in industrial goods. Its members have included Austria, Finland, Iceland, Norway, Sweden, and Switzerland. By the 1990s, plans were being made to have EFTA members join the European Community.

2. Nicholas Owen, *Economies of Scale, Competitiveness, and Trade Patterns Within the European Community* (New York: Oxford University Press, 1983), pp. 119–139.

3. Mordechai E. Kreinin, *Trade Relations of the EEC: An Empirical Approach* (New York: Praeger, 1974), chap. 3.

4. "EEC Effects on the Foreign Trade of EEC Member Countries," *EFTA Bulletin* (June 1972), pp. 14–21.

5. *U.S.–Canada Free Trade Agreement: Summary of Major Provisions, 1987* (Washington, D.C.: Office of Public Affairs, Office of the Trade Representative).

6. Canadian Department of Finance, *The Canada–U.S. Free Trade Agreement: An Economic Assessment* (Ottawa: Author, 1989), p. 32.

Chapter 10

1. See Robert Carbaugh and Darwin Wassink, "International Joint Ventures and the U.S. Auto Industry," *The International Trade Journal* (Fall 1986).

2. The value of the marginal product of labor (*VMP*) refers to the amount of money producers receive from selling the quantity that was produced by the last worker hired; in other words, *VMP* = product price × the marginal product of labor. The *VMP* curve is the labor demand schedule. This follows from an application of the rule that a business hiring under competitive conditions finds it most profitable to hire labor up to the point at which the price of labor (wage rate) equals its *VMP*. The location of the *VMP* curve depends on the marginal productivity of labor and the price of the product that it produces. Under pure competition, price is constant. Therefore, it is because of diminishing marginal productivity that the labor demand schedule is downward-sloping.

3. How do we know that area *c* represents the income accruing to U.S. owners of capital? Our analysis assumes two productive factors, labor and capital. The total income (value of output) that results from using a given quantity of labor with a fixed amount of capital equals the area under the *VMP* curve of labor for that particular quantity of labor. Labor's share of that area is calculated by multiplying the wage rate times the quantity of labor hired. The remaining area under the *VMP* curve is the income accruing to the owners of capital.

4. Wage-rate equalization assumes unrestricted labor mobility in which workers are concerned only about their incomes. It also assumes that migration is costless for labor. In reality, there are economic and psychological costs of migrating to another country. Such costs may result in only a small number of persons' finding the wage gains in the immigrating country high enough to compensate them for their migration

costs. Thus, complete wage equalization may not occur.

5. George Borgas et al., *On the Labor Market Effects of Immigration and Trade*, Working Paper No. 3761 (Cambridge, Mass.: National Bureau of Economic Research, June 1991). See also Richard Freeman, ed., *Immigration, Trade, and the Labor Market* (Cambridge, Mass.: National Bureau of Economic Research, 1988).

Chapter 12

1. This chapter considers the foreign exchange market in the absence of government restrictions. In practice, foreign exchange markets for many currencies are controlled by governments; therefore, the range of foreign exchange activities discussed in this chapter are not all possible.

2. In commodity markets, the *close* is a period of time, generally less than two minutes, during which a large number of transactions can occur. To obtain a single closing price, exchanges must calculate what the last price of the day would be, if there were one. A common method is to take a single average of the highest and lowest prices during the closing period.

Chapter 13

1. This chapter presents the so-called *relative version* of the purchasing-power-parity theory, which addresses changes in prices and exchange rates over a period of time. Another variant is the *absolute version*, which states that the equilibrium exchange rate will equal the ratio of domestic to foreign prices of an appropriate market basket of goods and services at one point in time.

2. J. Frenkel, "International Capital Mobility and Crowding Out in the U.S. Economy," in R. Hafer, ed., *How Open Is the U.S. Economy?* (Springfield, Mass.: Lexington Books/Heath, 1986).

3. Stated more technically, demand schedule D_0 is downward-sloping because a lower current exchange rate suggests a higher expected appreciation of the dollar, a higher expected return on dollar assets compared with foreign assets, and thus a higher quantity of dollar assets demanded. See F. S. Mishkin, *The Economics of Money, Banking, and Financial Markets* (Boston: Little, Brown, 1986), pp. 636–638.

4. In practice, virtually all exchange-market intervention is carried out by central banks of other nations and not by the Federal Reserve; hence, this example is somewhat unrealistic. However, the Federal Reserve occasionally conducts for-

eign exchange market operations, and we continue to use the United States as the home country to maintain consistency with the rest of this section.

5. R. Levich, "Currency Forecasters Lose Their Way," *Euromoney* (August 1983), pp. 140–147.

Chapter 14

1. Under a fixed exchange-rate system, the supply of and demand for foreign exchange reflects credit and debit transactions in the balance of payments. These forces of supply and demand, however, are not permitted to determine the exchange rate. Instead, government officials peg, or fix, the exchange rate at a stipulated level by intervening in the foreign exchange markets to purchase and sell currencies. This topic is examined further in the next chapter.

2. David Hume, "Of the Balance of Trade." Reprinted in Richard N. Cooper, ed., *International Finance: Selected Readings* (Harmondsworth, England: Penguin Books, 1969), chap. 1.

3. John Maynard Keynes, *The General Theory of Employment, Interest, and Money* (London: Macmillan, 1936).

4. The monetary approach to the balance of payments had its intellectual background at the University of Chicago. It originated with Robert Mundell, *International Economics* (New York: Macmillan, 1968), and Harry Johnson, "The Monetary Approach to Balance of Payments Theory," *Journal of Financial and Quantitative Analysis* (March 1972).

5. An import quota would promote payments equilibrium by restricting the supply of Canadian imports and increasing their price. The quantity of money demanded by Canadians rises, reducing the excess money supply and the payments deficit. As discussed in the next chapter, a currency devaluation also leads to higher-priced imports. This generates higher quantities of money demanded and a shrinking payments deficit, according to the monetary approach.

Chapter 15

1. Helen Junz and Rudolf R. Rhomberg, "Price Competitiveness in Export Trade Among Industrial Countries," *American Economic Review* (May 1973), pp. 412–419.

2. Sidney S. Alexander, "Effects of a Devaluation on a Trade Balance," *IMF Staff Papers* (April 1952), pp. 263–278.

3. See Donald S. Kemp, "A Monetary View of the Balance of Payments," *Review,* Federal Reserve Bank of St. Louis (April 1975), pp. 14–22; and Thomas M. Humphrey, "The Monetary Approach to Exchange Rates: Its Historical Evolution and Role in Policy Debates," *Economic Review,* Federal Reserve Bank of Richmond (July–August 1978), pp. 2–9.

Chapter 17

1. Recall from Chapter 11 that BOP transactions are grouped into two categories: the current account and the capital account. Private-sector transactions and official (central bank) transactions are included in the capital account. With double-entry accounting, total debits equal total credits in the BOP statement. This implies that a current-account deficit (surplus) will equal a capital account surplus (deficit).

   In this chapter, we assume that BOP equilibrium occurs when the current-account deficit (surplus) is equal to the surplus (deficit) on private-sector capital transactions; the balance on official capital transactions thus equals zero. This measure is known as the official reserve transaction balance; it emphasizes the role of all private-sector transactions in a nation's international payments position. It follows that a BOP deficit (surplus) occurs if the deficit (surplus) on current-account transactions exceeds the surplus (deficit) on private-sector capital transactions.

2. See A. C. Day, "Institutional Constraints and the International Monetary System," in R. Mundell and A. Swoboda, eds., *Monetary Problems of the International Economy* (Chicago: University of Chicago Press, 1969), pp. 333–342.

3. See S. Fischer, "International Macroeconomic Policy Coordination," in M. Feldstein, *International Economic Cooperation* (Chicago: University of Chicago Press, 1988), p. 19.

6. See R. Putnam and C. R. Henning, "The Bonn Summit of 1978: A Case Study in Coordination," in R. Cooper et al., *Can Nations Agree?* (Washington, D.C.: The Brookings Institution, 1989), p. 17.

Index